HARDY GERANIUMS

Peter F. Yeo

BATSFORD

This new edition first published in 2001
First published in paperback 2005

The first edition was published by Croom Helm (later
Christopher Helm) in 1985 and was twice reprinted. In 1988
it was published in German by Ulmer as *Geranium:
Freiland-Geranien für Garten u. Park* in translation by
Marion Zerbst, and with an additional chapter by Dr Hans
Simon on the horticultural utility of geraniums in Central
Europe. The English edition was then re-published by
Batsford with minor corrections and a new jacket in 1992.

ISBN 0 7134 8928 6

A CIP catalogue record for this book is available from the British Library.

Printed in Malaysia

for the publishers

B T Batsford
Chrysalis Books Group
The Chrysalis Building
Bramley Road
London W10 6SP

www.chrysalisbooks.co.uk

An imprint of **Chrysalis** Books Group plc

Contents

Preface

The expression 'hardy geraniums' is the favoured one in horticultural circles for distinguishing *Geranium* of the botanists from *Pelargonium*, and it therefore forms the title of this book, but within its covers they are usually referred to as cranesbills. The title calls for a small apology, in that I have included some species that can stand only a few degrees of frost.

In the preface to the first edition of this book I claimed that nothing had previously appeared that would permit confident identification of cultivated cranesbills. With my book I aimed to fill that gap. I wanted to help converted geraniophils and to entice others to explore the beauty expressed in their apparently endless variation. In the 15 years preceding *Hardy Geraniums* (1985) there had already been an upsurge of horticultural interest in them, partly promoted by a trial by the Royal Horticultural Society at Wisley. This has continued to snowball in an extraordinary way, and I frequently have chance encounters with people who know about the variety and versatility of these plants in the garden.

In parallel with the spread of knowledge about cranesbills there has been continual growth in the number of forms available. In this edition of *Hardy Geraniums* I have included nearly 40 additional species that have been introduced from the wild. Apart from this there has been a complete transformation in the position with regard to hybrids, mainly due to the work of one person, Alan Bremner of Kirkwall, Orkney. He has done some 24,000 cross-pollinations of *Geranium* over 14 years up to the beginning of 1999. The hybrids raised by Mr Bremner and others are important horticulturally but they add enormously to the difficulty of writing a diagnostic key (as further explained in Chapter 8). I have decided to compromise between covering everything and leaving out the hybrids altogether. The latter course would be unthinkable in the case of *G. x magnificum* and some others. Also, it seems pointless to discard information that was in the first edition, though sometimes I have shortened it. Individual treatment of hybrids in Chapter 9 is now, with one exception, confined to those that have received validly published and legitimate binary Latin names. Hybrids are dealt with in varying detail under the treatment of one or other parent species. The text is at the end of the species-account, but there is no longer a separate heading for hybrids in the discussion of species. A list of hybrids is presented in Appendix III.

Interesting new developments are micro-propagation and trade-marking under legislation on plant variety rights. Both have been involved in the marketing of *Geranium* 'Rozanne' by Blooms of Bressingham. A distinctive large-flowered hybrid between *G. himalayense* and *G. wallichianum* occurred spontaneously but could only be increased quickly by micro-propagation. The trade-marked cultivar was then released through Blooms' many retail outlets, accompanied by a glossy leaflet in colour giving the plant's history and horticultural qualities.

I came to know the cranesbills in the course of duty at the University Botanic Garden, Cambridge, but my interest in them is sustained by my delight in them as garden plants. The conditions of my employment in the University helped in several ways to make the writing of the first edition possible. I had at my disposal the combined resources of the University and Departmental Libraries and had an entitlement to Study Leave, which I took for two terms in 1983. My colleagues in the Botany School and University Botanic Garden willingly undertook to cover my teaching and other responsibilities in those two terms. In addition I had the services of Miss J.A. Hulyer of the University Department of Botany to photograph the leaf-silhouettes.

For this edition additional leaf-silhouettes have been made by scanning into a computer and the whole text was scanned and made into word-process files for editing. This facility has been made available to me by Dr Mark Winfield of the Department of Plant Sciences, University of Cambridge, who has generously and patiently given his time when I have needed help.

I am deeply grateful to all concerned.

Essential to the writing of the book has been the generosity of many plantsmen, gardeners and garden curators who have given me plants, shared their knowledge and in many cases given their hospitality, and I have pleasure in offering hearty thanks to them. Their names, or the names of the gardens for which they work, are mentioned as sources of plants or information, and I hope they will accept this collective acknowledgement. However, I would like to record the great contribution of plants by the late Jan Stephens, as evidenced in the captions to the illustrations of leaf-silhouettes.

Additional gardens visited for this edition are those of David and Pat Victor at Hockliffe, Bedfordshire; Bleddyn and Sue Wynn-Jones at Crûg Farm Plants near Caernarfon; and Judith Bradshaw at Catforth Gardens near Preston, Lancashire. Much use has been made of the Victors' collection and I thank them for repeatedly welcoming my wife and me on visits to them. They also very kindly took me to the above-named gardens, and David has amplified my cultural recommendations in Chapter 2.

In addition I am indebted to the authorities of the Kew Herbarium for facilities and to the Council of the Linnean Society of London for permission to use figures published in the Botanical Journal of the Linnean Society in 1973 and 1984. Philip Oswald very kindly provided the Latin description given in Appendix II. Much other help is acknowledged in the first edition.

I thank my wife, Elizabeth, for her interest in and support for my work on both editions and for criticising parts of the text, helping to select photographs, generously giving much time to work on the typescript and proofs and driving me on visits to gardens.

The photographs for colour plates 4, 33 and 48 were taken by the late F.T.N. Elborn, the rest by me. The line-drawings are by Dr Frances Kupicha.

ABBREVIATIONS

BG = botanic garden (some botanic gardens are indicated simply by their place-names)

CUBG = University Botanic Garden, Cambridge, UK

CGG = international code for CUBG herbarium

HCC = Horticultural Colour Chart (see page 26)

RHSCC = Royal Horticultural Colour Chart (see page 26)

edn.1 = *Hardy Geraniums*, first edition, 1985 and reprints

f. = forma

sect. = section

subg. = subgenus

subsect. =subsection

subsp. or ssp. = subspecies

var. = variety

Chapter 1
History

THE SCOPE OF THE BOOK

This book deals only with those plants covered by the scientific name *Geranium*. However, 'geranium', as a word in the English language, applies to the group which botanists call *Pelargonium*. This anomaly is a source of frequent bewilderment to the layman and it stems from changes in botanical classification, as will be explained below. The plants included in this book are a selection from those species of *Geranium* that are in cultivation at the present time in the British Isles and their named variants and hybrids. Because nearly all *Geranium* species have some ornamental value the enthusiast is liable to try any that can be obtained, and this means that a few species of minimal garden value are in circulation and need to be included. Several species are native to the British Isles and among these too are some weedy species; they have also been included as they are liable to be encountered in gardens even though their presence is unintended by the owner. Finally, a few species that are not in cultivation but whose names are in circulation, misapplied to other species, are briefly dealt with for the purpose of clarification, as well as a few others that are likely to be introduced or re-introduced.

GERANIUM, PELARGONIUM AND *ERODIUM*: THE NAMES

Geranium belongs to the botanical family Geraniaceae. Botanists have differed in their opinion as to what genera should be included in this family, but the present tendency, which I support, is to restrict it to the five genera: *Geranium*, *Pelargonium*, *Erodium*, *Monsonia* and *Sarcocaulon*. In all of them there is a narrow beak-like structure at the top of the fruit and this has inspired the naming of the first three genera after birds. *Geranium* comes from the Greek *geranion*, a diminutive form of *geranos*, a crane. *Geranion* has been in use for members of the family since the time of Dioscorides in the first century AD. By analogy, *Pelargonium* was coined from the Greek *pelargos*, a stork, and *Erodium* from *erodios*, a heron. However, vernacular usage does not correspond with these derivations because, although *Geranium* is called cranesbill, it is *Erodium* that we call storksbill.

The confusion between *Geranium* and *Pelargonium* arose as follows. *Pelargonium* species are mostly native to southern Africa. They began to be cultivated in Europe early in the seventeenth century. In the early eighteenth century J.J. Dillenius's book *Hortus Elthamensis* (published in England in 1732) described seven species of *Pelargonium*, but they were all referred to as *Geranium africanum*, with additional names to separate them from one another. Unlike the European cranesbills, also called *Geranium*, they had irregular flowers and the awn of the fruit always carried a plume of hairs. Dillenius considered that if, for this reason, a separate generic name was needed, they could be called *Pelargonia*. Shortly afterwards the name *Pelargonium* was adopted formally for these plants by Joannis Burman (in *Rariorum Africanorum Plantarum*, Amsterdam, 1738–9). But Linnaeus, in his *Species Plantarum* (1753), which we take as the starting point for the nomenclature of flowering plants, did not accept *Pelargonium* as distinct from *Geranium*. So all the species we now place in *Pelargonium* were called by him *Geranium*, in which he also included the plants we now call *Erodium*. There was a considerable influx of southern African plants to Europe in the eighteenth century and the pelargoniums were sufficiently numerous and striking to catch the public's attention. In view of Linnaeus' reputation and the importance of his publications, they were inevitably called *Geranium*.

It was the French magistrate and distinguished amateur botanist Charles-Louis L'Héritier de Brutelle who asserted that *Pelargonium* ought to be recognised as a separate genus and he now carried the botanical world with him. L'Héritier's work on the family achieved first publication in William Aiton's *Hortus Kewensis* (1789), in which his new genus *Erodium* was also published. This, alas, was too late to change the public's notions, and the more popular kinds of *Pelargonium* are still known as geraniums.

PUBLICATIONS ON *GERANIUM*

There has only been one world monograph of *Geranium* – that of R. Knuth (1912), published in the series *Das Pflanzenreich* and forming part of a treatment of the whole family Geraniaceae. A dip into the introduction to this work, or the account of the Geraniaceae in Hegi's *Illustrierte Flora von Mittel-Europa* (Gams, 1923–4), will show that a great deal has been written about *Geranium* – on its morphology, anatomy and physiology – and that it is nearly all in German, like these two great works in which one may trace the references. More recently, bibliographies of both *Geranium* and Geraniaceae have been published by Robertson (1972).

For taxonomic accounts of *Geranium* we must look first to two early attempts to cover all plants: Linnaeus' *Species Plantarum* (1753) (*Geranium* on pp. 676–83) and A.P. De Candolle's *Prodromus Systematis Naturalis Regni Vegetabilis* vol. 1 (1824) (*Geranium* on pp. 639–44). After these, and apart from Knuth's monograph, we have to rely mainly on regional monographs and Floras (the works in which all the plants of a country or region are described). In *Species Plantarum* there were 15 species of what we now call *Geranium*, while in the *Prodromus* there were 66. Knuth included 260-odd species and many more have been described since. Not all of these are really distinct species, but a global check-list by Aedo, Muñoz Garmendia & Pando (1998) recognises 420 species. Noteworthy regional monographs are one for Mexico and Central America by Moore (1943; additional species in Moore, 1963), one for Australasia by Carolin (1964), one for the perennials of North America by Jones and Jones (1943), one for East Africa by Kokwaro (1971), one for southern Africa by Hilliard & Burtt (1985), one for south-west China by Yeo (1992) and one for Malaysia by Veldkamp & Moerman (1978), but not all of these are of much importance for the horticulturist. In addition there is a revision of the Tuberosum Group by Davis (1970), one of the subgenus Erodioidea by Aedo (1996) and one for sections Batrachioidea and Divaricata of subgenus Robertium by Aedo, Aldasoro & Navarro (1998). The annuals of North America, including aliens from elsewhere, have been treated by Aedo (2000).

Knuth's monograph, although quite essential for the researcher, is in some ways defective. Knuth failed to classify the species satisfactorily, which means that many closely related species are described far apart in the text. In his key to the sections one may have to decide simultaneously between as many as 13 different possibilities, and the keys to species of the various sections contain frequent contradictions. Added to all this is the fact that the keys and descriptions are in Latin. Knuth's species-descriptions are, however, usually good.

Nearly all modern Floras provide quite effectively for the identification of their included species of *Geranium*.

The report of the trial of *Geranium* in the Royal Horticultural Society's Garden at Wisley, Surrey, mentioned in the Preface, appears in *The Garden*, vol. 103, Proceedings, pp. 67–71 (1978). Several authors have tried to help the horticulturist and plantsman by means of fairly cheaply produced leaflets. The non-British ones are *Hardy Geraniums*, compiled by Dennis Thompson of Seattle (1982), *Growing Geraniums and Pelargoniums in Australia and New Zealand* (Llewellyn, Hudson & Morrison, 1981), *L'essentiel sur les géraniums vivaces* by Dominique Évrard (of the Societé Nationale d'Horticulture de France, 1997) and *Geranium* by Urs Baltensperger (1997). The British ones have been supplanted by *Hardy Geraniums for the Garden* by Joy Jones *et al.* (1992), and *Hardy Geraniums, a Wisley Handbook* by David Hibberd (1994). A general view of cranesbills as garden plants is provided by *The Gardener's Guide to Growing Hardy Geraniums* by Trevor Bath and Joy Jones (David & Charles, 1994) and *Geranium für den Garten* by Coen Jansen (1997). Both are lavishly illustrated with beautiful colour plates. Books by Buczacki (1998) and Felton (2001) devote about half their space to *Geranium* and half to *Pelargonium*; they contain much information for the grower but no reliance can be placed on them for identification.

There are two check-lists available. *Geranium Family, Species Check List, edn. 4, part 2, Geranium* (1992), compiled by R.T.F. Clifton, is published by the British Pelargonium and Geranium Society (BPGS). It is a full list of names with annotations, mostly descriptive, where possible. The check-list by Aedo, Muñoz Garmendia & Pando (1998, already cited) lists the names of what are believed to be good species in the framework of a classification of the genus; the distribution of each is given by standardised geographical codes, and maps of the occurrence of the taxonomic sections are provided.

THE NATURAL OCCURRENCE OF *GERANIUM*

Whereas *Pelargonium* is essentially a genus of warm–temperate conditions, with very few species being hardy in Britain, *Geranium* is equally characteristic of cool–temperate conditions, and very few are tender in Britain. As aridity is rare in the cool–temperate parts of the world, so most cranesbills are adapted to well-watered soils. The great majority of the species, therefore, come from the temperate northern part of Eurasia and its more southerly mountain regions, and from the temperate and mountainous parts of North and South America. But practically everywhere that suitable climates are to be found *Geranium* will be found, too, including South Africa, the Arabian peninsula, the Indian peninsula, Taiwan, Indonesia, New Guinea and the Hawaiian Islands. In addition it is found in Australia (including Tasmania), New Zealand, the Azores, Canary Islands and Madeira. In the warmer parts of these regions annual species become more prevalent, as in the Mediterranean region, tropical East Africa, the Arabian peninsula and the southern part of Iran. In these areas annuals will usually pass the summer as seeds and grow through the winter. Also in the Mediterranean region and south-west Asia there are perennial species with more or less well-developed tubers and these become dormant in summer. Depending on the severity of the winters to which they are subjected the summer-dormant species begin growth either in the autumn or in the spring, and in the latter case they may have a very short growing season.

The great majority of perennial species of *Geranium* range from 30 to 120cm in height and grow in grassland and tall-herb communities such as meadows, roadsides and woodland margins, and in open woodland or low scrub (which is often an indication of rocky ground with little topsoil). Alpine species, which are usually less than 30cm tall, and always bear most of their foliage much below that height, are quite uncommon. In Europe they are represented only by the Cinereum Group. Several alpines exist in the eastern Himalayas and the mountains of western China, tropical East Africa and Central America, and in the northern Andes. It is in the last-named area that the alpine growth habit is at its most extreme.

The *Geranium* species of oceanic islands are specialised in two different ways: those of the North Atlantic islands are giant rosette herbs, with large leaves, whereas those of the Hawaiian Islands are bushy in habit and have small leaves with simplified shapes and, sometimes, veining.

THE INTRODUCTION OF CRANESBILLS INTO CULTIVATION

No one seems to have established when cranesbills were first cultivated and it seems unlikely that they ever will. The species that probably has the longest recorded history is *G. robertianum*, Herb Robert. This is because, of all European species, it is the one that has been most used for medicinal purposes. In medieval Latin it was called Herba Roberti, and the English form, 'herbe Robert', was already in use in the thirteenth century (Grigson, 1955). Gams (1923–4) states that Saint Robert or Ruprecht is said to have taught its use in medicine, but Gams suspects that all the names for *G. robertianum* which are based

on Robert or Ruprecht represent corruptions of 'herba rubra'. Grigson, however, suggests that the German name Ruprechtskraut refers to Knecht Ruprecht, a mythical servant who will protect the house if well treated (a German 'Robin Goodfellow'). Grigson shows that the species has an unusually large number of common names, so for whatever reason or reasons, it is a plant that has long attracted people's attention, and the history of the names still in use is, therefore, unlikely to be unravelled. As it is such a common plant, readily appearing around the house (at least in rural conditions) (Grigson, 1955) it is unlikely that it was deliberately cultivated, and if it was encouraged it would have been for the purpose of maintaining a supply for medicinal use. According to Gams it is, or was, used for treatment of conjunctivitis, nosebleeds, rashes, bruises, all kinds of swellings, toothache, fevers, gout and afflictions of the kidneys, lungs and genitalia. Today, *G. robertianum* is tolerated rather than cultivated (except for one or two of its variations).

Naturally enough, the longer a plant has been in cultivation, the less likely we are to have a record of when it was first introduced. Nobody can know when the first Briton placed a piece of Meadow Cranesbill (*G. pratense*), one of our finest wild flowers, in his garden simply for the joy of having it close at hand – and there are two other British natives of real garden value to which the same applies: *G. sanguineum* and *G. sylvaticum*.

It was in the late eighteenth century and the nineteenth century that authors began to seek out the earliest records of cultivation of our garden plants, and a typical example of a publication in which such dates are given is J.C. Loudon's *Hortus Britannicus* (1830, 2nd edn. 1832). In the latter there are 24 *Geranium* species which, I allow, have some garden value, and dates of first recorded cultivation are given for 21 of these. Two fall into the sixteenth century, two into the seventeenth and six into the eighteenth. The four earliest are *G. macrorrhizum* (1576), which must have been grown for its herbal or perfumery value, *G. tuberosum* (1596), *G. versicolor* (syn. *G. striatum*) (1629) and *G. argenteum* (1699). Two others which must have come in before the eighteenth century are *G. pyrenaicum*, which has become well naturalised in Britain, and *G. phaeum* (Mourning Widow). All these are European. Of the six eighteenth-century introductions, four are European, one South African and one North American. But even Loudon was able to record eleven nineteenth-century introductions, five from south-east Europe and the Caucasus, three from north and east Asia and three from the Himalayas. A trickle of new species has continued to arrive from these regions right up to the present time. One really productive area that had not been touched by the time of *Hortus Britannicus* was south-west China. The plants from this area began to come in at the beginning of the twentieth century, through the expeditions of William Purdom, George Forrest and E.H. Wilson, though the number of species was small. Surprisingly, few species from this rich area are at present in cultivation in the West, though with the re-opening of China to outside visitors some more species have been introduced from there.

A striking contribution to the geranium population of British gardens has been made by the arrival of many species from South Africa, another rich area. Their success has probably been helped by the absence of severe weather in Britain in most recent winters, but even so

they are hardier than might have been expected. They include some beautiful species of distinctive habit and foliage.

The Andean region has so far contributed little to our stock of garden cranesbills. I suspect that in the first place this is due to the difficulty of finding plants with ripe seed attached. Another factor is the notorious difficulty of cultivation of Andean alpines. However, I have grown some of Robin Parer's Peruvian alpine geraniums, and although all are now lost they should be growable, given the right kind of attention (they had silvery leaves and white flowers but they are not yet satisfactorily named).

The horticultural history of *Geranium* also includes the origin of garden hybrids, but this subject is dealt with in Chapter 7.

EARLY AND LATE

Most cranesbills begin to flower in June or early July. Those beginning to flower earlier (May or even late April) or later (mid-July onwards) are as follows:

Earlier

albiflorum (13)
antrorsum (61)
atlanticum (9)
caeruleatum (11)
deltoideum (83)
erianthum (23)
flanaganii (71)
libani (98)
linearilobum (90)
lucidum (117)
macrorrhizum (119)
macrostylum (89)
maculatum (73)
malviflorum (91)
peloponnesiacum (97)
phaeum (128)
phaeum x reflexum (129)
platyanthum (some forms) (22)
pratense var. stewartianum (16)
pseudosibiricum (12)
reflexum (130)
rivulare (10)
sylvaticum (8)
tuberosum (88)

Later

caffrum (69)
christensenianum (26)
koreanum (41)
krameri (44)
lambertii (25)
pogonanthum (34)
procurrens (27)
pulchrum (66)
robustum (64)
rubifolium (29)
sinense (31)
soboliferum (43)
swatense (30)
thunbergii (52)
wallichianum (most forms) (24)
yoshinoi (54)

Numbering of species in Chapter 9 is shown in parentheses ( ).

TALL AND SHORT

Lists of taller and shorter species are given below. Some trailing or scrambling species may be less than 25cm or more than 50cm high, according to the availability of support. A list of these is supplied as well. Annuals and biennials are omitted from these lists.

Tall

(usually more than 50cm)
atlanticum (9)
californicum (81)
maculatum (73)
maderense (127)
nervosum (some forms) (77)
palmatum (126)
phaeum (some forms) (128)
pratense (some forms) (16)
psilostemon (14)
pulchrum (66)
rubescens (96)

Extensively Trailing or Scrambling

albanum (112)
asphodeloides subsp. asphodeloides (86a)
christensenianum (26)
deltoideum (83)
lambertii (25)
lambertii x procurrens
papuanum (62)
procurrens (27)
procurrens x psilostemon (14)
robustum (64)
suzukii (57)
swatense (30)

Short

(usually less than 25cm)
sessiliflorum x traversii (59) (x antipodeum)
antrorsum (61)
caeruleatum (11)
Cinereum Group (132–148)
dalmaticum (121)
dalmaticum x macrorrhizum (x cantabrigense) (120)
endressii x sessiliflorum
endressii x traversii (x oxonianum) (2)
farreri (36)
glaberrimum (118)
incanum (68)
macrostylum (89)
nakaoanum (103)
nepalense (55)
orientali-tibeticum (49)
papuanum (62)
polyanthes (102)
pylzowianum (48)
schiedeanum (82)
sessiliflorum (60)
sibiricum (56)
stapfianum (42)
strictipes (104)
thunbergii (52)
traversii (58)

Numbering of species in Chapter 9 is shown in parentheses ( ).

"RED, WHITE AND BLUE"

The majority of *Geranium* species are some shade of pink or purplish blue. Lists of plants with deeper purplish red flowers, white flowers and blue flowers (these always lean towards violet) are given below. By no means all cranesbills fit into these groups, some having different shades, or varying patterns and combinations of colours. Some small-flowered species are omitted.

Purplish Red

argenteum x subcaulescens
   (x lindavicum):
   'Gypsy' (133)
biuncinatum (dark eye)
   (108)
caespitosum (sometimes)
   (79a)
endressii x traversii:
   'Russell Prichard' (3)
incanum (68)
kishtvariense (28)
macrorrhizum 'Bevan's
   Var.' (119)
nakaoanum (103)
ocellatum (dark eye) (81)
palustre (37)
papuanum (62)
phaeum var. phaeum x
   reflexum (129)
polyanthes (102)
procurrens (dark eye) (27)
procurrens x psilostemon
   (dark eye)
psilostemon (dark eye)
   (14)
pulchrum (66)
sanguineum (50)
stapfianum (42)
strictipes (104)
subcaulescens (dark eye)
   (140)

White

albiflorum (13)
asphodeloides (some
   forms) (86)
christensenianum (with
   purple veins) (26)
cinereum 'Album' (137)
clarkei 'Kashmir White'
   (19)
dalmaticum 'Album' (pink
   sepals) (121)
dalmaticum x
   macrorrhizum: 'Biokovo'
   (pink sepals) (120)
ibericum, white form
   (with violet veins) (93)
lambertii 'Swansdown'
   (crimson eye) (25)
macrorrhizum 'Album'
   (pink sepals) (119)
maculatum 'Album' (73)
phaeum 'Album' (128)
potentilloides (63)
pratense 'Galactic' (16)
pratense 'Plenum Album'
   (16)
pyrenaicum forma
   albiflorum (113)
refractum (some forms)
   (33)
richardsonii (80)
rivulare (10)
robertianum 'Album'
   (brown sepals) (123)
robertianum 'Celtic
   White' (123)
sanguineum 'Album' (55)
sessiliflorum (60)
sylvaticum forma
   albiflorum (8)
sylvaticum 'Album' (8)
thunbergii (some forms)
   (52)

Blue

erianthum (23)
gymnocaulon (95)
himalayense (20)
himalayense x pratense
libani (98)
malviflorum (some forms)
   (91)
peloponnesiacum (97)

platypetalum (92)
pratense (16)
pseudosibiricum (12)
saxatile (21)

Numbering of species in
Chapter 9 is shown in
parentheses ( ).

NORTH AND SOUTH

The majority of the larger-growing species of *Geranium* are likely to flourish better where summers are cooler, or rainfall is higher, than in the hotter south-east of England. I observed long ago that some of the more popular species grow well in the railway station gardens of Inverness-shire and I am told by Mr Alan Bremner that some, at least, grow well in the Orkney Isles, where *G. pratense* has escaped from cultivation into the wild. Mr Jack Drake, of Aviemore, Inverness-shire, was experienced with the lower-growing species and hybrids and found that many grow well, including *G. sanguineum* forms and the Cinereum Group. It is probably about this latitude, however, that noticeable limitations on what can be grown compared with southern England begin to make themselves felt. *G. wallichianum* has been a failure at Aviemore though I have seen it at the University Botanic Garden of Aberdeen. Mr Drake found that *G. dalmaticum* only flowers well at Aviemore if grown on the sunny side of a wall, and *G. himalayense* does not produce enough flowers to make it worth growing.

Although most species are in fact hardy in at least the greater part of the British Isles, a few are marginally hardy or slightly tender and in the colder parts of the country these species will be impossible, or will be lost intermittently. Plants in these categories are some *G. traversii* hybrids, *G. incanum*, *G. palmatum*, *G. polyanthes* and *G. suzukii*. The charming dwarf trailing species, *G. papuanum*, hardly stands any frost at all.

I suspect there is nowhere in the inhabited parts of the British Isles where some *Geranium* species cannot be grown, and it seems that over a considerable part of this area climatic variation does not noticeably limit the possibilities.

OUTSIDE THE BRITISH ISLES

Most of the inland parts of the British Isles come into Hardiness Zone H4 of *The European Garden Flora* (Walters *et al.*, 1984), with a mean minimum of $-5°C$ to $-10°C$; the extreme minimum in the

British Isles is around -20°C. As most *Geranium* species are considered generally hardy in the British Isles they will survive at least this minimum. This places them in hardiness Zone 4 of the United States Department of Agriculture, in which temperatures down to -18°C may be expected for up to a week at a time. Many will survive a lower minimum; *Geranium* species native to the United States and Canada, eastern Europe and most of northern Asia together with many from the Himalayas and western China will be among these hardier plants. In any case, conditions for the plants are ameliorated if there is a good cover of snow.

Species which do not always survive the winter in inland Britain are *G. incanum*, *G. suzukii*, *G. traversii* (and also its hybrids), *G. palmatum*, *G. canariense* and *G. maderense*. These will only be reasonably safe in Zone H5 for Europe (mean winter minimum down to -5°C) or Zone 6 in North America, except perhaps *G. maderense* which can probably survive -5°C if hardened off progressively but would not survive the coldest winters experienced in this zone. A few other species, among them *G. polyanthes*, are suspected of not being very hardy in Britain.

Most *Geranium* species are certain to be winter-hardy in the lowlands of the cooler parts of Australia and New Zealand. In the parts of these countries (and the USA) where frost is rare, summers are likely to be too hot or too dry or both (unless lack of frost is due to oceanic westerly winds). I give below a list of species mentioned for California, the warmer parts of New Zealand, and for Australia (Sydney, New South Wales, and Stirling, South Australia) by my correspondents in these areas as being at least reasonably easy to grow:

G. cinereum x subcaulescens: 'Ballerina' (141)
G. dalmaticum (121)
G. incanum (68)
G. macrorrhizum (119)
G. maculatum (73)
G. pratense (16)
G. sanguineum (50)
G. thunbergii (52)

It will be noticed that these include some of the species that are not fully winter-hardy in Britain, together with *G. sanguineum* which grows in hot dry situations, and some Mediterranean species. Mr Trevor Nottle, of Stirling, South Australia, where the winter temperature is rarely below 0°C, and the summer temperature goes to $34\text{--}38^\circ$C, has succeeded with a much wider range of *Geranium* species and hybrids, in some cases using the shade of a wall or an insulating layer of cobbles.

PROPAGATION

Most perennial *Geranium* species have fibrous root systems and so are easily propagated by division of the rootstock, as with most other perennial herbaceous plants. Those with tuberous roots are easily propagated by separating the tubers. Pieces of rhizome of the rhizomatous species can be broken or cut away and potted up; they will soon put up new leaves and roots and grow away. A fourth group, those with thick woody rootstocks, are a little more difficult. In these, leafy shoots should be taken at or just below soil level in early spring or summer. Any flower buds and lower leaves should be stripped from the shoots and they should then be placed in a well-drained rooting mixture, such as Perlite and sharp sand, in a shady spot. Rooting should occur in a few weeks and they can then be potted on. In the Cinereum Group root-cuttings may be tried. If this does not succeed it may be necessary to sow seed, but this should be done with cognisance of the possibilities of hybridisation.

As explained in Chapter 4, the branching, short-lived, above-ground stems of *Geranium* are really inflorescences and in most species they cannot be rooted. In a few, however, there is no rosette and nearly all the foliage leaves are borne on these flowering stems, which are more persistent than is the rule and can be rooted. Examples are *G. sanguineum*, most South African species and *G. wallichianum*. As some South African species are not quite hardy in most of Britain and *G. wallichianum* is difficult to move, propagation by cuttings may be a useful method. Flowering pieces of *G. x antipodeum* can be rooted even though the plant is not without a rosette; the rooted pieces simply continue to flower until winter and then form a rosette. *G. procurrens* is most unusual in that its flowering stems run along the ground and take root; *G. christensemianum* is similar. Plenty of new plants can be obtained in this way. However, the *procurrens* hybrid, 'Ann Folkard', does not root itself readily.

Seed of *Geranium* is not difficult to collect provided one looks for those fruits in which the rostrum is turning brown but has not yet exploded. Collect them after early morning dew has cleared. Place them in a large puffed-out envelope or a cardboard box where they can explode and release their seeds. In most cases the seeds need a few months of after-ripening before germination is possible. At this period keep them in paper bags in cool conditions (say, the salad compartment of a refrigerator). Sow in early winter in a cool house or in early spring in the open. Germination may be prolonged, and the main flush may not take place until spring. A very few species may be reluctant to germinate at all. The seeds of the blue-flowered biennial, *G. bohemicum*, mostly germinate after fires. If seed in the soil is reluctant to germinate, light a small fire over the site and soon afterwards there will be a new crop of seedlings.

To check for any other special requirements as to use or propagation, refer to the account of the species concerned.

DISEASES AND PESTS

Geranium is relatively disease-free. *G. canariense* occasionally seems to carry a virus causing distortion of the flowers, and this may be transferred to such related plants as *G. rubescens* and *G. maderense*. Affected plants should be destroyed and new stock grown from seed; any deformed plants in the progeny should also be destroyed. Some species may serve as hosts for white-fly and aphides but infestations of plants out of doors are not usually serious. The thick rootstocks and frequently thick roots provide an ideal habitat for the larvae of craneflies (Tipulids), the yellow-underwing moth and certain beetles such as the vine weevil (*Otiorrhynchus sulcatus*) (Clifton, 1979). These may seriously weaken plants in pots or may even kill them. Wilted or snipped-off leaves and poor growth are the symptoms. Infested pots should be tipped out and the insects removed. Plants should be re-potted in fresh soil with added insecticide. For plants in the open one should take the precaution of establishing a number of separate plants as soon as possible after acquisition. Another pest which I have observed is a small caterpillar which lives on the undersides of the leaves and eats numerous elliptical holes in them. I have no remedy for this.

AWARD OF GARDEN MERIT

Current lists of plants that have received the Award of Garden Merit can be found in *The AGM Handbook*. The Award is given to plants "of outstanding excellence for garden decoration or use" that are "available in the trade", are "of good constitution" and "require neither highly specialised growing conditions nor care". The

labels of AGM plants for sale to the public should show an icon in the form of a two-handled cup trophy. The list is maintained by the Royal Horticultural Society and is obtainable from RHS Enterprises, RHS Garden Wisley, Woking, Surrey, GU23 6QB, UK. The AGM list is also available on CD–ROM (see below).

SOURCES

Information technology has seen immense changes since 1985, and they are continuing. Huge amounts of information can be stored on laser disk (and new forms of magnetic disk) which means bulky annual references like *The RHS Plant Finder* can be made available manageably. This massive directory of British and Irish nurseries and the plants they stock is now available on a compact disc (CD–ROM). Earlier editions of the CD–ROM were called *The Plant Finder Reference Library*, and also embraced *The National Plant Collections Directory*, detailing the current holders of National Collections under the auspices of the National Council for the Conservation of Plants and Gardens, *The Seed Search*, compiled, edited and published by Karen Platt, Sheffield, and several other data files, including UK and International Garden Societies. A recent edition incorporates *Award of Garden Merit Plants* (see above), the *RHS Good Plant Guide, Garden Societies* and *UK Gardens* open to the public. Cultivar registers (ICNCP – see Chapter 3), the *National Plant Collections Directory* (NCCPG) and some other files are available on the *Professional Edition* to which the standard edition can be upgraded at extra cost. The publisher is The Plant Press, Freepost, Lewes, BN7 2ZZ.

At the time of writing, *The National Plant Collections Directory* also has a website: http://www.nccp.org.uk and an E-mail address: collections@nccpg.org.uk).

In 2000 Mr Andrew Norton, holder of one of the national collections of *Geranium*, started up a website, which contains illustrations and information under a variety of headings and provides the opportunity to 'talk' to other enthusiasts. The address of the site is http://www. hardygeraniums.org

Chapter 3
Nomenclature

Classification consists of putting objects into groups. In biological classification – but not only in biological classification – similar individuals are placed in groups and similar groups are arranged into higher groups, and so on. The process continues upwards, forming a hierarchy embracing, in the case of a biological classification, all living things. The groups at the different levels are called categories; for example, "species", "genus" and "family" are categories. Each category is said to have a rank; thus a genus has a lower rank than a family but a higher rank than a species. The two words "family" and "variety" are commonly used in a loose sense by laymen in talking about plants and animals, and it is important to remember that in biology these words are used for particular categories with their own definite ranks. Note that "species" is the same in both the singular and plural and that the plural of "genus" is "genera".

Nomenclature is the process of putting names to the various groups which one wishes to recognise at the various ranks. Named groups are called *"taxa"* (singular *"taxon"*). Nomenclature makes classification explicit, and as classifications vary, so names change. Thus, what for Linnaeus was *Geranium* became for L'Héritier *Geranium*, *Pelargonium* and *Erodium*. Similarly, what for Boissier was *G. crenophilum* became for Bornmüller *G. asphodeloides* subspecies *crenophilum*; where Rydberg saw a distinct species, *G. strigosum*, and Royle another, *G. lindleyanum*, most botanists nowadays see only *G. nervosum* and *G. robertianum* respectively. On the other hand, although Knuth took a similar view of *G. canariense*, equating it with *G. anemonifolium*, which was first described from Madeira, those who have seen the Madeiran plant and its Canarian counterpart in the living state have no doubt that the two are distinct species. The freedom to reclassify is essential in order that we may take into account new knowledge, and to annul the excesses or rectify the faults of observation of our predecessors. But whatever the facts at our disposal, the use we make of them in producing a classification is the result of a series of personal decisions. Sometimes we feel we have to annul the excesses and rectify the faults even of our

contemporaries! Contemporary classifications can and do differ, and the bystander who has not time to make his own detailed studies must make some more or less arbitrary decision as to which of them to follow. The process of classification is called taxonomy, and the changes of name, and of the sense of names, mentioned above are taxonomic changes. Taxonomy is never correct or incorrect; it is merely more or less reasonable or acceptable.

A kind of mistake which deserves separate mention is the misapplication of names. For example, cultivated plants from Kingdon Ward's collection, no. 22796, from Burma, were at first thought by me and other botanists to be *G. yunnanense*. Now, however, I am sure they are *G. pogonanthum*. Another case is that of *G. malviflorum* which was depicted in *Curtis's Botanical Magazine* as *G. atlanticum*. This kind of error can quite easily be corrected by re-labelling the specimens which exist in a few great herbaria, but it will probably persist in the naming of the plants in cultivation for a very long time (as in fact happened with the second example). Although in these cases (professional) botanists were implicated in the original misapplication of the name, it is a kind of error that is easily made by the amateur botanist or horticulturist in attempting his own identifications, or even by the gardener who lets his labels become switched when sowing his seeds or some time thereafter. Misapplied names are not synonyms and are not shown as such in this book.

The application of scientific names of plants is regulated by the *International Code of Botanical Nomenclature 2000* (Greuter, *et al.*, 2000). This states that for a name to be acceptable it must meet certain conditions of publication ("effective publication"), so as to make sure it is available to the botanical public, and certain conditions for "valid publication", so that others may verify how the name is to be applied. The two most important conditions for valid publication are that the name be accompanied by or related to an effectively published description, and that a "type" (usually a *"type-specimen"*) be indicated. Within this framework the principle of priority is maintained. Thus, the earliest name which fulfils all the conditions laid down is the correct one (i.e. nomenclaturally correct).

Priority does, however, imply a starting point, and for most plants this is the publication date of Linnaeus' *Species Plantarum* in 1753; in that work binary names (two-word names, see next paragraph) for species were first consistently adopted. There is no doubt that we must have a Code, but a code should, ideally, be unchanging. Unfortunately, so much plant nomenclature was already in existence by the time people started to frame rules that there was no alternative to trying to legalise the best practice of the time. So the Code has evolved over a long time, incorporating many changes in an attempt to take care of previously unforeseen contingencies as well as being subject to occasional major changes of policy. Although the intention of the *International Code of Botanical Nomenclature* is to promote stability, name-changes for "nomenclatural" reasons (i.e. non-taxonomic reasons) do take place, and they have four main causes: (1) a previously overlooked prior name is discovered; (2) the Code is changed; (3) a long-used name is for the first time examined in the light of the Code and found to infringe the rules; and (4) an author infringes the rules embodied in the Code in force at the time of writing; this may happen through more or less blatant disregard for the Code or by an honest failure to interpret rules correctly. Similar to (1) is the case where fresh information comes to light about precise dates of publication of two names for the same plant, whereby their priority is reversed. Names overthrown for any of the reasons given above become synonyms of the correct name.

The name of a species consists of two words, the generic name (written with a capital initial letter) and the specific epithet (written with a small initial letter). Sometimes it is felt necessary taxonomically to divide a species, and the principal categories of lower rank used for this purpose are, in order of descending rank, subspecies ("subsp." or "ssp."), variety ("var.") forma ("f."). (However, when the English "form" is used in this book it means a variant of unspecified rank.) When a plant in one of these so-called "infraspecific" categories is named, a term denoting the category must always be included, as was done in the example above of *G. asphodeloides* subsp. *crenophilum*.

The species of a genus may be arranged in groups of lower rank than genus; several categories are available for this purpose, those used in this book being subgenus ("subg."), section ("sect.") and subsection ("subsect."). Here the term denoting the category must be included in the name, for example *Geranium* sect. *Tuberosa*. The epithet of a subdivision of a genus always has a capital initial letter.

Hybrids are of great importance in horticulture, and they may be referred to by the use of a hybrid formula, thus: *G. ibericum* x *G. platypetalum*. It may be convenient, however, to have a name for a hybrid, and the name *G.* x *magnificum* has been provided for this particular hybrid. Such names are in Latin form and subject to the regulations of the *International Code of Botanical Nomenclature*. They are part of the corpus of botanical nomenclature, which means that they must conform to all the rules, and the name for a hybrid cannot be the same as the name of a non-hybrid group (for example, species) of the same rank. All this means that after a new hybrid has arisen, its naming must await the decision of someone conversant with the rules to get on with the job of describing it in Latin and publishing it in a suitable place. However, this delay may be avoided by the use of cultivar names (see below).

When different individuals from the same two parent species are crossed, the progeny are likely to be different. Some hybrids are fertile, and when they are self-fertilised, crossed with their sisters, or crossed back to their parents, a burst of much more extreme variation is usually released. Nevertheless, the formula, or the name of the interspecific hybrid, covers all individuals which are known or reasonably believed to be descended from the crossing of the two named parent species. This does not mean, however, that such variation has to go unrecognised, as will be explained shortly.

This rule about the applicability of botanical names for hybrids interacts with taxonomic changes. Thus when *G. cinereum* was circumscribed as comprising a number of botanical varieties, as in edn.1, the name *G.* x *lindavicum* covered hybrids of any of them with *G. argenteum*. Now that the *cinereum* parent is treated as a species in its own right, namely *G. subcaulescens* (as, in fact, it was when *G.* x *lindavicum* was described), only crosses between *G. argenteum* and *G. subcaulescens* can be included.

The exact meaning of the word 'hybrid' depends on the context. A hybrid can be the result of a cross between any two individuals which differ genetically. To make matters more precise, we can talk about an interspecific hybrid, for example. If we refer to a hybrid between *Geranium ibericum* and *G. platypetalum* it probably means we are talking about a single individual (of an interspecific hybrid). If we say "*Geranium* x *magnificum* is a hybrid between *G. ibericum* and *G. platypetalum*", we are talking about all the individuals which might ever arise from the crossing of the two named parent species. However, in the 1983 edition of the *International Code of Botanical Nomenclature* (Voss, *et al.*, 1983) a new term for such an assemblage of individuals was introduced, namely "Nothospecies" (literally "hybrid-species"). Similarly, it will be possible to refer, for example, to "nothosubspecies" or, in general, "nothotaxa". There is, however, absolutely no requirement to publish nothospecies names for interspecific crosses; cases should be considered on their own merits, bearing in mind that confusion rather than clarity might be the result of having too many "notho-" names (note that only one has been added in this book).

The use of authors' names after plant names makes the name complete, preventing confusion in instances where the same name has been published for two or more different species. For example, Knuth (1912) included in his monograph both *G. platypetalum* Fischer & Meyer, and *G. platypetalum* Franchet. This, naturally enough, is not allowed by the Code. Knuth apparently spotted the mistake at the last moment and in the addenda at the end of the monograph he supplied a fresh name, *G. sinense* Knuth, as a replacement for *G. platypetalum* Franchet which is the later of the two identical names ("homonyms"). A similar case is provided by the name *G. grandiflorum* Edgeworth. Before Edgeworth described this Himalayan plant which has become so well known in gardens, the same name had been used for different plants by several authors, of whom the earliest was Linnaeus. Linnaeus' *G. grandiflorum* is not even a member of the family Geraniaceae so it will never be used for a *Geranium* again: nevertheless the rules say that the later homonyms may not be used. The author citation for our cranesbill is, therefore, *G. grandiflorum* Edgeworth not Linnaeus. That this name infringed the rules was first noticed by Hylander; he dealt with the matter by seeking an independently published name for the same plant, and he found *G. meeboldii* Briquet. He therefore stated (Hylander, 1960) that this was the correct name for *G. grandiflorum* Edgeworth. However, some time later Schönbeck-Temesy (1970) took the view that the name *G. himalayense* Klotzsch also applied to the same plant and, as it was of earlier date, it should therefore be adopted. The problem with this name is that there is no type specimen and the original description and illustration are very incomplete. Knuth (1912) had considered it to be a synonym of *G. pratense*. However, on the evidence available, I support Schönbeck-Temesy's view, so *G. himalayense* is the name adopted in this book. By tradition many author-names are abbreviated and so may appear cryptic to the outsider; in this book, therefore, they are not abbreviated. To find out if a name already exists, botanists refer to *Index Kewensis*, a serial publication which shows the names that have been published for seed plants since the starting date in 1753. *Index Kewensis* (which initially did not list names in ranks below that of species) is now available on compact disc

and on-line. In both cases, it has been combined with two other major plant-name catalogues under the title *International Plant Names Index*, web-site: http:/www.uk.ipni.org/

Frequently the reader will encounter double author citations, that is, a name or names within parentheses and another name or other names outside them, thus (taking a plant name already mentioned): *G. asphodeloides* N.L. Burman subsp. *crenophilum* (Boissier) Bornmüller. This reflects the fact that Boissier described the plant as a species and Bornmüller regarded it as a subspecies (that is, he changed its rank downwards). Such double citations are required also for upward changes of rank and for "sideways" movements, for example the transfer of a subspecies out of one species and into another.

The kind of variation which is found among individuals arising from the crossing of two named species (or other taxa) is dealt with – in the case of cultivated plants – by the *International Code of Nomenclature for Cultivated Plants* (ICNCP) (Trehane, *et al.*, 1995). As far as this book is concerned, the only category in this code which we need to use is that of "cultivar". The definition of cultivar can vary according to the nature of the plants concerned. Thus for annuals and biennials it is normally a sexually reproducing group in which certain specified characters are maintained from generation to generation. In woody plants and perennial herbs a cultivar is normally a clone and there is not much point in trying to apply cultivar nomenclature unless the clones are distinguishable. However, there are cases in *Geranium* where perennials which vary within narrow limits when grown from seed are treated as cultivars (examples are *G.* x *oxonianum* 'Claridge Druce' and *G. wallichianum* 'Buxton's Variety'). As is shown by the second of these examples, cultivar nomenclature is applicable not only to the results of hybridisation but also to variants of species (or indeed taxa of other ranks) which may arise in cultivation or are brought into cultivation from the wild (see the interesting case of *G. wallichianum* 'Syabru', species number 24, in Chapter 9). Like the botanical code, the code for cultivated plants adopts the principle of priority and lays down certain requirements for the publication of names and the ways in which names are to be formed. Cultivar epithets must be names in common language unless they were published before 1 January 1959 (in which case they may be in Latin) or unless they were published in conformity with the botanical code for plants which are now considered to be cultivars. In all cases they must be typographically distinguished from botanical names and this is normally done by giving them capital initial letters, by placing single quotation marks around them and by not printing them in italics. The cultivar epithet has to be attached to what is called a "collective name" and this is most often a botanical name in the rank of genus or below. In *Geranium* the collective name is nearly always that of a species or interspecific hybrid (nothospecies) or is a hybrid formula (in which case it is a good idea to place a colon between the formula and the cultivar epithet).

Typical examples of cultivar names appear in the preceding paragraph. Attachment of the cultivar epithet to the generic name is seen in *Geranium* 'Russell Prichard', a hybrid of which the parents have long been doubt. The current proliferation of cultivars, often hybrids of doubtful and/or complex parentage, means that names of this form are being used increasingly.

The freedom to attach a cultivar epithet to a collective name in any of the above forms means that when a new hybrid arises it may be named as a cultivar even if there is no Latin name for the hybrid as such. The conditions for valid publication laid down by the code for cultivated plants are easier to meet than those in the botanical code, and anyone who studies the ICNCP carefully should be able to carry out valid publication of new cultivar names.

The ICNCP provides for the establishment of International Registration Authorities which keep lists of cultivar names (valid and invalid) for particular groups of plants. One for *Geranium* and *Erodium* has been set up under the auspices of the Geraniaceae Group of the British Pelargonium and Geranium Society. The Registrar is Mr David Victor, The Old Stables, Church Lane, Hockliffe, Leighton Buzzard, Bedfordshire, LU7 9NL, England. New cultivars should be registered; suitable publication is one step in this process. Anyone wishing to publish a new cultivar epithet in *Geranium* should consult the Registrar.

I have deliberately kept this chapter very brief because more detailed explanations of the rules of nomenclature are readily available elsewhere. The most complete coverage is in Jeffrey (1989). Accounts directed especially at the horticulturist are those of McClintock (1980) and Rowley (1980: chapter entitled "How plants are named"). More detailed information based on both codes is found in *The RHS Plant Finder* mentioned at the end of Chapter 2 (section on *The Naming of Plants*; in the CD–ROM version you may have to use the "Help" file in the body of the directory to access it). The practice of taxonomy is described by Jeffrey (1982).

Chapter 4
Structure and Terminology

CONSTRUCTION OF THE *GERANIUM* PLANT

Those aspects of the structure of the *Geranium* plant most relevant to its identification are described here. The description of the structure does not attempt to cover every variation, and exceptions to some of the statements will easily be discovered by anyone deeply involved with cranesbills. Many of these will be accounted for in the individual species-descriptions.

It is necessary to read the whole of this chapter to prepare oneself to use the later parts of the book. A pocket lens with a magnification of about eight times is required for looking at hairs on the plant and the sculpture of the ripe carpels.

Terms and expressions which are defined here are italicised. Definitions of other technical terms used in this chapter will be found in the glossary. Although my plant descriptions are long and detailed, I have tried to keep the language as simple and familiar as possible.

ROOTS AND STEMS

The plant consists essentially of roots, a vegetative stem and a flowering stem. The difference between the two types of stem is best understood by considering one of the overwintering annual species such as *G. robertianum* in the early stages of flowering. The plant will be found to have a

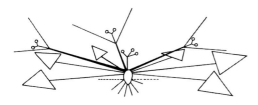

Figure 4.1 Diagram of a rosette-forming annual *Geranium* plant. The short central stem produces many leaves crowded into a rosette; these leaves are shown as triangles. Flowering stems grow out from the axils of the upper rosette-leaves; each internode terminates in a pair of leaves (not shown), two axillary branches and a cymule. The central stem bears a three-flowered cymule (see p. 22)

rosette of leaves crowded on to a much abbreviated rooted stem (Figure 4.1). From the axils of the uppermost leaves arises a group of radiating flowering branches. Each of these begins with an internode which bears a pair of *opposite* leaves at the top. Between the bases of these leaves (that is, in their axils) arises a pair of branches and between these a pair of flowers. The branches behave in exactly the same way as the first group of branches (Figure 4.4). Indefinite continuation of this system of forking would double the number of branches at every node, producing a dense and tangled branch system and probable overcrowding of leaves and flowers. However, in *G. robertianum* possible congestion is often reduced by inequality in thickness and length of the branches of a pair; this inequality increases upwards until the stage is reached at which one branch remains as a dormant bud. In some perennial species there are only a few forking nodes and the leaves diminish in size very rapidly, becoming mere *bracts*, with a simplified outline.

An alternative way for annual species to develop is by the production of a few extended internodes below the group of radiating branches (Figure 4.2). In some annual species, such as *G. ocellatum*, there is no rosette and no visible differentiation into the two types of stem described above.

Although the forking stems potentially bear a pair of flowers at every node, those at the first node, or the first few nodes, are often suppressed. Nevertheless, it seems that the forking stems are in fact the flowering stems, being essentially different in their behaviour and shorter life span from the first-formed, rosette-bearing stems. However, I shall, in this book, use the term *inflorescence* for that part of the branch system which bears flowers – that is, omitting those nodes in which the potential flowers do not develop.

In perennial species the roots sent out by the initially formed, rosette-bearing stem often pull it into an oblique or horizontal attitude. The stem continues to grow in length, and it goes on producing leaves after the emission of the flowering stems (Figure 4.3). Then, when it is ready to flower again, more flowering stems

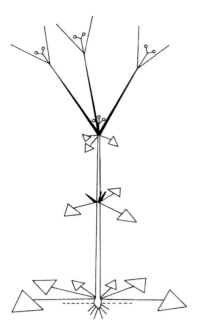

Figure 4.2 Diagrammatic representation of a rosette-forming annual *Geranium* plant that produces an elongated central stem from which the flowering branches arise. Note the three-flowered cymule at the top of the central stem

appear in the axils of some of the newer leaves. The rooted stem forms the *rootstock*, which is often woody. This usually grows slowly, with very short internodes, but with longer internodes it can vary to become a stout rhizome or tuber or, in extreme cases, a far-creeping under-ground stolon. In some perennial species, for example *G. sanguineum* and *G. wallichianum*, there are so few leaves on the rootstock that one cannot talk

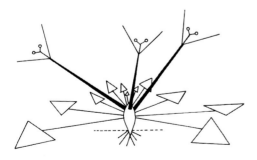

Figure 4.3 Diagrammatic representation of a rosette-forming perennial *Geranium* of compact growth. The short central stem continues to grow after the flowering stems have developed, producing more leaves and eventually more flowering stems (not shown); it usually becomes horizontal or oblique

of a rosette and most of the foliage is borne on the flowering stems. In many South African species there is no real cessation of growth in winter and here again the distinction between the vegetative and the flowering stems is not evident.

There are several ways in which the basic plan of branching in *Geranium* is modified. Sometimes the internode of one member of each pair of branches is suppressed (Figure 4.4); this is not tantamount to the suppression of that shoot, for the pair of leaves which should be produced at the top of the internode unfolds and rests against the preceding leaf. From its axils

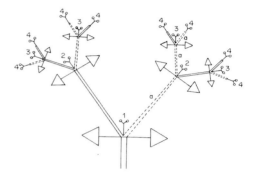

Figure 4.4 Basic plan of *Geranium* inflorescence. Leaves and lateral branches are omitted after the third level of branching. The system is capable of indefinite continuation; in its natural condition it is three-dimensional. Internodes shown by dashed lines may be suppressed

arise one normal shoot and one with a suppressed internode, and so on. Some species produce single-leaved nodes and in this book the leaves so borne are described as *solitary*; at such nodes there may be one branch or two, or one branch and a flower-pair.

The production of flowers in pairs is characteristic of *Geranium*. The two flower-stalks (*pedicels*) arise at the top of a common stalk, the *peduncle*, where there are four *bracteoles* (lesser bracts). The two-flowered unit is referred to as a *cymule*. Some species occasionally or consistently produce one-flowered cymules. In *G. sanguineum* these always have a peduncle, whereas in *G. sibiricum* the peduncle is sometimes suppressed, and the flower is then borne on a stalk with no joint and no bracteoles. Occasionally, three-flowered cymules may be seen.

The type of inflorescence seen in *G. robertianum* may be described as *diffuse*, for the shoot has a prolonged development, producing a succession of flower-pairs over a long period. Flowering finally

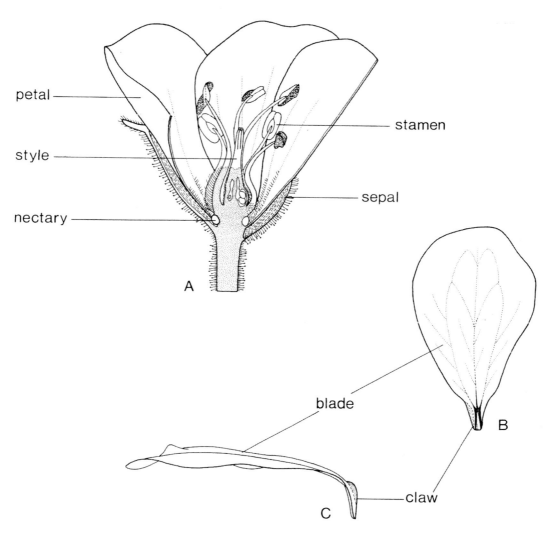

petal —

style —

nectary —

stamen

sepal

A

blade

B

claw

C

Figure 4.5 (A) Section through flower of *Geranium sylvaticum* in which the stigmas have not yet diverged; note the pinheaded glandular hairs on the pedicel (stalk) and sepals; (B) & (C) side and surface views of a petal which has a claw and a blade (*G. palmatum*), the claw being distinguished mainly by structure and its angle with the blade (usually the junction of claw and blade is more obvious in the outline than here)

ceases when neither of the two axillary buds flanking a cymule grows out. In diffuse inflorescences, the leaves become very gradually reduced in size and complexity of lobing. Contrasted with the diffuse inflorescence is the *dense* type. This makes a striking display of flowers over a relatively short period. Various modifications may contribute to this. Where there is suppression of internodes, as described above, some of the flower-pairs are inevitably brought closer together; if the later ones become increasingly advanced in their development, they flower in quick succession and before they can be smothered by the growth of the shoots which did not have suppressed internodes. In more normal systems a similar advance in the timing of flowers at later nodes, combined with a rapid decrease of leaf-size and internode-length, can also give rise to a dense inflorescence. The end of

flowering in dense inflorescences may result from the non-growth of an axillary bud but sometimes cymules take the place of ordinary branches. In some species the peduncles of the later cymules, and apparently some of the internodes supporting them, are suppressed. We then find a cluster of unjointed flower-stalks (pedicels) arising from a single point, producing an *umbel-like* grouping (this happens in *G. erianthum*).

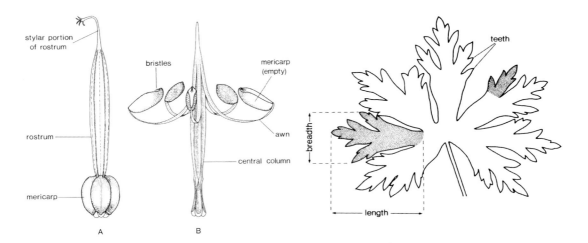

Figure 4.6 The parts of the fruit of *Geranium*: (A) when nearly mature; (B) after discharge. This is a seed-ejecting type with retention of the seed in the pre-explosive interval by a tuft of bristles (see Chapter 5)

Figure 4.7 Leaf-blade of *Geranium* with a *division* shaded on the left and a *lobe* shaded on the right; in this example the divisions are palmato-pinnately lobed

FLOWERS AND FRUITS

The flower structure in *Geranium* is very uniform (Figure 4.5). There are five sepals, five petals, 10 stamens in two whorls and five carpels. The sepals are overlapping and unequal, usually differing in the size of their papery margins. They always have a projecting point (the *mucro*) at the tip. The petals are variously shaped and may or may not have an apical notch. In a few cases the petal is divisible into a stalk (or *claw*) and a blade (Figure 4.5 B, C). The stamens in the outer whorl are placed opposite the petals. At the base of each inner stamen is a swollen gland, the *nectary*. These can be exposed to view by detaching the sepals and petals, and each will usually be found to be encased in a glistening drop of nectar. The five carpels are joined to a central column but not to each other; they are topped by a common style, which is thickened at the base and divided at the top into five stigmatic branches with the receptive (stigmatic) surface on the inner side (the branches are referred to as *stigmas* in this book). The five carpel-chambers each contain two ovules, of which only one normally develops into a seed. The fruit is dry when ripe.

When the flower has opened, the anthers of the five outer stamens soon burst. Later (perhaps the next day) the other five burst. After this (often after another day's delay) the stigmas, which have hitherto remained straight and pressed against each other (Figure 4.5), curl back and are for the first time receptive to pollen (Figure 9.69D). The flower

therefore has definite *male and female stages*. However, this applies only to the larger-flowered species which are adapted to cross-pollination by insects. In small-flowered species the inner anthers may burst only an hour or two later than the outer, and the stigmas spread at about the same time as the flower opens. Such flowers are mainly self-pollinated, though they retain the potentiality for being cross-pollinated.

After fertilisation there is a rapid growth in length of the thickened base of the style to form the *rostrum* (Figure 4.6A). The seeds are dispersed by the explosive break-up of the rostrum as it dries out: five horny strips (the *awns*) – one for each carpel – suddenly peel away from the bottom upwards, leaving behind a *central column* (Figure 4.6B). Before this happens, the carpel is gently freed from the lower part of the central column and then remains attached only to the lower end of its awn. Thus, when the awns move, the carpels move. The genus is sharply divided into three groups according to the manner in which the seeds are despatched; the details will be found in Chapter 5. The separated carpels derived from a fruit which splits up as in *Geranium* are called *mericarps*.

DESCRIPTIVE CONVENTIONS

The following conventions have been adopted for the description of plants in Chapter 9 and for use in the keys in Chapter 8.

Dimensions. An unqualified measurement always refers to length.

The Leaf. In all our species the leaf is palmate and stipules are present. The primary segments are each called *divisions*. Each division is usually *lobed* and the lobes bear *teeth*. If the cutting of the divisions is very uniform it is considered that they have teeth but no lobes. In a few species the lobes have no teeth. The ways of reckoning the length and breadth of lobes are shown in Figure 4.7. It will be seen that the width of a division includes the lobes and the width of a lobe includes the teeth. When counting the teeth on a lobe the tip of the lobe should be ignored.

Where the lobes are very narrow they are not contiguously arranged on the division, and the same applies to narrow teeth on the lobes (Figure 9.57). When this is the case the width of the divisions (defined as above) is irrelevant; what is significant is the width of the portions of the divisions lying between successive pairs of lobes. The same applies to parts of lobes between successive pairs of teeth. These widths are not likely to differ much within the leaf. In this case *all* these parts are referred to as *segments*. (The use of the terms division, lobe, tooth and segment as explained here is standardised in this way only in this book.)

Each leaf-division has a broadest point somewhere above the base. If it is at the apex, the latter has a more or less cut-off or rounded appearance and the overall outline of the leaf will be rather even, and rounded, kidney-shaped or weakly angled (Figures 9.8 and 9.47 show examples). More usually the broadest point is below the apex and the division is then tapered in both directions. The nearer the widest point is to the apex, the more briefly and abruptly is the division tapered beyond its widest point.

A consequence of having the broadest point at or near the apex is that the lobes are apical; in fact they have a palmate arrangement, to the extent that this is possible in a relatively narrow organ. Other arrangements of the lobes occur when the widest point is some way down from the apex. Occasionally, but usually only when the lobing extends down the sides of the division below the widest point, the lobing is pinnate. Most commonly, however, the lobing is confined to the portion beyond the widest part and is of an intermediate type: *palmato-pinnate* (as in Figure 4.7).

Leaf-size. This is measured by width which is sometimes indicated approximately as a range based on units of 5 or 10cm, e.g.

not more than 5cm
between 5 and 10cm
between 10 and 20cm
more than 20cm.

Size is given for the largest leaves, which are usually the basal (rosette) leaves or the lower stem leaves. If the largest leaves are usually on the borderline between two ranges the size is given as "about 10cm" (etc., as the case may be). As leaf-size is very flexible, allowance has to be made for exceptional sizes resulting from exceptional growing conditions. Most gardeners will probably find that my measurements for leaf size are usually on the low side.

Hairs. The only parts of a *Geranium* plant which never seem to have hairs are the anthers, the stigmatic surfaces and the seed-coats. Descriptions of the hair-covering are therefore sometimes omitted. The hair-distribution on petals or stamens will, in fact, almost always be mentioned, because it is more or less characteristic for the species. *Glandular hairs* are those with a rounded, usually spherically swollen and often red tip (Figure 4.5A). Hairs without this are called *eglandular*. Examination with a strong lens will often show that a *Geranium* plant is beset with very tiny glandular hairs. These are not usually mentioned in the descriptions, and if glandular hairs are mentioned, one should look for sizeable ones, similar in size to the pointed eglandular hairs which will usually also be present.

Flower Posture. The posture of the flower bud is not very important, although there are exceptions to the usual nodding posture. The commonest posture of the open flower is upwardly inclined. There are also some species in which the flower is held strictly erect, but distinguishing between these classes will not be necessary for identification within this book. In some species the flowers are approximately horizontal (good examples are *G. pratense* and *G. farreri*), which means that the petals are vertical. To avoid confusion, therefore, this condition will be indicated by the phrase "*floral axis horizontal*". A distinction will also sometimes be made between *inverted* flowers, which face vertically downwards, and *nodding* flowers, which have the floral axis below the horizontal but not vertical. When the fruit is ripe it is upright (except in some members of subgenus *Robertium*). In the interval between flowering and the ripening of the fruit the posture of the pedicels and of the immature fruit is important. When the posture of the immature fruit differs from that of its pedicel, the pedicel is bent under the fruit (Fig. 15B).

Sepal-length. This is always given without including the mucro. The collective term for the sepals of one flower, *calyx*, is sometimes used but not where length is under consideration. At fruiting-time the sepals are always larger than at flowering-time; the sepal-length given covers both stages unless the increase is conspicuous.

Petal-size. This may be given in millimetres or treated like leaf-size, on a scale of three different length ranges (or their borderline areas) thus:

not more than 8mm
8–16mm
more than 16mm.

The apex of the petal may or may not have a central notch. As an aberration, often temporary, there may be a number of unequal narrow incisions, obscuring the true shape. For notched petals, the length given is the overall length.

Flower-colour. A range of flower colours from a not-quite true blue to a deep pinkish red occurs in *Geranium*. The description of shades in this range is subjective because people's perception of them differs. However, for me most shades appear to fall to one side or other of a line which divides blue from pink and pinkish red, and I shall endeavour to indicate this distinction in my descriptions. On the borderline is violet, and a *Geranium* which is on this borderline is *G. sylvaticum* in its prevalent form. Sometimes the colour is somewhat greyed, and the greyed hues are represented by a range from bluish lilac (in some forms of *G. phaeum*) to dark maroon (in *G. sinense*). Where an exact description of colour is necessary, as is especially the case in characterising cultivars, colour-chart readings are given. Where possible the *Royal Horticultural Society Colour Chart* (1966) has been used (it is referred to as RHSCC). Sometimes it has been necessary to refer to the *Horticultural Colour Chart* (HCC) (Wilson, 1939 and 1942). Both of these have cross-references to other charts. The cross-references in RHSCC to HCC were obtained using a standardised light source. Under the conditions in which I work, however, I get different matchings between the two charts and have here recorded my own readings.

Anther-colour. When this is pale, the lines along which the anthers burst are often the most strongly coloured part. These lines are called the edges of the anthers, though they form their edges only after bursting.

Length of Stamens, Style and Rostrum. Stamen length will usually be given in comparison with sepal-length. If it lies between $2/3$ and $1^{1}/3$ times the length of the sepal (excluding the mucro) it is unremarkable and may not be mentioned. Stamens are usually measurable until the fruit is nearly ripe, but there is a slight increase in their length during the flowering period and immediately after petal-fall. *Style-length* is usually about the same as stamen-length and, as with stamens, if it is not mentioned, it can be assumed that the style attains between $2/3$ and $1^{1}/3$ times the length of the sepals. However, its length will sometimes be given in millimetres, taken from the base of the ovary (young carpels) to the base of the stigmas. The *rostrum* is at its full length when the fruit is ripe and slightly before. It is measured from the top of the mericarps to the base of the stigmas. It thus includes the slender tip which formed the style (or most of it) at flowering time. The length of this *stylar portion* is usually stated in the descriptions, though sometimes it cannot be determined because the rostrum is too gradually tapered.

Carpels and Seeds. In order to avoid confusion between a seed and a detached mericarp with a seed inside, please see Chapter 5. The fruit-discharge types, described there, are indicated in Chapter 9 for all species. The term 'mericarp' will be applied in this book to the ripe seed-containing part of the carpel, although technically it is probable that the awn is part of the carpel.

Chapter 5
Classification

THE DIFFERENCE BETWEEN *GERANIUM* AND RELATED GENERA

Of the four other genera in the family Geraniaceae, perhaps the most similar to *Geranium* is *Monsonia*. Its leaves are simple and in some cases palmately lobed, the cymules are sometimes two-flowered and the flowers are radially symmetric. The number of stamens, however, is 15, not 10. Another genus, *Sarcocaulon*, also has radially symmetric flowers and 15 stamens, but the flowers are solitary; it is a desert plant with succulent stems and reduced leaves. In *Erodium* the leaves may be simple, lobed or pinnate, the inflorescence is often umbel-like and the flowers are slightly irregular (bilaterally symmetric); the five inner stamens are normal but the five outer, opposite the petals, are without anthers. *Pelargonium* is similar to *Erodium* in its great range of leaf-shapes and in usually having the flowers in umbels. The flower is usually rather strongly irregular (bilaterally symmetric) and the number of stamens with anthers ranges from seven to two. All species of *Pelargonium* also have a narrow and often long nectarial tube running back from the flower along the upper side of the pedicel.

All four of the genera related to *Geranium* are alike in the way the ripe fruit breaks up: each mericarp, complete with awn, is thrown clear by a small explosion resulting from the release of tension built up in the rostrum during drying out (Figure 5.1). The seed remains in the mericarp. In *Monsonia* and *Erodium* the awn is either plumed for wind-dispersal, or it is coiled and apparently able to drive the mericarp body into the ground (Figure 5.1, above). The awn of *Sarcocaulon* is plumed. That of *Pelargonium* is also plumed, but it is helically twisted as well (Figure 5.1, below).

CLASSIFICATION OF *GERANIUM* SPECIES

There are three different ways in which the fruit breaks up in *Geranium* and this provides a convenient basis for dividing the genus into three subgenera.

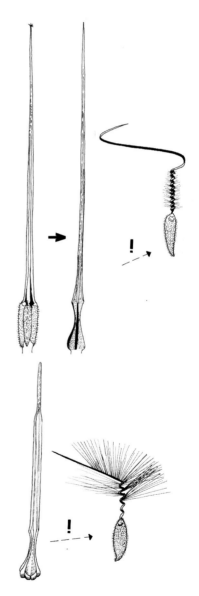

Figure 5.1 Above: fruit of *Erodium* before and after discharge, with one separated mericarp. Below: central column of fruit of *Pelargonium* after discharge, with one separated mericarp

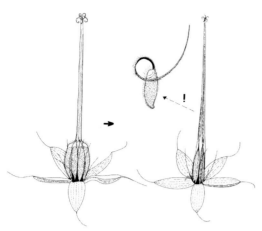

Figure 5.2 Fruit of *Geranium* subgenus *Erodioidea* with "*Erodium*-type" discharge. Left: in pre-explosive interval. Right: after discharge (one detached mericarp with awn shown). After discharge the central column is naked

One method of break-up of the fruit is that just described: the mericarp with the seed inside and the awn attached comes away from the central column, being thrown a short distance by the explosion (Figure 5.2). The awn becomes coiled but is not plumed. I have called this type of discharge the *Erodium*-type, though in fact the awn coils more or less at right angles to the mericarp and not in line with it as it does in *Erodium*. Species of *Geranium* with this type of fruit-discharge are placed in subgenus *Erodioidea*.

The second method is termed carpel projection, for the mericarp without the awn is thrown off to a distance of a few feet and the awn simply drops away at the moment of discharge (Figure 5.3). Species with this type of discharge constitute the subgenus *Robertium* which, as its name suggests, includes *G. robertianum* (Herb Robert).

The third method is called *seed-ejection*, because on discharge the awn curls back and the seed is thrown out of the mericarp (Figure 4.6). The mechanism is very like that of a Roman ballista, but it is upside-down compared with that. Species with seed-ejection are placed in subgenus *Geranium*.

It will be recalled from the description of the fruit in Chapter 4 that before discharge the mericarps separate from the central column so that each is then attached only to its awn. The mericarps of subgenus *Geranium* have to have a hole big enough to let the seed out, and the elevation of the mericarp just before discharge could permit the seed to fall out prematurely if there were no arrangements to prevent it. There are in fact three different ways of doing this, and subgenus *Geranium* is split into three according to the method of seed-retention in the pre-explosive

interval. The commonest method is to have a cluster of stiff hairs at the lower end of the carpel-orifice; these can bend under the pressure from the seed when the mericarp changes direction as its awn curls up during the explosion (Figure 4.6). These bristles are always borne on a horny tubercle which projects a short distance below the lower end of the mericarp; they are attached along its sides and change direction at the beginning of the pre-explosive interval so as to support the seed. Species with this arrangement are placed in section *Geranium*.

The second kind of arrangement for seed retention is a flexible prong on the lower edge of the orifice of the mericarp, in a position corresponding to that of the bristles in the previously-described type. The prong has the same texture as the rest of the mericarp wall and it functions in the same way as the bristles. The prong is cut out from the mericarp wall by the specially curved line of cleavage, which leaves a distinctively shaped residue attached to the central column (Figure 5.4). Species with this type of seed-retention constitute the section *Dissecta*.

Figure 5.3 Fruit of *Geranium* subgenus *Robertium* with "carpel-projection" discharge. The fruit is shown partly in the pre-explosive interval but with one awn and mericarp separated. After discharge the central column is naked

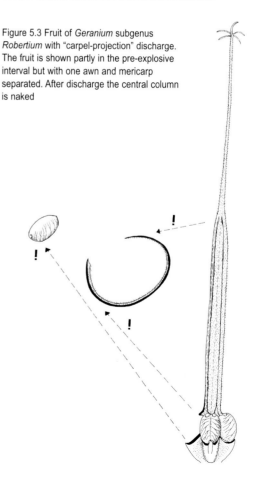

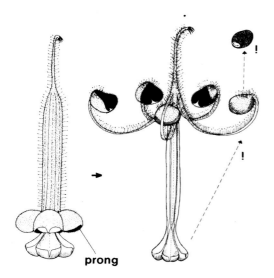

Figure 5.4 Fruit of *Geranium* subgenus *Geranium* section *Dissecta* with 'seed-ejection' discharge. Retention of the seed in the pre-explosive interval is by a prong. The carpels remain attached to the central column by their awns after discharge. The true trajectory of the seed is obliquely upwards

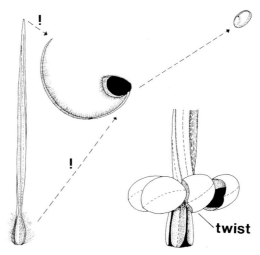

Figure 5.5 Fruit of *Geranium* subgenus *Geranium* section *Tuberosa* with "seed-ejection" discharge. Retention of the seed in the pre-explosive interval is due to twisting of the mericarps in this phase (right) and is assisted by the stamens (not shown). After discharge the central column is naked (left, on a smaller scale)

The third arrangement is quite different from the others, in that retention is achieved by a twist at the point where the mericarp joins the awn, bringing the open side of the mericarp into a sideways-facing position (Figure 5.5). This in itself must reduce the likelihood of the seed's dropping out but additional security is provided by the persistent stamen-filaments, every other one of which bars a carpel-orifice. In all species with this type of retention the mericarp and awn drop away at the end of the explosion, immediately after the seed has been ejected. Thus the familiar candelabrum-like appearance of the discharged cranesbill fruit is in fact restricted to subgenus *Geranium*, sections *Geranium* and *Dissecta*. Species with the twist-method of seed retention belong to section *Tuberosa*, which contains the Tuberosum Group and the Platypetalum Group.

All the different fruit-types described so far are quite easily observed and they can be of considerable assistance in identification. The fruits (and seeds) of the European and Caucasian species of *Geranium* have been excellently illustrated by Tokarski (1972). The classification based on them (Yeo, 1984b) is quite different from that of Knuth (1912) who put most of the annuals together and relied considerably on the type of rootstock to classify the perennials.

Among the sections of subgenus *Geranium*, there is evident correlation of characters with that of fruit-type in section *Tuberosa*. Section *Dissecta*,

however, is too small for such correlation to be apparent and section *Geranium* too large.

Various groups of correlated characters, including some from the fruit, can be used to divide up the two smaller subgenera. Taking into account new discoveries and a change of opinion, the classification of these used here is slightly changed compared with edn.1. The characters of the sections of these two subgenera are outlined in Chapter 9, where the species are dealt with in systematic order. This is preferable to alphabetical order as it has the effect of putting similar species near each other and separating dissimilar species. Similarity, of course, is a subjective concept, but systematic botany takes into account as many characters as possible in order to determine overall similarity. The nature of plant variation is such that occasionally plants with pronounced differences in inconspicuous characters look superficially alike. Examples of pairs of species which look similar, but differ in their type of fruit discharge, are *G. phaeum* and *G. sinense*, and *G. nodosum* and *G. gracile*. A modicum of application should suffice to convince the doubtful reader of the basic dissimilarity of the members of these pairs.

The hierarchical classification outlined so far is set out overleaf, with indications of the approximate numbers of species in the sections (from Aedo, Muñoz Garmendia & Pando, 1998, in the case of larger groups) and the name of one well-known species included in each. The subgenera are placed in order of size (number of included species).

GERANIUM LINNAEUS

Subgenus *Geranium*
    Section *Geranium*: 348 species (*G. pratense*)
    Section *Dissecta* Yeo: 4 species (*G. asphodeloides*)
    Section *Tuberosa* Reiche: 19 species (*G. platypetalum*)
Subgenus *Robertium* Picard
    Section *Polyantha* Reiche: 8 species (*G. polyanthes*)
    Section *Trilopha* Yeo: 6 species (*G. trilophum*)
    Section *Divaricata* Rouy & Foucaud: 2 species (*G. albanum*)
    Section *Batrachioides* W.D.J. Koch: 4 species (*G. pyrenaicum*)
    Section *Unguiculata* Reiche: 2 species (*G. macrorrhizum*)
    Section *Lucida* Knuth: 3 species (*G. lucidum*)
    Section *Ruberta* Dumortier: 6 species (*G. robertianum*)
Subgenus *Erodioidea* Yeo
    Section *Erodioidea* Picard: 3 species (*G. phaeum*)
    Section *Subacaulia* Reiche: 6-12 species (*G. cinereum*)
    Section *Aculeolata* Yeo
    Section *Brasiliensia* Knuth

This statement reveals the big snag with this classification: the existence of about 350 species in section *Geranium*. This needs to be divided up into smaller groups but at present I do not see how such groups can be defined. In Chapter 9, therefore, I have not used the botanical categories of subsection or series for section *Geranium*, but have arranged the species as best I can in informally named groups. Within these groups there are certainly some species that I believe are closely related, but I am not sure that every species is rightly placed with its near relatives (see also Chapter 7). Even more difficult than forming these groups is the problem of their sequence; there is very little to go on here, and it will be evident that geographical distribution has played some part in determining the sequence I have adopted in Chapter 9.

The existence of two groups belonging to subgenus *Erodioidea* that are not dealt with in this book is shown in the above list. One is section *Aculeolata*, which accommodates a small-flowered East African species (*G. aculeolatum*), and the other is section *Brasiliensia* Knuth, which Dr Aedo (Aedo, *et al.*, 1998) has discovered to have the same type of fruit discharge, and therefore also belongs in this subgenus (its three species remain together as a section in their new position). Section *Anemonifolia* has been included in section *Ruberta*.

Chapter 6
Structure in Relation to Function

The relation of structure to function on the level of the organ or the whole plant has been subject to relatively little scientific investigation. These notes are therefore necessarily largely conjectural, but they should serve to show that the variations found within a genus of plants have their functions. This will perhaps add another dimension of interest to the making of a collection of *Geranium* species in cultivation.

ROOTS AND ROOTSTOCKS

Many species of *Geranium* produce remarkably thick roots which penetrate deeply into the soil. These are often accompanied by finer roots near the surface. Little is known about the way *Geranium* roots exploit the soil, however. The rootstock is made up of the permanent stem and the roots it bears. The compact type of rootstock is usually associated with plants which produce plenty of basal leaves and have erect, self-supporting stems. These rootstocks hold water and nutrients during the unfavourable season, which may be summer or winter. Such plants are *G. sylvaticum, G. pratense, G. maculatum, G. oreganum* and *G. platypetalum*, which grow in stable soils. Especially if summer is the unfavourable season, the rootstock may be tuberous, as in *G. peloponnesiacum* and, even more so, in the related Tuberosum Group. Some species in the latter group have invaded cultivated land and their tubers then function also as organs of dispersal. A stout, slow-growing rootstock which develops on the surface is found in *G. phaeum*, producing a mass of rhizomes reminiscent of those of the Bearded Iris (*Iris germanica*). They probably get winter protection from snow in their natural habitat and their function might be to swamp competition or to allow slow migration away from exhausted soil. The woody rootstock of the North American *G. nervosum* perhaps suits it to the dry shade of pine woods where it often grows.

European examples of species with far-creeping rhizomes or stolons are *G. macrorrhizum* and *G. dalmaticum*. These tend to grow on cliffs and in rock crevices, and their rhizomes presumably help them to spread along crevices and into cracks. Some of the Chinese high-mountain species (*G. stapfianum, G. pylzowianum, G. orientali-tibeticum*) have slender rhizomes which seem to be related to growing in turf affected by frost-heaving or to scree conditions.

An interesting contrast in rootstocks is presented by two closely related species from Kashmir, *G. rubifolium*, which is almost tuberous, and *G. kishtvariense*, which has rather slender, rapidly spreading underground stolons. To what differences of habitat these variations are related, we do not yet know.

ABOVE-GROUND HABIT

Plants of medium or large stature with little or no ability to spread underground fall into two main types above ground. Some produce a strong flush of basal leaves in the spring and then erect flowering stems. Examples are *G. sylvaticum, G. pratense* (Figures 9.9 and 9.21) and many others. Others produce few or no rosette leaves and have stems which are not self-supporting (Figure 9.37). In our gardens they may trail on the ground, but if we let them grow among other plants, we see what is probably their natural habit: they scramble up through small shrubs or keep pace with other herbaceous perennials which give them support. Thus these two growth habits are apparently two ways of dealing with competition. In the first case the basal leaves compete by shading adjacent plants; in the second the plant is always climbing up to the light and producing new leaves favourably placed to receive it. The first type of habit is compatible with having a dense inflorescence of many flowers produced in a short time, whereas the second is not, and all species with this habit have diffuse inflorescences. Sometimes, as in *G. albanum*, the scrambling growth-habit is combined with the production of abundant basal leaves.

What seems to be a rather different habit is that seen in *G. sanguineum* and, perhaps less markedly, in *G. dahuricum* and *G. yesoense*. Here the plant often finds itself without support and its thin but stiff branches diverge at wide angles so that a bushy growth with numerous contact points with the soil is formed. If other, taller plants are available, however, these species can scramble through them. There are bulbous thickenings (pulvini) at the nodes of the stems and the bases of the leaf-stalks. These can alter the angles between internodes and between leaf and stem, an adaptation which is useful if the supporting structures shift.

LEAVES AND HAIRS

Little is known about the ways in which the varied attributes of the leaves function, but there is a clear correlation between leaf-type and habitat. The shadier the habitat, the more likely is the leaf of *Geranium* to have shallow divisions and lobes and numerous small teeth; the texture tends to be wrinkled, the colour yellowish and the hairiness moderate (Figures 9.40 and 9.110). At the other extreme are plants of dry places usually with darker green leaves which have very narrow leaf segments. Examples are *G. sanguineum* (Figure 9.61), the Mexican *G. schiedeanum* (Figure 9.90) and the South African *G. incanum* (Figure 9.77), the last two of which have the leaf-edges recurved and the channelled undersides of the segments more or less filled up with hairs.

Alpines, and many annuals, have small leaves with the divisions broadest at or near the apex and terminally lobed, so that the overall outline of the leaf is a nearly smooth curve (Figures 9.63 and 9.8). Some members of the Cinereum Group, with leaves of this kind, have a silvery covering of appressed hairs whose reflective properties may protect the leaf from excessive heating.

Plants of moderately sunny habitats have leaves intermediate in lobing, texture and hairiness (Figure 9.84).

The hairs that clothe the leaves, and vary in density in approximate agreement with the exposure of the plants to sun, are eglandular. Some species also have glandular hairs. These are almost always more abundant on the upper parts of the plant and are more often found on stems and sepals than on the leaves. They usually make the plant sticky to the touch and may, therefore, be a protection against infestation by aphides and an impediment to access by ants, which often encourage and protect aphides. Most lowland species of *Geranium* have glandular hairs, whereas most alpine species lack them, probably because such small insect pests are less important in the alpine climate.

INFLORESCENCES

Most annual species have relatively small flowers which, as mentioned in Chapter 4, are essentially adapted to self-pollination. They do not make a big display individually, and there would seem to be no point in their being massed into dense inflorescences if insect-pollination is relatively unimportant.

Among large-flowered species we have seen how the trailing and climbing growth-habit restricts its possessors to a diffuse type of inflorescence. Dense inflorescences are found in the self-supporting species – examples are *G. pratense* (Plate 10), *G. sylvaticum*, *G. maculatum*, *G. erianthum* and *G. palmatum*. Whether the density of the inflorescence is primarily adapted to attracting insects effectively or is related to some other aspect of the plant's life which perhaps demands concentrated seed-maturation is not known.

The posture of the unripe fruits and their pedicels shows interesting variations (Figures 9.9, 9.18 and 9.20). These are probably concerned with keeping the unripe fruits away from open flowers, the method varying according to the form of the inflorescence and the posture of the open flowers.

FLOWERS

The life of the flower has four stages: bud, open flower, unripe fruit and ripe fruit. Buds are often nodding, and the mucros of the sepals in many cases probably act as 'drip-tips', helping to discharge rainwater from the surface.

The open flower is involved in several functions: it has to present pollen for removal by pollinators or, in self-pollinating species, for transfer to the stigmas; it has to receive pollen on its stigmas; if it is insect-pollinated, it has to attract insects and reward them so that they will visit a succession of flowers; it then also has to ensure that they make the right movements to carry out pollination; and it has to prevent insects which are too small to cause pollination from stealing the reward. The attraction is provided by the petals, which in many species have coloured marks that either increase the attractiveness of the flower to the insect or act as guide-marks, signalling the centre of the flower where the nectar is. In a few species of *Geranium* with inconspicuous guide-marks, photography with ultra-violet filters has shown distinct patterns of ultra-violet absorption in the flower. As insects can see ultra-violet light, these UV-free areas look different to them. Therefore, it may be expected that further investigation will show that the number of species with insect-visible guide-marks is much greater than the number with human-visible guide-marks. At present we know little of the significance of the different flower colours and their patterns in *Geranium*.

The reward offered by *Geranium* is always nectar, and at least some of even the very small-flowered species produce it. The pollen is usually accessible and much must be taken by the bees which are the principal pollinators of *Geranium*. They could either take it directly or stow it in their pollen baskets after grooming themselves between flower-visits. Thus the floral economy has to allow for the diversion of some pollen from its proper function.

Certainly there are some specialisations in pollination as between the different species of *Geranium*, and these involve not only petal colour but the colours of other floral parts. In addition flower size and shape (i.e. hollow, flat or convex), posture (from erect to inverted) and the size, position and curvature of the stamens and stigmas are all involved. The petals and stamens bear hairs; here again there is doubt about the exact functions of the different arrangements, but obvious possibilities are to improve the foothold for pollinators or to influence the directions from which they probe the flowers, and to exclude very small insects from the nectaries.

We may now look at some examples of these adaptive types. Bumble-bees are large and have moderately to extremely long tongues. In general, the plants most conspicuously adapted to them have long tubular flowers (for example, Labiatae and some Boraginaceae) or petals formed into long nectar spurs, as in *Aquilegia*, columbine. These possibilities are not open to *Geranium* but it has been noted that bumble-bees are more ready than some other insects to cling upside-down to flowers. Hence, some *Geranium* species with a strong adaptation to bumble-bees have a horizontal or nodding floral axis and long stamens held near the centre of the flower on which the bees alight. Examples are *G. pratense* (Plate 10) and *G. erianthum* (Plates 16 and 17). More strongly nodding flowers, flat or convex, are found in *G. phaeum* and *G. reflexum* (Plate 50). The sombre colouring of *G. phaeum* var. *phaeum* suggests, by analogy with similarly coloured flowers in other families, that these flowers are wasp-pollinated. However, the flowers are produced very early, when only queen wasps are available, and they seem readily to attract bees. The extremely similar but unrelated *G. sinense* (Plate 21), from China, flowers later and really does attract wasps, though in England in some years great numbers of hoverflies visit it. Both types of insect cling to the stamens. It is interesting to note that the floral hairs in *G.*

sinense are rudimentary and the nectaries are fused into a prominent ring around the flower. As wasps have very short and relatively broad tongues, these floral characteristics would seem to be adapted to their needs.

The above-mentioned nodding flowers with centrally positioned stamens usually have white or pale and translucent petal bases. This gives the flower a pale centre which is sometimes strikingly illuminated from behind by the sun, as in *G. phaeum* var. *phaeum*.

When the flower is pendent but has diverging stamens, as in *G. lambertii*, *G. pogonanthum* and *G. yunnanense*, it seems probable that the pollinators alight on the petals.

The opposite extreme from these types is found in the pink-flowered *G. nervosum* and *G. fremontii* of North America (Plate 30). Here the flower is strictly upright and the stamens with rather long anthers curve outwards near their tips. Bees, often the shorter-tongued species of bumble-bee, walk round the flower on the petals, contacting the anthers with their backs. When the flower reaches the female stage, long curving stigmas stand at the level formerly occupied by the anthers.

Some *Geranium* species have found a way of demanding a long reach by the insect's tongue and so specialising more exclusively on the long-tongued insects. In *G. dalmaticum* and *G. macrorrhizum* there is a bladdery calyx, clawed petals and a narrow throat (Plate 47). The stamens and style are curved downwards and are used as an alighting place by bumble-bees. A further refinement is found in *G. robertianum* and its allies. Each petal claw bears a channelled ridge which fits against a stamen filament. The claws are flanged on either side of the ridge in such a way that two neighbouring petals form a narrow passage leading to the nectary situated between their points of attachment. The visiting insect has to probe each in turn. Bumble-bees and the long-tongued hoverfly, *Rhingia*, visit *G. robertianum*. This species is rather anomalous in possessing such an arrangement because the stigmas are receptive when the flower opens and self-pollination readily occurs. Among the allied species with this construction is *G. palmatum*, in which the nectar passages have a slit-like, instead of a circular, entrance. I suspect this makes the flowers attractive to butterflies. The related *G. maderense* has slightly less slit-like entrances, upright instead of horizontal flowers, and overarching stamens, suggesting that it is visited by rather small bees which are touched on their backs by the anthers and stigmas.

It is only in this group that slight zygomorphy (bilateral symmetry) of the flowers occurs, being evident in *G. dalmaticum*, *G. macrorrhizum* and *G. palmatum*.

Though greatly outnumbered in individuals by honey-bees and bumble-bees, there are numerous species of solitary bees of varying sizes which may provide pollinators for many of the species of *Geranium* which are without extreme specialisations of floral form and colour. On the mixed collection of *Geranium* plants that I grow together in pots at Cambridge, the mason bee, *Osmia rufa*, is sometimes common; it has a long tongue but visits the different species readily.

A final possible specialisation of *Geranium* flower is towards beetle-pollination. This is generally more important in warm conditions. When I collected *G. richardsonii* in Colorado, several beetles came out of the flowers, which are unusual in being white and in having a great quantity of hair on the upper surface of the petals (Plate 31). Whether such features can be related to beetle-pollination remains to be seen.

At the stage of the immature fruit the sepals usually close over the developing carpels. When the fruit is ripe they diverge again, thereby making way for the operation of the explosive discharge mechanism. At the same time the fruit assumes an upright position, regardless of its posture during development, so putting the carpels into the best position for seed dispersal. This does not hold for section *Ruberta*, an exception for which I have no explanation.

Geranium must be classed as a heavy-seeded genus, and the role of its discharge mechanism is presumably simply to get the seeds clear of the parent plant. Long-distance dispersal must then be left to chance.

A possible exception to this rule is found in *G. robertianum* and *G. purpureum*. In these species each mericarp, when shot off, trails "tangle-strands" (see p. 177), by which it frequently gets caught up on surrounding vegetation. A possible function for this is to assist consumption by browsing mammals which would, if the seeds are resistant to the animals' digestive enzymes, cause dispersal over longer distances. It is perhaps significant that *G. robertianum* is a woodland plant with an enormous distribution from western Europe to China and Japan. Plants with fruits or seeds dispersed by animals (usually externally) are particularly prevalent in woodland.

The remarkable inflexed wings on the fruits of *G. trilophum* and *G. biuncinatum* suggest adaptation to wind-dispersal, but *G. biuncinatum* (Plate 43) also has a pair of hooks on each mericarp which is probably an arrangement for adhesion to the fur of animals, in which case this species has both "belt and braces". The small rounded fruits of the little weed, *G. molle*, if tipped out on to a table, roll about as if with a life of their own. This probably helps them to find a crevice in the soil before they come to rest after discharge.

Chapter 7
Chromosome Numbers
and Hybrids

CHROMOSOME NUMBERS

Chromosome numbers sometimes give indications of relationships and the possibilities for hybridisation, and they may govern the outcome of hybridisation if it occurs. However, the chromosome number is only one of several factors that can determine whether a cross-pollination leads to the formation of a viable hybrid, and whether such a hybrid is in some degree fertile. Nevertheless, one can say that hybridisation is less likely to take place if the chromosome numbers of the parents are unequal than if they are equal, and that hybrids between parents differing in chromosome number are usually more or less completely sterile. A knowledge of chromosome numbers is, therefore, helpful background to a survey of hybrids or for any programme of deliberate hybridisation.

The diploid (2n) chromosome numbers found in the various taxonomic subdivisions of the genus *Geranium* are listed below (sometimes the haploid condition was observed; in these cases the count has been doubled). References to the sources of most of this information are in Yeo (1984b, Tables 2 and 3) or, for later records, in Goldblatt and co-authors (1985–1996). It should be mentioned that mistakes are sometimes made in counting chromosomes. The chromosomes of *Geranium* are relatively small and do not stain well, and some erroneous counts appear to have been published, though in fact it is rarely possible to prove that an error has been made. Because most species of plants have a single characteristic chromosome number, the finding of a number different from one already reported needs to be particularly well substantiated. Erroneous reports can arise not only from miscounts but also from misidentification. These can easily be cleared up if voucher specimens are kept, something which has frequently been neglected. In the following paragraphs I have indicated my doubts about some counts and a few

of the more recently published counts have actually been omitted. (The classification used in this book is set out on page 30 in Chapter 5 and, in more detail, on pages 57–60 in Chapter 9.)

Subgenus *Geranium*, with about 370 species, displays 11 different chromosome numbers. Section *Geranium*, with about 350 species, most commonly shows 28 chromosomes – a number found so far in about 40 species from Europe, Continental Asia, Japan and New Zealand (*G. traversii*). Tetraploids, that is, species with exactly double this number (56 chromosomes), are rare; the following are reported: *G. sessiliflorum* (probably of Australasian rather than South American origin); the related *G. hyperacrion*, from New Guinea; and *G. wlassovianum* from north and east Asia (28 is now also reported for this (Goldblatt, 1985–96, no. 51)). Another species from New Guinea, *G. niuginiense*, has 36 chromosomes, a number also found in subgenus *Robertium* but not known elsewhere in subgenus *Geranium*. A record of 56 chromosomes is also available for *G. palustre* but there are three records of 28 for this species. A higher multiple of 28, namely 84 (hexaploid), also exists in this section, having been found repeatedly in *G. sanguineum*, for which, however, there is also one count of approximately 56; there are also two counts of 82.

The number 26, found also in two sections of subgenus *Robertium*, is found in section *Geranium* of subgenus *Geranium*. It has been reported twice for the perennial *G. endressii*, for which 28 has also been reported, and it is the only number reported for *G. rotundifolium*, in which it has been found several times.

The tetraploid number corresponding to 26, namely 52, is found in the only two known North American annuals and in seven perennials ranging from Canada to Argentina. The only other number reported in North America is 28. For *G. erianthum* this is expected, as it is a species of the far north-west which also occurs in north-east Asia, and there has 28. However, 28 is also reported for

G. richardsonii, a species with no evident connections outside the Americas, and for which 52 chromosomes have previously been recorded.

Counts of 24 have been published for two species, *G. pratense* and *G. sylvaticum*, which usually have 28. These should be regarded with caution.

The only count known to me from a southern African species is of 22 for *G. caffrum* (supplied by Dr Mary Gibby of the Natural History Museum, London, in year 2000).

The only other chromosome number known in this section is 18, found repeatedly in the annual species, *G. columbinum*.

In section *Dissecta* of subgenus *Geranium* the number 28 shows up again, in *G. asphodeloides*, which is, however, the most variable in chromosome number of all *Geranium* species, showing also 30, 26 and 24. *G. asphodeloides* is perennial or biennial. The related annual species, *G. dissectum*, has 22 chromosomes. As this species is in a different section of the genus from *G. caffrum*, their common chromosome number is presumably the result of evolutionary convergence.

Finally in this subgenus, we come to section *Tuberosa*. Here, 28 is the number known for two species of the Tuberosum Group, and two of the Platypetalum Group, namely *G. platypetalum* itself and *G. gymnocaulon*. However, the investigator of the latter also found 56 chromosomes in the same species. *G. ibericum* has 56 chromosomes. Reports of 42 in *G. platypetalum* are based on the misidentification of *G.* x *magnificum*, a sterile hybrid between *G. platypetalum* and *G. ibericum*. There are two annual or biennial species in this group, *G. bohemicum* with 28 and *G. lanuginosum* with 48 chromosomes.

Subgenus *Robertium* is the most diverse in chromosome number, with 13 numbers showing in 27 species (not counting aberrant numbers in *G. lucidum*).

From section *Polyantha* only *G. polyanthes* has been counted: it has 28 chromosomes.

In section *Trilopha* there is an old count of 50 for *G. favosum* and a more recent one of 56 for *G. ocellatum* of West African origin.

In section *Divaricata* the perennial species *G. albanum* has 28 and there are recent counts of both 26 and 28 for the annual species *G. divaricatum*, though there are four of 26 and one of 28. (The surprising count of 20 given by Van Loon (1984b) for *G. albanum* surely deserves comment from the author; its absence could be the result of a typesetting error.)

In section *Batrachioidea* there are several reports of both 26 and 28 for the perennial *G.*

pyrenaicum and of 26 for the three annuals, *G. brutium*, *G. molle* and *G. pusillum*. The solitary report of 34 for the latter is believed to be an error.

In section *Unguiculata* (as revised), *G. dalmaticum* and *G. macrorrhizum* both have 46. For the latter there are reliable counts also of 87–93, but there are several of 46.

Section *Lucida* (as revised) contains *G. glaberrimum* with 30 chromosomes and the annual *G. lucidum*, for which both 20 and 40 have been counted more than once and 60 once. Van Loon (1984b) found 40 in Europe, along with the so-called dysploid numbers 41, 42, 43 and 44. The chromosome number of *G. lasiopus*, also perennial, is unknown.

In section *Ruberta* (as revised), *G. cataractarum* has 36 (reported for both southern Spanish and north-west African plants), *G. purpureum* has 32, *G. robertianum* 64, and *G. rubescens* and *G. canariense* 128. Reports of 32, 54 and 56 for *G. robertianum* have not been substantiated in the extensive work of Baker (1957, and personal communication: see Yeo, 1973) or of Van Loon (1984b). The two species of the formerly recognised section Anemonifolia, *G. palmatum* and *G. maderense*, both have 68 chromosomes. The report of 128 for the former arose from editorial error; it really refers to *G. canariense*.

In subgenus *Erodioidea*, section *Erodioidea*, all three species have 28 chromosomes. The number 14 has been reported twice for *G. phaeum*, but in an incidental manner and not in the affirmative way that one requires for a number that is known in no other species and is at variance with three independent counts of 28. In section *Subacaulia*, 28 has been reported for *G. argenteum*, *G. cazorlense*, *G. cinereum* and *G. subcaulescens*, as well as for *G. nanum* (refuting an earlier count of 26). In addition a tetraploid (56) variant has been found in *G. subcaulescens*.

To summarise: a diploid number of 28 is found in all sections of subgenera *Erodioidea* and *Geranium*, and in three sections of subgenus *Robertium*; multiples of this number are rare but involve one additional section of subgenus *Robertium*; of the five annuals in subgenus *Geranium*, three have numbers below 28; all species confined to the Americas, whether annual or perennial, have 52 chromosomes, as far as is known; the chromosome number is highly variable in subgenus *Robertium*.

Changes in chromosome number may occur in small steps in addition to the doubling and summation described in the next section, and they can be upwards or downwards. In flowering plants in general there is a tendency for short-lived species to have fewer chromosomes than their closest longer-lived relatives. The annual species *G. molle* (26), *G. rotundifolium* (26), *G. dissectum* (22) and *G. columbinum* (18) exemplify the tendency. Probably only one or two pairs are lost at a time. *Geranium* is curious in that what looks like a reduction is sometimes reversed. Thus *G. lanuginosum*, a spring annual, has 48 chromosomes, as against 28 in its nearest relative, *G. bohemicum*, an overwintering annual. *G. lanuginosum* seems to have dropped its basic number from 14 to 12 and then changed from diploidy with 24 chromosomes to tetraploidy with 48. A similar process, but with the loss of only one chromosome pair, could account for the number 52 in North American species. But here the annuals and perennials all have this number.

It is quite noticeable that the species that have more than one number on the same ploidy level are perennials with little root-protection and are possibly short-lived: *G. endressii*, *G. pyrenaicum* and *G. asphodeloides* , for example. Polyploidy itself can facilitate chromosome loss, since most of the genes will be duplicated when the polyploid is evolutionarily young. Loss of a chromosome will then be largely compensated for by its duplicate. This may account for reports of 82 instead of 84 in *G. sanguineum* and variations around 46 and 92 in *G. macrorrhizum*, although with large numbers of chromosomes difficulty of counting may be the reason for reported variation.

Extra chromosomes on top of 40 found in *G. lucidum* by Van Loon (1984b) are probably not very significant genetically and are probably tolerated because there is a tetraploid complement anyway. Van Loon often found from two to four different numbers in the same population. He worked entirely with root tips, and sometimes found two different numbers in the same plant.

Chromosome numbers may have a role in classification but, in *Geranium* (as we have just seen), each of the taxonomic groups that has been proposed on the basis of fruit-type includes some species with 28 chromosomes. Therefore, the chromosome number does not differentiate these groups and is of no use in classification. However, it is of some interest at sectional level within subgenus *Robertium* and at lower levels in subgenus *Geranium*.

CHROMOSOME DOUBLING AND SUMMATION IN THE ORIGIN OF NEW SPECIES

Species whose chromosome number is an exact multiple of some other number found in the

genus (polyploids) have already been mentioned. The way this comes about is usually as follows. A hybrid is formed between two species with the same chromosome number. The parents are sufficiently distantly related that their chromosomes, when brought together in the hybrid, do not form pairs at reduction division (meiosis), the process in which the sex cells are formed. (It is a simplification to say that the products of meiosis are sex cells, but full details are unnecessary here.) If the chromosomes do not pair, the sex cells do not receive a complete and correct set of chromosomes. They are then either inviable or give rise, after taking part in fertilisation, to inviable embryos. The hybrid is, accordingly, sterile. Then, by one of a number of methods, an individual containing a double set of chromosomes (complete set from each of the two original parent species) arises from the hybrid. When this individual comes to form sex cells, every chromosome finds a suitable partner and the plant produces progeny. These will be similar to the original hybrid but will probably show a little more variation than did either parent, but nothing like as much as the progeny of an initially fertile hybrid. If they succeed in the struggle for existence, a new species will have come into existence instantaneously. This fertile tetraploid is genetically isolated from its parents because, if it crosses with them, the progeny will have an odd number of chromosome sets (it will be a triploid) and will be sterile. This is the probable origin of *Geranium* species such as *G. ibericum* and *G. wlassovianum* with 56 chromosomes instead of the usual 28. The sterility of the triploid back-cross is due to the fact that only half the chromosomes derived from the tetraploid hybrid can find partners at meiosis.

Exactly this situation is found in the sterile garden hybrid, *G. x magnificum*; it has 42 chromosomes, and at meiosis in the anthers, approximately 14 pairs of chromosomes and 14 odd chromosomes can be seen. On grounds of its external characters it was inferred that this hybrid was a cross between *G. ibericum* (56) and *G. platypetalum* (28). The observations on chromosome behaviour in the hybrid suggest that one of the progenitors of *G. ibericum* was *G. platypetalum* or something closely related to it. If the chromosome set of *G. x magnificum* was doubled we should have a plant with 84 chromosomes. This might or might not be fertile depending on whether there was preferential pairing among the *platypetalum* chromosomes and the *platypetalum*-like chromosomes derived from *G. ibericum*. If pairing can take place among chromosome sets of different origin, the chromosomes can join up to form groups of three and four and this leads to incorrect segregation and sterility. However, a tetraploid might cross with a distantly related diploid, and if the triploid resulting doubled its chromosome number, we might expect the hexaploid to be fertile. There is one *Geranium* with 84 chromosomes, namely *G. sanguineum*. One is always tempted with polyploids to speculate on their likely origin, and we have seen that there is evidence of involvement of *G. platypetalum* in the origin of *G. ibericum*. There might have been three species involved in the origin of *G. sanguineum*, but I can offer no suggestions as to what they were. Possibly its ancestors no longer survive. These considerations cast suspicion on the report of about 56 chromosomes for *G. sanguineum*, mentioned earlier.

The situation found in *G. ibericum* is also found in *G. robertianum* (64 chromosomes) in relation to *G. purpureum* (32). There presumably is or was another species with 32 chromosomes that joined up with *G. purpureum* to make *G. robertianum*. There is, however, evidence for the idea that *G. canariense* and *G. rubescens* (each with 128 chromosomes) arose on different occasions by the doubling of the chromosomes of *G. robertianum*, and not by the involvement of a further species (Widler-Kiefer & Yeo, 1987). This process is less likely to lead to the development of a new species than the one where a hybrid arises first, and is less common.

A fertile version of a hybrid that is normally sterile has cropped up among Alan Bremner's hybrids (see later, this page). The parent species are *G. traversii* (white-flowered) and *G. versicolor* (white form illegitimately called 'Album'). Both have 28 chromosomes but *traversii* is from New Zealand and *versicolor* from southern Europe. The fertile form is referred to as TWVA. Both the sterile and the fertile plants exhibit distortion of the leaves and flowers that affects part of the plant and fluctuates over time. Plants grown from seed produced by flowers on normal parts of TWVA are more stable. When TWVA is back-crossed to either parent, the resulting progeny are sterile. These facts suggest that we may have here a newly derived allotetraploid (tetraploid derived from a hybrid) comparable in origin to *G. ibericum*. A chromosome count could decide the issue.

The origin of new species by hybridisation followed by chromosome doubling can take place with any combination of parental chromosome numbers. It has already been indicated that it can happen when a diploid and a tetraploid cross. It can also happen with numbers which are neither equal nor multiples of the same number. *G. maderense* and *G. palmatum* have 68 chromosomes, which is rather puzzling in view

of the occurrence of 64 in the related *G. robertianum*. When it became known that *G. cataractarum* had 36 chromosomes, I noticed that 68 could be obtained by adding 36 and 32. Accordingly *G. maderense* was crossed with *G. cataractarum* and *G. purpureum*. The first of these crosses produced a hybrid, in the meiosis of which approximately 18 chromosome-pairs were formed. *G. maderense* is thus probably of hybrid origin, one of the parents being *G. cataractarum*.

THE HYBRIDISATION WORK OF ALAN BREMNER

In the 14 years to the beginning of 1999 Alan Bremner carried out some 24,000 pollinations of *Geranium*. He has very kindly lent me all his records. There is a huge table showing the results of each batch of pollinations, quantified throughout, beginning with growth of the rostrum and listing various responses through to the production of reasonably vigorous flowering progeny. Always the best result is shown, but commonly a range of responses actually occurred among the flowers used in a particular cross. The basis of this table is a list of all the batches of pollinations, giving details of the parent stocks and the responses to pollination. There is a further list dealing with all the crosses that produced offspring, from seedlings with albino cotyledons that only survived a few days, through to vigorous flowering hybrids; the more successful progeny are described and details are given of their introduction to horticulture and under what cultivar name. There is a large batch of 35-mm transparencies, showing a leaf and a flower. Usually, several hybrids are included in each frame. The information contained in all this material has been used in writing the following paragraphs.

THE KNOWN HYBRIDS OF *GERANIUM*

In describing the origin of new species by chromosome doubling I have mentioned the occurrence of distantly related species which can form hybrids that are sterile because their chromosomes cannot pair up when the sex cells are being formed. This inability to pair is normally the consequence of a long sequence of generations in isolation, during which the chromosomes are rearranged and the genes have mutated (both these types of change being a matter of chance initially and influenced thereafter by natural selection). The accompanying morphological and physiological changes may reach the point at which we recognise their bearers as representatives of different species. Eventually this genetic divergence reaches the point at which hybrids cannot be formed at all.

In edn.1 I listed all the reported hybrids in *Geranium*. There were 39 of them, but six were doubtfully correctly reported, leaving 33 reasonably safe hybrid combinations. Thanks to the monumental work of Alan Bremner (see above), we now know a lot about which species of *Geranium* can cross and which apparently cannot, but it is no longer possible to comment on every hybrid. Instead, all the known hybrids that reached maturity are listed in Appendix III under five headings; these include about 160 binary hybrids and a further 30 [2 Jan. 2000] in which one or both parents were binary hybrids already. The first total includes 16 binary crosses. General comments on the range of hybrids are made in the present chapter, while in Chapter 9 a note on hybrids that have occurred is provided for most species and sometimes their garden value is indicated. In addition, the hybrids that have received validly published binary names are treated on a par with the species.

If we look at the results of Bremner's attempts to make crosses at the higher taxonomic levels, we find, firstly, that there were no successful crosses between members of subgenus *Robertium* and members of either of the other two subgenera. The best results were very thin seeds that did not germinate. These were produced when *G. pyrenaicum* was crossed with two New World species (one of which was *G. carolinianum*), and a seed germinating to give a short-lived albino seedling when *G. albanum* was pollinated with the New World *G. carolinianum*. *G. albanum* has an inoperative fruit discharge mechanism and its position is somewhat speculative. With *G. albanum* excluded, subgenus *Robertium* would be totally isolated from the other subgenera. This is the group, variously delimited, that some authors have raised to generic rank, as an entity separate from *Geranium* (*Robertium* Picard and *Robertiella* Hanks). To me they are still *Geranium* but they do seem to be the most remote group in the evolution of the genus.

Secondly, the sections within subgenus *Geranium* are effectively isolated from each other. Between section *Geranium* and section *Tuberosa* the best result was in the cross between *G. platypetalum* and *G. carolinianum* which produced seven fat seeds that did not germinate, while the two species of section *Dissecta* could not be crossed with those of section *Tuberosa* or those of section *Geranium*.

In view of these barriers to interbreeding it was at first surprising to me to find that crosses between subgenus *Geranium* section *Geranium* and subgenus *Erodioidea* section *Subacaulia* are viable. This was proved by Bremner's crosses and by spontaneous production at Cambridge of hybrids by open-pollinated plants of *G. traversii* x *G. sessiliflorum* (*G.* x *antipodeum*), the pollen parents of which were evidently members of the Cinereum Group (subgenus *Erodioidea*). However, it is not so surprising if one looks at the morphology of the fruit rather than how it functions. The bristly tubercle present in these two groups is clearly homologous (Yeo, 1984 & 1990), though functioning in quite a different way (see Chapter 5). The fruits of sections *Dissecta* and *Tuberosa* function like those of section *Geranium* but they do not have the bristly tubercle. It has long been a mystery to me that there should be three different variants of the seed-ejection method of dispersal, but one possibility has been independent origin of all three (as opposed to evolution of one version to another). The apparent genetic isolation of the groups expressing them gives weight to this hypothesis, which itself would be rather remarkable if true.

An indication that some of the barriers that Bremner found might have been breached in nature is presented by two crosses. These are *G. asphodeloides* x *G. bohemicum* and *G. phaeum* x *G. sylvaticum*; unfortunately the records are unsubstantiated.

A classification that takes greater account of the sterility barriers could be proposed as an alternative to the one in Chapter 5, as shown below without author-names and exemplars.

GERANIUM LINNAEUS

Subgenus I *Geranium*
    Section (1) *Geranium*
    Section (2) *Erodioidea*
        Subsection (2a) *Erodioidea*
        Subsection (2b) *Subacaulia*
        Subsection (2c) *Aculeolata*
        Subsection (2d) *Brasiliensia*
Subgenus II *Tuberosa*
    Section (3) *Tuberosa*
    Section (4) *Mediterranea*
Subgenus III *Dissecta*
    Section (5) *Dissecta*
Subgenus IV *Robertium*
    Section (6) *Polyantha*
    Section (7) *Trilopha*
    Section (8) *Divaricata*
    Section (9) *Batrachioidea*
    Section (10) *Unguiculata*
    Section (11) *Lucida*
    Section (12) *Ruberta* (including *Anemonifolia*)

This may better reflect evolutionary relationships but there are practical considerations against its adoption. It makes the numerical disparity between the groups even greater, and it might need further alteration if definite evidence was obtained against a close relationship of the subsections *Subacaulia* and *Erodioidea*, which have not yet been successfully crossed with each other. (Although the two groups – I hereafter revert to treating them as sections of a subgenus – are very different except in fruit-type, this result is rather surprising.)

Continuing to look at sterility barriers at the lower level of section, we find a total barrier between the remodelled sections of subgenus *Robertium*, which is not really surprising because the sections are mostly rather distinct. There is also apparently no hybridisation between subsections *Tuberosa* and *Mediterranea* (both in subgenus *Geranium*), though only two crosses were attempted (with respectively three and 48 flowers pollinated).

The very large section *Geranium* of subgenus *Geranium* is the source of most of the known inter-specific hybrids (and here I resort to the informal classification into groups used in Chapter 9). We find a profusion of hybrids in the European and west to central Himalayan species. There are fewer hybrids in the north-east Asian Groups but many involving the small-flowered eastern Asian Sibiricum Group and the Sessiliflorum and Potentilloides Groups of Australasia.

The existence of species that have good "combining ability" (an *ad hoc* expression used by plant breeders) when crossed with geographically remote or morphologically dissimilar species is very evident, and hybrids seem to be particularly numerous when two such species or groups are crossed. It is not known what allows these species to retain their cross-compatibility but its occurrence seems to be arbitrary and it creates an element of "noise" in the relationship between degree of incompatibility and apparent external similarity. For example, *G. endressii* crosses readily with members of the Sessiliflorum Group, though it comes from western Europe, while the Sessiliflorum Group comes from Australasia, and there is no particular similarity between them.

Other "good combiners" are *G. psilostemon* in the Sylvaticum Group, the species of the Wallichianum Group, the Potentilloides Group (a group of small-flowered species now represented in Chapter 9 that must be closely related to the Sessiliflorum Group) and *G. carolinianum* of the Maculatum Group. The last case is remarkable because it is a North American annual with 52 chromosomes, and because it has crossed with a wide range of species from the New and Old Worlds.

I also recognise a set of mainly small-flowered New World species, chiefly on the basis of distribution, as the Cordilleran Group. They extend from Mexico into and throughout the Andes and seem to be rather closely related to the Sessiliflorum Group (which is itself in part Cordilleran), but they have wide-ranging crossability relationships.

Bremner did six crosses among South African species which were already noted for the ease with which they cross in gardens, and some hybrids have been noted in the field. These species often express characters approaching those of other, closely related species, which may be the result of hybridisation. Both the readiness to hybridise, and the formation of intermediate characters suggest that they constitute an evolutionarily young group. (They all share the character of deeply slashed stipules.) South African species account for three of the six new groups treated in Chapter 9.

Because of the above-mentioned "noise" in crossability, the crossing results are of limited value in substantiating a taxonomic classification. The Groups near the beginning of the classification – Endressii, Rotundifolium, Sylvaticum, Collinum and Pratense – seem to be genuinely quite closely related. *G. collinum* and *G. pratense* have long been known to cross with each other; now we can say that their crossing relationships with other species are similar, for Bremner found that *G. pratense* could be crossed with seven species aside from *G. collinum*, and *G. collinum* could cross with five of these. In a more strictly botanical treatment the Pratense and Collinum Groups should probably be united, but to do this would make it more difficult to characterise the Pratense Group; there are other species or varieties related to *G. collinum*, that are not yet known to me in cultivation, for which a separate Collinum Group would be useful. It is satisfactory that there is nothing against my placing of *G. rotundifolium*. In the Endressii Group *G. nodosum* failed to cross with anything else, but there seem to be no other species to which it might be joined on morphological grounds. The Wallichianum Group seems to be held together rather well by internal cross-compatibilies, the Refractum Group rather less so. *G. farreri* has crossed with two species of the former but does not share the short style of that group. *G. sanguineum*, seemingly isolated by not resembling any other species and by having a hexaploid chromosome complement, has crossed with the Sylvaticum and Wallichianum Groups, but these are "good combiners".

In Bremner's work successful crossing was the rule within those of my groups that comprise more than one species, although often only certain members were involved. For these members such crosses provide some support for my classification. Internal crosses were not tried in the Palustre Group, while in the adjacent Krameri Group the barely distinguishable *G. dahuricum* and *G. yesoense* produced viable hybrids. In addition these two groups intercrossed in the form of *G. soboliferum* and *G. wlassovianum. G. krameri* itself was not used in this work.

An important aspect of hybrids is their fertility. Alan Bremner has gathered some information on this subject but it cannot be reproduced in detail in this book. Observations on the fertility of hybrids obviously come at the end of all the other work involved in performing and recording cross-fertility on a large scale. In fact Bremner had to confine himself to working on open-pollinated plants in the garden or the greenhouse which was open to potentially pollinating insects, so the fertility of a hybrid exclusively to its own pollen could not be estimated. The level of fertility of these open-pollinated plants varied from high, with good seed-setting, to very low, with perhaps a few seeds produced in a season's flowering, as well as the ultimate of no seeds being seen at all.

Using a survey of Bremner's results, the following have "medium to high" seed-set. From the horticultural point of view low fertility in a plant will suggest hybridity and indicate that this possibility must be considered when using the keys in this book (see Chapter 8). From a plant-breeding point of view even very low fertilities can be important in opening the way to raising later generations.

argenteum x *cinereum*
canariense x *rubescens*
collinum x *pratense*
dahuricum x *pratense*
endressii x *versicolor* (x *oxonianum*)
kishtvariense x *rubifolium*
maderense x *palmatum*
phaeum x *reflexum* (x *monacense*)
sessiliflorum x *traversii* (x *antipodeum*)
subulato-stipulatum x *vulcanicola*

In each case except that of *G. dahuricum* x *G. pratense* the parents are obviously closely related. Rather surprisingly, some evidently closely related species have produced hybrids which are sterile, for example *G. pusillum* and *G. pyrenaicum, G. dalmaticum* and *G. macrorrhizum,* and *G. bicknellii* and *G. carolinianum.* Where the chromosome number is

markedly different, hybrids between even closely related species may be expected to be sterile. *G. himalayense* forms a sterile hybrid with *G. pratense* though it is more similar to *G. pratense* than is *G. collinum,* and it would not be surprising if it turned out to have 56 chromosomes. Anomalously, the hybrid *G. sessiliflorum* x *G. traversii* is partly fertile, although the first parent is a tetraploid and the second a diploid. It can only be supposed that one of the counts is wrong, or that one of the parents exists in more than one chromosome race.

Dr Helen Kiefer, in her hybridisation experiments at Cambridge with species of subgenus Robertium, found that in all reciprocal pollinations the response was highly unequal, and in all cases where progeny arose they were obtained by crossing in one direction only (Widler-Kiefer & Yeo, 1987). When successful crosses within subgenus *Geranium* were achieved by Bremner, failure in the other direction also seems to have been frequent.

A peculiarity of the stamens of some sterile hybrids of *Geranium* is the varying extent of their development, even in the same plant at different times. I have seen this in *G.* x *magnificum* and in hybrids of the Pratense Group. The most extreme indication of male-sterility is severe, early abortion of the anthers and drastic reduction in the length of the filaments. A less extreme manifestation is expressed in normal or slightly shortened filaments, and normal-sized but mustard-coloured anthers which do not open. Then sometimes one finds superficially normal anthers which burst to produce normal-sized pollen grains of a normal blue colour. Microscopic examination of these reveals that they are empty.

RAISING AND FINDING NEW HYBRIDS

Controlled crossing of *Geranium* is not at all difficult, though it is much less hazardous if a greenhouse is available. As the anthers mature before the stigmas (see Chapter 4), it is easy to remove them with fine scissors or forceps before the stigmas are receptive. A lens should be used to inspect the flower after this operation to make sure no pollen has been scattered. If only a few grains have been scattered, it will be worthwhile trying to remove them. The flower is then covered with a small translucent envelope which can be secured with one or two paper-clips. A day or two later the bag is removed, and if the stigmas are spreading, they are touched with a freshly opened anther from the intended male parent. The bag is then reinstated and it has to stay in position until after the fruit is ripe to prevent the loss of the seeds. Paper bags will not last out of doors unless one is exceptionally lucky with the weather. If hybridising has to be done in the open, it may be possible to enclose the flowers in plastic tubing with gauze over the top for ventilation and wadding round the flower-stalk. The tubing would have to be wired to a stick. An excellent brief guide to plant-breeding is that of Lawrence (1948). Careful written records of attempts at crossing should always be kept; not only will they guard against lapses of memory but, even if the object is to produce interesting new plants for the garden, the records will have scientific value.

As to what crosses are likely to succeed, Bremner has shown that closely or distantly related species may cross but that, as described above, the boundaries between the main taxonomic groups are rarely breached.

Nature can experiment on an even bigger scale than we can, so field botanists and horticulturists should look out for hybrids. *G. pratense* x *G. sylvaticum* was found in the Alps by Richard Nutt, but the hybrid does not seem to have been raised artificially yet. Anybody who finds a spontaneous hybrid should take all possible steps to obtain evidence, preferably by collecting a portion of the plant and carefully pressing it, by taking measurements of floral parts while still fresh, and by photographing it. A portion of the plant should be taken for propagation if that can be done without injuring the remainder (unlikely with annuals but these will die anyway).

For more information on hybrids in horticulture, see literature cited in Chapter 1 and the illustrated articles by Hibberd (1992), Moss (1997) and Bremner (1997).

Chapter 8
Identification

This book is mainly about identification and readers are most strongly urged to try to identify specimens for themselves. However, for one reason or another, the would-be identifier may from time to time fail to arrive at a convincing identification, and may then need outside help, hence the two sections of this chapter.

GETTING IT DONE FOR YOU

Experts, professional and otherwise, are usually willing to identify specimens submitted in good condition. Specimens to be sent fresh should be sealed in a polythene bag as soon as they are cut. Polythene transmits oxygen and carbon dioxide but not water or water-vapour. Excess water in a polythene bag merely sets up rot, and no water should be added unless the specimen is collected in hot sunshine when the sparsest possible sprinkling of water should be added, or you can breathe into the bag before sealing it. If the journey to the expert is likely to take more than two days, it is better to make a pressed specimen. This also has the advantage that if the expert is away from base, the specimen will not have deteriorated by the time he or she gets back.

If you do not have a plant press, place the specimen in the middle of 12–20 thicknesses of newspaper and cover with a pile of books. Change the newspaper after 24 hours and again later if conditions are cool and humid. Some *Geranium* species are slightly succulent and take unusually long to dry. Dry specimens are for the most part quite stiff.

The specimen should include a good length of stem and basal leaves if available, and unripe and ripe fruit if possible. If the dimensions of the plant seem to require it, cut the top off and place it in the press as an additional layer with extra paper. If the branching is prolific, discard some of the branches. If the leaves are complex in outline, detach one or two from the plant and flatten them carefully before closing the press. Allow a few petals to lie detached in the press and include one or two flowers from which two or three sepals and petals have been removed from one side so as to expose the stamens. Take a note of any leaf-markings and the colour of sepals, petals, stamens and stigmas.

DOING IT YOURSELF

Gardeners will normally have fresh specimens to hand but there is no reason why they should not work from specimens they have pressed themselves (see above). Please do not rush to identify an unknown plant the moment the first flower opens. A delay of a week or two will see the immature fruits in being, and four or five weeks will give you a ripe fruit, making available many more useful characters. Some species may finish flowering before the first fruits are ripe, in which case dried specimens of the flowers will be needed.

It is necessary to read chapters 4 and 5 before embarking on identifications. Those with little or no botanical experience are advised to take one or two species, the names of which they know, and see if they can get the right answer using one or other of the diagnostic keys, before starting on an unknown specimen. Keys get easier to use the more you use them.

Two keys are provided: a multi-access and a dichotomous key. The multi-access key makes minimal use of the characters of the ripe fruit. The dichotomous key (which is broken up into sections) makes full use of fruit characters. If you have ripe fruit, the dichotomous key may be preferable because more than one-third of the species fall into the smaller groups with relatively short keys. If fruit is not fully developed, identification with the dichotomous key may still be attempted, following the list of hints given at the beginning of the key. In any case the sculpture of the fruit, mentioned in couplet 2 of the dichotomous key to groups, is visible some time before the fruit is ripe. Although in most species fruit-discharge is explosive, resulting in the disappearance of the seeds or the carpels, it is usually possible to find some fruits that are just ripe and which can be induced to explode and of which the discharge-products can be collected. For this purpose, look for rostra which are drying out and turning brown.

Do not forget that the keys cover only the species and hybrids which I have decided to include in the book.

PLANTS WITH DOUBLE FLOWERS

These cannot be identified with the keys but they are known in only four species (or hybrids), as numbered in Chapter 9:

2. G. x oxonianum (double-flowered forms also have narrow and strap-shaped petals or ones with triangular lobes)
16. G. pratense
20. G. himalayense
50. G. sanguineum

HOW TO USE THE MULTI-ACCESS KEY

For each of the eleven characters listed below choose the letter of the character-state corresponding to your plant and write it down (put the letters in groups, as in the key beginning on p. 46, to make it easier to read the resulting formula). If a character-state is not observable, write alternative formulae with all possible states for the group concerned. Plants that have been in flower for some time without showing any development of the fruit may be sterile hybrids and, for these, blanks should be left in the formula for the last three characters. For technical terms see

Chapters 4 and 5 and the Glossary. Trace the formula in the alphabetically arranged list, turn up the species indicated (see Chapter 9) and check the description (the short one, if provided, will usually show whether you are right or not). If a species has two formulae differing in only one character, so that the formulae would be adjacent in the list, the two states of the character are shown one above the other, thus $0/p$. If two species have the same formula, it will be necessary to check both; if more than two species have the same formula, there is a reference to the diagnostic notes given at the end of the key (before using these it is essential to understand the terms 'division', 'lobe' and 'tooth' as applied to the leaves; see Chapter 4, especially Figure 4.7). If the key has clearly failed, go through the list of characters again looking for borderline cases and prepare alternative formulae for any that you find. This type of key requires you to answer most of the necessary questions about your specimen as a first step, whereas a dichotomous (forking) key requires attention to the plant and the key alternately throughout the entire process of identification. If the answers to some questions are uncertain, it is easier to try alternative possibilities with this key than with a dichotomous key, which acts like a maze in these circumstances.

**Characters and character-states
used in the multi-access key**

CHARACTER 1

A. Main leaves with deepest incisions not reaching more than $2/3$ of the way to the top of the leaf-stalk

B. Main leaves with deepest incisions reaching more than $2/3$ of the way to the top of the leaf-stalk but not all the way

C. Main leaves with deepest incisions reaching top of leaf-stalk

CHARACTER 2

D. Divisions of main leaves broadest at or very close to apex, lobes apical

E. Divisions of main leaves broadest well below apex, lobing pinnate or palmato-pinnate

CHARACTER 3

F. Glandular hairs present, at least on upper parts

G. Glandular hairs not present

CHARACTER 4

H. Floral axis above the horizontal (flowers erect or upwardly inclined)

I. Floral axis horizontal or below the horizontal (flowers directed horizontally or nodding)

CHARACTER 5

J. Sepal mucro not more than $1/8$ length of sepal

K. Sepal mucro more than $1/8$ length of sepal

NOTES

1. Main leaves are the basal leaves (if any) and/or lower stem-leaves

2. See Note 1

3. Check pedicels, sepals, mericarps and base of rostrum

4. Ignore very small hairs difficult to see at 8x magnification

5. Length of sepal does not include mucro. The ratio can usually be judged by eye

CHARACTER 6

L. Petals not over 8mm long

M. Petals over 8mm but not over 16mm long

N. Petals over 16mm long

CHARACTER 7

O. Petals with a distinct central apical notch

P. Petals feebly or not at all notched at apex

CHARACTER 8

Q. Petal base without hairs on central part of front surface

R. Petal base with hairs on central part of front surface

CHARACTER 9

S. Immature fruit horizontal or drooping

T. Immature fruit upwardly inclined or erect

CHARACTER 10

U. Rostrum with stylar portion not more than 4mm, sometimes none

V. Rostrum with stylar portion more than 4mm

6. Include length of claw if any

7. As an aberration the petals may have a number of narrow incisions; if so, try 'P'

8. The petal base usually has lateral hair-tufts which may extend on to surface; look for surface hairs between the tufts or a continuous hair tract right across petal; in *G. macrorrhizum* hairless part may be restricted to the central channel, overhung by hairs on the ridges of the claw

9. This can be observed as soon as obvious development of the rostrum has begun; the *ripe* fruit is usually upright and ripeness is first shown by the browning of the rostrum

10. This character can be observed long before the fruit is ripe or on ripe fruit if not broken; in a few species it may not be possible to use this character because the transition from thick rostrum to thin stylar portion is too indefinite

CHARACTER 11   11.Specimens
W. Mericarps with a   qualifying as 'X'
   pattern of raised   may have one or
   ribs, at least at the   two conspicuous
   top, or with crests   but thin and
   near top   scarcely raised
X. Mericarps without a   transverse veins
   pattern of raised   near top
   ribs, without crests

THE MULTI-ACCESS KEY

ADF HJLO RTUX	7.	rotundifolium
ADF HJLP QTUW	117.	lucidum
Trilophum Group, p. 163		
ADF HJLP QTVW	117.	lucidum
ADF HJMO QTUW	102.	polyanthes
	115.	brutium
ADF HJMO QTUX	113.	pyrenaicum
ADF HJMO QTVW	112.	albanum
ADF HJMP QTUW		
Trilophum Group, p. 163		
ADF HKLO QTUX	76.	carolinianum
ADF HKMO QTUW	102.	polyanthes
ADF HK$^{L/}_{M}$P QTUW		
Trilophum Group, p. 163		
ADF HKMP QTUX	86.	asphodeloides
ADF HKMP RTUW	105.	hispidissimum
ADF IJNO QT$^{U/}_{V}$X	96.	renardii
ADF IKN$^{O/}_{P}$ QTVX	92.	platypetalum
ADG HJLO QTUW	114.	pusillum
ADG HJLO QTUX	116.	molle
ADG HJMO QTVW	112.	albanum
ADG HJMO RTU$^{W/}_{X}$		
Cinereum Group, p. 187		
ADG HJMP $^{Q/}_{R}$TUX	62.	papuanum
	58.	traversii
ADG HJNP QTUW		
Cinereum Group, p. 187		
ADG HKLP $^{Q/}_{R}$TUX	60.	sessiliflorum
	61.	antrosrsum
ADG HKMP $^{Q/}_{R}$TUX	51.	sessiliflorum
		x traversii
		(G. x antipodeum)
	61.	antrorsum
ADG IJNO QT$^{U/}_{V}$X	96.	renardii
ADG IJNP RTUX	25.	lambertii
AEF HJM$^{O/}$P $^{Q/}_{R}$TUX	70.	schlechteri
AEF HJMP QTUW		
Trilophum Group, p. 163		
AEF HJNO QTUX	97.	peloponnesiacum
AEF HJNP RTUX	27.	procurrens
AEF HKLP RTUX	52.	thunbergii
AEF HK$^{L/}_{M}$P QTUX		
Trilophum Group, p. 163		
AEF HKMP RSUX	29.	rubifolium
AEF HKMP RTUX	52.	thunbergii
AEF HKNO QTUX	101.	gracile

AEF HKNP RSUX	28.	kishtvariense
	29.	rubifolium
AEF IKMP QTVW	119.	macrorrhizum
AEF IKMP QTVX	22.	platyanthum
	23.	erianthum
AEF IKNP QTVW	119.	macrorrhizum
AEF IKNP QTVX	23.	erianthum
AEG HJ$^{M/}_{N}$P R—-	3.	x riversleaianum
AEG HK$^{M/}_{N}$P R—-	3.	x riversleaianum
AEG HKNO RSUX	5.	nodosum
AEG HKNO RTUX	24.	wallichianum
AEG HKNO RTVX	4.	versicolor
AEG HKNP RTUX	24.	wallichianum
AEG IJNO QTUX	98.	libani
AEG IJNO RTUX	25.	lambertii
BDF HJMP QTUW	102.	polyanthes
	103.	nakaoanum
BDF HJMP RTUX	30.	swatense
BDF HJNO RTUX	79.	fremontii
BDF HJNP RTUX	30.	swatense
BDF HJNP QTVW	118.	glaberrimum
BDF HJNP RTUX	79.	fremontii
BDF HKLO QTUX	76.	carolinianum
	87.	dissectum
BDF HKMO QTUW	102.	polyanthes
BDF HKMP QSVX	21.	saxatile
BDF HKMP QTUW		
Trilophum Group, p. 163		
BDF HKMP QTUX	85.	patagonicum
	86.	asphodeloides
BDF HKMP RTUW	105.	hispidissimum
BDF HKNP RTVX	81.	californicum
BDF IJNP QSVX	18.	regelii
BDF IKNP RTVW	121.	dalmaticum
BDF IKNP R—	120.	x cantabrigiense
BDG HJLO QTUW	114.	pusillum
BDG HJLO QTUX	116.	molle
BDG HJMO QTUW		
Cinereum Group, p. 187		
BDG HJMO QTUX	42.	stapfianum
BDG HJMO RTUW		
Cinereum Group, p. 187		
BDG HJMO RTUX	39.	donianum
BDG HJMP QTUW	103.	nakaoanum
Cinereum Group, p. 187		
BDG HJMP QTUX	57.	suzukii
BDG HJMP RTUW		
Cinereum Group, p. 187		
BDG HJMP RTUX	39.	donianum
BDG HJNO QTUW		
Cinereum Group, p. 187		
BDG HJNO QTUX	42.	stapfianum
BDG HJNO RTUW		
Cinereum Group, p. 187		
BDG HJNO RTUX	39.	donianum
BDG HJNP QTUW		
Cinereum Group, p. 187		
BDG HJNP QTVW	118.	glaberrimum

BDG HJNP RTUW
   Cinereum Group, p. 187
BDG HJNP RTUX   See diagnostic notes
BDG HK$^{L/}_{m}$P QTUX   See diagnostic notes
BDG HKMO $^{Q/}_{R}$TUW
   Cinereum Group, p. 187
BDG HKMP $^{Q/}_{R}$TUW
   Cinereum Group, p. 187
BDG HKMP RTUX   45. dahuricum
                  37. palustre
BDG HKNO $^{Q/}_{R}$TUW
   Cinereum Group, p. 187
BDG HKNP RTUX   37. palustre
                  57. hayatanum
BDG IJMP RSVX   36. farreri
BEF HJLP QTUW
   Trilophum Group, p. 163
BEF HJM$^{O/}_{P}$ QTUX   67. harveyi
BEF HJMP RTUW   128. phaeum
BEF HJMP RTUX   27. procurrens
                  30. swatense
BEF HJMP RTVX   77. nervosum
BEF HJNP RTUX   27. procurrens
                  30. swatense
                  65. brycei
                  77. nervosum
BEF HJNP RTVX   77. nervosum
BEF HKLO RSUX   13. albiflorum
BEF HKLO RTUX   75. bicknellii
                  12. pseudosibiricum
BEF HKLP RTUX   12. pseudosibiricum
                  52. thunbergii
BEF HKMO QTUX   99. bohemicum
                100. lanuginosum
BEF HKMO RSUX   13. albiflorum
                  30. swatense
BEF HKMP RTUW   104. strictipes
BEF HKMP QTUW
   Trilophum Group, p. 163
BEF HKMP RTUX   See diagnostic notes
BEF HKMP RTVX   77. nervosum
BEF HKNO QT$^{U/}_{V}$X   See diagnostic notes
BEF HKNO RSUX   30. swatense
BEF HKNO RTUX   1. endressii
                  2. x oxonianum
BEF HKNP RT–X   83. deltoideum
BEF HKNP RTUX   66. pulchrum
BEF HKNP QSVX   19. clarkei
BEF HKNP QTUX   See diagnostic notes
BEF HKNP QTVX   16. pratense
                     (var.
                     stewartianum)
BEF HKNP QTVC   15. collinum
BEF HKNP RTUX   See diagnostic notes
BEF HKNP RTVX   77. nervosum
                  78. viscosissimum
BEF IJMP QSUW   129. x monacense
                130. reflexum

BEF IJMP QSUX   32. delavayi
BEF IJMP QSVX   32. delavayi
                  33. refractum
BEF IJMP QTUW   129. x monacense
BEF IJMP RTUW   128. phaeum
BEF IJMP RTUX   26. christensenianum
BEF IJNP QSVX   20. himalayense
BEF IKMP QSUX   31. sinense
BEF IKMP QSVX   31. sinense
                  33. refractum
BEF IKMP QTUW   131. aristatum
BEF IKMP QTVW   119. macrorrhizum
BEF IKMP QTVX   22. platyanthum
                  23. erianthum
BEF IKMP RTUX   26. christensenianum
BEF IKMP RSVX   33. refractum
BEF IKNP QSVX   16. pratense
BEF IKNP QTVW   119. macrorrhizum
BEF IKNP QTVX   93. ibericum
                     subsp. jubatum
                  23. erianthum
BEG HJLP RTUX   11. caeruleatum
BEG HJMO QTUX   67. harveyi
BEG HJMO RTUX   50. sanguineum
BEG HJMP QTUX   67. harveyi
BEG HJMP RTUW   128. phaeum
BEG HJMP RTUX   44. krameri
                  50. sanguineum
BEG HJNP QTUX   43. soboliferum
BEG HJNP QTVX   9. atlanticum
BEG HJNP RTUX   38. wlassovianum
                  43. soboliferum
BEG HKLO QTUX   56. sibiricum
BEG HKLO RSUX   13. albiflorum
BEG HKLO RTUX   12. pseudosibiricum
                  55. nepalense
BEG HKLP QTUX   53. wilfordii
                  56. sibiricum
BEG HKLP RTUX   12. pseudosibiricum
                  55. nepalense
BEG HKMO QTUX   51. columbinum
BEG HKMO RSUX   6. rectum
                  13. albiflorum
BEG HKMO RTUX   See diagnostic notes
BEG HKMP QTUX   51. columbinum
                  54. yoshinoi
BEG HKMP RTUX   See diagnostic notes
BEG HKNO QTVX   93. ibericum
                     subsp. ibericum
BEG HKNO RSUX   6. rectum
BEG HKNO RTUX   See diagnostic notes
BEG HKNO RTVX   4. versicolor
BEG HKNO QTUX   40. shikokianum
BEG HKNP QTUX   73. maculatum
BEG HKNP QTVX   9. atlanticum
                  15. collinum
BEG HKNP RTUX   See diagnostic notes

BEG IJMP Q$^{S/}_{T}$UW   129. x monacense
                                 130. reflexum
BEG IJMP RSVX   35. yunnanense
BEG IJMP RTUW   128. phaeum
BEG IJNO QTUX   98. libani
BEG IJNP RSVX   35. yunnanense
BEG IKMP RSVX   34. pogonanthum
BEG IKNO QTUX   95. gymnocaulon
CEF HJLO QTUX   89. macrostylum
CEF HJM$^{O/}_{P}$ QTUX   69. caffrum
                                  89. macrostylum
CEF HJMP QTVX   122. cataractarum
CEF HJN$^{O/}_{P}$ QTUX   64. robustum
                                  69. caffrum
CEF HJNP QTVW   127. maderense
CEF HKMP QTVW   123. robertianum
CEF HKN$^{O/}_{P}$ QTUX   69. caffrum
CEF HKNP QTVW   124. rubescens
CEF IJNP QSVW   125. canariense
CEF IKNP QSVW   126. palmatum
CEG HKMO QTUX   88. tuberosum
                                  90. linearilobum
CEG HKMO RTUX   68. incanum
CEG HKNO QTUX   65. tuberosum
                                  91. malviflorum
CEG HKNO QTVX   91. malviflorum
CEG HKNO RTUX   68. incanum

Diagnostic notes for multi-access key (stop when you reach a description that fits the specimen)

BDG HJNP RTUX
1. Rootstock not composed of small tubers joined by lengths of slender rhizome, 39. *donianum*
2. Leaves conspicuously marbled; stigmas 3–6mm, 49. *orientali-tibeticum*
3. Leaves not or scarcely marbled; stigmas less than 3mm, 48. *pylzowianum*

BDG HK$^{L/}_{M}$P QTUX
1. Stems trailing and rooting, 57. *suzukii*
2. Flowers in cymules spaced along the leafy stems, 63. *potentilloides*
3. Flowers near the ground, below the blades of the basal leaves or just above 61. *antrorsum*

BEF HKMP QTUX
1. Stipules entire, stigmas 3.5–4mm, 82. *schiedeanum*
2. Stipules split, sepals 6–8mm, 71. *flanaganii*
3. Stipules split, sepals 4–5.5mm, 72. *ornithopodon*

BEF HKMP RTUX
1. Sides of leaf-divisions with lobes and teeth extending nearly to base and far below broadest part of division, 8. *sylvaticum*
2. Flowers funnel-shaped, petals white, 10. *rivulare*
3. Erect; petals notched, pink; stigmas 4–6mm, 77. *nervosum*
4. Erect; petals not notched, white or nearly so; stigmas 3–4mm, 80. *richardsonii*
5. Sprawling; petals not

more than 10.5mm,
52. *thunbergii*
6.Sprawling; petals
15–16mm,
82. *schiedeanum*
7. Erect, flowers
funnel/trumpet-shaped,
petals blue to violet,
fruiting pedicels erect,
12. *pseudosibiricum*
8.Stipules split; petals
to 15mm long,
71. *flanaganii*

BEF HKNO QT$^{U/v}$X

1.Flowering period
short, April–May;
petals rather pale blue,
97. *peloponnesiacum*
2.Flowering period
short, June–July; petals
deep blue or purple,
94. x *magnificum*
3. Flowering period
long, June onwards;
flowers funnel-shaped;
petals pink, 101.
gracile

BEF HKNP QTUX

1.Petals magenta with
blackish base,
14. *psilostemon*
2.Erect; flowers about
30mm in diameter,
partly in umbel-like
clusters,
73. *maculatum*
3.Erect; flowers more
than 40mm in
diameter,
not in umbel-like
clusters, 74. *oreganum*
4.Sprawling; sepal
mucro not more than
1.5mm,
82. *schiedeanum*

BEF HKNP RTUX

1.Erect; petals notched,
pink, 77. *nervosum*
2.Erect; petals not
notched, white or
nearly so, 80.
richardsonii
3.Sprawling; petals
bluish lilac,
82. *schiedeanum*

BEG HKMO RTUX

1.Cymules 1-flowered;
petals more than
12mm, 50. *sanguineum*
2.Cymules 2-flowered;
petals more than
12mm, 6. *rectum*
3.Petals less than
10mm, 55. *nepalense*

BEG HKMP RTUX

1.Cymules 1-flowered,
petals not less than
12mm, 50. *sanguineum*
2.Erect; sides of leaf-
divisions with
lobes and teeth
extending nearly to
base, and far below
broadest part of
division,
8. *sylvaticum*
3.Sprawling; petals
brilliant purplish
pink, 37. *palustre*
4.Sprawling; leaf-lobes
2–3 times as long
as broad, 46. *yesoense*
5.Sprawling or erect;
petals less than
10mm, 55. *nepalense*

BEG HKNO RTUX

1.Cymules 1-flowered,
50. *sanguineum*
2.Flowers saucer-
shaped; anthers and
stigmas blackish,
24. *wallichianum*
3.Flowers funnel-
shaped; anthers and
stigmas not blackish,
6. *rectum*

BEG HKNP RTUX

1.Cymules 1-flowered,
50. *sanguineum*
2.Leaf-divisions deep,
deeply cut,
46. *yesoense*
3.Anthers and stigmas
blackish,
24. *wallichianum*
4.Petals brilliant
purplish pink; stigmas
up to 3mm,
37. *palustre*
5.Petals not brilliantly
coloured; stigmas
more than 3.5mm,
38. *wlassovianum*

How to Use the Dichotomous Keys

The key is broken up into sections; the first section is a key to groups. Each number in the left-hand margin is linked with two descriptions (a couplet) of some character of the plant, lettered "a" and "b". Start with couplet "1" and decide whether your plant corresponds with "a" or "b". The next step is indicated in the right-hand margin. If there is a number, go to the couplet of that number; if a group is mentioned, go to the group indicated and proceed in the same way. In the groups you either go to another couplet or arrive at the name of a species or other taxon, numbered as in Chapter 9. In the latter case, verify your identification with the description in Chapter 9, as with the multi-access key.

A dichotomous key forces you to take the characters in a pre-arranged sequence. However, if a character is missing or doubtful it is often worth trying both leads in a couplet successively, although if this happens more than once or twice one tends to lose heart!

What to do if the Characters of the Fruit are not Available

This may be because the fruit is unripe or is failing to develop for some reason, the most likely being that the plant is a hybrid; it may be possible to arrive at an identification with the aid of the following hints (which cover only a few of the possibilities if lack of fruit is due to hybridity).

(1) If the flowers are more or less nodding and have widely spreading or reflexed petals and the pedicels of immature fruits are not erect, consider Group B and Group F, couplet 6 onwards.

(2) If the plant is erect and the flowers are strongly inclined to reddish colouring and have a black centre, then the plant will be 27. *G. procurrens* or a hybrid of *G. psilostemon* (go to no. 14)

(3) If the petals have a clearly defined claw, the plant will probably be found in Group C.

(4) If the stamens are twice or more as long as the sepals, go to Group C.

(5) If the flower is funnel-shaped but without sharply defined or strongly keeled petal-claws go to Group F or species 101. *G. gracile*.

(6) If the leaf-blades are divided to the base (incisions reaching leaf-stalk), try Groups C and D before F.

(7) If the anthers are scarlet before they burst, go to Group C.

(8) If the petals are blue, lavender or white with feathered veins and are notched at the apex, go to Group D.

(9) If the plant is an annual not fulfilling condition (7), try Groups C and E.

(10) If none of these conditions holds, the plant is most likely to be a member of Group F and although this has the longest key, it is probably best to try this first.

The dichotomous key

KEY TO GROUPS

1a. Fruit-discharge mechanism inoperative, carpels shed when ripe or after a long delay, not thrown off; rostrum remaining thin   Group A, p. 51

b.   Fruit forcibly disrupted at maturity; rostrum soon thick   2

2a. Mericarps thrown off with the seed inside, frequently prominently sculptured   3

b.   Seeds ejected from mericarps, the latter often remaining attached by the awn to the rostrum; mericarps not sculptured   4

3a. Mericarps thrown off with awn (which becomes coiled) attached (Figure 5.1) Group B, p. 51

b.   Mericarps separating from the awn at the moment of explosion, awns falling to the ground (Figure 5.3)   Group C, p. 51

4a. Mericarp without a seed-retaining structure at lower end of orifice, falling after discharge (Figure 5.5)   Group D, p. 52

b.   Mericarp with a prong or tuft of bristles at lower end of orifice for temporary retention of seed in pre-explosive interval, nearly always remaining attached to rostrum after discharge   5

5a. Mericarp with a prong at lower end of orifice, usually bent so as to be inside the chamber after the seed has been expelled (Figure 5.4); rare   Group E, p. 52

b.   Mericarp with a tuft of bristles seated on a horny tubercle at lower end of orifice (Figure 4.6B); common   Group F, p. 52

GROUP A

1a. Flowers more than 20mm in diameter; plant perennial *112. albanum*

b. Flowers 10mm in diameter or less; plant annual *G. divaricatum* (see p. 166)

GROUP B

1a. Usually more than 30cm in height; floral axis below the horizontal; petals widely spreading (flower flat) or reflexed (the Phaeum Group) 2

b. Usually less than 30cm in height; flowers more or less erect, saucer-shaped or bowl-shaped (the Cinereum Group: key to species is on p. 188)

2a. Sepal mucro more than half as long as sepal body *131. aristatum*

b. Sepal mucro much less than half as long as sepal body 3

3a. Petals nearly as wide as long or wider, widely spreading; filaments with long hairs *128. phaeum*

b. Petals about $^2/_3$ as wide as long or less, evidently reflexed just above the base 4

4a. Petals about $^2/_3$ as wide as long (detach them for examination); filaments with long spreading glistening hairs on lower half *129. x monacense*

b. Petals about $^1/_2$ as wide as long; filaments with only very fine hairs on the edges at the base *130. reflexum*

GROUP C

1a. Leaf-blades divided to the base 2

b. Leaf-blades not divided as far as the base 7

2a. Stamens about twice as long as sepals 3

b. Stamens not nearly twice as long as sepals 4

3a. Central division of leaf-blade wedge-shaped, not stalked *125. canariense*

b. Central division of leaf-blade constricted into a distinct stalk *126. palmatum*

4a. Leaf-blades mostly much more than 20cm wide, readily reaching 40cm in width; petals 13–18mm wide with claw only 2.5mm *127. maderense*

b. Leaf-blades not much more than 20cm wide, if that; petals not more than 13mm wide with claw 5mm long or more 5

5a. Flowers 11–16mm in diameter; detached mericarps with long hair-like fibres attached at top *123. robertianum*

b. Flowers 17mm in diameter or more; detached mericarps without long hair-like fibres attached at top 6

6a. Biennial; sepal mucro $^1/_4$–$^1/_3$ as long as sepal body *124. rubescens*

b. Perennial; sepal mucro $^1/_8$–$^1/_6$ as long as sepal body *122. cataractarum*

7a. Stamens nearly twice as long as sepals or more 8

b. Stamens much less than twice as long as sepals 11

8a. Calyx not bladdery; flowers upwardly inclined; stamens and style straight *118. glaberrimum*

b. Calyx bladdery; floral axis horizontal; stamens and style sinuous 9

9a. Blades of lower leaves less than 5cm wide *121. dalmaticum*

b. Blades of lower leaves more than 5cm wide (sometimes less in no. 120) 10

10a. Some of the lower leaves more than 10cm wide; fruit developing and seed normally ripening *119. macrorrhizum*

b. Lower leaves not more than about 7cm wide; fruit sometimes not enlarging; seed not ripening *120. x cantabrigiense*

11a. Cymules one-flowered *103. nakaoanum*

b. Cymules two- or three-flowered, or flowers arranged in umbel-like clusters 12

12a. Flowers (except the first few) in tight umbel-like clusters; (lower leaves alternate) *102. polyanthes*

b. Flowers mostly in cymules 13

13a. Plant perennial with a thick fleshy rootstock 14

b. Plant annual or perennial but with a scanty rootstock 15

14a. Sepals 8mm long or more; leaves paired or in threes *104. strictipes*

b. Sepals not more than 7.5mm; leaves paired *105. hispidissimum*

15a. Most of the flowers on each plant cleistogamous (without petals and producing fruit without ever opening) (the Trilophum Group: key to species is on p. 163)

b. None of the flowers cleistogamous 16

16a. Plant glossy and fleshy; sepals with deep keels and cross-ribs; petals clawed *117. lucidum*

b. Plant with dull hairy surface, not fleshy; sepals only ordinarily ribbed; petals not clawed 17

17a. Mericarps hairy, not extensively ribbed 18

b. Mericarps hairless, closely ribbed 19

18a. Perennial; flowers 12–27mm in diameter *113. pyrenaicum*

b. Annual, often overwintering; flowers about 6mm in diameter *114. pusillum*

19a. Petals 8–12.5mm *115. brutium*

b. Petals 4–6mm *116. molle*

GROUP D

1a. Blades of main leaves divided to the base 2
  b. Blades of main leaves not divided to the base 5
2a. Sepals 7–9mm; petals 16–22mm; stylar portion of rostrum 3–5mm *91. malviflorum*
  b. Sepals 4–7mm; petals 8–17mm; stylar portion of rostrum less than 3mm 3
3a. Upper parts of plant freely clothed with glandular hairs *89. macrostylum*
  b. Plant without conspicuous glandular hairs 4
4a. Basal leaves with divisions lobed from just below the middle and beyond, or with few lobes, or with both these conditions; lateral divisions of basal leaves joined for $^1/_6$ –$^1/_4$ of their length *90. linearilobum*
  b. Basal leaves with divisions lobed for most of their length, lobes numerous; lateral divisions free or nearly so except for outermost pair on each side which may be joined for up to $^1/_6$ of their length *88. tuberosum*
5a. Flowers funnel-shaped; petals pink *101. gracile*
  b. Flowers not funnel-shaped; petals not pink 6
6a. Leaves sage-textured, greyish; petals whitish or pale lavender with strong violet-blue veins *96. renardii*
  b. Leaves not sage-textured and greyish, though sometimes wrinkled; petals blue 7
7a. Sprawling annuals or biennials with diffuse inflorescences; flowers not more than 23mm in diameter 8
  b. Erect perennials with dense inflorescences; flowers 28mm or more in diameter 9
8a. Biennial; petals about 9–11 x 8–9mm, ground-colour not whitish at base; seeds mottled in light and dark brown *99. bohemicum*
  b. Annual; petals about 8–9 x 6–7mm, ground-colour nearly white at base; seeds uniformly brown *100. lanuginosum*
9a. Basal leaves scarcely angled in outline, divided about halfway to the base, their divisions broadest near the apex, palmately lobed (lobes apical) *92. platypetalum*
  b. Basal leaves distinctly angled in outline, divided as far as $^2/_3$ or more, their divisions broadest well below the apex, palmato-pinnately lobed (lobes on the sides) 10
10a. Plant with conspicuous glandular hairs on upper parts 11
  b. Plant without conspicuous glandular hairs 13
11a. Basal leaves with sides of divisions lobed and toothed nearly to the base; plant

flowering in June, leafy all summer; stylar portion of rostrum 4–7mm 12
  b. Basal leaves with sides of divisions not lobed and toothed below the widest part; plant flowering in May, leaves disappearing in summer; stylar portion of rostrum 2–3mm *97. peloponnesiacum*
12a. A sterile hybrid, never producing good seeds *94. x magnificum*
  b. A naturally-occurring fertile plant *93. ibericum* subsp. *jubatum*
13a. Plant flowering in May, leaves disappearing in summer *98. libani*
  b. Plant flowering in June or later, leafy all summer 14
14a. Noticeably hairy plant with wrinkled leaves and upwardly inclined flowers 40–48mm in diameter *93. ibericum* subsp. *ibericum*
  b. Inconspicuously hairy plant with unwrinkled leaves and horizontal floral axis; flowers about 35mm in diameter *95. gymnocaulon*

GROUP E

1a. Petals between 8 and 16mm *63. asphodeloides*
  b. Petals not more than 8mm *64. dissectum*

GROUP F

This is divided into two for the purpose of the diagnostic key, as follows:
    a. Stipules deeply cut into two or more long acute, usually narrow, lobes (species of southern Africa) Group F(1)
    b. Stipules entire or slightly lobed (when the stipules are joined in pairs the tips may be separate but each point represents a whole stipule)
(species of other regions than southern Africa) Group F(2) (page 53)

GROUP F(1)

1a. Lowest leaves cut to the base 2
  b. Lowest leaves not cut to the base 4
2a. Leaf-segments not more than 2mm wide *68. incanum*
  b. Leaf-segments more than 2mm wide 3
3a. Leaf-segments not more than 5mm wide *69. caffrum*
  b. Leaf-segments (at least some of them) more than 5mm wide (a much-branched grey-hairy shrub with profusely segmented leaves) *64. robustum*
4a. Leaves mostly 0.5–3cm wide; divisions

with lobes $1-2\frac{1}{2}$ times as long as broad
67. *harveyi*

b. Leaves mostly 6cm wide or more; divisions with lobes mostly not more than $1\frac{1}{2}$ times as long as broad 5

5a. Plant grey-hairy; leaf-divisions pinnately lobed, with numerous segments 6

b. Plant not grey-hairy; leaf-divisions palmately or palmato-pinnately lobed, usually rather sparsely segmented 7

6a. Leaf-divisions elliptic or lanceolate or oblanceolate, shallowly lobed and toothed; lobes and teeth not spreading 66. *pulchrum*

b. Leaf-divisions rhombic, lobed nearly halfway to the midrib; lobes and teeth mostly spreading 65. *brycei*

7a. Teeth and tips of lobes usually numerous and crowded 70. *schlechteri*

b. Teeth and tips of lobes few, not crowded 8

8a. Flowers larger (sepals 6–8mm, petals 10–16mm) 71. *flanaganii*

b. Flowers smaller (sepals 4–5.5mm, petals 7–10mm) 72. *ornithopodon*

GROUP F(2)

1a. Annuals, easily pulled up complete with root system 2

b. Perennials, usually breaking from the root system when pulled up 5

2a. Immature fruits erect on reflexed pedicels 3

b. Immature fruits erect on erect pedicels 4

3a. Leaf-blades divided nearly to base; sepals 6–8mm, enlarging to 8–9mm
51. *columbinum*

b. Leaf-blades not divided nearly to base; sepals 3.5–5mm 7. *rotundifolium*

4a. One fruiting pedicel in each cymule twice as long as sepals or more; rostrum with stylar portion 2–3mm 75. *bicknellii*

b. Fruiting pedicels at most $1\frac{1}{2}$ times as long as sepals; rostrum with stylar portion about 1.5mm 76. *carolinianum*

5a. Flowers nodding or inverted 6

b. Flowers not nodding 12

6a. Tips of filaments, anthers and stigmas blackish; stigmas 5–6mm 25. *lambertii*

b. Tips of filaments, anthers and stigmas paler though sometimes rather dark red or the anthers inky blue; stigmas not more than 4.5mm 7

7a. Upper part of plant with coarse, dense, entirely purple glandular hairs 33. *refractum*

b. Glandular hairs of upper part of plant colourless or sometimes red-tipped, dense to sparse or sometimes absent 8

8a. Petals with very few hairs on edges at base, none on surface; nectary forming a ring all

round the flower; petals blackish
31. *sinense*

b. Petals with numerous hairs on the edge at base; nectaries five, separate; petals rarely blackish 9

9a. Flowers light violet-blue, mostly in dense umbel-like clusters; immature fruits erect, standing above the currently open flowers
22. *platyanthum*

b. Flowers not violet-blue, in 2-flowered cymules; immature fruits nodding 10

10a. Filaments almost without hairs 32. *delavayi*

b. Filaments profusely hairy at base 11

11a. Petals not more than $1\frac{1}{3}$ times as long as broad, forming a bowl-shaped or saucer-shaped flower 35. *yunnanense*

b. Petals about twice as long as wide, curling backwards gently between the sepals
34. *pogonanthum*

12a. Sprawling or trailing plants; flowers small (petals 15mm or less), dispersed amongst the leaves, usually pale (but bright pink in one species) 13

b. Plants not with this combination of characters; petals usually more than 10.5mm but plant sometimes trailing 22

13a. Plant unisexual 11. *caeruleatum*

b. Plant with bisexual flowers 14

14a. Leaf-divisions toothed rather than lobed and toothed 53. *wilfordii*

b. Leaf-divisions clearly both lobed and toothed 15

15a. Anthers violet-blue 16

b. Anthers pale pink, cream or whitish, sometimes with blue edges 19

16a. Flowers 12–15mm in diameter; some glandular hairs nearly always present on sepals, rostrum, mericarps and, sometimes, pedicels 52. *thunbergii*

b. Flowers 9–12mm in diameter; plant without glandular hairs 17

17a. Plant with massive taproot to 12mm thick
84. *herrerae*

b. Plants with slender root system 18

18a. Leaf-divisions short, broad, rather abruptly tapered; cymules 2-flowered or a mixture of 1-flowered and 2-flowered 55. *nepalense*

b. Leaf-divisions long, narrow, gradually tapered; cymules 1-flowered 56. *sibiricum*

19a. Stems regularly rooting at nodes; stalks of the 1-flowered cymules holding the flowers well above the leaves (flowers funnel-shaped, white) 57. *suzukii*

b. Stems not or occasionally rooting at nodes; flowers borne only just above the leaves 20

20a. Flowers about 10mm in diameter, white, scarcely raised above the foliage 21

b. Flowers about 15mm in diameter, white or pink, conspicuous
   59. x antipodeum (sessiliflorum x traversii)

21a. Rostrum about 9mm; lower internodes very short so that spread of plant is usually less than 20cm   *60. sessiliflorum*

b. Rostrum 11–16mm; habit loose, plant readily spreading beyond a diameter of 20cm   *63. potentilloides*

22a. Rootstock a system of tubers up to 10 x 6mm interlinked by lengths of slender stolon (underground rhizome); plant usually small, inflorescence few-flowered   23

b. Rootstock not so constructed; plant stature variable   24

23a. Leaves marbled, tips of teeth and lobes more or less obtuse; flowers purplish pink with a cup-shaped white centre; stigmas 3–6mm   *49. orientali-tibeticum*

b. Leaves not marbled, tips of teeth and lobes more or less acute; flowers deep rose-pink, trumpet-shaped, with petals white only at extreme base; stigmas less than 3mm
   48. pylzowianum

24a. Petals deep magenta; plant without glandular hairs (bushy)   *37. palustre*

b. Plant not both magenta-flowered and without glandular hairs   25

25a. Petals with few hairs on basal margins and none on front surface; plant with glandular hairs (other plants with similarly few petal hairs do not have glandular hairs); flowers weakly trumpet-shaped   *85. patagonicum*

b. Petal-base with numerous hairs or, if very few, plant is without glandular hairs   26

26a. Flowers funnel-shaped or trumpet-shaped (view them from the side; some borderline species are keyed under both alternatives) 27

b. Flowers not funnel-shaped or trumpet-shaped   38

27a. Pedicels of immature fruits spreading on or just above the horizontal or below the horizontal   28

b. Pedicels of immature fruits erect   33

28a. Divisions of leaf-blades toothed but not lobed   *5. nodosum*

b. Divisions of leaf-blades clearly lobed as well as toothed   29

29a. Rosette-leaves numerous at flowering time 30

b. Rosette-leaves few or none at flowering time   32

30a. One pedicel in each pair usually shorter than sepals   *13. albiflorum*

b. Pedicels usually $1^1/_2$–4 times as long as sepals   31

31a. Basal leaves to 12cm wide with rhombic-obovate divisions; plant weakly hairy; petals with coloured veins   *54. yoshinoi*

b. Basal leaves to 6cm wide with broadly wedge-shaped divisions that are broadest at the apex; plant rather strongly appressed-hairy; petal-veins not distinctively coloured
   59. x antipodeum (sessiliflorum x traversii)

32a. Plant bushy; leaves not wrinkled; stigmas 4.5mm   *40. shikokianum*

b. Plant erect; leaves wrinkled; stigmas 2.5–3.5mm   *6. rectum*

33a. Lobes of main leaf-blades mostly 2–4 times as long as broad; blades not usually divided less than $^4/_5$ and often nearly to base   34

b. Lobes of main leaf-blades not more than about $1^1/_2$ times as long as broad; blades not usually divided beyond $^4/_5$, occasionally to $^5/_6$ 35

34a. Main leaves with divisions broadest near the middle; inflorescence dense; flowers white   *10. rivulare*

b. Main leaves with divisions broadest at or near apex; inflorescence diffuse; flowers deep reddish purple or magenta   *39. donianum*

35a. Petals net-veined   36

b. Petals not net-veined   37

36a. Ground-colour of petals white; flowers usually 25–30mm in diameter *4. versicolor*

b. Ground-colour of petals pink; flowers usually more than 30mm in diameter, or petals aberrant, linear   *2. x oxonianum*

37a. Plant hoary on account of its dense clothing of appressed hairs   *3. x riversleaianum*

b. Plant without a hoary hair-clothing
   1. endressii and *2. x oxonianum* or veinless state of *4. versicolor*

38a. Plant trailing   39

b. Plant not trailing   54

39a. Cymules all 1-flowered; flowers not in umbel-like clusters   40

b. Cymules all or mostly 2-flowered or flowers in umbel-like clusters   45

40a. Divisions of leaf-blades deeply cut with more or less spear-like lobes and, sometimes, teeth   41

b. Divisions of leaf-blades shallowly cut with lobes broader than long and with the teeth small or none   42

41a. Stipules not more than 7mm, free or united in pairs, ovate or triangular, mostly reflexed
   50. sanguineum

b. Stipules 8–9mm, broadly ovate, mostly united in pairs, erect   *47. hayatanum*

42a. Dwarf alpine plant with pink petals held below or just above the leaves; basal leaf-segments tending to be much reduced
   61. antrorsum

b. Plant without this combination of characters   43

43a. Leaves clothed with fine greyish hairs;

flowers pale pink to white, held just above
the leaves 58. *traversii*

b. Leaves not grey-hairy; flowers held well
above the leaves 44

44a. Flowers white or nearly so 57. *suzukii*

b. Flowers purple 62. *papuanum*

45a. Stamens and stigmas blackish 46

b. Stamens and stigmas not blackish 49

46a. Petal bases blackish like the stamens and
stigmas 27. *procurrens*

b. Petal bases white or pink 47

47a. Petals mainly pink or blue with darker
veins; floral axis vertical 48

b. Petals mainly white with darker veins;
floral axis horizontal 26. *christensenianum*

48a. Stigmas 5.5–7mm; rootstock short and
stout; teeth and tips of lobes of leaves quite
shallow and coarse 4. *wallichianum*

b. Stigmas to 4.5mm; rootstock composed of
slender rhizomes; teeth and tips of lobes of
leaves finer, narrow and deep
28. *kishtvariense*

49a. Leaf-segments diverging strongly from one
another, giving a latticed effect
82. *schiedeanum*

b. Leaf-segments weakly divergent 50

50a. Divisions of lower stem-leaves with longest
lateral lobes not more than $1^{1}/_{2}$ times as
long as broad; plant with glandular hairs
52

b. Divisions of lower stem-leaves with longest
lateral lobes 2 or more times as long as
broad; plant without glandular hairs 51

51.a. Divisions of main leaves broadest just
below apex 45. *dahuricum*

b. Divisions of main leaves broadest just
above middle 46. *yesoense*

52a. Petals bearded on margins and front surface
only at the base 53

b. Petals bearded on the front surface except
in the apical one-fifth 83. *deltoideum*

53a. Peduncles 1.5–8cm, pedicels 1.5–3cm
38. *wlassovianum*

b. Peduncles mostly 4–16cm, pedicels 3–6cm
30. *swatense*

54a. Flowers partly in umbel-like clusters 55

b. Flowers not in umbel-like clusters 59

55a. Floral axis horizontal; stamens appressed to
style; petals bluish 56

b. Floral axis more or less erect; stamens
curving away from style; petals pink 57

56a. Eglandular hairs of lower or middle part of
stem spreading 22. *platyanthum*

b. Eglandular hairs of lower or middle part of
stem appressed 23. *erianthum*

57a. Leaf-divisions pinnately lobed down the
sides nearly to the base; leaf ferny (many
segments) 9. *atlanticum*

b. Leaf-divisions lobed mainly near the
middle; leaf not ferny (segments not very
numerous) 58

58a. Sepal mucro 2–3.5mm; petals without hairs
all across front surface at base; pedicels of
immature fruits erect 73. *maculatum*

b. Sepal mucro 1–1.5mm; petals with hairs all
across front surface at base; pedicels of
immature fruits reflexed 78. *viscosissimum*

59a. Floral axis approximately horizontal 60

b. Floral axis upwardly inclined or vertically
erect 63

60a. Dwarf alpine plants up to about 25cm; leaf-
lobes and divisions not very narrow 61

b. Plants usually more than 30cm tall; if
smaller, then with very narrow leaf-lobes
and divisions 62

61a. Leaf-divisions tapered towards apex; petals
blue; immature fruits reflexed on reflexed
pedicels 18. *regelii*

b. Leaf-divisions broadest at apex; petals pale
pink; immature fruits spreading or lying on
the ground 36. *farreri*

62a. Main leaves divided as far as $^{4}/_{5}$ or less;
rootstock more or less creeping
underground; inflorescence diffuse; flowers
40–60mm in diameter 20. *himalayense*

b. Main leaves divided as far as $^{6}/_{7}$ or more;
rootstock compact, not creeping;
inflorescence dense; flowers 35-45mm in
diameter 16. *pratense*

63a. Petals not more than 10mm 53. *wilfordii*

b. Petals more than 10mm 64

64a. Petals purplish red with a black spot at the
base 14. *psilostemon*

b. Petals otherwise coloured 65

65a. Immature fruits spreading or nodding (on
spreading or reflexed pedicels) 66

b. Immature fruits erect (on erect or reflexed
pedicels) 69

66a. Stylar portion of rostrum 7–8mm 67

b. Stylar portion of rostrum absent or up to
1.5mm 68

67a. Petals 22–29mm; leaf-divisions with
numerous narrow lobes 2–3 times as long
as broad; leaves 5–13cm wide 19. *clarkei*

b. Petals not more than 17mm; leaf-divisions
with few short lobes; leaves not more than
5.5cm wide 21. *saxatile*

68a. Plant without rosette leaves; petals purple,
14–18mm 29. *rubifolium*

b. Plant producing rosette leaves; ground
colour of petals nearly white; petals about
10mm 54. *yoshinoi*

69a. All stipules completely united in pairs
(without free tips); stigmas and tips of
stamens blackish or dark violet; (stigmas
5.5–7mm) 24. *wallichianum*

b. Stipules free or some of them incompletely united in pairs (free at tips); stigmas and tips of stamens not blackish or dark violet   70

70a. Dwarf alpine plant with slender underground stolons; petals deep pink with red base, notched at apex; sepals reddish
42. stapfianum

b. Plant without the above combination of characters   71

71a. Petals without hairs all across front at base 72

b. Petals with hairs all across front at base 73

72a. Petals about 23mm, nearly as broad as long; immature fruits erect on erect pedicels   *74. oreganum*

b. Petals not more than 20mm, $1^{1}/_{4}$–2 times as long as broad; immature fruits erect on more or less reflexed pedicels *15. collinum*

73a. Plant with glandular hairs   74

b. Plant without glandular hairs   77

74a. Divisions of main leaves with lobes and teeth extending down the sides nearly to base; inflorescence dense; stigmas 2–3mm; pedicels erect   *8. sylvaticum*

b. Divisions of main leaves with lobes and teeth extending down the sides only to the middle or just beyond; inflorescence diffuse; stigmas 3–6mm; pedicels usually spreading or reflexed   75

75a. Petals white or pale lilac, not notched, 12–18mm; stigmas 3–4mm
80. richardsonii

b. Petals pink, 13–22mm, more or less notched; stigmas 4–6mm   76

76a. Flowering stems usually clustered, branching from near the ground, profusely branched; stem-leaves numerous   *79. fremontii*

b. Flowering stems usually solitary, branching high up, not profusely; stem-leaves few
77. nervosum

77a. Pedicels of immature fruits erect   78

b. Pedicels of immature fruits spreading or reflexed   79

78a. Leaves divided as far as about $^{6}/_{7}$ or less; stigmas 2–3mm   *8. sylvaticum*

b. Leaves divided nearly to the base on either side of the central division; stigmas 5–6mm
43. soboliferum

79a. Petals not more than 16mm, $1^{1}/_{3}$ times as long as broad, with hairs on front surface extending above basal tuft over basal $^{1}/_{3}$ or $^{1}/_{2}$; stylar portion of rostrum about 1.5mm
44. krameri

b. Petals 17–22mm, more than $1^{1}/_{2}$ times as long as broad, with hairs on front surface confined to basal tuft; stylar portion of rostrum 2–3mm   *38. wlassovianum*

Chapter 9
The Cultivated Cranesbills

INTRODUCTION AND EXPLANATIONS

The standard treatment for each species in this chapter includes a summary description and a full botanical description. The first gives the full range of flower colours, whereas the second gives only the typical colour, provided any variations are covered in descriptions of varieties, cultivars, etc. (Some species receive a non-standard treatment: a shorter main description and no summary description.) Hybrids are mostly dealt with under parent species but the treatment is selective (see Preface). Most of the known hybrids are listed in Appendix III.

The range of material on which the descriptions are based varies widely, and some allowance must be made for this. The emphasis, however, has been on plants that are in cultivation.

Important information contained in the descriptions of the subdivisions of the genus (see Chapter 5) and of the informal groups is repeated in the species-descriptions except in the cases of section Tuberosa and of groups represented by only one species.

Synonyms that are current in horticultural circles are given in parentheses after the current name at the beginning of each description. Other synonyms are given when it seems useful to do so. Misapplied names (see Chapter 3) are not shown as synonyms but are dealt with in the discussion sections and, like the synonyms, can be traced in the index.

Terminology, conventions and abbreviated references to colour charts cited as RHSCC and HCC are explained in the second part of Chapter 4. In the present chapter I use place-names to indicate certain important British gardens, thus "Cambridge" means the University Botanic Garden, Cambridge; "Edinburgh" the Royal Botanic Garden, Edinburgh; "Kew" the Royal Botanic Gardens, Kew, London; and "Wisley", the Garden of the Royal Horticultural Society, Wisley, near Woking, Surrey. "Cambridge" is sometimes followed by an accession number, consisting of four digits for the year and four for a serial number for that year; for ease of reading I have added a dot after the first four digits. The Cambridge University Botanic Garden herbarium is referred to as CUBG herbarium (its official code in *Index Herbariorum* is CGG). "The Wisley Trial 1973–6" means the trial held at Wisley for horticultural evaluation of *Geranium* in the years 1973–6. "The Report of the Wisley Trial" means the report in Proceedings of the Royal Horticultural Society, 103, 67–71 (1978) (in library copies the proceedings are usually bound with *The Garden* (formerly *Journal of the Royal Horticultural Society*) for the same year, which has the same volume number).

THE ILLUSTRATIONS

The silhouettes or line-drawings of leaves show the basal leaves or lower stem-leaves unless otherwise indicated. In all cranesbills there is variation according to the part of the plant on which the leaves are borne and the climatic conditions under which they unfolded, as well as variation between plants on account of their varying genetic constitutions; the illustrations on their own should therefore not be relied upon for identification, but used for confirmation.

Most specimens illustrated were cultivated at the University Botanic Garden, Cambridge. For these the caption gives the donor and date of donation, if known (a few have lost their accession numbers and their ultimate source is unknown). A few specimens were obtained from other gardens and for these the name of the grower appears, preceded by "cult.", and followed by the date of collection of the specimen. "B.G." means "botanic garden". Collecting-numbers and collector's names (when differing from the name of the donor) are given in parentheses after the locality. Captions to colour plates are mostly comparable to those of leaf-silhouettes, but include the month in which the photograph was taken. "Cult." here means a photograph taken in a garden other than Cambridge B.G.

CLASSIFICATION AND ARRANGEMENT OF SPECIES

The following list shows at a glance how the species treated in this chapter are grouped. A more condensed presentation of the classification of the genus *Geranium* is given in Chapter 5.

GERANIUM LINNAEUS
SUBGENUS I GERANIUM

Section Geranium
The Sylvaticum Section

The Endressii Group

1. G. endressii Gay
2. G. x oxonianum Yeo (G. endressii x G. versicolor)
3. G. x riversleaianum Yeo (G. endressii x G. traversii)
4. G. versicolor Linnaeus
5. G. nodosum Linnaeus
6. G. rectum Trautvetter

The Rotundifolium Group

7. G. rotundifolium Linnaeus

The Sylvaticum Group

8. G. sylvaticum Linnaeus
9. G. atlanticum Boissier
10. G. rivulare Villars
11. G. caeruleatum Schur
12. G. pseudosibiricum J. Mayer
13. G. albiflorum Ledebour
14. G. psilostemon Ledebour

The Collinum Group

15. G. collinum Willdenow

The Pratense Group

16. G. pratense Linnaeus (var. pratense & var. stewartianum Y.J. Nasir)
17. G. transbaicalicum Sergievskaya
18. G. regelii Nevski
19. G. clarkei Yeo
20. G. himalayense Klotzsch
21. G. saxatile Karelin & Kirilow

The Erianthum Group

22. G. platyanthum Duthie
23. G. erianthum De Candolle

The Wallichianum Group

24. G. wallichianum D. Don
25. G. lambertii Sweet
26. G. christensenianum Handel-Mazzetti
27. G. procurrens Yeo
28. G. kishtvariense Knuth

29. G. rubifolium Lindley
30. G. swatense Schönbeck-Temesy

The Refractum Group

31. G. sinense Knuth
32. G. delavayi Franchet
33. G. refractum Edgeworth & J.D. Hooker
34. G. pogonanthum Franchet
35. G. yunnanense Franchet

The Farreri Group

36. G. farreri Stapf

The Palustre Group

37. G. palustre Linnaeus
38. G. wlassovianum Link
39. G. donianum Sweet
40. G. shikokianum Matsumura
41. G. koreanum Komarov

The Stapfianum Group

42. G. stapfianum Handel-Mazzetti

The Krameri Group

43. G. soboliferum Komarov
44. G. krameri Franchet & Savatier
45. G. dahuricum De Candolle
46. G. yesoense Franchet & Savatier
47. G. hayatanum Ohwi

The Pylzowianum Group

48. G. pylzowianum Maximowicz
49. G. orientali-tibeticum Knuth

The Sanguineum Group

50. G. sanguineum Linnaeus (var. sanguineum & var. striatum Weston)

The Columbinum Group

51. G. columbinum Linnaeus

The Sibiricum Group

52. G. thunbergii Lindley & Paxton
53. G. wilfordii Maximowicz
54. G. yoshinoi Nakai
55. G. nepalense Sweet
56. G. sibiricum Linnaeus
57. G. suzukii Masamune

The Sessiliflorum Group

58. G. traversii J.D. Hooker
59. G. x antipodeum Yeo (G. sessiliflorum x G. traversii)
60. G. sessiliflorum Cavanilles (subsp. sessiliflorum & subsp. novaezelandiae Carolin)
61. G. antrorsum Carolin
62. G. papuanum Ridley

The Potentilloides Group

63. G. potentilloides De Candolle

The Robustum Group

64. G. robustum Kuntze
65. G. brycei N.E. Brown
66. G. pulchrum N.E. Brown

The Harveyi Group

67. G. harveyi Briquet

The Incanum Group

68. G. incanum N.L. Burman (var. incanum & var. multifidum (Sweet) Hilliard & Burtt)
69. G. caffrum Ecklon & Zeyher

The Schlechteri Group

70. G. schlechteri Knuth
71. G. flanaganii Knuth
72. G. ornithopodon Ecklon & Zeyher

The Maculatum Group

73. G. maculatum Linnaeus
74. G. oreganum Howell
75. G. bicknellii Britton
76. G. carolinianum Linnaeus

The Fremontii Group

77. G. nervosum Rydberg
78. G. viscosissimum Fischer & Meyer
79. G. fremontii Gray (*with*
   a. G. caespitosum E. James
   and b. G. atropurpureum
   A. Heller)

The Richardsonii Group

80. G. richardsonii Fischer & Trautvetter
81. G. californicum Jones & Jones

The Bellum Group

82. G. schiedeanum Schlechtendal

The Deltoideum Group

83. G. deltoideum Hanks & Small

The Cordilleran Group

84. G. herrerae Knuth
85. G. patagonicum J.D. Hooker

Section Dissecta Yeo,
  The Dissectum Section

86. G. asphodeloides N.L. Burman (subsp. asphodeloides, subsp. crenophilum (Boissier) Bornmüller & subsp. sintenisii (Freyn) Davis)
87. G. dissectum Linnaeus

Section Tuberosa Reiche,
  The Tuberosum Section

Subsection Tuberosa,
  The Tuberosum Group

88. G. tuberosum Linnaeus (*and* subsp. linearifolium (Boissier) Davis)
89. G. macrostylum Boissier
90. G. linearilobum De Candolle
91. G. malviflorum Boissier & Reuter

Subsection Mediterranea Knuth,
  The Platypetalum Group

92. G. platypetalum Fischer & Meyer
93. G. ibericum Cavanilles (subsp. ibericum & subsp. jubatum (Handel-Mazzetti) Davis)
94. G. x magnificum Hylander
95. G. gymnocaulon De Candolle
96. G. renardii Trautvetter
97. G. peloponnesiacum Boissier
98. G. libani Davis
99. G. bohemicum Linnaeus
100. G. lanuginosum Lamarck
101. G. gracile Nordmann

SUBGENUS II ROBERTIUM (PICARD)
  Rouy & Foucaud
  Section Polyantha Reiche,
  The Polyanthes Group

102. G. polyanthes Edgeworth & J.D. Hooker
103. G. nakaoanum Hara
104. G. strictipes Knuth
105. G. hispidissimum (Franchet) Knuth

Section Trilopha Yeo, The Trilophum Group

106. G. omphalodeum Lange
107. G. trilophum Boissier
108. G. biuncinatum Kokwaro
109. G. ocellatum Cambessèdes
110. G. mascatense Boissier
111. G. favosum A. Richard

Section Divaricata Rouy & Foucaud, The Albanum Group

112. G. albanum Bieberstein

Section Batrachioidea W.D.J. Koch, The Pyrenaicum Group

113. G. pyrenaicum Burman
114. G. pusillum Linnaeus
115. G. brutium Gasparrini
116. G. molle Linnaeus

Section Lucida Knuth, The Lucidum Group

117. G. lucidum Linnaeus
118. G. glaberrimum Boissier & Heldreich

Section Unguiculata Reiche, The Macrorrhizum Group

119. G. macrorrhizum Linnaeus
120. G. x cantabrigiense Yeo
121. G. dalmaticum (Beck) Rechinger

Section Ruberta Dumortier, The Robertianum Group

122. G. cataractarum Cosson (subsp. cataractarum & subsp. pitardii Maire)
123. G. robertianum Linnaeus
124. G. rubescens Yeo
125. G. canariense Reuter
126. G. palmatum Cavanilles
127. G. maderense Yeo

SUBGENUS III ERODIOIDEA YEO

Section Erodioidea Picard, The Phaeum Group

128. G. phaeum Linnaeus
129. G. x monacense Harz (nvar. anglicum Yeo & nvar. monacense)
130. G. reflexum Linnaeus
131. G. aristatum Freyn

Section Subacaulia Reiche, The Cinereum Group

132. G. argenteum Linnaeus
133. G. x lindavicum Knuth (G. argenteum x G. subcaulescens)
134. G. nanum Battandier
135. G. cazorlense Heywood
136. G. subacutum (Boissier) Aedo
137. G. cinereum Cavanilles
138. G. subargenteum Lange
139. G. dolomiticum Rothmaler
140. G. subcaulescens De Candolle
141. G. cinereum x G. subcaulescens
142. G. austro-apenninum Aedo
143. G. thessalum Franzén
144. G. ponticum (Davis & Roberts) Aedo
145. G. lazicum (Woronow) Aedo
146. G. makmelicum Aedo
147. G. petri-davisii Aedo
148. G. palmatipartitum Knuth

CULTIVATED CRANESBILLS: THE DESCRIPTIONS

SUBGENUS I GERANIUM

Plants annual or perennial. Fruit discharge by seed-ejection: each carpel has a hole big enough to allow the seed to escape, which it does during the explosive recurvature of the awn. The carpel does not separate from the awn. The awn may or may not remain attached to the central column of the rostrum. Mericarps not sculptured.

SECTION GERANIUM, THE SYLVATICUM SECTION

Plants annual or perennial. Retention of seed in mericarp during the pre-explosive interval by bristles attached to a horny tubercle at the lower end of the mericarp. Awn remaining attached to central column of rostrum after discharge.

This section forms the major part of the subgenus and is worldwide in distribution. The species dealt with here are assigned to 28 informally named groups.

THE ENDRESSII GROUP

Perennials with compact or creeping rootstock. Leaves with diamond-shaped or elliptic divisions. Stipules slender-pointed. Flowers erect, funnel-shaped, with more or less notched petals which are hairy across front at base. Immature fruits and their pedicels erect, spreading or reflexed.

Four species from S. Europe and W. Asia, all cultivated. (Two hybrids of 1. *G. endressii* are also described here and others are mentioned under that species; most involve members of other groups.)

1. G. endressii Gay (Figure 9.1)

Rather small perennial with moderately deeply cut, pointed leaf-divisions and bright pink or salmon-pink upright funnel-shaped flowers, 30–37mm in diameter, with notched petals. Border, woodland, ground-cover. Leafy in winter. June to September.

Plant with extensive elongated rhizomes on or just below the surface, and stems usually 25–50cm tall. Blades of basal leaves between 5 and 10cm wide, light green, wrinkled, divided as far as $^4/_5$–$^5/_6$ into 5; divisions gently tapered both ways from about the middle, palmato-pinnately lobed about halfway to the midrib, the lobes 1–1$^1/_2$ times as long as broad, usually with 2 or 3 teeth. Teeth and tips of lobes acute. Lowest one or two stem-leaves solitary. Stem-leaves gradually diminishing in size and length of stalk upwards, changing little in shape. Plant conspicuously hairy, some of the hairs on the sepals, and sometimes also pedicels and peduncles,

glandular. Inflorescence rather dense. Pedicels up to 2$^1/_2$ times as long as sepals. Flowers erect, funnel-shaped. Sepals 7–9mm; mucro 1–2mm. Petals more than 16mm, about twice as long as broad, more or less notched at apex, broadest above the middle, bright deep pink, becoming darker and redder with age; base and lower parts of veins colourless, translucent; apical parts of veins slightly darker than ground-colour and slightly netted; base with hairs extending across front surface and on margins, hardly tufted. Stamens about $^2/_3$ as long as sepals to nearly equalling them; filaments curving outwards at tips, white, tinged with pink, hairy in the lower half; anthers yellow or purplish. Stigmas 2.5–3.5mm, pink or reddish, bristly on the backs. Immature fruits and their pedicels erect. Rostrum 18–21mm, including stylar portion 2.5–3mm, with dense minute hairs and sparse longer bristles. Mericarps 3.5mm. Discharge: seed-ejection (bristles).

Western half of Basses-Pyrénées, mainly in France but just extending into Spain. Naturalised further north.

A strongly colonising evergreen perennial, tolerating shade or sun. The bright pink flowers are colourful for a long period; E.A. Bowles (1914) described the colour as "raspberry-ice pink" to which A.T. Johnson (1937) added "chalky", the chalkiness being imparted by a silvery sheen. The petal colour intensifies with age and becomes slightly redder. Thus the colour progresses from HCC Mallow Purple, slightly paler than 630/1, through Cyclamen Purple 30/2 to Rhodamine Purple 29/2 and, in the withering flower, Fuchsia Purple, between 28/2 and 28/1. I have also seen a plant with magenta flowers (HCC 27/1) that do not fade. (HCC 30/2 approximates to RHSCC Red-Purple Group 74C, HCC 28/1–2 is near Red-Purple Group 67B and C

Figure 9.1. *G. endressii*: from Mrs O. Vaughan, 1975, coll. Britain: Devon (naturalised); 7.5cm wide

and HCC 27/1 is near Red-Purple group 68A: the other shades cannot be approximated in RHSCC.)

G. endressii differs from 101. *G. gracile* in the jagged edges of the leaf-divisions, in fruit discharge type and in many less conspicuous characters; for differences from 4. *G. versicolor* see that species. It is a notably promiscuous hybridiser. It is easily propagated by separation of the rhizomes.

G. endressii 'Wargrave Pink' ('Wargrave') has petals of a light salmon-pink, (RHSCC Red Group 55B), though a little bluer at the extreme edge in young flowers; towards the tips a slightly darker network of veins is visible. The petals change colour with age only slightly. Petals are distinctly notched; stigmas scarcely 2.5mm long. It grows to about twice the height of *G. endressii* when in the sun. It might be a cross with 4. *G. versicolor* (i.e. belong to 2. *G.* x *oxonianum*) but in most details it is nearly the same as *G. endressii*; it was introduced by Waterer, Sons & Crisp in 1930, having been found in their nursery by their foreman, Mr W. Wright (Clifton, 1979). Because of its colour it is best planted away from most pinkish geraniums.

G. endressii has formed a number of hybrids spontaneously and as a result of artificial pollination. They include the important 2. *G.* x *oxonianum* (*G. endressii* x 4. *G. versicolor*) and 3. *G.* x *riversleaianum* (*G. endressii* x 58. *G. traversii*). Its many other hybrids include crosses with the massive 14. *G. psilostemon* and the tiny 60. *G. sessiliflorum* (Figure 9.4, page 64).

2. *G.* x *oxonianum* Yeo (Figure 9.2, Plate 2)
Leafy perennial, up to about 80cm, combining in various ways the characters of 1. *G. endressii* and 4. *G. versicolor*, and usually recognisable by the funnel-shaped flowers, up to 40mm in diameter, and the pink petals with darker net-veining, notched at the apex. Border, woodland, ground-cover. June onwards.

Often taller than either parent. Leaf blades between 5 and 20cm wide, sometimes brown-blotched, more or less wrinkled; divisions usually with the more solid outline, greater relative breadth and abrupt tapering of *G. versicolor* but lobing a little deeper and coarser, as in *G. endressii*. Flowers (at least in the named cultivars) larger than in either parent, with sepals to 11mm and petals to 26mm long and 15mm wide, in some cases more than half as wide as long. Plants with aberrant narrow petals sometimes occurring. Petals usually pink with a network of dark veins but sometimes without the latter; ground colour often intensifying with age. Rostrum to 27mm, its stylar portion 3–4mm. Discharge: seed-ejection (bristles).

A fertile hybrid between 1. *G. endressii* and 4. *G. versicolor*. Has escaped into the wild in Britain and France in the absence of the parents.

This hybrid arises readily when the parents grow together. Being fertile it is able to produce a great range of variants, many of which have been named. One of these is 'Claridge Druce', a specimen of which has been designated as the type of the nothospecies (hybrid) *G.* x *oxonianum*. This cultivar "was named in memory of the noted botanist who discovered it" in 1960 by Mr Graham Thomas and the then curator of the University Botanic Garden, Oxford, Mr G.W. Robinson, when the former was on a visit to Oxford (Thomas, 1970, 1976). The cultivars should normally be propagated by division. Many cultivars have been named, and Hibberd (1994) includes twelve that are not in this book.

In those cultivars which have normal petals that are not heavily veined (i.e. excluding 'Claridge Druce') the veining shows up more strongly when the light falls in such a way as to bring out the silvery sheen on the surface, against which they make a contrast.

G. x *oxonianum* 'Armitageae' (*G. endressii* var. *armitageae* Turrill), with abnormal petals, 16–17 x 4–4.5mm, is best included with 'Thurstonianum'.

G. x *oxonianum* 'A.T. Johnson' (*G. endressii* 'A.T. Johnson's Var.') is one of two cultivars presented by A.T. Johnson to the firm of Ingwersen which were named, described and distributed by the latter (the other one is 'Rose Clair'). The descriptions of them given by Ingwersen (1946) clearly relate them to the first two of three described by Johnson (1937, p. 179). 'A.T. Johnson' was said to be dwarfer than typical *G. endressii*, similar to it in foliage, and with "the blossoms ... a beautiful shade of silvery-pink". It would seem from this that it should not have the salmon tint of 'Rose Clair' and should therefore be bluer. However, plants with salmon-pink petals (HCC 23/2 or 23/3, RHSCC Red Group 55B or the

Figure 9.2. *G.* x *oxonianum* 'Claridge Druce': from G.S. Thomas, 1974; 9.5cm wide

very similar Red-Purple Group 62A) are in circulation under the name 'A.T. Johnson' and one was submitted to the Wisley Trial (1973–6) under that name. It may be doubted whether the true 'A.T. Johnson' is still in cultivation. Readers should not expect agreement on 'A.T. Johnson' and 'Rose Clair' in the nursery trade.

G. x *oxonianum* 'Claridge Druce' (Figure 9.2) is a very vigorous and rather tall, strongly hairy plant with dark, slightly glossy foliage, large trumpet-shaped flowers, the petals of which are lightly notched, up to 26 x 14mm and rosy pink in colour: HCC Petunia Purple 32/2, RHSCC Purple-Violet Group 90C, with a strong network of darker veins, fading to unveined white in the basal $^1/_5$–$^1/_4$. Thomas (1982) states that it seems to come true from seed. In fact, plants show some variation, but many are so similar that it is certainly necessary to accept that 'Claridge Druce' is a name not restricted to one clone, but applicable to any clone having approximately the characters given above.

G. x *oxonianum* 'Rose Clair' (*G. endressii* 'Rose Clair'): see *G.* x *oxonianum* 'A.T. Johnson'.

G. x *oxonianum* 'Southcombe Double' has petaloid stamens and reduced petals that form a small irregular but quite dense double shrimp-pink flower, though the first and last of the season may be more normal.

G. x *oxonianum* 'Thurstonianum' (*G. endressii* var. *thurstonianum* Turrill) has aberrant flowers with extremely narrow, strap-shaped purple petals and the stamens more or less petaloid (i.e. like the abnormal petals). For discussion and further references (going back to Bowles, 1914), see McClintock in Stace (1975). Plants vary as to presence or absence of leaf-blotching and in leaf-shape and pedicel length; the petal width also varies, and when it lies between about 3 and 6mm, netted veins are clearly visible showing that a failure of lateral expansion has made the veins crowded, thereby causing the colour to seem dark. This is another instance where it is inappropriate to limit the cultivar name to a single clone. Turrill gave the maximum petal-width as 3mm but it varies continuously up to 6mm. *G. endressii* var. *armitageae* Turrill is therefore best included in 'Thurstonianum'.

G. x *oxonianum* 'Walter's Gift' has a brown-purple blotch on either side of each incision between the leaf-divisions and between the leaf-lobes. The cultivar is the result of crossing *G.* x *oxonianum* 'Claridge Druce' with 4. *G. versicolor* (and it is therefore a back-cross) and its name is the name of Mary Ramsdale's garden in Essex (Évrard, 1997).

G. x *oxonianum* 'Winscombe' (Plate 2) is near *G. endressii* but is distinguished by a greater change in petal colour during the life of the flower, from nearly white to moderately deep pink. The petals are noticeably net-veined when old. Colour chart readings are, for youngest flowers, HCC Rhodamine Pink 527/2, for older flowers, HCC Persian Rose 628/2, and finally HCC 628/1 and 628 (the first three of these approximate to RHSCC Red-Purple Group 62C, 73C and 68B respectively).

G. x *oxonianum* has itself produced many hybrids (see Appendix III and discussion of 14. *G. psilostemon*).

3. *G.* x *riversleaianum* Yeo (Figure 9.3, Plate 3)
Trailing hoary perennials; leaves angular with divisions more or less tapered to the tip; flowers pink to deep magenta, 20–32mm in diameter, with faintly notched petals; sterile. Rock garden, ground-cover. June onwards.

Plant with a short stout rootstock. Blades of basal leaves between 5 and 10cm wide, divided as far as $^2/_3$ or $^3/_4$ into 7; divisions tapered both ways from above the middle, rather abruptly so to the tip, mostly lobed for about $^1/_3$ of their length, the lobes about as long as broad, few-toothed; teeth and tips of lobes obtuse or acute. Lower stem-leaves paired or solitary, upper paired, stalked, reduced in size gradually upwards. Flowering stems form a diffuse inflorescence, ascending or trailing, up to 1m long. Whole plant covered in rather short more or less appressed hairs, enhancing the naturally greyish component in the colour of the leaves. Cymules 2-flowered. Flowers more or less erect, widely funnel-shaped. Sepals 6–7mm; mucro 1mm or less. Petals 14–17mm, slightly longer than broad, lightly notched at apex, light pink, with faint darker unbranched veins, to deep magenta, with obscure darker feathering; base slightly hairy on front surface and margins.

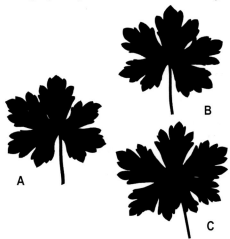

Figure 9.3. *G.* x *riversleaianum*: (A) & (B) 'Russell Prichard', from G.S. Thomas, 1974; (C) 'Mavis Simpson', from G.S. Thomas, 1981; 4–5cm wide

Filaments shorter than sepals, white or nearly so, hairy; anthers yellow or purplish, usually empty and failing to burst. Stigmas 2–3.5mm, pink to crimson, outer surfaces with few or many bristles. Rostrum and carpels not developing.

Hybrids between 1. *G. endressii* and 58. *G. traversii*.

This hybrid seems to arise fairly easily when the parents occur together in gardens, despite the fact that *G. endressii* is Pyrenean and *G. traversii* comes from Chatham Island, off New Zealand. It makes extensive, abundantly flowering carpets which die back to the rootstock in winter. Thomas (1977) says 'Russell Prichard' is not reliably hardy except in the warmer counties of the British Isles, but Ingwersen (1946) found it hardy in the Weald of Sussex; in my experience the rootstock benefits by division and replanting every few years. The petal colour may fade slightly with age, unlike that of 2. *G. x oxonianum*, which intensifies. The name is explained below under 'Russell Prichard'. 'Mavis Simpson' is a good garden plant.

G. x riversleaianum 'Chapel End Pink' and 'Chapel End Red' were raised by Mr Jan Stephens (see Stephens, 1967) but have probably been lost to cultivation. The first had "shell-pink" flowers 2.5cm in diameter and the second crimson flowers, "rather paler and brighter than the colour of the 'Russell Prichard' flower". There are dried specimens of 'Chapel End Pink', dated 1967, in the CUBG herbarium.

G. x riversleaianum 'Mavis Simpson' (Figure 9.3C) has the leaf-divisions and lobes broader in relation to their length than those of 'Chapel End Pink' and 'Russell Prichard', and in spring faint brown blotches are present in the notches; petals light pink ("shell-pink"): darkest parts of darkest flowers HCC Phlox Purple 632/2 (in RHSCC this is between Red-Purple Group 73B and 75A–B but is remote from both), pale centrally and becoming paler with age, with a silvery sheen and conspicuous dark purple, slightly feathered veins; stigmas crimson. The plant is named after the staff member at Kew who found it growing as a chance seedling in the Royal Botanic Gardens. The brown blotches on the leaves suggest that this may be a triple hybrid, *G. x oxonianum* x *G.*

traversii, but Mr Brian Halliwell, of Kew, tells me that *G. traversii* var. *elegans* and *G. endressii* were growing near the spot where it was found.

G. x riversleaianum 'Russell Prichard' (Figures 9.3A & B, Plate 3) has flowers fully 3cm in diameter, of a rich magenta, and sharply toothed leaf-divisions. The flower colour is much more intense than in either parent and this, apparently, led to the supposition, held formerly, that the plant is *G. sanguineum* x *G. traversii*. It is named after a member of the family which owned the now defunct Riverslea Nursery in Hampshire.

4. *G. versicolor* Linnaeus (*G. striatum* Linnaeus) (Figure 9.5, Plate 4)

Rather low-growing perennial with blotched leaves, shallowly cut and broadly pointed leaf-divisions and strongly net-veined (sometimes veinless) white trumpet-shaped flowers, 25–30mm in diameter, with clearly notched petals. Rock garden, woodland, ground-cover. Leafy in winter. May to October.

Plant with a rather compact rootstock, with stems up to 60cm in length but spreading so that the plant is usually low and bushy. Blades of basal leaves between 5 and 20cm wide, usually brown-blotched between the divisions, divided as far as $^2/_3$ or $^4/_5$ into 5; divisions abruptly tapered both ways from about the middle, palmato-pinnately lobed about $^1/_3$ of the way to the midrib; lobes as long as broad or less, with 1–3 teeth. Teeth and tips of lobes obtuse or acute. Stem-leaves paired, gradually diminishing in size and length of stalk upwards, changing little in shape. Plant covered with bristly hairs, sometimes densely, but in any case sparsely on peduncles and pedicels. Inflorescence diffuse. Pedicels up to about $1^1/_2$ times as long as sepals but one of each pair nearly always shorter than sepals. Flowers erect,

Figure 9.4. *G. endressi* x *G. sessiliflorum*: 'Kate', O.G. Folkard, 1979; 1.8 and 2.2cm wide

Figure 9.5. *G. versicolor*; 5.5 and 9cm wide

trumpet-shaped. Sepals 7–9mm, erect but not appressed to petal-bases, recurved at tips, with a few long hairs; mucro about 1.5mm. Petals slightly more than 16mm, twice as long as broad, notched, broadest near apex, erect at base, spreading above and recurved at tips, white with a close network of fine magenta-coloured veins which fades in age; base thinly hairy on margins and front surface, the hairs not tufted. Stamens slightly longer than sepals; filaments white with pink tips, sparsely hairy to beyond the middle; anthers bluish. Stigmas 3.5mm, red with whitish receptive surface, not bristly. Immature fruits and their pedicels erect. Rostrum about 18mm, including stylar portion about 6mm, with dense minute hairs and no bristles. Mericarps 3.5mm. Discharge: seed-ejection (bristles).

Central and S. Italy, Sicily, southern part of Balkan Peninsula (including Greece, Yugoslavia and Albania).

This species is attractive in its unusual net-veined flowers and its crop of fresh-looking leaves held through the winter. Plants vary in their density of hair-covering and obtuseness of leaf-teeth. As well as differing from 1. *G. endressii* in the obvious characters of the leaves and petals, *G. versicolor* differs also in the much more compact rootstock, the sparseness of the hairs on the peduncles, pedicels and calyx, the absence of large glandular hairs on these parts (not always present in *G. endressii*, however), lack of long hairs on the rostrum, the shorter pedicels and longer stamens (other floral parts are remarkably similar in size). This list may assist in the diagnosis of hybrids. In the dried state *G. versicolor* may resemble 101. *G. gracile*; the latter, however, has glandular hairs, smaller sepals, a different fruit-discharge type and other differences.
G. versicolor 'Snow White' (incorrectly 'White Lady') has the petal-veins uncoloured, leaving the flower silvery white.

G. versicolor has crossed with 1. *G. endressii* to produce the fertile hybrid 2. *G. x oxonianum*, and has produced both fertile and sterile hybrids with 58. *G. traversii* (Bremner, specimen in CUBG herbarium).

5. G. nodosum Linnaeus (Figure 9.6)
Perennial with swellings above the nodes of the stems and bright green leaves with 3 or 5 elliptic or lanceolate divisions, which are toothed but scarcely lobed; flowers about 2.5–3cm in diameter, erect, funnel-shaped, in a diffuse inflorescence, with bright purplish pink to extremely dark purple, slightly veiny and distinctly notched petals. Young fruits horizontal. Woodland and wild garden. June to October.
Plant with elongated rhizomes on or just below the surface, and stems usually 20–50cm tall. Blades

Figure 9.6. *G. nodosum*: (A) origin unknown; (B) from Will Ingwersen, 1976; both 9cm wide
(difference partly genetic, partly environmental)

of basal leaves between 5 and 20cm wide, bright green and slightly glossy above, glossy beneath, divided as far as about $^2/_3$ into 5; divisions more or less elliptic with gradually tapered tips, scarcely lobed, unevenly toothed except at base, the basal pair widely splayed; teeth and tips of divisions acute. Stem-leaves paired, decreasing gradually in size and length of stalk upwards, mostly with 3 lanceolate divisions, the upper nearly stalkless. Inflorescence unequally forked, diffuse. Stems, leaf-stalks and sepals with more or less numerous small appressed hairs; leaf-blades with scattered larger spreading hairs. Flowers erect. Sepals 8–9mm; mucro 1.5–2mm. Petals more than 16mm, twice as long as broad or more, wedge-shaped, broadest near the deeply notched apex, bright purplish pink or tending to violet with carmine veins at base, which are slightly branched above; base with rather numerous hairs across front surface and on margins. Stamens longer than sepals; filaments white, hairy for $^2/_3$ of their length; anthers blue. Styles red. Stigmas about 2mm, red, hairless. Immature fruits and their pedicels horizontal or slightly nodding. Rostrum about 22mm, including stylar portion about 3mm, with minute hairs only. Mericarps 3.5mm. Discharge: seed-ejection (bristles).

Central France to Pyrenees, to C. Italy and to C. Yugoslavia.

G. nodosum grows naturally in mountain woods, and is an attractive subject for the woodland and wild garden, mainly on account of its glossy leaves with virtually unlobed but saw-toothed divisions. It differs from 101. *G. gracile* in fruit-discharge type, absence of glandular hairs, posture of immature fruit, etc. It is easily propagated by seed or by division. It is variable in leaf-shape (see Figure 9.6) and in flower-colour, some tints being much more attractive than others. The case of the following cultivar is unusual in *Geranium*.

G. nodosum 'Whiteleaf' has extremely dark petals (especially inwards from the relatively pale edge) marked with nearly black feathered veins; the petal apices are more or less 3-lobed. This was raised by Mr A.W.A. Baker; having collected a plant in the Alpes Maritimes that was showing a tendency in the direction of the described colour, he then intensified it by selective breeding.

6. G. rectum Trautvetter (Figure 9.7)
Perennial with sharply toothed and lobed leaf divisions, a very diffuse inflorescence and bright pink, funnel-shaped or trumpet-shaped flowers about 25mm in diameter, with slightly veiny, more or less notched petals. Woodland. June to October.

Rootstock thick, compact. Basal leaves on flowering shoots few or none. Leaves like those of 1. *G. endressii* or similar but with shorter and broader divisions, lobes and teeth, sometimes slightly marbled. Hair-clothing like that of 5. *G. nodosum*. Inflorescence very diffuse. Pedicels mostly $1^{1}/_{2}$–4 times as long as sepals. Sepals 7–8mm; mucro 1.5mm. Petals about 16mm, twice as long as broad or less, broadest above the middle, rounded or distinctly notched at apex, bright rose-pink with white base and dark crimson, scarcely branched veins; base hairy across front and on margins. Stamens longer than sepals; filaments white, hairy to beyond the middle; anthers whitish with blue margins. Stigmas 2.5–3.5mm, pink to crimson. Immature fruits erect or deflexed on pedicels spreading just above the horizontal. Rostrum about 20mm, including stylar portion 2–3mm. Mericarps 4.5mm. Discharge: seed-ejection (bristles).

Central Asia: Kirgizstan (Tian Shan), Kazakhstan (Tarbagatai), Chinese Turkestan (Dzungaria/Songaria), N.W. Himalayas.

A plant of little horticultural interest with leaves more or less like those of 1. *G. endressii* in shape, with hair-clothing sparse and like that of 5. *G. nodosum*, and with floral details very similar to those

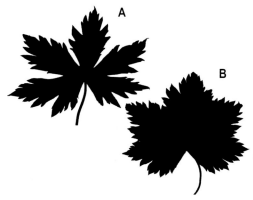

Figure 9.7. *G. rectum*: (A) from Mrs J. Forty (Joy Jones), 1973 (probably from former USSR); (B) from Moscow Acad. Sci. B.G., 1980; 7cm wide

of the latter. It differs from both species in its compact rootstock and long pedicels. The variation noted in the description reflects a rather pronounced divergence between two stocks grown at Cambridge which, nevertheless, clearly belong to the same species. It is propagated by seed or by division of the rootstock.

THE ROTUNDIFOLIUM GROUP

Only one species.

7. G. rotundifolium Linnaeus (Figure 9.8)
Annual with blades of lower leaves less than 5 or up to 10cm wide, rounded in outline, divided nearly as far as half into 7 or 9; divisions lobed for $^{1}/_{3}$ of their length; lobes sparsely toothed; lobes and teeth obtuse; notches marked with a small crimson spot; stipules and bracteoles crimson; stem-leaves paired, stalked, the upper with acute lobes and teeth; glandular hairs present on most parts of the plant. Sepals about 3.5–5mm, nearly erect, with a very short mucro. Petals up to about 7 x 3mm, erect with spreading tips, wedge-shaped, almost clawed, weakly notched at apex, terminal $^{1}/_{3}$ pink, otherwise white or sometimes with an intense purple mark where the ground colour changes; base with a few small hairs on front surface and margins. Anthers bluish. Style evident, about 1.5mm long; style and outer surfaces of stigmas hairy. Immature fruits erect on sharply reflexed pedicels. Rostrum 13–14mm, including stylar portion 2.5mm. Discharge: seed-ejection (bristles).

Europe, Asia, N. Africa.

A weed, sometimes troublesome, overwintering or flowering in the season of germination, normally found in tilled ground. Easily

Figure 9.8. *G. rotundifolium*; 4.5 and 7cm wide

distinguished from 114. *G. pusillum* and 116. *G. molle* by the abundant glandular hairs and the fruit type. From *G. molle* it differs also in the scarcely notched petals with erect base and from *G. pusillum* in the larger, bright pink petals.

On the supposition that the erect, slightly notched petals and distinctly developed style are vestiges retained from a larger-flowered ancestor, I have concluded that this species may be related to the Endressii Group. Glandular hairs, surface hairs on the petals and hairy stigmas also occur in that group, but not deflexed pedicels with upturned tips.

Annuals often have stronger sterility barriers than related perennials, but *G. rotundifolium* has been successfully crossed with other species. These are the readily hybridising 76. *G. carolinianum* and the species 14. *G. psilostemon*, that I have classified in the other group which is adjacent to the Rotundifolium Group.

THE SYLVATICUM GROUP

Perennials with a compact rootstock. Leaves generally with freely lobed and toothed divisions of moderate to narrow width. Flowers more or less erect, medium-sized or small. Fruits erect on usually erect pedicels. Stylar portion of rostrum short (to 3mm) except in *G. atlanticum*.

Seven species of Europe and N. and W. Asia are placed in this group. They are linked by groups of characters, very few of which hold for all species. Hybridisation with species outside the group is due mainly to 14. *G. psilostemon*.

8. *G. sylvaticum* Linnaeus (Figures 9.9 & 9.10)
Medium-sized perennial with rather deeply divided leaves with the divisions profusely lobed and toothed nearly to the base, flowers 22–30mm in diameter, borne in a dense inflorescence, and usually violet-blue with a white centre but also pink or white, and with immature fruits erect on

erect pedicels. Sun or light shade or in the wild garden. May and June.

Plant erect, 30–70cm tall, with compact rootstock. Basal leaves 10–20cm wide or more, divided as far as $^4/_5$ or more into 7 or 9; divisions tapered both ways from a point above the middle, rather solid in outline, with lobing and toothing continued down the sides nearly to the base; lobes up to twice as long as broad, with up to 4 teeth. Teeth and tips of lobes acute. Stipules of basal leaves to 2cm, light brown, hairless or minutely hairy at the tip, ovate or oblong-ovate. Lowest one or two stem leaves solitary. Length of leaf-stalks diminishing rapidly upwards so that upper leaves are almost stalkless. Stipules of stem leaves to about 15mm, ovate-acuminate to lanceolate. Upper stems, peduncles, pedicels, sepals and rostrum usually with glandular hairs. Inflorescence dense. Flowers numerous, erect, saucer-shaped. Sepals 5–7mm; mucro about $^1/_5$ as long as sepal. Petals slightly less than 16mm, not more than $1^1/_2$ times as long as broad, rounded or slightly notched at apex, usually purplish violet with white base; base with hairs all across front surface. Filaments divergent, arched outwards in female stage of flower, pinkish; anthers bluish. Stigmas 2–3mm, purplish. Immature fruits and their pedicels erect. Rostrum 17–21mm, including stylar portion 1.5–2.5mm. Mericarps about 4mm. Discharge: seed-ejection (bristles).

Most of Europe; N. Turkey.

G. sylvaticum is common in meadows in the mountains of southern Europe; further north and east it occurs down to sea level. It is native in Britain, being common from Yorkshire northwards to about the Great Glen in Scotland. It may be found not only in meadows but on roadsides, in stream gullies and in lightly shaded situations. It is a reasonably

Figure 9.9. *G. sylvaticum*: from Miss M.McC. Webster, 1965, coll. Britain: E. Scotland; 12.5cm wide

Figure 9.10. *G. sylvaticum*: from Miss M.McC. Webster, 1965, coll. Britain: E. Scotland. (A) shoot beginning to flower, x $^2/_3$; (B) portion of inflorescence with mature and immature fruit, x $^2/_3$; (C) petal, with pigmentation, x 2; (D) base of front surface of petal, x 4; (E) flower in male stage with petals and two sepals removed, x 4; (F) stamen of outer whorl, seen from back, x 4; (C) ripe fruit, x 2; (H) seed, x 4

showy plant for the garden in early summer. There is a very effective mass-planting of it under hazel at Sissinghurst Castle, Kent.

G. sylvaticum var. *alpestre* Domin & Podpera (*G. alpestre* Schur, not Chaix) has no glandular hairs and has purplish pink petals; it is endemic to the Carpathian mountains; plants grown at Cambridge, obtained as seed named *G. alpestre* from the Botanic Garden of Lvov, Ukraine, have a dense hoary hair-covering on the upper stems but also an admixture of glandular hairs; although thus differing from the description of the variety, they also have thicker leaves than western European plants of *G. sylvaticum* in general, as does a plant from the north side of the Caucasus (Rix 2533, year 1976), also grown at Cambridge. Another thick-leaved plant has been collected in Greece by J.C. Archibald (96 528 500); it has foreshortened and relatively blunt leaf segmentation, but is distinguished also by a hoary appearance in the inflorescence and deep purplish rose flowers with a large, well-defined white eye and a diameter up to only 24mm.

Of particular interest to the gardener are the colour forms. In north-east Europe pink and white flowers become more prevalent as one goes north, so that populations with all three colours, or pink and white, or white only, may be found. Pink-flowered, and probably white-flowered, forms occur occasionally elsewhere in the range of the species.

The following are colour-variants:

G. sylvaticum forma *albiflorum* A.C. Blytt is the naturally occurring white-petalled variant that retains pink colouring in the sepals, stamens and stigmas (not the same as *G. albiflorum* Ledebour).

G. sylvaticum 'Album' is a pale-leaved, entirely anthocyanin-free, white-flowered cultivar, which comes true from seed.

G. sylvaticum 'Amy Doncaster' has flowers of a beautiful deep blue with a clear white centre; named after the lady in whose garden it first appeared.

G. sylvaticum 'Angulatum' (*G. angulatum* Curtis) is the same in its petal colour as *G. sylvaticum* var. *wanneri* but the petals are large and broad, and slightly notched. When it was described in Curtis's Botanical Magazine in 1792 (type specimen – in poor condition – in Natural History Museum, London), no indication of its occurrence in the wild was given and I therefore treat it as a cultivar. It was known to Bowles (1914) who confirmed the large petal-size, saying the flower was the size of a four-shilling piece which was about 4cm in diameter. I was surprised and delighted to find it, unnamed, in 1989 in Rosemary Lee's garden, Coombland, in Sussex. The epithet *angulatum* refers to the angled stems, hardly the plant's most striking feature.

G. sylvaticum 'Baker's Pink' is a particularly beautiful pale pink-flowered plant introduced to cultivation from near Wengen in the Swiss Alps by Mr A.W.A. Baker. It is rather tall and large of flower for this species. See also forma *roseum*.

G. sylvaticum 'Mayflower' is an improved clone with flowers of a specially good rich violet-blue, the white centres of which are small; it was introduced by Alan Bloom about 1972.

G. sylvaticum forma *roseum* Murray is the naturally-occurring pink-petalled variant.

G. sylvaticum var. *wanneri* Briquet has pale rose-pink petals with bright rose veins. The original dried specimens, which I have seen, have the sepal mucro half as long as the sepal or nearly so. They were collected from Mont Billiat and a few other localities in the Genevan alps, and the original collection was reported to be constant in cultivation. The specimens do not resemble 10. *G. rivulare*, although Briquet said they did. In edn.1 I mentioned that the sepal

mucro of the plant grown under this name at Edinburgh in 1983 was not particularly long, implying doubt as to its identity. I later found that I had misjudged the length of the mucro; it is in fact about as in the authentic material and there is thus no reason to doubt the identity of the British-grown stocks. The darker veins on the petals are feathered and looped. (See also *G. sylvaticum* 'Angulatum'.)

Crosses have been reported with two other species in the same group, 13. *G. albiflorum* and 10. *G. rivulare* respectively. A sterile plant submitted to the Wisley Trial and later presented to Cambridge by Mr R.D. Nutt appears to be 16. *G. pratense* x 8. *G. sylvaticum*: it is anomalous in that the petals are white with a pale lilac network and are drawn out into a point at the base to a greater extent than in either supposed parent. More detail is given in edn.1. Another cross overstepping the group boundaries is with 37. *G. palustre*. A seedling appeared in Mr. A.W.A. Baker's garden that looks very like *G. sylvaticum* in habit but it flowers later and has richly purple flowers, a colour that suggests *G. palustre*. The leaf-outline also deviates in the direction of *G. palustre*, and I have now concluded that this is what it is, though the tendency to glossiness of that species is missing. The flowers are 25mm in diameter and the petals are marked with strong purple veins. Cultivar name: 'Tidmarsh' (village where Mr Baker lived).

9. *G. atlanticum* Boissier (Figure 9.11, Plate 5) Perennial to 70cm, winter-green and summer-dormant. Basal leaves profusely cut (ferny), often brown-stained, almost circular. Flowers numerous, upright, mostly on short and crowded stalks, about 3.5–4.5cm wide. Sepals purple and petals violet or pinkish with no lightening in colour towards the centre of the flower. Filaments and stigmas are crimson or dark red, as are the upper stipules, bracts and bracteoles. Immature fruits erect on erect pedicels. Glandular hairs normally absent. Probably tolerant of light shade. April, May.

Compact perennial to 70cm tall with crowns to 1.5cm thick, dormant after flowering and producing new leaves in autumn. Basal leaves to about 11–15cm wide, almost circular in outline, divided as far as $^4/_5$ or nearly to the base into 5 or 7; divisions broadly rhombic, overlapping, with pinnate lobing down the sides nearly to the base; lobes mostly 2–3 times as long as broad with several shorter bluntish to acute teeth, or themselves pinnately lobed and with a few to

Figure 9.11. *G. atlanticum*: cult. Reading Univ., coll. Morocco (Dr S.L. Jury, of Reading Univ., with M. Ait Lafkih and B. Tahiri: 15120); 9cm wide

several teeth; upper surface dark green, slightly glossy, the segments centrally pale green towards the base and sometimes in winter more or less strongly blotched with brown-purple in the sinuses; veins heavily impressed; lower surface paler, uniform. Stipules 7–15mm long, ovate or oblong-ovate, hairless. Stem-leaves 1–3 at each node, rapidly reduced and simplified upwards. Upper surface of leaves with hairs more or less appressed, lower with longer hairs that are densest on the veins. Plant usually without glandular hairs. Stipules to about 8mm, tailed, base pink. Stems stout, branching above, densely covered with mainly spreading hairs. Upper stipules, bracts and bracteoles crimson. Inflorescence rather dense, flat-topped, probably flowering for only a short time. Peduncles mostly less than 2cm long or suppressed, occasionally to 5cm; pedicels mostly 1cm or less but sometimes to 1.5 or 3cm, eglandular-hairy. Flowers varied in orientation (nodding in bud). Sepals about 6–8mm, with long appressed or loose hairs, purple on inner surface and at base on outer, or throughout; mucro 1–2mm. Petals usually 20–22 x 15–21mm, rounded, squarish or faintly notched at apex, overlapping or not (individual plants vary), with a dense tuft of silky hairs on either margin at base and some hairs on base of veins on back, bluish violet to pink, with up to 7 slender darker veins in the basal third (no lightening of colour at base). Stamens with filaments darker and redder than the petals, widened at base, with a few long hairs and a fringe of small ones on the enlargement, slightly spreading at the tips; anthers blue-black. Pollen dull greyish. Style purple, hairless except at base; stigmas about 1.5–2mm, purple. Pedicels after flowering erect. Rostrum 26–36mm with stylar portion

about 8mm. Rostrum and carpels very shortly hairy. Carpels probably about 4mm. Discharge: seed-ejection (bristles).

N. Algeria (Constantine) *[Knuth]*, N. Morocco *[Jury et al., see below]*, Tunisia *[Clifton [anon.], 1997]*.

Vigorous shade-grown autumn leaves may have shallower, coarser and more bluntly tipped leaf-segmentation.

This tall handsome plant is reminiscent of 126. *G. palmatum*. Its early flowering may restrict its outdoor cultivation in the British Isles to western coastal areas, but this remains to be seen.

G. atlanticum differs from 8. *G. sylvaticum* in its narrower, more overlapping (but equally profuse) leaf-segments, absence of glandular hairs, larger, redder flowers, larger fruit and long style, and from 16. *G. pratense* (also with a long style) by the more ferny leaves, absence of glandular hairs, the erect floral axis, redder flower colour and erect fruits.

J.D. Hooker's misidentification of *G. malviflorum* as *G. atlanticum* (1879) was recognised at Kew by 1902, as shown in the Hand-List of Herbaceous Plants, edn. 2 (cited in this book under 'Royal'). However, the misapplication continued to be frequent in horticultural circles until about 1985.

G. atlanticum was introduced to cultivation by Dr Stephen Jury (Reading University), M. Ait Lafkih and B. Tahiri, no. 15120, from Jebel Zerhoun, 1230m, and from Beni Snassen, 960m, both in northern Morocco. Four clones raised by Dr Jury have been grown at Blooms of Bressingham for trial. Their staff showed them to me in April 1999; one had broader, overlapping petals, giving a handsomer effect than the others. The blue-violet forms gave a colour-chart match of RHS CC74A 'Cyclamen Purple' (Jury, 1996).

10. G. rivulare Villars (*G. aconitifolium* L'Héritier; *G. sylvaticum* Linnaeus subsp. *rivulare* (Villars) Rouy) (Figure 9.12, Plate 6)
Compact perennial with deeply divided and narrowly lobed leaves, and medium-sized, erect, funnel-shaped flowers 15–25mm in diameter, borne in a dense inflorescence; petals white with violet veins. Sun or light shade. May and June.

Erect perennial, 20–45cm, with compact rootstock. Basal leaves between 5 and 20cm wide, divided nearly to the base into 7 or 9; divisions tapered both ways from near the middle, broken in outline; lobes 2–4 times as long as broad, sometimes with several teeth which may be bent outwards and/or widely separated from one another. Lowest one or two stem-leaves solitary.

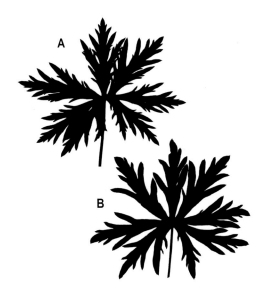

Figure 9.12. *G. rivulare*: (A) from J. Stephens, 1960; (B) from W.J.N. Warner, 1966; 7.5 and 9cm wide

Stem-leaves, and some of the basal, differing much from those of *G. sylvaticum* in having the divisions deeply cut into long, narrow, sometimes spreading, almost toothless lobes. Tips of lobes and teeth acute. Length of leaf-stalks diminishing rapidly upwards so that the upper leaves are almost stalkless. Plant without glandular hairs except on the mericarps and lower part of rostrum. Inflorescence dense. Flowers fairly numerous, erect, funnel-shaped. Sepals about 5–7mm; mucro about $\frac{1}{6}$ as long as sepal. Petals slightly less than 16mm, more than $1\frac{1}{2}$ times as long as broad, white with fine violet veins extending nearly to tip; base with hairs all across front surface. Stamens with white filaments and violet anthers. Stigmas about 2mm, deep pink. Immature fruits and their pedicels erect. Rostrum 22–25mm, with stylar portion 2mm. Mericarps about 4mm, bearing long glandular hairs. Discharge: seed-ejection (bristles).

W. and centre of the European Alps.

Grows in poor alpine meadows, dwarf-shrub heaths and woods of larch and Arolla pine.

A tidily growing, rather inconspicuous plant, not without a modest – though short-lived – charm when in flower. It is not particular about its cultural conditions, despite its name.

The similarity of *G. rivulare* to 8. *G. sylvaticum*, under which it is placed as a subspecies in *Flora Europaea* (Webb & Ferguson,

1968), lies mainly in the habit, with a rather regular dense inflorescence of many erect flowers borne on pedicels that remain erect after flowering, and in the presence of hairs across the width of the upper surface of the petal-base. *G. rivulare* has a more obvious resemblance to 11. *G. caeruleatum* Schur, the latter differing in its very low growth, violet-blue flowers and the absence of glandular hairs on the fruit.

11. G. caeruleatum Schur (*G. sylvaticum* subsp. *caeruleatum* (Schur) Webb & Ferguson) (Figure 9.13, Plate 7)
A neat, low-growing perennial increasing rapidly by short rhizomes. Leaves deeply and finely cut, sometimes pressed to the soil. Flowers to 16mm wide, erect, pale milky blue, quite numerous. Fruit erect. Sun or shade. May (also June and July in nature).

Tufted perennial to 25cm (sometimes to 30cm). Basal leaves with blades to 10.5cm wide, divided nearly to the base into 7; divisions broadly rhombic, broadest just above the middle, overlapping, palmato-pinnately lobed; lobes about $1\frac{1}{4}$–3 times as long as broad, almost parallel-sided, with 1–4 teeth; teeth 1–$2\frac{1}{2}$ times as long as broad, like the tips of the lobes acute. Hairs of the blades appressed, rather coarse, those on the underside concentrated along the veins. Leaf-stalks to $2\frac{1}{2}$ times as long as blades, backwardly appressed-hairy. Stipules to about 1cm, ovate-lanceolate, soon dry and brown, hair-fringed at the tip. Stem-leaves to about 4cm wide, paired except sometimes the first, very similar to the basal, but with stipules 3–5mm. Stems clothed as the leaf-stalks. Plant without

Figure 9.13. *G. caeruleatum*: from H. Walsweer, 1985; 9cm wide

glandular hairs. Inflorescence with branches at 2 or 3 successive leafy nodes and one or two bracteate nodes. Flowers opening in quick succession. Peduncles 1.5–4cm, erect, densely recurved-hairy. Pedicels erect, 6–10mm, woolly. Flowers widely campanulate, unisexual; females to 16mm wide. Sepals 4–5mm, with mucro 0.5mm or less, tinged with purple, the outer shaggy. Petals 7–8mm, obovate, pale violet with white basal third to half, with or without darker veins, hairy at base on the front, the hairs extending across the width of the petal but more abundant towards the edges. Filaments of female flowers widened at base. Style 3mm; stigmas 2.5mm, deep pink outside, flesh-pink on the receptive surface. Immature and ripe fruit erect. Rostrum 11–13mm, including stylar portion of only 0.5mm. Discharge: seed-ejection (bristles).

Mountains of the Balkan Peninsula and the Carpathians.

A female clone reached me in 1985 from Mr H. Walsweer, of Heerde, Netherlands, and the above description is based mainly on this. Young fruits were obtained for descriptive purposes by pollinating it with 10. *G. rivulare*. The species is placed in The Sylvaticum Group on account of its stipules, inflorescence form, petal hairs and small rounded carpels. It was treated as a subspecies of *G. sylvaticum* in *Flora Europaea* (Webb & Ferguson, 1968), though it is superficially quite unlike that. It has some resemblance to 10. *G. rivulare* in foliage but the leaves are smaller and more regularly toothed and lobed, and the flowers are not funnel-shaped. It is a dainty early-flowering species.

12. G. pseudosibiricum J. Mayer (*G. sylvaticum* Linnaeus subsp. *pseudosibiricum* (J. Mayer) Webb & Ferguson) (Figure 9.14)

Dioecious perennial to 40cm with freely toothed leaves to 17cm wide, deeply divided into 7 and slightly grey-hairy. Flowers of a beautiful blue (but see discussion) with crimson stigmas, the male to 25mm wide, the female to 15mm. Flowers erect but the males nodding after flowering. Flowering in May and then commonly repeatedly through the summer.

Erect dioecious perennial, to about 40cm tall. Stems slender, firm, with opposite leaves, or the first one solitary, with usually two branches and a cymule at twin-leaved nodes. Stems, leaf-stalks and stipules clothed with very small backwardly and closely appressed hairs. Blades of basal leaves to about 10cm wide (sometimes to 17cm), divided

Figure 9.14. *G. pseudosibiricum*: from Halle B.G., 1987; 9cm wide

as far as $^6/_7$–$^9/_{10}$ into 7; divisions broadest above the middle, palmato-pinnately lobed from below the middle; lobes $1^1/_2$–$2^1/_2$ times as long as broad, usually with 1–4 teeth; teeth and lateral lobes sometimes turned outwards; teeth and tips of lobes acute; leaf-stalks $1^1/_2$–2 times as long as blades. Stem-leaves with stalks as long as blade or shorter, blades decreasing upwards and becoming simplified, the lower slightly more finely cut than the basal; stipules to about 10mm, ovate-lanceolate. Leaf-blades all appressed-hairy above and green or flushed with purple, moderately to densely clothed with loose hairs and pale green beneath. Inflorescence loose, but with many flowers open simultaneously, sometimes with glandular hairs. Peduncles to 6cm; pedicels from shorter than calyx to three times as long as calyx. Peduncles and pedicels densely clothed with backwardly more or less appressed eglandular hairs. Flowers nodding in bud, erect when open. Male flowers trumpet-shaped, nodding after flowering. Sepals 5.5mm, green with purple base, and with mucro about 0.75mm. Petals to 16 x 7.5mm, rounded or straight at apex, deep blue with white basal zone and red-purple veins, slightly paler on the back, hairy at the base, at the sides and across the front surface. Stamens longer than the sepals; filaments white, pale pink at tips, strongly widened and hairy-margined towards the base; anthers coloured as the petals. Style and stigmas red-purple, about equalling the stamens, stigmas not separating until about the time of petal-drop. Female flowers funnel-shaped, erect after flowering. Sepals 4.5–5mm, otherwise as in male flowers. Petals to 9 x 4.5mm, deep violet-blue to pale violet, otherwise as in male flowers. Stamens with base as in male plant but the slender terminal part much shortened. Style and stigmas purple; stigmas separating as the flower opens. Immature and ripe fruit erect. Rostrum 12–16mm, hairy, abruptly tapered into a stylar portion of about 2.5mm. Carpels about 3mm, with long glandular hairs. Discharge: seed-ejection (bristles).

Ural Mountains and Siberia.

Two stocks have been cultivated at Cambridge. One came from Halle Botanic Garden, Germany, as seed in 1987; this was grown in a number of generations and always several plants so as to provide females that can keep up the possibility of raising it from seed, despite the fact that the female flowers are smaller. The second was a female plant from Mr Walsweer of Heerde, The Netherlands, in 1989. This has more finely cut leaves and the whole plant is suffused with brown-purple, but the flowers are not pretty. In the short description above I have referred to the flower colour of only the Halle stock.

The species epithet is evidently based on a superficial resemblance to *G. sibiricum* in leaf-shape and in the small flower-size, apparently sometimes much smaller than described here.

13. *G. albiflorum* Ledebour (Figure 9.15)
A low perennial, with the stems, leaf-edges and sepals purplish brown; leaves rather like those of 8. *G. sylvaticum*. Inflorescence loose. Petals less than 8mm or sometimes more, white with violet veins or pale lilac, notched. May and June, and usually again later. Semi-shade.

Perennial, with the stems usually inclined, 20–60cm, with compact rootstock. Basal leaves between 5 and 20cm wide, divided as far as $^4/_5$ or slightly more into 7; divisions tapered both ways from a point above the middle, rather solid in outline; lobes not more than twice as long as broad, with 1–3 teeth; tips of lobes and teeth rather blunt or acute. Upper leaves sometimes with more space between the divisions, and fewer teeth on the lobes, more or less stalked. Stems and leaf-margins purplish brown. Branches diverging rather widely. Glandular hairs absent or sometimes present on peduncles and pedicels. Inflorescence diffuse. One pedicel of each pair often shorter than sepals. Flowers rather few, upwardly inclined, widely funnel-shaped. Sepals about 4.5mm, flushed with purplish brown; mucro 0.5–1mm. Petals less than 8mm or sometimes more, more than $1^1/_2$ times as long as broad, notched at apex, white or pale lilac with violet veins; base with hairs all across front surface. Stigmas between 1.5 and 2mm, pale pink. Immature fruits and their pedicels slightly nodding. Rostrum about 18mm including stylar portion about 2mm. Mericarps just under 4mm. Discharge: seed-ejection (bristles).

N. and Central Asia and north-eastern part of European Russia.

Grows in similar habitats to those of 10. *G. rivulare*.

I grew a group of plants of this species in pots from 1979, when I received the seed from the Botanic Garden of the Academy of Sciences, Moscow, and my description is based mainly on these, all of which are female. Later they were planted out in semi-shade where they made strong leafy clumps with delicate, attractively coloured but not showy inflorescences.

G. albiflorum has basal leaves rather like those of 8. *G. sylvaticum* but less profusely toothed, and petals like those of 10. *G. rivulare* but smaller. The brown tinting of stems and leaves, the loose branching, notched petals and the slightly nodding immature fruits are distinctive.

Figure 9.15. *G. albiflorum*: from Moscow Acad. Sci. B.G., 1979; 8 and 12cm wide

Figure 9.16. *G. psilostemon*: from John Innes Hort. Inst., 1922; 21cm wide

14. *G. psilostemon* Ledebour (*G. armenum* Boissier; *G. backhouseanum* Regel) (Figure 9.16, Plate 8)

Tall perennial with very large basal leaves and a rather loose inflorescence of flowers about 35mm in diameter, bright magenta with a black centre and black veins. Border, wild garden, sun or shade. June–August.

Erect perennial, 80–120cm tall, with compact rootstock. Blades of basal leaves more than 20cm wide, divided as far as $^4/_5$ into 7; divisions tapered both ways from beyond the middle; lobes slightly longer than broad, with several teeth, some of them deep. Teeth and tips of lobes acute. Stem-leaves paired, mostly with 5 divisions, diminishing gradually in size and length of stalk upwards. Leaf-blades sparsely hairy; upper stems, peduncles and pedicels with dense short hairs and longer glandular hairs; hairs of sepals and rostrum mostly glandular. Inflorescence erect, diffuse. Flowers erect, shallowly bowl-shaped. Sepals 8–9mm; mucro about 3mm. Petals about 18mm long and nearly as wide, rounded or lightly notched at apex (see above for colour); base with a few hairs at either edge. Filaments divergent towards their tips, mainly blackish but with pale dilations on either side at base; anthers blackish. Stigmas 2.5–3mm, dark red-purple. Immature fruits erect on more or less reflexed pedicels. Rostrum 27–30mm, including stylar portion about 3mm. Mericarps 5mm. Discharge: seed-ejection (bristles).

N.E. Turkey, S.W. Caucasus Region.

A stately plant best grown in broken shade against a dark background; the sunlit flowers will then appear intensely luminous. The stems usually need support. Its first sign of life in spring is the production of crimson stipular sheaths; it ends its season of growth with fine autumn colour. Propagated by division and seeds.

G. psilostemon 'Bressingham Flair' (Plate 8) is less tall-growing and has rather less intensely coloured petals which are somewhat crumpled and lightly notched; it was introduced by Bloom's of Bressingham, Norfolk, in 1973.

G. psilostemon crosses with several other species to give sterile progeny. The cross with 27. *G. procurrens* occurred spontaneously in seed gathered from *G. procurrens* by the Rev. O.G. Folkard about 1973 in his garden at Sleaford, Lincolnshire. This is a popular garden plant under the name 'Ann Folkard' (Figure 9.17, Plate 9). It forms a mound of golden-green foliage borne on a tangled mass of stems, surmounted by dusky-purple black-centred flowers 35–40mm in diameter, with velvety-looking petals, from June to October, and likes sun. It is propagated by division of the rootstock. More seedlings of this cross have been obtained by Alan Bremner, one of which is more compact than 'Ann Folkard' and has been named 'Anne Thompson' (Bremner, 1997).

Figure 9.17. *G. procurrens* x *G. psilostemon*: 'Ann Folkard': from O.G. Folkard, 1975; 16cm wide

Other named hybrids of *G. psilostemon* raised by Alan Bremner are 'Patricia' (with 1. *G. endressii*), 'Nicola' (with 2. *G. x oxonianum*) and 'Eva' (with 16. *G. pratense*). A striking product of the cross *G. psilostemon* x *G. x oxonianum* raised by Mr H.J. Mazza of Leeds has three-lobed petals, the central lobe being the largest and pointed, the others pointed or blunt (Mazza, 2000).

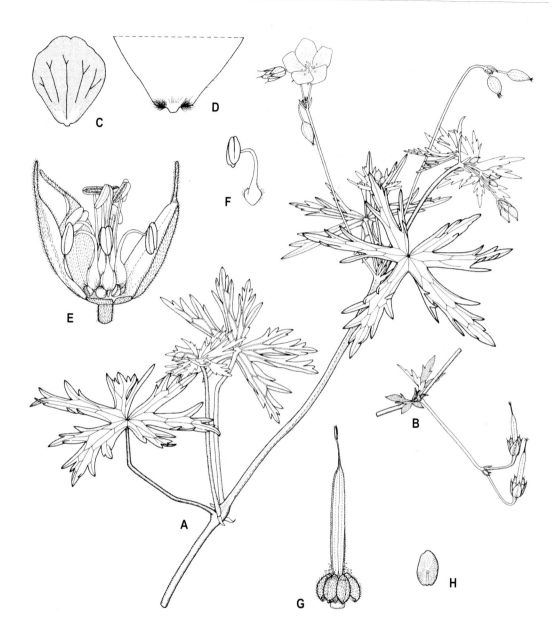

THE COLLINUM GROUP

Perennials with compact rootstock and diffuse habit. Stipules of basal leaves long, slender, acute. Leaf-divisions more or less pinnately lobed with lobes more than twice as long as broad, sharply toothed. Flowers about 25–30mm in diameter, saucer-shaped; petals without hairs across front surface at base. Style well-developed.

Figure 9.18. *G. collinum*: from P.H. Davis, 1955, coll. Turkey: Van Prov., no. D 23804. (A) shoot beginning to flower, x ²/₃; (B) cymule with immature fruit, x ²/₃; (C) petal, with pigmentation, x 2; (D) base of front surface of petal (the occurrence of hairs between the tufts is most unusual in this species), x 4; (E) flower in male stage with petals and two sepals removed, x 4 ; (F) stamen of outer whorl, seen from back, x 4; (G) ripe fruit in pre-explosive interval, x 2; (H) seed, x 4

Figure 9.19. *G. collinum*: (A) from C.D. Brickell, 1980, coll. Iran: Elburz Mts; (B) from P.H. Davis, 1955, coll. Turkey: Van Prov. (D 23804); (C) from J. Stephens, 1966, coll. Iran: Marand (Furse 9091); 9–16cm wide

One widespread species, *G. collinum*, in S.E. Europe and W. and C. Asia; other species have been segregated from *G. collinum* in C. Asia but I have not formed definite opinions about their distinctness.

15. *G. collinum* Willdenow (Figures 9.18 & 9.19)
Bushy perennial with sharply toothed leaves and diffuse habit, producing saucer-shaped bright pink to pale bluish pink flowers 25–30mm in diameter over a long period; petals rounded, weakly veiny. Border, wild garden, sun. June to September.

Rootstock compact, producing very thick roots. Young leaves in spring often yellowish and flushed with pink. Blades of basal leaves between 5 and 20cm wide, divided as far as $^4/_5$–$^5/_6$ into 7; divisions tapered both ways from well above the middle, palmato-pinnately lobed for nearly $^1/_2$ their length; lobes rather far apart, some of them 2–3 times as long as broad, with few to several teeth; teeth up to about $2^1/_2$ times as long as broad. Teeth and tips of lobes acute or rarely obtusish. Stipules of basal leaves up to 3cm, narrow, tapered to a fine point. Stem-leaves paired, decreasing gradually in size and length of stalk upwards, lobing becoming more pinnate and leaf outline less rounded, more angular, uppermost greatly reduced and nearly stalkless. Plant generally covered with small appressed hairs but

undersides of leaves with larger, more spreading hairs; glandular hairs often present on upper peduncles, pedicels, sepal-bases and rostra. Inflorescence diffuse, branches usually paired and unequal. Peduncles mostly 4–14cm. Pedicels mostly 1.5–3.5cm. Sepals 7–12mm, gradually tapered at apex; mucro usually 2–3mm, occasionally shorter. Petals 13–20mm, broadest above the middle, about $1^1/_4$–2 times as long as broad, rounded at apex, usually medium pink, sometimes paler or darker, sometimes with red simple or feathered veins; base with a dense tuft of white hairs at either side and above this a fringe of hairs, but without hairs extending across front surface. Filaments abruptly widened at base, lilac or pink at tips, finely fringed with hairs in lower part; anthers yellowish or pinkish, usually appearing greyish after opening. Nectaries topped with a tuft of hairs. Stigmas 1.5–2.5mm, pinkish or reddish. Immature fruits erect on more or less reflexed pedicels. Rostrum 20–27mm including the distinct stylar portion 4–5mm long. Mericarps about 3–4mm. Discharge: seed ejection (bristles).

S.E. Europe, C. and E. Turkey, W. and C. Asia, extending to Siberia and N.W. Himalayas.

A widespread and somewhat variable species, usually easily recognised by its bushy habit, medium-sized pink flowers and sharply toothed leaves slightly recalling those of 16. *G. pratense* but with fewer, coarser teeth and lobes. It is not of great garden value but is fairly frequently included in the collections of expeditions. In nature it is often found in damp meadows but it grows well in dry conditions in British gardens. It has virtually no superficial resemblance to 16. *G. pratense* but it forms fertile hybrids with it and has strong resemblance in floral details: the rounded petals, the hairs over the nectaries, the enlarged stamen-bases, the distinct style and rather short stigmas. It is distinguished from 46. *G. yesoense* by the tuft of hairs over the nectaries and the lack of hairs across the front surface of the petal-bases; there are also differences in the leaves.

G. collinum has crossed spontaneously or been crossed (by Alan Bremner) with all available members of the Pratense Group and with 45. *G. dahuricum* (Lundström, 1914). The resulting hybrids range from sterile to fairly fertile. (The hybrid with *G. dahuricum*, *G.* x *bergianum* Lundström, was found in the Stockholm Botanic Garden; Lundström referred to *G. collinum* as *G. londesii* Link). A chance hybrid with 19. *G. clarkei* found at Cambridge is established as a useful garden plant under the name 'Nimbus'; it has fairly small, finely and decoratively cut leaves and medium-violet petals suggestive of a stormy sky. It is fertile under open-pollination, producing progeny that clearly express their parentage.

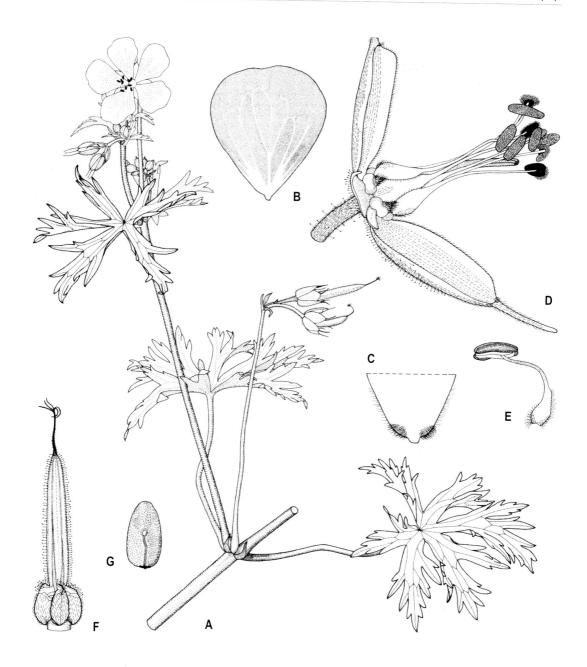

THE PRATENSE GROUP

Perennials with a compact or creeping rootstock. Inflorescence usually with glandular hairs. Flowers large; floral axis usually horizontal; petals blue or pink, not notched; petals without hairs across front surface at base; style (stylar portion of rostrum) long; immature fruits and their pedicels

Figure 9.20. *G. pratense* "European Form": from Halle B.G., 1974, coll. Germany: Röblingen See. (A) portion of shoot beginning to flower, x $^2/_3$, (immature fruit is normally distinctly nodding); (B) petal, with pigmentation, x 2; (C) base of front surface of petal, x 4; (D) flower in male stage with petals and three sepals removed, x 4; (E) stamen of outer whorl, seen from back, x 4; (F) ripe fruit, x 2; (G) seed, x 4

Figure 9.21. *G. pratense* "European Form": from P.F. Yeo, 1966, coll. Britain: Somerset; 13.5cm wide

downwardly inclined or reflexed; pedicels short or very short in relation to sepals.

An uncertain number of species in C. Asia and N.W. Himalayas, and one, *G. pratense,* occurring from W. Europe to W. China.

The various components of *G. pratense* treated here, and closely related species with binary names, can cross with most others. Other hybrids of *G. pratense* are dealt with at the end of the alliance, and not at the end of the account of the European form.

16. *G. pratense* Linnaeus (Figures 9.20 & 9.21)
More or less tall perennial with rather finely cut leaves; inflorescence dense; flowers 35–45mm in diameter, saucer-shaped, with horizontal axis; petals not notched, blue to white; style long; immature fruits and their pedicels reflexed. Border, wild garden, sun or light shade. June to July and often again.

Rootstock compact, about 2cm thick. Plant usually about 75cm tall but up to 130cm. Blades of basal leaves often more than 20cm wide, divided as far as $^6/_7$–$^9/_{10}$ into 7 or 9, sometimes broader than long; divisions tapered both ways from above the middle, pinnately lobed, rather open in outline; lobes mostly 2–3 times as long as broad, curving outwards, with several teeth, usually very unequal in number on the two sides. Teeth and tips of lobes acute or obtusish. Stipules of basal leaves up to about 3cm, narrow, tapered to a fine point. Stem-leaves paired, decreasing gradually in size and length of stalk upwards, their divisions tapered from about the middle, those of the middle leaves often with the terminal part more or less evenly and deeply cut into toothless lobes. Upper surfaces of leaves with small

appressed hairs; lower surface with similar or more divergent hairs on the veins; stems and leaf-stalks with larger reflexed hairs diverging weakly or strongly; upper part of inflorescence with dense glandular hairs. Flowering stems bearing peduncles only in the upper part, these becoming very short or suppressed at high nodes, forming a dense inflorescence. Peduncles mostly 2–10cm. Pedicels short, one or both in each cymule shorter than the sepals. Floral axis horizontal. Sepals 7–12mm, usually tapered at apex, forming a slightly bladdery calyx after flowering; mucro 1.5–3.5mm. Petals 16–24 x 13–20mm, only slightly longer than broad, rounded at apex, deep violet-blue or campanula-blue, varying to white, usually white at extreme base, with translucent, sometimes pinkish, veins; base with a dense tuft of hairs on either side and a fine fringe above this, but without hairs extending across front surface. Stamens slightly longer than sepals; filaments abruptly widened at base, more or less deep pink, finely fringed with hairs in lower part; anthers dark violet or blue-black. Nectaries topped with a tuft of hairs. Stigmas 2–2.5mm, greenish, tinged with pink, or brownish, dull purple or crimson. Immature fruits reflexed on reflexed pedicels. Rostrum 23–29mm including the distinct stylar portion 7 or 8mm long. Mericarps 4.5–5mm. Discharge: seed-ejection (bristles).

This description applies to plants from Europe and the Altai Mountains of C. Asia, and from W. China and possibly W. and E. Siberia.

In England this species, Meadow Cranesbill, occurs in great abundance on the carboniferous and Jurassic limestones, on chalk in the south-west and more sparsely on clay in East Anglia; it usually grows on roadsides. In Europe, where it is widespread, it often grows in meadows and is not confined to calcareous soils. It readily establishes colonies outside its native range, and has done so in eastern North America. As a colonist it is usually found near houses. It does not grow naturally in shade.

The plants covered by the above description will eventually become known as var. *pratense* but because few other varieties of *G. pratense* have been defined, it seems preferable in this book to refer to it as the "European Form" despite the inclusion of plants from the Altai region of C. Asia and beyond. The latter, when grown in Cambridge, become dormant in autumn in the normal way but their dormancy is easily broken by mild weather; the leaves that then come up are usually frosted sooner or later and the damage may even be severe enough to prevent flowering at the normal time. Apart from such plants, *G. pratense* is easily grown and may be propagated by division or seed. Not only is it one of

Britain's finest wild flowers but it is a lovely garden plant, valuable especially in herbaceous borders and making its main effect in June, July and sometimes August. The petals of a typical British form of wild origin gave a colour chart reading near RHSCC Violet-Blue Group 93C (actually HCC Hyacinth Blue 40/1, becoming Methyl Violet 39/1); readings for the Altai plants taken with HCC and matched by me with RHSCC are Violet-Blue Group 90D, 91A and 92A, i.e. less blue.

The species as a whole extends outside the area already indicated into the Caucasus, the south-west of W. Siberia in the Russian Federation, together with Kirgizstan and Uzbekistan, and thence into the Himalayas. There seem to be considerable taxonomic difficulties in these areas but two more or less well-marked forms are dealt with below within 16. *G. pratense*. Three more very close relatives of *G. pratense* are thereafter treated as species (numbers 17, 18 and 19).

First, however, I deal with the variants of the "European Form". It may be mentioned that pale-flowered or white-flowered plants are not infrequent in nature. For all double-flowered cultivars I have placed 'Plenum' as the first word of the cultivar epithet, following Thomas (1976, 1982).

G. pratense forma *albiflorum* Opiz is the botanical name for white-petalled plants and need not be reserved for plants which are strictly anthocyanin-free. It may be used for white-flowered plants growing wild or brought into cultivation from the wild (see also *G. pratense* 'Galactic').

G. pratense 'Bicolor' is a synonym of 'Striatum'.

G. pratense 'Galactic' is a name proposed for an anthocyanin-free plant grown at Cambridge, having been received from Mrs Joy Forty (Joy Jones) in 1971; in a dry situation it grows to about 75cm in height and has a flat-topped inflorescence; the flowers are 40–48mm in diameter with overlapping petals which sometimes have a hint of a notch (there are dried specimens in the CUBG herbarium, dated 3 July 1973 and 30 June 1978). It is probably the same as the plant which received an Award of Merit at Wisley Trial as "*G. pratense album*". Ingwersen's (1946) description of *G. pratense* var. *album* suggests the same plant; he was probably unaware of the botanically validly published name *G. pratense* var. *album* Weston, which is best treated as a synonym of *G. pratense* forma *albiflorum* (see above), as its description reads merely "with white flowers".

G. pratense 'Mrs Kendall Clark' is a name which now seems indissolubly tied to the plant illustrated in Plate 10; the plant was submitted to the Wisley Trial under this name and described in the report as 75cm tall, with a petal colour of RHSCC Violet-blue Group 91A (a moderately pale colour) with white veining (which could make it seem paler). The name was probably applied originally to a different plant, otherwise it is difficult to see how Ingwersen (1946) could describe it without mentioning the veiny petals. Mr Graham Thomas has told me that the true 'Mrs Kendall Clark' was not in the Wisley Trial, but we now have to accept that the name has been usurped.

G. pratense 'Plenum Album' is a double white with rather small flowers. Ingwersen (1946 states that the flowers deteriorate noticeably in old clumps.

G. pratense 'Plenum Caeruleum' (Plate 11) has rather small, light lavender-blue double flowers tinged with lilac (RHSCC Violet-Blue Group 94B), loosely petalled according to Thomas (1982). It was misdescribed in the Report of the Wisley Trial. The flower-form is less regular than in 'Plenum Violaceum'.

G. pratense 'Plenum Violaceum' has rather small rich deep violet-blue (RHSCC Violet Group 87–89) double flowers tinged with purple (RHSCC Violet Group 86B) in the centre and petals "arranged in a cup-formation so that each flower is an exquisite rosette" (Thomas, 1976, 1982). Flowering in July.

G. pratense 'Purpureum Plenum' is probably the same as the preceding.

G. pratense 'Silver Queen' was raised by A.T. Johnson and is a tall plant with large "silver-blue" flowers (Ingwersen, 1946). The Wisley Trial Report gives its height as 130cm and the flower-colour as white with a slight tinge of very pale violet.

G. pratense [names including the word] 'Reiter' have dark brown-purple foliage as a result of artificial selection carried out in the USA by Victor Reiter. (They are named at a rank higher than that of cultivar which is not used in this book; it seems that no cultivar epithets are yet available for them.) *G. pratense* 'Striatum' ('Bicolor') has white petals spotted and streaked with violet-blue in varying intensities and to very varying extents. At least a proportion of the seedlings come true (Ingwersen, 1946). This kind of variegation is attributed to an unstable gene.

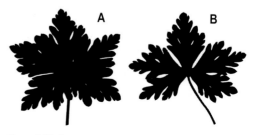

Figure 9.22. *G. pratense* "Nepal Form": (A) from J. Stephens, 1968; (B) from Wisley, 1971; 8cm wide

16. *G. pratense* continued: the two distinct regional variants that I separate from the "European Form" (p.79a, second paragraph) follow here.

G. pratense Linnaeus "Nepal Form" (lacks a formal scientific name) (Figure 9.22)
Differs from "European Form" in the following points: blades of basal leaves often less than 20cm wide, with 7 divisions; all leaves with divisions rather abruptly tapered both ways from about the middle, with a much more solid outline because the lobes and teeth are broader and, though more or less acute, abruptly tapered; paired branches more unequal and the upper internodes of the inflorescence longer, so that rather elongated and one-sided shoots are formed.

W. and C. Nepal, Kashmir, perhaps N.E. Afghanistan.

Two stocks of the "Nepal Form" have been grown at Cambridge. One was received from Mr Jan Stephens in 1968; it had softly hairy leaves with pale marbling on the upper surface; the petals were flushed with a purple tinge in the lower half but faded to white at the base. The other I found growing at Wisley in 1971; the leaves were not marbled and they had a coarser hair-covering; the petal colour was rather intense but white at the extreme base; the petal-veins were purple for about $^2/_3$ the length of the petal; it never had many flowers out at once and was of little garden value. A colour chart reading on the Stephens stock was redder than for the European form at equivalent of RHSCC Violet Group 86C–D, becoming Purple-Violet Group 82B–C.

Figure 9.23. *G. pratense* var. *stewartianum*: from S.K. Raina, 1981–2, coll. India: Jammu, clone selected as 'Elizabeth Yeo'; 21cm wide

At first glance the "Nepal Form" might not be recognised as *G. pratense* because the leaves are so different, but the blue flowers with horizontal axis, the minor floral details and reflexed immature fruits with bladdery calyx are essentially *G. pratense*.

G. pratense var. *stewartianum* Y.J. Nasir (Figure 9.23, Plate 12)
A large branching plant to about 1.5m, thus similar in stature and vigour to the European form but more bushy and flowering earlier (May). Petal colour variable, from purple to pink (not approaching blue).
The largest basal leaves may be 9cm wide in a constrained plant but up to 24cm in open ground; the divisions, lobes and teeth are as numerous as in the European form but wider, giving a much more solid effect when pressed out flat (in life they sometimes curl up at the sides). Usually the leaf-divisions overlap as in the European form but sometimes the sinuses between them are open. The stem-leaves are usually pentagonal, resembling the basal leaves of the "Nepal Form" (Figure 22). The pedicels (and their developing fruits) are not reflexed but erect or spreading (and then bent upwards under the flower), and even the shorter pedicel of each pair is longer than the calyx. The flowers differ from those of the European form in being upwardly inclined (as in 19. *G. clarkei*) and in having a non-bladdery calyx and pink to violet or purple petals (with or without darker veins); when well-developed they may be 32–45mm in width, much as in the European form.

N. Pakistan, Kashmir.

I received three samples of seed of this from S.K. Raina in 1981 and 1982; all the plants raised (specimens of 8 were dried and preserved) were distinguishable from one another by differences in leaf-size, flower-size and colour and by subtle variations in the leaf segments. Chadwell no. 31 (1986) from Sonamarg, Kashmir, represents this variety. The most horticulturally obvious characteristics are the coarse foliage, solid leaf-outline, the varying but not blue petal colour and the early date of flowering.
I have selected for naming as cultivars the two pinkest of Raina's clones:
G. pratense var. *stewartianum* 'Elizabeth Yeo' (after my wife) with colourless petal veins, and
G. pratense var. *stewartianum* 'Raina' (after the collector) with the veins darker than the background.

The name *G. pratense* subsp. *stewartianum* Y.J. Nasir embraces two varieties, var. *stewartianum* and var. *schmidii* Y.J. Nasir. The latter has petals only 12mm long and these have hairs all over the surface at the base. Its true affinity may lie elsewhere, but I have not seen good material of it. For the plant in cultivation it is therefore important to stick to varietal rank.

G. pratense has spontaneously formed fertile hybrids with 15. *G. collinum* and 45. *G. dahuricum* and sterile ones with 8. *G. sylvaticum* and 20. *G. himalayense* (see the latter parent for details). I once found *G. pratense* x *G. thunbergii* (52.) (with white flowers) and Alan Bremner has raised *G. pratense* x

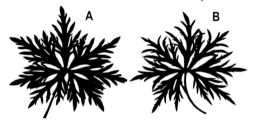

Figure 9.24. (A) *G. pratense*: form with slender leaf-segments, from Yakutsk Acad. Sci. B.G., 1973; 12cm wide
(B) *G. transbaicalicum*, from Moscow Acad. Sci. B.G., 1975; 6.5cm wide (different reductions)

G. swatense (30.) and *G. pratense* x *G. psilostemon* (14.): 'Eva'. For crosses with closer relatives see description of the Pratense Group and Appendix III.

17. *G. transbaicalicum* Sergievskaya (Figure 9.24B, Plate 13)
Plants about 25cm tall, slender, with darkly pigmented stems. Basal leaf-stalks more or less prostrate. Blades of basal leaves often less than 20cm wide with numerous narrow lobes and teeth; basal and stem-leaves edged with red or brown, the segments more or less channelled; petals often a darker tint of the colour usual in *G. pratense*. Otherwise as in 16. *G. pratense* "European Form".

Siberia, in the regions to E. and W. of Lake Baikal.

Two samples with such low growth and finely cut leaves have been grown at Cambridge, having been received from the Botanic Gardens of the Academy of Sciences in Moscow in 1975 and Yakutsk in 1973 respectively. In the former, named *G. transbaicalicum,* the leaf-divisions are freely pinnately lobed with the lobes spaced out along a narrow central portion, starting just above the base. This is a most distinctive and attractive plant. In the latter the divisions are less narrow, are palmato-pinnately lobed, starting just below the middle, and the lobes and teeth are correspondingly broader. In some plants of the Yakutsk stock there is a slight

chlorophyll deficiency giving a golden tinge to the centres of the leaf-divisions.

There is in fact a series of plants progressively more like the "European Form" of *G. pratense* that makes me reluctant to accept *G. transbaicalicum* as deserving specific rank. However, it is convenient to retain the binary name and in any case subspecific rank is not easy to apply until the whole of the variation in this alliance has been mapped out. All these stocks break their dormancy too early in Britain; the attractive Moscow one would be suitable for rock gardens in parts of Europe with a continental climate, and is the one I have made available to nurserymen and collectors.

18. *G. regelii* Nevski
A slightly creeping perennial with flowers like those of *G. pratense* but plant of smaller stature (to 55cm), with slenderer stems and smaller leaves (to 10cm wide) with simpler, blunter segmentation. Inflorescence very loose in cultivation. Mayonwards.

Tufted perennial with crowded shoots and rhizomatous offsets. Stems to about 55cm tall. Blades of basal leaves to 10cm wide, divided as far as $^4/_5$ into 5 or 7; divisions rhombic or wedge-shaped, with rather open sinuses between them, coarsely 3-lobed at the apex; lobes mostly about as long as broad, with one or two teeth; lobes and teeth often turned outwards, obtuse and mucronate to acute; leaf-stalks 3–4 times as long as blades; stipules about 8mm, ovate, downy. Stem leaves paired, with blades to 7.5cm wide, usually divided as far as $^9/_{10}$ into 5; divisions to $1^1/_2$ times as long as broad, sometimes acute, the lobes of the upper with no teeth; leaf-stalks of the lowermost longer than the blades. All leaves thinly clothed with appressed hairs above and with more spreading hairs, mainly on the veins, beneath. Inflorescence very loose. Peduncles and pedicels as in *G. pratense* except that pedicels are up to $1^1/_2$ times as long as sepals. Flowers as in *G. pratense*, to 4cm wide, but sepals only 7–8mm and mucro 0.5–1mm. Petals with purple veins. Fruit is in *G. pratense*.

Mountains of Tien Shan and Pamir Alai, N.E. Afghanistan, W. Himalayas (Chitral in Pakistan, Himachal Pradesh in India [the specimen cited below]).

This species seems to have local variations resulting from evolution (parallel or divergent) on different mountain ranges, as photographs taken in nature in the former USSR and Afghanistan show different leaf-shapes. The similarity of the flowers and fruits to those of *G. pratense* raises doubts about its entitlement to specific rank. The description here is based on Kirkpatrick

Figure 9.25. *G. clarkei*: from J. Stephens, 1969, as *G. bergianum*; 10cm wide

& McBeath 1882, Patsio, Lahul, Himachal Pradesh, India, 3800m, Cambridge accessions, 1986.0324 Edinburgh and 1988.0147 Edinburgh. This has very long internodes and leaf-stalks but when collected in India was only 15cm tall. The petal colour is rather pale.

19. G. clarkei Yeo (Figure 9.25)

Rhizomatous perennial up to about 50cm tall. Blades of basal leaves deeply divided, the divisions with numerous, deep, few-toothed or entire lobes. Inflorescence looser than in 16. *G. pratense* with longer pedicels. Flowers upwardly inclined, 42–48mm in diameter, purplish violet, pink or white, and then with lilac-pink veins. Border, sun. June onwards.

Basal leaves numerous, long-stalked, with narrow acute stipules up to 2cm long and with a blade 5–13cm wide, divided almost to the base into 7. Divisions broadest about the middle, deeply palmato-pinnately or pinnately lobed; lobes usually 2–3 times as long as wide, with 1 or 2 teeth. Teeth and tips of lobes acute. Stem-leaves similar, opposite. Stems up to about 50cm tall, forming a branched, many-flowered but not dense inflorescence. Hair-clothing of the lower parts rather densely felted or almost none, of the upper branches and parts of the flowers glandular. Peduncles 1.5–12cm; pedicels not shorter than the calyx. Flowers with axis upwardly inclined and with widely divergent sepals and petals. Sepals about 11mm; mucro *c.* 1.5–2.5mm, violet at base. Petals 22–29 x 18–22mm, broadly wedge-shaped at the base, rounded at the apex, of a fine purplish violet colour or white with delicate pale lilac net-veining. Bases of the petals provided with dense

hairs on the margins and sometimes a very few on the surface. Filaments ovately enlarged and finely hairy at the base. Stigmas 1.5–2mm. Immature fruits and their pedicels spreading and ascending or slightly nodding. Rostrum 24–28mm, including stylar portion 6–8mm. Mericarps 4–5mm. Discharge: seed-ejection (bristles).

Kashmir.

This plant is named after C.B. Clarke (1832–1906), Superintendent of the Calcutta Botanic Gardens, President of the Linnean Society of London and substantial contributor to *Flora of British India*; he collected the earliest specimen of this *Geranium* that I could find in the Kew Herbarium, which I have designated as the type.

The species occurs naturally at altitudes from 2,100 to 4,200m. It was brought to my notice by Mr Jan Stephens when, in 1968, he gave me the violet-flowered form under the name *G. bergianum* and the white as *G. rectum*, under which names they had been growing at Kew. I sought specimens in herbaria and matched these plants with many specimens from Kashmir (two of them actually labelled *G. rectum*). (*G.* x *bergianum* Lundström is 15. *G. collinum* x 45. *G. dahuricum*.) Later I received two samples of this species collected in nature, one from Mr Roy Lancaster (L. 158, 1982) and one from Dr S.K. Raina (no. 949, 1983), both from Gulmarg in Kashmir. Both have purple flowers (in Lancaster's plant RHSCC Violet Group 81B, with suffusion of 82C; in Raina's, bluer, RHSCC Violet Group 88B), but the name 'Kashmir Purple' should be restricted to the clone to which it originally applied and its selfed progeny (see below). The description from edn.1 has now been revised to cover these.

Because of their obvious relationship with 16. *G. pratense* Mr Stephens's plants were treated in the Wisley Trial, 1973–6, as cultivars of that species, and named respectively 'Kashmir Purple' and 'Kashmir White'.

It was clear that they represented a distinct species very different from *G. pratense* in habit, being of lower growth, producing a carpet of basal leaves, and having a more diffuse inflorescence, although still with abundant flowers. They also differ in the longer pedicels, ascending floral axis and larger violet, or white and net-veined, petals. Some growers find the spread of *G. clarkei* by means of rhizomes too invasive, but the slightly less vigorous 'Kashmir White' may be more acceptable in this respect, and it has become widely grown in gardens.

G. clarkei differs from *G. himalayense* in the erect habit, more narrowly cut leaves, the upturned flowers and colour of the petals.

The part of *Flora of Pakistan* dealing with Geraniaceae (Nasir, 1983) does not account for *G. clarkei*, although it describes two new taxa in the *G. pratense* alliance (see 16. *G. pratense* var. *stewartianum*).

G. clarkei 'Kashmir Pink' has pink petals; it did not actually arise in Kashmir.

G. clarkei 'Kashmir Purple' (*G. pratense* 'Kashmir Purple') has the petal-colour RHSCC Purple-Violet Group near 82B–C, becoming 81A (less blue than *G. pratense* "Nepal Form" and still less blue than *G. pratense* "European Form"). This plant appears to come true from seed.

G. clarkei 'Kashmir White' (*G. pratense* 'Kashmir White') (Plate 14) is rather less vigorous than 'Kashmir Purple' and has white petals with pale lilac-pink veins which appear greyish at a distance. Miss Elizabeth Strangman raised plants from seed and found a proportion of them to be purple-flowered, even though 'Kashmir Purple' was not growing in the same garden.

G. clarkei has hybridised rather freely within its group and with the closely related Collinum Group (for hybrids with the latter, see 15. *G. collinum*). A sterile hybrid with 20. *G. himalayense* appeared spontaneously at Cambridge and Dr Helen Kiefer produced a hybrid at Cambridge with 16. *G. pratense* ("European Form") using the white-flowered *G. clarkei*; this was nearly sterile as was a spontaneous hybrid between this species and what was probably 16. *G. pratense* "Nepal Form" that has now become a popular garden plant under the name 'Brookside'. The flower is a lovely clear blue with a small white eye and the inflorescence is hoary with white hairs. (It was first found in 1982; specimens collected on 1 August 1987 were placed in the CUBG herbarium under accession number 1987.0219.)

20. *G. himalayense* Klotzsch (*G. grandiflorum* Edgeworth, not Linnaeus; *G. meeboldii* Briquet) (Figures 9.26, 9.27 & 9.28, Plate 15)
A carpeting plant with angularly cut leaves and long-stalked usually deep blue to whitish flowers, generally 40–60mm in diameter. Border, ground-cover, sun or partial shade. June, sometimes continuing to October.

Perennial spreading by underground rhizomes. Blades of basal leaves between 5 and 20cm wide, divided as far as $^3/_4$ or $^4/_5$ into 7; divisions shortly tapered both ways from about the middle, rather solid in outline, 3-lobed at the apex; lobes about as broad as long, usually somewhat spreading, sometimes strongly so, with a few teeth. Teeth and

Figure 9.26. *G. himalayense*: from Alan Bloom, 1956, one division separated; 12.5cm wide

Figure 9.27. *G. himalayense*, from Sino-Himalayan Plant Association (Chadwell 31); 8cm wide

tips of lobes obtuse or obtusish. Stipules rather narrow, acute, up to 2cm long. Stem-leaves paired, gradually diminishing in size and length of stalk upwards and becoming slightly more broken in outline and more sharply toothed. Plant rather uniformly covered with small, more or less appressed hairs, those of the undersides of the leaves sometimes longer and more spreading; glandular hairs present on upper stems, calyces and rostra. Peduncles mostly 4–18cm. Pedicels short, one in each cymule usually no longer than the calyx. Floral axis horizontal (rarely upwardly inclined). Flowers saucer-shaped. Sepals 8–12mm, often stained with purplish at base; mucro 0.5–1.5mm. Petals 20–31 x 18–25mm, $1^1/_3$ times as long as broad to nearly equal in length and breadth,

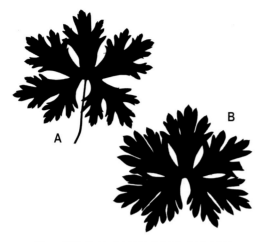

Figure 9.28. *G. himalayense*: 2 clones received as *G. grandiflorum alpinum*, either of which might be 'Gravetye': (A) from J.E. Raven, 1976; 9.5cm wide (B) from J. Stephens, 1969; 7cm wide (different reductions)

rounded at apex, deep campanula-blue, often flushed with pinkish near base and white at extreme base; base with a short dense tuft of hairs at either side and a fringe above this, but without hairs all across front surface. Filaments usually tinged with pink, abruptly enlarged at base, which is fringed with fine hairs; anthers dark blue. Stigmas 2–3.5mm, pink to purplish. Immature fruits reflexed on reflexed pedicels. Rostrum 27–30mm, including stylar portion 7–10mm. Mericarps 4.5–5mm. Discharge: seed-ejection (bristles).

Himalayas from N.E. Afghanistan to C. Nepal; Tadzhikistan (Pamir Region).

This is the largest-flowered of all species of *Geranium* and a fine garden plant, with a long flowering season and good ground-covering (and weed-smothering) ability. Colour-chart readings are bluer than those of 16. *G. pratense*, around RHSCC Violet-Blue Group 94B (HCC Hyacinth Blue 40/1–2 to Lobelia Blue 41/1–2). It occurs with various leaf-shapes and flower-sizes; one with broad leaf-lobes is distributed by Bloom's of Bressingham, Norfolk, and is perhaps the same as the subject of H.G. Moon's painting in *Flora and Sylva*, vol. 1, 1903, opposite p. 54, and reproduced on the cover of Dr Evrard's book (1997) (though that portrait was thought by Johnson (1937) to represent 'Gravetye'). A plant with upwardly inclined flowers was noted in 1983 at the Northern Horticultural Society's Garden, Harlow Car, Harrogate, Yorkshire.

Floral and fruit details are closely similar to those of 16. *G. pratense*, making clear the rather close relationship of these two species.

G. himalayense 'Derrick Cook' is a fine white form with the petals bearing feathered purple veins. It was collected in Nepal by Mr Cook in 1985. I was shown cut material of it by Mr John Norton, of 'Plantstuff', in 1998 (dried specimen 20.v.1998 in CUBG herbarium).

G. himalayense 'Gravetye' (Figure 9.29, Plate 15) has smaller foliage with sharper and narrower lobes and teeth than other stocks and is slightly lower-growing; it has larger flowers with a stronger purplish flush in the centre, a disadvantage in the eyes of some. I have received two clones under the name *G. grandiflorum* var. *alpinum*, to both of which the above description applies, and I do not know whether it is feasible to restrict the name 'Gravetye' to one; if it is, it should be used for the clone which received an Award of Merit in the Wisley Trial, 1973–6, and was submitted by Messrs. Ingwersen. The principal colour of its flowers is RHSCC Violet-Blue Group 94B. (The name *G. grandiflorum* Edgeworth var. *alpinum* (Regel) Knuth has been commonly misapplied to this plant; in its original sense it is a synonym of 18. *G. regelii*.)

G. himalayense 'Irish Blue' has flowers 35mm in diameter and paler than usual (RHSCC 94C), a difference which makes them look less blue, and with a still larger central purplish area than in 'Gravetye'; the petals are faintly notched at the apex. The plant was found by Mr Graham Thomas in Eire about 1947 (Clifton, 1979). A plant with the same flower-colour is grown at Edinburgh under a collector's number which I have investigated and found to be erroneous; possibly it is this same clone.

G. himalayense 'Plenum' ('Birch Double') has purplish double flowers not more than 35mm in diameter with narrow petals sometimes lobed on the surface and with a second calyx inside the outer petals. The petals are purplish pink (RHSCC Purple-Violet Group 80A) with blue shades (Violet Group 86C) and darker veins (colour-chart readings from Wisley Trial Report). The leaves are small with short, relatively rounded segments. The plant is much less vigorous than single-flowered stocks. Records of this plant go back to 1928 (Clifton, 1979), but the name 'Birch Double' (referring to Ingwersens' Birch Farm Nursery) was introduced in the Report of the Wisley Trial. However, as Ingwersens themselves were still using the epithet 'Plenum' in 1984 there seems to be no case for adopting the later name.

Blooms of Bressingham have introduced *G. himalayense* x *G. wallichianum* (24.): 'Rozanne' with a brochure in colour including a picture of the plant (see also Preface). Otherwise the parentage of known hybrids falls within the Pratense Group. A sterile hybrid with 19. *G. clarkei* occurred spontaneously at Cambridge before 1984. In 1975 Dr Helen Kiefer crossed *G. pratense* "European Form" with *G. himalayense* 'Gravetye' at Cambridge and raised two seedlings. At least one has garden value and has been named 'Helen' (see below). The same parentage has been inferred for the deservedly popular sterile clone 'Johnson's Blue'; this seems to have appeared about 1950 among plants raised by Mr B. Ruys, of Dedemsvaart in The Netherlands, from seed of *G. pratense* sent him by Mr A.T. Johnson, of Tyn-y-Groes, North Wales, who had selected an improved strain of that species (Thomas, 1976; Johnson, 1937). Evidently, with numerous clones of *G. himalayense* in cultivation, and diverse forms of *G. pratense*, there are possibilities for raising further distinct and perhaps valuable hybrids.

Figure 9.29. *G. himalayense* x *G. pratense*: 'Johnson's Blue', from G.F. Clark, 1971, *ex* Knightshayes Garden *per* D. Wright; 6 and 7cm wide

G. himalayense x *G. pratense*: 'Helen' shows a stronger palmate tendency in the leaf-divisions than 'Johnson's Blue' (which is almost perfectly pinnate); its flowers are 4.5cm wide and its petals are of a deeper colour than those of 'Johnson's Blue', abruptly fading to white at the base. (There are dried specimens in the CUBG herbarium with accession number 1975.0288, and dated 30.vi.78 and 29.v.80; details of origin are given above.)

G. himalayense x *G. pratense*: 'Johnson's Blue' (Figure 9.29) is a fairly exact intermediate between the putative parents. It is a somewhat creeping perennial with leafy stems to about 70cm (more graceful than those of *G. pratense*). The blue flowers with horizontal floral axis are about 50mm

in diameter and are held well above the foliage. It is suitable for the border in sun and flowers from June onwards. It flowers persistently because it is unable to set seed, but with the continual branching of the inflorescence it eventually becomes untidy. Despite this, it is a really valuable garden plant. The principal colour of the petals is bluer than that of *G. pratense* and about as blue as *G. himalayense* (Report of the Wisley Trial, 1973–6).

21. *G. saxatile* Karelin & Kirilow (Figure 9.30A & B)
Perennial to about 40cm with crowded short, erect rootstocks, spreading by slender underground rhizomes. Crowns with small crowded leaves having slender stalks mostly 4–6 times as long as blades. Flowers to 3.5cm wide, blue, nearly erect. Border, sun. June onwards.

Blades of basal leaves to 5.5cm wide, divided as far as $^2/_3$–$^4/_5$ into 5 or 7; divisions more or less rhombic, palmately or palmato-pinnately lobed in the upper half approximately; lobes about 1–1$^1/_2$ times as long as broad, with one or two teeth; teeth and tips of lobes acute; upper surface slightly marbled, both surfaces with partially spreading hairs, those beneath mainly on the veins. Leaf-stalks slender, with sparse backwardly appressed hairs. Stipules to about 14mm, ovate, distinctly bristle-tipped, hairless. Stems clothed as the leaf-stalks, usually with a short basal internode followed by a long one up to 16cm, with leaves in pairs. Lowest stem leaves with 5 divisions, with ovate-attenuate stipules to about 8mm and petioles about 3–3$^1/_2$ times as long as blades; upper rapidly diminishing in

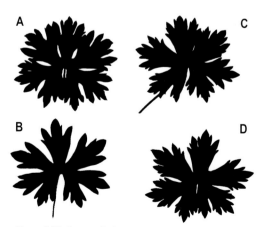

Figure 9.30. *G. saxatile*: from Elizabeth Strangman, CUBG accession 1987.0186 (identical with Dr A.C. Leslie 6/80B); (C) & (D) plant related to the preceding from Dr A.C. Leslie, 1980 (ACL 6/80A, coll. Chimgan, N.E. of Tashkent); larger of each is 6cm wide

size, complexity and petiole length. Inflorescence very loose; peduncles to 17cm, with large glandular hairs; pedicels about $2^{1}/_{2}$–6 times as long as sepals, clothed as the peduncles. Flowers to 3.5cm wide, nearly erect. Sepals 6–7mm, glandular-hairy, with base and veins violet; mucro 1–1.5mm. Petals to 17 x 16mm, widely spreading, mid-blue-violet at first, becoming mid-purple, with a small white area and a tuft of hairs on either side, not extending across the front surface, at the base. Stamens with filaments white and strongly widened at base, slender and lilac above, the enlargement minutely hair-fringed. Tufts of hairs present above the nectaries. Anthers greyish blue; pollen pale yellow. Style deflexed in the first stage of flowering. Stigmas about 2mm. Pedicels after flowering usually spreading almost horizontally and sometimes slightly bent under the calyx. Immature fruits held more or less in line with the pedicels. Rostrum about 22mm including stylar portion of about 8mm, glandular-hairy on the thickened part. Carpels about 3.5mm, with minute eglandular hairs and at the top a few large glandular hairs. Discharge: seed ejection (bristles).

This description is of a plant that was collected in Uzbekistan in 1980 by Dr A.C. Leslie (no. ACL 6/80B, CUBG accession 1980.0497) (locality: mts above Khamzaabad, S.W. of Fergana). Within a year the same plant was received at Cambridge from Mr A.W.A. Baker, who had also been to the Fergana area with the Alpine Garden Society at about the same time (grown at Cambridge under no. 1981.0285). Miss Elizabeth Strangman has also supplied it, no. 1987.0186. It is probably the plant known as "*Geranium* sp., Pamirs", though the Pamir mountains are far to the south-east of Khamzaabad. The reasons for thinking it is *G. saxatile* are given in Appendix II, where an account is given of another similar plant in which the post-floral pedicels are reflexed (Figure 9.30C & D).

THE ERIANTHUM GROUP

Perennials with few solitary lower stem-leaves, few paired upper stem-leaves and very dense, partly umbel-like inflorescences. Floral axis horizontal or nodding. Flowers flat. Petals not notched, without hairs across front surface at base. Stamens appressed to the style, filaments moderately enlarged at base and covered with long spreading or recurved hairs in lower part. Immature fruits erect.

Three species of N.E. Asia (one extending into N.W. America) (but see reference to Tsyrenova under *G. erianthum*). Two are cultivated; the third is Chinese and known only from the type specimen.

Figure 9.31. *G. platyanthum* (*G. eriostemon*): from Mrs J. Forty (Joy Jones), 1972; 12cm wide

22. G. platyanthum Duthie (*G. eriostemon* De Candolle not Poiret) (Figure 9.31)
Strongly hairy perennial with pale green, sometimes wrinkled leaf-blades which are cut halfway or slightly more into broad shallowly lobed divisions, and very crowded horizontal or nodding white or pale violet flowers which are 25–32mm in diameter and flat or nearly so; stamens appressed to the style, dark-tipped; fruits erect, held above the flowers. Woodland and wild garden. April, May or June, often flowering again.

Plant usually 30–50cm tall, with a thick, compact rootstock. Blades of basal leaves between 5 and 20cm wide, sometimes more, divided as far as $^{1}/_{2}$ or $^{3}/_{5}$ into 5 or 7, upper surface light green, sometimes wrinkled, sometimes narrowly red-edged; divisions shortly tapered to the apex from above the middle, hardly tapered towards the base, shallowly 3-lobed at apex with toothed lobes or merely unevenly toothed. Teeth and tips of lobes very short but more or less acute. Stem-leaves similar, few, with 3 or 5 divisions which are less abruptly tapered at the tip, lowest few solitary, others paired; length of stalks decreasing upwards rapidly. Plant covered with coarse, more or less spreading, eglandular hairs, with an admixture of glandular hairs throughout or in upper parts. Inflorescence very dense, with a large proportion of the flowers in umbel-like clusters, though some of the suppressed peduncles may develop during the maturation of the fruit. Floral axis horizontal or strongly nodding. Flowers flat or nearly so. Sepals 7–10.5mm, flushed with brownish red, widely spreading; mucro 0.5–1mm. Petals not more than 16mm, nearly as broad as long, rounded or shallowly and irregularly lobed at apex, flat except for waved margins, widely spreading, rather light violet-blue fading to white at base; base with a dense tuft of hairs on either side and a fringe beyond this, but without hairs across front surface (many on the back). Filaments appressed to the style, moderately enlarged at base, enlargement white, remainder blackish purple, basal half covered with long coarse spreading hairs with recurved tips; anthers dull bluish. Style 8.5–10.5mm, mostly hairless. Stigmas 1.5–3mm, greenish to dull red. Immature fruits erect on erect pedicels, standing above the currently open flowers. Rostrum 22–28mm, including stylar portion 5–6mm. Mericarps 3.5–4mm, nearly black. Discharge: seed-ejection (bristles).

N.E. Asia from E. Siberia eastwards, E. Tibet and W. China, Korea, Japan.

G. platyanthum is a rather thick-set plant, described unmistakably by A.T. Johnson (1937) in the following words: "with leaves like a hollyhock that colour well in autumn and a stature of over two feet (it) crests this massive pyramid with down-turned blooms the size of a shilling (22.5mm in diameter) in cool violet." He said it came to him as *G. sinense*, which he rightly thought it was not. I first met it at Wisley in 1971 as *"chinense"*, and in 1984 Cambridge had it under that name from Munich B.G., Germany. It is curious that it should be so misnamed, as it was introduced into cultivation as *G. platyanthum* Duthie, described in 1906 on the basis of E.H. Wilson's nos. 1948 and 3298 from, respectively, Western Hubei (Hupeh) and Sichuan, China. This was listed by the UK nursery firm of Veitch in their "Novelties for 1906". Duthie did not compare *G. platyanthum* with *G. eriostemon* but Knuth (1912) synonymised the two without comment, unfortunately adopting the wrong epithet (the name *G. eriostemon* having been used for another plant before De Candolle used it). In nature *G. platyanthum* grows in woodland habitats and mountain meadows.

At Cambridge I have grown the Wisley plant, and one from Mrs Joy Forty (Joy Jones), together with plants raised from seed under the name 23. *G. erianthum* from the Botanic Garden of the Academy of Sciences, Vladivostok, on the Russian Pacific coast. The last differs slightly from the first two in the shape and relative sizes of the leaf-divisions, in flowering first in April or May rather than in June, and in having the floral axis horizontal rather than nodding. *G. platyanthum* is easily propagated by division of the rootstock or from seed.

The short, shallowly lobed leaf-divisions and spreading hairs on the lower stems and undersides of the veins of the lower leaves are the best characters for distinguishing *G. platyanthum* from 23. *G. erianthum*.

G. reinii Franchet & Savatier and *G. onoei* Franchet & Savatier, recognised by Knuth, are treated as infraspecific taxa under *G. eriostemon* in Japanese Floras, with forma *onoei* (Fr. & Sav.) Hara subordinate to variety *reinii* (Fr. & Sav.) Maximowicz which embraces all Japanese material; if this treatment is to be retained, the nomenclature will have to be revised. Variety *reinii* has been collected in N.E. China by Roy Lancaster (his number 1211, from Changbai Shan, 1,600m, Jilin Province, cultivated specimen in CUBG herbarium, viii.1985). In the variety all the leaf segments are comparatively elongated and acute at the tips, leaving only the hair-clothing of the stems for reliable separation from *G. erianthum*, though the leaves of the latter are more profusely lobed and toothed.

G. platyanthum forma *albiflorum* [authority] is a comparatively short form with white petals and yellow anthers.

Figure 9.32. *G. erianthum*: from Uppsala B.G., 1973, *ex* Sapporo B.G.; 11cm wide

23. G. erianthum De Candolle (Figures 9.32 & 9.33, Plates 16 & 17)
Plant similar to 22. *G. platyanthum* but lower stems with eglandular hairs not spreading, and with more deeply divided and more acutely and profusely lobed and toothed leaves; flowers 27–37mm in diameter, more variable in ground-colour, often veiny, with horizontal axis. Border, wild garden, sun or partial shade. May to June and often once or twice again.

Similar to 22. *G. platyanthum* in habit, flowers and fruits, differing as follows: blades of basal leaves divided as far as $^2/_3$–$^4/_5$ into 7 or 9; divisions tapered both ways from the middle, overlapping their neighbours (even the basal pair), freely lobed; lobes about as long as broad with rather numerous teeth; teeth and tips of lobes acute; upper leaves like lower but with 5 or 7 narrower divisions; eglandular hairs of the stem

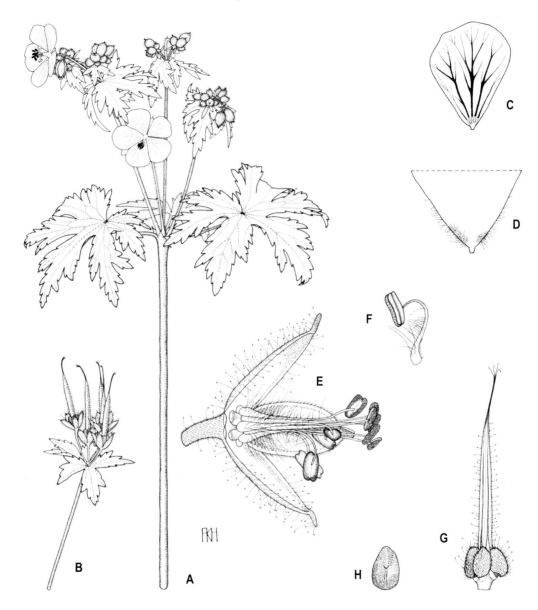

Figure 9.33. *G. erianthum*: from Moscow Acad. Sci. B.G., 1973. (A) shoot beginning to flower, x $^2/_3$; (B) portion of inflorescence with immature fruit, x $^2/_3$; (C) petal, showing pigmentation of veins, x 2; (D) base of front surface of petal, x 4; (E) flower in male stage with petals and two sepals removed, x 4; (F) stamen of outer whorl, seen from back, x 4; (G) ripe fruit in pre-explosive interval x 2; (H) seed, x 4

fine and appressed, those of undersides of leaf-veins directed forwards; floral axis horizontal; petals from less than 16mm to considerably more, nearly triangular, white or light to deep violet-blue, darkly veined, veins sometimes feathered. Rostrum to 35mm, with stylar portion 6–10mm. Discharge: seed-ejection (bristles).

E. Siberia, Kuril Isles and Sakhalin Island, Japan, Alaska, Aleutian Isles, Canada (N. British Columbia).

A showier plant than *G. platyanthum*, like it in producing good autumn colour in the foliage, but probably more tolerant of full sun. The production of opposite leaves on short stalks gives these two species a distinctive habit that is shown in Figure 9.32.

As well as the cultivars named below and other Asian stocks, a New World stock has been introduced to European gardens by Mr Thomas Schulz (CUBG accession 1991.1150, from Chugach Mountains, Anchorage, Alaska). Individual flowers, to 32mm in diameter, are superb, of a good campanula-violet colour, slightly graded, with unfeathered purple veins. The fruits are at the upper limit of size for the species and the leaves are dark green and firm.

G. erianthum 'Calm Sea' (Plate 17) combines very pale ground colour and strong smudgy blue veining in the petals; it is low in stature and has leaves of a darker green and firmer texture than other Far Eastern specimens. It was received at Cambridge from the Botanic Garden of the Academy of Sciences in Vladivostok, on the Russian Pacific coast, incorrectly named *G. maximowiczii*.

G. erianthum 'Neptune' (Plate 16) is a plant of vigorous growth and large deep blue flowers, easily the finest stock I have seen at Cambridge. It came from Uppsala University B.G., Sweden. They received it from Sapporo B.G., Japan, incorrectly named *G. eriostemon* forma *onoei* (see under 22. *G. platyanthum*).

G. erianthum 'Undine' has pure white petals and yellow anthers; growth habit is low.

A revision of *G. erianthum* by Tsyrenova (1985) proposes the recognition of three species which, she says, have been confused until now. They are *G. erianthum*, *G. orientale* (Maximowicz) Freyn and *G. elatum* (Maximowicz) Knuth. I have not been able to allocate cultivated material to these entities. New World material is assigned by Tsyrenova to *G. erianthum*. Knuth accepted *G. elatum* but placed it apart from *G. erianthum*.

THE WALLICHIANUM GROUP

Leaves divided as far as $^3/_4$ or less into 3 or 5; basal rosettes scarcely developed, stems usually trailing or scrambling. Petals with hairs all across front surface at base. Style very short, about $^2/_3$ as long as sepals. Stigmas very long (4mm or more).

I have assembled five Himalayan species together with the recently introduced Chinese species, *G. christensenianum*, to make this group.

24. *G. wallichianum* D. Don (Figure 9.34, Plates 18 & 19)

Variable perennial with no rosette-leaves, trailing stems with leaves divided into 5, and conspicuous blunt stipules, all united in pairs for the whole of their length; flowers 27–36mm in diameter, purplish pink to blue, often with a more or less

Figure 9.34. *G. wallichianum*: (A) from J. Stephens, 1968; (B) 'Buxton's Variety', from G.W.T. White, 1973; 6.5 and 10.5cm wide

circular or angular white centre, or almost white, with rounded or slightly notched petals and blackish stamens and stigmas. Rock garden, patio, shrubbery. July to October.

Rootstock stout. Stems sometimes erect when young, otherwise trailing or scrambling. Blades of main leaves between 5 and 15cm wide, more or less wrinkled and marbled on upper surface, divided as far as $^2/_3$ or $^3/_4$ into 5 or sometimes 3; divisions abruptly or gently tapered both ways from about the middle, often with a slender tip, shallowly or very shallowly lobed; lobes toothed. Teeth and tips of lobes acute. Leaves paired, the 4 stipules of a pair joined to make two, broadly ovate, obtuse, conspicuous; branches occasionally paired but many nodes with only one branch or a branch and a cymule. Hair-clothing variable, eglandular. Inflorescence diffuse, leafy. Peduncles 3–14cm. Pedicels mostly 2–6 times as long as sepals. Flowers upwardly inclined, saucer-shaped or nearly flat. Sepals 6–9mm, the base and the lower parts of the veins purplish; mucro 1.5–3.5mm. Petals 16–17 x 13–16mm, approximately heart-shaped or triangular, rounded to more or less notched at apex, rather deep pink or purplish pink to blue, marked with dark, simple or feathered veins, especially on the back, and often with a fairly sharply marked basal white area, or almost white, usually $^1/_4$–$^1/_2$ as long as petal; base with a dense tuft of hairs at either side and usually a belt of erect hairs on front surface between them. Stamens $^2/_3$ as long as or equalling sepals; filaments curving outwards, blackish to red-purple at tip with whitish flanges forming the basal enlargement, or almost entirely blackish, lower part fringed with fine hairs, base with a more or less distinct tuft; anthers black. Style 5–6mm. Stigmas 5.5–7mm, black to dark red-purple, sometimes with minute hairs on outer surface. Immature fruits erect on deflexed pedicels. Rostrum 22–32mm, including stylar portion 1–2mm. Mericarps 4–5mm, unusually widely open at base. Discharge: seed-ejection (bristles).

Himalayas from N.E. Afghanistan to Kashmir.

A variable species, distinguishable from most others by its very large, fused stipules. Similar stipules are found in *G. koreanum* but they have two short points and the plant has more ovate leaf-lobes and teeth, and lighter-coloured stamens and stigmas.

The extremes of variation mentioned above in, for example, extent of white on petals, length of mucro and length of rostrum, are represented in different plants, not in the same one, but the colour variations can occur within a single colony. This has been shown in a remarkable photograph taken in N.W. India by Mr Henry Taylor, in which he laid out about 20 different flowers from one colony, several types of which have not yet been seen in the species as cultivated in Britain (Taylor, 1999; Clifton, [anon.] 2000). The trailing habit makes *G. wallichianum* suitable for retaining-walls and patios provided the plants are cool and moist at the roots, but it is also happy scrambling upwards through dwarf shrubs. The plant forms a deep taproot and there are no rosette-bearing shoots, which makes it difficult to divide; it is therefore usually propagated by seed. The individual flowers of most stocks are beautiful but in general *G. wallichianum* is not of great garden merit, except in 'Buxton's Variety', which is quite outstanding. Some of the flower forms in Mr Taylor's photograph look desirable.

G. wallichianum 'Buxton's Variety' ('Buxton's Blue') (Figure 9.34B, Plate 18) has compact, closely creeping growth, small marbled leaves with very short and shallowly lobed divisions, medium campanula-blue flowers, delicately veined and with a very large white centre. To indicate its value, I cannot do better than quote Thomas (1976): "It is a pearl beyond price, producing a non-stop display from the end of June onwards of lovely Spode-blue flowers with large white centres and dark stamens over a luxuriantly leafed plant." The name commemorates E.C. Buxton of Bettws-y-Coed, in whose garden it appeared about 1920 (Clifton,

1979). The selection of Nemophila-blue forms and the elimination of other colours was, however, described earlier by Wolley Dod (1903) and Clifton (1979) points out that a plant called 'Shirley Blue' received an RHS award in 1890. Wolley Dod noted that as the weather gets cooler in autumn, the flowers become bluer. The plant we have today is distinctive in its vegetative parts, as I have indicated above, even though it is propagated by seed. (McBeath 1703, from Kulu, Himachal Pradesh, India, with blue flowers similar to those of 'Buxton's Variety' is tall and vigorous, with acuminate or very acute leaf-segments.)

G. wallichianum 'Syabru' has slightly downy leaves with a hint of lime-green marbling and deep purple flowers with still darker veins and no lightening of the colour at the centre. The petals are notched. This was collected in the Trisuli Valley of Nepal by Edward Needham and named after the village where it was found; in fact this is a re-introduction, because the plate accompanying the original description in the first volume of Sweet's *Geraniaceae* (1821) depicts this form.

Within its group *G. wallichianum* has crossed with 28. *G. kishtvariense* and 29. *G. rubifolium* (including 'Nora Bremner') and outside it with 36. *G. farreri*, 1. *G. endressii*, 2. *G.* x *oxonianum* and 14. *G. psilostemon* (Bremner's results).

25. *G. lambertii* Sweet (*G. grevilleanum* Wallich; *G. chumbiense* Knuth) (Figure 9.35)
Trailing and scrambling perennial with leaves divided into 5 and nodding or inverted flowers 30–35mm in diameter, either pale pink, or virtually white, then usually with a dull crimson stain at the base of each petal; stamens, at least at the tips, blackish, very hairy in the lower half; stigmas black. Wild garden, ground-cover, partial shade. July, August.

Figure 9.35. *G. lambertii*: from Leeds B.G., 1980; 10cm wide

Plant with very few basal leaves. Blades of main leaves between 5 and 15cm wide, somewhat wrinkled above, divided just beyond halfway into 5; divisions broad, tapered both ways from well above the middle, the tips therefore very abruptly tapered, 3-lobed; lobes about as long as broad or rather less, toothed. Teeth and tips of lobes acute. Leaves paired, the upper similar to the lower or with slightly narrower divisions with the lobes curved outwards. Stipules 10–15mm, ovate, acute, not united. Plant moderately hairy; glandular hairs usually present at the base of the calyx and on the rostrum. Branches usually paired and unequal, sometimes solitary in the inflorescence. Inflorescence diffuse. Peduncles mostly 5–15cm. Pedicels 1–3 times as long as sepals. Flowers with horizontal axis or, more usually, nodding or inverted, saucer-shaped or shallowly bowl-shaped. Sepals 9–11mm, broad, purplish at base; mucro 1–2mm. Petals 20–24mm long and nearly as broad, broadest near the rounded apex, more or less strongly narrowed at the base, pale pink or white and then usually with a crimson stain at the base running out somewhat into the veins (white petals may turn faint lilac on drying); base with a dense tuft of hairs on either side and some spread across front surface. Stamens about as long as sepals; filaments curving outwards, dull crimson at the base which is only gradually enlarged, black at the tips, covered densely at the base with spreading white hairs, more sparsely so above, hairless in the upper $^1/_4$; anthers black. Style 6–8mm. Stigmas 5–6mm, black, with bristly hairs on the outside, at least at the base. Immature fruits erect on reflexed pedicels. Mericarps 5mm. Mature rostrum 26–30mm, including stylar portion about 4mm. Discharge: seed-ejection (bristles).

Himalayas from C. Nepal to Bhutan and adjacent parts of Tibet; reports of occurrence from further west are probably erroneous.

The pink form of this species, which is the one described by Sweet, is an attractive carpeter. The white form usually has a crimson stain at the base of each petal ('Swansdown', see below), but I have seen it without; it has flatter, more strongly inverted flowers than the pink (even sometimes slightly reflexed petals). The species seems to like growing up through small shrubs. In the Cambridge Botanic Garden the white form, when unsupported and in the open, hardly blooms, producing a few flowers and then going back to leaf-production. However, *G. lambertii* does not seem to give problems elsewhere in East Anglia. *G. candicans* Knuth, a name often misapplied to the white form of *G. lambertii*, is a white-flowered form of 35. *G. yunnanense*, not in cultivation (Yeo, 1983). Edgeworth and Hooker (1874) noted the occurrence in Sikkim of a very pale

Figure 9.36. *G. christensenianum*: cult. David Victor, Hockliffe, Bedfordshire, *ex* Heronswood Nursery, 2000; 7cm wide

form (probably white in life) with a purplish eye. When writing about 27. *G. procurrens* (Yeo, 1973) I incorrectly assumed this was a misinterpretation of C.B. Clarke's notes on a specimen of that species. *G. lambertii* 'Swansdown' is the name published by Clifton (1979) for the white form with deep rose or crimson centre (RHSCC about 53A); veins of petals faintly pink; bases of the stamens the same colour as the petal-bases; leaves moss-green, marbled in lighter and darker shades. Comes true from seed.

G. lambertii has been found to form a variety of hybrids. Within its group it has been crossed by Alan Bremner with 30. *G. swatense* and 27. *G. procurrens*, while a hybrid of the latter parentage had appeared in the garden of Miss Elizabeth Strangman, Washfield Nursery, Hawkhurst, Kent, about 1981 and received the name 'Salome'. The stems are trailing and scrambling but not rooting, and the leaf-blades are slightly marbled. The flower colour represents a novelty in *Geranium*: the petals have a dark violet base and heavy dark violet veins running out on a nearly white ground, and the stamens and stigmas are dark. This hybrid flowers from mid-July onwards.

Outside its group *G. lambertii* has crossed with several members of the small-flowered Sibiricum Group and Sessiliflorum Group. Some have been named, for example 'Joy', an attractive low-spreading plant with pale flowers (*G. lambertii* x *G. traversii*).

26. *G. christensenianum* Handel-Mazzetti (Figure 9.36)

A scrambling or trailing plant whose leaves have five or three divisions. Flowers to 37mm wide, with horizontal axis. Petals white with purplish red veins; filaments largely and anthers and stigmas wholly very dark. Mainly autumn, continuing late.

Stems trailing, reaching a metre in length, rooting and scrambling, with glandular hairs, at least above.

Leaf-blades to 5.5cm wide, divided nearly as far as $^3/_4$ into 3 or 5; divisions ovate or rhomboidal, sometimes with wide sinuses between them, shallowly and sparsely lobed and toothed; lobes and teeth ovate, acute, sometimes conspicuously mucronate. Blades and stalks hairy with eglandular and some glandular hairs. Stipules to 11mm. Flower-pairs borne in axils of foliage leaves. Peduncles to 6cm; pedicels at flowering about as long as sepals, later $1^1/_2$–2 times as long. Peduncles and pedicels with long glandular hairs with colourless stalks and pigmented heads. Flowers with horizontal axis. Sepals 9–11mm, with glandular hairs as on pedicels; mucro 1–2.5mm. Petals to 16 x 13mm, broadly obovate, white or nearly so, with fine dark purplish red and slightly feathered veins, hairy at base on edges and front surface. Filaments blackish-violet except on their edges at the base, curved outwards at first, hairy on lower $^1/_3$–$^2/_3$, scarcely widened at base. Anthers and stigmas black. Style purplish violet to black, hairy; stigmas 5mm. Immature fruits and their pedicels erect. Rostrum 18–20mm (perhaps more), including stylar portion of 4mm, with long glandular hairs. Discharge: seed-ejection (bristles).

China (Yunnan).

This species was discovered at Pe Tsao-lin in 1917, and specimens were sent to Copenhagen. These had only leaves with three divisions, but in the cultivated material the lower leaves have five. The plant's habit recalls *G. procurrens*, while the white ground colour of the petals recalls *G. lambertii*.

It was collected again on Longzhou Shan, Sichuan, by Eric Hammond jointly with Kunming University in the 1990s. From this source it was first cultivated in the USA by Dan Hinkley, Heronswood Nursery, Oregon, and then sent to David Victor in England in 1999. A photograph by David Victor appeared in *Geraniaceae Group News*, Spring 2000, issue no. 77, p. 11.

27. *G. procurrens* Yeo (Figures 9.37 & 9.38)

Stems red, trailing for long distances and rooting; leaf-divisions 5, lobed about halfway to the midrib; flowers more or less erect, 25–35mm in diameter, dull pinkish purple with black centre; petals not overlapping; stamens and stigmas black. Wild garden, ground-cover, preferably in shade. July to October or November.

Plant with few basal leaves and trailing stems extending to 1m or more in a season's growth, rooting at the nodes. Blades of earlier leaves of the season between 5 and 10cm wide, divided as far as $^2/_3$ into 5 or rarely 7, upper surface slightly wrinkled and faintly marbled; divisions tapered both ways from above the middle or near the tip, apex 3-lobed;

Figure 9.37. *G. procurrens*: from Wisley, 1971, ex O.G. Folkard; 9cm wide

lobes as long as broad or less, toothless or with one or two teeth. Teeth and tips of lobes obtuse or acute. Leaves paired, some of their stipules free, some united in pairs for part of their length, acute; divisions of upper leaves narrower than those of the lower and with a more broken outline. Plant moderately hairy; glandular hairs present on upper parts including leaf-stalks, sepals and rostra. Inflorescence very diffuse. Peduncles mostly 5–8cm. Pedicels 3–5 times as long as sepals. Sepals 6–9mm, reddish at base; mucro 1mm or less. Petals 16–18 x 8.5–12mm, enlarging noticeably with age, rather dull deep pinkish purple with V-shaped black area at base and black veins; base with a dense tuft of hairs on each side running out into an extensive fringe and with hairs all across front surface between the tufts. Stamens about as long as sepals, black; filaments not enlarged at base, with relatively sparse long white bristly hairs at base. Style about 5.5mm. Stigmas 4–4.5mm, black, with some bristly hairs on the outside at the base. Immature fruits erect on erect pedicels. Rostrum about 18mm, including stylar portion about 1.5mm. Mericarps about 4mm, black with black hairs. Discharge: seed-ejection (bristles).

Himalayas (E. Nepal, Sikkim).

The history of this plant has been told by Yeo (1973). Specimens were collected in the 1840s but were generally thought to be *G. lambertii* (for which the name *G. grevilleanum* was in use). It was cultivated at Kew in 1931 and may have lingered on, little known, in some gardens. However, it was again introduced by Dr G.A.C. Herklots in 1967, and after that it rapidly became widely distributed in British gardens. On its re-introduction it was unfortunately misidentified as 15. *G. collinum*. Its trailing habit and

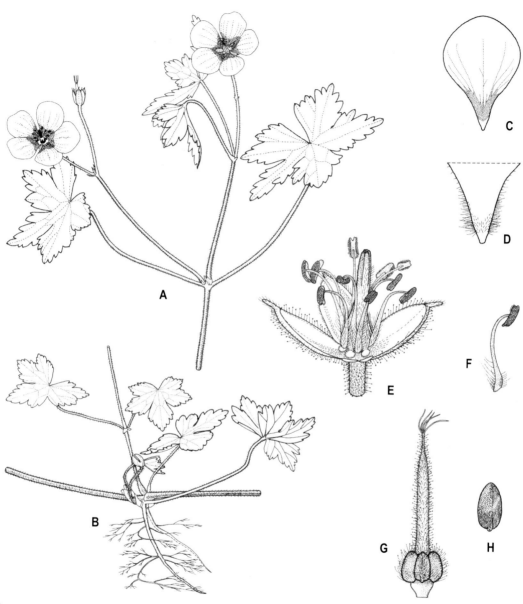

late production of slightly sombre flowers makes it a somewhat specialised plant for gardens. Its runners may be tied up to a wall; they die off in autumn and if they have been allowed to sprawl, they leave behind young rooted plants. Propagation is therefore easy. I have never seen a seedling of this species.

Its hybrid with 14. *G. psilostemon* has proved to be an outstanding garden plant. A hybrid with 25. *G. lambertii* has occurred spontaneously. (See respective parent species for details.)

Figure 9.38. *G. procurrens*: from Wisley, 1971, *ex* O.G. Folkard. (A) portion of flowering shoot, x $^2/_3$; (B) portion of trailing shoot formed early in season, with roots at node, x $^2/_3$; (C) petal, showing dark pigmentation, x 2; (D) base of front surface of petal, x 4; (E) flower in male stage with petals and two sepals removed, x 4; (F) stamen of outer whorl, seen obliquely from back, x 4; (G) mature fruit, x 2; (H) seed, x 4

28. *G. kishtvariense* Knuth (Figure 9.39, Plate 20) Rhizomatous plant with bushy growth, bright green wrinkled leaves with 3 or 5 serrated divisions, swollen nodes and leaf-stalk bases; flowers nearly 40mm in diameter, of a rich royal purple (see also discussion); petals with a V-shaped white patch at base, finely veined; stigmas and tips of stamens blackish red. Immature fruits reflexed. Woodland and semi-shade. June to September.

Perennial with extensively creeping, rather slender, underground stolons. Blades of basal leaves (often not produced on flowering shoots) and lower stem-leaves mostly 4–9cm wide, bright green, wrinkled, divided as far as about $^2/_3$ into 5; divisions tapered both ways from about the middle, moderately wide, rather shallowly lobed; lobes broader than long, with one or several teeth. Teeth and tips of lobes finely acute. Lowest leaves solitary, others paired, gradually changing upwards to a 3-lobed condition, with predominance of the middle lobe. Stems slender, with internodes of very variable length, producing bushy growth; nodes and bases of leaf-stalks swollen. Stipules free or joined in pairs. Plant with rather bristly more or less appressed hairs and with glandular hairs on upper parts including sepals and rostra. Peduncles mostly 3–6cm. Pedicels about $1^1/_2$–4 times as long as sepals. Flowers upwardly inclined. Sepals 7–9mm, purple at base; mucro 2–3mm. Petals about 21 x 17mm, broadest above the middle, rounded at apex, deep pinkish purple with fine, slightly feathered, purple veins and a V-shaped white area at the base; base with a dense tuft of short hairs near each margin, a fringe on the margin, and rather dense hairs on front surface between the tufts. Stamens about $^2/_3$ as long as sepals; filaments white and strongly enlarged at

Figure 9.39. *G. kishtvariense*: from R. Lancaster, 1980, coll. India: Gulmarg, Kashmir (L 159); 11cm wide

base, blackish red and curving outwards at apex, with a tuft of hairs at extreme base and hairs on back and margins of the enlarged part, minutely fringed above this to about half their height; anthers blackish. Style about 5mm. Stigmas about 4.5mm, blackish red, finely bristly on the outside. Immature fruits reflexed on reflexed pedicels. Rostrum 17–18mm, without a stylar portion. Mericarps about 3.5mm. Discharge: seed-ejection (bristles).

Kashmir.

The introduction of this species into cultivation is due to Mr Roy Lancaster, who collected the plant described above in 1978 (no. L. 159) on the perimeter track, Gulmarg, near Srinagar, and another plant at the upper edge of the forest between Gulmarg and Khillanmarg (L. 177). L. 159 has finely formed flowers of a splendid colour (RHSCC Purple Group near 78, between A and B; HCC Petunia Purple 32/1, approaching 32/2 in age – Plate 20); botanically it is distinctive in its rhizomes, swollen nodes, very short stamens, more or less obliterated style and reflexed immature fruits. In some characters it recalls 6. *G. rectum* but it more strongly resembles 29. *G. rubifolium*. It is easily increased by division.

A form with slightly paler and less purplish petal colour is in cultivation; I am not sure whether this is L. 177.

When Mr Lancaster's L. 159 was introduced in 1978, I already knew of the plant from specimens in the Kew Herbarium collected at Gulmarg and from a colour photograph taken by Mr O. Polunin at Apharwat; I considered that it was related to 6. *G. rectum* but did not recognise it as *G. kishtvariense*, which I thought was an unintentional re-description of the little-known *G. rubifolium*. However, on comparing L. 159 in cultivation with the subsequently acquired *G. rubifolium* (no. 29), I found that, although the two plants were extraordinarily similar, their underground parts were completely different and there was a corresponding difference in the number of stems produced. Knuth said that *G. kishtvariense* has a rhizome, while for *G. rubifolium* he indicated a compact rootstock (by stating that the rhizome and stems are like those of *G. wallichianum* and then that the latter has a short vertical rootstock ['caudex']). By this, the possibility that the description of *G. kishtvariense* applies to *G. rubifolium* is eliminated, albeit deviously.

G. kishtvariense has hybridised within its group with 29. *G. rubifolium* and 24. *G. wallichianum* and outside it with 59. *G. x antipodeum* and 2. *G. x oxonianum*.

29. G. rubifolium Lindley (Figure 9.40)

A stately perennial with compact rootstock, erect stems, bright green wrinkled leaves divided about halfway or as far as $^2/_3$ into 3 or 5 broad serrated divisions, and swollen nodes; flowers about 25–30mm in diameter; petals purplish violet or violet with V-shaped white patch at base, finely veined; stigmas reddish to blackish. Woodland margin in partial shade. June to September.

Rootstock compact with swollen roots. Stems few, erect, to 70cm main leaves mostly 5–14cm wide, with scarcely lobed divisions which are very broad on the lower leaves but distinctly elongated on the upper; with flowers similar to those of 28. *G. kishtvariense* but slightly smaller, sepals with mucro about 1–1.5mm, smaller, petals, 14–18mm long, purplish violet or violet in colour with faintly notched apex, filaments about as long as sepals, usually merely purplish pink at tips, anthers greyish violet to blackish, and sometimes reddish stigmas; the rostrum has a distinct stylar portion 1–1.5mm long, and the mericarps are about 4.5mm long. Discharge: seed-ejection (bristles).

Kashmir.

The characters given above for distinguishing the above-ground parts of *G. rubifolium* from those of 28. *G. kishtvariense* apply only to the plants known to me in cultivation. A survey of specimens in the Kew Herbarium suggests that the floral differences are inconstant.

This species was described from plants raised in the garden of the Horticultural Society of London in 1839, from seed sent by J.F. Royle from the Himalayas. Lindley, when describing it, stated that "it should be planted in light soil, or on rock work, as it is soon destroyed by the wet in winter". In fact it seems soon to have died out. However, I raised plants from seed sent in 1981 by Dr S.K. Raina, collected at Duchsum in Kashmir. Their growth was at first sluggish and intermittent, but several plants grew well and flowered in 1983. In most of my plants the petal colour is RHSCC Purple Violet Group 80B–81B, but in one they switched to Violet Group 84A during the 1983 growing season and later reverted to the original colour; in this plant the upper parts of the stamens are dark whereas in the purple-petalled plants they may be dark or pale. Although the flowers of this species are usually less brilliant than 28. *G. kishtvariense*, Mr David Victor grows a form that is at least as brilliant as the latter (while not showing any sign of hybridisation with that).

G. rubifolium has crossed within its group with 28. *G. kishtvariense* and 24. *G. wallichianum* and outside it with members of the Sessiliflorum Group.

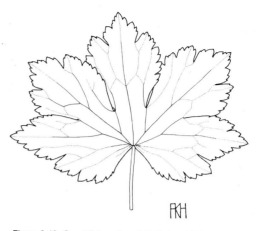

Figure 9.40. *G. rubifolium*: from S.K. Raina, 1981, coll. India: Duchsum, Kashmir; 12cm wide

Figure 9.41. *G. swatense*: cult. D. Victor, 1998, Berlin introduction from Cambridge; 8cm wide

30. G. swatense Schönbeck-Temesy (Figure 9.41)

Trailing glandular-hairy perennial with thickened roots, loosely hairy leaves, those of the stem to 6cm wide, pentagonal. Flowers 25–40mm wide, on long stalks above the low-lying leaves, pink. Rock garden or low border. Summer.

Perennial with carrot-like root about 13mm thick. Stems thin, freely branched, soon sprawling, with spreading eglandular and small-headed glandular hairs and paired leaves; internodes about 1.5–10cm. Basal leaves (produced by non-flowering plants or crowns) with blades to 8.5cm wide, divided as far as $^3/_4 - ^4/_5$ into 7, more or less kidney-shaped in outline; divisions wedge-shaped, more or less palmately lobed in the apical $^1/_3$, sometimes overlapping; lobes $1-1^1/_2$ times as long as broad, with 1–3 teeth, the outer lobes usually turned outwards; teeth as long as broad or less; teeth and tips of lobes obtuse, mucronate or some of them acute; upper surface green, sometimes with pale marbling and sometimes a red edge, both surfaces hairy, some of the hairs being very long. Leaf-stalks 1–2 times as long as blade, clothed as the stem. Stipules 4–6mm, apparently wider than long. Blades of stem-leaves mostly 2.5–6cm wide, differing from the basal in having 5 divisions that are more rhombic (making the blade pentagonal) and that may have sharper lobes and teeth; stipules to 5mm, 2–3-pronged, very hairy. Cymules far exceeding the leaves, carrying their flowers well clear of the mainly prostrate foliage. Peduncles mostly 4–16cm; pedicels 3–6cm, peduncles and pedicels clothed as the stems. Flower buds nodding. Flowers 25–40mm wide, funnel-shaped when young, turning towards the sun. Sepals 8–11mm, noticeably narrow, sometimes recurved, with purple veins and a purple blotch at the base, tapered into a mucro 1–1.5mm long, densely covered with long glandular and eglandular hairs. Petals to 20 x 18mm, rounded at apex, purplish pink to bluish pink or white, with a small white area at base and with slightly darkened veins, bearded on the margins and front surface at the base. Stamen filaments with a strongly widened white hair-fringed base, and a narrow purple part; no hairs near the nectaries. Anthers grey-blue. Style, excluding the stigmas, much shorter than the sepals; stigmas 3–4.5mm, red. Pedicels spreading or reflexed under the erect immature fruits. Rostrum 16–25mm, clothed at the base as the stem, gradually glabrous to the apex, with slender stylar portion about 3mm. Carpels about 4mm; seeds to 3mm. Discharge: seed-ejection (bristles).

N. Pakistan, N.E. Afghanistan, N.W. India (Kashmir).

This species was introduced from Pakistan simultaneously by two expeditions (as reported by Ross, 1989, and Yeo, 1989): one by Ern & Prelaz from the botanic garden of Berlin-Dahlem and one by members of the Swedish Expedition to Pakistan, 1983 (SEP). Both were sent to Cambridge as seed in 1985, the second from Edinburgh. A detailed account of the Edinburgh stock was published by John Ross in 1989. Collection details are (1) Ern & Prelaz 7525,

Cambridge accession 1985.0284, N.W. Frontier, Swat Division, Utror Tal near Utror, 2400m. (2) SEP 131, Edinburgh accession 84.0146, Cambridge accession 1985.0314, Gilgit (Chilas): Babusar Valley, N. of Babusar Village, 2878m, dry meadows on a N.W. slope (Ross, 1989). SEP 131 flowered at Cambridge but soon died and I do not have a complete comparison of it with the Berlin stock, though the latter is the more attractive.

The low habit of *G. swatense* makes it suitable for use on the rock garden, provided adequate space is available. A white-flowered form is reported to occur but I do not know of its being in cultivation.

G. swatense has crossed with 25. *G. lambertii* within its group and 16. *G. pratense*, 14. *G. psilostemon*, 50. *G. sanguineum* and members of the Sessiliflorum Group outside it.

THE REFRACTUM GROUP

Perennials with a thick compact rootstock. Basal rosettes present. Lower leaves usually divided beyond $^3/_4$; divisions 5 or 7. Some of the stipules usually united in pairs. Inflorescence diffuse. Flowers nodding or fully inverted. Pollen more or less yellow. Style more than 7mm long. Stigmas 4.5mm or less. Immature fruits reflexed on more or less reflexed pedicels.

Five species of the Himalayas, S.W. China and N. Burma.

***31. G. sinense* Knuth** (*G. platypetalum* Franchet, not Fischer & Meyer) (Figure 9.42, Plate 21)
Late-flowering perennial with inverted flowers less than 2cm in diameter; petals reflexed, blackish maroon with a coral-pink base; stamens crimson, appressed to the style; immature fruits reflexed. Woodland. July, August.

Figure 9.42. *G. sinense*: from Oxford B.G., 1971; 13cm wide

1. *G. macrorrhizum* cultivars in the rose garden, Sizergh Castle, Cumbria (National Trust); June

2. *G.* x *oxonianum* 'Winscombe', cult. R.P. Dales, Sussex, 1983; July

3. *G.* x *riversleaianum* 'Russell Prichard', cult. Cherry Hinton Hall, Cambridge (NCCPG)

4. *G. versicolor*, posed, with one flower dismembered; September

5. *G. atlanticum*, cult. Blooms of Bressingham, Norfolk, 1999; April (greenhouse)

6. *G. rivulare*, from Jan Stephens, 1960; May

7. *G. caeruleatum*, female, from H. Walsweer, 1989; May

8. *G. psilostemon* 'Bressingham Flair', cult. Alan Bloom, 1974; June

9. *G. procurrens* x *G. psilostemon*, from O.G. Folkard, 1973; July

10. *G. pratense* 'Mrs Kendall Clark', cult. Mrs J. Forty (Joy Jones), Surrey, 1981; June

11. *G. pratense* 'Plenum Caeruleum', cult. R.P. Dales, Sussex, 1983; July

12. *G. pratense* var. *stewartianum*, from S.K. Raina, 1981; 'Raina' at left with veiny petals, 'Elizabeth Yeo' on right with veins not evident; May

13. *G. transbaicalicum*, from Moscow Acad. Sciences B.G., 1975: May

14. *G. clarkei* 'Kashmir White', from Jan Stephens, 1986; June

15. *G. himalayense*, probably 'Gravetye', from J.E. Raven, 1970; June

16. *G. erianthum* 'Neptune'; May

17. *G. erianthum* 'Calm Sea'; August

18. *G. wallichianum* 'Buxton's Variety', cult. P. F. Yeo, Cambridge, 1984; August

19. *G. wallichianum* 'Syabru', from Edward Needham, 1986; August

20. *G. kishtvariense*, from Roy Lancaster, 1980; coll. Kashmir; July

21. *G. sinense*, from Jan Stephens, 1969; July

22. *G. delavayi*, from Roy Lancaster, 1990; June

23. *G. pogonanthum*, white form, from Edinburgh, June; 1993

24. *G. stapfianum*, from Jan Stephens, 1969; May

25. *G. orientali-tibeticum*, foliage, from H.E. Guinness, 1960; May

26. *G. sanguineum* var. *striatum*, cult. Sizergh Castle, Cumbria (National Trust), 1983; June

27. *G. antrorsum*, from P. Hammond, 1992, coll. Australia; May

28. *G. robustum*, cult. The Nursery Far Afield, near Buckingham, 1990; June

29. *G. schlechteri*, from J. Compton, 1989, Compton, d'Arcy & Rix, 217; July

30. *G. fremontii*, from H.E. Moore, 1973, coll. Colorado; June

31. *G. richardsonii*, from P.F. Yeo, 1973, coll. Colorado; June

32. *G. herrerae*, posed, from D. McClintock, 1975

33. *G. deltoideum* from Kew B.G., 1987, coll. Mexico by K.D. Rushforth; March (greenhouse)

34. *G. asphodeloides* subsp. *asphodeloides*, white form, from E.M. Rix, 1971, coll. Turkey by C.R. Fraser-Jenkins; June

35. *G. malviflorum*, from Jan Stephens, 1966; May

36. *G. ibericum* subsp. *ibericum*; June

37. *G.* x *magnificum* 'Peter Yeo' (formerly "clone C"), cult. Mrs J. Forty (Joy Jones), Surrey, 1983; June

38. *G. renardii*, from T. Watson, Munich B.G., 1955; May

39. *G. gracile* x *G. ibericum*: 'Sirak', from Hans Simon, 1990; June [Under sp. 101, last para.]

40. *G. peloponnesiacum*, from Wisley, 1971, coll. Richard Gorer in Greece; May

41. *G. polyanthes*, from Mrs B.C. Rogers, 1960; July

42. *G. strictipes*, from Edinburgh, 1992; coll. Lijiang, Yunnan; July

43. *G. biuncinatum*, Kew, flower (above) and fruit (right), coll. Yemen by J.R.I. Wood, 1982; flower March (greenhouse)

44. *G. albanum*, from Jan Stephens, 1968; June

45. *G. glaberrimum*, from G.G. Guittonneau, 1976; coll. Turkey; May (greenhouse)

46. *G.* x *cantabrigiense* 'Cambridge', from H. Widler-Kiefer, 1974; June

47. *G. dalmaticum*, cult. P.F. Yeo, Cambridge, 1980; June

48. *G. cataractarum* subsp. *cataractarum*, with one flower dismembered, from R.C. Barneby, 1970; coll. S. Spain; April (greenhouse)

49. *G. maderense*; March (greenhouse)

51. *G. aristatum*, from Kew, 1976; June

50. Upper row: left, *G. phaeum* var. *phaeum*, from Dresden B.G.; middle, *G. reflexum*, from Marburg B.G.; right, *G. phaeum* var. *lividum*, from B. Wurzell. Lower row: left, *G. x monacense* nothovar. *monacense*, from Graham Thomas; right, *G. x monacense* nothovar. *anglicum*, from R.P. Dales; all posed, May

52. *G. nanum*, from Dr. Charles Aitchison, 1995, coll. Morocco; May (greenhouse)

53. *G. cinereum*, from Spetchley Park Gardens, 1960; June

54. *G. cinereum* x *G. subcaulescens*, cult. Cambridge City Parks Dept., NCCPG coll., 1986: left, 'Ballerina', right, 'Laurence Flatman'; June

55. *G. subcaulescens*, 'Splendens', cult. Rogers' Nursery, Pickering, Yorks., 1991; June

56. *G.* x *lindavicum* 'Gypsy', cult. Mrs J. Forty (Joy Jones), Surrey, 1983; June

Perennial with a thick compact rootstock and widely spreading branches. Blades of basal leaves between 5 and 20cm wide, rich green, slightly glossy and slightly marbled, divided as far as $^3/_4$–$^7/_8$ into 7, the central pair of incisions noticeably longer than the others; divisions rather elongated, tapered both ways from above the middle, lobed or merely unequally toothed, the untoothed sides straight; lobes usually broader than long. Teeth and tips of lobes rounded in profile but usually more or less acute. Stem-leaves partly solitary, partly paired, with widely splayed basal divisions, gradually diminishing in size upwards, lower sometimes larger than the basal, with 5 or 7 divisions, upper with 3, and with abruptly shorter stalks; lobes and teeth acute; stipules 8–18mm long, conspicuous, brown, pointed, those of paired leaves united in pairs for part or most of their length. Glandular hairs present in the inflorescence but not on the rostrum. Inflorescence diffuse. Peduncles mostly 1.5–6cm but some of the upper suppressed. Pedicels mostly 2–3 times as long as sepals. Flowers inverted. Sepals 5.5–7.5mm, reflexed, green with reddish base; mucro about 0.75–1.5mm. Petals 9–10 x 6mm, broadest slightly above the middle, rounded but with irregular lobes at apex, sharply reflexed just above the base, slightly more spreading at tips where appressed to sepals, blackish maroon with a dull pink base, the basal half of which is fleshy and translucent; base with a handful of hairs on each margin and sometimes on front surface. Nectary one, forming a ring round the flower with a recess for the attachment of each petal, greenish. Stamens about $1^1/_3$ times as long as sepals; filaments appressed to the style, deep red with a pale base, feebly and evenly enlarged towards the base and hairless or with scattered bristly hairs in the lower half; anthers blackish. Style 8–9mm. Stigmas 1.5–2mm, dark red. Immature fruits reflexed on spreading or reflexed pedicels. Rostrum 18–22mm, including stylar portion about 4mm. Mericarps about 3.5mm. Discharge: seed-ejection (bristles).

S.W. China (Yunnan, Sichuan).

The flowers of *G. sinense* are objects of curiosity which only reveal their beauty on close examination. It is thus something of a connoisseur's plant, and as such its praises have been sung both by Johnson (1937) and Ingwersen (1946) (in both cases as *G. delavayi*). It is a rather uniform species, at one time usually grown under the name of its variable close ally, 32. *G. delavayi*. The nectary in the form of a ring round the flower is unique in the genus, as far as I know. The freely accessible nectar attracts wasps and in some years great numbers of hoverflies of the *Syrphus balteatus* group.

Propagation is by division of the rootstock or by seed.

This species and *G. delavayi* show a strong resemblance in their flowers to members of the Phaeum Group (nos. 128–131) from Europe, but the difference in fruit-discharge mechanism shows that this is the result of convergent evolution.

In S.W. China many intermediates between *G. sinense* and 32. *G. delavayi* have been collected, suggesting that natural hybridisation is occurring. *G. sinense* has been crossed by Alan Bremner with 35. *G. yunnanense* to produce a remarkable deep red hybrid named 'Pagoda'.

32. G. delavayi Franchet (*G. forrestii* Knuth; *G. kariense* Knuth) (Figure 9.43, Plate 22)
Similar to 31. *G. sinense* but with broader, more or less overlapping leaf-divisions, larger flowers, hairier petals, usually (but not always) of much paler colour, and separate nectaries. Summer, partial shade.

Figure 9.43. *G. delavayi*: from R. Lancaster,1990.0772, coll. China: N.W. Yunnan (L 1681); 12cm wide

Other differences from *G. sinense* are as follows: leaf-divisions more distinctly lobed, all incisions more or less closed; blades of stem-leaves not larger than those of basal leaves, decreasing in size abruptly after the first 2 or 3 nodes but their stalks decreasing gradually in length; sepals 6–10mm; base of petal with a dense tuft of (usually straight) hairs on either edge; filaments with a small basal tuft of hairs; nectaries 5, separate; mericarps 5mm. Variable characters are glandular hairs (sometimes absent), petal size and shape (8–12mm or rarely to 16mm long and $1^1/_4$–$1^1/_2$ or rarely to $3^1/_2$ times as long as broad), petal colour (blackish red to pale pink or rarely white, whitish at base, sometimes with a dark area above or below the whitish zone), hairs on petal-base between the lateral tufts (often absent) and stamen filaments bright purplish pink to nearly black. Mericarps 5mm. Discharge: seed-ejection (bristles).

S.W. China (Yunnan, Sichuan).

The name of this plant was formerly commonly applied in gardens to 31. *G. sinense*, probably as a result of misidentification of the field-collections from which the seed came. Typically, it differs from *G. sinense* in leaf-shape, petal-colour and in the separate nectaries. It is variable in floral details. It differs from 34. *G. pogonanthum* to some extent in leaf-shape and in the less hairy reflexed rather than recurved petals, less hairy stamens and the filaments which are longer in relation to the sepals.

Two importations of it were made to Britain about 1990. Cambridge accession 1990.0772 is Roy Lancaster's L. 1681, Yulongshan (Jade Dragon Mountain), above Lijiang, N.W. Yunnan, 3350m, and Cambridge accession 1992.0664 is Long, McBeath & Peterson, CLD 430, Chungtien, Na Pa Hai, Yunnan, 3550m. Both are quite attractive with mid-pink, white-zoned petals that have hairs on the front surface at the base. Lancaster's plant is the larger-flowered and the extreme base of the petal is dark in colour. Mr David Victor has a stock with similarly coloured flowers supplied by Kilo Chin nursery as *G. batangense* (a synonym of *G. refractum*).

The occurrence of possible natural hybrids is mentioned under 31. *G. sinense*.

33. *G. refractum* Edgeworth & J.D. Hooker (*G. melanandrum* Franchet)
Perennial with deeply divided leaves having the teeth and lobes turned outwards, rather blunt, and inverted or nodding white or pink flowers with narrow, reflexed, petals, borne in an inflorescence covered with conspicuous, wholly purple, glandular hairs. Probably best in sun.

Rootstock compact. Blades of basal leaves between 5 and 10cm wide, often marbled, divided as far as $^5/_6$ or $^9/_{10}$ into 5; divisions broadest near the apex, palmato-pinnately lobed, middle one often relatively short; lobes mostly $1–2^1/_2$ times as long as broad, with 1–3 teeth. Teeth and tips of lobes usually curved outwards, more or less obtuse. Stem-leaves gradually decreasing in size upwards, mostly stalked. Large glandular hairs, with the stalk and the head purple, present on the upper leaves and in the inflorescence but not on the rostrum. Inflorescence sparse. Flowers inverted. Sepals usually 8–11mm, flushed with purple and with a dark purple base. Petals mostly 12–16mm long and 2–3 times as long as broad, reflexed just above the base, rounded at

apex, white, pale pink or, rarely, red-purple; base with a dense tuft of silvery crisped hairs on either side, similar hairs sometimes spread across front surface. Filaments 11–14mm, appressed to the style, rather evenly enlarged towards base, reddish purple at tips and pale at base, or uniformly pink, usually with fine hairs on lower part; anthers blue-black. Style 7.5–12mm. Stigmas usually 2–3mm, pink to purplish red. Immature fruits reflexed on reflexed pedicels. Rostrum 15–22mm, including stylar portion 5–8mm. Mericarps 3.5–4mm, Discharge: seed-ejection (bristles).

Himalayas (Nepal to Bhutan), N. Burma, S.W. China (Yunnan, Sichuan).

It is rather strange that this widespread species was not in cultivation when edn.1 was in preparation. Since then it has been brought in by the Edinburgh B.G. (Long, McBeath & Paterson, CLD 226, Central North Yunnan, Chungtien Bi Ta Hai forest, 3540m, Cambridge accession 1992.0663). Among the species with nodding flowers and reflexed petals it is immediately distinguished by the coarse, wholly purple, glandular hairs. It was originally described from the Himalayas, where the flowers are white, whereas Chinese plants, usually pink-flowered, were given another name, *G. melanandrum*. However, the Edinburgh botanist W. Edgar Evans (d. 1940) recognised that *G. melanandrum* was a synonym of *G. refractum* and E.H. Wilson named all his Chinese specimens of this species *G. refractum*.

34. *G. pogonanthum* Franchet (Figure 9.44, Plate 23)
Perennial with a compact rootstock and marbled leaves with sharply toothed and deeply lobed divisions; flowers inverted, about 25–35mm in diameter; petals pink to white, rather narrow, gently recurved, conspicuously bearded; filaments crimson, divergent at the tips; anthers blackish. Rock garden, wild garden, sun or shade. July to September.

Rootstock thick and compact. Blades of basal leaves between 5 and 10cm wide or occasionally more, marbled above, divided as far as $^2/_3$ or $^9/_{10}$ into 5 or 7; divisions tapered both ways from above the middle, palmato-pinnately lobed, the untoothed sides straight or slightly concave; lobes prominently toothed. Teeth and tips of lobes acute. Stem-leaves paired, decreasing gradually in size and length of stalk upwards, the upper relatively long-stalked. Stipules acute, some of them fused in pairs. Glandular hairs sometimes present on upper parts of plant, but not the rostrum, colourless or with only the head reddish. Branches paired or the upper solitary. Inflorescence diffuse. Peduncles mostly 4–8cm. Pedicels $1^1/_2$–3 times as long as sepals. Sepals 7–10mm, purple at base; mucro 1–1.5mm or

A

B

Figure 9.44. *G. pogonanthum*: (A) from Wisley, 1971; (B) from Edinburgh, 1973; both coll. Burma: Mt. Victoria (Kingdon Ward 22796); 9 and 7cm wide (different reductions)

sometimes to 2mm. Petals 8–16mm or sometimes to 20mm, usually about twice as long as broad, rounded at apex, widely spreading from the base and recurved between the sepals towards the tip, pink or purple or nearly white; base with a dense tuft of long, somewhat wavy, white hairs on each side and longer, less dense hairs across the front surface. Stamens slightly longer than sepals; filaments 8–10mm, curving outwards at the tips, feebly but evenly enlarged towards base, purplish red with paler base, the lower $^1/_3$–$^2/_3$ covered with long spreading hairs; anthers blue-black. Style 8–11mm. Stigmas 2.5–4mm. Immature fruits reflexed on reflexed pedicels. Rostrum 18–23mm, including stylar portion about 6mm. Mericarps 3.5–4.5mm. Discharge: seed-ejection (bristles).

S.W. China (Yunnan, Sichuan), W. Central and N. Burma.

This species was introduced into cultivation by F. Kingdon Ward after his last expedition, which was to Mount Victoria, in west central Burma, in 1956. The collecting number was 22796, but there was also a

seed number: U Maung Gale (local collector) 5897. Ward noted "petals reflexed like a Martagon lily's, the nodding pink flowers also suggest a miniature *Nomocharis* at first sight". An introduction from China, with white-petalled flowers, has been made by the Edinburgh B.G. (Long, McBeath & Paterson, CLD 149, Chungtien Wo Fang Shan, 3350m), Cambridge accession 1992.0663. Two other stocks from Yunnan, Brickell & Leslie 12101 and 12115, have small, rather pale, scarcely recurved petals and lack garden value (Cambridge accession from Wisley 1988.0010 and 1988.0011).

G. pogonanthum is usually a graceful plant with beautiful and unique flowers and the Kingdon Ward introduction is now quite widely grown. It is tolerant of various conditions but does not thrive in open ground at Cambridge. It makes a very thick rootstock which becomes built up above soil level and if the plants show signs of ailing, they should be divided up and the pieces that are healthy replanted. It is also easily raised from seed.

After its introduction it was identified, I believe at Kew, as *G. yunnanense* and I later published a detailed description of it under that name (Yeo, 1975). However, as explained elsewhere (Yeo, 1983), I have since then reviewed a large amount of herbarium material from S.W. China, and have learnt to distinguish this plant from 35. *G. yunnanense*. Although it was described in 1889, I discovered only a single specimen identified with it up to the time of writing edn.1, and that identification was mistaken.

G. delavayi (no. 32) sometimes resembles *G. pogonanthum*: distinctions are given under the former species.

G. pogonanthum has been crossed by Alan Bremner with 31. *G. sinense* and 35. *G. yunnanense*.

35. G. yunnanense Franchet (*G. candicans* Knuth, not of gardens) (Figure 9.45)
Perennial with a compact rootstock, marbled and rather bluntly toothed and lobed leaves and a diffuse, few-flowered inflorescence; flowers 25–35mm in diameter, nodding or almost fully inverted, bowl-shaped, with rather broad pink (rarely white) petals, pale filaments diverging from the base and blackish anthers. June, July.

Rootstock thick and compact. Blades of basal leaves between 5 and 10cm wide, marbled above, divided as far as $^4/_5$ or $^6/_7$ into 5; divisions tapered both ways from above the middle, palmato-pinnately lobed; lobes 1–2 times as long as broad, few-toothed. Teeth and tips of lobes more or less acute. Stipules acute, the middle ones sometimes united in pairs. Glandular hairs absent or sparsely present on undersides of leaves. Inflorescence diffuse, usually with fewer flowers

Figure 9.45. *G. yunnanense*: from Edinburgh (no. 812574/0611), 1981, coll. China: Yunnan Prov.; 8cm wide (the separation of the lateral lobes from the middle one is not characteristic)

than in 34. *G. pogonanthum*. Flowers nodding to almost inverted, shallowly bowl-shaped. Sepals 10–12mm; mucro 1–1.5mm. Petals 15–20mm long and not more than $1^1/_3$ times as long as broad, rounded at apex, divergent, usually pink; base with a dense tuft of straight hairs on either side and hairs across front surface. Filaments 11–15mm, slightly divergent at base, more so at tips, feebly but evenly enlarged towards base, white or greenish at base, pink or purplish at tips, with long spreading hairs; anthers blue-black. Style 10–14mm or even as little as 5mm. Stigmas 2.5–4.5mm. Immature fruits nodding on spreading or reflexed pedicels. Rostrum 15mm (stylar portion 2–3mm) or up to 23mm. Mericarps 3–4mm. Discharge: seed-ejection (bristles).

S.W. China (Yunnan), N. Burma.

Although it has often been collected, I have no evidence that *G. yunnanense* was cultivated until the 1981 Sino-British Expedition to Cangshan brought it back. A plant was kindly presented by Edinburgh to Cambridge that year and it flowered there in 1982 (Yeo, 1983). *G. yunnanense* differs from 34. *G. pogonanthum* in having more sparsely and less acutely lobed and toothed leaves, fewer, larger, bowl-shaped flowers with broad, non-recurved petals, and more divergent stamens. The individual flowers are beautiful but *G. yunnanense* has proved difficult to grow in southern England. The plant cultivated has rather short styles, style-length being a character in which the species is unusually variable.

The name *G. candicans* is a synonym of *G. yunnanense*; it refers to a white-flowered form of it which occurs rather rarely. However, in gardens the name has been misapplied to 23. *G. lambertii*.

For hybrids, see 31. *G. sinense* and 34. *G. pogonanthum*.

THE FARRERI GROUP

Plant dwarf, without tubers or stolons. Hairs eglandular. Floral axis horizontal. Petals with hair-tufts on margins at base and a small tuft on front surface. Filaments enlarged at base. Stamens slightly diverging at the functional stage. Style long; stigmas short. Immature fruits lying on the ground or more or less horizontal.

One species from W. China, which seems to have no close relationships with other dwarf alpine species in its geographical area. The pink petals with hairs on the front surface at the base, and the contrasted blue-black anthers on slightly divergent filaments, agree with 35. *G. yunnanense*. Connections with the Palustre and Krameri Groups seem to be totally ruled out by the pollination system of *G. farreri* which involves a long style, short stigmas and weakly divergent stamens which are probably used as an alighting place (as in 16. *G. pratense*). The same is true of the Wallichianum Group but *G. farreri* has hybridised with two of these.

36. *G. farreri* Stapf (Figure 9.46)

Dwarf alpine plant with shallowly lobed leaf-divisions, reddish stems, leaf-stalks and leaf-margins, and flowers about 30–35mm in diameter

Figure 9.46. *G. farreri*: from Uppsala B.G., 1969; 4cm wide

with horizontal axis; petals and filaments very pale pink; anthers blue-black. Alpine house, rock garden. Late May, June.

Perennial with small rootstock which apparently splits up, each crown usually with a taproot thicker than the other roots. Plant to about 12cm high with stems, leaf-stalks and margins of leaves more or less red. Blades of basal leaves not more than 5cm wide, rounded or kidney-shaped in outline, faintly marbled on upper surface, divided as far as $^3/_4$ or $^5/_6$ into 7; divisions broadest near the apex where they are 3-lobed for about $^1/_4$–$^1/_3$ of their length; lobes as broad as long or broader, with an occasional tooth. Teeth acute, tips of lobes obtuse or acutish. Stem-leaves paired, those of a pair often unequal, their divisions somewhat tapered from above the middle, decreasing in size gradually upwards. Hairs eglandular. Stem usually oblique or sprawling with short lower internodes, so that most of the foliage, including the long-stalked basal leaves, is at about the same level. Branches solitary or paired. Peduncles mostly 2–4cm and pedicels about $2^{1}/_{2}$ times as long as sepals, holding the flowers well above the leaves. Sepals 7–9mm; mucro 0.5–1mm. Petals 13–15 x 10–15mm, abruptly expanded at the base into a short broad claw, with a rounded blade and crinkled margin, very pale pink; base with a dense tuft of hairs on either side and a fringe beyond this, and a small tuft in middle on the front surface, not connected with the lateral tufts. Filaments 9–11mm, slightly diverging, distinctly enlarged at the extreme base, white with a pink tinge at tips, with a few small, mainly marginal hairs at base; anthers blue-black. Style 10–13mm, pink, hairless. Stigmas 1.5mm, pinkish. Immature fruits lying on the ground or spreading horizontally on deflexed pedicels attached to horizontal peduncles. Rostrum about 23mm, including stylar portion 7–9mm. Mericarps 3.5–4mm. Discharge: seed-ejection (bristles).

W. China (Gansu).

Farrer (1917) found this plant in 1914 at 3,600m and above on the Red Ridge of the Min-Shan in Western Kansu (Gansu), but he states that Purdom had collected it there before him. According to Stapf (1926) the effective introduction of the species to cultivation was by seed mixed with seed of 48. *G. pylzowianum* under Farrer's number F. 170, and consequently plants were, at first, grown under that name. Much more persistently it has been known as *G. napuligerum* Franchet, with which it was tentatively identified when the species received an Award of Merit of the Royal Horticultural Society in May 1924 (*Journ. RHS.*, 50, page 1, 1925). The identity of the plant can be ascertained from the photograph in *Gardeners' Chronicle*, 75, 333 (1924). (I have encountered no evidence that the glandular-haired *G. napuligerum* has ever been in cultivation – though it is now claimed that it is being grown in Norway (Olsen, 2000).)

Although Stapf may have been right about the reason that *G. farreri* was referred to *G. pylzowianum*, his story is incomplete. *G. farreri* was raised at Farrer's home at Ingleborough in Yorkshire from his collection no. F. 201 (see below) and progeny from this source were distributed at latest by 1920 (Bowles, 1921).

In 1986 I found a specimen of *G. farreri* in the Herbarium of the Royal Botanic Garden, Edinburgh, that was labelled as either from Farrer's Expedition to Burma in 1919, or that to Kansu/Tibet 1914–1915. There can be little doubt that this corresponds with the seed-sample F. 201 (Yeo, 1992). The only other wild-collected herbarium specimen of *G. farreri* that I have seen is Joseph Rock's no. 13184, from the T'ao River Basin, which lies on the north-east flank of the Min-Shan with valleys running towards the crest of the latter.

G. farreri is by far the most charming of all alpine species of *Geranium*. Farrer (1917, p. 172) is irresistibly quotable: "All the wide wilderness of shingle and scree was tufted and carpet-bedded with this new treasure. No other plant or flower was there at all; the Geranium fills the whole stage with its profusion of large and very pale pink flowers springing all over the close and matted tufts that ramify through the shingle ... [there was a] crowded dance of its faintly flushing blossoms, silvery in the cold pale air that day."

I am not certain how the rootstock splits up but it is probably as follows: a tap-rooted rosette produces another rosette from the side and this develops its own taproot; then, perhaps, the connection of the rosettes decays and perhaps also the roots have some contractile power. The drawing in Stapf (1926) is consistent with this suggestion. The plant has no power of spreading by rhizomes. When grown in pots *G. farreri* seems to benefit from frequent re-potting.

For the relationships of *G. farreri*, see above under the Farreri Group. The species has crossed with 24. *G. wallichianum*.

THE PALUSTRE GROUP

Perennials of bushy habit. Main leaves divided about as far as $^{5}/_{6}$ or less into 5 or 7, their lobes not more than $1^{1}/_{2}$ times as long as broad. Hairs eglandular. Pedicels $1^{1}/_{2}$ times as long as sepals or more. Petals pink to purple, with or without hairs on front surface between basal tufts; without hairs more extensively scattered over front surface. Filaments enlarged at base, with or without a tuft of hairs above each nectary. Style more or less distinctly shorter than sepals. Stigmas 2.5–5.5mm. Immature fruits erect on spreading or reflexed pedicels.

This group is tentatively assembled for the purpose of this book and consists of five species, one East European, one Himalayan and three East Asian. At least the latter seem very closely related to the Krameri Group (p. 107). The Palustre Group is distinguished from the latter mainly by the absence of hairs over an extensive area of the front surface of the petal-base. Both groups have the styles rather short in relation to the sepals and the stigmas long in relation to the size of the flower.

37. *G. palustre* Linnaeus (Figure 9.47)

A low, bushy perennial with bright green coarsely

Figure 9.47. *G. palustre*: from Halle B.G., 1974, coll. Germany: Harz; 9.5cm wide

lobed and toothed leaves; flowers about 30–35mm in diameter, in a diffuse inflorescence; petals deep magenta, not overlapping, rounded at apex. Border, wild garden. June to August.

Perennial with a stout, compact rootstock; bushy, reaching about 40cm. Blades of basal leaves between 5 and 10cm wide, thickish, rather smooth above, often glossy beneath, divided as far as $2/3$ or $5/6$ into 7; divisions tapered both ways from the middle or above, occasionally broadest near apex and sometimes nearly parallel-sided, coarsely pinnately lobed; lobes about as broad as long, with 1–3 teeth. Teeth and tips of lobes obtuse or acute, usually with strongly curved margins. Stem-leaves paired, numerous, decreasing in size upwards gradually, with 3 or 5 divisions. Plant covered with rather bristly eglandular hairs, those of upper surfaces of leaves and those of the sepals and pedicels appressed, the latter reflexed, others more or less spreading. Stems and branches thin; branches mostly paired, forming a diffuse inflorescence of long duration. Peduncles 2–7cm. Pedicels $2^{1}/_{2}$–4 times as long as sepals. Flowers widely trumpet-shaped. Sepals 6.5–8mm; mucro about 1mm. Petals 16–18 x 9–10mm, about $1^{1}/_{2}$ to nearly 2 times as long as broad, broadest near the top, evenly tapered to the base, rounded at apex, brilliant deep magenta with very dark purplish, slightly feathered veins, white at extreme base; base with rather coarse loose hairs on margins and all across front surface. Filaments with a narrowly

triangular enlargement at base, coloured like the petals but paler at base, or mainly pale and tinged with pink at tips, lower part with bristly hairs on the margins; anthers violet or cream, becoming violet. Nectaries not topped by hair-tufts. Style about 6mm. Stigmas 2.5–3mm, flesh-coloured to dark red. Immature fruits erect on deflexed pedicels. Rostrum about 17mm, including stylar portion about 2.5mm. Mericarps about 3.5mm. Discharge: seed-ejection (bristles).

E. and C. Europe (with only scattered occurrences W. of the Rhine valley).

In nature *G. palustre* is often associated with ditches and small river valleys but it also grows in drier situations in scrub and on wood margins. In the garden it tolerates dry soil and full sun. The flowers are brilliantly but rather harshly coloured, and the plant lacks distinction of habit. An apparent garden hybrid with 8. *G. sylvaticum* is described under that species.

38. *G. wlassovianum* Link (Figure 9.48)

Bushy perennial with softly greyish-hairy leaves,

Figure 9.48. *G. wlassovianum*: from Hull B.G, 1971; 8cm wide

rather shallowly but sharply cut, and dusky magenta-purple or sometimes pink, heavily veined flowers in a diffuse inflorescence; petals rounded at apex. Wild garden or border, sun or partial shade. July, August.

Rootstock stout, compact. Plant growing to about 30cm in height. All leaves relatively short-stalked, blades often flushed with brown above, the basal few in number, their blades mostly 5–15cm wide, divided as far as $2/3$–$5/6$ into 7; divisions broadest at the middle or above, shortly tapered to the apex, only slightly tapered below the widest point, palmato-pinnately lobed for about $1/4$ of their length; lobes mostly broader than long, the lowest often bent outwards, with a few teeth. Teeth and tips of lobes acute. Stem-leaves paired, gradually decreasing in size upwards, usually with 5 divisions, their stipules sometimes united in pairs for part of their length. Plant rather densely covered with soft eglandular hairs. Branches paired or solitary. Inflorescence diffuse. Peduncles 1.5–10cm. Pedicels mostly $1^{1}/_{2}$–3 times as long as sepals. Flowers slightly recessed in the centre. Sepals 9–12mm; mucro 1–2mm. Petals 17–22 x 9–13mm, just over $1^{1}/_{2}$ times as long as broad, broadest above the middle, tapered evenly or nearly so to base, rounded at apex, deep purplish magenta with dark violet feathered veins almost throughout, white at base, or the ground-colour sometimes much paler; base with a tuft of hairs from side to side across front surface and with marginal fringes beyond this. Stamens longer than sepals, curving outwards when functional; filaments rather abruptly enlarged at extreme base, base white, otherwise coloured like the petals, with a fine even hair fringe on margins in lower $^{1}/_{3}$–$^{1}/_{2}$, becoming coarse at bases of outer filaments, inner with a row of bristly hairs down the middle at extreme base; anthers bluish. Each nectary topped by a hair-tuft. Style 7–10mm. Stigmas 3.5–5.5mm, deep red to pink. Immature fruits erect on spreading or deflexed pedicels. Rostrum 20–24mm, including stylar portion 2–3mm. Mericarps 3.5–4.5mm. Discharge: seed-ejection (bristles).

E. Siberia, Mongolia, Far Eastern part of Russia, N. China.

In its native lands this species grows in damp situations. In cultivation in Britain it grows moderately well even in dry ground in full sun. The form of it in general cultivation in Britain is rather compact in growth and has deep purplish flowers of slightly varying shades, but usually rather a sombre colour. At Cambridge we also have a looser-growing plant (less satisfactory in this respect) with larger pale pink, white-centred flowers in which the strong veining of the petals is retained. It came from Tomsk University B.G., W. Siberia.

The hair-clothing and much more veiny petals distinguish *G. wlassovianum* from 37. *G. palustre*. It also has some resemblance to 24. *G. wallichianum* but does not have the black anthers and stigmas of that species, nor the large, fully united stipules.

G. wlassovianum has crossed with *G. soboliferum*, from the nearby Krameri Group.

39. G. donianum Sweet (*G. multifidum* D. Don,

Figure 9.49. *G. donianum*: cult. Jack Drake, 1983, coll. Nepal: Iswa Khola (L.W. Beer); 6cm wide

not Sweet; *G. stenorrhizum* Stapf) (Figure 9.49) A non-creeping dwarf perennial with most of its foliage near the base. Leaves finely cut, kidney-shaped to circular in outline, marbled with paler green. Inflorescence rather open. Flowers medium-sized, funnel-shaped, with more or less intensely red-purple petals. Rock garden. Sun.

Perennial up to 40cm tall but sometimes dwarfed, with thick compact rootstock. Leaves 5–10cm wide, marbled, divided at least as far as $^{4}/_{5}$ and often to within 2 or 3mm of the leaf-stalk into 5 or 7; divisions broadest at or near apex, palmately lobed; lobes usually 2 to 4 times as long as wide, with a few teeth. Teeth and tips of lobes acute or sometimes obtuse. Stem-leaves similar to the basal, few, paired. Hairs eglandular, coarse, sparse or sometimes dense enough to give a silky effect. Inflorescence diffuse. Flowers erect or upwardly inclined, funnel-shaped. Sepals about 8–11mm; mucro about 1mm. Petals about 13–19mm, varying from $1^{1}/_{4}$ to more than $1^{1}/_{2}$ times as long as broad, rounded or notched at apex, attenuate at base, deep reddish purple or magenta; base with hairs on margin and front surface. Filaments more or less abruptly enlarged and hairy at base, dark purple. Style about 6mm. Stigmas about 3–4mm. Immature fruits erect on widely spreading or reflexed pedicels. Rostrum not more than 12mm, mericarps between 2 and 4mm. Discharge: seed-ejection (bristles).

Himalayas (widespread), S.W. China (Dadjiang lu in Sichuan), Tibet.

There are two dried specimens of cultivated material of this species in the Kew Herbarium, and a painting made from one of them. One was grown at Kew in 1934, and the other, the subject of the painting, was grown by Sir Frederick Stern at Highdown, Goring-by-Sea, Sussex, in 1932. The species was introduced again by L.W. Beer from Iswa Khola, Nepal, probably collected during his reconnaissance for the Beer, Lancaster and Morris expedition of 1971. Although some early collections have died out, more have been introduced. *G. donianum* is widespread and variable, so possibilities exist for the introduction of more amenable stocks. It is a desirable plant for the rock garden. Wild-flower seed merchants in India and Sikkim offer seed of *G. donianum* but in my experience send only 102. *G. polyanthes*.

The name *G. multifidum* was published by different authors for different species on the very same day, so one species had to be re-named. Later, Dr Otto Stapf of Kew attempted to separate dwarf alpine states with relatively obtuse leaf-lobes as a separate species under the name *G. stenorrhizum*, but other Kew botanists did not support the distinction, and nor can I. The leaves of *G. donianum* recall those of 48. *G. pylzowianum* but the habit is different, both above-ground and below. *G. donianum* differs from 15. *G. collinum* in the intensely coloured funnel-shaped flowers, the hairs spread across the front surface of the petals, and in the small leaves with the divisions broadest near the apex.

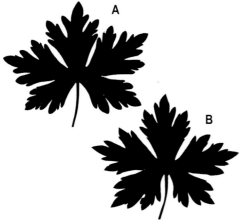

Figure 9.50. *G. shikokianum*: (A) var. *shikokianum* from Wisley, 1975, *ex* Dr Rokujo, *per* K.A. Beckett; (B) var. *quelpaertense*, from Wisley, 1975, coll. Japan: Quelpart Island (Dr Rokujo, *per* K.A. Beckett); 8 and 6.5cm respectively (different reductions)

40. G. shikokianum Matsumura (Figure 9.50)
Bushy perennial with leaves rather deeply and coarsely lobed and cut, sometimes marbled; flowers more or less funnel-shaped, 25–30mm in diameter, pink with large white centre and a network of fine purple veins. Sun or partial shade. June to September.

Perennial usually 20–40cm tall, with compact rootstock. Leaf-blades matt and faintly or distinctly marbled above, very shiny beneath. Basal leaves few. Blades of main leaves mostly between 5 and 10cm wide, divided as far as about $^5/_6$ into 5 or 7; divisions tapered both ways from about the middle, or sometimes very abruptly to the apex from above the middle, lobed halfway to the midrib or for $^1/_3$ of their length; lobes about $1^1/_2$ times as long as broad, with 1–3 teeth, the outermost teeth curving outwards. Teeth and tips of lobes more or less acute. Stem-leaves paired, decreasing gradually in size and length of stalk upwards, their stipules fused in pairs for most of their length, green. Hairs eglandular. Branches paired or solitary, forming a diffuse inflorescence. Peduncles mostly 4–6cm but lowest up to 16cm. Pedicels $2–3^1/_2$ times as long as sepals. Flowers funnel-shaped. Sepals 8–9mm with scattered, long, fine, tapered, bristly hairs; mucro 1.5–2mm. Petals $16–18 \times 10–12$mm, broadest above the middle, rounded at apex, evenly tapered to base, pink with $^1/_3$ or more of their length at the base white, with reddish purple net-veining; base without hairs all across front surface, margins with a dense tuft and beyond this a fringe. Stamens divergent; filaments abruptly widened at base, white or tinged with pink towards tips, with or without a fringe of fine hairs in the lower part, inner with a tuft of hairs at base over each nectary; anthers bluish. Style 6mm. Stigmas 4.5mm, green, yellowish or pinkish. Immature fruits erect on reflexed pedicels. Rostrum 18mm, including stylar portion 1–2mm. Mericarps 4.5mm. Discharge: seed-ejection (bristles).

S. Japan, Korea (Quelpart Island).

G. shikokianum is probably best suited to partial shade. It is easily propagated by division and at times the rootstock seems to break up spontaneously. The white-centred, net-veined flowers are pleasing. This character of the petals is stated by Ohwi (1965) to occur only in 44. *G. krameri* and 54. *G. yoshinoi* among Japanese species, though it does not occur in our stock of the latter, whereas it is clear from the leaves that our plant really is *G. shikokianum*. Varieties *shikokianum* and *quelpaertense* were introduced to Britain by Mr K.A. Beckett, two stocks having been given him by the Japanese horticulturist Dr Rokujo, and variety *yoshiianum* was more recently intoduced by the Wynn-Joneses.

G. shikokianum var. *shikokianum* from the mainland of Japan is loose in growth and less hairy than the other varieties; it has very attractive leaf-marbling.

G. shikokianum var. *yoshiianum* (Koidzumi) Hara is a dwarf form to 30cm tall from the island of Yakushima at the extreme south of Japan. The Wynn-Jones introduction (BSWJ 1234) has well-marbled leaves.

G. shikokianum var. *quelpaertense* Nakai, (Figure 9.41B), described as smaller, lower-growing, more densely covered with spreading hairs than var. *shikokianum* and found only in Quelpart Island between Japan and Korea.

41. G. koreanum Komarov (Figure 9.51)

Tall, probably scrambling, or bushy perennial from a compact rootstock. Lower leaves with 5 or 7 wide, shallowly toothed and lobed divisions, giving a solid outline. Stem-leaves with more open segmentation. All leaves very weakly hairy, glossy beneath. Flowers loosely arranged, about 2.2–4cm wide, bright pink with usually a large white eye and finely feathered darker veins on the pink part. Pedicels reflexed and hooked under the immature fruit. Summer. Partial shade.

Perennial with stiffly spreading shoots to about 80cm from a compact rootstock. Stems and leaf-stalks downy with dense short backwardly directed hairs, sometimes red, internodes to 23cm. Blades of basal leaves to about 25cm wide, scarcely angled in outline, divided as far as $\frac{1}{2}$–$\frac{2}{3}$ into 5 or 7; divisions almost oblong to broadly rhomboidal or almost circular, 3-lobed at the apex to a depth of $\frac{1}{4}$–$\frac{1}{3}$, the lobes shallowly toothed. Teeth and tips of lobes obtuse or broadly pointed, or the smallest teeth acute. Stalks of basal leaves to about twice as long as blades, stipules to 13mm, linear-lanceolate, finely pointed, hairless. Stem-leaves paired, with blades to about 8cm wide, divided as far as $\frac{2}{3}$–$\frac{3}{4}$ into 5, or the upper into 3; divisions rhomboidal or ovate, broadest at or above the middle, rather shallowly lobed and toothed. Teeth and tips of lobes about as long as broad, ovate, acute. Stipules of stem-leaves 8–18mm, united in pairs completely or with separate tips, broadly oblong to ovate, herbaceous, hairy on the veins or hairless, the lower sometimes free and narrowly triangular. Blades of all the leaves dull above and with sparse appressed hairs, pale and glossy beneath and with sparse looser hairs mainly on the veins. Inflorescence loose, rather leafy, with solitary or paired branches. Peduncles mostly 3–9cm. Pedicels 1–4 times as long as calyx, downy, like the peduncles. Sepals 8–11mm, green or flushed with red, strongly ribbed, almost hairless, with mucro 1–3mm. Petals 12–19 x 8–12mm, obovate,

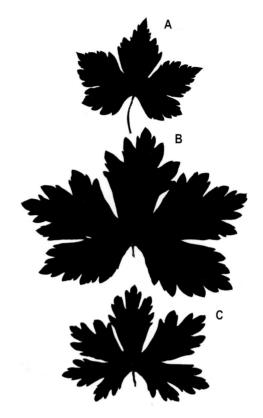

Figure 9.51. *G. koreanum*: (A) from M. Fillan, 1991.1149, collected by him in South Korea, at 1,250m alt., leaf 9cm wide; (B) & (C) cult. B. & S. Wynn-Jones, coll. South Korea (BSWJ 602), 14cm wide (larger)

bright pink, usually with extensive white base and narrow, finely feathered, dark veins, tapered to a narrow base where there is a dense tuft of hairs at the sides and sometimes on the front surface; hairs extend up the margin sparsely to about $\frac{1}{3}$ or $\frac{1}{4}$ the length of the petal. Filaments white or greenish at base, pink at apex, tapered gradually from the base, slightly downy at base or hairless, curving outwards when functional. Anthers bluish. Nectaries each with a tuft of hairs on top. Stigmas about 5mm, greenish or straw-coloured to dull red, shortly hairy on the backs or hairless. Pedicels reflexed and bent upwards under the calyx after flowering, thickened under the calyx in fruit. Rostrum 18–25mm, minutely downy, with a few long glandular hairs at the base. Mericarps about 4.5mm, minutely downy and with long glandular hairs at the apex. Discharge: seed-ejection (bristles).

Korea.

This variable species is suitable for shade and tends to be chlorotic in the open. Some clones may be worth having in a shady corner or wild garden.

I have based my description on (1) Cambridge accession no. 1991.1149 Fillan, collected by Mark Fillan in Chisi National Park, Nogodan-san, S. Korea, at 1250m; (2) Cambridge accession no. 1993.0606 Compton, Compton, D'Arcy & Coke 222, from N. Korea; and (3) Bleddyn & Sue Wynn-Jones, BSWJ 602, from S. Korea (dried non-flowering shoots in Cambridge Botanic Garden herbarium, and a plant in my garden). Fillan's plant appears to be a single clone (though it may well breed true), and it is quite attractive. Six clones of CDC 222 were raised at Cambridge, all visibly different: they vary in vigour of growth, leaf-shape and thickness of stems, peduncles and pedicels. BSWJ 602 is quite similar to the Fillan plant but whereas the latter has hairs all across the front of the petal base, the Wynn-Jones one has only the marginal tufts. The variation in the CDC stock is so great that I have wondered whether two species could be represented (the plants can be sorted into two groups of three each on leaf-shape) or whether natural hybridisation has occurred. If our plants are hybrids, the other parent might be *G. maximowiczii* Regel (not in cultivation and not very well known to me). However, I have provisionally assigned all these plants to *G. koreanum*.

All our plants have some stipules united in pairs, but there is much variation as to how many nodes at the base of the stem have leaves with free stipules. In fact, *G. koreanum* was first described as having the stipules free, but Nakai (1912) keyed it on the possession of united stipules! This character is set against having free stipules except at the uppermost nodes but there is no definition of how high up the fusion of stipules sets in. This branch of Nakai's key leads to the unfortunately named *G. koraiense* Nakai (1911), which is supposed to have the stamen-filaments densely bearded and the front of the petal base hairy along the veins. The Wynn-Joneses have collected in South Korea a plant which they believe to be the latter species (BSWJ 797, T'aepacksan, Taegu Province; it has much more acute and deeper leaf cutting).

Knuth (1912) cited *G. wallichianum* from Korea but these specimens must have been *G. koreanum* with united stipules (see 24. *G. wallichianum* for differences). There is a little authentic material at Kew, and this has united stipules.

THE STAPFIANUM GROUP

Plant dwarf with slender underground stolons. Hairs eglandular. Petals notched at apex, with a tuft and a fringe of hairs on each edge at the base but without hairs spread across surface. Filaments not enlarged at base. Nectary surmounted by a tuft of hairs. Style not longer than sepals. Stigmas rather long. Immature fruits erect on spreading or reflexed pedicels.

One species in S.W. China.

G. stapfianum is difficult to place in relation to any other species. It is here positioned after the Palustre Group because that group includes one species (40. *G. shikokianum*) without hairs across the front surface of the petals and one with notched petals (39. *G. donianum*); its long stigmas associate it with both the Palustre Group and the Krameri Group.

42. *G. stapfianum* Handel-Mazzetti (*G. forrestii* Stapf, not Knuth) (Figure 9.52, Plate 24)
Dwarf alpine plant with marbled leaves, red stems, leaf-stalks and leaf-margins and upwardly inclined flowers 25–35mm in diameter; petals notched, reddish purple, with red veins converging to a red patch at base. Alpine house, rock garden. June.

Perennial with an elongated scaly rootstock and extensive slender underground stolons; roots not thickened. Plant to about 15cm high with stems, leaf-stalks and margins of leaves red. Blades of basal leaves not more than 5cm wide, kidney-shaped in outline, marbled above, divided as far as $^4/_5$ into 5 or 7; divisions broadest at apex, sometimes overlapping, lobed at apex for $^1/_4$ to nearly $^1/_2$ their length; lobes up to twice as long as broad, sometimes with 1 or 2 teeth. Teeth and tips of lobes obtuse or acute. Stem-leaves similar, only one or two pairs present or sometimes none. Plant without glandular hairs. Inflorescence of only 1 or 2 cymules, sometimes emerging directly from the rosette. Peduncles 2–10cm. Pedicels 2–3 times as long as sepals. Flowers saucer-shaped. Sepals 7.5–9mm, more or less flushed with dark red; mucro about 0.5mm. Petals 12–20 x 11–14mm, almost oblong in shape, notched at apex, deep

Figure 9.52. *G. stapfianum*: from J. Stephens, 1969, *ex* Wisley; 3cm wide

magenta with darker red, slightly feathered veins reaching nearly to apex and converging at base to form a red patch; base with a dense tuft of hairs on either edge and a sparse fringe above this, without hairs all across front surface. Stamens as long as sepals, uniformly tapered from base to apex, diverging from near the base, dark red but paler towards base, finely hairy at base; anthers dark reddish. Nectaries each surmounted by a tuft of hairs. Style 6–9mm, deep red. Stigmas 3.5–4mm, dark red. Immature fruits erect on spreading or reflexed pedicels. Rostrum 15–16mm, including stylar portion 2–3mm. Mericarps 2.5mm. Discharge: seed-ejection (bristles).

S.W. China (Yunnan, Sichuan), S.E. Tibet.

G. stapfianum occurs in open stony alpine pastures and on boulders and cliffs at altitudes from 3,200 to 5,200m. It has been abundantly collected and looks most striking on the herbarium sheet. In cultivation it is disappointing in that its flowers are few and produced over a short period. It should, however, be tried out in scree conditions in the cooler parts of the British Isles.

The Cambridge stock of *G. stapfianum* was obtained from Mr Jan Stephens in 1969. He had received it from Wisley as 15. *G. collinum*, said to have been collected in Nepal, which must have been a mistake. Because of its rhizomatous growth it is easy to work up a large stock of it quickly but some unknown affliction destroyed all but a vestige of my stock one autumn. It recovered and was planted out on some rock-work, but disappeared in a dry summer. Seeds had been saved and it was started off again but it then gradually and finally died out. Roy Lancaster tells me that his reported re-introduction of this species (in Bath & Jones, 1994) is an error. The species was known in cultivation to Stapf (1926) and a photograph of it under the name *G. pylzowianum* (no. 48) appeared in *Gardeners' Chronicle*, 90: 361 (1931). The main colour of the petals is HCC 32/1 Petunia Purple, which best matches RHSCC Purple Group 78B.

THE KRAMERI GROUP

Perennials with compact rootstock and usually weak stems. Main leaves divided as far as $^5/_6$ or more into 5 or 7, their lobes about twice as long as broad or more. Hairs eglandular. Cymules usually two-flowered (one-flowered in *G. hayatanum*). Pedicel-length variable. Petals pink to reddish, usually with hairs on front surface at base between lateral tufts and scattered more extensively over front surface. Stamen-filaments enlarged at base, with or without a tuft of hairs over each nectary.

Style considerably shorter than sepals (except, apparently, in small-flowered forms of 45. *G. dahuricum*). Stigmas 3–6mm. Immature fruits erect on usually spreading or reflexed pedicels.

Like the Palustre Group, this group has been tentatively assembled for the purpose of this book. The species are native to E. Asia, including Japan in some cases. All five species included here have (or can have) hairs scattered over the front surface of the petal well above the base, unlike those of the Palustre Group, but like those of the Pylzowianum Group. Other species which are probably to be included are several Chinese species, some of which were described as new by Yeo (1992).

43. *G. soboliferum* Komarov (Figure 9.53)

Small compact perennial with ferny leaves and deep magenta, somewhat veiny, flowers about 30mm in diameter; petals rounded at apex; stigmas about 5mm long; pedicels of immature fruits erect. Rock garden, perhaps water garden. July to September.

Figure 9.53. *G. soboliferum*: from T. Shimizu, 1976, coll. Japan: Nagamo Pref.; 7.5cm wide

Rootstock thick, compact. Plant usually about 30–40cm in cultivation. Blades of basal leaves to 12cm wide, divided nearly or quite to the base into 7; divisions broadest below or above the middle, usually overlapping their neighbours, pinnately dissected into segments only 3–9mm wide; lobes 4–6 times as long as broad, parallel-sided, with teeth up to about 6 times as long as wide. Teeth and tips of lobes acute. Stem-leaves similar, paired, decreasing gradually in size and abruptly in length of stalk upwards, their stipules united in pairs, more or less persistently green. Hairs eglandular. Branches mostly paired. Inflorescence rather dense. Peduncles 4–6cm (or the lowest to 15cm). Pedicels mostly $1–2^1/_2$ times as long as sepals. Flowers saucer-shaped. Sepals 8–9mm; mucro 1–2mm. Petals 16–18mm, $1^1/_2$ times to nearly twice as long as broad, broadest above the middle, rounded at apex, rather sharply widened just above base, deep reddish purple with darker veins; base with a tuft of hairs towards either edge and none or few on front surface between tufts, but with scattered long hairs arising from the veins on the front surface for nearly half the length of the petal. Filaments strongly curved outwards, more or less abruptly enlarged at base, similar in colour to petals, pale at base, edges in basal $1/3$ with a fringe of fine hairs, bases of inner with a tuft of hairs over each nectary; anthers bluish. Style 5–6mm, red. Stigmas 5–6mm, red. Immature fruits erect on erect pedicels. Rostrum 14–16mm, including stylar portion about 1mm. Mericarps 2.5mm. Discharge: seed-ejection (bristles).

Russian Federation (Ussuria, on Pacific coast), Manchuria, mountains of C. and S. Japan.

The name of this species refers to its ability to produce some kind of runner. These I have never seen and Bobrov (1949) says they are rarely seen in herbaria. At Cambridge it has hitherto been grown mainly in a shady plunging bed and its habit in full sun is unknown. Several clones derived from seed sent from Japan by Professor T. Shimizu have been maintained. Other accessions are being grown in Britain.

The showy inflorescence and finely cut leaves make this plant distinctive and it may have garden value, though the flower colour is rather harsh. It is propagated by division or from seed.

44. *G. krameri* Franchet & Savatier (Figure 9.54)
Perennial with compact rootstock. Stems up to 80cm but usually collapsing at base. Basal leaves between 5 and 20cm wide, broader than long, divided as far as $4/5$–$6/7$ into 5 or 7. Stem-leaves

Figure 9.54. *G. krameri*: from Aritaki Arboretum, 1978, coll. Japan: Yamanashi Pref.; 13cm wide

decreasing abruptly in length of stalk upwards, mostly stalkless or nearly so, distinctive in shape; lower stem-leaves divided as far as about $5/6$ into 5 or 7; divisions long, rather narrow, the basal widely splayed, all with 3 elliptic or triangular lobes at apex, the middle lobe much the longest and usually shallowly 2-toothed, the lateral toothless, bent outwards, margins of untoothed part of divisions straight or concave; upper stem-leaves divided into 3, middle division much the largest. Teeth and tips of lobes acute. Hairs eglandular. Flowers flat. Petals about 11–14mm, about $1^1/3$ times as long as broad, slightly concave, rounded at apex, light pink with darker, scarcely feathered veins; base with a dense tuft of erect white hairs on front surface, lower $1/3$–$1/2$ with scattered hairs on front surface. Style about 5mm. Stigmas 4.5–5mm. Immature fruits erect on reflexed pedicels. Rostrum 18–22mm, its stylar portion about 1.5mm. Mericarps 2.5mm. Discharge: seed-ejection (bristles). Partial shade. July to September.

N. China (S. to W. Hubei), Far Eastern part of Russian Federation (S.), Korea, Japan (C. and S.).

I know this species from herbarium specimens and a single cultivated accession that arrived in 1978; a single plant was raised initially and open-pollinated seedlings from this. It was eventually lost at Cambridge but other accessions have arrived in Britain recently. It makes long internodes and then tends to collapse, and it seems unlikely that it has garden value. It is distinctive in its leaf-shape and in the straight line of erect hairs across the petal-bases that forms a pentagonal palisade around the stamens.

45. *G. dahuricum* De Candolle (Figure 9.55)
Slender sprawling perennial with small finely cut leaves and a diffuse inflorescence; flowers on very slender pedicels, about 28mm in diameter; petals light pink, with fine dark red unfeathered veins; stigmas 3–3.5mm. Wild garden, rock garden, sun. June to August.

Rootstock thick; stems thin, attaining about 50cm in length but collapsing before this to make a low bushy plant. Undersides of leaf-blades matt. Basal leaves few at flowering time, often red-edged, between 5 and 10cm wide, divided as far as $3/4$ or $6/7$ into 7; divisions broadest just below the apex, 3-lobed for more than $1/3$ of their length, the middle division often small and the basal pair particularly large; lobes up to $2^1/2$ times as long as broad, with 0–2 teeth, not bent outwards. Teeth and tips of lobes acute, or tips of lobes bluntish. Stem-leaves sometimes less than 5cm wide, paired, numerous, divided as far as

Figure 9.55. *G. dahuricum*: from Uppsala B.G., 1973, coll. China: Chihli Prov. (Harry Smith 21569); 7.5cm wide

$^6/_7$ into 5 or 7; divisions tapered both ways from above the middle, their lobes often far apart, the lateral bent outwards; segments usually 3–5mm wide, rather narrower than those of basal leaves. Upper leaves with the basal divisions widely splayed, the uppermost stalkless. Stipules of stem-leaves sometimes united in pairs. Hairs eglandular, rather dense on the leaves, but everywhere fine, appressed on the veins beneath and nowhere widely spreading except sometimes on sepals when old. Branches paired or solitary. Inflorescence diffuse. Peduncles mostly 2–5cm. Pedicels 3–6 times as long as sepals and sometimes longer than peduncles. Flowers saucer-shaped. Sepals 5–9mm; mucro 0.75–1.75mm. Petals 13–14 x 9–10mm, not more than $1^1/_2$ times as long as broad, broadest above the middle, rounded at apex, rather broad at base, light pink with fine dark red veins over about $^4/_5$ of their length; base densely hairy on front surface and margins, the hairs extending upwards on the surface for $^1/_4$–$^1/_2$ the length of the petal and on the edge for half its length or all round. Filaments abruptly enlarged at the base, with fine hairs on the margin in the lower part and a few hairs on the back at the extreme base of at least the inner filaments; anthers bluish. Style 6–7mm. Stigmas 3–3.5mm, reddish. Immature fruits erect on spreading or reflexed pedicels. Rostrum 14–17mm, without an evident stylar portion. Mericarps about 2.5mm. Discharge: seed-ejection (bristles).

Continental •N.E. Asia from E. Siberia and Mongolia to the Pacific, extending southwards in W. China to Sichuan.

G. dahuricum is one of those persistent flowerers that scarcely draw attention to themselves but may be of some use for the sake of having something in flower in the rock garden at an awkward season. With its slender stems and deeply cut leaves it never approaches coarseness. The newly emerging leaves come up pink and yellow. The rootstock is easily divided and plants can be raised from seed. My description is based on one stock in cultivation and a moderate number of herbarium specimens which suggest that the species is rather uniform. Further introductions have taken place since edn.1.

G. dahuricum is so similar to 46. *G. yesoense* that I have not been able to provide a satisfactory distinguishing character in the dichotomous key (Chapter 8). Representatives of the two entities have been successfully crossed by Bremner. The relationship of the two plants is further discussed under 46. *G. yesoense*.

46. G. yesoense Franchet & Savatier (Figure 9.56)
Perennial of more or less bushy growth with leaves sharply and deeply cut, and scattered pink or rarely white flowers about 22–28mm in diameter; petals, if coloured, with darker veins, rounded at apex; stigmas 3.5–4.5mm. Wild garden, water garden. June to August.

Perennial similar to 45. *G. dahuricum*, to about 40cm high with compact rootstock. Undersides of leaf-blades usually shiny. Blades of

Figure 9.56. *G. yesoense*: (A) from Sendai B.G., 1980; (B) from T. Shimizu, 1976, coll. Japan: Nagamo Pref.; 7.5 and 7cm

basal leaves between 5 and 10cm wide, divided as far as $5/6$ or more into 7; divisions tapered both ways from above the middle, pinnately or palmato-pinnately lobed, varying from rather narrow to very wide and overlapping their neighbours; lobes mostly 2–3 times as long as broad, with 0–4 teeth which are up to 3 times as long as broad, the lateral lobes or their outer teeth bent outwards. Teeth and tips of lobes acute. Stem-leaves similar to basal, changing gradually upwards, their stipules free or some of them united in pairs. Hairs of the lower and middle stems reflexed and appressed, those of the leaf-undersides spreading, usually coarser than those of 45. *G. dahuricum.* Flowers saucer-shaped or slightly funnel-shaped. Sepals 6–10mm; mucro 1–2mm. Petals 15–20 x 8–13mm, $1^{1/3}$–2 times as long as broad, tapered almost uniformly to the base, pink with fine darker veins or white; base hairy across front surface and on margins, a few hairs sometimes scattered some way along the veins and margins. Style 5–6mm, usually red. Stigmas 3.5–4.5mm, red or pink. Rostrum 15–29mm, including stylar portion about 1mm. Mericarps 2.5–4.5mm. Discharge: seed-ejection (bristles). Other characters as in 45. *G. dahuricum,*

Central and N. Japan, Kuril Isles.

G. yesoense has deeply cut foliage and often a bushy habit, in both of which characters it recalls 50. *G. sanguineum.* It differs from it, however, in having paired flowers and no hair-tufts over the nectaries, like 37. *G. palustre,* as well as in the paler flowers. It is a plant of no great horticultural interest, but certainly does not deserve Ingwersen's (1946) ferocious condemnation which, judging by the description, could have been based on 52. *G. thunbergii,* another Japanese species.

I have grown six stocks of *G. yesoense*: five had pink flowers and varied in flower and fruit size, habit and the nature of the leaf-cutting. The sixth is white-flowered and has broad crumpled petals; it is low-growing and its leaves and sepals are densely covered with the kind of hairs found on the sepals of 40. *G. shikokianum.* It was sent by Dr V.I. Safonov of the Sakhalin Complex Research Institute, Novoalexandrovsk, who collected it on the South Kuril Isles (immediately north of Japan). Ohwi (1965) recognises three varieties of *G. yesoense*; my white-flowered one belongs to var. *yesoense,* while the pink ones, being less hairy, are probably referable to var. *nipponicum* Nakai.

For distinctions between *G. yesoense* and 15. *G. collinum,* see under the latter. Although it is normally possible to distinguish *G. yesoense* from

45. *G. dahuricum* without difficulty, the differences are quite trivial and few of them are constant. Plants of *G. yesoense* are usually coarser; the basal leaves differ from those of the stem less than in *G. dahuricum,* their divisions having spreading lobes, while the upper leaves do not usually have splayed basal divisions; the hairs of the undersides of the leaves are coarse and spreading and the surface is usually shiny; the petals are often longer and relatively narrower; the stigmas are longer on average; and the rostrum includes a short stylar portion instead of none. These differences do not justify specific separation but I consider it inadvisable to make the necessary nomenclatural combinations of the varietal names of *G. yesoense* with the specific name *G. dahuricum* without personally studying the variation in *G. yesoense.* The *status quo* must therefore remain for the time being and it will not cause problems in horticulture if it does.

47. *G. hayatanum* Ohwi (Figure 9.57)
Trailing and ascending perennial, becoming bushy, with leaf-blades cut nearly to the base and divisions lobed for $1/3$ to $2/3$ of their length. Leaves mostly paired. Cymules 1-flowered. Flowers to 30mm in diameter, light purplish pink with darker veins. Plant without glandular hairs. Flower stalks erect in flower and immature fruit.

Perennial with stems to 50cm, trailing and ascending. Stems and leaf-stalks with sparse or scattered long recurved eglandular hairs, denser at top of leaf-stalks. First or second stem internode 2–3 times as long as lower leaf-blades. Leaves mostly paired. Basal and lower stem leaves to 6.5cm wide, kidney-shaped or slightly angular, often with wide basal sinus, divided as far as $5/6$ or $6/7$ into 5; divisions wedge-shaped or

Figure 9.57. *G. hayatanum*: cult. B. Wynn-Jones (Crûg Farm Plants), 1999, coll. Taiwan (BSWJ 164); 10cm wide

fan-shaped, 2-lobed or 3-lobed for $^1/_3$–$^2/_3$ their length, the lobes turned outwards, overlapping those of neighbouring divisions, mostly with 1 or 2 teeth; teeth and tips of lobes very acute. Upper surface of leaf-blades dark green, sometimes purplish, lightly marbled, sparsely hairy with long, forwardly appressed hairs; lower surface much paler, slightly glossy, with long hairs mainly on the veins. Stipules 8–9mm, mostly, if not all, completely united in pairs, broadly ovate or nearly circular in outline. Flowers scattered among the upper leaves, in 1-flowered cymules. Flower stalks 1–3.5cm, without bracts or with rather wide bracts in the upper half, more or less erect throughout, densely clothed with backwardly appressed hairs. Sepals 6–7mm, green or flushed with purple at base, with loose, forwardly directed hairs; mucro 1–1.5mm. Petals 16–17 x 9–10mm, wedge-shaped, rounded at apex, not overlapping, light purplish pink with the basal third or half white, almost the whole traversed by slightly branched deep purple veins; base with a dense tuft of hairs on the margins, extending less densely across the surface front and back. Stamens with purple, white-based filaments moderately enlarged and hairy towards the base; anthers bluish. Stigmas 3–3.5mm, deep pink. Fruits erect. Rostrum about 22mm, including stylar portion about 3mm, densely clothed with forwardly appressed hairs. Carpels hairy. Discharge: seed-ejection (bristles).

Taiwan (endemic).

Introduced by Bleddyn and Sue Wynn-Jones (BSWJ 164). Found in Taroko National Park, clambering over dwarf bamboo at 3,300m (not occurring below 3,000m). Cultivated in open ground it makes a neat mound of foliage. It is hardy in Scotland. Mr Wynn-Jones tells me that it hybridises readily.

THE PYLZOWIANUM GROUP

Small alpine plants with small underground tubers interlinked by slender stolons; stems and leaf-stalks slender, sinuous, coming up from the buried tubers. Stem-leaves mostly solitary. Hairs eglandular. Flowers few. Petals with hairs on front surface in basal $^1/_4$ or more. Filaments enlarged at base. Immature fruits erect on more or less reflexed pedicels.

Apparently three species from W. China, two described here, the other (*G. canopurpureum* Yeo) known to me from a single herbarium sheet. The absence of glandular hairs and the development of hairs on the front surface of the petals in all three species, and the long stigmas of *G. orientali-*

tibeticum suggest a close relationship with the Krameri Group. The shortness of the stigmas in *G. pylzowianum* is probably connected with a rather specialised pollination arrangement, in which the clawed petals and narrow base of the flower also participate (see under 49. *G. orientali-tibeticum*).

48. *G. pylzowianum* Maximowicz (Figure 9.58) Dwarf perennial with underground runners and

Figure 9.58. *G. pylzowianum*: from J. Stephens, 1966; 5.5cm wide

tiny tubers; blades of basal leaves not much more than 5cm wide, divided nearly to the base, divisions wedge-shaped, deeply cut into narrow lobes and teeth; flowers few to a stem, 27–32mm in diameter, trumpet-shaped, deep rose-pink with a greenish centre, with short stamens and stigmas. Rock garden, sun. May, June.

Plant reaching 12–25cm, with small tubers, about 5 x 3mm, deep underground and connected in chains by thread-like stolons. Leaf-stalks and stems coming up individually from the tubers, slender, sinuous. Blades of basal leaves less than or little more than 5cm wide, divided nearly to the base into 5 or 7, kidney-shaped or semicircular with basal divisions widely splayed and the middle one short, or pentagonal with the divisions more evenly arranged and more equal in size; divisions broadest near apex, palmato-pinnately lobed; lobes mostly $1^1/_2$–4 times as long as broad, with 0–3 teeth. Teeth and tips of lobes acute or sometimes obtuse. Stem-leaves mostly solitary, stalked, smaller than the basal. Hairs eglandular. Inflorescence composed usually of up to 3 cymules, cymules occasionally emerging direct from tubers. Peduncles mostly 4–10cm. Pedicels mostly $3^1/_2$–6 times as long as sepals. Flowers widely trumpet-shaped. Sepals 7–9mm, moderately divergent; mucro 0.5–1mm. Petals 16–23mm and $1^1/_2$ times to nearly twice as long as broad, narrowed into a claw at base, blade broad with rounded or faintly notched apex, deep rose-pink except for a whitish base, with fine dark almost unbranched veins; base with rather long hairs on front surface and margins for about $1/4$ the length of the petal, densest below. Filaments 6–8mm, curving outwards at tip when functional, distinctly but evenly enlarged towards base, white, sometimes pink towards tips, lower part. generally covered with small hairs. Anthers before bursting cream with violet-blue edges. Style 5–7mm. Stigmas 2.3–2.8mm, pink to orange-red. Immature fruits erect on more or less reflexed pedicels. Rostrum 16–18mm, including stylar portion 1–2mm. Mericarps about 2.5mm. Discharge: seed-ejection (bristles).

W. China (Gansu, Shaanxi, Sichuan, Yunnan).

This is a charming scree-plant, dwarf, with large rose-pink flowers (RHSCC Purple-Violet Group 80C) in which the small stamens and stigmas are crowded into the narrow throat. The green colour of the sepals is visible through the petal-bases. Although not a dominating plant, it will invade its neighbours, and Ingwersen (1946) recommends putting it in a self-contained pocket in the rock garden.

At Cambridge we at one time had two significantly different stocks. The one now lost was the smaller in leaf, with elliptic, obtusish, rather than linear, acute leaf-lobes and teeth. According to Stapf (1926) *G. pylzowianum* was introduced into cultivation by Messrs. Veitch, having been collected by William Purdom in the Taipei Shan (Tsin Ling range) in Shensi (Shaanxi) in 1910; one might suspect that as it grew to a large size in cultivation (up to 30cm high), it was really the next species, *G. orientali-tibeticum*. However, I have seen Purdom's original specimen in the Kew Herbarium and identified it as *G. pylzowianum*. Later introductions were made by Farrer (his no. 170, from Kansu, 1914, which was mixed with 36. *G. farreri* (Stapf, 1926)) and by Dr Alan Leslie (in 1981).

G. pylzowianum is sometimes named *Geranium* 'Frances Perry', apparently because Mrs Perry grew it and did not know what it was.

The natural habitat of *G. pylzowianum* is alpine pastures and meadows and rock ledges, at an altitude of 2,400 to 4,250m.

49. G. orientali-tibeticum Knuth (Figures 9.59 & 9.60, Plate 25)

Dwarf perennial with underground runners and small tubers like those of 48. *G. pylzowianum* but larger; leaf-blades deeply cut and strongly marbled in two shades of green, those of basal leaves up to 10cm wide; flowers few to a stem, 23–27mm in

Figure 9.59. *G. orientali-tibeticum*: from H.E. Guinness, 1960; 6cm wide

diameter, flat but with a cup-shaped white centre, the outer parts of the petals rather deep purplish pink; stamens and stigmas longer than in 48. *G. pylzowianum*. Rock garden, sun. June, July.

Plant similar to 48. *G. pylzowianum* but with tubers 5–10 x 4–6mm, and usually 20–35cm tall; leaf-blades strongly marbled, with lobes not more than $2^{1}/2$ times as long as broad, their tips and teeth often more or less obtuse; with up to 5 cymules in the inflorescence; pedicels mostly $2–3^{1}/2$ times as long as sepals; petals 16–22mm, $1^{1}/4–1^{1}/3$ times as long as broad, triangular at base, not clawed, crumpled, basal $1/3$ white, remainder purplish pink, hairs on front surface spread all over the white area and beyond for $1/3–1/2$ the length of the petal; filaments 7.5–9.5mm; style 6mm, stigmas 3–6mm, rostrum 19–21mm, mericarps 3–4mm. Discharge: seed-ejection (bristles).

S.W. China (Sichuan, in the neighbourhood of Dajian lu).

A scree-plant, closely related to 48. *G. pylzowianum*, differing from it in its mostly larger vegetative parts and fruits, marbled leaves with broader, blunter lobes, smaller flowers of a deeper pink, with a bowl-shaped white centre and longer stamens and stigmas, the petals being claw-less. Compared with *G. pylzowianum*, it is more likely to smother other plants on the rock garden if allowed to invade them. It grows in scrub at altitudes of 2,250 to 2,750m and is found only in the neighbourhood of Tatsien lu (Dajian lu) which is also called Kangding (variously spelt). The petal colour appears to me bluer than

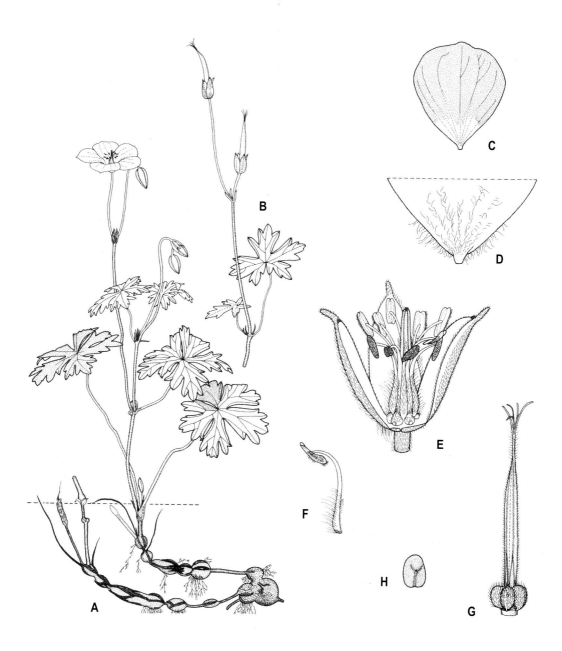

that of *G. pylzowianum* but reference to a colour chart has shown that it is merely darker (RHSCC Purple Violet Group 80B).

I have received *G. orientali-tibeticum* from a number of sources, usually named *G. stapfianum roseum*, a name which is scarcely to be found in the literature, and which certainly has no botanical standing. Its only resemblance to 42. *G. stapfianum* is in the marbled leaves. After making

Figure 9.60. *G. orientali-tibeticum*: from J. Stephens, 1968. (A) plant beginning to flower, x $^2/_3$; (B) portion of inflorescence with mature fruit, x $^2/_3$; (C) petal, with pigmentation, x 2; (D) base of front surface of petal, x 4; (E) flower in male stage with petals and two sepals removed, x 4; (F) stamen of outer whorl, seen obliquely from back, x 4; (G) mature fruit, x 2; (H) seed, x 4

allowance for certain deficiencies in the original description, I have concluded that this plant is the mysterious *G. orientali-tibeticum* (Yeo, 1984a, in which the captions to the colour plates have been interchanged). Knuth must have had a specimen without the characteristic stolons and tubers, while the leaf-marbling is easily lost in drying; also, he must have had an exceptionally tall specimen because he gives the height as 50cm (I have a shade-grown specimen over 40cm). The type specimen was burnt in Berlin in 1945 but there are other specimens from the same area and collector, namely J.-A. Soulié, which are this species. These are labelled 'Thibet Oriental', because Dajian lu was at that time in Tibet. I am breaking up the specific epithet with a hyphen, as Knuth originally had it, because the word is confusing to read and to write with its string of two-letter syllables in the middle: *alitibet*. This is contrary to the International Code of Botanical Nomenclature, but the infringement is minor and computer software does not seem to take any notice of the hyphen!

Like 48. *G. pylzowianum*, *G. orientali-tibeticum* was introduced into cultivation by Messrs. Veitch, there being a specimen in the Kew Herbarium cultivated at Glasnevin Botanic Garden, Dublin, the label of which states that the plant (seed) came from Veitch in 1914. Possibly it was E.H. Wilson's no. 3300, collected in July 1903, which I have seen in herbaria.

The differences in floral details between this species and 48. *G. pylzowianum* clearly relate to differences in pollination arrangements. I suspect that the short stamens and stigmas crowded into the narrow throat of the flower of the former are intended to brush the face of a short-tongued insect, whereas the stamens and stigmas over-arching the central bowl of the flower of *G. orientali-tibeticum* may act by rubbing the proboscis of some larger insect, thrust between them.

THE SANGUINEUM GROUP

Rhizomatous perennials with very few basal leaves and bushy growth of long-lived leafy and wiry flowering stems. Hairs eglandular. Leaf-blades deeply and rather narrowly divided and lobed; lobes and teeth few. Cymules 1-flowered. Flowers large; petals usually slightly notched and with hairs all across front surface between lateral tufts at base; stamens shorter than sepals, with filaments enlarged at base; style shorter than stamens, with long stigmas.

One species from Europe (including Caucasia) and adjacent Turkey. It has much in common with the Krameri Group (nos. 43–47) but has no scattered hairs on the front surfaces of the petals,

Figure 9.61. *G. sanguineum*; 7cm wide

thus resembling the Palustre Group (nos. 37–41). It is one of the few large-flowered species of *Geranium* which consistently has 1-flowered cymules (others in this book, are the Taiwanese 47. *G. hayatanum* and the hoary-leaved 58. *G. traversii*).

50. *G. sanguineum* Linnaeus (Figure 9.61)
Low bushy perennial with leaves cut nearly to the base into rather narrow, deeply lobed divisions; inflorescence diffuse, leafy; cymules 1-flowered; flowers 25–42mm in diameter, erect, purplish red or various shades of pink or white. Border, rock garden, sun. May to August.

Perennial with shortly spreading underground rhizomes. Rosette leaves few, differing from stem-leaves in being less deeply divided and in having obtuse tips of lobes. Stem-leaves paired, stalked, their blades less than 5cm wide or between 5 and 10cm, divided as far as $^3/_4$ or $^7/_8$ into 5 or 7; divisions mostly deeply 3-lobed for $^1/_3$ or $^1/_2$ their length, the lobes entire or with 1 or 2 teeth, 2–4 times as long as broad, the middle lobe much the longest, the laterals curving outwards. Tips of teeth and lobes acute. Stipules mostly not more than 4mm, sometimes to 7mm, mostly reflexed, some of them fused in pairs for most of their length. Hair-clothing bristly, eglandular. Branches solitary or paired, forming a very diffuse and leafy inflorescence of long duration. Cymules 1-flowered. Peduncles mostly 4–7cm. Pedicels mostly 2–5 times as long as sepals. Flowers saucer-shaped, more or less erect. Sepals 6.5–10mm; mucro 1.5–3.5mm. Petals 14–21 x 13–17mm, not much longer than broad, heart-shaped, usually with a shallow notch at apex, less commonly with a deep one or none, tapered almost evenly to the base, intense purplish red, white at extreme base, usually with darker veins; base with a dense tuft of hairs on either edge and usually with hairs across front surface between the tufts. Stamens shorter than sepals; filaments considerably but gradually enlarged towards the base, coloured more or less like the petals at their tips, edges fringed with hairs, sometimes minute, in the lower half, and with a few hairs on the back; anthers bluish. Style about 5mm. Stigmas 3.5–4.5mm, red or flesh-coloured. Immature fruits erect on erect pedicels. Rostrum 22–32mm, including stylar portion 1–2mm. Mericarps 4–4.5mm. Discharge: seed-ejection (bristles).

Most of Europe, Caucasus, N. Turkey.

A plant of dry scrubby situations in nature, and in the British Isles found chiefly on limestones and coastal rocks and dunes. *G. sanguineum* has few basal leaves, most of its foliage being in the inflorescence, which continues to grow even after flowering has ceased, sometimes sending out new shoots from nodes that earlier bore only one branch. It varies greatly in the size of the flowers, the form of the leaves, density of hair-clothing and compactness of habit. It is difficult to pin down what it is in the leaf-form that renders this plant always recognisable despite the variation. The foliage of *G. sanguineum* usually colours well in autumn. The largest-flowered plant of normal colouring known to me is an old stock at Cambridge, with flowers up to 42mm in diameter (this could be the same as 'Cedric Morris', listed below).

The typical flower-colour of *G. sanguineum* (RHSCC Purple Group 78C) is too fierce for the taste of many gardeners, but a good range of other shades is now available. Of these, 'Jubilee Pink' and 'Shepherd's Warning' were raised by Mr Jack Drake, of Inshriach Nursery, Aviemore, Inverness-shire, from open-pollinated seed of var. *striatum*, which itself is flesh-pink, and which was growing in the nursery with the typically coloured forms. *G. sanguineum* var. *striatum* is the correct name for the plant usually known as var. *lancastriense*. Soft pink forms like 'Glenluce' (below) are frequent in some wild populations.
G. sanguineum 'Album' is white-flowered, with no trace of pink or purple in any part of the flower; flower diameter up to 42mm; begins flowering in June and is of relatively tall, loose habit.
G. sanguineum 'Betty Ellis' forms neat mounds of slightly glossy foliage and close above it produces a generous crop of intensely coloured medium-sized flowers (3–4cm wide according to age) that are given some elegance of form by the recurvature

of the petals near the apex. This was presented to Cambridge Botanic Garden by Mrs Betty Ellis, of Coton, near Cambridge, where she used to run a nursery. First described by Yeo (2000).
G. sanguineum 'Cedric Morris' is a large-flowered cultivar (Hibberd, 1994); see discussion of the species above.
G. sanguineum 'Elsbeth', of Continental origin, is large-flowered like 'Cedric Morris' but has hairier leaves and more vividly coloured flowers (Hibberd, 1994).
G. sanguineum 'Glenluce' was found on a cliff near Glenluce, Wigtownshire, Scotland, by A.T. Johnson (Johnson, 1937); it has "large blooms of an exquisite wild-rose pink"; Johnson says it is 50cm tall with silky leaves, but his garden was shady and Thomas (1976, 1982) says it is of compact growth. Nevertheless, my plants reached a considerable size with age. Petal colour: HCC Mauve, 633/1, RHSCC Violet Group 84B.
G. sanguineum 'Holden' has a spreading habit, small leaves and bright rose-pink flowers; it was raised before 1975 by Mr R. Milne-Redhead (Clifton, 1979) at Holden Clough Nursery, Bolton-by-Bowland, Lancashire.
G. sanguineum 'Jubilee Pink' is a rather compact plant with flowers 38mm in diameter of a magenta-pink (RHSCC Red-Purple Group 68A), beginning to flower in June. At the Wisley Trial in 1976 it received a First Class Certificate, the only variant of *G. sanguineum* to receive this highest award (see, however, 'Shepherd's Warning'); it was raised by Mr Jack Drake (see above under *G. sanguineum*).
G. sanguineum lancastriense is a synonym of *G. sanguineum* var. *striatum*.
G. sanguineum 'Minutum' grows only a few cm high and has leaves 1–2.5cm wide and flowers 3cm wide; it has been offered by Ingwersen's of East Grinstead, Sussex. The Latin-form cultivar epithet may be illegitimate (see also the next).
G. sanguineum 'Nanum', offered formerly by Ingwersen's, was described as dwarf and compact, with rose-red salver-shaped flowers (Clifton, 1979). The name is apparently illegitimate. 'Minutum' is said to be more compact and to come true from seed.
G. sanguineum 'Nyewood' is small-leaved and medium-sized in its intensely coloured flowers (Hibberd, 1994).
G. sanguineum 'Plenum' is dwarf, dark-flowered, and with wrinkled petals; it has some extra petals but is not a full double; I saw it at Bloom's of Bressingham, Norfolk, in 1979.
G. sanguineum 'Roseum' is a name first published by J. Stormonth in his 1928 catalogue of plants with a spreading habit and bright rose flowers (Clifton, 1979).

G. *sanguineum* 'Shepherd's Warning' has flowers of RHSCC Red-Purple Group 67C, flushed with 67B (deeper), that is, they are a little deeper and redder than in 'Jubilee Pink'. Its origin is the same as that of 'Jubilee Pink' but at the Wisley Trial it received an inferior award (Highly Commended). However, Mr Drake, writing to Mr Clifton in 1979, said that he now considered 'Shepherd's Warning' superior because of its compact habit (it was apparently less compact at Wisley) and he mentioned that it is a marvellous wall plant.

G. *sanguineum* var. *striatum* Weston (G. *sanguineum lancastriense* G. Nicholson; G. *sanguineum* var. *lancastrense* (Miller) Druce) (Plate 26) is quite distinct in its pale flesh-pink flowers (the colour is HCC Roseine Purple, 629/3, which matches RHSCC Red-Purple Group 73D); this colour is produced by rather faint, diffuse veining on a blush ground. The Wisley Trial Report assesses the colour of the veins (RHSCC Red-Purple Group 72D), not the overall effect; the Report makes clear the wide variation in habit and leaf-colour within the variety, which is native to Walney Island and other sites on the Cumbrian coast, England. The habit varies from dwarf to very dwarf. Plants begin to flower in May. Another name sometimes applied to the Walney Island plant is G. *sanguineum* var. *prostratum* (Cavanilles) Persoon, but it is also sometimes applied to dwarf plants regardless of flower-colour and it does not have priority over var. *striatum*.

G. *sanguineum* var. *striatum* 'Farrer's Form' (var. *lancastrense* [sic] 'Farrer's Form') is, according to Clifton (1979), the same as 'Form 1' in the Wisley Trial Report; it combines compactness (20cm tall) with dark green leaves. I saw it at Kew in 1971 and noted its compactness.

G. *sanguineum* var. *striatum* 'Splendens' (var. *lancastrense* [sic] 'Splendens') was described in the Wisley Trial Report as 45cm tall with very slightly serrated petals, pale pink with deep pink main veins, and with secondary veins RHSCC Red-Purple Group 72D, and beginning to flower in June.

Despite the fact that it has no very close relatives, as indicated by my giving it a Group to itself, G. *sanguineum* has formed a number of hybrids at the hands of Alan Bremner; they show strong predominance of G. *sanguineum* in their habit and foliage (probably because of a preponderance of contributed chromosomes – see Chapter 7), but on close examination the foliage is always found to lack the spear-like or dagger-like segments of *sanguineum*. They are with G. *lambertii* x G. *procurrens*, G. *procurrens* (producing 'Dilys'), G. *psilostemon* (producing 'Little David') and G. *swatense* (producing 'Diva').

THE COLUMBINUM GROUP

Annuals with deeply and finely divided leaves, cymules longer than subtending leaves, funnel-shaped flowers with broad-based sepals which enlarge conspicuously in fruit, narrow petals with a tuft of hairs on each margin at the base, stamen-filaments enlarged at base and a distinct style.

Perhaps two species in Europe and W. Asia, although G. *schrenkianum* Becker (mainly in Kazakhstan), which is smaller-flowered and more delicate than 51. G. *columbinum*, is included within the latter in *Flora Europaea* (Webb & Ferguson, 1968).

51. G. *columbinum* Linnaeus (Figure 9.62)
Annual with blades of basal leaves less than 5cm wide or a little more, divided to the base or nearly so into 5 or 7; divisions broadest at or above the middle, deeply lobed; lobes rather few, mostly 2–4 times as long as broad, widely spreading except in some of the first-produced leaves, with a few widely spreading teeth, some of which are deep. Leaf-segments of all orders nearly parallel-sided. Teeth and tips of lobes more or less obtuse. Stem-leaves paired, similar, smaller, with narrower and more acute lobes and teeth. Hairs eglandular, mostly appressed. Inflorescence diffuse. Cymules much longer than the subtending leaves. Flowers funnel-shaped. Sepals 6–8mm, enlarging to 8–9mm in fruit; mucro 2mm. Petals 8.5–12mm, wedge-shaped, about 3 times as long as broad, blunt or notched at apex, pale to deep reddish pink, white at base, veins sometimes darker. Stamens $^2/_3$ as long as sepals; filaments greatly enlarged at base, slightly hairy. Anthers bluish. Stigmas reddish, hairy. Rostrum 16–17mm, with a distinct stylar part 4mm long. Mericarps 3–4mm. Discharge: seed-ejection (bristles).

Europe, W. Asia.

A graceful annual with sometimes moderately conspicuous flowers. It is a native of local occurrence on limestones in Britain and colonises

Figure 9.62. G. *columbinum*: from P.F. Yeo, 1977, coll. Corsica: central valley: (A) stem-leaf; (B) basal leaf; 5.5 and 5cm wide

open communities in artificial habitats. Another annual with similar leaves is 87. *G. dissectum*; this has some of the hairs glandular, cymules shorter than the subtending leaves, much shorter petals and different seed-retention (prong).

THE SIBIRICUM GROUP

Perennials with ill-defined and ill-protected rootstock. Leaf-blades divided into 3, 5 or 7. Stipules broad-based and drawn out into long points. Glandular hairs confined to the inflorescence or absent. Flowers small, with petals 10.5mm or less (larger in 54. *G. yoshinoi*). Petal-bases with hairs on margins and sometimes also on front surface. Stamens and style very short. Stamen-filaments much enlarged at base, hairy. Stigmas short, hairy on outer surfaces. Immature fruits erect on usually spreading or reflexed pedicels. Pedicels thickened under the calyx when fruit is ripe.

Six species in S. and E. Asia and one in Africa (extending into S.W. Asia). The whitish-flowered forms of these often have a 'red-white-and-blue' effect because the anthers are blue and the stigmas red.

52. *G. thunbergii* Lindley & Paxton (*G. nepalense* Sweet var. *thunbergii* (Lindley & Paxton) Kudo) (Figure 9.63)

Sprawling, noticeably hairy perennial, with usually light green leaves; blades of stem-leaves mostly between 5 and 10cm wide, with 5 broad, pointed divisions, the basal widely splayed, or the upper with 3 almost diamond-shaped divisions; inflorescence diffuse; flowers normally 12–15mm in diameter; petals rounded or scarcely notched, white to deep pinkish purple; anthers blue; stigmas red. Ground-cover. July or August to October.

Perennial with a small rootstock. Stems trailing, sometimes rooting. Leaves mostly light green; some present in winter, these being darker green and almost always with bold brownish purple marks in the notches. Blades of basal leaves divided as far as $^2/_3$ or $^3/_4$ into 5; divisions broad, shortly tapered both ways from about the middle, coarsely and shallowly lobed in the apical $^1/_3$ or $^1/_4$; lobes not longer than broad, shallowly toothed. Teeth and tips of lobes obtuse with a small point, or acute. Stem-leaves paired, the lower with 5 divisions, of which the basal pair are usually rather small and widely splayed; upper with 3 broadly elliptic but pointed divisions with a few coarse lobes and sometimes shallow teeth, those of a pair noticeably unequal. Plant covered with spreading eglandular hairs;

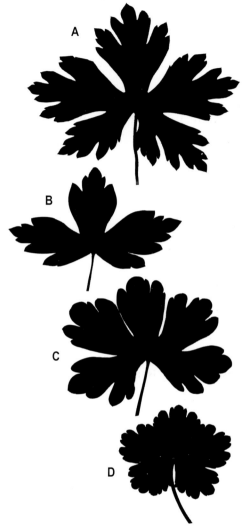

Figure 9.63. *G. thunbergii*: (A) from Kyoto B.G., 1965: basal leaf; (B) the same: stem-leaf; (C) from Y. Fukuda, 1975, coll. Japan: Shiobara Pref.; (D) from Mrs E. Smallbone, 1981, cult. in Sydney area, NSW, Australia; 5–9.5cm wide

some glandular hairs usually present on sepals, rostrum and mericarps, and sometimes the pedicels. Inflorescence diffuse; cymules 2-flowered, longer than the subtending leaves. Sepals 5–6mm, enlarging to 6.5–7mm in fruit; mucro 1mm or less. Petals 7–10.5 x 4–6mm, rounded or scarcely notched at apex, white or pale to deep purplish pink, with purple veins; base with a hair-fringe on either edge and a few hairs across the front surface. Filaments 4–5mm, enlarged at base, with numerous hairs on back and margins. Anthers violet-blue. Stigmas 1–2mm, flesh-pink or red. Immature fruits erect on erect, spreading or rarely reflexed pedicels. Rostrum 13–18mm with virtually no stylar portion. Mericarps 2.5–3mm. Discharge: seed-ejection (bristles).

N. China, Taiwan, Japan and neighbouring archipelagoes.

G. thunbergii is an almost weedy species, the seed of which is frequently 'traded' among botanic gardens. It just deserves to gain a place in the flower garden, preferably as ground-cover. Although it produces great quantities of seed, I have never seen much spontaneous germination in Cambridge. It is closely related to 55. *G. nepalense* and has been treated as a variety of it. Named thus, it sometimes loses its varietal name and becomes "*G. nepalense*". I have received it under this name from Mrs E. Smallbone of Strathfield, New South Wales, where it was one of the few *Geranium* species found to have garden value in the Sydney area up to that time (early 1980s). This particular form is more compact and has darker green leaves than usual, and deep purplish pink flowers. Some plants recently found as garden escapes in the English West Midlands entirely lack glandular hairs. For a comparison of *G. thunbergii* with *G. nepalense*, see under the latter; for confusion with another species see 54. *G. yoshinoi*.

G. thunbergii has been in circulation also under the name of the next species, 53. *G. wilfordii*.

This species is one of the many that can cross with 25. *G. lambertii* (q.v.); within its group it has also crossed with 56. *G. sibiricum* (Bremner).

53. *G. wilfordii* Maximowicz (Figure 9.64)
Related to 52. *G. thunbergii* but with initially erect stems and long internodes (mostly 5–15cm). Leaves to 11cm wide, with only 3 well-developed divisions which are tapered to a rather long triangular point and are evenly toothed rather than lobed and toothed; middle division rapidly becoming predominant upwards over the laterals. Plant less hairy than *G. thunbergii* and without glandular hairs. Sepal mucro more than 1mm long. Petals smaller than those of *G. thunbergii* and flowers insignificant. The immature fruits erect on sharply reflexed pedicels.

E. Asia, Japan.

This has been grown at Cambridge where it was received as an impurity in seed of 56. *G. sibiricum* sent by Dr Safonov of Sakhalin. *G. wilfordii* has been found as an alien in the Warsaw Province of Poland and a nicely illustrated account of its

Figure 9.64. *G. wilfordii*: from Dr V.I. Safonov, 1985; to 11cm wide

occurrence there has been published (Rostanski & Tokarski, 1973).

G. wilfordii has crossed with two species in the nearby Sessiliflorum Group, and *G. herrerae*, a member of the Cordilleran Group (see Chapter 7) that is probably closely related to the Sessiliflorum Group.

54. *G. yoshinoi* Nakai (Figure 9.65)
A stiff perennial to 60cm with spreading upper branches. Upper leaves mostly divided into 3. Flowers medium-sized (18–23mm wide), white to pale pink with darker veins. Pedicels of immature fruits spreading or reflexed, bent under calyx. Summer and autumn.

An umbrageous perennial to 60cm, with stout stems and leaves solitary below, paired above. Internodes to 20cm, rigid, dull red, or only the nodes red, with some backwardly appressed hairs and a band of backwardly curled hairs. Blades of basal leaves to 12cm wide, divided as far as $^4/_5$ into 5 or 7; divisions rhombic-obovate, broadest above the middle, shallowly lobed above the widest part; lobes with one or two shallow teeth; profile of lobes and teeth convex, acute; upper surface with appressed hairs, lower with short spreading hairs on the veins, flushed with purple in early spring. Leaf-stalks $1–1^1/_2$ times as long as blade with

Figure 9.65. *G. yoshinoi*: earlier and later stem-leaves of a young plant, from Wisley, and cult. P.F. Yeo, same source; later one 11cm wide

backwardly appressed or backwardly spreading hairs. Stipules about 6mm, lanceolate, minutely hairy. Stem leaves smaller, divided as far as $^3/_4$ or $^2/_3$ into 5 or 3; divisions elliptic, the central one increasingly predominant higher up the stem, sharply toothed in the upper half or third. Stipules 3–5mm, almost thread-like, soon drying out, minutely hairy. Inflorescence prolifically branched; peduncles 2–4cm, much longer than the leaves. Peduncles and pedicels very slender hirsute. Flower buds very slender. Flowers about 18–23mm wide, erect, shortly trumpet-shaped. Sepals 6–7mm, narrow, minutely appressed-hairy on the veins; mucro 1–2mm. Petals about 10–6mm, entire at apex, pink or nearly white with darker veins, each edged with a few small hairs at the base. Stamens with filaments enlarged and hair-fringed at the base, slender and pink at the apex. Stigmas 2.5mm, red. Immature fruits erect on reflexed or spreading pedicels bent under the calyx. Fruit about 27mm. Rostrum minutely hairy. Carpels with long bristly hairs. Discharge: seed-ejection (bristles).

Japan.

The plant described was introduced by seed from Unitopia Sasayama, Hyogo, Japan, to Wisley under the name *G. yesoense* var. *lobatodentatum* Takeda; it had been offered in the 1991 seed-list of the Japanese garden and was identified by me in 1996 (Yeo, 1998). Coincidentally, Wisley had received seeds about the same time under the name *G. yoshinoi*

from another Japanese source but the plants to which they gave rise are *G. thunbergii*.

This plant makes much foliage from a profusion of stiff branches before producing its thinly scattered flowers. It has some details in common with 53. *G. wilfordii*, and I have now accordingly placed it in the Sibiricum Group, a decision supported by the appearance in 2001 of an obvious hybrid with 52. *G. thunbergii*.

Our plant keys out unambiguously to *G. yoshinoi* in Ohwi (1965) and agrees with most of his description, but he says the stipules are usually united, stigmas 3–3.5mm, petals with basal hairs across the front surface. Some of these discrepancies are rather worrying. However, the discrepancies between our plant and the original description and key characters in Nakai (1912) are worse. Here the stipules are again said to be united (completely or with two points, sometimes the lower nearly free), and also green and leathery, elliptic and striped; the stems and leaf-stalks are said to be very slender and the stems ascending or rooting; finally, the appearance of the plant is said to recall 43. *G. soboliferum* and 45. *G. dahuricum*, which ours certainly does not. However, the illustrations of *G. yoshinoi* in Makino (1961) and Kitamura & Murata (1961), respectively a line-drawing and a painting, show no obvious disagreement with the characters of our plant, and the latter is quite like it.

G. yesoense var. *lobatodentatum* Takeda is not mentioned by Ohwi (1965) but was illustrated by Kitamura & Murata (1961).

55. G. nepalense Sweet (Figure 9.66)
Similar in habit to 52. *G. thunbergii* but with a slenderer stem, usually becoming bushy, and with

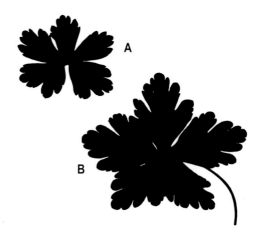

Figure 9.66. *G. nepalense*: (A) from R. Gorer, 1974, coll. by G. Ghose of Darjeeling, India; (B) from S.K. Raina, 1981, coll. India: Srinagar, Kashmir; 4 and 8cm wide

smaller darker green leaves. Leaves often slightly marbled, and often purple beneath and brownish above but not blotched in the notches. Blades of basal leaves divided as far as $^3/_4$ or $^5/_6$ into 5 or 7; divisions shortly tapered both ways from above the middle, with 3 or 5 lobes at apex; lobes not longer than broad, toothed. Teeth and tips of lobes acute or obtuse. Stem-leaves paired, stalked, with 3 or 5 more gradually tapered divisions and usually acute teeth and tips of lobes. Hairs eglandular. At least some cymules in each plant 2-flowered but 1-flowered cymules not infrequent. Flowers 10–12mm in diameter. Sepals 4.5–5mm, becoming 5–6.5mm in fruit. Petals 5–8.5mm long, rounded or notched at apex, white to pale pink, rarely deep pink, with darker veins. Anthers violet-blue. Stigmas 0.5–1mm, red. Immature fruits erect on reflexed pedicels. Rostrum 10–13mm with stylar portion about 0.5mm. Mericarps 3–3.5mm. Discharge: seed-ejection (bristles).

E. Afghanistan, Himalayas, peninsular India, China (Yunnan, Sichuan, Hubei, Henan, Guangxi).

This species is sometimes introduced by purchase of wild-flower seed from commercial collectors in the Himalayan region but it is a weed and can be quite persistent out of doors in Cambridge. The flower colour may range from pale pink to white in the same plant according to environmental conditions, but there is some inherent variation also. When the name *G. nepalense* was first published, it was accompanied by a not very good plate of a plant with deep red flowers (which I have never seen in this species).

G. nepalense differs from 52. *G. thunbergii* in being slenderer, smaller-leaved and slightly smaller-flowered. Also, *G. thunbergii* usually has glandular hairs. *G. nepalense* is rather variable in stature and leaf-form, certain forms approaching *G. thunbergii* in these characters (see Figure 9.66).

56. G. sibiricum Linnaeus (Figure 9.67)

Perennial with slender rootstock and sprawling stems. Foliage pale green. Basal leaves few. Lower stem-leaves between 5 and 10cm wide, divided as far as about $^5/_6$ (sometimes much more); divisions rather narrow, gradually tapered both ways from about the middle, with rather numerous lobes, nearly straight-sided in the unlobed part; lobes divergent from midrib of the division at a small angle, up to about twice as long as broad, rather shallowly toothed. Teeth and tips of lobes acute. Divisions of upper stem-leaves untoothed and with the lobes forming a coarse saw-edge. Stem-leaves paired, stalked. Hairs eglandular. Cymules 1-flowered, sometimes with no pedicel. Flowers 9–10mm wide. Sepals 4mm, enlarging to 5 or 6mm in fruit; mucro about

Figure 9.67. *G. sibiricum*: from J. Rishbeth, 1978, coll. China: Kirin Prov.: (A) middle leaf; (B) lower leaf; 6 and 7cm wide

0.75–1.25mm. Petals about 5–7mm, wedge-shaped, rounded or notched at apex, white or pale pink with purple veins. Anthers violet-blue. Stigmas about 1mm, pink. Rostrum 10–13mm, the stylar portion about 1mm. Mericarps 3–3.5mm. Discharge: seed-ejection (bristles).

E. and C. Europe (where it is spreading westwards), most of northern Asia, China, Japan, W. Himalayas; introduced into N. America.

G. sibiricum is a weed, resembling an annual in habit though in fact a perennial. It grows in disturbed ground and, in continental climates, in lawns. In its small whitish flowers it resembles 55. *G. nepalense* but is distinguished from it by the sharply lobed, narrow leaf-divisions and constantly 1-flowered cymules. Even when grown in the greenhouse this species goes dormant in winter. Has formed hybrids with 76. *G. carolinianum*, 1. *G. endressii* and 2. *G. x oxonianum* from groups remote in my classification, and with 63. *G. potentilloides*, 60. *G. sessiliflorum* and 84. *G. herrerae* from groups placed near it in my classification (Bremner).

57. G. suzukii Masamune (Figure 9.68)

Almost prostrate carpeting plant with small leaves cut into 3 or 5 divisions. Lobes of winter leaves shallow, blunt, scarcely toothed, those of summer-leaves obovate or semi-ovate, longer,

Figure 9.68. *G. suzukii*: cult. P.F. Yeo, 2000, coll. B. & S. Wynn-Jones in Taiwan (BSWJ 016); left: winter leaf; right: summer leaf which is 30mm wide

more unequal. Flowers scattered, 12mm (perhaps to 20mm) in diameter, white.

Ground-hugging, weakly hairy perennial spreading by reddish, thread-like stolons (rooting at nodes). Hairs small, those of the stipules appressed and forwardly directed, those of the leaf-blades forwardly divergent, those of the leaf-stalks appressed and backwardly directed. Leaves to 4.5cm wide, paired, divided as far as $^3/_4 – ^5/_6$ into 3 or 5. Autumn/winter leaves kidney-shaped or nearly circular, with 5 divisions each with three very short and broad and nearly equal lobes. Spring/summer leaves with the divisions approximately obovate or semi-ovate, mostly 3-lobed at the apex, without or with a very few teeth; lobes about as wide as long or wider, the middle one overtopping the laterals, bluntly pointed or obtuse and mucronate. Upper surface matt, dark green with extensive pale green blotches more or less centrally on the divisions (but these can be hardly noticeable), lower surface glossy, sometimes suffused with red-purple. Leaf-stalks about $1^1/_2–3$ times as long as blade, reddish. Stipules to about 5mm, narrowly triangular, drawn out into a hair-like point. Flowers scattered. Cymules 1-flowered, borne at the nodes and in axils of leaves of condensed side-shoots, so that there appears to be a succession of flowers from one node, their stalks 2.5–9cm, with the bracteoles above or below the middle. Pedicels after flowering reflexed and bent upwards under the calyx. Sepals 5–9.5mm, green, pale between the ribs, with mucro 1mm. Petals 9–15mm, rounded at apex, white, with fine violet veins that become colourless towards the base, weakly hair-fringed at base, the hairs not extending all across front surface. Stamens about $^2/_3$ as long as sepals; filaments white, with thread-like terminal bristly part and strongly widened base without hairs; anthers tinged with violet. Stigmas about 1.5mm, greenish. Rostrum probably 18–22mm, with very short stylar portion, minutely hairy. Mericarps about 3mm, hairy. Discharge: seed-ejection (bristles).

Taiwan (endemic).

Introduced by Bleddyn and Sue Wynn-Jones (BSWJ 016) from Taroko National Park at an altitude of 2,400m (though it occurs up to 3,000m). In nature it forms shallowly rooted carpets in partial or full shade and in cultivation it must be kept moist. It is not fully hardy in Britain (but more so than 62. *G. papuanum*) and may never exceed the status of a curiosity. This plant gives the impression of a prostrate nearly hairless 56. *G. sibiricum* with broader leaf-segments and larger-than-usual flowers. In habit it is very like 62. *G. papuanum*.

Has been crossed with 60. *G. sessiliflorum* by Alan Bremner.

THE SESSILIFLORUM GROUP

Perennials with well-developed basal rosette leaves or forming rosettes at rooted nodes, and with bushy or trailing, diffuse inflorescences. Blades of lower leaves rounded in outline with divisions broadest at or near apex and with shallow lobes and teeth. Hairs eglandular. Cymules 1-flowered. Pedicels longer than peduncles. Stamen-filaments enlarged at base. Stamens and style distinctly shorter than the sepals. Rostrum often without a distinct stylar portion.

This description covers only the species actually included in this book. They come from Australia, New Zealand (including Chatham Islands) and Papua–New Guinea, while one has a subspecies in South America. They are probably closely related to other species of Australasia.

58. *G. traversii* J.D. Hooker (Figure 9.69A)
Greyish-hairy, low-growing; basal leaves long-stalked, rounded in outline with shallow obtuse lobes and teeth; cymules 1-flowered; flowers held just above basal leaves, 26–29mm in diameter, white or opaque (milky) pink. Rock garden. Sun. June to September.

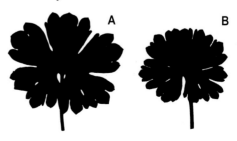

Figure 9.69. *(A) G. traversii*: from F. Beanland, 1982; (B) *G. sessiliflorum* subsp. *novaezelandiae* x *G. traversii* (*G.* x *antipodeum*), K.A. Beckett, 1981; 5 and 4cm wide

Perennial with compact rootstock. Basal leaves numerous, long-stalked, their blades between 5 and 10cm wide, often broader than long, divided as far as $^3/_5$ into 7; divisions broadest almost at the apex, giving a scarcely angled outline to the whole blade, 3-lobed for about $^1/_4 - ^1/_3$ of their length; lobes broader than long, often with 1 or 2 small teeth. Teeth acutish, tips of lobes obtuse or broadly pointed. Stem-leaves paired, becoming reduced in size rather rapidly upwards, the upper with 5 divisions which are less enlarged towards the tip than those of basal leaves, giving the blade a more angular outline. Stipules not united, finely tapered. Hairs eglandular, dense, fine, clothing the whole plant in a greyish hoariness. Branches mostly paired, forming a diffuse inflorescence which becomes bushy and collapses, so that flowers are carried only a little above the basal leaves. Cymules 1-flowered. Flowers saucer-shaped. Sepals about 6.5–8mm; mucro 0.5–1mm. Petals 12–13mm long and almost as broad, rounded at apex, contracted at base into a short triangular claw, white or opaque (milky) pink, fading at the edges, with fine darker veins on lower half of blade and a whitish claw; base with evident hairs at the sides and a few fine hairs on veins of front surface of claw and base of blade (difficult to see). Stamens about $^2/_3$ as long as sepals; filaments enlarged at base, white, finely hairy in lower part; anthers yellow with pink edges. Stigmas 1.5mm, pinkish, hairy on outer surfaces. Immature fruits erect on erect pedicels. Rostrum 8–11mm, without a distinct stylar portion. Mericarps about 3mm. Discharge: seed-ejection (bristles).

Chatham Islands (nearly 640km east of New Zealand).

In nature *G. traversii* grows on coastal cliffs. When first discovered it was described as having white flowers and the white form was known to Bowles (1914) and to Ingwersen (1946); then it seemed to be ousted by the pink form. The botanical name of the pink-flowered form is var. *elegans* Cockayne and of the white var. *traversii*. Although plants cultivated in Britain are very uniform, Dr David Given has told me that in nature *G. traversii* shows great variation in vigour, in the shape and colour of the leaves and in the size and colour of the flowers. The pink-flowered var. *elegans* would therefore be better treated at the rank of forma or even regarded as a cultivar, but this matter had best be handled by New Zealand botanists.

G. traversii grows well in England but it is easily lost in severe winters and perhaps also through winter damp. However, it regenerates naturally from seed as a rule. The old inflorescences are said to bend down and take root, giving a "hen-and-chickens" effect (Allan, 1961). I have not seen this but Farrer (1919) mentions striking cuttings in autumn as a precaution against loss in winter.

G. traversii is on the whole coarser in growth than the grey-leaved members of the Cinereum Group (nos. 104–110) and it differs from them in fruit-discharge type.

G. traversii has crossed spontaneously with the European 1. *G. endressii* to produce *G. x riversleaianum* (no. 3), and with 60. *G. sessiliflorum* to produce 59. *G. x antipodeum* and these two crosses have been made deliberately also by Alan Bremner. As mentioned under *G. x antipodeum* this species can cross outside the subgeneric boundary into the Cinereum Group.

59. *G. x antipodeum* Yeo, see Appendix II (Figure 9.69B)
Plant with basal leaves slightly smaller than those of 58. *G. traversii* and with tiny stem-leaves 2cm or less wide in a profusely branched trailing inflorescence; upper leaf surface bright green or flushed with brown; flowers 15–20mm in diameter, white, more or less flushed with rose. Rock garden. June to autumn.

Tufted perennial with numerous basal leaves and many leafy stems to 20cm. Basal leaves with blade to 6cm wide, divided about as far as $^3/_5$ into 7; divisions crowded and not lying flat, broadly wedge-shaped, widest at the apex where they are shallowly and obtusely 3-lobed; most lobes with one or two small obtuse teeth. Stem leaves paired, very unequal, or sometimes solitary, mostly 7–20mm wide, with mostly elliptic divisions and lobes, the uppermost sometimes unlobed. Stems, leaf-stalks, peduncles and pedicels felted with backwardly appressed hairs. Leaf-blades shortly appressed-hairy, bright green or flushed with brown. Hair-clothing of plant less dense than in 58. *G. traversii*. Cymules 1-flowered, the stalks mostly 3–5cm with the bracts well below the middle. Flowers shallowly funnel-shaped. Sepals 5–6mm, acuminate, flushed with brown or purplish brown, outer surface felted and with some very long hairs, mucro about 1mm. Petals 10 x 6–8mm, pale pink, with white base, to opaquely white, rounded at apex, clawed at base, with a few marginal hairs. Filaments white, considerably widened and finely hair-fringed from the middle down; anthers pale violet or violet-edged. Stigmas about 1.5mm, whitish, yellowish or flesh-pink. Pedicels sometimes reflexed and bent upwards under the immature fruit. Rostrum 11–14mm, with hardly any stylar portion, felted. Discharge: seed-ejection (bristles).

Hybrids between 60. *G. sessiliflorum* and 58. *G. traversii*, arising in gardens.

This hybrid readily arises in gardens where the parents grow together. My description is based partly on specimens gathered in Mr and Mrs K.A. Beckett's garden at Stanhoe, near King's Lynn, Norfolk (later grown at Cambridge and named 'Stanhoe' (Yeo, 1988)), and partly on Alan Bremner's deliberate cross using the brown-leaved 'Nigricans' cultivar of *G. sessiliflorum* as one parent ('Sea Spray'). I have also seen the hybrid at Kew (in 1971) and at Bloom's of Bressingham, Norfolk (in 1979 and 1980) and in both places it appeared to be fertile, with variable progeny. 'Stanhoe' produces a small amount of seed which is viable and gives rise to some plants very like the F1 (and these have also been used in making my description). The plants described have the hybrid formula *G. sessiliflorum* Cavanilles subsp. *novaezelandiae* Carolin x *G. traversii* J.D. Hooker var. *elegans* Cockayne (except possibly some of Alan Bremner's), though the name *G. x antipodeum* legally applies to crosses of any form of either parent.

G. x antipodeum 'Sea Spray' has brown-green foliage and makes plants of up to 1.2m wide. See preceding paragraph for history of this and next cultivar.

G. x antipodeum 'Stanhoe' has slightly hoary green foliage and is less vigorous.

Any degree of fertility is surprising in a cross between a diploid (*G. traversii*) and a tetraploid (*G. sessiliflorum*), and a check on the chromosomes of both parents and the hybrids is desirable.

The petal colour may change from pale pink in cool weather to white in hot.

The botanical name has been supplied for this hybrid (in Appendix II) because it has itself given rise to so many further hybrids, and referring to them becomes difficult, especially if the infraspecific elements in the parental names are specified.

Like its parent *G. traversii*, *G. x antipodeum* has also crossed with 25. *G. lambertii*, but it has made not only this cross but also those with 28. *G. kishtvariense*, 29. *G. rubifolium* and 30. *G. swatense*. All four are large-flowered species placed in the Wallichianum Group (nos. 24–30). Then it has made several crosses with species in groups placed near to its own, including 84. *G. herrerae* in the Cordilleran Group. Like its

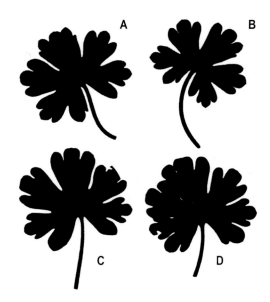

Figure 9.70. *G. sessiliflorum* subsp. *novaezelandiae*: (A) & (B) from Lausanne B.G.; (C) & (D) 'Nigricans', from J. Stephens, 1964; 2 to 2.5cm wide

parents, it can also cross beyond the subgeneric boundary into subgenus Erodioidea (species of the Cinereum Group).

60. *G. sessiliflorum* Cavanilles (Figure 9.70)
Dwarf perennial, sometimes carpeting, with green to dark brown leaves and white or pale pink flowers 10–18mm in diameter, held at or around the level of the foliage. Rock garden. June onwards.

Perennial with a compact rootstock, stout for the size of the plant. Blades of basal leaves about 1.5–4.5cm wide, circular or kidney-shaped in outline, divided as far as $^1/_2$ to $^5/_6$ into 5 or 7; divisions broadest at the apex, shallowly 3-lobed at apex; lobes broader than long, obtuse, rarely toothed. Stem-leaves mostly 1–2.5cm wide, usually slightly angular, with 5 or 7 divisions, some of which may be unlobed; lobes obtuse or bluntly pointed. Hairs eglandular. Inflorescence diffuse, upper internodes short, causing flowers to be held at about the level of the blades of the basal and lower stem-leaves; cymules 1-flowered, the first ones often arising from the rosette; flowers erect, funnel-shaped. Sepals 3.5–7mm, brownish green, covered with long spreading hairs. Petals 6.5–9 x 3–4mm, broadest at apex, white; base with a few hairs on each edge and an occasional hair on the front surface; filaments shorter than sepals, enlarged at base, white, fringed with minute hairs in the lower part; anthers yellowish. Stigmas 1.5mm, whitish. Rostrum about 8mm, with no stylar part. Mericarps about 2.5mm. Discharge: seed-ejection (bristles),

South America (Andes and cool-temperate lowlands), New Zealand (N. and S. Islands) and Australia (Tasmania and S.E. highlands of the continent).

Florally, this is usually an insignificant species. However, there is considerable horticultural interest in forms of subsp. *novaezelandiae* with brown pigment in the leaves and in the large number of slightly larger-flowered hybrids that it has produced.

Three subspecies were recognised by Carolin (1965): *sessiliflorum* from South America, *novae-zelandiae* Carolin from New Zealand (North and South Islands) and *brevicaule* (J.D. Hooker) Carolin from Australia/Tasmania. Carolin gave only the scantiest of diagnostic characters. However, as I have grown a number of Mrs Robin Parer's Peruvian samples of *G. sessiliflorum*, I feel the time has come to recognise subsp. *sessiliflorum* and to try to distinguish it from the frequently grown subsp. *novaezelandiae*. My account is based on some notes made in the Kew Herbarium as well as Mrs Parer's samples.

G. sessiliflorum subsp. *sessiliflorum* has the leaves mostly paired, with the blades divided as far as $^4/_5$–$^5/_6$; hairs of stems and petioles usually backwardly spreading, those of the blades sufficiently numerous to impart a downy or velvety texture. Leaf-divisions are more wedge-shaped than in subsp. *novaezelandiae* (a consequence of having deeper incisions). Flowers sometimes more than 10mm in diameter. Immature fruits erect on erect pedicels. One of Robin Parer's Peruvian plants (see above) had forwardly appressed hairs on the petioles and stems. Unfortunately all the Peruvian plants I grew were kept in a greenhouse and all are now dead. They showed significant variation in flower-size.

G. sessiliflorum subsp. *novaezelandiae* Carolin has the leaves mostly solitary, with the blades divided as far as $^1/_2$–$^3/_5$; hairs of stems and petioles usually backwardly more or less appressed, those of the blades not dense enough to impart a downy or velvety texture. Leaf-divisions more oblong (because shallower). Stem-leaves not usually more than 1.5cm wide. Flowers not more than 10mm in diameter and petals not more than 7.5mm long. Immature fruits erect on mostly spreading or reflexed pedicels.

The cultivars listed below belong to this subspecies.

G. sessiliflorum 'Nigricans'. Soon after they unfold, the leaves become olive green or bronzy

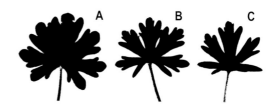

Figure 9.71. *G. antrorsum*: (A) from P. Hammond, 1992.0381, coll. New South Wales (HMNB 3329); (B) & (C) from Alan Wood, 1991.1180, coll. T. Carter; 45mm wide

above and when dying they turn orange. Brownish-leaved plants were mentioned by Allan (1961), who says that where the brown and the green occur together in nature, intermediate colours may be found. When I wrote edn.1 I knew of only one brown-pigmented stock, and for that I took up the already existing cultivar epithet 'Nigricans'. This name appeared in the autumn supplement to the 1967 catalogue of The Plantsmen, Sherborne, Dorset, but it was applied to a plant received at Cambridge from Mr Jan Stephens in 1964; if it was published before 1959, it will be legitimate.

G. sessiliflorum 'Porter's Pass'. Since 1985 a range of brown-tinted plants has been brought to Europe from New Zealand, mostly being coppery rather than bronzy, and some stocks have been named, for example 'Porter's Pass', which has deep reddish leaves (not all plants from Porter's Pass fall within the cultivar).

G. sessiliflorum subsp. *novaezelandiae* has been crossed successfully with nearly all its nearest relatives (i.e. those in its own group and the Sibiricum and the Potentilloides Groups). Among the many others with which it has crossed is the South American *G. herrerae*. This gives rise to low carpeting plants with flowers about 1.5cm in diameter which seem to have considerable garden value. Similar plants also arise when *sessiliflorum*'s hybrid 59. *G. x antipodeum* crosses with 84. *G. herrerae*. As mentioned under *G. x antipodeum* the present species can cross outside the subgeneric boundary into the Cinereum Group.

61. *G. antrorsum* Carolin (Figure 9.71, Plate 27)
A dwarf tufted alpine with 1-flowered cymules of deep pink or pink flowers opening near ground level or just above the leaves. Plant bristly. Leaves of distinctive shape, rather light green. Largest flowers 12–20mm wide (varying according to stock).

Perennial to about 20cm, of tufted habit from a thick but not swollen taproot. First leaves smaller than the main ones, divided as far as $^1/_2$

into 5; basal divisions with a single lobe on the outside. Main leaves to 4.5cm wide, divided as far as $^1/_2$–$^4/_5$, with a very wide basal sinus and closed or moderately open lateral sinuses; divisions widest just below the apex, the median and laterals lobed for $^1/_5$ –$^1/_3$ of their length, the lobes usually with one or two small lateral teeth; teeth and tips of lobes obtuse and mucronate to acute. (There is a tendency for the basal lobes and their teeth to be smaller and narrower than the others, giving a distinctive shape; this is most pronounced in the leaves of the inflorescence.) All leaves rather pale green, slightly glossy, slightly recurved at the edges and strongly coarsely hairy; hairs of the stalks spreading, of the blades forwardly appressed. Stipules to about 12mm, ovate-lanceolate, with the margins inrolled to form a long fine point, sparsely and finely hairy, largely pink or red. Flowering stems with forwardly directed hairs, their internodes suppressed or nearly so, the cymules appearing more or less basal. Cymules 1-flowered, bristly, with bracteoles below the middle, sometimes near the base, carrying the flowers below or just above the leaves. Flowers erect. Sepals 5–9mm (perhaps to 11mm), green, bristly, with mucro 2–3mm long. Petals to 11 x 9mm, rounded, milky pink or deep pink, with deep red scarcely branched veins; almost hairless. Filaments 2–4mm, considerably widened in the lower $^2/_3$, pale pink, hairless or nearly so; anthers partially purple. Stigmas 1.5–2mm, bristly on the back, dark red. Immature fruits on pedicels spreading on, or arched over, the ground, growing above the leaves suddenly just before maturity (unless the flowers themselves were above the leaves from the first). Fruit bristly with rostrum 14–16mm and no stylar part; mericarps about 3mm, bristly. Seeds about 2.5mm, finely reticulate. Discharge: seed-ejection (bristles).

S.E. Australia.

The showiest form that I have seen is represented in cultivation at Cambridge by HMWB 3329 (Hammond, Minter, Walsh & Belling; Cambridge accession 1992.0381 Hammond); it has flowers nearly 2cm wide and rising above the leaves. Alan Wood's stock – 1991.1180 Wood at Cambridge (collected by Tim Carter in the Snowy Mountains, S.E. Australia) – has flowers to 14mm wide, while HMWB 3355 (1992.0338 Hammond at Cambridge) has smaller flowers still (to 12mm wide) and darker in colour; they are more or less at ground level and partly hidden. HMWB 3329 was collected at Yarrangobilly Caves, Kosciusko National Park, and HMWB 3355 at Digger's Creek, Kosciusko National Park (Yeo, 1995).

The original description gives the stipules as only 6mm long and obtuse and the sepals as attaining 11mm (only 9mm in my experience). It also says the pedicels are swollen below the calyx. The range of petal lengths from 6 to 12mm given by Carolin is consistent with the range of flower sizes that I have seen in cultivation.

This species seems to be short-lived but it produces a lot of seed that germinates readily. The largest-flowered form is moderately ornamental.

62. G. papuanum Ridley (Figure 9.72)

A small prostrate species, with attractive glossy foliage and deep pink flowers about 27mm wide. Probably flowering most of the year. Not hardy.

Trailing perennial. Stems thin, reddish, readily rooting at the nodes, hirsute, with unequal paired leaves and paired branches, one branch of each pair with expanded internodes, continuing in the direction of the previous internode, the other appearing lateral and having its first few internodes suppressed, so that it forms a leaf-cluster. Leaf-blades to about 2cm wide, divided just beyond half their radius into 5 or 7; divisions widest at the apex, with convex marginal profile, the central one shallowly 3-lobed, with the middle lobe the shortest, or unlobed, the others mostly shallowly 2-lobed with occasionally a tooth; teeth and tips of lobes obtuse or very bluntly pointed. Divisions of leaf-blades crowded, not lying flat, rather thick, glossy green and with spaced-out appressed hairs above, purple beneath with the veins picked out by dense forwardly directed bristly hairs. Leaf-stalks densely clothed with backwardly directed hairs. Stipules about 4mm, very narrow, acute, hairy. Cymules 1-flowered, borne erect at the nodes, much longer than the leaves. Peduncles 2–4cm; pedicels 1.5–3cm. Peduncles and pedicels clothed as the stem. Flowers erect, salverform (i.e. with a narrow tubular base). Sepals 6–7mm, green, with hairy veins; mucro about 0.5mm. Petals presumably at

Figure 9.72. *G. papuanum*: from R.F. Beeston, 1988, collected by the Rev. N. Cruttwell in New Guinea; 18mm wide

least 15mm, broadly rounded and tapered at base into a claw about 2mm long; blade deep purplish pink, claw white with a few fine hairs on each edge. Stamens about 5mm, basal half widened, white, finely hair-fringed, apical half pink-tinged; anthers small, yellow. Stigmas about 1.5mm, green. Immature fruit erect. Rostrum about 12mm, hairy, with stylar portion up to 2.5mm. Carpels about 2mm, hairy. Discharge: seed-ejection (bristles).

Papua New Guinea.

A distinctive species in its closely prostrate habit, glossy leaves and brightly coloured flowers. The details of its introduction and a colour photograph, supplied by its introducer, the Rev. Norman Crutwell, were published in the *Alpine Garden Society Bulletin* 56: 192–194 (1988). It is not hardy in S.E. England but is easily rooted from cuttings or raised from seed. Its native altitudinal range is from 2,500m to 3,500m, and it probably experiences frosts briefly down to -6°C. I have placed it in the Sessiliflorum Group on the ground of its stem-rooting ability, shallowly divided leaves, lack of glandular hairs and medium-sized flowers in 1-flowered cymules. *G. papuanum* lacks the basal rosette of 60. *G. sessiliflorum* and 58. *G. traversii* but forms little rosetted clusters at the nodes where it roots. On these criteria 57. *G. suzukii* ought to be placed here, too, and my placing it in the Sibiricum Group is debatable.

THE POTENTILLOIDES GROUP

Perennials without distinct resting buds, forming freely branched stems. Lower leaves rounded or weakly angled, their divisions lobed mainly at the apex. Cymules borne among the leaves. Flowers small, white or pale pink.

Several species in Australasia and Indonesia.

Apart from *G. potentilloides* three species have been grown at Cambridge: *G. homeanum* Turczaninov, *G. retrorsum* De Candolle and *G. solanderi* Carolin. Several more species recognised by Carolin (1965) might fall into this group.

A plant naturalised at Bordon, Hampshire, in the south of England, (Cambridge accession 1988.0463 Brewis: Lady Anne Brewis) has been grown in Cambridge and confirmed as *G. retrorsum* by me, using Carolin's revision (Carolin, 1965). It was originally thought to be this species by Lousley (1962) but this was disputed by Townsend (1964) (compare the history of 59. *G. herrerae*). A second stock of *G. retrorsum* cultivated at Cambridge was perceptibly different but clearly of the same species (1987.0185 Smallbone: Mrs E. Smallbone, Strathfield, New South Wales). *G. solanderi* has the smallest flowers of any *Geranium* I know but some stocks produce larger flowers.

63. *G. potentilloides* De Candolle (Figure 9.73)
Low bushy perennial without distinct resting buds. Stems to 40cm, with paired leaves. Main leaves to 6cm wide, divided as far as $^3/_4 - ^5/_6$ into 7, kidney-shaped to slightly angled in outline; divisions broadest near the apex, with the entire part of the margin concave, palmately lobed for $^1/_4$ to nearly $^1/_2$ their length; lobes obtuse, teeth often acute and turned outwards. Stipules about 8mm, ovate-lanceolate, tailed. Upper leaves divided into 5 or 7, with divisions more wedge-shaped, the central having predominance over the others. Inflorescence diffuse. Cymules 1-flowered. Peduncles and pedicels densely clothed with reflexed hairs, or downy with minute curly hairs. Flowers 11–16mm wide, more or less erect. Sepals 3–6mm, minutely downy and with larger, more bristly, hairs, with mucro 0.5–1mm. Petals white or pale pink with white base, fringed with a few hairs on either side at the base, not or faintly notched. Stamen filaments white, strongly widened at the base and there with hairy margins; anthers pale yellow. Stigmas about 1mm, pale yellow or crimson. Pedicels reflexed and turned up at the tips after flowering. Rostrum about 11–16mm, hirsute, with stylar portion 0.5–1mm or none. Carpels 2.75–4mm. Discharge: seed-ejection (bristles).

Australia, New Zealand, Indonesia.

A mainly weedy species, but white-petalled plants with maximal flower size can be quite attractive.

Hybrids between *G. potentilloides* and 60. *G. sessiliflorum* have been found in New South Wales by Carolin (1965) and created artificially by Alan Bremner. Bremner has also crossed *G. potentilloides* with 56. *G. sibiricum* and 58. *G. traversii*, which are close to it in the classification, and with 4. *G. versicolor*, 1. *G. endressii* and 25. *G. lambertii*, which are remote from it but all more or less "good combiners".

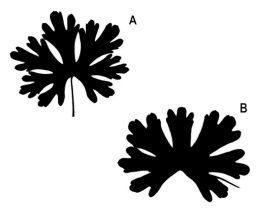

Figure 9.73. *G. potentilloides* : (A) upper & (B) lower stem-leaves, from Kew, 1987, coll. Arthur's Lake, Tasmania (B. Halliwell 2206); 5cm wide

THE ROBUSTUM GROUP

Robust, basally woody perennials, without resting buds. Stipules deeply divided. Leaf-blades felted beneath. Leaf-segments wide compared with those of the Incanum Group and the Harveyi Group (below). Flowers 32–42mm wide, violet to pink. Petals and filaments densely hairy at base, the latter moderately widened. Pedicels usually more or less spreading or reflexed after flowering and bent upwards under the calyx.

Apparently only shoots of the previous year can flower.

Southern Africa.

The southern African geraniums have been revised by Hilliard & Burtt (1985). As they all have deeply split stipules they appear to constitute a single evolutionary branch of Section Geranium. When growing together they readily produce hybrids. As with other species in this book I have grouped them informally.

64. G. robustum Kuntze (Figure 9.74, Plate 28)
Bushy perennial with the stems woody at the base, large-growing and very leafy. Leaves profusely, elegantly and deeply cut, green above and more or less white-felted beneath. Flowers numerous, held above the foliage on old shoots, 32–42mm wide; petals violet with a large white basal area. Glandular hairs present. Summer.

Large bushy, very leafy evergreen perennial. Stems to about 8mm in diameter and 1.75m long, but normally collapsing, giving a plant height of about 60cm, woody at the base, downy with a dense covering of reflexed hairs, with solitary leaves below and paired ones above. Internodes 1.5–2.5cm in non-flowering parts of plant, 8–14cm in the flowering part and there glandular-hairy. Blades of main leaves to 12cm wide, divided to the base into 5; divisions rhombic, more or less overlapping, deeply pinnately lobed from near the base upwards, the lobes mostly twice as long as broad and freely toothed; lobes and teeth mostly turned outwards, obtuse to acute, slightly recurved at the edges; upper surface with impressed veins and clothed with fine appressed hairs, green, lower velvety with dense hairs and appearing grey-green to nearly white; stalks mostly 1–3 times as long as blades, densely covered with recurved or reflexed hairs. Stipules to about 12mm, cut from just above the base into 2 or more linear-attenuate lobes, hairy. Leaves becoming smaller upwards and ultimately simplified. Inflorescence very loose, many-flowered. Peduncles 4–12cm, pedicels 2.5–9cm, like the peduncles eglandular and velvety or glandular-hairy and shaggy. Flowers nodding in bud, opening erect. Sepals 6–9mm, recurved at tips, green, flushed with purple except at

Figure 9.74. *G. robustum*: from R. Parer, 1987, cult. P.F. Yeo; 10cm wide

base outside, becoming red inside, clothed like the pedicels; mucro 0.5–1mm. Petals 19–21 x 11–13mm, notched, sometimes overlapping, violet with large white basal area extending further at the sides than at the middle, violet area with darker veins, margins at the base with a strong tuft of hairs not extending across either surface. Stamen filaments moderately widened and strongly hairy at the base, whitish; anthers grey-blue. Stigmas 2.5–4.5mm, red. Pedicels more or less spreading and curved upwards under the flower and fruit. Rostrum 15–22mm, including the very slender stylar portion of 2.5–4mm; hairs eglandular or glandular and eglandular. Carpels 4mm, densely bristly; seeds 3.5mm. Discharge: seed-ejection (bristles).

South Africa (Transvaal, Natal, Orange Free State, Transkei and Cape), Lesotho.

This species was introduced into cultivation outside South Africa by Mrs Robin Parer before edn.1 was published but I knew little of it then. It has been introduced repeatedly and is now widely cultivated in Britain and is reasonably hardy. It is attractive in leaf and showy in flower.

G. robustum has crossed spontaneously with 65. *G. brycei* and artificially with 66. *G. pulchrum* (Bremner) and 71. *G. flanaganii* (Bremner). The existence of the cross with *G. brycei* may make identification of the parents difficult. The cross between 68. *G. incanum* and *G. robustum*, called 'Rambling Robin', has been raised by Bleddyn Wynn-Jones.

65. *G. brycei* N.E. Brown (Figure 9.75)
Bushy perennial with the stems woody at the base. Glandular hairs present. Similar to 64. *G. robustum* in shape of leaf segments and flowers but leaves less deeply cut and with a more solid outline, velvety above and closely grey-woolly beneath. Not growing so tall as *G. robustum*. Flowers 35–45mm wide, rich purplish blue with a white centre. Stamens and style small. Summer.

Evergreen with semi-woody stems to about 1m tall. Internodes 0.5–1.5cm long in non-flowering part of plant, 5–15cm in the flowering part, densely and finely hairy; upper branches glandular-hairy. Lower leaves solitary, to 11cm wide, divided as far as $^3/_4$–$^4/_5$ into 5 or 7; divisions broadest above the middle, their margins lobed or toothed above the middle or nearly to the base, the lobes about 1–1$^1/_2$ times as long as broad, tending to turn outwards, usually with 1–5 teeth; teeth and tips of lobes obtuse or bluntly pointed. Upper leaves opposite, reduced gradually in size and in the relative width of their segments. Upper surfaces of all leaves greyish green on account of dense clothing of forwardly directed hairs; lower surfaces pale grey-green, woolly. Leaf-stalks up to 4 times as long as blades, with backwardly spreading hairs. Stipules to about 12mm, cut for half their length or more into 3 or 4 linear-lanceolate segments, usually more or less red. Inflorescence large and loose. Flowers nodding in bud, erect in flower. Sepals 6–9mm, green with brownish red base, densely glandular-hairy, glossy within; mucro less than 1mm. Petals 17–20 x 12–19mm, rounded or irregularly lobed

Figure 9.75. *G. brycei*: from D. Victor, Cambridge 1998.0465, and cult. D. Victor; one division of one leaf separated; 12cm wide

at apex, overlapping, purplish violet, redder on back, white at base, with a dense tuft of white hairs all across upper surface at base. Stamen filaments pink at extreme tip, elsewhere white, moderately widened towards the base, densely hairy at base; anthers edged with lilac. Stigmas 2–2.5mm, pink to red. Immature fruits erect, their pedicels erect or slightly bent under the calyx. Rostrum 16–18mm, more or less red, glandular-hairy, sharply contracted into the hairless stylar portion of about 5mm. Carpels about 4mm; seeds nearly 3mm. Discharge: seed-ejection (bristles).

South Africa (Orange Free State, Natal, Transkei), Lesotho.

Introduced soon after 64. *G. robustum* by Sir Peter Watkin-Williams and others. Has a finer flower-colour than *G. robustum*. Has crossed spontaneously with 64. *G. robustum* in Britain.

66. *G. pulchrum* N.E. Brown (Figure 9.76)
A large bushy perennial with the stems woody at the base. Handsome in foliage. Leaves heavily felted, at least beneath, with distinctive rather narrow divisions with a comparatively solid outline. Flowers to 35mm wide in a large open inflorescence held above the leaves, rather deep pink. Summer.

Bushy perennial to 1.2m. Stems to 12mm in diameter, woody at the base, downy with a dense clothing of recurved hairs, with crowded (but not rosetted) alternate leaves below. Main leaves with blade to 14cm wide, divided as far as $^6/_7$–$^7/_8$ into 5 (incipiently to 7); divisions narrowly rhombic to lanceolate, more or less pinnately lobed about halfway to the midrib over most of their length; lobes with more or less numerous small teeth; teeth and tips of lobes semi-ovate, mucronate; upper surface hoary green, densely covered with appressed hairs, or less hairy and deep green, lower surface pale grey-green on account of a dense woolly coat of hairs; leaf-stalks mostly 1$^1/_2$–2$^1/_2$ times as long as blade, clothed as the blades; stipules about 2cm, hairy, with a small entire basal part and about 6 linear, almost thread-like, lobes. Upper stem internodes attaining 5–8cm, more or less glandular-hairy, their leaves divided into 5, with oblong or lanceolate divisions with wide sinuses between them. Inflorescence loose and very large, with internodes reaching 9cm or sometimes more, and becoming glandular upwards with purple-tipped hairs, the lower leaves alternate, the upper paired and much reduced. Peduncles mostly 3.5–5.5cm; pedicels usually about same length as peduncles,

Figure 9.76. *G. pulchrum*: from Mr Pearn, Isle of Man, 1988.0145; 12cm wide

sometimes shorter at first. Flowers nodding in bud, erect when open. Sepals 7–9mm, narrow, grey-green with purple veins, glandular-hairy; mucro about 1.5mm. Petals to about 18 x 15mm, weakly heart-shaped, overlapping, rather deep pink with a V-shaped greenish area at the base, with strong, fine, somewhat feathered purple veins, and with a tuft of hairs on the edges and front surface at the extreme base. Stamen filaments white, slightly widened and strongly hairy at the extreme base; anthers lilac. Style before opening equalling the stamens, yellowish; stigmas about 3.5mm, deep purple on their backs. Pedicels spreading or reflexed after flowering and turned up at the tip. Rostrum 27mm including stylar portion about 3.5mm, glandular-hairy. Carpels 4mm, glandular-hairy. Discharge: seed-ejection (bristles).

South Africa (Drakensberg in southern Natal).

A superb foliage plant that also makes a show with its flowers. Surprisingly hardy in Britain (in view of its hairy leaves). In the Drakensberg it occurs over a wide altitudinal range (Hilliard & Burtt, 1985). In nature it grows in damp gullies but it seems to have no special soil requirements in Britain. Different stocks show variation in density of hair-clothing, redness of upper stems and date of flowering.

Has been crossed with 64. *G. robustum* (Bremner).

THE HARVEYI GROUP

Perennial without winter resting buds, bushy, woody at base. Part or whole of the growth with felt hairs. Leaves small, with deeply pinnatifid divisions. Leaf-segments usually wider than in the Incanum Group. Stipules deeply lobed. Flowers of medium size. Sepal mucro of minimal size. Stamen-filaments widened at the base.

This group has been formed to accommodate *G. harveyi*. A few other South African species might be sufficiently similar to be included in it but none is covered in this book.

67. *G. harveyi* Briquet

Bushy perennial, woody below. Foliage felted; leaf-blades to only 3cm wide, deeply divided but solid in outline, on long stalks. Glandular hairs sometimes present above. Sepal mucro very short. Petals magenta or purplish blue, of moderate size. Summer.

Bushy, usually low-growing, clump-forming perennial, woody below. Stems slender, downy, with the leaves alternate or the uppermost paired. Leaf-blades mostly 0.5–3cm wide, divided as far as $^{4}/_{5}$–$^{5}/_{6}$ into 5; divisions broadly rhombic, deeply pinnatifid or palmato-pinnately lobed; lobes $1–2^{1}/_{2}$ times as long as broad, ovate to narrow-linear, toothless. Both surfaces densely clothed with silvery hairs though the upper surface may appear green. Leaf-stalks mostly 3–6 times as long as the blade, felted with backwardly directed hairs. Stipules to about 8mm, cut into two linear-acute segments. Inflorescence diffuse. Peduncles mostly 4–12cm, pedicels 2.5–5cm, these axes felted like the leaf-stalks; glandular hairs sometimes also present on pedicels. Sepals 4.5–7mm, felted and sometimes also with glandular hairs, sometimes purple within, with mucro 0.25–0.5mm. Petals 12–15 x 6.5–9mm, notched at apex, wedge-shaped at base with a weak tuft of hairs on either edge, magenta or purple-blue. Stamens distinctly longer than the sepals, enlarged towards base and there sparsely hair-fringed. Stigmas 2–2.5mm, crimson. Immature fruit more or less erect. Rostrum about 2cm, including stylar portion about 2mm, clothed like the sepals. Discharge: seed-ejection (bristles).

South Africa (Transkei, Cape).

Suitable for the rock garden.

THE INCANUM GROUP

Similar to the Harveyi Group but with narrower, generally linear, leaf-segments.

This group covers about four southern African species that have the narrowest leaf-segments of all.

68. G. incanum N.L. Burman (Figure 9.77)
Bushy perennial with all leaves divided to the base and their divisions, lobes and teeth all 1mm or less in width; inflorescence diffuse; flowers 27–35mm in diameter; petals white (var. *incanum*) or violet to deep reddish purple with darker veins (var. *multifidum*) and a narrow apical notch. Rock garden, patio, sun. June to autumn.

Perennial with aromatic herbage and no clear distinction between flowering and non-flowering shoots; stems branched below and becoming woody, closely leafy below, less so above. Leaves mostly solitary, some of the upper paired; blades less than or slightly more than 5cm wide, divided to the base into 5, green above, silky white-hairy beneath; divisions pinnately lobed and some of the lobes toothed; segments about 1mm wide or less. Stipules narrow, acute, deeply cut into 2 or 3 segments. Hairs eglandular, appressed. Peduncles mostly 6–14cm. Pedicels mostly 3–7cm. Sepals 5–6mm, silvery-silky; mucro 1mm. Petals 13–18 x 9–14mm, approximately heart-shaped, with a narrow notch, deep magenta-pink with darker veins and a white V-shaped mark at the base; base with a dense tuft of hairs at either edge and a small group of hairs on middle of front surface between the tufts. Filaments enlarged and hairy on the edges below, white at base, pink above; anthers cream with purple edges. Stigmas 3–3.5mm, flesh-pink, hairy on outsides. Immature fruits erect on more or less reflexed pedicels. Rostrum about 22mm, including stylar portion 2–2.5mm. Mericarps about 4.5mm. Discharge: seed-ejection (bristles).

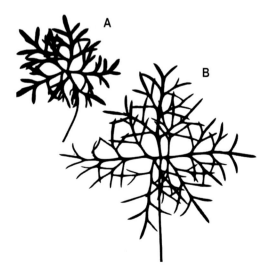

Figure 9.77. *G. incanum*: from R. Gorer, 1975: (A) coll. in June; (B) coll. in November; 3 and 6cm wide

South Africa.

This is a distinctive and showy species for a warm situation. It is not hardy in severe winters in Britain but regenerates reliably from seed. It may also be propagated from stem-cuttings and maintained under glass through the winter.
G. incanum var. *multifidum* (Sweet) Hilliard & Burtt. This is the form commonly cultivated in Britain, and to which the above description applies. *G. incanum* var. *incanum* has smaller, usually white, flowers and is highly ornamental.
    Has hybridised with 64. *G. robustum, q.v.*

Two other plants which I have grown belong to two closely related species briefly dealt with below. I am grateful to Mr B.L. Burtt for the identification of the first three representatives of the Incanum Group described here.

68a. G. magniflorum Knuth
Rootstock producing crowded short stems with rosette-like clusters of leaves. Divisions of leaves with central segments about 2mm wide; lobes about 1.5mm wide, few, toothless. Stipules cut into 3 or more segments. Glandular hairs present on upper stems, cymules, sepals and rostra. Inflorescence with branches and peduncles often widely divergent. Peduncles 1.5–7cm. Pedicels 1.5–4cm. Sepals about 5.5mm; mucro almost none. Petals about 10 x 8mm, heart-shaped with a wide notch, plum-purple with darker veins and a very clear white or greenish basal area; base with very weak hair-tufts at the sides and a few hairs in middle of front surface. Filaments white; anthers bluish. Stigmas 2mm, reddish. Rostrum about 18–22mm including stylar portion about 3mm. Mericarps about 3.5mm. Discharge: seed-ejection (bristles).

South Africa (Drakensberg in southern Natal).

This was received from Mr Jan Stephens in 1967 as *G. thodei* Knuth. The petal colour matches HCC 31 Orchid Purple, a very intense colour, not far from RHSCC Purple Group 87A. The plant is quite dwarf and is suitable for the rock garden. It has finally been lost at Cambridge after dying and being re-started several times from seed.

68b. G. drakensbergense Hilliard & Burtt. Compared with *G. magniflorum*, this had larger flowers that were sparser and less intensely coloured and were produced in October. Its petal-bases had distinctive features.

South Africa (Drakensberg in southern Natal).

Figure 9.78. *G. caffrum*: from D. Victor 1998 and cult. D. Victor, 1998; 11cm wide

The stock cultivated was collected at 2,750m on the Drakensberg in 1970 by Sir Peter Watkin-Williams. It had a much shorter life at Cambridge than *G. magniflorum*.

69. G. caffrum Ecklon & Zeyher (Figure 9.78)
Bushy and very leafy perennial with finely cut leaves which lack silky hairs. Flowers 22–31mm wide, pink or white, numerous and held well above the leaves. Sun. Summer.

Large, loose, bushy evergreen perennial, becoming woody at the base. Stems to 50cm and probably sometimes to 1m, with internodes mostly 3.5–12cm, clothed with backwardly appressed hairs and sometimes also spreading red-tipped glandular hairs. Leaves alternate or the upper opposite. Lower leaves with blade to about 10cm wide, divided to the base or nearly so into 5 or 7; divisions pinnately lobed $^3/_4$–$^5/_6$ of the way to the midrib; some of the lobes with 1 or 2 teeth. Upper leaves smaller, sometimes divided into 3. All leaf segments 1.5–5mm wide and 2–6 times as long as wide. All leaf-blades tending to redden, with rather small appressed hairs, those of the undersides mostly on the veins. Leaf-stalks with backwardly appressed hairs. Stipules to about 8mm, usually split into two, slightly hairy. Inflorescence diffuse. Peduncles about 1.5–15cm, erect, clothed as the stem. Pedicels about 1.5–3cm, erect or divergent and then bent below the calyx, clothed as the stem. Flowers erect, shallowly funnel-shaped. Sepals 5–9mm, felted with fine, forwardly directed, appressed hairs and with glandular hairs in addition; mucro about 1mm. Petals to 17 x 12mm, rounded or notched at apex, mid-pink with white base, sometimes with darker veins,

with a weak tuft of hairs on either edge near the base. Filaments enlarged at base, white with red tip, hairless. Anthers cream with red sutures and pink back. Style 5–6mm. Stigmas from just over 2mm to 3.5mm, dark red. Fruit erect. Rostrum 17–18mm including stylar portion about 4mm, with glandular and eglandular hairs. Carpels about 3.5mm, shaggy, with glandular and eglandular hairs. Discharge: seed-ejection (bristles).

South Africa (Natal and Cape).

Although the inflorescence of *G. caffrum* is very loose, the flowers held well above the bushy base of the plant on long stalks can make quite a good show. Hilliard & Burtt (1985) say the petals are usually white, and give a smaller size-range for the floral parts. *G. caffrum* may be damaged by frost but sows its seeds readily. It differs from *G. incanum* in its lack of silvery hairs on the backs of the leaves and on the sepals, and in the presence of some glandular hairs. It is less beautiful than *G. incanum*.

In nature it may root at the nodes, and it is subject to hybridisation.

THE SCHLECHTERI GROUP

Perennials without winter resting buds, sometimes woody at the base. Leaves various but not very elaborately cut, with broad segments, not noticeably thick. Presence of hairs on front surface of petal bases inconstant. Stamen-filaments slightly or moderately widened towards the base. Flowers white to pink, sometimes with a distinctively coloured centre. Immature fruit erect on spreading or reflexed pedicels.

Apparently several species would constitute this last group of southern African species in this book.

70. G. schlechteri Knuth (Figure 9.79, Plate 29)
Bushy glandular-hairy perennial to 30cm tall and with leaves to 6.5cm, sometimes to 8cm, wide. Flowers to 24mm wide, funnel-shaped. Highly variable; the best form available has pretty pink flowers with a very well-defined white eye and notched petals. Summer.

Densely branched, slender-stemmed perennial to about 30cm in height, without resting buds. Stem-internodes mostly 4–8cm, often red with copious red-tipped glandular hairs. Leaves mostly solitary, the uppermost paired. Blades of main leaves to 8cm wide, divided as far as $^1/_2$–$^2/_3$ into 5 or 7, weakly 5-angled in outline

Figure 9.79. *G. schlechteri*: from James Compton, 1989, coll. Sani Pass (Compton, D'Arcy & Rix [CDR] 217); 5cm wide

(even when 7-parted); divisions widely rhombic, sometimes overlapping, profusely or sparsely palmato-pinnately lobed in the apical half for $^{1}/_{4}$–$^{1}/_{3}$ their length, often red-edged; lobes as long as broad or less, toothed; teeth and tips of lobes obtuse or shortly pointed, weakly mucronate; upper surface dark green, with appressed eglandular hairs and sometimes, near the edge, loose glandular hairs; lower surface much paler, with eglandular and, sometimes, glandular hairs; leaf-stalks 3–4 times as long as blade; stipules to about 5mm, with 2–3 ovate-lanceolate glandular-hairy lobes. Upper leaves gradually smaller, simpler and with more open sinuses. Inflorescence diffuse, profusely branched, leafy. Peduncles 2–8cm; pedicels 1.5–3.4cm; both glandular-hairy. Flowers nodding in bud. Open flowers erect, funnel-shaped. Sepals 4–5.5mm, green, glandular-hairy; mucro 0.5mm or less. Petals to about 13 x 9mm, wedge-shaped or obovate, overlapping or separated, entire or notched, from just below the middle pale or deep pink with or without dark red veins, basal part white, extreme base with a weak tuft of hairs on the edges and front surface (the latter perhaps sometimes lacking). Stamen filaments white, slightly enlarged and slightly hairy at the base; anthers flesh-coloured with lilac sutures. Stigmas 1.5mm, yellowish-flesh-coloured. Pedicels spreading or reflexed, bent under the developing fruit. Fruit erect. Rostrum 16–19mm, glandular-hairy, with slender stylar portion about 1.5mm. Carpels about 3mm, bristly and with a few glandular hairs. Seeds about 2mm. Discharge: seed-ejection (bristles).

South Africa (Transvaal, Natal, Cape, Orange Free State), Lesotho.

My description of this variable plant is based on Hilliard & Burtt's revision (including dried specimens from South Africa supplied by Hilliard & Burtt – their numbers 15517 and 13489) and on two cultivated stocks: Compton, D'Arcy & Rix 217, Sani Pass (Cambridge accession 1989.0534 Compton) and Rachel Saunders, without collecting number (Silverhill Seeds, Cape Town), at 1,800–2,000m on Cathedral Peak, Drakensberg, Natal (Cambridge accession 1998.0466 Victor).

CDR 217 has been identified by Dr Hilliard as *G. schlechteri*. It has very attractive bright pink flowers with a sharply defined white eye and notched petals, while Victor's plant has a very pale pink flower with an ill-defined white eye and rounded petals. The notched petal is not normal for this species but is characteristic of *G. wakkerstroomianum* Knuth, a species which CDR 217 approaches in some other points! However, that differs in having no glandular hairs or, rarely, a few, and it seems best to allow this character to be the deciding one. I have seen a third stock in cultivation: it was raised by Alan Bremner from seed of MW (Michael Wickenden) 83 (locality details awaited). This has leaves with few, shallow obtuse teeth and petals about 8 x 5mm; it has no garden value.

71. G. flanaganii Knuth (Figure 9.80)
Bushy perennial with woody base, without any striking features. Leaves rather shallowly cut, with 3 or 5 divisions, wrinkled, with tips of lobes and teeth bluntly pointed or obtuse and mucronate, sometimes attractively red-edged. Glandular hairs present above. Flowers 25–31mm wide, pink. Early summer.

Straggling perennial from a bushy and woody base. Stems finely spreading-hairy, sometimes reddish. Leaves mostly alternate but

Figure 9.80. *G. flanaganii*: from F. & D. Hibberd (Axletree Nursery), Cambridge 1987.0141; 7cm wide

the uppermost paired. Lower leaves with blade to about 7cm wide, divided as far as $^2/_3$–$^3/_4$ into 5; mostly with broadly rhombic palmato-pinnately lobed divisions; lobes about as long as broad, entire or sparingly toothed. Teeth and tips of lobes bluntly pointed or obtuse and mucronate. Upper leaves gradually smaller, becoming trifid. All leaves matt green, wrinkled and appressed-bristly above, sometimes red-edged, paler beneath with spreading or appressed hairs. Leaf-stalks usually $1^1/_2$–$2^1/_2$ times as long as leaf-blade, with fine, sometimes dense, recurved hairs. Stipules to about 6mm, bristly, bifid or trifid with linear segments. Inflorescence diffuse. Peduncles mostly 2.5–12cm, hairy. Pedicels mostly 2.5–5cm, with eglandular and glandular hairs, the latter dark-tipped or clear-tipped. Flowers erect. Sepals 6–8mm, green, glandular, with mucro to about 1.5mm. Petals to 15 x 11mm, rounded or notched at apex, pink, with or without pale base and darker veins, with a weak tuft of hairs on either side at the base (and all across the front surface or not). Stamens with pale pink outwardly curved filaments that are moderately and evenly widened towards the hairy base, and blue or blue-edged anthers. Stigmas 1.5–2mm, pink. Pedicels usually spreading and turned upwards below the calyx. Rostrum 17–20mm, including stylar portion of 3mm, glandular-hairy. Carpels unknown. Discharge: seed-ejection (bristles). Early summer.

South Africa (Transkei, Cape).

Characters separating this from the generally smaller-flowered *G. ornithopodon* tend to break down. Introduced by Axletree Nursery. May scramble if supporting vegetation is available.

72. *G. ornithopodon* Ecklon & Zeyher
Similar to 71. *G. flanaganii* but the leaf divisions almost oblong, not rhombic, the central one with only two (sometimes three) pairs of pinnately arranged lobes, these only occasionally with a small tooth on the outer edge, the sepals smaller (4–5.5mm) and the petals smaller (7–8, sometimes to 10mm), sometimes white. Filaments slightly widened towards the base. Style probably 1.5–2mm. Discharge: seed-ejection (bristles).

South Africa (Cape).

A plant of untidy habit and low decorative value. Another similar South African species is *G. ornithopodioides* Hilliard & Burtt; it is immediately recognisable by its peltate leaves.

THE MACULATUM GROUP

Annuals or perennials. Upper parts usually with glandular hairs. Blades of basal leaves usually divided more than $^4/_5$. Sepal mucro $^1/_5$ or more as long as sepal. Petals without hairs across front surface (except in 75. *G. bicknellii*). Stamen-filaments enlarged at base. Pedicels of immature fruits erect. Rostrum with an evident stylar portion.

The group comprises the four species described here and one additional annual species closely related to 76. *G. carolinianum* (Aedo, 2000).

73. *G. maculatum* Linnaeus (Figure 9.81)
Perennial 50–70cm tall, sparsely leafy; main leaves with the divisions narrowly diamond-shaped and with very acute lobes and teeth; flowers partly in umbel-like clusters, about 30mm in diameter; petals pale to deep pink or white, rounded or slightly notched at apex; pedicels of immature fruits erect. Border, wild garden, sun or partial shade. May to July.

Rootstock compact and stout. Blades of basal leaves 5–20cm wide, divided as far as about $^9/_{10}$ into 5 or perhaps 7; divisions rather solid in outline but with rather wide notches between them, gradually tapered both ways from about the middle, the basal untoothed part of the margin long and nearly straight; lobes about $1^1/_2$ times as long as broad, diverging from midrib of the division at a narrow angle, toothed. Teeth and tips of lobes very acute. Stem-leaves paired, few, lowest sometimes more than 20cm wide, widely spaced by the long stem-internodes, decreasing rapidly in size and length of stalk upwards, the uppermost stalkless and with 3 divisions. Hairs mostly eglandular, those of the stem appressed to the surface; very long, small-headed glandular hairs sometimes present on sepals and at base of rostrum.

Figure 9.81. *G. maculatum*: from Alpine Garden Soc., 1969, coll. USA: N. Carolina; 13.5cm wide

Inflorescence of a few very long-peduncled lower cymules and groups of flowers without peduncles. Flowers upwardly inclined, shallowly bowl-shaped. Sepals 8–10mm; mucro 2–3.5mm. Petals 18–19 x 10–12mm, broadest near the tip, apex rounded or shallowly notched, base abruptly widened, bright or pale pink, fading to white at base, veins translucent; base with a tuft of hairs at either side, fringed above the tufts, without hairs all across front surface. Stamens loosely spreading when functional; filaments slightly shorter than sepals, pink, abruptly enlarged and with marginal hair-fringes at the base; anthers greyish. Each nectary with a tuft of hairs at the top. Style about 8.5mm. Stigmas 2–3mm, flesh-pink. Immature fruits erect on erect pedicels. Rostrum 23–25mm, including stylar portion about 4mm. Mericarps 4–5mm, blackish. Discharge: seed-ejection (bristles).

E. North America (westwards to Manitoba and Kansas).

A rather tall perennial of moderate appeal. Usually seen as pale-flowered plants, but a deeper-coloured one grown at Cambridge seems preferable. Its natural habitat is "fields, meadows and open woods" (Jones & Jones, 1943). The rootstock is easily divided.

On comparing the short description with that of 8. *G. sylvaticum* it will be seen that *G. maculatum* differs in being sparsely leafy and in having narrowly diamond-shaped leaf-divisions. These are also untoothed from about the broadest part downwards. Apart from this, *G. maculatum* has larger, typically pink, petals, without hairs across the front surface. There is virtually no resemblance to 16. *G. pratense*.

G. maculatum var. *album* Lauman. Plant without anthocyanin. Petals white. A beautiful plant.

74. G. oreganum Howell (Figure 9.82)
Perennial about 60cm tall with leaves recalling those of 16. *G. pratense*; inflorescence not very dense; flowers 43–47mm in diameter; petals deep purplish pink, rounded at apex; immature fruits erect on erect pedicels. Border. June, July.

Perennial with a compact rootstock. Blades of basal leaves 10–20cm wide, divided nearly to the base into 7; divisions tapered both ways from above the middle, broad but rather open in outline, deeply and coarsely pinnately lobed; lobes up to 2 or $2\frac{1}{2}$ times as long as broad, sometimes curving outwards, with few or several teeth. Teeth and tips of lobes acute. Stem-leaves paired, decreasing in size abruptly after the first few pairs. Glandular hairs present on upper stems, sepals and rostra. Inflorescence rather diffuse.

Figure 9.82. *G. oreganum*: from Edinburgh, 1959; 10.5cm wide

Flowers saucer-shaped, upwardly inclined. Peduncles mostly 4–11cm. Pedicels mostly $1\frac{1}{2}$–$2\frac{1}{2}$ times as long as sepals. Sepals about 10mm; mucro 2.5–4.5mm. Petals up to 23 x 21mm, rather evenly tapered to the base, deep purplish pink; base with a dense tuft of hairs on either edge and beyond that a fringe, but without hairs across front surface. Filaments curving outwards, abruptly enlarged at base and there with minute hair-fringes, pink; anthers yellow with purple edges. Each nectary topped by a dense hair-tuft. Style 9–11mm. Stigmas 2.5–3mm, reddish. Immature fruits erect on erect pedicels. Rostrum about 30mm, including stylar portion 3–4mm. Mericarps 4.5mm. Discharge: seed-ejection (bristles).

W. United States (S. Washington, Oregon, N. California).

The above description is taken from plants growing at Cambridge which were received as seed in 1959 from Edinburgh. This is a lovely species with very large flowers, and should be better known. I have raised new plants from seed, but the species should be easy to propagate by division.

G. oreganum has some resemblance to 16. *G. pratense* but the leaf-cutting is coarser, the typical flower colour is different (HCC 32/1 Petunia Purple, similar to RHSCC Purple Group, between 78B and 78C), the stamens curve outwards all the time the flower is open, the flower is upwardly inclined and the immature fruits are erect on erect pedicels.

75. G. bicknellii Britton (Figure 9.83A)
Spring annual or overwintering annual. Blades of basal leaves not more than 10cm wide, dark green,

firm in texture, divided nearly to the base into 7; divisions broadest above the middle, deeply 3-lobed; lobes about twice as long as broad, with several more or less deep teeth. Teeth and lobes almost parallel-sided, obtuse or acute at tips, the teeth often bent outwards. Stem-leaves similar to the basal. Stems usually three from the rosette or from a short erect central stem, regularly forked, producing a diffuse leafy inflorescence. Glandular hairs present on upper stems, sepals and rostra. Cymules in fruit normally with at least one pedicel twice as long as sepals. Flowers somewhat funnel-shaped, about 9mm in diameter. Sepals 4–5mm; mucro about 1mm. Petals about 7 x 3.5mm, notched, pale pink with darker forked and almost looped veins; base with a tuft of hairs on either side and hairs between tufts across front surface. Filaments enlarged and with fine hair-fringes at base; anthers bluish. Stigmas less than 1mm, crimson. Immature fruits erect on erect pedicels. Rostrum 16–17mm, including a distinct stylar portion 2–3mm. Mericarps about 2.5mm, black. Discharge: seed-ejection (bristles).

North America (Canada, E. United States).

A species with small pink flowers and distinctive thickish, dark green, slightly shiny leaves. The leaf-divisions are not as blunt as those of the round-leaved Eurasian annuals, 116. *G. molle*, 114. *G. pusillum* and 7. *G. rotundifolium*, and not as finely dissected as those of 51. *G. columbinum* and 87. *G. dissectum*. The flowers appear quite deep reddish pink because of the strong veining.

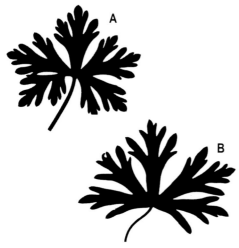

Figure 9.83. (A) *G. bicknellii*: from Vancouver B.G., 1978; (B) *G. carolinianum*: Antwerp B.G., 1971; 4 and 4.5cm wide

A hybrid with 76. *G. carolinianum* was found in the Cambridge Botanic Garden in 1981. The upper leaves appeared intermediate between those of *G. bicknellii* and the upper rosette leaves of *G. carolinianum*. There was no fruit development whatever.

76. *G. carolinianum* Linnaeus (Figure 9.83B)

Annual, usually behaving as a spring annual. Blades of basal leaves about 5cm wide, those produced first rounded in outline, divided as far as about $^1/_2$ into 7; divisions broadest at the apex, some unlobed, some very shallowly 3-lobed. Blades of later rosette-leaves and of stem-leaves divided as far as $^3/_4$ or $^6/_7$ into 5 or 7; divisions like those of 75. *G. bicknellii*. Stem with a very long first internode, then a few solitary and paired, or only paired, leaves. The paired leaves subtend branches producing dense umbel-like clusters of flowers, sometimes with one or two perfect cymules. Glandular hairs present on pedicels, sepals and rostra. Pedicels in fruit about $^1/_2$–$1^1/_2$ times as long as sepals. Flowers funnel-shaped. Sepals 5–8mm, sometimes very broad; mucro about 1.25mm. Petals 5 x 2mm or sometimes considerably larger, white or pale pink; base with a few hairs on the margins. Stigmas about 1mm. Immature fruits erect on erect pedicels. Rostrum about 12–13mm including a distinct stylar portion 1.5mm long. Mericarps 3–3.5mm, black. Discharge: seed-ejection (bristles), empty mericarps usually shed.

North America (Canada, E. and S. United States, N.W. Mexico). Introduced in China.

This annual usually has insignificant white flowers but is sometimes grown by collectors. It differs considerably from 75. *G. bicknellii* in habit though certainly closely related to it. In readily shedding its empty mericarps it resembles the Tuberosum Group and the Platypetalum Group. This condition has probably evolved independently in this case; it prevents the interference with discharge in other flowers in the crowded inflorescence that would be caused by retention of empty mericarps.
G. carolinianum var. *confertiflorum* Fernald has dense inflorescences and is the plant described above.
G. carolinianum var. *carolinianum* has a more open inflorescence. A revision by Aedo (2000) does not recognise this difference taxonomically.

G. carolinianum has shown astonishing hybridising ability in the hands of Alan Bremner (see Appendix III).

THE FREMONTII GROUP

Perennials with a thick rootstock. Blades of basal leaves divided as far as about $^6/_7$ or less; divisions rather broad, with few coarse shallow lobes and teeth. At least the upper parts of the plant strongly glandular-hairy (except in 79b. *G. atropurpureum*). Flowers strictly erect, usually pink or purplish, their stamens and long stigmas (4–6mm) curving outwards above the petals which are hairy across the front surface for about $^1/_4$ to $^1/_2$ their length. Sepals with mucro not more than $^1/_8$ of their length. Immature fruits erect on spreading or reflexed pedicels.

Western North America, mainly in the Rocky Mountains but in the south spreading westwards and entering Mexico in Baja California. There are several species but the taxonomy of the group is difficult. The five species covered here are all said to have the hairs on the front surface of the petals restricted to the basal quarter (Jones & Jones, 1943) but this limit is commonly exceeded. The Richardsonii Group, which follows, is closely related.

77. *G. nervosum* Rydberg (*G. strigosum* Rydberg not N.L. Burman; *G. strigosius* St John; *G. viscosissimum* Fischer & Meyer var. *nervosum* (Rydberg) Hitchcock) (Figure 9.84)

Sticky-hairy aromatic perennial with rather broad leaf-divisions, usually with a single flowering stem, forking above; inflorescence diffuse; flowers erect, 24–40mm in diameter, pink or purplish red; petals notched, with dark veins and with hairs across front surface for about $^1/_3$ of their length; stamens and stigmas curving outwards above the petals; immature fruits erect on erect, spreading or reflexed pedicels. Border, wild garden, sun. May onwards.

Perennial with a very stout, deep, woody rootstock. Blades of basal leaves 5–20cm wide, light green, divided as far as about $^4/_5$ into 7; divisions broadest above the middle, palmately lobed at apex, unlobed part of margin nearly straight; lobes up to $1^1/_2$ times, or the central lobe twice, as long as broad, toothed, the outer teeth often bent outwards. Teeth and tips of lobes acute. Stem-leaves few, paired or the first two solitary, much smaller than the basal, the lowest with 5 divisions which are broadest about the middle, their lobes and teeth spreading or incurved, sometimes both on the same plant. Plant rather strongly hairy, hairs on upper parts mostly glandular and sticky, not purple. Stem solitary with a very long first internode, forming a diffusely branched inflorescence above. Peduncles mostly 1–3cm. Pedicels mostly 1–2 times as long as sepals. Flowers erect, flat. Sepals 7–10mm; mucro about 0.5–1.25mm. Petals 13–22 x 7–16mm, from about $1^1/_4$–2 times as long as broad, some of them more or less notched at apex, abruptly enlarged just above the base, pale or deep pink, usually fading

Figure 9.84. *G. nervosum*: from Vancouver B.G., 1978, coll. Canada: Botanic Valley, British Columbia; 13.5 and 8cm wide

to white at base, with weak or strong darker, forking veins; base with a dense tuft of hairs on the sides and on front surface and with more scattered hairs extending over basal $^1/_3$–$^1/_2$ of front surface. Filaments slightly longer than sepals, curving outwards above, slightly and evenly enlarged towards base, pink, bearing rather coarse hairs over most of their length; anthers yellow with purple edges, or pink. A more or less distinct tuft of hairs present over each nectary. Style about as long as sepals; stigmas 4–6mm, reddish, widely spreading. Immature fruits erect on erect, spreading or reflexed pedicels. Rostrum 21–35mm, including stylar portion 2–5mm. Mericarps about 5.5mm. Discharge: seed-ejection (bristles).

W. North America (British Columbia and Alberta to N. California and Colorado).

This species is of moderate interest for the border and, in its smaller forms, for the larger rock garden. It is very variable; thus the leaf-shape may vary, the lower stem hairs may be spreading or appressed, and the petals have a large range in size and they vary in shape independently of this. The name *G. incisum* (Torrey & Gray) Brewer & Watson belongs strictly to 74. *G. oreganum*, but for a long period American authors applied it in error to the present plant, which

Figure 9.85. *G. viscosissimum*: from Alpine Garden Soc., 1965, coll. USA: Wyoming; 9cm wide

doubtless explains why Bloom's of Bressingham, Norfolk, at one time offered *G. nervosum* as *G. incisum*. Bloom's stock is a rather small neat form with the hairs of the lower parts appressed, those of the upper parts short, and with well-coloured flowers of moderate size; it is certainly the most garden-worthy variant out of four that I have seen. I have had it in flower as early as May and as late as November.

Propagation of *G. nervosum* is by seed or by division of the rootstock; it may not be possible to obtain pieces with adequate young root-growth, and careful nursing will then be necessary.

78. *G. viscosissimum* Fischer & Meyer (Figure 9.85)
Similar to 77. *G. nervosum* but stems glandular-hairy from the base up, basal leaves apparently larger; inflorescence beyond the first fork with some greatly contracted branches and suppressed peduncles, producing umbel-like clusters of flowers accompanied by cymules with more or less reduced peduncles; pedicels longer, 4–8 times as long as sepals, strongly reflexed under the erect immature fruits; sepals to 12mm, with mucro 1–1.5mm. Stylar portion of rostrum about 6mm. Discharge: seed-ejection (bristles). June and again later.

West North America (British Columbia and Alberta to N. California and South Dakota).

My acquaintance with this species is limited to one stock obtained from the Alpine Garden Society in 1965, originating from seed collected in Wyoming, and plants seen at Foston Nursery, Lincolnshire. It is a most beautiful plant, at least in the earlier stages of flowering, as it has large flattish pale pink, finely veined flowers with a white centre. The petals are up to 23 x 19mm. It may flower repeatedly through the season. Because of the

amount of variation in both *G. viscosissimum* and 77. *G. nervosum*, it is said by American authors that the two cannot always be distinguished, and some prefer to treat *G. nervosum* as a variety of *G. viscosissimum*.

79. *G. fremontii* Gray (Figure 9.86, Plate 30)
Sticky-hairy, unpleasantly scented perennial; blades of main leaves divided as far as $^3/_4$; divisions with few coarse lobes and teeth at apex; inflorescence diffuse, leafy, prolifically branched; flowers 35–40mm in diameter, like those of 77. *G. nervosum*. Border, sun. June onwards.

Perennial with thick rootstock, more branched than in 77. *G. nervosum* and 78. *G. viscosissimum*. Blades of basal leaves 5–10cm wide, divided as far as $^5/_6$ into 5 or 7; divisions broadest near apex, sides of the three middle ones concave in the lower unlobed part, lobed at apex for $^1/_5 - ^1/_4$ of their length; lobes mostly broader than long, usually with one or two teeth of which the outermost on each division are bent outwards. Teeth and tips of lobes obtuse or acute. Stem-leaves numerous, paired or the first one or two solitary, decreasing gradually in size and length of stalk upwards, with 3 or 5 very coarsely lobed divisions. Hairs glandular except on upper leaf-surfaces and sometimes stalks of basal leaves and lower internodes. Flowering stems usually several together, with mostly paired branches, forming an extensive and diffuse inflorescence. Cymules sometimes 3-flowered, upper often with short or suppressed peduncles. Pedicels mostly $2^1/_2$–4 times as long as sepals. Flowers the same as those of 77. *G. nervosum*, with petals not less than 16mm, sometimes clearly

Figure 9.86. *G. fremontii*: from P.F. Yeo, 1973, coll. USA: Colorado; x $^2/_3$

notched. Immature fruits erect on spreading or strongly reflexed pedicels. Rostrum about 18mm, including stylar portion about 3mm. Mericarps 4.5mm. Discharge: seed-ejection (bristles).

West North America (Wyoming to New Mexico and Arizona).

I have grown two stocks of this species from the Rocky Mountains in the neighbourhood of Boulder, Colorado, one collected by me in 1973 and one by Professor H.E. Moore at the same time; the first had strongly coloured and veined flowers, and the second rather washy pink flowers. I have only grown them in open beds in dry Cambridge soil. They make big rootstocks, partly above the ground, and these tend to die off in parts, sometimes leaving the surviving crowns imperfectly rooted. Frequent replanting therefore seems advisable to keep the plants in good growth. *G. fremontii* can be quite showy, and flowers for a long time, but is rather ungainly in habit.

As a result of introductions since edn.1 the two following specific names have to be accounted for; these names have been much in dispute.

79a. G. caespitosum E. James (Figure 9.87)
Differing from *G. fremontii* in that the stems become trailing or scrambling and that, usually, the petals are dark purple.

79b. G. atropurpureum A. Heller (*G. caespitosum* in the sense of A. Gray, 1849)
Trailing and scrambling like *G. caespitosum* but without glandular hairs and usually with pink petals (but Moore, 1943, thought darker red to purple the more normal condition).

Moore (1943) amplifies the above description of the habit by saying that the cymules are scattered in the axils of the leaves.

Both occur in the Rocky Mountains of the United States, but *G. atropurpureum* also extends into Mexico. *G. caespitosum* was unrecognisable from its scanty original description in 1823 and its author had collected no specimens of it. Thus the application of the name was only settled as a result of visits by botanists to the type locality in 1921. Meanwhile the same plant had been described as *G. fremontii* var. *parryi* Engelmann and then raised to specific rank as *G. parryi* (Engelmann) A. Heller, on the mistaken supposition that *G. caespitosum* James was not validly published. These names are now synonyms of *G. caespitosum* James.

Holmgren (1997) treats all three taxa as belonging to one species, the name of which on grounds of priority is *G. caespitosum*. *G. fremontii* is then a synonym of this, though it may be recognised at varietal rank, as *G. caespitosum* var. *fremontii* (A.

Figure 9.87. *G. caespitosum*: cult. P.F. Yeo (from D. Victor, 1999); see 79. *G. fremontii*; 6cm wide

Gray) Dorn. Although it is clear that the three species that I am recognising have only minor distinctions, I prefer to keep them up so as not to upset the nomenclature of *G. fremontii*.

The existence of a small-flowered form of *G. caespitosum* with very strongly coloured narrow and recurved petals was mentioned by Mrs Robin Parer at a meeting in England in 1999.

THE RICHARDSONII GROUP

Similar to the Fremontii Group but leaf-divisions tending to be more gradually tapered beyond the widest part, and with lobes and teeth not curved outwards. Sepal mucro usually more than $1/8$ the length of the sepal. Petals white to lavender or pink, hairs on front surface extending from base for $1/2$–$3/4$ the length of the petal.

Jones & Jones (1943) deal with two Californian species that they consider closely related to *G. richardsonii*. Moore (1943) mentions one Mexican species (*G. albidum* Hanks & Small) as being closely related to *G. richardsonii*; this itself is a member of his series Lata, containing four species. Thus there could be seven species in the group. The white petals of *G. richardsonii* turn pale yellow on drying, but I do not know whether this is true of other white-flowered members of the group.

80. G. richardsonii Fischer & Trautvetter (Figure 9.88, Plate 31)
Perennial, 30–60cm tall, with bright green, slightly glossy and inconspicuously hairy leaves. Inflorescence diffuse. Flowers about 24–28mm in diameter; petals white or tinged with pink, usually lightly purple-veined, not usually notched. Stigmas greenish or yellowish. Wild garden, water garden, sun. May onwards.

Figure 9.88. *G. richardsonii*: from P.F. Yeo, 1973, coll. USA: Colorado; 9cm wide

Perennial with a thick rootstock. Blades of basal leaves 5–10cm wide, divided as far as $^2/_3$ or $^5/_6$ into 5 or 7; divisions tapered gradually or abruptly both ways from above the middle, lobed at apex for $^1/_3$ of their length or slightly more; lobes slightly shorter to slightly longer than broad, sparsely toothed. Teeth and tips of lobes broadly pointed to acute, rather symmetric. Stem-leaves paired or the first one solitary, numerous, decreasing gradually to a very small size, divisions 5 or 3, then with the middle one much the largest. Plant less hairy than the species of the Fremontii Group (numbers 77–79); non-glandular hairs more or less appressed; glandular hairs red-tipped, dense in the inflorescence. Stems solitary or few together, rather regularly forking, forming an extensive and diffuse inflorescence. Peduncles mostly 2–6cm. Pedicels mostly $1^1/_2$–4 times as long as sepals. Flowers erect, flat. Sepals about 6mm; mucro about 1.5mm. Petals 12 x 6–18 x 15mm (i.e. variable in shape), rounded at apex, white or sometimes pale pink, with or without faint purple veins; base strongly hairy all over front surface, hairs sparser upwards but extending $^1/_2$–$^3/_4$ the length of the petal. Filaments curving outwards above, moderately and evenly enlarged towards base, bearing rather coarse hairs over most of their length. Anthers lilac or greyish. Stigmas 3–4mm, greenish or yellowish. Immature fruits erect on erect, spreading or reflexed pedicels. Rostrum 13–17mm, including stylar portion about 1mm. Mericarps about 3.5mm. Discharge: seed-ejection (bristles).

West North America (British Columbia and Saskatchewan to South Dakota, New Mexico and California).

In nature *G. richardsonii* is decidedly variable; I collected a good form as seed in Colorado in 1973; it has broad rounded petals and a taller habit than plants I have received from horticultural sources.

The species grows in damp places and should be tried in waterside situations in gardens. The rootstock tends to develop in the same way as that of 77. *G. fremontii* and re-planting should therefore be carried out with similar frequency.

81. G. californicum Jones & Jones (Figure 9.89)
A tall, straggling glandular-hairy perennial. Leaves with 5 wedge-shaped or rhombic divisions that have lobes but very few teeth. Flowers to 40mm wide, numerous, pink with a white centre. Hairs present over half the length of the petals. Stamens and stigmas curving outwards.

Straggling perennial to at least 60cm. Rootstock stout. Blades of basal leaves to 8cm wide, divided as far as $^3/_4$ –$^4/_5$ into 5, with a more or less narrow basal sinus; divisions rhombic or wedge-shaped, 3-lobed at apex, the lobes as long as broad or a little more, occasionally with a tooth on one side; tips of lobes and teeth bluntly pointed. Leaf-stalks about 3 times as long as blade, with glandular and longer eglandular hairs. Stipules to 20mm, lanceolate, tapered into a thread-like tip, densely eglandular-hairy. Stem leaves numerous, stalked, their blades divided as far as $^5/_6$ into 5; basal divisions entire, lanceolate, others with 2 or 3 lobes; lobes rarely toothed, acuminate. Leaf-stalks clothed as those of basal leaves. Stipules to 10mm, like the basal. The upper leaves shorter still and

Figure 9.89. *G. californicum*: from D. Victor, cult. Yeo; 9cm wide

broader. Stems with the leaves (mostly) paired and with the same hair-types as the leaf-stalks, rather slender, with middle internodes to 15cm, upper shorter but still relatively long, so that the inflorescence is very· loose. Peduncles to 13cm, glandular-hairy, erect; pedicels to 5.5cm, glandular-hairy, erect. Flowers erect, saucer-shaped. Sepals about 8mm, green or purplish, densely glandular-hairy, with some longer eglandular hairs, and mucro about 1.5mm. Petals to 21 x 14mm, weakly notched at apex, deep pink fading to white in basal $^1/_3$, with fine darker feathered veins (or petals white), with a dense tuft of hairs all across the base and scattered hairs over the remainder of the basal $^1/_2$ of the upper surface. Filaments slightly longer than the sepals, curving outwards, pale pink, widened evenly towards the base, with long, straight, rather coarse hairs towards the base; anthers pink. Style purple; stigmas 5.5mm (6–9mm according to Munz's *California Flora*), divergent, yellow outside, pink inside. Fruit erect. Rostrum 18–22mm, including stylar portion of 5–6mm, which has short simple forwardly divergent hairs. Carpels 5mm, with glandular and eglandular hairs. Discharge: seed-ejection (bristles).

United States (California).

Related to 80. *G. richardsonii* and with similar leaves but a very loose inflorescence. Differing mainly in the larger, more strongly coloured flowers, longer stylar portion of the rostrum and longer stigmas. Also related to 77. *G. nervosum* and differing from that in its almost toothless leaves, longer internodes, pale-centred flowers with longer stigmas and longer stylar portion of rostrum. My description is based on a plant from David Victor: NNS 98 303, from Slate Mountain, Tulare County, California. Plants vary in the intensity of petal-colouring.

THE BELLUM GROUP

Perennials with few or no basal leaves. Blades of main leaves divided nearly to the base into 3, 5 or 7; divisions pinnately lobed; lobes sometimes pinnately toothed. Hairs eglandular. Inflorescence diffuse. Petals rounded or slightly notched; hairs at the base variable. Stigmas 3–7mm.

S. and Central Mexico and Guatemala.

Moore (1943) named informally a series Bella comprising seven species including *G. schiedeanum*, described here. I have followed him in basing the name of this group on *G. bellum* Rose. Some other species of this group, together with *G. alpicola* Loesener in Moore's series Nivea, could be useful rock garden plants.

Figure 9.90. *G. schiedeanum*: from Logan B.G., 1974; 5 and 6cm wide

82. *G. schiedeanum* Schlechtendal (*G. purpusii* Knuth) (Figure 9.90)

Rather low-growing perennial; blades of principal leaves 5–10cm wide, their divisions narrow at base and enormously widened at the middle or above, pinnately lobed and with the teeth arranged pinnately on the lobes, wrinkled and slightly glossy above, very pale beneath and usually made more so by the dense hair-clothing; flowers about 30mm in diameter; petals not notched, lavender. Rock garden, front of border, ground-cover, sun. June to September.

Rootstock thick, forming short horizontal rhizomes and bearing large swollen roots. Basal leaves few; basal and lower stem-leaves rounded or kidney-shaped in outline, divided into 5 or 7, the middle division free nearly to the base, the others separated for $^2/_3$–$^3/_4$ of their length; divisions overlapping one another, broadest near the middle, pinnately lobed, margins of unlobed portion with concave profile; lobes about $1^1/_2$ times as long as wide, widely spreading, enormously increasing the width of the division, most of them pinnately toothed with teeth of almost equal size on either side; upper surface slightly glossy, wrinkled, recurved at edges, lower very pale, not entirely on account of the dense hair-covering running along veins and margins. Teeth and tips of lobes acute or blunt with a small point. Stem leaves mostly paired, upper similar to lower, lobes of basal divisions often without teeth. Plant without glandular hairs. Stems slender, reddish; branches solitary, paired or in threes, forming a diffuse inflorescence. Cymules with one or, usually, two flowers. Peduncles mostly 6–12cm but up to 18 or even 28cm. Pedicels 1–4 times as long as sepals. Flowers erect. Sepals 6–7mm; mucro 1–1.5mm. Petals about 15–16 x 12–13mm, broadest near apex, rounded or faintly notched, evenly tapered to base, medium purplish violet, white at extreme base, veins pink; base with a well-developed tuft of hairs on either edge and sometimes a few hairs in a narrow band across front surface. Filaments slightly longer than sepals, curving outwards above, white, slightly enlarged at base and here stiffly hairy. Style less than $^2/_3$ as long as sepals. Stigmas 3.5–4mm, pink and with a few coarse hairs on back, yellowish on front. Immature fruits erect on usually erect pedicels. Rostrum about 18mm, with stylar portion scarcely 1mm. Mericarps 3–4mm. Discharge: seed-ejection (bristles).

South Mexico (San Luis Potosi to Vera Cruz and Oaxaca).

The natural altitudinal range of *G. schiedeanum* is 1,050–3,350m, with most occurrences between 1,800 and 3,050m.

Moore (1943) described considerable variation in *G. schiedeanum* and placed four other specific names as synonyms of it. The leaves are not always twice pinnately cut, as described here, and the flower colour can be purple, red-purple, and perhaps white, as well as lavender as in our plant (which is near RHSCC Violet Group 87B). The cultivated plant was first seen by me in 1974; it was then growing unlabelled at Logan Botanic Garden, Wigtownshire, Scotland, a satellite of Edinburgh B.G. The above description is almost entirely based on this cultivated material but another stock with less hair on the underside of the leaves has been collected by a Cambridge expedition to Mexico (accession 1996.0414, Kerley, Pigott & Pigott no. V.29).

G. schiedeanum is a rather attractive plant, and suitable for a warm situation on the rock garden. In the spring of 1979 it was very late in starting into growth; as we had had severe cold and a long period of repeated thawing and freezing, I suspect the only surviving growth at the end of the winter was several centimetres below ground. In 1982 the plant came up at a normal time despite lower temperatures in the preceding winter, and I believe this was caused by the long-lasting snow-cover. The rootstock can easily be divided. I have never been able to obtain viable seed from plants of the Logan stock growing at Cambridge.

A plant with leaves like ours was cultivated at Darmstadt, Germany, early in the twentieth century, and was made the basis of *G. purpusii* Knuth, one of the names reduced to the synonymy of *G. schiedeanum* by Moore (1943).

THE DELTOIDEUM GROUP

Perennials with a stout rootstock producing few basal leaves and trailing stems. Leaf-blades with 3 or 5 rhomboidal, sharply toothed, divisions. Peduncles very long. Petals hairy almost throughout, notched, reflexed beyond the sepals. Pedicels spreading or reflexed when fruit is immature.

Moore (1943) assigned *G. deltoideum* to his informally published Series Deltoidea which, after revision (Moore, 1951), comprises seven Mexican species.

83. *G. deltoideum* Hanks & Small (Figure 9.91, Plate 32)
Perennial with trailing stems bearing marbled leaves with 3 or 5 rhomboidal, blunt-toothed divisions. Flowers rising above the leaves on long stalks, pink, with very hairy petals that are turned back beyond the tips of the sepals as if wilting (because the petals are reflexed a flower-diameter is not given). Spring and early summer.

Perennial with slender much-branched trailing red stems clothed with recurved eglandular hairs and very small glandular hairs, the lower internodes mostly less than 4cm, so that the plant is bushy, upper to 7.5cm. Basal leaves few, absent in flowering plants. Main leaves paired, with blade to 6.5cm wide, divided as far as $^4/_5$–$^5/_6$ into 3 or 5; divisions mainly rhomboidal, pinnately or palmato-pinnately lobed, very unequal, the terminal usually predominant, the basal so much smaller than the laterals that the leaf may be considered to have only 3 divisions; lobes ovate, not longer than broad, few-toothed; teeth and tips of lobes mostly obtuse and mucronate; upper surface clothed with forwardly

Figure 9.91. *G. deltoideum*: from Kew, 1987, coll. K.D. Rushforth (Mexico); 7cm wide

directed hairs, bright matt green marbled with large yellow-green patches, sometimes red-edged, lower surface much paler, similarly hairy to the upper. Stipules to 7mm, ovate-lanceolate and tailed, hairy, soon brown. Leaf-stalks about as long as the blades, clothed as the stems, red. Peduncles 12–14cm, arising from the prostrate stem, about $3/4$ –$2^1/4$ times as long as the adjacent leaves, clothed as the stems except that the eglandular hairs are straight. Pedicels 2–3 times as long as the sepal bodies, their glandular hairs not so short as on the stem. Flowers turned towards the light. Sepals about 8mm, green, tinged with brown at the base, with large and small eglandular hairs and glandular hairs nearly as long as the longest eglandular; mucro about 1.5mm. Petals to 19 x 13mm, crumpled, reflexed vertically over the tips of the sepals, not overlapping, deeply notched, mid-pink with paler base which is drawn out into a densely bearded claw with hairs all across the front surface, these extending over all but the apical $1/5$ of the petal. Stamens $1/2$ as long again as the sepals; filaments curving outwards, with sparse long hairs, slightly widened towards the base, flesh-pink above; anthers greyish. Styles at first shorter than stamens, then elongating to equal them. Stigmas about 4.5mm, red with whitish receptive surfaces, spreading when receptive. Pedicels spreading or reflexed while fruit is ripening and hooked under the young fruit. Rostrum 2–2.5cm, tapered gradually into a slender stylar portion, hairy. Carpels about 3.5mm, hairy. Discharge: seed-ejection (bristles).

Mexico (Jalisco province).

This was introduced by Mr Keith Rushforth and first raised at Kew. Derivatives of this importation at Cambridge died out, owing to my being unable to deal with the needs of all my plants. It does appear to need some special care, probably just prompt propagation (by seed or cuttings) when it is looking unhappy. If it has been lost, it would be well worth reintroduction. Mr Rushforth found it in maize fields under *Abies* and *Pinus* at 3,400m. In habit it shows some resemblance to the Asiatic species 30. *G. swatense*. The centre of the flower is like that of 77. *G. nervosum* and 78. *G. viscosissimum*. The manner in which the petals are reflexed is, as far as is known, unique in this genus. However, this may be a feature of this sample alone, as it is not mentioned by Moore (1943).

THE CORDILLERAN GROUP

Mainly small-flowered species of the Mexican and Andean cordillera.

I have very little understanding of the numerous species of the Andes, never having attempted a taxonomic revision of them. However, two of them need inclusion here and several have been used widely in crossing experiments by Alan Bremner. The results of these indicate close relationships among them and with other groups. These might lead eventually to a taxonomic grouping of Cordilleran species together with members of the Sessiliflorum Group and the Potentilloides Group. One species, 60. *G. sessiliflorum*, is already recognised as spanning the Australasian and the Andean geographical areas.

Of species not treated in this edition I have grown three named ones from Mexico collected by Utrera and others, one unidentified from Costa Rica collected by Thomas Schulz (perhaps also grown by Bremner) and one unidentified from Peru from Mrs Robin Parer. Alan Bremner's work covers another unidentified species from Chile. The three Mexican ones, all quite distinct in the living state, were *G. subulato-stipulatum* Knuth, *G. kerberi* Knuth and *G. vulcanicola* Small.

84. G. herrerae Knuth (Figure 9.92, Plate 33)
Small-leaved bushy perennial without winter resting buds. Leaf-divisions three-lobed at the tip, giving a rounded outline to the whole blade. Cymules two-flowered, borne among the leaves. Flowers 11–12mm wide, deep ruby red, with white centre, devoid of darker veins.

Stems arising from a long taproot, to 12mm thick but constricted at the neck in young plants. Habit bushy with much-branched stems reaching at least 50cm, but only 3mm thick when dried. Stems thinly backwardly appressed-hairy. Basal leaves with lamina commonly to 5cm wide, exceptionally to 6.5cm wide, divided as far as $2/3$–$3/4$ into 5; divisions with the undivided part having straight or slightly concave margins, palmately lobed at the apex for $1/2$ their length or less, giving the blade a kidney-shaped or occasionally nearly circular outline; lobes with 0–2 teeth; teeth and tips of lobes very obtuse, even straight across the top; surfaces bright green, sparsely hairy, with hairs of the underside somewhat spreading. Basal stipules apparently to 15mm, acute, minutely hairy. Petioles to about 5 times as long as blade, not more than 1mm thick when dried, with sparse backwardly appressed hairs, especially towards the apex. Stem-leaves paired, unequal, gradually smaller and shorter-stalked upwards, with hairier stalks, more pentagonal blades and deeper incisions (to about $5/6$). Stipules of stem-leaves to 3–6mm, lanceolate, downy. Most nodes with a branch and, except the very lowest, a cymule; internodes mainly in the range 5–10cm; inflorescence therefore large, loose and leafy. Lower peduncles 2.5–3.5cm and longer than the

Figure 9.92. *G. herrerae*: from D. McClintock, Cambridge 1975.0027; 5cm wide

pedicels; upper less than 1cm and shorter than the pedicels. Pedicels 10–25mm. Flowers cup-shaped and so less wide than would be expected from the petal-length, more or less erect. Sepals 3.5mm, enlarging to 5mm in fruit, with 3 main veins, moderately to sparsely clothed with small appressed hairs; mucro 0.5–1mm. Petals 5–6mm, to about 3.5mm wide, weakly notched at apex and contracted into a short claw at the base, rather deep pink with 5 colourless veins and rather extensive white base; claw with a few long fine hairs on each edge. Stamen filaments white, considerably widened at base and there with a few hairs. Nectaries noticeably large. Anthers whitish. Stigmas 1mm or less, yellow-green. Pedicels spreading or reflexed after flowering and bent beneath the erect calyx. Rostrum 11–15mm, clothed with fine forwardly directed hairs. Carpels nearly 3mm, dark brown, shortly hairy. Discharge: seed-ejection (bristles).

South America (Chile, Peru, Bolivia).

This rather weedy species is somewhat redeemed by its tiny bright purplish pink flowers, the petal veins being uncoloured.

It came into garden cultivation through its chance appearance as an alien in Alderney (Channel Islands). It was first found there in June 1938 and another collection of it was made from about the same place by three botanists in 1957 (Lousley, 1962; Kent, 1959). One of the collectors on the second occasion, David McClintock, grew it in Kent and in 1975 sent some to Cambridge (accession 1975.0027). Kent's report states that the plant was identified as *G. retrorsum* L'Hérit. ex DC. by E.F. Warburg.

Two further notes (Townsend, 1961 and 1964) resulted in the introduction of *G. submolle* Steudel as a possible name for this plant. Townsend was in fact very tentative about this but this is the name usually applied to the plant. Dr H. Heine later saw the type and stated that *G. submolle* was not our plant (Yeo, in preparation).

Mrs B. Halfdan Nielsen, of Copenhagen, saw dried specimens of our plant loaned from Cambridge in 1995 and considered it to be *G. herrerae* Knuth (1930). There is a specimen in the Kew Herbarium that matches our plant and has been named *G. herrerae* by its collectors and by Halfdan Nielsen. The type of *G. herrerae* was in Berlin and will therefore have been destroyed. Thus an easy confirmation of the plant's identity is ruled out. I am by no means convinced of this determination but there are points in its favour. It seems better to adopt it provisionally rather than describe a new species which will probably later be reduced to the synonymy of one of the many other specific names of South American geraniums.

Other specimens at Kew and the Natural History Museum, London, substantiate the distribution given above.

The importance of *G. herrerae* in horticulture is through its contribution to hybrids. At Cambridge I have found that some of the progeny of open-pollinated seed from 59. *G.* x *antipodeum* (*G. sessiliflorum* x *G. traversii*) were apparently hybrids with the present species. These plants have garden value; they have enormous productivity, covering the ground with their profusely branched stems and decking themselves with small flowers in various shades of pink, rather in the manner of a small 3. *G.* x *riversleaianum*, as the growth dies back in winter. The foliage may show the influence of *G. sessiliflorum* 'Nigricans'. Our plant has also hybridised with the apparently related 60. *G. sessiliflorum* (subsp. *novaezelandiae*) and *G. retrorsum* De Candolle (in the Potentilloides Group) (Alan Bremner). In addition, Alan Bremner has obtained hybrids of it with 76. *G. carolinianum*, 65. *G. sibiricum*, 1. *G. endressii*, 2. *G.* x *oxonianum* and 49. *G. orientali-tibeticum*.

85. *G. patagonicum* J.D. Hooker

Perennial without distinct resting buds. Stems to 80cm with internodes 10–12cm, erect but collapsing. Basal leaves with blades to 5.5cm wide, nearly circular in outline, divided as far as $^3/_4$–$^4/_5$ into 7; divisions crowded, widest at the apex, 3-lobed; lobes usually each with one or two teeth; upper surface with sparse appressed hairs, lower with looser hairs; leaf-stalks $2^1/_2$–$3^1/_2$ times as long as blade, with fine, spreading eglandular hairs; stipules to 8 (perhaps 10)mm. Upper leaves with blades mostly divided nearly to the base into 5; divisions rhombic, surfaces clothed as in basal leaves; stipules lanceolate. Cymules 2-flowered, spaced along the leafy stems, exceeding subtending leaves, glandular-hairy. Flowers 18–25mm wide, more or less erect, weakly funnel-shaped. Sepals 5–6mm, noticeably wide, with mucro about 0.5mm. Petals wedge-shaped, slightly notched, medium-pink with slightly feathered dark veins; margins towards the base with a few hairs. Filaments considerably widened in basal $^3/_5$. Stigmas about 1.5mm. Fruit erect. Rostrum 18–20mm, abruptly contracted into a stylar portion 1.5–2mm long, glandular-hairy. Carpels about 4mm, eglandular-hairy. Discharge: seed-ejection (bristles).

Andes and temperate South America.

Introduced (to Belgium) by Ivan Louette. This description is based on a seedling of Ivan Louette's stock and a mature plant provided by Dr Dominique Évrard. Although the flowers are medium-sized, the plant is unlikely to have much garden value. It belongs to a group of supposed species that have been very poorly characterised by the botanists who described them.

There is a run of fairly uniform *G. patagonicum*, including the type, in the Kew Herbarium. When present, the glandular hairs are often difficult to see because the heads are very small and the eglandular hairs are long and interfere with the view. I am not sure whether they are present on the type specimen. However, the peduncles, pedicels and rostrum are described as having a partly glandular hair-clothing by Barboza & Correa (1988).

SECTION DISSECTA YEO, THE DISSECTUM SECTION

Plants annual, biennial or perennial. Retention of seed in mericarp during the pre-explosive interval by a part of the mericarp wall which projects as a prong. Awn remaining attached to central column of rostrum after discharge.

Two species of Europe and W. Asia, possibly one or two more.

86. *G. asphodeloides* N.L. Burman (*G. pallens* Bieberstein)

Biennial or perennial with stout rootstock and many thick roots. Blades of leaves divided as far as $^2/_3$ or $^5/_6$ into 5 or 7; divisions broadest above the middle, sometimes at the apex. Stem-leaves paired. Plant with at least some glandular hairs. Inflorescence diffuse, leafy. Flowers 23–34mm in diameter. Sepals 6–8mm, noticeably narrow; mucro from less than 1mm to 2mm. Petals $1^1/_2$–$2^1/_2$ times as long as wide; base with a dense

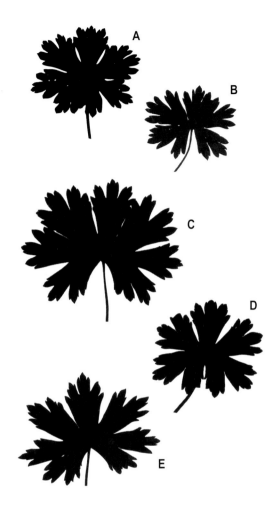

Figure 9.93. *G. asphodeloides* subsp. *asphodeloides*: from E.M. Rix, 1971, coll. Turkey: Cankiri Prov. (Fraser-Jenkins 2188); (A) & (B) two plants, May; (C) & (D) two plants November; (E) from R. Gorer, 1974, coll. Greece: Lower Pindus; 4–7cm wide

tuft of hairs on either edge but without hairs across front surface. Filaments distinctly enlarged below and with fine hair-fringes towards the base. Stigmas about 1mm or less. Rostrum 14–19mm including distinct stylar portion 4–5mm long. Immature fruits erect on spreading or reflexed pedicels. Mericarps 2.5–3mm. Discharge: seed-ejection (prong).

G. asphodeloides is easily distinguishable as being the larger-flowered of the only two widespread species with the prong arrangement for retention of the seed in the pre-explosive phase of discharge. However, it is also distinctive in the narrow sepals which, together with the stamens and style, seem small in relation to the size of the petals, and in its short stigmas. The plant forms big clumps, easily divided up. It flowers abundantly despite the diffuse inflorescence, and has a long season.

As this species is divisible into three subspecies, a condensed description, intended to distinguish it from other species, is given above. The three subspecies are treated below in accordance with their horticultural importance.

G. asphodeloides 'Starlight' is a cross between subsp. *asphodeloides* and subsp. *crenophilum* having entirely white flowers and rather wider petals than 'Prince Regent' (see subspecies *asphodeloides*). It arose on the Geranium Display Bed at Cambridge in 1980. Subspecies *asphodeloides* was represented by both pink- and white-flowered plants, and both colours were represented among the hybrids, which were quite numerous. Three of each colour were removed and kept growing elsewhere in the Garden. The white ones were given to Dr David Hibberd who provided the cultivar name; he found the three plants and their progeny to be so uniform that the use of the name could not be restricted to one clone. (The pink-flowered hybrids are displayed at the time of writing in the Cambridge Botanic Garden; they are densely flowered and attractive.) Except in flower-colour, these hybrids are intermediate between the parents; their glandular hairs are partly red-tipped and partly not.

84a. *G. asphodeloides* subsp. *asphodeloides*
(Figure 9.93, Plate 34)
Perennial with bushy growth; stem-leaves with irregularly and sharply cut divisions; petals usually 2–3 times as long as broad, pale to deep pink, with usually strong darker veins, or white. Rock garden, wild garden, sun. June to August.

Basal leaves few, their blades up to about 8cm wide, divided as far as $^2/_3-^3/_4$ into 5 or 7; divisions broadest at or near apex, lobed at apex for about $^1/_3$ of their length, broad, straight-sided; lobes shallowly toothed. Teeth and tips of lobes obtuse or obtusish. Stem-leaves numerous, usually divided as far as $^4/_5-^5/_6$ into 5; divisions broadest above the middle, usually 3-lobed; lobes up to about $2^1/_2$ times as long as wide, acute, more or less toothed; teeth acute. Eglandular hairs mostly small and appressed; glandular hairs with red tips present on pedicels, sepals and rostra, sometimes also on peduncles or all stems and leaf-stalks. Flowers flat. Sepals 6–7mm, widely spreading, more or less flushed with pink; mucro usually 1mm or less. Petals 10–15 x 4.5–7mm, twice as long as wide or

more, rarely up to 8.5mm wide and only $1^1/_2$ times as long as wide, not so widely spreading as sepals, rounded or faintly notched at apex, broadest at middle or apex, usually pale pink with darker veins running most of their length but also deep pink or white. Filaments coloured as the petals; anthers bluish. Stigmas red.

South Europe from Sicily eastwards to Crimea and Caucasus; N. Iran; Turkey; absent from Crete and Cyprus.

Subspecies *asphodeloides* is the most common and widespread subspecies of *G. asphodeloides* and is highly variable. In a sample grown from seed collected in Çankiri Province, Turkey, by Dr C.R. Fraser-Jenkins, in 1970, I raised plants with pink petals of differing shades and with white petals, and with varying shapes, colours and textures in the leaves. Mr Richard Gorer collected a vigorous, dark-flowered, broad-petalled plant at Karpenisi in the Lower Pindus of Greece and presented it to Cambridge in 1974.

Perhaps the most beautiful member of the group is the following:
G. asphodeloides (subsp. *asphodeloides*) 'Prince Regent': it has pale lilac petals with fine dark stripes. It is unusual in that its stems and leaf-stalks are glandular-hairy throughout. It was described without a cultivar name in edn.1. It was obtained by Mr Jan Stephens from Mrs B.C. Rogers as *G. pallens* and passed on to Cambridge in 1970; *G. pallens* is the name used for *G. asphodeloides* in *Flora of the USSR* (Bobrov, 1949).

A reported natural hybrid of *G. asphodeloides* (subspecies *asphodeloides*) with 99. *G. bohemicum* (in section Tuberosa) is mentioned in Chapter 7.

86b. *G. asphodeloides* subsp. *crenophilum*
(Boissier) Bornmüller (Figures 9.94 A & B)
Differs from 86a. subsp. *asphodeloides* in having more erect stems, numerous basal leaves, often more than 10cm wide, with blades almost circular in outline, and stem-leaves similar to the basal, with divisions broadest at the apex and lobes up to only about $1^1/_2$ times as long as broad; in having glandular hairs on all vegetative parts and on the sepals and rostra, the hairs not being tipped with red; and in having the flowers slightly funnel-shaped at the base, the sepals 7–8mm long and the petals broad and deep rose-pink.

Lebanon, Syria.

Superficially quite a lot different from subsp. *asphodeloides*, this subspecies tends to build its

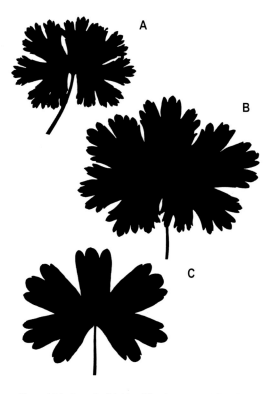

Figure 9.94. *G. asphodeloides*: (A) subsp. *crenophilum*, from J. Stephens, 1969, coll. Lebanon: Kidisha Gorge (W.K. Aslet), March (greenhouse); (B) the same, a larger leaf, May (greenhouse); (C) subsp. *sintenisii*, from Mrs J. Forty (Joy Jones), 1980, from a young fast-growing plant; 5.5, 11 and 6.5cm wide (unequal reductions)

rootstock up above ground and needs re-planting from time to time. It can be propagated by division or seed. It seems quite hardy out of doors at Cambridge. In the form of its flowers it might be judged better than the starry subsp. *asphodeloides* but it lacks the individuality of the latter. It was twice collected in the Kidisha Gorge, Lebanon, by Mr W.K. Aslet, but may not be in cultivation now.

86c. *G. asphodeloides* subsp. *sintenisii* (Freyn) Davis (Figure 9.94C)
Perennial, forming a mass of leaves with blades between 5 and 20cm wide. Basal leaves rather like those of subsp. *crenophilum*, stem-leaves more different from the basal than in the latter, less so than in subsp. *asphodeloides*; stems, leaf-stalks, undersides of leaves, sepals and rostra more or less covered with red-tipped glandular hairs. Inflorescence very prolific. Petals up to 13mm long, pale pink or sometimes deep purple.

North Turkey.

I received seeds of the pink form of this from Mrs J. Forty (Joy Jones) in 1980. They were sown that autumn and some plants were exposed to the winter but none flowered in 1981, though all did in 1982. However, seeds sown in 1982 produced flowering plants in 1983. The flowers were pale pink and the petals wrinkled.

87. *G. dissectum* Linnaeus
A low-growing annual with stem-leaves deeply cut into narrow segments. Cymules not longer than subtending leaves (a distinction from 51. *G. columbinum*). Glandular hairs usually present above. Petals 6mm or less, deeply notched, usually deep pink. Rostrum 12–13mm, with a distinct stylar portion 1–2mm long. Discharge: seed-ejection (prong).

Europe and W. Asia; widely naturalised elsewhere.

G. dissectum is reliably distinguished from other small species with similar leaves which occur in various parts of the world by the fruit-type. It is a weed with no garden value, extremely common in Britain.

SECTION TUBEROSA REICHE,
THE TUBEROSUM SECTION

Annual, biennial or perennial. Eglandular hairs of sepals much longer than half the width of the sepal. Petals more or less notched, base without hairs across front surface but with a tuft of fine hairs (rarely a mere fringe) on either edge. Stamen filaments with large hairs. Immature fruits erect on erect pedicels. Stigmas not more than 2.5mm. Retention of seed in the mericarp during the pre-explosive interval by a twist at the junction of awn and mericarp, so that the orifice faces sideways. Awn not remaining attached to central column after discharge.

Mediterranean region, W. Asia as far as Kashmir; annual and biennial species extending north to S. Scandinavia.

The section is easily divided into two groups which are best characterised separately.

SUBSECTION TUBEROSA, THE TUBEROSUM GROUP

Perennial. Rootstock an underground tuber, usually horizontal; adjacent tubers linked together by slenderer sections of rhizome. Plants becoming dormant in summer after flowering. Leaf-blades deeply cut into mostly narrow segments, at least the incisions on either side of the middle division usually reaching to top of leaf-stalk, middle division usually distinctly smaller than those on either side of it. Most of the cymules without peduncles. Petals usually pink or purplish. Filaments rather evenly enlarged towards base, usually with moderate-sized hairs on margins in addition to the large ones.

Up to ten species in the Mediterranean region and W. Asia. Some are sometimes treated as subspecies, as here, reducing the number to a minimum of six. Of these, four are treated here. None was used in Alan Bremner's hybridising experiments.

The members of this group occur naturally in areas of summer drought; they are precociously flowering, coming up rapidly in spring or autumn and typically producing the first cymule (in spring) at the first or second node. Examples grown at Cambridge seem to be infertile to their own pollen. Davis (1970) states that several species are composed of both normal, hermaphrodite, plants and female plants (the condition called gynodioecy). In this connection, see remarks under 88. *G. tuberosum*.

88. *G. tuberosum* Linnaeus (*G. stepporum* Davis) (Figure 9.95A)

Leaves with at least the three middle divisions free to the base or nearly so; divisions deeply cut into numerous narrow entire or narrowly toothed lobes; flowers about 20–30mm in diameter; petals purplish rose with darker veins, notched; stylar portion of rostrum about 1mm. Leafy in spring. Rock garden. May.

Tuber 7–15mm thick. Blades of basal leaves 5–10cm wide, with 5 or 7 divisions, the middle one free to the base, and usually also those either side of it, deeply cut into segments 3mm wide or less; divisions broadest about the middle, overlapping, pinnately lobed throughout most of their length; lobes numerous, about 2–4 times as long as broad, the larger ones with scattered narrow teeth. Teeth and tips of lobes acute. Stem-leaves paired, those at the first or first and second nodes usually similar to the basal, thereafter nearly or quite stalkless and with narrowly lanceolate divisions with scattered narrow lobes or close-set short lobes forming a saw-edge, decreasing in size gradually. Plant without glandular hairs. Stems erect. Branches partly paired and partly solitary. All or most of the cymules with the peduncle suppressed. Pedicels about $1\frac{1}{2}$–$3\frac{1}{2}$ times as long as sepals. Sepals 5–8mm, flushed with purple, especially within; mucro 1mm or less. Petals 9–17 x 7–13mm, broadest well above the middle, deeply notched between rounded lobes, bright rose-purple, with dark veins slightly forking at tips; base with a

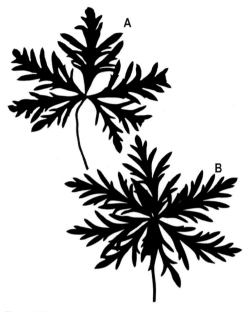

Figure 9.95. *(A) G. tuberosum:* from Dr A.P. Vlasto, 1963, coll. Yugoslavia: Zaroukhla valley; (B) *G. macrostylum*, from Miss J. Robinson, 1980, *ex* Sir Cedric Morris; 6cm wide

tuft of hairs on either edge but without hairs across front surface. Filaments considerably but evenly enlarged towards base, about the same colour as veins of petals, with rather sparse large hairs. Fertile anthers dark bluish. Stigmas about 2.5mm, usually strongly coiled, crimson. Rostrum about 17mm, stylar portion about 1mm, indistinct. Discharge: seed-ejection (twist).

Mediterranean region eastwards to W. Iran.

This is a common and variable species which behaves as a weed in cornfields and vineyards. The tubers multiply rapidly, and in Turkey are used for food. The above description is based on plants at Cambridge collected by Dr A.P. Vlasto in 1963 at Zaroukhla in Yugoslavia. A wide range of petal-sizes has been observed in this stock, which is probably one clone. The smallest flowers which I have seen on it appeared in 1971; none of them had well-formed anthers. In 1972 all flowers were larger than those of 1971 but some which had most of the anthers fertile were larger than the others. In this stock the petals do not overlap and are somewhat contracted towards the base, revealing the coloured sepals between them.

European plants belong to subsp. *tuberosum* which, however, occupies most of the range of the species. Overlapping with its W. Asiatic range, but extending further east, is:

Figure 9.96. *G. tuberosum* subsp. *linearifolium*: cult. D. Victor; 12cm wide

G. tuberosum subsp. *linearifolium* (Boissier) Davis (Figure 9.96), in which the divisions of the basal leaves are completely separated, the lobes of the basal leaves are shorter and the first pair of stem-

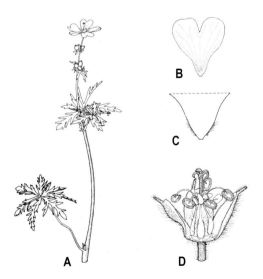

Figure 9.97. *G. macrostylum*: from Miss J. Robinson, 1980, *ex* Sir Cedric Morris. (A) shoot at beginning of flowering, x $^1/_2$; (B) petal, showing dark pigmentation, x $1^1/_2$; (C) base of front surface of petal, x $3^1/_2$; (D) flower with petals and two sepals removed, x $3^1/_2$; the anthers of the outer whorl of this flower were abortive

leaves does not have a pair of branches, though there may be a cymule at this point. The name *G. stepporum* Davis refers to this plant, but after publishing it the author chose, on the basis of further study, to treat it as a subspecies (Davis, 1967).

Another subspecies, *G. tuberosum* subsp. *micranthum* Schönbeck-Temesy, was described in *Flora Iranica* (Schönbeck-Temesy, 1970).

89. G. macrostylum Boissier (Figures 9.95B & 9.97)
Similar to 88. *G. tuberosum*, but tubers mostly elongated, 5–10mm thick, upper parts of plant with red-tipped glandular hairs, stylar portion of rostrum 1.5–2.5mm long, sepals 4–5mm. Discharge: seed-ejection (twist). Leafy in autumn, winter and spring. Rock garden. May.

Greece, Albania, S. Yugoslavia, C. and S.W. Turkey.

A pretty species which, however, was regarded as a pest by Miss J. Robinson of Boxford, Suffolk, the tubers being small and easily scattered. The same stock was naturalised in the garden of Sir Cedric Morris at Hadleigh, Suffolk.

Flower colouring takes two forms. In one the petals are pale pink with indistinct veins converging to form a darker reddish zone at the base; in the other the colour is purplish, much pinker in the centre than at the edges of the petals, which are heavily marked with purple veins, the flower being not at all darkened in the centre, and overall very like that of 88. *G. tuberosum*. The first pattern characterises Miss Robinson's stock and Professor Peter Davis's rather more vigorous collection no. 41771 (Turkey: N. side of Samsun Da., Izmir, 1965, cultivated at Edinburgh). The second is found in H. & B. 580, Cambridge accession 1984.0377 Hunter, also from Turkey (at the Sinekcibeli Pass south of Elmali, cultivated at Cambridge).

90. G. linearilobum De Candolle (Figure 9.98)
Blades of basal leaves with the middle division free to the base and often particularly small, the lateral joined for about $^1/_6$–$^1/_4$ of their length, divisions very variable; stem with one or two solitary leaves before the first pair, flowers about 36mm in diameter; petals deeply notched, purplish pink, strongly veined; rostrum with stylar portion 1.5–3mm. Leaves present in spring. Rock garden. May.

Blades of basal leaves up to 10cm wide, with 7 or 9 divisions, middle one particularly small, free to the base, others joined for about $^1/_6$–$^1/_4$ of their length; divisions either (a) pinnately lobed with few, widely

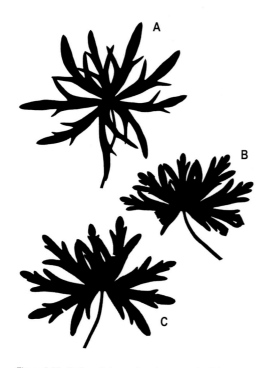

Figure 9.98. *G. linearilobum* subsp. *transversale*: (A) from R.F. Hunter, 1980, coll. Kazakhstan: S. of Alma Ata; (B) & (C) from R.F. Hunter, 1980, coll. Uzbekistan: Tschim Gan (Chimgan), near Tashkent; 6.5–8cm wide

divergent untoothed lobes up to about 6 times as long as wide, the lowest lateral ones arising just below the middle of the division and being not more than half as long as the central one, or (b) pinnately lobed only above the middle with less divergent lobes up to about 4 times as long as wide and usually toothed, the lateral much more than half as long as the central. First one or two stem-leaves solitary, others paired, usually changing gradually in form, size and length of stalk upwards, their lobes without teeth, the divisions of the uppermost without lobes. Plant without glandular hairs. Cymules mostly or all stalkless. Sepals about 6.5mm, green; mucro 1mm or less. Petals 13–15 x 12–13mm, overlapping at their widest part, bright pink with bold, slightly forked, darker veining. Stamens, when not aborted, pink. Stigmas dark red. Rostrum up to 18mm with stylar portion 1.5–3mm. Discharge: seed-ejection (twist).

Southern Russia, Caucasus, N. and W. Iran, E. Turkey, Central Asia.

This species was introduced by Mr R.F. Hunter in 1980; he collected it in the Tschim Gan (Chimgan) Valley near Tashkent (Cambridge accession 1980.0318), and again about 10km south of Alma Ata (Cambridge accession 1980.0359). Dr Martyn Rix took a photograph of it at the former locality (see Rix & Phillips, 1981, p. 65); this shows basal leaves of the type (b) of my description, but extraordinarily different stem-leaves with entire divisions 10 or 12 times as long as wide, which have not appeared on the plant in cultivation (and are not mentioned in the above description). The basal leaves are the same as on the cultivated plant and fall within the range of variation described by Davis (1970) for *G. linearilobum* subsp. *transversale* (Karelin & Kirilow) Davis. The leaves of type (a) in my description are found on Mr Hunter's Alma Ata plant; they correspond with Davis' description of subsp. *linearilobum*, but that subspecies occurs only in the western part of the range of the species, and these specimens were collected near its eastern limit. However, I have not studied herbarium specimens of this subspecies and, on account of their origin, both cultivated stocks ought to be referred to subsp. *transversale* for the present. For horticultural purposes it may eventually prove unimportant to distinguish subspecies within *G. linearilobum* (which, incidentally, is not to be confused with *G. tuberosum* subsp. *linearifolium* (Boissier) Davis).

Figure 9.99. *G. malviflorum*: from J. Stephens, 1966: (A) March; (B) November; 10.5cm wide

91. G. malviflorum Boissier & Reuter (Figure 9.99, Plate 35)

Blades of basal leaves mostly 6–10cm wide (larger than in most other members of the Tuberosum Group), the middle division free to the base, the others shortly joined; divisions freely pinnately lobed from near the base, and the lowest lobes pinnately toothed; flowers about 35–45mm in diameter; petals heart-shaped, violet-blue or purplish, veiny. Leaves present in spring, sometimes also in autumn and winter. Rock garden, border. April, May.

Tubers up to 6 x 1.5cm, spindle-shaped. Blades of basal leaves mostly between 10 and 15cm wide, with 7 divisions, the middle one free to the base; divisions broadest about the middle, overlapping, pinnately lobed to within 3–1.5mm of the midrib for most of their length or from just below the middle; lobes numerous, mostly 2–5 times as long as broad, the lower ones pinnately toothed, some without teeth. Stem-leaves paired, the first pair similar to the basal, thereafter abruptly reduced in size and in complexity of lobing, and stalkless or nearly so. Plant without glandular hairs. Stems erect. Branches paired, the first pair subtended by the first leaves. Many of the cymules without peduncles. Pedicels up to about 3 times as long as sepals. Flowers saucer-shaped at first. Sepals 7–9mm, flushed with violet; mucro about 1.5mm. Petals 16–22mm, about $^4/_5$ as broad as long, heart-shaped, overlapping or contiguous, violet-blue or violet, with strong darker veins forking near tips, obliterated towards the base; base with a tuft of hairs on either edge but without hairs across front surface. Filaments purplish, evenly enlarged towards base, with rather sparse large hairs. Anthers cream with black edges, becoming blue-black. Stigmas about 1.5mm, deep red. Rostrum 20–22mm, with stylar portion 3–5mm. Mericarps about 4mm, nearly black, with white bristles. Discharge: seed-ejection (twist).

South Spain, Morocco, Algeria.

This magnificent blue-flowered species was for long commonly misnamed *G. atlanticum* in gardens, having been illustrated under that name in error in the authoritative *Curtis's Botanical Magazine* (Hooker, 1879) (see 9. *G. atlanticum*). Most plants in cultivation, including a stock at Cambridge, are probably a clone descended from the Algerian plant there depicted. Leaf-divisions which are pinnately lobed only from just below the middle upwards instead of from near the base appear on these plants in autumn. A second clone grown at Cambridge was collected by Mr Richard Gorer in Ronda, S. Spain. It differs in not sending up its leaves until early spring, and in having the sides of the lobes and teeth edged with purplish brown, in flowering later and in having the flowers less blue. Regardless of when the leaves come up, *G. malviflorum* becomes dormant after flowering. The amount of flower produced in cultivation may vary from year to year, and in some situations is persistently small. Other introductions, by Professor P.H. Davis, are cultivated at Edinburgh and another, collected by Dr Stephen Jury and others, is grown at Reading University.

SUBSECTION MEDITERRANEA,
THE PLATYPETALUM GROUP

Annual, biennial or perennial, the last either green all summer or summer-dormant. Blades of main leaves not usually divided beyond $^7/_8$. Some of the cymules often without peduncles. Petals usually blue, with darker, usually feathered or netted veins. Filaments rather abruptly enlarged towards base, with minute hairs on enlarged part as well as the large, more generally distributed hairs.

Ten or eleven species, the perennials confined to Greece, Turkey, the Levant and the Caucasus; the one annual and one biennial scattered in S. and E. Europe and N.W. Africa. Hybrids occur rather freely in the group but no crosses outside the group have yet succeeded.

92. G. platypetalum Fischer & Meyer (Figures 9.100 & 9.101)

Noticeably hairy perennial, up to about 40cm; main leaves rounded in outline, divided about half-way into 7 or 9; divisions broadest near apex with short, broad, freely toothed lobes; inflorescence dense; floral axis horizontal; flowers 30–45mm in diameter; petals usually notched, deep violet-blue

Figure 9.100. *G. platypetalum*: from E.M. Rix, 1971, coll. Turkey: Rize Prov. (Fraser-Jenkins 2355); 12cm wide

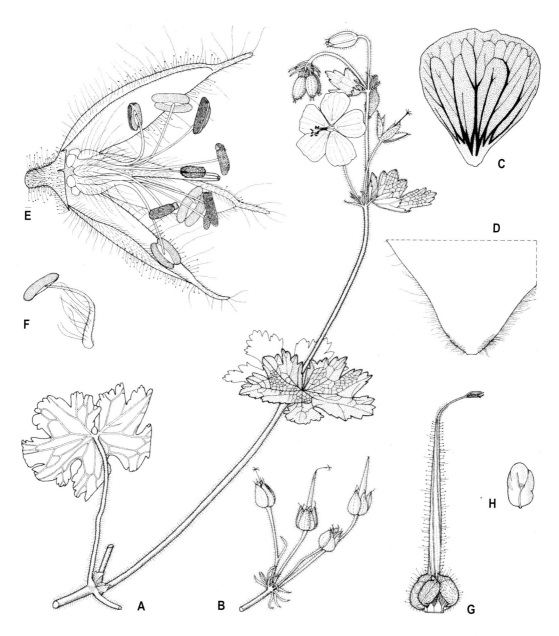

with darker veins. Border, sun or partial shade. June and sometimes later.

Perennial with thick compact rootstock. Blades of basal leaves between 10 and 20cm wide, rounded, sometimes broader than long, wrinkled above, divided as far as about $\frac{1}{2}$ into 7 or 9; divisions broadest near apex, broader than long, lobed at apex for about $\frac{1}{3}$ of their length, sides of

Figure 9.101. *G. platypetalum*: from J. Stephens, 1969, *ex* Kew; (A) portion of flowering shoot, x $\frac{2}{3}$; (B) portion of inflorescence with immature fruit, x $\frac{2}{3}$; (C) petal, with pigmentation, x 2; (D) base of front surface of petal, x 4; (E) flower in male stage with petals and two sepals removed, x 4; (F) stamen of outer whorl seen obliquely from the back, x 4; (G) fruit in pre-explosive interval, x 2; (H) seed, x 4

unlobed part convex to concave; lobes broader than long, mostly with a tooth on each side. Teeth and tips of lobes obtuse or broadly pointed. Stem-leaves paired, or a solitary one is sometimes present near base, the upper with 3 or 5 divisions broadest near the middle, gradually reduced in size and length of stalk upwards. Glandular hairs of mixed lengths, some very long, present on much of the plant, exceeded in length by the eglandular hairs, but these scarce in the more glandular parts except for the sepals. Inflorescence dense, some or all the peduncles suppressed, longest up to 8cm. Pedicels not more than 3 times as long as sepals, both in one cymule sometimes shorter than sepals. Bracteoles 7–15mm. Floral axis horizontal. Flowers flat or saucer-shaped. Sepals 9–12mm; mucro 2–4.5mm. Petals 16–22 x 13–19mm, notched or feebly 3-lobed at apex, broadest and sometimes recurved near apex, deep violet or blue-violet, usually slightly paler and pinkish at base, with very dark violet, embossed, glossy and forking veins. Filaments slightly curved outwards at tips at first, arching back towards petals later, with many long hairs, coloured like the petals, paler at base, which is distinctly enlarged and bears few or many minute hairs. Anthers blue-black. Stigmas about 2.5mm, dark red. Immature fruits erect on erect pedicels. Rostrum about 24–30mm, with stylar portion 4–5mm. Mericarps about 5mm. Discharge: seed-ejection (twist).

Caucasus region, including N.E. Turkey and N.W. Iran.

G. platypetalum in Turkey grows in spruce woods and hazel scrub (Davis, 1967). Certain forms of this species in which the flowers are not too flat or too sombre make attractive perennials which may flower two or three times in a season.

G. platypetalum is a parent of the very commonly grown sterile hybrid, 94. *G.* x *magnificum*; this appears to have arisen by chance on a number of occasions in gardens. A wild hybrid with 96. *G. renardii* (q.v.) has also been found. Recently, both these hybrids have been synthesised by Alan Bremner and, in the case of 94. *G.* x *magnificum*, in both directions. Two other crosses obtained by Bremner are 95. *G. gymnocaulon* x *G. platypetalum* and 93. *G. ibericum* x (*G. platypetalum* x 96. *G. renardii*). The second partner in this cross is mentioned under 96. *G. renardii* (q.v.).

93. *G. ibericum* Cavanilles subsp. ***ibericum*** (Figure 9.102, Plate 36)
Noticeably hairy perennial, up to about 50cm;

Figure 9.102. *G. ibericum* subsp. *ibericum*; 15cm wide

main leaves angular in outline, divided as far as $^2/_3$–$^7/_8$ into 9 or 11; divisions broadest near middle, overlapping, with deep complex lobing; flowers 40–48mm in diameter; petals notched, violet-blue with feathered purplish veins. Border, sun. June.

Differs from 92. *G. platypetalum* in having blades of basal leaves divided as far as $^3/_4$–$^7/_8$ (occasionally only $^2/_3$) into 9 or 11; divisions broadest just above the middle, palmato-pinnately lobed, the main lobes themselves lobed, the lobing and toothing continued down the sides of the divisions nearly to the base, the lobes about 1–2 times as long as broad, toothed, often turned outwards, teeth and tips of lobes acute; and in having stalkless upper stem-leaves, no glandular hairs, bracteoles 4.5–9mm long, few or no peduncles, upwardly inclined flowers, sepal mucro only 2–3mm, relatively narrower petals (about 24–26 x 16–17mm) and rostrum 27–35mm with stylar portion 4–7mm. Discharge: seed-ejection (twist).

North-east Turkey, Caucasus, perhaps N. Iran.

This plant is probably adapted to drier conditions than 92. *G. platypetalum*; it is perhaps handsomer, too, partly because the flowers face upwards; it was highly commended at the Wisley Trial, 1973–6. At Cambridge there is an old stock of unknown origin and another from western Armenia, supplied by the Erevan Botanic Garden. The latter tends to build its rootstock up above ground-level and to need occasional replanting.

G. ibericum subsp. *ibericum* is not difficult to distinguish from 92. *G. platypetalum* by its lack of glandular hairs but the situation is complicated by the existence of the hybrid between the two (94. *G. x magnificum*) and of *G. ibericum* subsp. *jubatum* (see below). The differences between subsp. *ibericum* and 94. *G. x magnificum* are mentioned under the latter.

93b. *G. ibericum* subsp. *jubatum* (Handel-Mazzetti) Davis is not much (if at all) different in its leaves from subsp. *ibericum*; the bracts and sepal mucros are about the same length as in that and the petals are the same shape (and can be nearly white). However, the hairs on the pedicels are like those of 94. *G. x magnificum* (with an admixture of glandular hairs among the very long eglandular hairs).

Northern Turkey.

The stock at Cambridge resembles the typical clone of 94. *G. x magnificum* additionally in having the floral axis horizontal and the petals bluer than in subsp. *ibericum*. The plant was collected in N.E. Turkey by Mr A.W.A. Baker, who presented a root to Cambridge in 1981.

G. ibericum subsp. *jubatum* 'White Zigana' has the petals not quite white, and retaining their violet venation. It was collected in the Zigana Pass, Turkey, by Mr Michael Baron of Alresford, Hampshire.

G. ibericum x *G. platypetalum* is dealt with next.

94. *G. x magnificum* Hylander (Figures 9.103, 9.104 & 9.105, Plate 37)

Very hairy perennial up to 50–70cm or even more; main leaves to 20cm wide, slightly angular in outline, with very wide, overlapping but relatively shallow, profusely lobed and toothed divisions; flowers crowded, 40–50mm wide, with rich purplish violet petals; pedicels with rather uniform-length glandular hairs, distinguished from 93. *G. ibericum* subsp. *ibericum* by possession of glandular hairs and from both subsp. *ibericum* and subsp. *jubatum* by its sterility and greater vigour. Border, ground-cover, sun or partial shade. June.

Blades of basal leaves to 20cm wide, less angular than in 93. *G. ibericum* subsp. *ibericum*, sometimes broader than long (thus approaching 92. *G. platypetalum*), divisions very like those of *G. ibericum*, sometimes more abruptly tapered beyond the the widest part. Upper parts of stem and pedicels covered with both very long eglandular hairs (such hairs very sparse in 92. *G. platypetalum*) and abundant glandular hairs less than half their length (not of very variable length, as in *G. platypetalum*). Bracteoles 5–9mm. Floral axis horizontal to nearly erect. Flowers saucer-

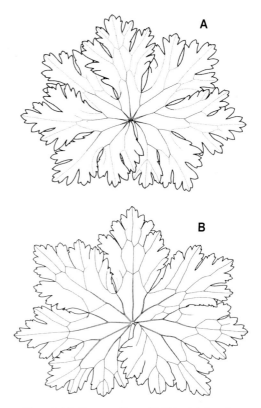

Figure 9.103. *G. x magnificum*: (A) 'Hylander', from B. Wurzell, 1972; (B) 'Peter Yeo', cult. P.F. Yeo, 1983; 11 and 12cm wide

shaped. Petals 22–24 x 16–22mm, often with a point in the notch (its presence or absence varies from flower to flower). Stamens either normal or sometimes with yellowish anthers which do not burst. Some of the rostra often partly developed but not usually reaching full size and seeds not ripening; stylar portion 4–7mm.

Evidently a hybrid between 92. *G. platypetalum* and 93. *G. ibericum* subsp. *ibericum*, but the time and place of its origin are unknown.

The foliage of this hybrid is very like that of *G. ibericum* and the plant is best distinguished by its failure to ripen seed. The mixture of moderately long glandular and very long eglandular hairs on the pedicels is also a good character provided one is comparing it with the eglandular 93. *G. ibericum* subsp. *ibericum* and not with 93. *G. ibericum* subsp. *jubatum*. 92. *G. platypetalum* is moderately distinct in its leaves; its pedicels bear glandular hairs of very variable length, while the eglandular hairs among them that are longer than

Figure 9.104. *G. x magnificum*: clone 'B', from Kew, 1972, *ex* G.S. Thomas, as *G. ibericum* var. *platypetalum*; 9.5 and 11cm wide

the glandular are very sparse. The petals of the hybrid range from a little wider than those of *G. ibericum* to about as wide as those of *G. platypetalum*. The very fine flower-colour no doubt reflects the qualities of both parents.

G. x magnificum is perhaps the commonest member of its genus in gardens. It will gradually spread to fill the space available and may be left for years without attention. It produces a magnificent display when it is in flower but the season is rather short and I have never seen it flower a second time (but see description of 'Rosemoor' below). The leaves may colour well in autumn, however. I know of three clones which I describe below after giving the history of the plant.

The name *G. x magnificum* was given to this plant in 1961 by Dr Nils Hylander, of the Uppsala Botanic Garden, Sweden. In the course of building up a collection of *Geranium* he repeatedly obtained it under the name *G. platypetalum*, while the true *G. platypetalum* arrived from various botanic

gardens under assorted names. Having noted its sterility and compared it with *G. platypetalum* and *G. ibericum*, he concluded that it was a hybrid between the two. His published account of his investigations (Hylander, 1961) includes valid publication of the name for the hybrid. He obtained evidence from his own observations and from books and periodicals that *G. x magnificum* was cultivated in various countries, including Britain. He could not find out when it first appeared but the earliest evidence for its existence was a herbarium specimen gathered in 1871 in the Botanic Garden of Geneva and preserved in the Botanical Museum at Uppsala.

Rather curiously, Hylander never went into the question of chromosome numbers, yet they had been investigated by Warburg (1938) working at Cambridge. Warburg found 28 chromosomes in *G. platypetalum* and 56 in a plant received as *G. ibericum* var. *talyshense* (this is a tetraploid but Warburg erroneously referred to it as a hexaploid). He also had what he called "sterile *platypetalum*", different from the one with 28 chromosomes and, he stated, known in gardens as *G. ibericum*, *G. ibericum* var. *platypetalum* or *G. platypetalum*. He said he had never observed seed on this plant, and had failed to induce seed formation by pollinating it with other species. He considered that it agreed with the description of *G. platypetalum* but I feel no doubt that he had *G. x magnificum*. It had 42 chromosomes (triploid) and from their behaviour Warburg thought it was a triploid derived by the crossing of two species (an allotriploid).

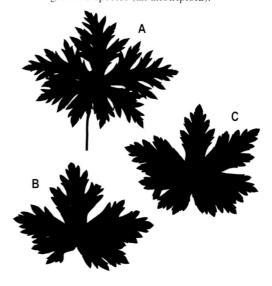

Figure 9.105. *G. x magnificum*, upper leaves: (A) 'Hylander' (clone 'A'); (B) clone 'B'; (C) 'Peter Yeo' (clone 'C'), sources as in Figs 9.103 & 9.104; 7–7.5cm wide

Hylander (1961) suspected that the photograph accompanying the report of the Award of Garden Merit to *G. ibericum* (*Journal of the Royal Horticultural Society*, 67, fig. 130, 1942) (also published in Synge & Platt, 1962) was truly that species, especially as there was mention of abundant seed-production. However, I am certain the plant illustrated is *G. x magnificum*, and while I consider that the latter deserves the A.G.M., I do not think *G. ibericum* does or would have obtained it.

In edn.1 I described three clones of *G. x magnificum* that I had recognised as distinct in cultivation. Afterwards I grew two further accessions for several years without being able to decide whether they represented additional clones. With levels of similarity so high it may not matter whether two plants represent one clone or two very similar ones. However, it seems that it will be informative to continue to include the three previously described clones to show the sort of points in which differences are found. Previously there was a problem with the naming of these clones and I designated them by the letters A, B, and C. Clifton (1979) had published the names 'Hylander' and 'Peter Yeo' for clones A and C respectively but had confused their characters and I was reluctant to use the names. Now, however, I have agreed with the International Registrar of cultivar names in *Geranium*, Mr D.X. Victor, that the names should be used in this sense.

Alan Bremner has crossed 93. *G. ibericum* with 92. *G. platypetalum* in both directions, but I have no detailed information about the plants raised.

G. x magnificum 'Hylander' (Figures 9.103A & 9.105A): blades of basal leaves very like those of *G. ibericum*, more deeply divided compared with clone 'B', with the divisions more gradually tapered beyond the widest part, deeper green, more wrinkled than in "B" and 'Peter Yeo'; flowers more obviously grouped into clusters than in these, with axis horizontal, petals broader and more overlapping than in "B", less so than in 'Peter Yeo', but slightly recurved towards apex and margins, their dark-coloured veins less bold and more profusely branched than in 'Peter Yeo'; filaments white at base.

This is apparently the most widely distributed clone (which Cambridge Botanic Garden had received from Bloom's of Bressingham, Norfolk). I am fairly certain it is the one on which Hylander based his account of *G. x magnificum* (he included a photograph of a herbarium specimen in his article). This opinion led to the choice of the epithet 'Hylander' for its cultivar name.

G. x magnificum Clone "B" (Figures 9.104 & 9.105B): blades of basal leaves having the divisions intermediate in shape between those of 'Hylander' and 'Peter Yeo', and perhaps less profusely toothed, less wrinkled and paler than those of 'Hylander'; flowers less obviously grouped into clusters than in 'Hylander', more like those of *G. ibericum* than are those of 'Hylander' and 'Peter Yeo', with axis upwardly inclined or erect and with narrower, scarcely recurved, straighter-sided petals, the veins of which are less profusely branched than those of 'Hylander', more so than those of 'Peter Yeo'; filaments almost white at base. I found the chromosome number to be triploid and the meiosis to show up to 14 bivalents (chromosome pairs) and 14 or more univalents (unpaired chromosomes), thus showing allotriploid behaviour as found for an unspecified clone by Warburg (1938, cited above).

I have found this plant only at the Royal Botanic Gardens, Kew, which had been given it by Mr Graham Thomas under the name *G. ibericum* var. *platypetalum*. From 1972 onwards it was grown at Cambridge.

G. x magnificum 'Peter Yeo' (Figures 9.103B & 9.105C, Plate 37): of the three clones, this has the basal leaves the most like those of *G. platypetalum*, the divisions being much more abruptly tapered beyond the middle (the middle ones apparently overlapping less) and the teeth and tips of lobes being blunter, and it shows an obvious corresponding difference in the upper leaves (Figure 9.105); the surface of the leaves is only shallowly wrinkled; the flowers are not obviously clustered and they have the axis horizontal; it has the broadest, most strongly overlapping petals with the most strongly curved sides of the three clones and they are often both lobulate and undulate at the apex; the petals are bluer, and have bolder but less profusely feathered veins than those of 'Hylander' and clone "B"; the filaments are pink at the base.

I first noticed this clone in Mrs J. Forty's (Joy Jones's) former garden at Woking. It is not uncommon.

G. x magnificum 'Rosemoor' is a more compact and repeat-flowering clone (Baltensperger, 1997).

95. *G. gymnocaulon* De Candolle

Inconspicuously hairy, slender perennial to about 35cm tall; blades of basal leaves not wrinkled, between 5 and 10cm wide, cut rather like those of 93. *G. ibericum* but less complexly; inflorescence dense; floral axis horizontal; flowers about 35mm in diameter; petals notched, violet-blue, with darker, slightly forked veins. Rock garden. July, August.

Perennial with thick rootstock, developing above ground for several centimetres. Blades of basal leaves between 5 and 10cm wide, angular in outline, divided as far as about $^6/_7$ into 7; divisions broadest about the middle, palmato-pinnately lobed, lobing and toothing continued down the sides below the middle but not nearly to the base; lobes about twice as long as broad, the lateral sometimes curving outwards, toothed, the teeth sometimes widely spreading. Teeth and tips of lobes very acute. Stem-leaves similar, decreasing gradually in size and length of stalk upwards, all stalked, the first one or two solitary, others paired. Sepals and rostrum with long eglandular hairs, hairs otherwise minute, crisped, eglandular. Stems slender, with the first two internodes very long, the solitary leaves accompanied by a pair of branches or a branch and a cymule, paired leaves mostly with a pair of branches and a cymule. Inflorescence dense but peduncles not suppressed, mostly not more than 4cm and often shorter than pedicels. Pedicels mostly $1–1^1/_2$ times as long as sepals. Floral axis more or less horizontal. Flowers almost flat. Sepals 7–10mm, flushed with purple; mucro 2–3mm. Petals up to 18 x 14mm, broadest near apex, notched, rather deep violet-blue with darker, forking veins, reaching about $^2/_3$ of the way to the apex, pale at extreme base. Filaments at first divergent, later recurved, lilac-pink with white base, with long coarse hairs and minute hairs on the enlarged base; anthers bluish. Stigmas about 1.5mm, dull pink. Rostrum about 25mm with stylar portion about 3mm. Mericarps about 4.5mm. Discharge: seed-ejection (twist).

North-east Turkey, S.W. Caucasus.

This species has probably been introduced on a number of occasions but is apt to die out. A group of plants was raised at Cambridge from seed from Nalchik Botanic Garden in the Caucasus in 1965; they did well on the rock garden until 1977 when they unaccountably died. Quantities of seeds were set in some years but I never saw any germinating near the parent plants. Some which I sowed produced only a handful of seedlings and I failed to raise any to maturity. It is an unassuming but quite attractive plant, flowering later than its allies.

This species has been crossed by Alan Bremner with 93. *G. ibericum.*

96. G. renardii Trautvetter (Figure 9.106, Plate 38)
Low-growing perennial with rounded sage-textured leaves, shallowly divided and lobed; inflorescence dense; petals wedge-shaped, notched, white or pale violet, with bold, slightly forked violet veins. Rock garden, wall, patio, sun or partial shade. June.

Figure 9.106. *G. renardii*: from T. Watson, 1955, *ex* Munich B.G.; 8.5cm wide

Perennial with thick woody rootstock trailing above ground. Blades of basal leaves up to 12cm wide, grey-green, finely wrinkled, divided as far as $^1/_2$ into 5 or 7; divisions broader than long, usually with spaces between them and with a wide space between the basal pair, scarcely tapered below the middle, roughly semi-circular above it, with shallowly 3-lobed or 5-lobed apex; lobes shorter than broad, toothed. Teeth and tips of lobes obtuse. Stem-leaves paired, sometimes one pair not much smaller than basal, otherwise abruptly reduced in size and length of stalk and much altered in shape. Hairs eglandular or those of the pedicels sometimes glandular, those of leaf-blades short, forming a deciduous felt on upper surfaces and a thick persistent felt on lower surfaces. Stems slender, usually once or twice forked, the tips of the branches bearing dense umbel-like clusters of flowers, usually without peduncles. Pedicels $1–1^1/_2$ times as long as sepals. Floral axis horizontal or upwardly inclined. Flowers flat. Sepals 7–9mm; mucro about 0.5mm. Petals about 15–18 x 9–10mm, $1^1/_2–2$ times as long as wide, wedge-shaped, notched, not contiguous, white or bluish white or inclining towards lavender or violet, boldly marked with violet feathered veins. Filaments with long coarse hairs below, moderately enlarged at base, there white, otherwise deep violet; anthers yellow with violet edges. Stigmas about 2mm, dull reddish, style the same colour. Immature fruits erect on erect pedicels. Rostrum about 25mm with stylar portion 4–5mm. Mericarps about 4mm. Discharge: seed-ejection (twist).

Caucasus.

An attractive and unmistakable plant, unique in its foliage and almost so in its flowers. It was introduced by Walter Ingwersen in 1935 (Ingwersen, 1946) and he says that the ground-colour of the petals is "pastel-lavender", while Bobrov (1949) says it is pale pink. Ingwersen found the plant on rock-cliffs and recommends that it should never be grown in "fat" soil, but should be provided with a meagre diet and wedged between rocks to maintain its dwarf and compact habit. Otherwise it becomes coarse and cabbagy. It grows and flowers particularly well in Scotland and northern England, and does not seem to disappoint, despite general neglect of Ingwersen's advice.

G. renardii 'Walter Ingwersen' is a name applied to the stock which received an Award of Merit at the Wisley Trial in 1976, as it was considered desirable to specify that it was Ingwersen's own introduction, though it was sent for trial by Mr Graham Thomas (the specific epithet was omitted from the name in the report of the trial). Ingwersen's "pastel lavender" notwithstanding, the report of the Wisley trial described the flowers as white with purple venation, and to me the ground colour of the petals of plants in cultivation up to the time of edn.1 is white. However, Hibberd (1994), while illustrating this form, describes the colour as "palest bluish purple", and Bath & Jones (1994) call it "opal white".

G. renardii 'Tschelda' has upwardly inclined flowers and light violet, heavily veined petals, the veins forking but not netted. It was introduced by Dr Hans Simon; Jansen (1997) states that it is *G. platypetalum* x *G. renardii* collected by Dr Simon in the Caucasus. However, its characters do not give much support for the idea that it is a hybrid.

G. renardii 'Whiteknights' was obtained by Reading University in 1975 through international seed exchange with Greifswald Botanic Garden in the then East Germany. The floral axis is upwardly inclined and the ground colour of the petals is "mid-bluish purple". The growth is looser, with longer flower-stalks, than in 'Walter Ingwersen' (Hibberd, 1994). It is named for the University of Reading estate, not for any colouring in the plant.

A description by Y.N. Woronow of a hybrid with 92. *G. platypetalum* is quoted by Bobrov (1949); the hybrid was found in nature at two localities. For another possible occurrence of this hybrid see above under *G. renardii* 'Tschelda'. More recently the cross was made artificially by both Ivan Louette in Belgium and Alan Bremner in Orkney. Louette's clone is called 'Philippe Vapelle' and the same name is being applied to Bremner's cross because these synthesised hybrids are very much alike, with leaves and flowers intermediate between those of the parents, the petal colour being a fairly deep blue-violet.

Other hybrids are with 101. *G. gracile*, 93. *G. ibericum*, 98. *G. libani* and 97. *G. peloponnesiacum* (Alan Bremner).

97. *G. peloponnesiacum* Boissier (Figure 9.107, Plate 39)

Perennial about 60cm tall with glandular hairs above; blades of basal leaves 10–20cm wide, divided as far as $^3/_4$ or less into 7; divisions diamond-shaped, with rather solid outline, cut half-way to the midrib; flowers 38–43mm in diameter, in loose umbel-like clusters on tall stems; petals notched, porcelain-blue, with slightly smudgy feathered or netted dark veins; plant dormant after flowering. Leaves present in winter. Border, rock garden. May.

Perennial from a thick rhizome. Basal leaves appearing in autumn; their blades (in spring) wrinkled, 10–20cm wide, divided as far as $^2/_3$ or $^3/_4$ into 5 or 7; divisions broad, tapered both ways from about the middle, with entire, straight or concave sides below the broadest part, palmato-pinnately lobed, edges of lobes and divisions often faintly marked with a wide brown band; lobes about as long as broad, toothed. Teeth and tips of lobes mostly obtuse. Stem-leaves paired, with 3 or 5 divisions, the lowest larger than the basal, gradually reduced in size and length of stalk upwards, the uppermost almost stalkless. Hairs mostly straight and spreading; upper parts of plant with glandular hairs but these few on the sepals. Stems with long internodes. Some peduncled cymules present but most flowers in umbel-like clusters and then on long

Figure 9.107. *G. peloponnesiacum*: from Wisley, 1971, coll. Greece: Lower Pindus (R. Gorer); 7 and 8.5cm wide

pedicels, 3–5 times as long as sepals, so that inflorescence is not dense. Flowers upwardly inclined, shallowly funnel-shaped. Sepals 9–12mm; mucro 1–1.5mm. Petals up to about 25 x 17mm, deeply notched, straight-sided, rather pale violet-blue with darker but not sharply drawn feathered or slightly netted veins, ground-colour often paler towards base, front surface with or without occasional hairs towards base. Filaments straight when anthers are functional, purplish pink. Anthers cream with blue edges. Stigmas about 1mm, greenish. Rostrum about 22mm including stylar portion 2–3mm. Discharge: seed–ejection (twist).

Greece.

This species was not introduced until about 1972 when Mr Richard Gorer collected seed at Karpenisi in the Lower Pindus mountains. I saw young plants at Wisley in 1973 and was allowed to take three back to Cambridge.

G. peloponnesiacum is a lovely plant, producing sprays of large pastel-blue flowers in May on long stalks which sway in the breeze.

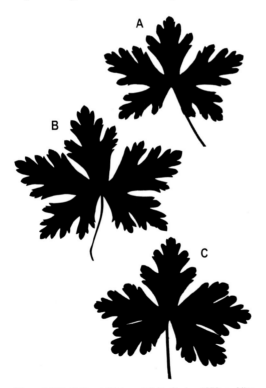

Figure 9.108. *G. libani*: (A) from A.R.M. Clarke, 1978, *ex* Miss J. Robinson (B) larger leaf of same stock, cult. Alan Bloom, 1983 (C) from Kew (202-74-01899), 1978, coll. Lebanon: Mt. Lebanon; 6, 13.5 and 7cm wide (unequal reductions)

Despite its height, I suggest that it may be acceptable on the rock garden because of its summer dormancy.

The species has crossed with 98. *G. libani* (its closest relative) and 96. *G. renardii*.

98. *G. libani* Davis (*G. libanoticum* (Boissier) Boissier, not Schenk; *G. peloponnesiacum* Boissier var. *libanoticum* Boissier) (Figure 9.108)
Perennial about 40cm tall; blades of basal leaves glossy above, divided as far as $^2/_3$ or $^4/_5$ into 5 or 7, with rather broken outline; flowers about 28–32mm in diameter; petals notched, medium violet-blue or violet, with more or less smudgy, slightly feathered veins. Plant dormant in summer. Leaves present in winter. Rock garden. April, May.

Differs from 97. *G. peloponnesiacum* in its lesser height, glossy upper leaf-surfaces, more open (gappy) leaf division and lobing, the lateral lobes of the divisions curving outwards, abrupt decrease in size of stem-leaves after the first pair, absence of glandular hairs, pedicels about twice as long as sepals, shorter sepals (7–9mm), shorter petals (17–20mm), and longer rostrum (30–35mm) with stylar portion only about 3mm. Discharge: seed-ejection (twist).

Lebanon, W. Syria, central S. Turkey.

This species reached Cambridge in 1978 from two sources, and the plants are rather different. Kew (Wakehurst) sent plants collected in 1974 at the source of the Kidisha River, Mount Lebanon, and Mr Andrew Clarke gave me a clone obtained from Miss J. Robinson. No locality is available for the latter but Miss Robinson received it from an acquaintance who was known to have visited Lebanon.

The Kew plant has broader leaf-divisions and lobes and broader, bluer, petals, making a more desirable type of flower. Mr Clarke's plant has narrower and more violet petals but is much more free-flowering. I saw a fine clump of it flowering in light shade at Bressingham Gardens, Norfolk, in 1983. The synonymy of this species shows, firstly, that it has been called *G. libanoticum*, a name which it cannot retain because *G. libanoticum* Schenck has priority (the name applies to a species that belongs to the Tuberosum Group which is not in cultivation) (Davis & Roberts, 1955) and, secondly, that Boissier considered it sufficiently similar to 97. *G. peloponnesiacum* to treat it as a variety of the latter.

This species has crossed with 97. *G. peloponnesiacum* and 96. *G. renardii*.

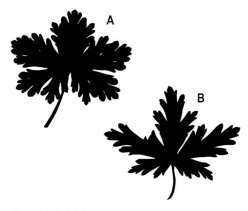

Figure 9.109. *(A) G. bohemicum*; (B) *G. lanuginosum*: from Antwerp B.G., 1971, (damaged); 5.5 and 6cm wide

99. G. bohemicum Linnaeus (Figure 9.109A)
Sprawling, hairy biennial; blades of main leaves wrinkled, divided as far as about $^3/_4$ into 5 or 7 broadly diamond-shaped, closely toothed and lobed divisions. Lobes and teeth very short, more or less acute. Glandular hairs present on leaf-stalks, stems, peduncles, pedicels, sepals and rostra. Inflorescence diffuse, leafy, with long-stalked leaves. Flowers up to about 23mm in diameter. Sepals about 6mm, enlarging to 9mm; mucro 1.5–2mm. Petals about 9–11 x 8–9mm, notched, moderately strongly violet-blue with darker, forked veins, these converging to a pinkish zone at base; base with hairs on each side forming a small tuft. Stamens and styles just under $^2/_3$ as long as sepals. Stigmas green or whitish. Rostrum about 22mm, without a distinct stylar portion. Mericarps about 5mm, black. Seeds mottled in light and dark brown. Cotyledons with a notch on each side. Discharge: seed-ejection (twist).

East and C. Europe, north to S. Scandinavia.

Among annual and biennial species of *Geranium* only two, *G. bohemicum* and 100. *G. lanuginosum*, have blue flowers. Those of *G. bohemicum* might be considered just big enough to give the plant some appeal, at least to the more ardent devotees of the genus. *G. bohemicum* was the subject of detailed investigation by the Swedish botanist Hedlund (1901) who studied specially its rather peculiar seed-ejection arrangement which, we now know (Tokarski, 1972), is common to the Tuberosum and Platypetalum Groups. He also noted that the occurrence of the plant is very sporadic and associated with the sites of fires (see Chapter 2). The character of the notched cotyledons is shared only with the two species of Section Divaricata in

Subgenus Robertium (see 112. *G. albanum*) and 131. *G. aristatum* of Subgenus Erodioidea.

Another Swedish botanist, K.V.O. Dahlgren (1923, 1925), carried out crossing experiments between *G. bohemicum* and 100. *G. lanuginosum* and obtained sterile hybrids with marbled leaves (see Chapter 7).

100. G. lanuginosum Lamarck (*G. bohemicum* Linnaeus subsp. *depraehensum* Almquist) (Figure 9.109B)
Sprawling, glandular-hairy annual, forming a rosette when over-wintering, similar to 99. *G. bohemicum*; leaves not wrinkled, marbled, with lobes and teeth finger-like, being deeper than those of *G. bohemicum* and parallel-sided with rounded tips. Flowers up to 16mm in diameter. Sepals 3.5–5mm in flower, enlarging to about 8mm. Petals 8–9 x 6–7mm, campanula-blue but pale pinkish white between veins in basal half; base with hairs on each side forming a sparse fringe. Stigmas purplish pink. Rostrum about 18mm. Seeds uniformly brown. Cotyledons not notched. Discharge: seed-ejection (twist).

Mediterranean region, including N.W. Africa, Sweden (where it is perhaps introduced).

This species, of no garden value, is included here because it is so like 99. *G. bohemicum* that it could be taken for it by anyone unaware that it existed. It has been artificially crossed with the preceding species, q.v.

101. G. gracile Nordmann (Figure 9.110)
Noticeably hairy perennial to about 40cm tall, with light green, wrinkled, slightly glossy leaf-blades, the basal divided as far as $^2/_3$ or $^3/_4$ into 5 or 7; divisions scarcely lobed, more or less saw-edged; flowers deeply funnel-shaped; petals narrow, notched, pale to deep pink, with white base and eyelash-like veins. Woodland. June onwards.

Plant with a thick, much-branched rootstock. Blades of basal leaves light green, wrinkled, up to 20cm wide, divided as far as $^2/_3$ or occasionally $^3/_4$ into 5 or 7; divisions diamond-shaped or broadly elliptic, tapered both ways from above the middle, with teeth continuing down the sides well below the broadest part, scarcely lobed but with numerous regular or alternately large and small teeth. Teeth incurved, highly asymmetric, more or less acute. (Another type of leaf with more distinct lobes and very few coarse teeth may be produced under conditions favouring very rapid growth.) Stem-leaves paired, similar to the prevalent type of basal leaf but with 3 or 5 divisions, decreasing

Figure 9.110. *G. gracile*: cult. P.F. Yeo, 1983, coll. Turkey: Trabzon Prov. (Lancaster 79); 19cm wide

gradually in size and length of stalk upwards. Upper parts of plant, apart from leaves, with glandular hairs. Stem forking repeatedly, forming inflorescences of prolonged growth, leafless in the upper parts, never densely flowered. Peduncles mostly 2–4cm. Pedicels about $1\frac{1}{2}$–$2\frac{1}{2}$ times as long as sepals. Flowers erect, funnel-shaped. Sepals 6–7mm; mucro 1.5–2mm. Petals about 21 x 9mm, wedge-shaped, notched, erect at base, flared above, pale pink gently shaded to white towards the base or bright deep pink with white basal third, the lower part of the coloured zone with short purple veins; base with a sparse hair-fringe on either side. Filaments of the inner and outer whorls more unequal than usual, tinged pink, basal enlargement inconspicuous, large hairs more restricted to base than in other members of the Platypetalum Group. Anthers cream with blue edges. Stigmas deep flesh-pink. Rostrum about 23–26mm with stylar portion about 4mm but not well demarcated. Mericarps about 4.5mm, dark brown. Discharge: seed-ejection (twist).

North-east Turkey, S. Caucasus, N. Iran.

Plants growing at Cambridge were collected by Mr Roy Lancaster in woodland below the Sumena Monastery, south of Trabzon, N.E. Turkey in 1977 (no. L. 79). I supposed this to be a new introduction but while writing this book I discovered a dried specimen cultivated at Cambridge in 1900 and

another grown at Kew in 1930. After edn.1 was published I found the pale form, now covered by my description, in two gardens in The Netherlands, and introduced it to Britain.

This species has attractive foliage and charming flowers (especially in clones with well-developed 'eyelash' marks on the petals); in hot dry conditions smaller flowers of paler colour are produced.

Superficially *G. gracile* is extraordinarily like a hairy version of 5. *G. nodosum* (of the Endressii Group) and quite unlike all other species of the Platypetalum Group. Like *G. nodosum* it is a woodland plant, and the similarity is a testimony to the forces of natural selection operating in similar environments. Presumably the type of leaf seen in these two plants is well adapted to woodland conditions, and the resemblance in the flowers suggests that both have been forced to adapt themselves to similar types of pollinating insect. Gone are the blues of the flowers of most members of the group, and their dense inflorescences (there is a long flowering period), while the hairs on the petals and filaments and the basal enlargements of the filaments are reduced, these being evidently unnecessary in the deeply funnel-shaped flowers.

G. gracile is unequivocally placed in the Platypetalum Group by its fruit, but it also shows resemblance to its true relatives in the form of the exceptional basal leaves mentioned in the description and in having very long hairs on its sepals. Although the fruit-type distinguishes it from members of the Endressii Group, additional characters are mentioned in discussion under nos. 1, 2, 4 and 5. Finally, its affinity with other members of the Platypetalum Group is shown by its hybrids with them (see below).

G. gracile 'Blanche', listed by Hibberd (1994), is probably the pale form described in my discussion. *G. gracile* 'Blush' is the rather inappropriate name for the deep pink form (Hibberd, 1994).

G. gracile has crossed with 93. *G. ibericum* and 96. *G. renardii*. The former cross was made by Dr Hans Simon and brought into commerce as 'Sirak'; Alan Bremner has made the same cross and it has been circulated under the same name. It clearly combines the characters of its parents but this knowledge does little to tell us what a superb plant these have produced (Plate 40). The latter cross goes under the name 'Chantilly' (Hibberd, 1994; Moss, 1997.

SUBGENUS II ROBERTIUM

Plants annual or perennial. Fruit-discharge by carpel projection: each carpel is thrown off explosively with the seed in it and the awn drops away at the moment of explosion. Base of mericarp rounded, without a horny point or blunt tubercle.

SECTION POLYANTHA, THE POLYANTHES GROUP

Perennial plants with a thick knobbly rootstock. Petals rounded at apex. Style not more than 6mm, stigmas less than 2mm. Mericarps 4–5mm, acute at apex, blunt at base, with netted ribs. Eight species from the Himalayas and the mountains of Burma and S.W. China.

102. G. polyanthes Edgeworth & J.D. Hooker
(Figure 9.111, Plate 41)
Perennial, 20–45cm tall, with slightly succulent rounded leaves, the lobes and teeth confined to the apices of the divisions. Flowers partly in umbel-like clusters, about 25mm wide, funnel-shaped, deep pink, reminiscent of *Oxalis*. Rock garden. July.

Rootstock thick, knobbly, tuber-like. Leaves slightly succulent, often narrowly edged with red. Blades of basal leaves up to 5cm wide, occasionally more, rounded in outline, divided as far as $^2/_3$ or $^4/_5$ into 7 or 9; divisions broadest at the apex where they are lobed for $^1/_5$ of their length; lobes mostly with a few small teeth. Teeth and tips of lobes acute or obtuse with a small point, all reaching about the same level. Stipules about 6mm broad, ovate, sometimes toothed at the top. Stem-leaves similar, but the upper with fewer and narrower divisions; lower solitary; uppermost paired, some of these almost without stalks and with unequal lobes. Cymules without peduncles; pedicels hairy; flowers partly in umbel-like clusters, erect, funnel-shaped. Sepals 6–7mm, hardly at all spreading, green, flushed with purplish red, densely covered with glandular hairs; mucro 0.75mm or less. Petals about 12–15mm, about $1^1/_2$ times as long as broad, bright purplish pink with fine, slightly feathered veins, a glistening texture and pale base, rounded at apex, gradually tapered at base; base with a tuft of fine hairs on margins but no hairs on front surface. Filaments 4.5mm, white. Anthers about 0.7mm, yellow. Style about 3mm; stigmas 1.5mm, yellowish, tipped with pink. Immature fruits and pedicels erect. Rostrum with no stylar portion. Mericarps 4mm, with a network of raised veins, finely hairy, acute at apex. Discharge: carpel-projection.

Figure 9.111. *G. polyanthes*: from O. Polunin, 1978, coll. India: Sikkim/Nepal border, Uttar Pradesh; 8cm wide

Himalayas from Nepal eastwards, S.W. China (Yunnan).

This is an attractive plant but it seems to be temperamental in cultivation, though not difficult to establish initially, nor to increase by division. Its natural habitat is alpine meadows. It begins growth very late – perhaps in May.

Sometimes some of the flowers are cleistogamous.

G. polyanthes has been repeatedly introduced from the Himalayas, and is often sold by local dealers in wild-flower seeds, sometimes as 39. *G. donianum*. The two species can be distinguished by their seeds, *G. donianum* having seeds that are ejected from the carpel and appear smooth, whereas *G. polyanthes* seeds are shed (and therefore despatched) in their carpels, showing the raised network of veins and coat of fine hairs. *G. donianum* differs also in having deeply lobed leaf-divisions.

103. G. nakaoanum Hara
Low-growing, apparently tuberous alpine producing rounded leaves with 7 or 9 divisions. Cymules 1-flowered. Flowers to 35mm wide, intense pinkish red, like those of *102. G. polyanthes*.

Perennial from a probably tuberous rootstock with stems to about 12cm. Leaves mostly basal, the blades of these not more than 3cm wide, divided as far as about $^5/_6$ into 7 or 9; divisions broadest at the apex, giving the blade a kidney-shaped outline, 3-lobed at the apex for about $^1/_3$ of their length, the lobes occasionally toothed. Inflorescence loose. Cymules 1-flowered, with peduncles to 15cm, pedicels to 6.5cm, both with small recurved hairs. Flowers similar to those of *G. polyanthes* (that is, medium-sized, with intensely coloured petals and very small, *Oxalis*-like, male and female organs). Sepals 5–7mm with mucro 0.5mm and very small hairs. Fruit like that of 102. *G. polyanthes*. Discharge: carpel projection.

Himalayas (C. and E. Nepal, Sikkim, Bhutan).

Mr B. Wynn-Jones tells me that 'HWJCM 504', collected at an altitude of 4,000m, is in cultivation and represents this species. There have been other reported introductions but I have not seen it in flower. Photographs taken in the field show the resemblance of the flowers to those of 102. *G. polyanthes*. Most of the specimens in the Natural History Museum, London, lack fruits, suggesting that some animal eats them. Because of this I assigned *G. nakaoanum* to subgenus *Geranium* when contributing notes to the *Flora of Nepal*. Later I found a misplaced specimen at the Museum that bore one ripe fruit, which showed clearly that the species belongs to subgenus Robertium.

104. G. strictipes Knuth (*G. strigosum* Franchet, not Burman) (Plate 42)
High-altitude perennial with thick rootstock, with flowering shoots lacking basal leaves and sometimes with the lowest leaves in a whorl of three. Flowers about 20mm wide, in 2-flowered cymules, erect, more or less funnel-shaped, deep purplish pink. Lower leaves rounded, deeply divided. Glandular hairs present. Summer.

Perennial with a massive rootstock to 2.5cm thick. Stems to about 30cm, erect or ascending, reddish, the first node sometimes producing 2 or 3 leaves and 2 or 3 branches, those above producing paired unequal leaves and paired or solitary branches; eglandular hairs either small and curved or large and straight; glandular hairs several-celled, with conspicuous heads; internodes sometimes rapidly decreasing upwards. Basal leaves absent from flowering shoots. Lower stem leaves to 7cm wide, their blades firm, divided as far as $^3/_4$ or nearly to the base into 5 or 7, circular to kidney-shaped in outline; divisions broadly rhombic, palmato-pinnately lobed for $^1/_4$–$^1/_2$ their length; lobes with one or two teeth. Teeth and tips of lobes ovate, acuminate, usually curving outwards. Upper surface of blades dull, red-edged, with larger and smaller appressed eglandular hairs, lower surface much paler, with loose large eglandular hairs. Leaf-stalks to 4 times as long as blade, clothed as the stem. Stipules 8–10mm, lanceolate, tailed, red, hairy. Upper stem leaves reduced, divided into 3 or 5. Inflorescence loose. Lowest peduncles 5–15cm, upper 4–6cm. Pedicels mostly 1–2.5cm. Peduncles and pedicels clothed as the leaves, erect. Flowers nodding in bud, about 2cm wide, erect and deeply saucer-shaped to funnel-shaped when open. Sepals 6–8mm, green, with glandular and eglandular hairs; mucro 1.5–2.5mm. Petals 11–15mm, triangular, often weakly notched at

apex, slightly clawed at base, deep purplish pink with colourless or pale green base, with fine dark purple feathered veins, strongly bearded at the base, the hairs extending across front and back surfaces. Stamens 5–6mm, expanded at base, curving outwards at tips, white, those over the nectaries hairy at base; anthers purplish. Styles and stigmas slightly exceeding the sepals; stigmas about 2mm, reddish on the outside or flesh-coloured. Fruit erect, hairy, with glandular-hairy rostrum about 2.5cm. Carpels 6mm, acute at apex, with a network of raised ribs, minutely hairy. Discharge: carpel projection.

China (Sichuan, Yunnan).

In this description some of the ranges are given as less than in my revision of Chinese species (Yeo, 1992) to make it more closely applicable to stocks in cultivation at the time of writing. These are Lancaster 1685B, N.W. Yunnan: Nandian, N. of Dali, 2,350m (Cambridge accession no. 1989.0744) and Sino-British Lijiang Expedition, SBLE 603, Central N. Yunnan: Lijiang Yulong Shan, Ganghoba, 3,250m (Cambridge accession no. 1992.0665 Edinburgh). This interesting species has quite showy flowers. When the rootstock gets too thick it may rot off, but this may be forestalled by timely division and removal of dead tissue. Its nearest relative in cultivation is 105. *G. hispidissimum*.

105. G. hispidissimum (Franchet) Knuth (Figure 9.112)
Perennial with a thick rootstock and strongly rounded and shallowly cut leaves. Herbage more or less shaggy-hairy. Flowers scattered, to 22mm wide, with white to purplish hairy-based petals. Summer.

Figure 9.112. *G. hispidissimum*: cult. R. Lancaster, 1987, coll. China (Lancaster 1685A); 10cm wide

Perennial with a massive rootstock to 2cm thick. Stems to about 30cm, erect or ascending, with paired leaves and branches below, and paired leaves and solitary branches above, with recurved eglandular hairs and long, many-celled, small-headed glandular hairs. Blades of basal leaves to 11cm wide, divided as far as $^1/_2-^4/_5$ into 5 or 7, circular to kidney-shaped in outline; divisions wedge-shaped or waisted, widest at the apex or shortly tapered, 3-lobed at the apex, with the lobes about as long as wide, with notably unequal teeth; teeth and tips of lobes sometimes curving outwards, acute, acuminate or rounded and cuspidate. Upper surface of leaf-blades sometimes stained with purple in the sinuses, with appressed glandular hairs, lower surface pale, prominently veined, sometimes flushed with purple, with denser and looser hairs than the upper. Leaf-stalks clothed as the stems, $1^1/_2-2^1/_2$ times as long as the blade. Basal stipules unknown. Stem leaves smaller, divided as far as $^2/_3-^3/_4$ into 3 or 5, tips of lobes and teeth acute or acuminate, with hairy ovate-lanceolate to linear stipules 8–12mm long. Inflorescence loose. Lowest peduncles 7–14cm, even the upper 3cm long or more. Pedicels mostly 1.5–3.5cm. Peduncles and pedicels clothed as the stems. Flowers more or less erect, shallowly bowl-shaped or shallowly funnel-shaped. Sepals about 5.5mm, glandular-hairy, with mucro 1.5–2mm. Petals 9–12mm, $1^1/_2$ times as long as broad or less, rounded at apex, white, pink with paler base and paler back, or purplish red, their margins and upper surface hairy at extreme base, the margins also hairy for $^1/_4$ length of petal. Stamen filaments about 4.5mm, white, widened and hairy at base, curving outwards at tips. Stigmas 1–1.5mm, crimson on the back, flesh-pink on the receptive surface. Fruit erect, hairy, with rostrum 16–22mm, including stylar portion about 1.5mm. Mericarps 4–4.5mm, acute at apex, net-veined on either side of midrib, minutely hairy. Discharge: carpel projection.

China (Sichuan and Yunnan, mainly the latter).

This plant was introduced to cultivation in Britain by Roy Lancaster (L 1658A). It is interesting as a member of the Polyanthes Group but so far has not shown signs of garden value. Its relative, 104. *G. strictipes*, has finer flowers. A more recent introduction to Britain was mediated by Chen Yi of the Chinese nursery firm of Kai Chen; the condition of the rootstocks that I have seen suggested that the exporters (or their suppliers) are digging plants from the wild. This material was misidentified as *G. dahuricum*.

SECTION TRILOPHA, THE TRILOPHUM GROUP

Annuals with no rosette, the stem internodes all elongated. Inflorescence diffuse. Flowering precociously, most of the flowers being cleistogamous (i.e. self-fertilised in the bud and never opening), these with shortened pedicels and no peduncles. Open (chasmogamous) flowers usually with a dark eye and always with dark stamens and stigmas. Pollen white or dark. Mericarps either with a pattern of ribs and an acute apex, or with a large toothed crest round the edge.

Six species of East and West Africa and the Arabian Peninsula, South Iran; one species re-appears in the Himalayas and S.W. China. They are not important in general horticulture but are interesting for their specialised features.

Germination is sometimes very poor but can be induced by scratching the seeds (not the mericarps).

Key to species of the Trilophum Group (see How to Use the Dichotomous Keys, p. 50)

1a. Mericarp with a saw-edged wing, on each side of the midrib, that is rolled so that the two rows of teeth are directed towards each other (mericarp very much larger than the seed) 2

b. Mericarp without toothed wings (not much larger than the seed) 4

2a. Each wing of mericarp drawn out into a hook at the apex *108. biuncinatum*

b. Mericarp without hooks 3

3a. Mericarps less than 5mm; leaves deeply cut (Fig. 9.113A) *106. omphalodeum*

b. Mericarps 5–5.5mm; leaves shallowly cut (Fig. 9.113B) *107. trilophum*

4a. Mericarps with strong horizontal ribs and, sometimes, weaker vertical ribs *109. ocellatum*

b. Mericarps with deep horizontal and vertical folds 5

5a. Leaves shallowly cut (like Fig. 9.113B); chasmogamous flowers with a nearly black centre *110. mascatense*

b. Leaves deeply and finely cut (Fig. 9.116); petals merely darkened near base by convergence of dark veins *111. favosum*

106. G. omphalodeum Lange (Figure 9.113A)
Leaf-blades not more than 5cm wide, divided as far as $^5/_6$ into 5; divisions coarsely and deeply pinnately lobed; lobes with an occasional tooth. Flowers 14mm in diameter; petals 8mm long, strongly overlapping, deep pink, slightly paler towards base, with dark veins in basal half which become much stronger at base. Stamens (except at extreme base) and stigmas deep purplish violet. Mericarps 4–4.75mm, with a toothed ridge down the middle and a wide recurved and toothed wing round the edge, rather dark brown to nearly black, apex extending beyond the lateral wings. Discharge: carpel projection.

This plant is in circulation among botanic gardens under the name *G. trilophum* (no. 107), where it was placed by Knuth (1912). It rarely produces open flowers in Cambridge but I once saw a clump of it flowering freely in the Copenhagen Botanic Garden (this stock has been tried at Cambridge) so at least somewhere in Europe it will behave as a decorative annual. *G. omphalodeum* was described from plants in the Copenhagen Botanic Garden in 1865, and it has every appearance of being specifically distinct but I cannot match it with wild plants in herbaria. Recognition of its distinctness here may lead to its rediscovery in nature.

107. G. trilophum Boissier (Figure 9.113B)
Leaf-blades often more than 5cm but less than 10cm wide, divided as far as $^1/_2$ or just beyond into 5; divisions shallowly 3-lobed at the top; lobes frequently toothed. Flowers 18–22mm in diameter; petals 10mm, not or only slightly overlapping, deep pink with a black base or rose-pink with a transverse band of white just below the middle and below this a lilac-pink area darkened by diffuse veins; stamens blackish except at base; stigmas blackish with nearly white tips. Mericarps 6mm, with a toothed ridge down the middle and a wide recurved and toothed wing round the edge, pale brown or orange-brown, apex overtopped by lateral wings. Discharge: carpel projection.

S. Red Sea region, Oman, S.W. Iran.

The form with paler petals, received at Cambridge in 1981, was collected by Dr A.G. Miller of Edinburgh Botanic Garden, at Dhofar, Oman, at an altitude of 900m. Also in the 1980s I grew five samples of this species collected in the mountains of Saudi Arabia by Mrs Sheila Collenette. Their flowers had black centres, suggesting that Dr Miller's pale form was a minor aberration. Their mericarps showed colour variation (see description).

108. G. biuncinatum Kokwaro (*G. yemense* in the sense of Knuth) (Figure 9.114, Plate 43)
Similar in habit and foliage to the Arabian (Yemeni) form of 109. *G. ocellatum* but with petals up to 10.5mm, $^3/_4$ as wide as long, overlapping, the basal triangle with a fine white border, and with the mericarp body 6.5mm long (excluding the hooks), with raised midrib and a wide recurved and toothed wing round the edge like that of 107. *G. trilophum*, but continued at the top into a hook on either side looking like a pair of horns. Discharge: carpel-projection.

Figure 9.113. (A) *G. omphalodeum*: from Amsterdam B.G., 1970; (B) *G. trilophum*: from Dr A.G. Miller, 1981, coll. Oman: Jebel Qara, Dhofar (Miller 2376); x $^2/_3$

Figure 9.114. *G. biuncinatum*: from Kew, 1981, coll. Yemen Arab Republic: Jebel Bura' (Wood 3126); x $^2/_3$

Southern Red Sea region.

G. biuncinatum flowers quite freely at the beginning of the year in the greenhouse and has relatively large flowers, as well as most remarkable fruits. I have grown three stocks at Cambridge: one from J.R.I. Wood, collected at Jebel Bura', Yemen, and given to Cambridge in 1981 by Kew Botanic Garden, and two from mountain localities in Saudi Arabia collected by Mrs Sheila Collenette, nos. 6112 and 6231.

109. *G. ocellatum* Cambessèdes (Figure 9.115)
Leaf-blades not more than 10cm wide, rather profusely lobed and toothed, divided as far as $2/3$ or slightly more into 5 or 7; divisions tapered both ways from above the middle; lobes about as long as broad, usually with 2 teeth; tips of lobes and teeth obtuse to acute. Flowers 10–22mm in diameter, deep pink with a black eye. Mericarps horizontally ribbed.

Mountains of W. Africa (Cameroon, S.W. Angola), E. Africa, Arabian Peninsula, Himalayas, S.W. China.

I have grown examples from Angola, Tanzania, Yemen and India. The Asian form is prostrate and I believe this holds throughout the Himalayan and Chinese parts of the distribution. The Arabian and African forms are more or less erect. The Angolan sample (Figure 9.115C) rarely produces its small chasmogamous flowers; the chasmogamous flowers of the East African sample (acquired only in 1996) have not yet been seen. The Yemeni and Indian stocks are described here.

109a. *G. ocellatum* Cambessèdes Yemen stock
(Figure 9.115D)
Petals about 9.5mm, about $1^{1/2}$ times as long as wide, not overlapping, deep pink with a black triangle at the base; stamens blackish except at extreme base; stigmas dark red. Mericarps about 2.5mm, with a raised midrib and about 9 transverse ribs on either side, all ribs covered with minute hairs.

This stock was received at Cambridge in 1981 from Dr A.G. Miller of Edinburgh. He collected it at Shibam in the Yemen Arab Republic (Miller & Long 3372). It produces a small number of open (chasmogamous) flowers out of doors and perhaps rather more in the greenhouse.

**109b. *G. ocellatum* Cambessèdes Jammu (India)
stock** (Figure 9.115A & B)
Flowers 19–22 mm in diameter. Petals to 11mm, almost as broad as long, slightly heart-shaped,

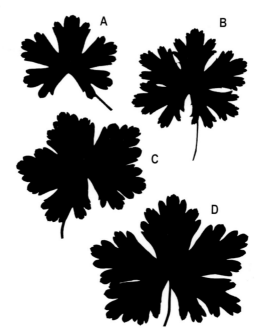

Figure 9.115. *G. ocellatum*: (A) from S.K. Raina, 1981, coll. India: Udampur, Jammu, grown in cool conditions; (B) the same, tropical conditions; (C) from Stockholm B.G., 1972, coll. Angola: Huila Distr. (Kers 3298); (D) from Dr A.G. Miller, 1981, coll. Yemen Arab Republic: Shibam (Miller & Long 3372); unequal reductions: A is 4cm wide, B 4.5cm, C 6.5cm and D 8cm

overlapping, deep purplish pink with a large blackish basal spot. Stamens blackish, with rather dark pollen. Stigmas dark red. Mericarps about 2mm, with a raised midrib and usually 10–12 transverse ribs on either side, hairless.

This stock, collected at Udamphur, in Jammu, India, by S.K. Raina, was received at Cambridge in 1981 and was grown in temperate and tropical greenhouses and out of doors for five years before it produced chasmogamous flowers. It has now done so in the temperate greenhouse in spring in a number of seasons, but I do not know what triggers it.

Chasmogamy in this sample is foreshadowed by the formation of larger leaves on the affected shoots and by the development of peduncles and pedicels. With its large well-formed flowers held above the prostrate foliage, it is very pretty. In 1986 I found that some flowers were only about 14mm in diameter and had only 5 stamens; in addition some such smaller flowers had petals and stamens unequal in size or even had a petal missing. Peduncle/pedicel development is also unstable; sometimes it occurs in cleistogamous cymules, and sometimes chasmogamous cymules are one-flowered or mixed.

110. G. mascatense Boissier
Similar in habit and foliage to 108. *G. biuncinatum* and the Arabian (Yemeni) form of 109. *G. ocellatum*. Petals 7–10 x 5–7mm, not overlapping, purplish pink with a black base and with or without a white boundary line. Mericarps with deep horizontal and vertical folds, as in 111. *G. favosum*.

Red Sea region, Oman, Iranian side of Persian Gulf region.

Grown at Cambridge from seed from Dr A.G. Miller (collected between Jeddah and Taif in the mountains of Saudi Arabia by Mrs Sheila Collenette – no. 1715 – and from Goat Island, Oman by M.D. Gallagher – no. 6398/12); also another Saudi mountain sample from Mrs Collenette (near Jabal Ibrahim – no. 6071) and another Omani sample (from Mr R.P. Whitcombe, collected at 1970m, Sayq).
This species was featured on an Omani postage stamp of the mid-1980s.

111. G. favosum A. Richard (Figure 9.116)
Similar in habit and foliage to 106. *G. omphalodeum* but more robust, and with larger (to 10.5cm wide) leaves. Flowers similar in size and colour to those of 106. *G. omphalodeum*. Mericarps like those of 110. *G. mascatense*.

Figure 9.116. *G. favosum*: from Kew, 1987, coll. Ethiopia, Tissat Falls, S.E. of Bhir Dar (Mesfin, Tadessa & Kagnew, no. 1740); 10cm wide

Sudan, Ethiopia, TFIA, Somalia.

This was grown at Cambridge from seed donated by Kew Botanic Garden It was collected in Ethiopia (Gojjam Region, Tissat Falls, 32km S.E. of Bhir Dar, collectors Mesfin, Tadessa & Kagnew, no. 1740). It has maintained itself for some years on the Geranium Display Bed at Cambridge.

SECTION DIVARICATA, THE ALBANUM GROUP

Annual or perennial plants. Cotyledons notched. Petals more or less notched at apex. Pollen bluish. Rostrum of fruit slender; discharge mechanism inoperative. Mericarps bristly, ribbed or crested.

Two species of N.W. Africa, S. Europe and W. and C. Asia: a perennial, described below, and an annual with very small flowers, *G. divaricatum* Ehrhart. Other species of *Geranium* known to have notched cotyledons are 99. *G. bohemicum* and 131. *G. aristatum*.

112. G. albanum Bieberstein (Figure 9.117, Plate 44)
Perennial with leaves present through the winter. Leaves rounded in outline. Inflorescence diffuse, flowers 22–25mm in diameter with pink, veiny, slightly notched petals. Herbaceous border, ground-cover, wild garden. June, July.

Rootstock compact, much branched. Blades of basal leaves 10–20cm wide, rounded in outline, divided as far as about $^1/_2$ into 9; divisions broad, tapered towards base from near the slightly rounded apex, lobed at the apex for $^1/_4$–$^1/_3$ of their length; lobes with up to about 5 unequal teeth. Tips of teeth and lobes obtuse or some of the teeth acute. Stipules of basal leaves thin, blunt, brown. Stem leaves paired, stalked, divided more deeply than the basal into 5 or 7, with rather narrower, often divergent, lobes and teeth. Plant conspicuously clothed with spreading eglandular hairs; glandular hairs sometimes also present. Stems trailing to more than 1m, forming diffuse inflorescences. Peduncles commonly 4–8cm; pedicels commonly 2.5–4cm, widely divergent. Flowers more or less erect. Sepals 6–7.5mm at flowering time, with mucro about 0.5mm, 7–9mm

Figure 9.117. *G. albanum*; 10cm wide

in fruit, green, flushed with purplish red. Petals about 10–12mm, lightly notched at apex, bright pink with slightly branched deep magenta veins; base with a few hairs on the surface and a small dense tuft at either side. Filaments magenta-pink; anthers violet-blue. Stigmas 1.5mm, deep pink. Immature fruits erect on more or less reflexed pedicels. Rostrum not becoming thickened, 6–8mm. Mericarps 4–4.5mm, broadest near the apex, upper half with a network of raised veins, produced into a crest of bristly teeth at the top. Mericarps, containing the seeds, remaining on plant long after death of calyx and rostrum.

South-east Caucasus and the adjacent part of Iran.

Grows in shrubby vegetation below the treeline. An undistinguished but very reliable and reasonably floriferous plant with a long flowering period. When among tall herbs or shrubs it scrambles and there may be genetic variation in its tendency to scramble. The name of the species derives from Albania, the Latin name for the Caspian province of the Caucasus, today called Daghestan.

SECTION BATRACHIOIDES, THE PYRENAICUM GROUP

Annual or perennial, softly hairy plants. Sepal mucro very small. Petals notched. Pollen bluish. Immature fruits erect on reflexed pedicels. Mericarps ribbed, though sometimes only faintly and only near the midrib at the top.

Four or perhaps five species in Europe and W. Asia.

113. G. pyrenaicum N.L. Burman (Figure 9.118A) Slender perennial with leaves present throughout the year. Leaves rounded in outline. Inflorescence diffuse, flowers about 12–18mm in diameter, with purplish pink (occasionally white) deeply notched petals. Woodland and wild garden. May–October.

Perennial with ill-defined and ill-protected rootstock. Blades of basal leaves up to about 10cm wide, rounded in outline, sometimes broader than long, divided as far as about $^1/_2$–$^2/_3$ into 7 or perhaps 9; divisions broadest at the apex, lobed at the apex for about $^1/_3$ of their length; lobes as broad as or broader than long, usually with 2 lateral teeth but in earliest leaves without teeth. Teeth and tips of lobes obtuse. Stipules of basal leaves ovate, acute, crimson. Stem-leaves paired, like the basal, becoming gradually reduced in size and length of stalk upwards, the uppermost with narrower, acute, toothless lobes. Plant with a dense clothing

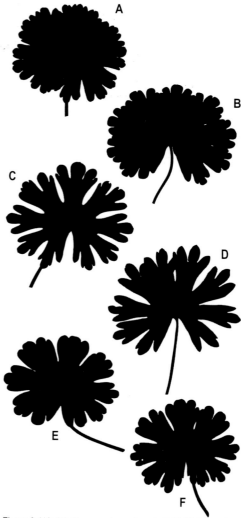

Figure 9.118. (A) *G. pyrenaicum*: from Dr S.M. Walters, 1975, coll. Georgia: Caucasus (SMW 75/457): (B) *G. brutium*, from K.A. Beckett, 1981, coll. Yugoslavia: Montenegro; (C) & (D) *G. pusillum*, weed in Cambridge B.G.; (E) & (F) *G. molle*, from P.F. Yeo, 1977, coll. Corsica: S.E. Mts; C and D 4cm wide, E and F 3cm wide; A and B with different magnifications, 5.5 and 7cm wide

of minute glandular and eglandular hairs, usually accompanied by an abundance of long eglandular hairs, but these sometimes absent except on leaf-blades. Stems trailing, up to about 70cm, forming a diffuse inflorescence. Peduncles mostly 1.5–5cm, slender; pedicels mostly 1–2cm, very slender. Sepals 4–5mm, green, with a very small mucro. Petals not more than 10mm, finely pointed at base, notched at apex for $^1/_3$–$^2/_5$ of their length, deep purplish pink, tending towards violet, except for white base; veins slightly darker than ground-colour; base with a small dense tuft of hairs towards either edge and a narrow hairless zone on the front surface between the tufts. Filaments pale pink, at least at the tips; anthers bluish. Stigmas about 1.5mm, pale yellow, sometimes tinged with pink. Immature fruits erect on sharply reflexed pedicels. Rostrum 12–13mm; stylar portion not more than 0.5mm. Mericarps about 2.5mm, with short appressed hairs and a few raised ribs in the immediate vicinity of the midrib at the top. Discharge: carpel-projection.

South-west and W. Europe, east to the Caucasus, introduced further north and naturalised in the British Isles.

Grows in meadows, on roadsides and on disturbed ground. A quite attractive plant for the wild garden, tolerant of moderate shade.

A large number of subspecies, varieties and formae has been described in *G. pyrenaicum*. Variants that I have encountered since writing edn.1 are added alongside forma *albiflorum* below, while the main description above is unaltered.

A full synonymy is given by Aedo *et al.* (1998) who divide the species into two subspecies. However, I do not think it safe to assume that all the variants outside subspecies *lusitanicum* are less significant than that, and I have adopted varietal rank (var. *majus* below).

In addition to the named variants I have to report two other interesting forms. In 1992 I visited the French department of Pyrénées Atlantiques and in the region of the Vallées d'Aspe and d'Ossau met with a dwarf form of the species with small deep reddish purple flowers – they were so small that I at first thought I was looking at a variant of 116. *G. molle*. I grew plants from seed in Cambridge (accession 1991.1177) and they retained their characters. Unlike var. *majus*, this plant does not have hairless carpels. The other variant was collected in 1998 by David Victor and John Anton-Smith on Erciyas Da. in Kayseri province, south central Turkey. This has leaves like those of 'Isparta' (below) and a light bluish purple petal colour like that of 'Isparta' but a slightly smaller petal with a relatively much larger – and bilobed – white basal area. This seems to be a very attractive garden plant.

G. pyrenaicum forma *albiflorum* Schur is a name that I presume applies to a plant common in British gardens having the petals and stamen-filaments white or, in cool weather, faintly tinged with pink. Gilmour & Stearn, having doubts about this, published a new name for it: *G. pyrenaicum* forma *pallidum* in *Journal of Botany* 70: Supplement, p. 6 (1932) ("flowers very pale pink, almost white").

G. pyrenaicum 'Bill Wallis' is distinguished by the intense anthocyanin colouring, making the stems and leaf-stalks deep purple, the leaf blades darker green than usual and the petals deep bluish purple. It is named after the deceased nurseryman who introduced it.

G. pyrenaicum 'Isparta' was found by me in the S.W. Turkish province of that name in 1989 (Clifton/Yeo, 1996) and is distinctive in cultivation; the plant tends to be larger than local British forms, with basal leaves to 19cm wide in Cambridge, the leaves paler and thicker, and the flowers larger, to 27mm wide, and also differently coloured – rather lighter and much bluer than usual, with a large white eye. This is now widespread in British gardens. (See also description of plant from Erciyas Da. in discussion of *G. pyrenaicum*).

G. pyrenaicum var. *majus* Merino (*G. pyrenaicum* subsp. *lusitanicum* (Sampaio) S. Ortiz) is found in N. Spain and N. Portugal and has long hairs on the pedicels and hairless carpels, features of no horticultural significance. I have included it here to show how I have disposed of *G. pyrenaicum* subsp. *lusitanicum*. I have grown one sample of this, received from a Spanish botanic garden under a wrong name; its flowers were only 13mm wide.

G. pyrenaicum is said to have hybridised naturally with 116. *G. molle* and 114. *G. pusillum* (see Chapter 7). The second of these crosses was raised by Alan Bremner; its parents have similar mericarps (unribbed).

114. *G. pusillum* Linnaeus (Figure 9.118C & D)
Annual with blades of lower leaves not more than 5cm wide, rounded in outline, divided as far as $^2/_3$ or $^3/_4$ into 9; divisions lobed for $^1/_3$–$^1/_2$ of their length; lobes toothed; lobes and teeth obtuse to acute, the lateral curved outwards; notches marked with a small crimson spot. Stem-leaves paired, stalked. Hairs eglandular, those of stems and leaf-stalks very short. Flowers extremely small; sepals about 2.5mm; petals about 4mm, notched at apex, lilac, not as widely spreading as the sepals; anthers only 5, bluish. Rostrum about 7mm, without a stylar portion. Mericarps about 2mm, otherwise like those of 113. *G. pyrenaicum*. Discharge: carpel-projection.

Europe, N. and W. Asia; introduced elsewhere.

A weed with an apparent preference for light soils. Superficially similar to 116. *G. molle* but differing in the short hairs on the stems, paired stem-leaves, smaller flowers and unribbed, hairy mericarps. Said to have hybridised naturally with 116. *G. molle* (see Chapter 7). See also hybrids listed for 113. *G. pyrenaicum*.

115. G. brutium Gasparrini (Figure 9.118B)
Annual with rounded leaves, with blades less deeply divided than those of 113. *G. pyrenaicum* but having more lobes and teeth when of comparable size. Flowers similar to those of *G. pyrenaicum* but up to 25mm in diameter and with bright rose-pink petals. Mericarps hairless, closely ribbed. Rock garden or border. Summer.

Stems to 80cm. Blades of basal leaves between 5 and 10cm wide, divided nearly as far as $^1/_2$ into 9; divisions lobed for $^1/_3$ or less of their length; lobes often with one tooth; teeth and tips of lobes blunt. Stem-leaves solitary, becoming rapidly reduced in size and length of stalk upwards. Hair-clothing nearly the same as in 113. *G. pyrenaicum*. Stems erect, up to about 30cm, becoming bushy, or up to 50cm and trailing, forming diffuse inflorescences which nevertheless produce a profusion of flowers. Peduncles and pedicels very slender. Sepals 4–6mm, with hardly any mucro. Petals 8–12.5mm (varying greatly according to conditions), gradually tapered or distinctly constricted at base, notched at apex for about $^1/_4$ of their length, with indistinct darker veins; base with a rather dense fringe of wavy hairs on either side. Filaments the same colour as the petals; anthers blue-black. Stigmas 1.5mm or slightly more, pink or purple. Immature fruits erect on sharply reflexed pedicels. Rostrum 7–9mm. Mericarps 2–2.5mm, acute at apex, hairless, densely covered with fine slanting ribs. Discharge: carpel-projection.

South Italy, Sicily, Balkan Peninsula, Turkey.

A showy and apparently easily grown annual. The above description is based on an introduction from the Pindus of Greece by Mr A.W.A. Baker, one from Yugoslavia (Montenegro) by Mr K.A. Beckett, and two that I collected, respectively in Greece (Corfu) and Yugoslavia (Serbia: Despotovac). In the solitary stem-leaves and ribbed mericarps it resembles 116. *G. molle*. In dry conditions, when the flowers are reduced in size, it may be difficult to distinguish it from that. It forms sterile hybrids with 116. *G. molle* (Appendix III).

116. G. molle *Linnaeus* (Figures 9.118E & F)
Annual with blades of lower leaves up to about 5cm wide, rounded in outline, divided as far as $^1/_2$ or $^3/_5$, into 9; divisions lobed for $^1/_3$–$^2/_5$ of their length; lobes often with 1 or 2 teeth on their sides, the lateral scarcely curved outwards; tips of lobes obtuse, teeth often acute. Lowest stem-leaves paired, others solitary, stalked. Hairs eglandular, many of them long. Sepals 3–5mm. Petals 4–6mm, notched at apex for about $^1/_5$ –$^1/_4$ of their length, purplish pink with white base, pale pink or white, widely divergent;

base with a fringe of wavy hairs on either side; anthers bluish. Stigmas about 1mm, crimson. Rostrum 5–8mm, stylar portion about 0.5mm. Mericarps like those of 115. *G. brutium* but only 1.5mm long and more nearly spherical. Discharge: carpel-projection.

Europe, W. Asia, extending to the Himalayas.

A weed of lawns and disturbed places on roadsides and hill pastures, *G. molle* is superficially similar to 114. *G. pusillum* but most of its stem-leaves are solitary and it has larger, spreading and more deeply notched petals and hairless, ribbed mericarps. Closely related to 115. *G. brutium* but smaller in all parts (except upper leaf-stalks) and less erect.

It is said to have hybridised naturally with 114. *G. pusillum* and 113. *G. pyrenaicum* (see Chapter 7).

SECTION LUCIDA, THE LUCIDUM GROUP

Plants annual or perennial. Stem and leaves slightly succulent. Leaves rounded, with shallow, obtuse divisions, lobes and teeth. Hairs mostly glandular. Sepals erect, with lengthwise keels and transverse flaps between these (in our species). Petals with a distinct claw and blade; claws ridged so as to form nectar-passages of circular cross-section; blade not notched at apex. Stamens slightly longer than sepals; pollen yellow. Immature fruits and their pedicels erect. Mericarps obtuse at apex, variously hairy.
Three species, two of them are dealt with here.

117. G. lucidum Linnaeus (Figure 9.119)
Erect annual up to 50cm tall, with succulent red stems and slightly succulent glossy leaves. Leaf-blades about 5cm wide, rounded in outline, divided as far as about $^2/_3$ into 5. Divisions broadest near the apex which is shallowly 3-lobed; lobes usually with a few teeth. Teeth and

Figure 9.119. *G. lucidum;* 6cm wide

tips of lobes obtuse. Stem-leaves paired, stalked. Flowers erect, not more than 10mm in diameter. Sepals about 5mm. Petals 8–9mm, with a very small deep pink (rarely white) blade shorter than the claw. Stamens and style reaching about 1mm beyond throat of flower. Rostrum about 11mm, its stylar portion 4mm. Mericarps about 2.2mm, broadest at the top, with a network of raised ribs which run parallel and vertically at the top. Discharge: carpel-projection. Wild garden, walls. Spring and summer.

Europe, N. Africa, S.W. and C. Asia.

This plant is attractive for its glossy green foliage and for the red colouring which develops when it is old. Plants arising from autumn germination form stronger rosettes and grow to a larger size than those germinating in spring.

118. *G. glaberrimum* Boissier & Heldreich
(Figure 9.120, Plate 45)
Dwarf aromatic perennial with small, almost hairless kidney-shaped leaves with blunt lobes and teeth. Flowers about 23mm in diameter, erect, bright pink. Petals with a claw at base. Stamens and style about twice as long as sepals. Alpine house and probably rock garden. April to June and sometimes again later.

Rootstock thick, developing above ground. Blades of main leaves not more than 5cm wide, wider than long, divided as far as $^3/_5$ or nearly so into 7 or 9; divisions more or less elliptic or tapered towards the base from near the rounded and shallowly 3-lobed apex; lobes mostly with a tooth on one side or both. Teeth and tips of lobes obtuse or acute. Upper stem-leaves similar, decreasing rapidly in size upwards, stalked; all stem-leaves paired, members of pairs unequal. Plant covered with minute glandular hairs but without large hairs. Stems forking regularly, forming inflorescences up to about 25cm tall. Sepals about 9mm long, erect, the outer ones with longitudinal ribs with small cross-connections; mucro 1mm or slightly more. Petals about 20mm, with a claw and a blade; blades less than 16mm, broadest near the tip, bright pink, with paler veins near base; claws hairy along the edges, each with a double ridge abutting a stamen so that the petals form 5 nectar-passages of approximately circular section. Filaments 17mm, deep pink; anthers red. Style 16mm, red; stigmas less than 1mm, red. Immature fruits and their pedicels more or less spreading. Rostrum about 17mm, including stylar portion 10mm. Mericarps 4–4.5mm, narrow, with a network of raised ribs or sparingly pinnately ribbed. Discharge: carpel-projection.

Figure 9.120. *G. glaberrimum*: from Prof. G.G. Guittonneau, 1976, coll. Turkey: Icel Prov. (73.06.26.03), 3.5 and 5.5cm wide

Mountains of S.W. Turkey.

Grows in rock fissures at 1,300–1,800m altitude. A very attractive plant for the alpine house which will probably prove itself satisfactory on the rock garden too. This plant has been established at Cambridge from a single seedling raised from seed sent by Professor Guittonneau in 1976 (his no. 73.06.26.03, from Mersin: between Anamur and Ermenek) and at Kew from a plant collected by Mr Brian Mathew in 1979 (Mathew, Baytop & Sütlüpinar no. 9613, from Antalya: Gunodogmus). The Kew plant has more acute leaf-teeth and more rounded and overlapping petal-blades than Guittonneau's. Another stock was collected by me in 1989 (Yeo no. 89.1, Cambridge accession 1989.0531, from Konya: S. of Lake Beysehir). This has sparingly pinnately ribbed mericarps, a contrast with the reticulate venation of the mericarps in Professor Guittonneau's sample. Such pronounced variation results from the scattered occurrence of the species on rock outcrops.

Pieces of the above-ground rootstock seem unwilling to root but the species can be increased by seed. I raised some plants from the original 1989 seed of my Konya sample by sowing in February 1998.

SECTION UNGUICULATA, THE MACRORRHIZUM GROUP

Plants perennial, with long rhizomes. Stems and leaves slightly succulent. Hairs mostly glandular. Sepals erect, forming a swollen calyx. Petals with a distinct claw and blade, not appreciably notched at apex. Pollen yellow. Floral axis horizontal. Flower slightly irregular. Stamens and style more than twice as long as calyx. Style hairless. Immature fruits and their pedicels erect. Mericarps with a pattern of ridges, obtuse at apex, hairless.

Two species in the mountains of the Mediterranean region, both cultivated, and hybrids between them.

119. *G. macrorrhizum* Linnaeus (Figure 9.121A)

Rhizomatous sticky and aromatic perennial. Leaves 10–20cm wide, with shallow rounded lobes. Flowers 20–25mm in diameter, with axis horizontal. Calyx reddish, inflated. Petals pink to purplish or white, with a claw at base. Stamens and style more than twice as long as sepals, sinuous. Rock garden, border, wild garden, ground-cover. Leafy in winter. May–June and usually again later.

Plant up to 30 or 50cm tall, with fleshy underground rhizomes and thick ascending, above-ground stems lasting several years. Lowest leaves 10–20cm wide, divided as far as $^2/_3$–$^3/_4$ into 7; divisions tapered both ways from above the middle, shallowly palmato-pinnately lobed; lobes about as long as broad, with several teeth. Teeth and tips of lobes obtuse or the teeth acute. Stems with 1–3 pairs of leaves, these similar to the lower but decreasing rapidly in size and length of stalk upwards. Plant densely clothed with minute glandular hairs and usually more or less densely covered also with long glandular and eglandular hairs, these occasionally almost absent. Inflorescence dense, usually with clusters above the first few flowering nodes. Pedicels shorter than or little longer than the sepals. Floral axis horizontal. Sepals 7–9mm, reddish, forming a bladdery calyx; mucro $^1/_4$–$^1/_2$ as long as sepal. Petals 15–18mm, with a claw and a blade; blades rounded, usually purple, slightly asymmetrically spreading in the flower; claws wedge-shaped, half the total length of the petal, with two rounded ridges and a central channel, hairy on the back and on the front at the sides, the hairs sometimes extending on to the tops of the ridges and overhanging the channel. Filaments 18–24mm, displaced to the lower side of the flower and slightly turned up at the tips, usually purplish red; anthers orange-red to dull red. Style about 22mm, growing rapidly, purplish red, displaced and curved like the filaments; stigmas 1–1.5mm, yellowish. Immature fruits and their pedicels erect. Rostrum about 30–34mm, stylar portion about

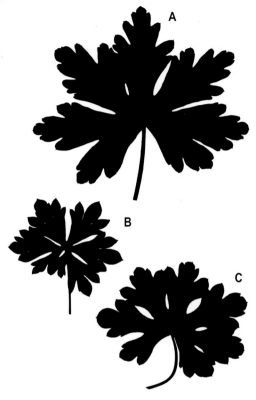

Figure 9.121. (A) *G. macrorrhizum* 'Bevan's Variety': from J. Stephens, 1969; (B) *G. dalmaticum*: from Miss E.M. Savory, 1958; (C) *G. x cantabrigiense*, raised by Dr. H. Widler-Kiefer, 1974; 10, 4 and 6cm wide

18mm. Mericarps 2.5–3mm, with wavy horizontal ribs. Discharge: carpel-projection.

S. side of the Alps, Apennines, Balkan Peninsula, S. and E. Carpathians; often naturalised elsewhere in Europe.

This species grows among rocks and scrub (usually in shade) in mountains and in subalpine woodlands, and has potential for drought-resistance. It has long been used for medicinal purposes and as a source of oil of geranium which is used in perfumery (now superseded in the latter role by *Pelargonium* species and hybrids). It has also been used in tanning. It is quite frequently introduced from the wild and the introductions show a good deal of variation in hair-clothing, petal colour and other details, which affect the plant's garden value. *G. macrorrhizum* is valuable for dry shady situations in the garden, but only certain of the cultivars qualify for a place in the herbaceous border or rock garden, though an Award of Merit was bestowed on the species at the Wisley Trial (1973–6). The first flower-buds are often damaged by late frosts. Easily propagated from the rhizomes or by using the rosette-bearing stems as cuttings.

G. macrorrhizum 'Album' has white petals and pink calyces and stamens; it was introduced by Walter Ingwersen from the Rhodope Mountains of Bulgaria, and is relatively large-flowered and a charming garden plant. White petals are mentioned as occurring occasionally in this species by Gams (1923–4). The name 'Album' will inevitably be used for white clones that appear indistinguishable from Ingwersen's. A supposedly distinguishable form is 'Spessart', below. Stocks at Cambridge lack hairs on the sides and front of the petal claws. See also *G. macrorrhizum* 'White-Ness'.

G. macrorrhizum 'Bevan's Variety' has deep red sepals and deep magenta petals of good form and size; it is about the most intensely coloured variant but the colours of the sepals and petals clash. First distributed by Washfield Nurseries, Hawkhurst, Kent, having been collected by Dr Roger Bevan while on an excursion with Dr Giuseppi.

G. macrorrhizum 'Czakor' is coloured almost as in the preceding but has the petals free of veining and of undulations, and thus of apparent firmer substance.

G. macrorrhizum 'Grandiflorum' was found by Ingwersen, having larger flowers than usual, but is apparently lost from cultivation.

G. macrorrhizum 'Ingwersen's Variety' a fine pale pink form (RHSCC Purple Group 75A) with rather pale green and slightly glossy foliage; it was found as a single plant among typically coloured plants on Mount Koprivnik, Montenegro, Yugoslavia, by Walter Ingwersen in 1929, and is the best form for the herbaceous border.

G. macrorrhizum 'Spessart' is a name that has been applied to a white form and a pink; in fact it belongs to the white. It is a selection from 'Album' made by the nurseryman Dr Hans Simon for its more strongly overlapping petals.

G. macrorrhizum 'Variegatum' has the leaves irregularly variegated with cream; the flowers are a fairly typical shade of purplish pink.

G. macrorrhizum 'White-Ness' lacks anthocyanin pigmentation, so the sepals are green and the other visible floral parts white, and is characterised also by small, glossy pale green leaves and upright habit; it was collected on Mount Olympus, Greece, in 1990 by Paul Matthews (no. PM 861) of Ness Botanic Garden, Cheshire (University of Liverpool) (Anton-Smith, 1997; Moss, 1997).

G. macrorrhizum crosses with its near relative *G. dalmaticum* to give sterile progeny, see 120. *G.* x *cantabrigiense*.

120. G. x *cantabrigiense* Yeo (Figure 9.121C, Plate 46)

Aromatic carpeting plant to about 30cm tall; foliage present in winter, light green, appearing hairless (the hairs present being minute); leaf-blades not more than 10cm wide, intermediate in size and shape between those of 119. *G. macrorrhizum* and 121. *G. dalmaticum*. Flowers about 25–28mm in diameter, formed and held like those of *G. macrorrhizum*; petals bright pink or white. Rock garden, front of border, ground-cover. Sun or shade. June to July.

Plant with long-lived trailing stems like those of 121. *G. dalmaticum*. Blades of main leaves 3–9cm wide, divided as far as $^3/_4$ or $^4/_5$ into 7; divisions broadest well above the middle, with 3 short broad lobes, each with 1 or 2 teeth, or some of them without teeth; teeth and tips of lobes rounded and mucronate. Flowering stems with leaves at the first and sometimes the second node; inflorescence of 1 cymule at the first fork and 5–10 flowers at the tip of each of the 2 branches. Flowers like those of 119. *G. macrorrhizum* and 121. *G. dalmaticum*, intermediate in most of the details in which these differ, but like *G. dalmaticum* in having hair-tipped teeth on the filaments. Petals bright pink or white and tinged with pink at base of blade. Sterile.

A hybrid between 119. *G. macrorrhizum* and 121. *G. dalmaticum*.

This hybrid has arisen independently on a number of occasions. In 1974 Dr Helen Kiefer, working at Cambridge, made reciprocal pollinations between the two parent species; 31 flowers were pollinated in each direction; with *G. dalmaticum* as the female parent three seeds were produced but none germinated, and with *G. macrorrhizum* as female parent five seeds were obtained, one of which germinated. This plant grew on and was finally planted in the Geranium Display Bed, where it grew extremely rapidly. It makes a more or less weed-proof carpet of pleasantly light green scented foliage and in some years the leaves can hardly be seen when it is in full flower. The colour of the petals is RHSCC Purple-Violet Group between 80B and 80C. In winter the leaves appear attractively glossy. The rostra mostly remain undeveloped. The description "Cambridge clone" has gradually evolved into cultivar 'Cambridge' which is now in general use (see below).

G. x *cantabrigiense* 'Biokovo' has runners that creep further than those of 'Cambridge' and consequently it forms a less dense mat; the petals are white with a tinge of pink at the base of the blade. The rostrum usually develops, but no seed is formed. This clone was found in 1977 near

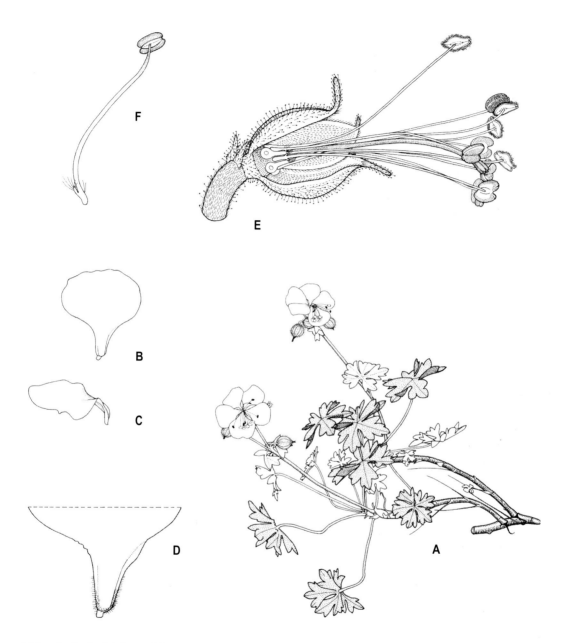

Makarska in the Biokova (Biokovo) mountains of southern Dalmatia, Yugoslavia, by the nurseryman Dr Hans Simon of Marktheidenfeld, Germany, who named it and introduced it into cultivation. Neither of the parent species was seen in the area; the locality is not very far from the type locality of 121. *G. dalmaticum* but this is extremely isolated on a mountain at the tip of a peninsula.

G. x *cantabrigiense* 'Cambridge' is the clone deliberately raised at Cambridge, as described

Figure 9.122. *G. dalmaticum*: from Miss E.M. Savory, 1958. (A) portion of plant beginning to flower, x $^2/_3$; (B) petal, x 2; (C) petal, seen from side, x 2; (D) base of front surface of petal, x 4; (E) flower in male stage with petals and two sepals removed, x 4; (F) stamen of outer whorl, x 4

above; at least one of the spontaneous clones differs by having a purple feathery blotch on each petal near the throat. Another clone has been named: see 'Karmina'.

G. x cantabrigiense 'Karmina' is listed by Hibberd (1994) merely as very similar to 'Cambridge'.

G. x cantabrigiense 'St. Ola' is similar to 'Biokovo', having been raised by Alan Bremner by crossing *G. dalmaticum* 'Album' with *G. macrorrhizum* 'Album'. It is said to have whiter flowers than 'Biokovo', rarely showing any pink, and broader, flatter petals and deeper green leaves (Hibberd, 1994).

121. *G. dalmaticum* (Beck) Rechinger (Figures 9.121B & 9.122, Plate 47)
Fragrant rhizomatous dwarf carpeting plant, with glossy hairless leaves not more than 4cm wide. Flowers formed and held like those of 119. *G. macrorrhizum* but calyx less red; petals shell-pink or white. Rock garden in sun or light shade, ground-cover. June–July.

Plant up to about 15cm tall, with trailing stems lasting several years which ascend at tips and bear leaf-rosettes. Almost leafless in winter. Blades of leaves up to 4cm wide, divided as far as $^4/_5$–$^6/_7$ into 5 or 7; divisions wedge-shaped, mostly 3-lobed for $^1/_4$–$^1/_3$ of their length, with the middle lobe the largest; lobes broad, abruptly pointed, usually without teeth. Flowering stems sometimes with one pair of leaves and with small bracts at higher nodes, or with bracts only. Plant hairless except for fine hairs on lower flowering stems and glandular hairs on pedicels and sepals. Inflorescence long-stalked, dense, few-flowered, many of the bracts barren. Pedicels shorter than calyx. Floral axis horizontal. Sepals 6–6.5mm, green with translucent pink margins, forming a bladdery calyx, the outer with raised ribs near the edges; mucro about $^1/_4$ as long as sepal. Petals 18mm long and up to 12mm wide, with a claw and a blade; blades broadly rounded, bright pink; claws wedge-shaped, about $^1/_3$ of the total length of the petal, woolly on back and sides and in a strip across the front above the base, without central ridges. Filaments 15mm, displaced to the lower side of the flower and slightly turned up at the tips, each with a pair of hair-tipped teeth at the base; anthers red. Style about 18mm, growing rapidly, crimson towards tip, displaced and curved like the stamens; stigmas 1.5mm, crimson. Rostrum about 33mm, including stylar portion 14mm. Mericarps 2.5–3mm, with lateral ribs slanting and occasionally forking or merging. Discharge: carpel-projection.

Coast of Montenegro (Dalmatia), N. Albania.

This species was introduced into cultivation in Britain by Mr Walter Ingwersen in 1947 and by 1949 it had already received an Award of Merit of the Royal Horticultural Society. The cultivar 'Album' was commercially introduced in 1956. It must have been a mutant of the original introduction. *G. dalmaticum* is a delightful plant, easy to grow and to propagate – by cuttings from the rhizomes. At Wisley it grows on the vertical face of a retaining wall. It is less floriferous in the north of Britain than in the south unless given maximum exposure to the sun.

The botanist O. Schwarz (1936) reported his surprise at finding *G. dalmaticum* in the garden of W. Liebmann in the German town of Arnstadt. It had been introduced by Liebmann from the type locality, Monte Vipera, on the peninsula of Sabioncello (now Pelješac) on the Dalmatian coast. Schwarz acquired it for the Berlin Botanic Garden and it was presumably from here that it was established at Munich, whence Dr Wilhelm Schacht gave material to Mr Ingwersen who brought it to England (note by W.T. Stearn on a specimen in the Natural History Museum, London). Soon after its discovery on Monte Vipera in 1894 it was discovered further south, in northern Albania, by Antonio Baldacci on his sixth and seventh journeys to Montenegro and Albania. The species was re-collected by Dr Mathias Baltisberger in northern Albania in 1983. Seed from this expedition was sent to Cambridge and plants were established on the limestone rock garden there and specimens were added to the CUBG herbarium. However, these plants died after some years. They differed from the plant from the type locality in being more robust and stiff in habit and having a more ordinary pink colour in the petals. They appeared to be much less vigorous in the production of rhizomes. The difference in habit is also visible in Baldacci's herbarium specimens at Kew and the Natural History Museum, London.

G. dalmaticum 'Album' has white petals and is slightly less vigorous than its progenitor (see above); it appears to have arisen in cultivation from the Ingwersen stock of the species and was shown at a Royal Horticultural Society meeting in July 1956 by Bloom's of Bressingham, Diss, Norfolk.

The hybrid between *G. dalmaticum* and *G. macrorrhizum* is 120. *G. x cantabrigiense*.

SECTION RUBERTA, THE ROBERTIANUM GROUP

Plants annual, biennial or perennial (in the latter case sometimes dying after flowering). Stems and leaves slightly succulent. Hairs mostly glandular.

Leaves divided to the base. Petals hairless, with a distinct claw and blade; claws ridged so as to form nectar-passages of approximately circular cross-section (except in 122. *G. cataractarum*); blade not appreciably notched at apex. Pollen yellow. Style hairy, at least at the base. Rostrum hairless. Mericarps with a pattern of ridges, obtuse at apex.

Section Ruberta now includes the former Section Anemonifolia (the Palmatum Group), and one species formerly in Section Unguiculata (the Macrorrhizum Group).

Seven species from the North Atlantic islands, Europe, Asia and Africa. The one species not described below is *G. purpureum* Villars, which is similar to *G. robertianum* but with much smaller flowers (petal-blades up to 2.5mm wide). Colour photographs of the four large North Atlantic island endemics appear in Yeo (1970).

122. *G. cataractarum* Cosson (Figure 9.123, Plate 48)

Dwarf aromatic perennial with leaves divided to the base into 3 and nearly into 5, recalling those of 123. *G. robertianum*. Flowers 17–19mm in diameter, funnel-shaped, inclined upwards. Calyx inflated. Petals deep to pale pink. Stamens less than twice as long as sepals. Leaves present in winter. Rock garden. June onwards.

Rootstock to about 12mm thick, developing above ground to about 2cm. Blades of basal leaves not more than 9cm wide, divided to the base into 3, and nearly to the base into 5; central division stalked, laterals on each side borne on a short common stalk, all broad, more or less fan-shaped, deeply pinnately lobed; lobes 1–1³/₄ times as long as broad, with several teeth. Teeth and tips of lobes obtuse or acute, mucronate. Stem-leaves paired, members of pairs unequal, lateral divisions stalkless. Plant more or less covered with very small-headed glandular hairs. Flowering stems with shorter eglandular hairs on one side, forking unequally, making a fairly dense inflorescence up to about 30cm tall. Flowers upwardly inclined. Sepals 5–6mm, enlarging to 7–8mm, making an inflated calyx; mucro 0.5mm or less. Petals 16 x 7–8mm, with a claw and a blade; blades bright pink, flat-ended; claws narrow, ¹/₃ of total length of petal, without hairs or central ridge. Filaments 7–9mm, projecting out of throat of flower, hairless, pink-tipped. Style about same length as filaments, reddish at tip; stigmas 1mm, flesh-pink on back and white on front. Rostrum 17mm; stylar portion 6–7mm. Mericarps about 3.5mm, with a network of ribs, those in the lower ²/₃ mostly directed lengthwise. Discharge: carpel-projection.

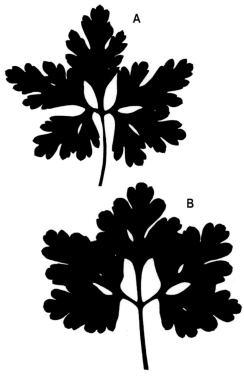

Figure 9.123. (A) *G. cataractarum* subsp. *cataractarum*: from Dr R.C. Barneby, 1970, coll. Spain: Jaén Prov. (B) *G. cataractarum* subsp. *pitardii*: from Prof. G.G. Guittonneau, 1977, coll. Morocco: Moyen Atlas (72.07.08.01); 5.5 and 6.5cm wide

S. Spain, Morocco.

G. cataractarum grows naturally on damp or shady limestone rocks. It was formerly grown on the limestone rock garden at Cambridge but it is short-lived. Its maintenance simply requires the conservation of self-sown seedlings. At Cambridge at the time of writing it is due for re-establishment from seed that has been in storage. *G. cataractarum* is also easily propagated by cuttings from the above-ground stock. The European and African components of this species are treated as subspecies (Guittonneau, 1974).

G. cataractarum subsp. *cataractarum*, from southern Spain, is slightly larger than subsp. *pitardii* in all parts (that is, attaining the maxima given in the species-description) and has the flowers less crowded; petals with the limb a strong deep purplish pink which does not become paler towards the throat; anthers scarlet. This has been grown at Cambridge from a stock originating from a cliff near the source of the Guadalquivir river, Province Jaén, Spain, collected by Dr Rupert C.

Barneby in 1967. The plant is completely hardy in Cambridge but has not proved as attractive on the rock garden there as it did in Dr Barneby's garden at Greenport, New York, as evidenced by a colour transparency he sent me. It would probably benefit from frequent renewal.

G. cataractarum subsp. *pitardii* Maire, from Morocco, is slightly smaller (to about 20cm) than subsp. *cataractarum* and smaller in all its parts (generally not reaching the maxima given in the species-description), with more crowded flowers and with narrower petal-blades of a soft pink, fading nearly to white towards the throat; anthers orange-red. My stock of the Moroccan representative of the species was received as seed in 1976. It was collected in the Middle Atlas by Professor Guittonneau in 1972 and cultivated by him. I grew a number of generations in the research section of Cambridge Botanic Garden. Pot-grown plants are very attractive. I now have it in paving in my own garden but the birds almost prevent its seeding.

A distinctive and attractive plant has been produced by crossing *G. cataractarum* (subsp. *cataractarum*) with *G. maderense*. This hybrid is almost exactly intermediate between the parents. It is a perennial with a rosette-bearing stem 10–20cm tall, branching after flowering, and having leaf-blades sometimes more than 20cm wide (Figure 9.124). The inflorescence is about 25cm tall, held well above the leaves (which become reflexed), with flowering stems forking regularly, borne in a group at the top of the rosette. Flowers 3cm in diameter at first, wider through splaying later. Petals about 18 x 12mm, with a claw about $^1/_5$ of their length; blades deep reddish pink with raised veins paler than the ground-colour, and a streak of darker red in the centre of the lower third.

It is quite sterile but can be propagated by the rooting of branches which form after flowering has taken place. Well-grown specimens are highly decorative, and if a system of management could be worked out, it might make a fine conservatory plant. It was raised at Cambridge, where it has been grown only under glass. The cross was made by me in 1971 and by Dr Helen Kiefer in 1974; it was successful only when *G. maderense* was the female parent. The main petal colour is HCC Phlox Purple, between 632 and 632/1.

123. *G. robertianum* Linnaeus (Figure 9.125)

A usually over-wintering, evil-smelling annual with leaves divided to the base into 3 and nearly to the base into 5, the divisions stalked, much cut. Flowers 11–16mm in diameter, pink or white. Petals with a claw at base. Wild garden, shade or sun, perhaps rock garden. Spring, summer, autumn.

A rosette-forming succulent annual, usually over-wintering, often strongly pigmented with red or brown. Blades of basal leaves up to about 11cm wide, divided to the base into 3 and nearly to the base into 5; divisions stalked, ovate or diamond-shaped, pinnately lobed almost or quite to the midrib; lobes less than twice as long as broad, toothed or with secondary, toothed, lobes. Teeth and tips of lobes obtuse, often with a distinct mucro. Stems leafy, the leaves decreasing gradually in size, complexity of lobing and length of stalk upwards, and becoming acutely toothed. Plant sparsely to densely beset with large, glistening, glandular and eglandular hairs.

Figure 9.124. *G. cataractarum* x *G. maderense*: raised by P.F. Yeo, 1971; 11cm wide

Figure 9.125. *G. robertianum*: from Besançon B.G., 1969, coll. France?; 7cm wide

Flowering stems arising in a cluster from the rosette or in one or more whorls on a central stem emerging from the rosette, forking regularly but slightly unequally below, more unequally above, forming a diffuse inflorescence. Sepals 4–6mm, erect; mucro about 0.75–1.25mm. Petals 10–14mm, with a claw and a blade; blades 3.5–5.5mm wide, deep pink with paler veins towards base; claws slightly shorter than the blades, each with a double ridge abutting a stamen so that 5 nectar passages of approximately circular cross-section are formed. Stamens projecting about 1.5mm from throat of flower; anthers red to pinkish orange. Stigmas 0.5–1.5mm. Rostrum 12–15mm; stylar portion 4–5mm. Immature fruits and their pedicels upwardly inclined. Mericarps 2–2.8mm, with a network of ribs, sparse towards the base, and 1 or 2, sometimes 3, collar-like rings round the apex, hairless or finely hairy, each with 2 bundles of hair-like fibres ("tangle-strands") near the top. Discharge: carpel-projection.

Europe, N.W. Africa, Canary Isles, Madeira, W. Asia, Himalayas, S.W. China, Taiwan. Probably an introduction in E. North America.

This is the familiar hedge-bank flower, Herb Robert. Some of its variation has been described by Yeo (1973) and Baker (1956) while more detailed researches are reported by Bøcher (1947) and Baker (1957). I found that different samples grown under similar conditions differed considerably in leaf-size and flower-size and somewhat in flower-colour. The smallest-flowered forms tend to be compact and prostrate, unlike the small-flowered *G. purpureum* (see under Section Ruberta), which tends to be erect or straggling. It is essentially a species for the wild garden and shady corners, though compact forms may be risked on the rock garden. All stocks which I have grown, except for cultivar 'Album', have to grow through the winter before they will flower. The species is mainly self-pollinating and different stocks grown near together remain distinct. This fact was noted by Bowles (1914) with regard to the two common white-flowered cultivars, now known as 'Album' and 'Celtic White'. However, when these are crossed, all the progeny in the first generation have the normal pink wild-type flower (see below).
G. robertianum has an enormous geographic range, and since edn.1 was written two Far Eastern stocks have been grown in Cambridge, Leslie 33.81 from Sichuan, and Wynn-Jones BSWJ 194 from Taiwan. They have weak pigmentation in the vegetative parts and petals, and the petal-size is in the lower part of the range shown in my description. They therefore have no horticultural interest.

G. robertianum 'Album' is a trailing, thin-stemmed plant, very strongly pigmented with red-brown in the vegetative parts, having rather large flowers with white or nearly white petals, attractively set off by the brown sepals; it flowers in the first year from seed and it may continue to flower late into the autumn, survive the winter and begin again early in spring. The botanical name *G. robertianum* forma *bernettii* A. Schwarz is said by Gams (1923–4) to apply to a plant with this colouring but whether it has the same growth behaviour is unknown. The cultivar name is that given by Ingwersen (1946). There are specimens of *G. robertianum* 'Album' in the CUBG herbarium. I have seen it from several sources. Mr E. Barrett sent me a plant similar to this which differs in requiring to be overwintered before it will flower. There are evidently other white or pale-flowered variants of this species in cultivation, some of them having been assembled by Mr Richard Clifton.
G. robertianum subsp. *celticum* Ostenfeld (*G. robertianum* var. *celticum* (Ostenfeld) Druce) occurs in W. Ireland and S. Wales; its red-brown pigmentation is restricted to nodes and bases of leaf-stalks, and its flowers are pale pink. It is apparently not at present in cultivation (but see next). Plants of *G. robertianum* that I saw on a short visit to the Burren, W. Ireland, were scarcely different from what one could find in England, so presumably they did not represent this subspecies.
G. robertianum 'Celtic White' is a dwarf, compact albino with at most a tinge of brown at the nodes, varying in its hairiness, and having bright green leaves and rather small flowers with pure white petals; it is called var. *celticum* in gardens but, as explained by Baker (1956), it is not that (see above), and I therefore proposed this cultivar name; there are specimens dated 10/6/1966, 14/6/1968 and 23/7/1970 in the CUBG herbarium. Bowles (1914), in attempting to trace the origin of this plant, was always led to one Sir Charles Isham, but he could not find out whence the latter got it. See 'Album' and 'Cygnus'.
G. robertianum 'Cygnus' is a name proposed by Clifton (1979) for white-flowered plants with rather little brown pigment, to which the botanical name *G. robertianum* forma *leucanthum* Beckhaus has been applied (Baker, 1956). The original description of the latter merely stated that the flowers were pure white with scarlet-red anthers and it was based on plants found in northern Germany; the application of the name is therefore uncertain.
G. robertianum subsp. *maritimum* (Babington) H.G. Baker is a name applied by Baker (1956) to coastal plants; the variation in the species seems, however, to cut across the coast/inland boundary.

I have crossed *G. robertianum* 'Album' with 'Celtic White' in both directions; the resulting plants are normal (like the wild form) in flower-size, flower-colour and in vegetative colouring; in genetical terms this can be explained by saying that the characters of each cultivar are determined by different recessive genes, the respective dominant ("wild-type") alleles of which are found in the other cultivar. Crossing 'Celtic White' with a normal wild form also gives only pink-flowered progeny. Sterile hybrids have been obtained by crossing this species with 127. *G. maderense*, *G. purpureum*, 124. *G. rubescens* and 125. *G. canariense* (see also Chapter 7).

124. G. rubescens Yeo (correct name *G. yeoi* Aedo & Muñoz Garmendia) (Figure 9.126)
A biennial, looking like a large form of 123. *G. robertianum*, with beetroot-red lower stems and leaf-stalks and with flowers 22–33mm in diameter. Sun or shade. May or June onwards.

Plant similar to 123. *G. robertianum* and having stems up to 60cm; stems and leaf-stalks much thicker than those of *G. robertianum*; leaf-blades up to 23cm wide with more generally acute teeth which are more prominently mucronate. Sepals

Figure 9.126. *G. rubescens*; piece shown 11cm wide

7–8mm, with mucro about 2mm. Petals 18–22mm; claws about half as long as blades; blades 7–13mm wide, bright purplish pink with paler veins near base; throat of flower dark red. Mericarps 3.3–3.7mm, with 1 or 2 collar-like rings at the top and no hairs or tangle-strands. Stylar portion of rostrum 6–7mm. Discharge: carpel-projection.

Madeira.

The evidence which justified the treatment of this plant, which has long been known, as a distinct species was collected by Mr W. Jackson and published by Yeo (1973) under the name that Jackson had proposed. Unfortunately the name *G. rubescens* Andrews had been published in the eighteenth century for a *Pelargonium* but the name had been disregarded by the compilers of Index Kewensis. Aedo & Muñoz Garmendia (1997) then chose a new epithet which does not convey anything about the plant. *G. rubescens* is very hardy and forms magnificent overwintering rosettes. It is useful for sheltered, partly shaded corners. In gardens it used often to be called *G. anemonifolium* (a synonym of 126. *G. palmatum*) or *G. lowei*, a name which has no botanical standing.

Sterile hybrids with 123. *G. robertianum* have been raised and have occurred spontaneously at Cambridge. Fertile hybrids with 125. *G. canariense* were raised at Cambridge and by Professor Herbert Baker at the University of California, Berkeley.

125. G. canariense Reuter (Figure 9.127) (correct name *G. reuteri* Aedo & Muñoz Garmendia)
A fragrant, evergreen, short-lived perennial with rosettes on a stem usually 5–15cm tall. Leaf-blades up to 25cm wide, succulent, divided to the base into 3 and nearly to the base into 5, divisions much cut, not stalked. Flowers 23–36mm in diameter, deep pink. Petals with a claw at base, not clasped by the sepals, and a narrow blade. Stamens about twice as long as sepals. Greenhouse or sheltered corners out of doors. Spring onwards.

Perennial with a rosette on a distinct above-ground stem which may become branched, and is commonly 5–15cm tall but in old, protected, plants up to 30cm. Flowering stems and leaves more or less succulent. Leaf-blades up to 25cm wide, divided to the base into 3 and nearly to the base into 5; divisions not stalked, deeply pinnately lobed; lobes $1\frac{1}{2}$–3 times as long as broad, themselves with secondary, toothed, lobes. Teeth and tips of lobes obtuse or acute. Leaf-stalks dull brownish to purplish. Stem-leaves paired, rapidly decreasing in size, complexity of lobing and length of stalk upwards. Flowering stems arising from neighbouring axils of the rosette or, in old plants, terminally, forming a dense inflorescence up to 45cm in height, its upper parts thickly covered with purple glandular hairs. Floral axis horizontal. Sepals 8–10mm, divergent; mucro about 1mm. Petals 17–24mm, with a claw and a blade; blades 6–9mm wide and $1^{3}/_{4}$–$2^{1}/_{2}$ times as long as wide, deep pink; claws half as long as blades or less, each with a double ridge abutting a stamen so that 5 nectar-passages of approximately circular cross-section are formed. Throat of flower pale or dark. Filaments about twice as long as sepals; anthers scarlet or dark red. Styles about as long as stamens, white; stigmas about 2mm long, pink or white. Immature fruits slightly nodding on spreading or deflexed pedicels. Rostrum about 30mm, including stylar portion 16–18mm. Mericarps about 3.5mm, with a uniform network of ribs and 1 or 2, sometimes 3, small collar-like rings at apex, hairless or with fine hairs at the top. Discharge: carpel-projection.

Canary Isles (Tenerife, Palma, Gomera and Hierro).

A plant for sheltered situations, preferably in the milder west, or for the greenhouse. I have had three accessions of *G. canariense* of known wild origin and two the same as each other from botanic gardens. The last was the neatest in habit and flower-form and is the one illustrated in colour by Yeo (1970). Some stocks are spoiled by minor deformities of the leaves and flowers, probably caused by a virus. Propagated by seed.

The name *Geranium canariense* Reuter was antedated by *G. canariense* (Willdenow) Poiret, a name published for a *Pelargonium* and omitted from Knuth's monograph (1912). Aedo & Muñoz Garmendia (1997) therefore proposed the name *G. reuteri*, a name which does not tell anything about the plant.

Fertile hybrids with 124. *G. rubescens* have been raised at Cambridge and by Professor Herbert Baker at the University of California, Berkeley. Other hybrids raised by Alan Bremner are with 126. *G. palmatum* and 123. *G. robertianum*.

126. *G. palmatum* Cavanilles (*G. anemonifolium* L'Héritier) (Figure 9.128)
Plant like 125. *G. canariense* but with hardly any development of stem except in old plants, and with leaves up to 35cm wide, their middle division stalked. Flowers distinctive, 33–45mm in diameter, with sepals clasping petal-claws and petals slightly oblique in posture, broad-bladed. Stamens twice as long as sepals. Greenhouse or sheltered corner out of doors. Summer.

Figure 9.127. *G. canariense*: from Barcelona B.G., 1966, *ex* La Orotava B.G.; piece shown 10cm wide

Figure 9.128. *G. palmatum*: from J. Stephens, 1964; piece shown 12.5cm wide

Perennial with a massive rosette on a condensed stem. Lower stems and leaves more or less succulent. Leaf-blades up to 35cm wide, divided and lobed much as in 125. *G. canariense* but with middle division distinctly stalked and the lobes up to 4 times as long as broad, light green. Leaf-stalks green or pink-flushed. Stem-leaves as in *G. canariense*. Flowering stems axillary, forming a dense inflorescence up to 1.2m in height, covered with purple glandular hairs except at the base. Floral axis horizontal. Sepals 7–10mm, appressed to the petal-bases and curved outwards at the tips; mucro 1–2mm. Petals 20–30mm long, arranged slightly obliquely, with a claw and a blade; blade 13–18mm wide and slightly longer than wide, purplish rose shading to deep crimson in the basal $1/5$, giving the flower a dark throat; claws $1/4$–$1/5$ as long as blade, each with a double ridge abutting a stamen so that 5 nectar passages of narrowly elongate cross-section are formed. Filaments about twice as long as sepals, slightly displaced to the lower side of the flower, deep magenta; anthers cream or yellow, sometimes tinged with pink. Styles like the filaments in length, position and colour. Stigmas 3–4mm, purplish crimson. Immature fruits and their pedicels downwardly inclined. Rostrum about 28mm, including stylar portion about 13mm. Mericarps 3.2–3.4mm, with a network of ribs, these closer towards apex where there are 1 or 2 collar-like rings, hairless. Discharge: carpel-projection.

Madeira

G. palmatum has been cultivated in Europe since the eighteenth century but has usually been known by the name *G. anemonifolium* which was published two years later than *G. palmatum*. The petal-colour is RHSCC Purple Group 77C, with base Red-Purple Group 71B. Different accessions received at Cambridge have differences in habit which affect the value of the plant. The best I have had, from this point of view, was received from Mr Jan Stephens in 1964, though I do not believe he introduced it from Madeira, as stated by Clifton (1979). The species may be used in the same way as *G. canariense* and propagation is by seed.

Fertile hybrids with 127. *G. maderense*, using the latter as female parent, have been raised at Cambridge. Alan Bremner has obtained a hybrid with *G. canariense*.

127. G. maderense Yeo (Figure 9.129, Plate 49)
A giant aromatic rosette plant, often dying after flowering, with a distinct erect rosette-stalk. Leaves even larger than in 126. *G. palmatum*, with distinctive pale brown stalks. Flowers about 35mm

Figure 9.129. *G. maderense*: from C.H.C. Pickering, 1967; piece shown 14.5cm wide

in diameter, with sepals clasping petal-claws; petals broad-bladed, purplish pink with a network of pale elevated veins, dark towards base. Stamens about as long as sepals. Greenhouse or sheltered position out of doors in areas with very mild winters. February or March onwards under glass.

Rosette-bearing stem up to 60cm tall and 6cm in diameter, either dying after flowering or continuing to grow by means of lateral branches. Flowering stems and leaves more or less succulent. Leaf-blades up to 60cm wide, divided and lobed much as in 125. *G. canariense* but with the middle division stalked, the lobes up to 4 times as long as broad and the secondary lobes rather far apart in the larger examples. Teeth and tips of lobes acute. Leaf-stalks dull reddish brown, hoary from the minute glandular hairs but without large hairs. Inflorescence arising from the centre of the rosette, consisting of a short central stem bearing 1 or 2 whorls of branches which give rise to a great mound of flowers above the leaves; lower parts coloured like the leaf-stalks, upper parts thickly covered with purple glandular hairs; branches regularly forking, sometimes some of the internodes suppressed. Stem-leaves decreasing in size rapidly upwards, becoming 3-lobed and the middle lobe becoming dominant. Floral orientation indefinite. Sepals 8–10mm, appressed to the petal-bases which are divergent; mucro about 1mm. Petals 19–21mm long, with a claw and a blade; blade 13–18mm wide and about as long or slightly longer, purplish pink with a network of pale elevated veins, darker towards throat which is blackish purple; claws only about 2.5mm, each with a double ridge abutting a stamen so that 5 nectar-passages of elongate cross-section are formed. Filaments about as long as sepals, purplish or dark red, curved outwards at the tips; anthers dark red. Styles and stigmas dark red; stigmas 2.5mm. Immature fruits indefinitely orientated, approximately in line with their pedicels. Rostrum about 20mm, including stylar portion 7mm. Mericarps 4–4.5mm, with a network of ribs and 1–3 collar-like rings at the top, hairless. Discharge: carpel-projection.

Madeira.

Except for *G. arboreum* A. Gray in Hawaii, this is the largest *Geranium* species, growing to about 1.5m in height, having the largest leaves of any species and producing an immense inflorescence of purplish flowers surrounded by the purple haze of its glandular hairs. The petal colour is RHSCC Purple Group 77C, passing through Red-Purple Group 72B towards the base which is 77A. In the parts of Britain where winters are cold it needs a greenhouse, but it may be grown out of doors on the Atlantic coast. It is naturalised in the Scilly Isles (Cornwall). In the greenhouse it requires two years to mature, and will only do this if potted on very rapidly or planted out. Some plants have been raised to flowering out of doors in 12 months. Its introduction is due to Major C.H.C. Pickering, who observed it in cultivation in Madeira and traced a natural population in the 1950s; only two or three restricted colonies are known. Pickering asked me for a taxonomic evaluation of it and I confirmed that it was specifically distinct from *G. palmatum;* he also sent it to many other countries and it is now widely cultivated (as well as escaping in some places). It grows mainly in the winter months and is able to withstand severe summer drought, so it would seem best suited to areas with a Mediterranean climate. The leaf-stalks are persistent and become reflexed, propping up the otherwise top-heavy rosette; they also store water and starch. To display this plant in a natural condition the leaf-stalks should not be tidied away.

Fertile hybrids have been raised at Cambridge by pollinating *G. maderense* with 126. *G. palmatum*, and sterile hybrids by pollinating it with 122. *G. cataractarum* (see under that species) and 95. *G. robertianum*.

SUBGENUS III ERODIOIDEA

Plants perennial. Fruit-discharge of the Erodium-type: carpel containing the seed discharged together with the awn as one unit; awn becoming coiled after discharge. Mericarps 5mm or more long; base tapered and terminating in a horny point which is glossy on the back and covered with bristles at the sides.

SECTION ERODIOIDEA, THE PHAEUM GROUP

Tall branching plants. Main leaves with the divisions tapered towards the tip, freely toothed. Flowers nodding, with widely spreading or reflexed petals. Apex of mericarp conical, with 3–5 keels or ridges around it.

Three species, all cultivated.

128. G. phaeum Linnaeus (Figures 9.130, 9.131 & 9.132, Plate 50)
A medium-sized leafy perennial with the leaves not deeply cut, but copiously toothed. Flowers about 22–25mm in diameter, nodding, flat, approximately circular, but often with a little point on each petal, in sombre shades of purplish red or a soft pale lilac, in either case with a white base, or entirely white; inflorescence-branches one-sided. Developing fruits upwardly inclined. Shade or semi-shade. Ground-cover. Leafy in winter. May–June and often again.

Perennial with stout rootstock growing on the soil surface, and oblique, often purple-dotted or even entirely blackish violet, stems reaching 40–80cm. Basal leaves mostly 10–20cm wide, divided as far as $^3/_5$ –$^2/_3$ or occasionally $^4/_5$ into 7 or 9, upper surface often blotched with purplish brown in the notches; divisions tapered both ways from about the middle, rather solid in outline; lobes about as long as broad, straight or curved outwards, with 2–5 or more teeth, a proportion of these usually very shallow. Teeth and tips of lobes acute or obtuse. Stipules of basal leaves large, thin and rounded. Stem-leaves, and sometimes the lower inflorescence leaves, solitary; upper inflorescence leaves paired, unequal, more or less stalkless, often with lobes up to $1^1/_2$ times as long as broad and very sharp teeth. Stipules of stem-leaves thin, brownish, conspicuous, usually slashed at the tip. Minute glandular hairs (see Chapter 4) larger than usual, dense. Inflorescence loose, with one or few long branches, with recurved tips, each with only one or two flowers open at a time, the flowers directed to one side. Peduncles and pedicels upwardly inclined. Flowers nodding or with axis horizontal. Sepals 6–11mm, usually

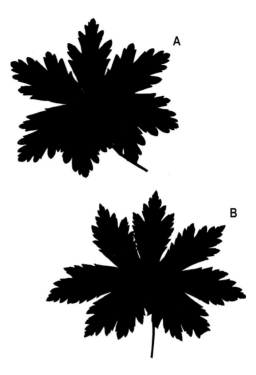

Figure 9.130. *G. phaeum* var. *lividum*: (A) from B. Wurzell, 1972; (B) 'Majus', from Mrs B.C. Rogers, 1966; 10 and 14cm wide

purplish at the base; mucro 0.5mm long or less. Petals usually 11–14mm, nearly as wide as long or wider, somewhat ruffled and/or lobulate round the edge, sometimes with a triangular point at the tip, widely spreading above the very shortly erect base, dull lilac or pinkish to deep violet, dull purple, maroon or nearly black, with a distinct whitish base; base with at least a few hairs across front surface and moderately tufted hairs at the sides. Filaments curved outwards at first, becoming appressed to the style as the anthers open but still spreading at the tips, coloured like the petals towards their tips, bearing very long spreading and glistening hairs with recurved tips in their lower halves. Anthers whitish with purplish edges. Stigmas 1.25–2mm, yellowish or greenish. Immature fruit upwardly inclined, pedicels likewise or sometimes more nearly horizontal. Mericarps 5–5.5mm, bristly, with 4 or 5 keels or ridges around the top. Stylar portion of rostrum 3–4mm. Discharge: Erodium-type.

Mountains of S. and C. Europe from the Pyrenees through the Alps to Croatia, Ukraine, Romania and Bulgaria. Often naturalised outside this range, especially northwards.

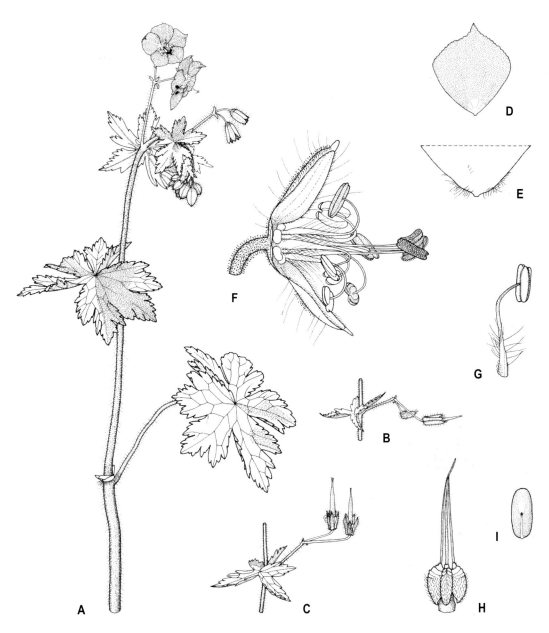

G. phaeum grows in damp meadows, and along wood margins and shady road verges in high hills and at the lower levels of the mountains. It is very suitable for cultivation in shade or semi-shade in Britain and its stout rhizomes enable it to withstand some dryness. It carries a good crop of basal leaves with which it covers the ground for most or all of the year. The flowers of var. *phaeum* are unusual in their dark colouring; the lighter flowers of var. *lividum* are more colourful but never vivid. A range

Figure 9.131. *G. phaeum* var. *phaeum*: from Liège B.G. 1979, coll. France: Hautes Pyrenées. (A) shoot beginning to flower, x $^2/_3$; (B) & (C) cymule with immature and mature fruit, respectively, x $^2/_3$; (D) petal, with pigmentation, x 2; (E) base of front surface of petal, x 4; (F) flower in male stage with petals and three sepals removed, x 4; (G) stamen of outer whorl seen obliquely from back, x 4; (H) fruit in pre-explosive interval, x 2; (I) seed, x 4

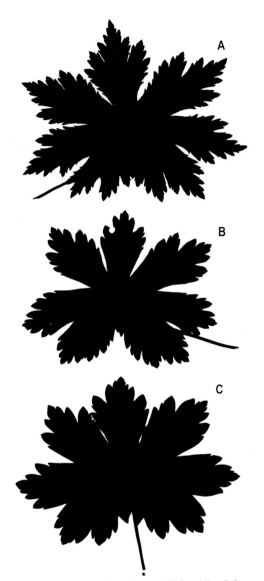

Figure 9.132. *G. phaeum* var. *phaeum*: (A) from Liège B.G., 1979, coll. France: Hautes Pyrenées; (B) from Dresden B.G., 1980, coll. Slovakia: Belaer Tatra; (C) from R.P. Dales, 1979, *ex* Margery Fish Nursery; 9–13.5cm wide

Switzerland, though it is not practicable to restrict it to this. White mutants appear among seedlings in cultivation occasionally. They appear to cross with var. *phaeum* or var. *lividum* to produce plants with faintly bluish flowers.

G. phaeum 'Lily Lovell' was raised and introduced by Trevor Bath (see Bath & Jones, 1994), and described as "larger and earlier than the type, the flowers a beautiful deep mauve, contrasting well with the distinctive light green leaves".

G. phaeum 'Rose Madder' has flowers an unusual shade of brownish pink.

G. phaeum var. *lividum* (L'Héritier) Persoon (Figure 9.130A, Plate 50) has the petals rounded and bluish, lilac or pink, rather pale, and with a white base smaller than in var. *phaeum*; the base and the lowest part of the coloured portion are traversed by short bluish or violet veins which become diffuse (smudged) as they enter the coloured zone, giving rise to a bluish halo, which forms a straight border with the white base; above the blue halo there is usually another whitish halo; in the principal colour there may be a noticeable change from pink towards blue during the life of each flower. This variety extends from Croatia westwards along the southern side of the alps, reaching the French Alps, and replacing var. *phaeum* throughout this area. The leaves are usually unblotched; Clifton (1979) notes that when dying they turn primrose yellow.

G. phaeum var. *lividum* 'Majus' (Figure 9.130) is the name under which a particularly tall and large-flowered clone (petals to 16mm long) was received at Cambridge from Mrs B.C. Rogers of Bromley, Kent, in 1966.

G. phaeum var. *phaeum* (Figures 9.131 & 9.132, Plate 50) has the petals cuspidate or sometimes lobulate and dark pinkish lilac to nearly black, with silvery white or nearly white bases; the white area has a jagged edge and the flower by transmitted light thus has a star-shaped white centre. In the least dark forms there may be dark veins just above the whitish base. The leaves may be blotched or unblotched. This variety occupies the greater part of the natural range of the species.

G. phaeum var. *phaeum* 'Samobor' has the basal half of each leaf-division dark purplish brown with each brown area traversed by a green mid-vein; it was collected near Samobor, Croatia, in 1990 by Miss Elizabeth Strangman, of Washfield Nursery, Hawkhurst, Kent.

G. phaeum var. *phaeum* 'Variegatum' has irregular pale yellow variegation towards the leaf-margins, the variegated areas usually somewhat curled; blotching of the borders of the sinuses may be brown, but is red if it falls on a patch of the yellow variegation. In the absence of a variegated form of var. *lividum* the name may be written as *G. phaeum* 'Variegatum'.

of intermediates between the two varieties can be seen in some gardens. Aedo (1996) does not find the distinction between the varieties clear enough for botanical use, but I feel it is worth keeping up for garden use.

G. phaeum 'Album' is a name applied by Ingwersen (1946) to a white-petalled *G. phaeum* of tall growth and large flower-size collected in

G. phaeum hybridises spontaneously in cultivation with the closely related 130. *G. reflexum* (see under 129. *G.* x *monacense*).

129. G. x **monacense** Harz (*G. punctatum* of gardens) (Figures 9.133 & 9.134, Plate 50)
Intermediate between 128. *G. phaeum* and 130. *G. reflexum* in colour and shape of petals (1¹/₂ times as long as broad) and the degree to which they are reflexed. Immature fruits and their pedicels upwardly inclined. Like 128. *G. phaeum* in requirements and behaviour.

Like 128. *G. phaeum* and 130. *G. reflexum* in vegetative parts, with or without brown blotches on the leaves. Petals 11–14mm, strongly reflexed, about 1¹/₂ times as long as broad, sometimes obscurely lobed at the tip, dark dull purplish red or pinkish lilac with a white basal zone and, above this, a dull bluish violet zone which is traversed by darker violet veins; margins at the base with a dense hair-tuft, as in *G. reflexum*. Stamens with long or very long hairs as in *G. phaeum*. Immature fruits and their pedicels slightly deflexed or the immature fruits inclined slightly upwards.

Evidently a spontaneous garden hybrid between 128. *G. phaeum* and 130. *G. reflexum*.

Plants of this hybrid were found growing near the parents by Dr K. Harz in his garden in Upper Bavaria, and named *G.* x *monacense* after the city of Munich (Harz, 1921). However, the hybrid has evidently arisen in different places and at different times, for different clones exist, as mentioned below, and apparent intermediates between *G. phaeum* and *G. reflexum* were noted by Bowles (1914).

The description above is based on three stocks grown at Cambridge. Two of these have purplish red petals, a little paler and more obviously purplish than those of *G. phaeum* var. *phaeum*, which is evidently one of their parents. One of them, which has strongly blotched leaves, was received from Mr G.S. Thomas in 1974 as *G. punctatum*, a name which is not to be found in botanical literature and rarely even in print (e.g. Johnson, 1937, p. 187) except in nursery catalogues. The other is like the first but with only weak blotches on the leaves. The third stock has lilac-pink petals (darkening slightly with age), and unblotched leaves. The petal-colour is intermediate between that of pink-flowered *G. reflexum* and *G. phaeum* var. *lividum* (as grown at Cambridge), and the latter is presumably one of its parents (it was given to me by Professor R.P. Dales of Horsham, East Sussex). The first two stocks (with darker flowers) represent nothovar. *monacense* and the

Figure 9.133. *G.* x *monacense* nothovar. *anglicum*: from R.P. Dales, 1979, *ex* Alan Bloom, as *G. phaeum*; 11cm wide

third represents nothovar. *anglicum*. Quite a lot of apparently good seed is produced by these hybrids but I have never sown any.

Figure 9.134. *G.* x *monacense* nothovar. *monacense*: from G.S. Thomas, 1974, as *G. punctatum*; 7 and 11cm wide (unequally reduced)

Attention was drawn to the name *G.* x *monacense* by Clement (1976, p. 24) as a result of the discovery by Mr Patrick Roper of a plant escaped from cultivation at Hurst Green, East Sussex. That plant was brought back into cultivation and has reached me via Mrs J. Forty (Joy Jones); it proves to be a second clone of nothovar. *anglicum.*

G. x *monacense* nothovar. *anglicum* Yeo (Figure 9.133, Plate 50) is the hybrid in which *G. phaeum* var. *lividum* has participated; the main petal colour is pinkish lilac and the whitish petal-base is small and straight-edged, while the bluish violet zone above it is wide, conspicuous and strongly veined. In the two clones known to me (see above) the leaves are unblotched, their divisions are comparatively long and narrow, each having the main pair of lobes noticeably divergent, and the teeth and tips of lobes are mostly obtuse. Professor Dales' plant was obtained by him from Bloom's of Bressingham, Diss, Norfolk (as *G. phaeum*) where I have seen it myself. The Hurst Green plant has been assigned a cultivar name (see below).

G. x *monacense* nothovar. *anglicum* Yeo 'Eric Clement' can be written "*G.* x*monacense* 'Eric Clement* '": it applies to the Hurst Green plant (Clifton, 1979, and ms notes). It differs from the Bressingham clone in being slightly more vigorous and in having slightly larger petals, more obviously lobed at the tip and with the edges curved forwards instead of being flat. The leaves do not turn yellow when dying (Clifton, 1979).

G. x *monacense* nothovar. *monacense* (Figure 9.134, Plate 50) is the hybrid in which *G. phaeum* var. *phaeum* has participated (this is indicated by the way in which Harz described *G. phaeum* when publishing *G.* x *monacense*). The main petal colour is purplish red (RHSCC Red-Purple Group 64B) and the whitish petal-base is relatively large and has a toothed edge, while the bluish violet zone above it is inconspicuous. Brown blotches are present in the notches of the leaves, the latter being conspicuously yellow when young.

G. x *monacense* nothovar. *monacense* 'Muldoon' Clifton, 1979) which may be shortened to "*G.* x *monacense* 'Muldoon' ", applies to a clone with strongly blotched leaves, presumably the one mentioned above that was received at Cambridge from Mr G.S. Thomas, and often called *G. punctatum.* (The name 'Muldoon' does not apply to the weakly spotted Cambridge clone.)

130. *G. reflexum* Linnaeus (Figure 9.135, Plate 50) Like 128. *G. phaeum* in vegetative characters. Petals much narrower (twice as long as broad), very strongly reflexed (making flowers only 13–16mm in diameter), rose-pink to dark violet with a more distinct white base. Immature fruits

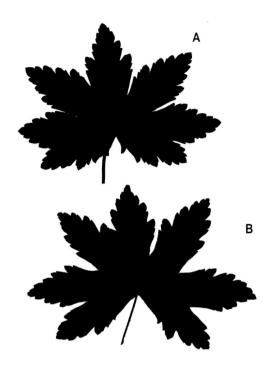

Figure 9.135. *G. reflexum*: (A) from Marburg B.G.; (B) from L. Bacon, 1989.0505 (coll. Pindus Mts, Greece); 9 and 14cm wide

downwardly inclined. Like *G. phaeum* in requirements and behaviour.

Vegetatively almost identical with 128. *G. phaeum*; leaves usually strongly blotched with brown where the divisions, and sometimes the lobes, meet. Flowers more or less inverted. Sepals like those of *G. phaeum* but more or less red-flushed. Petals 11–13mm, twice as long as broad or more, sometimes with a triangular point and often with one or more incisions at the tip, very strongly reflexed a short way above the erect base, the tips more spreading where they are pressed outwards by the sepals, bright rose-pink to dark violet, with a white base occupying about $^{1}/_{4}$ of the petal's length, and with a bluish band between the white and pink areas, without hairs across front surface at base but with a strong tuft or long fringe at either side. Filaments appressed to the style, bordered at the base with very small fine hairs. Immature fruits deflexed or horizontal on deflexed or horizontal pedicels. Mericarps with 3 or 4 keels or ridges around the top. Discharge: Erodium-type.

Italy (in the Apennines from Abruzzi to Marche and Umbria); Montenegro and Kosovo to N. Greece (Pindus and Thessaly), Bulgaria (Rhodope Mts.).

In its bright pink form this is a plant of similar garden value to 128. *G. phaeum*. The flowers are brighter in colour but appear rather small. A collection by Lionel Bacon from the Katara Pass in the Pindus mountains of Greece grown at Cambridge has dingy dark violet flowers and unspotted leaves. Because of the close similarity of *G. reflexum* to *G. phaeum* some authors have treated it as a variety of that. It is more distinct, however, from varieties *phaeum* and *lividum* than they are from one another.

G. reflexum is a parent of *G.* x *monacense*.

131. *G. aristatum* Freyn (Figure 9.136, Plate 51) A greyish-hairy perennial of medium size with rather large, coarsely lobed and toothed leaves. Flowers about 22–28mm in diameter, nodding with reflexed oblong petals, nearly white or lilac-pink at tips but with lilac veins becoming merged to a lilac zone at the base. Sepal mucro half as long as sepal body or more. Sun or light shade. Leafless in winter. June onwards.

Perennial with a stout rootstock emerging above the surface and nearly erect stems to about 60cm. Basal leaves mostly 15–20cm wide, divided as far as $^3/_4$ into 7 or 9, rather pale green; divisions tapered both ways from well above the middle, rather solid in outline; lobes about as long as broad, straight with V-shaped notches between them, and usually with 2–5 unequal teeth. Teeth and tips of lobes acute. Stipules of basal leaves about 2cm, very narrow, tapered to a long point. Stem-leaves paired, usually with five divisions diverging widely from each other, and few coarse lobes and teeth. Stem with branches mostly paired. Plant covered in long hairs, those of the upper parts mostly glandular. Inflorescence loose. Cymules often 3-flowered. Flowers nodding. Sepals 9mm, flushed with pink, reflexed, with a mucro $^1/_2$–$^3/_4$ as long as body of sepal. Petals 13–16mm, about twice as long as broad, strongly reflexed just above

Figure 9.136. *G. aristatum*: from Kew, 1976; 16.5cm wide

the base, nearly square-ended but slightly lobed or with a projecting triangular point at the tip, the greater part nearly white or lilac, with ill-defined, slightly netted, lilac-pink veining which coalesces to form a darker blotch on basal $^1/_3$ of petal, without hairs on front surface at base but a dense tuft on either side. Filaments pink at base, white towards tips, appressed to the style, with divergent stiff hairs in the lower half. Anthers cream, becoming pale brown. Nectaries each with a canopy of white hairs. Immature fruits erect on reflexed pedicels. Mericarps about 6mm, with 4 or 5 keels or ridges around the top. Stylar portion of rostrum not distinct. Discharge: Erodium-type.

Mountains of E. Albania, S. Yugoslavia and N. Greece (Pindus).

A fine plant, completely unmistakable, though evidently allied to 128. *G. phaeum*, etc. Old inflorescences may be cleared away through the long flowering season to keep it looking fresh. The one seedling I have seen had notched cotyledons.

SECTION SUBACAULIA, THE CINEREUM GROUP

Alpine perennials with a compact branching rootstock, the tips of the branches covered with stipules. Foliage silvery, hoary or greyish green. Main leaves with the divisions usually not or scarcely tapered to the tip. Stem leaves few and usually much reduced (not covered in the following descriptions). Plant without glandular hairs. Flowering peduncles emerging from the rootstock or borne on stems with solitary or paired branches. Pedicels spreading or reflexed after flowering, hooked under the calyx so as to hold the immature fruits upright. Flowers medium-sized, erect. Petals with hairs on the edges at the base and sometimes on front surface here. Mericarps at least 4mm long, hairy, compressed and 1–3-ribbed at the apex. Fruit discharge: Erodium-type.

The group occurs in the Atlas Mountains of Morocco, in S.E. and N. Spain, in the Pyrenees (perhaps French only), French Alps, Apennines, eastern Italian Alps and Balkan peninsula, and throughout Turkey, extending thence into Transcaucasia, Syria and Lebanon. In a central position is *G. argenteum*. Whereas variation east of this has traditionally been catered for with varietal names under *G. cinereum*, that in the west is covered by specific names. This anomaly has been removed by the provision of names at species-rank for all the distinguishable variants (Aedo, 1996). If all the 15 species of the group are not yet in cultivation, they probably soon will be. I have therefore included them all here, though there are some that I have not seen in the living state. The comparatively short species-descriptions should be read in conjunction with the Group description.

The key that I provide differs from that of Aedo (1996) because the characters that he uses do not always hold good, partly, no doubt, because of the effects of cultivation. In fact there are three species that I have been unable to separate. Apart from difficulties that I have encountered with the characterisation of species, anomalous specimens appear to be rather frequent in Turkey (Aedo, 1996).

Hybridisation between the species is frequent in gardens, but the resulting plants vary in their degree of sterility. The changed ranking of the naturally occurring members of the group results in a change to the application of the one valid binary name for a hybrid in this group: *G.* x *lindavicum* (no. 133). This hybrid and one that does not have a binary name receive treatment equivalent to that of the species of the group. Some of these hybrids have become popular garden subjects and more will in the future. Some of those raised by Alan Bremner involve *G.* x *lindavicum* and are thus triple hybrids (see Appendix III).

This group can also cross with members of Subgenus Geranium, Section Geranium (species 58, 59 and 60 in the Sessiliflorum Group and 84 in the Cordilleran Group; see also Appendix III and Chapter 7).

Key to the Geranium cinereum group (see How to Use the Dichotomous Keys, p. 50)

1a. Leaves silvery-silky on the underside or both sides, normally more than 2.5cm wide   2
b. Leaves not silvery-silky on either side, though sometimes grey-hairy (or, if so, leaves not more than 2.5cm wide)   4

2a. Leaves silvery-silky on both sides, the lateral incisions reaching the base or nearly so
132. argenteum
b. Leaves silvery-silky on underside, clearly not cut to the base   3

3a. Petals not very pale at base; lobes and teeth of leaves acute   *138. subargenteum*
b. Petals white at base; lobes and teeth of leaves obtuse   *145. lazicum*

4a. Vigorous plant with stems usually 30–50cm and leaves to 7cm wide; (petals pink with white base and purple confluence of veins; anthers and stigmas very dark)
147. petri-davisii
b. Less vigorous, with stems not more than 30cm (sometimes 35cm in *G. cinereum* which has net-veined petals and no pink or

purple colour in stamens and stigmas); leaves not more than 4cm wide   5

5a. Petals with a dark base and outside this completely covered by a strong network of dark purple veins; ground colour pinkish
141. cinereum x *subcaulescens*
b. Petal veins not particularly strong; ground colour deep purplish red   6

6a. Flowers intensely coloured, with blackish stigmas, anthers and filament tips; petals usually with a black spot or dark confluence of veins at the base
140. subcaulescens (and *133.* x *lindavicum*, and *144. ponticum*)
b. Flowers moderately dark to quite pale in colour; either without strong darkening of the petal-bases, or without dark stigmas and stamens, or both   7

7a. Expanded base of outer stamens produced into a lobe on either side of the filament; leaf-blades cut as far as about $^2/_3$ into shallowly and obtusely 3-lobed divisions
135. cazorlense
b. Expanded stamen-bases not lobed; divisions of leaf-blades more deeply cut or more acutely tipped   8

8a. Middle division of leaf-blade with the segments (lobes or teeth) numbering more than three
139. dolomiticum (and *140. subcaulescens* and *142. austro-apenninum*)
b. Middle division of leaf-blade with the segments not usually more than three   9

9a. Petals purplish pink (with darker veins)   10
b. Petals pale pink to almost white (often with darker veins)   11

10a. Petals with slightly lightened colour at base
140. subcaulescens
b. Petals with extensive white base
148. palmatipartitum (and *143. thessalum*)

11a. Petals with an even network of purple veins
137. cinereum
b. Petals without coloured net-veining   12

12a. Dwarf plants with short flowering stems (to *c.* 5.5cm) and with small flowers (sepals to 6mm, petals to 12mm) and small fruits (rostrum to 11mm)   *134. nanum*
b. Plants more robust, with flowering stems commonly longer than 5.5cm, and with larger flowers (sepals 6.5–10mm, petals

14–17mm) and larger fruits (rostrum 20–24mm)   13

13a.   Leaf-lobes obtuse   *146. makmelicum*
  b.   Leaf-lobes acute   *136. subacutum*

132. G. argenteum Linnaeus (Figure 9.137A)

Leaf-stalks and stems greyish with appressed hairs. Leaves not more than 5cm wide, divided nearly to the base into 7; divisions usually 3-lobed to beyond the middle; lobes more or less acute, without teeth, not lying flat. Leaf-blades silvery-silky on both sides, the lower surface slightly more thickly clad than the upper. Stems with 1 or 2 solitary leaves and 1 or 2 pairs of leaves. Inflorescence normally with fewer than 10 flowers. Sepals 5.5–8.5mm, silky; mucro about 1mm. Petals about 12–14mm, nearly as broad as long, more or less notched, pale pink to white, often with faint or distinct, more or less netted, darker veins. Filaments white or green; anthers pinkish orange. Stigmas 1–1.5mm, yellow. Rostrum 11–15mm. Mericarps 6–6.5mm.

French Alps (Depts. Hautes Alpes and Basses Alpes), Italy (S. Tyrol; Etruscan Apennines), Croatia (Julian Alps).

Somewhat variable in ways which affect its garden value. Propagation is by division, cuttings or root cuttings. One year at Cambridge we attempted to gather seeds from a clonal colony but could find none. Next year, when *G. cinereum* was placed beside it, many seeds were formed but all seedlings raised (about 10) proved to be hybrids with the latter.

This species sometimes confers silkiness to the leaves of its hybrids, which include 133. *G. x lindavicum*. The hybrid plants mentioned in the previous paragraph had the petals nearly as strongly net-veined as those of *G. cinereum*. The well-known cultivar 'Apple Blossom', considered to be of the same parentage, has almost uniformly pale pink petals.

133. G. x lindavicum Knuth

Plant more or less erect, up to 30cm tall. Leaves greyish-velvety, the divisions lobed for half their length or more. Inflorescences erect (at least at first), leafy, many-flowered. Petals 13–15mm, rounded or weakly notched at apex, rather strong purplish pink, with dark red, slightly feathered veins; these become more diffuse (smudgy) towards the base, broadening into a dark patch with a toothed edge. Filaments red-purple; anthers black. Stigmas dark red.

A garden hybrid: 132. *G. argenteum* x 140 *G. subcaulescens*.

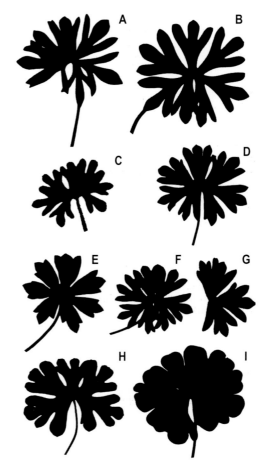

Figure 9.137. (A) *G. argenteum*: from Will Ingwersen, 1958; (B) *G. x lindavicum* 'Apple Blossom' (= A x E, probably again x A): cult. Harlow Car Gardens, 1983; (C) *G. nanum*: from Dr C. Aitchison, 1995, 16mm wide; (D) *G. cinereum* x *G. subcaulescens*: 'Ballerina' (= E x F): from R.F. Hunter, 1972; (E) *G. cinereum*: from Spetchley Park Gardens, 1960; (F) *G. subcaulescens*: from Alan Bloom, 1957; (G) the same, lateral divisions of one side removed; (H) *G. subcaulescens* 'Splendens': from Wisley, 1976; (I) *G. subcaulescens*: from J. Akeroyd, R. Mellors & C. Preston, 1976, coll. Greece: Mt Parnassos; 4.5–2.5cm wide [except C]

This description is based on plants raised in the Cambridge Botanic Garden in 1973 by Mr R.F. Hunter. The plants varied somewhat in habit and persistence but all are now dead. This suggests that if reliable plants are wanted, numerous progeny should be grown and tested. The cross was first raised by the nurseryman Sündermann at Lindau, on the German side of Lake Constance, and Knuth validated the name in 1912.

G. x *lindavicum* 'Alanah' (*G. argenteum* 'Alanah') was described by Ingwersen (1946) as just slightly less silvery in the foliage than *G. argenteum*, and extremely free in the production of its vivid crimson-purple flowers; he said it had been raised by Sir Jocelyn Gore-Booth in his garden at Lissadell in Ireland as a cross of *G. argenteum* with a very fine form of *G. subcaulescens*. There do not seem to be any plants in circulation under the name 'Alanah' at present, but it is mentioned here because Ingwersen thought it was the same as "the plant known as *G. argenteum* var. *purpureum*"(see below). Clifton (1979) gives a different story, apparently obtained from an early twentieth-century catalogue of J. Stormonth, according to which the parentage is *G. argenteum* 'Purpureum' x *G. traversii* (a member of Subgenus Geranium that is now known to be able to cross with members of the Cinereum Group). See also *G.* x *lindavicum* 'Lissadell'.

G. x *lindavicum* 'Gypsy' (Plate 55), is coloured unlike any other *Geranium* I know (though some recent *G. nanum* hybrids approach it). The petals are of a brilliant pink-cerise shot with carmine, fading to white just above the maroon, butterfly-shaped blotch at the base, and darkly net-veined. The upper surface of the grey-green leaf-blade is only sparsely hairy and the leaf-divisions are broad at the tips, similar to that in Figure 9.137D but more toothed. The plant was raised in the 1970s by Eric Smith, partner with J.C. Archibald in "The Plantsmen", a now defunct nursery firm; it is believed to be from *G.* x *lindavicum* 'Lissadell' pollinated with *G. subcaulescens* 'Splendens' (in which case it is a back-cross to *G. subcaulescens*). It may not be very hardy as it was for long thought to be lost, but it has now been re-found by Trevor Bath.

G. x *lindavicum* 'Lissadell' is similar to 'Alanah'; Clifton (1979) states that it has a beautiful silvery leaf and rich wine-coloured flowers. I have no detailed notes on 'Lissadell' but I saw it at Wisley in 1971 and observed that the leaf-segments were narrower than those of 'Purpureum' (below).

G. x *lindavicum* 'Purpureum' (*G. argenteum* 'Purpureum') was considered by Ingwersen (1946) to be the same as *G.* x *lindavicum* 'Alanah', in which case the description quoted above for that applies here. Plants are probably still current under the present name; one I saw at Wisley in 1971 appeared to be the present hybrid, and I noted that 'Lissadell' was very similar except in the width of the leaf-segments (see above).

134. *G. nanum* Battandier (Figure 137C, Plate 52)
Shoots crowded, more or less carpeting. Leaf-stalks pink towards base. Leaf-blades to 2.5cm wide, divided as far as about $^5/_6$ into 5 or 7;

divisions 3-lobed at the apex for $^1/_3$ to $^1/_2$ their length; lobes obtuse, without teeth, nearly equal, giving a rounded or kidney-shaped outline; both surfaces downy, grey-green, similar in colour. Leaf-segments crowded so that they cannot lie flat. Flowers carried just above the level of the leaves, funnel-shaped at first. Sepals 5–6mm, velvety, not strongly spreading, with hardly any mucro. Petals 10–13 x 6–8mm, rather oblong, faintly notched, not overlapping, pale pink or white with fine dark purple feathered and slightly netted veins. Filaments white, relatively longer than usual in the group and looped after anthers have opened; anthers white with blue lines of splitting or entirely purple. Stigmas greenish to pinkish brown; style striped with red. Mericarps 4.5–5mm. Rostrum about 10mm.

Morocco: High Atlas and Middle Atlas (one isolated locality).

This is the most compact species of the group and is suitable for the alpine house. The flower diameter varies from 18 to 22mm, according to the degree of expansion. White-flowered *G. nanum* was introduced into cultivation in Britain by Dr C. Aitchison in 1993 (Aitchison, 1994, 1995a) and is easily grown from seed or increased by division. A photograph of a pink-flowered plant taken in the High Atlas has also been published by Dr Aitchison (1997) and plants with strongly veined petals have been seen in the field but have not yet been introduced.

Hybrids of *G. nanum*, probably with *G. subcaulescens*, have flowers reminiscent of *G.* x *lindavicum* 'Gypsy'.

135. *G. cazorlense* Heywood
Leaf-blades not more than 2.2cm wide, divided as far as $^2/_3$–$^4/_5$ into 5 or 7. Divisions broadly wedge-shaped, broadest just about at the apex, making the leaf rounded, 3-lobed for about $^1/_4$–$^1/_2$ their length; lobes obtuse. Upper and lower leaf-surfaces similar in colour, with short appressed hairs. Sepals 6.5–7mm, shortly hairy, with mucro 0.3mm. Petals about 12 x 6mm, notched, white or pale purplish pink, without a dark basal spot. Filaments light yellow; expanded bases of outer filaments produced into a lobe on either side; anthers dark purplish brown. Stigmas light yellow. Mericarps 4mm. Rostrum 12–14mm.

Sierra de Cazorla, S.E. Spain.

Very rare; known only from two localities, 2km apart. Cultivated in England and illustrated by a beautiful photograph and a line-drawing by Lionel

Bacon (Bacon, 1993), showing it to be neat and low-growing. Flower said to be 25mm wide. The dark-coloured anthers are probably more than usually persistent. Reintroduced by Dr D. Évrard and Dr E.M. Rix in 1997 (but this importation not seen by me).

136. *G. subacutum* (Boissier) Aedo
Plant usually not more than about 10cm. Leaf-blades to 3.6cm wide, divided as far as $\frac{1}{2}-\frac{3}{4}$ into 5 or 7; divisions broadest at apex, giving a kidney-shaped outline, wedge-shaped with more or less open sinuses between them, palmately 3-lobed at the apex; lobes as long as broad or less, entire or with an occasional tooth; teeth and tips of lobes acute; upper and lower surfaces similar in colour. Flowers few. Sepals 6–9mm. Petals 13–15 x 8–10mm, slightly notched, white or pale pink with dark veins. Filaments apparently pale or unpigmented; anthers yellowish to brown or purple. Stigmas pink to purple. Mericarps about 4.5mm. Rostrum about 18mm.

Central Turkey, and possibly S.W. Turkey (depending on the ultimate assignment of specimens included in *G. subacutum* by Aedo).

As explained under 148. *G. palmatipartitum*, I exclude plants with strongly coloured petals from *G. subacutum*.

137. *G. cinereum* Cavanilles (Figures 9.137E & 9.138, Plate 53)
Leaf-blades not more than 5cm wide, divided as far as $\frac{3}{4}$ or $\frac{4}{5}$ into 5 or 7; divisions wedge-shaped, usually 3-lobed for $\frac{1}{5}-\frac{1}{3}$ of their length, the lobes about as broad as long, more or less acute, without teeth, the lateral more or less bent upwards. Leaf-blades greyish green, an effect not produced by hairs, which are small and sparse. Stems with up to 5 pairs of leaves but inflorescence usually with 10 or fewer flowers. Sepals 7.5–9.5mm; mucro 1mm or less. Petals about 17mm, notched, translucent white or pale pink

Figure 9.138. *G. cinereum*: from Spetchley Park Gardens, 1960. (A) plant beginning to flower, x $\frac{2}{3}$; (B) branch bearing cymule with immature fruit, x $\frac{2}{3}$; (C) petal, with pigmentation, x 2; (D) base of front surface of petal, x 4; (E) flower in male stage with petals and two sepals removed, x 4; (F) stamen of outer whorl, x 4; (G) fruit in pre-explosive interval, x 2; (H) seed, x 4

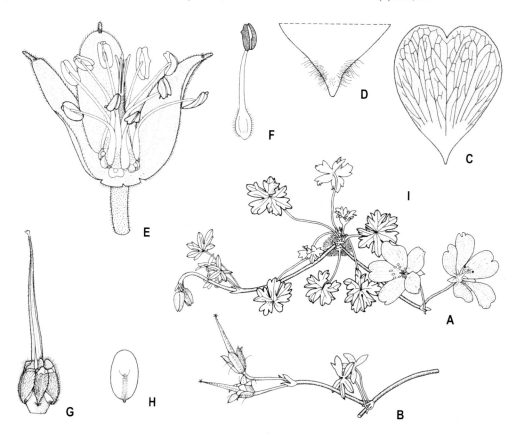

with a dense network of fine, sharply defined, pinkish purple veins. Filaments white; anthers yellowish. Stigmas 2mm, green. Mericarps about 5.5mm. Rostrum 1.7–1.9cm.

Central Pyrenees.

Can be propagated by division or from seeds if grown in isolation from other members of the *G. cinereum* group. The strongly coloured plants which are recommended to be grown by Ingwersen (1946) must be hybrids, though a degree of variation in the ground-colour occurs naturally.
G. cinereum 'Album' has completely white flowers.

For hybrids see 141. *G. cinereum* x *G. subcaulescens* ('Ballerina' etc.) and remarks on the Cinereum Group.

138. *G. subargenteum* Lange (Figure 139A)
Stems to 60cm but trailing. Leaf-blades to 8cm wide, divided as far as $^5/_6 - ^7/_8$ into 5 or 7; divisions broadest at or near apex, giving a nearly rounded outline, overlapping, with partly open or closed sinuses, more or less palmately lobed for about $^1/_3$ to nearly $^1/_2$ their length, toothed; teeth 1–2 times as long as broad; teeth and tips of lobes acute; lower surface velvety or silky, greyish, upper very finely and more sparsely hairy, much greener. Inflorescences with several pairs of small leaves and up to about 10 pairs of flowers. Sepals 8–9mm, finely hairy to greyish velvety-hairy, mucro 1–1.5mm. Petals to 21 x 13mm, distinctly notched, medium purple with fine dark occasionally forking or closely netted veins. Filaments white at base, same colour as petals at apex, anthers violet or bluish. Stigmas pink or yellowish-pink. Mericarps 5.5mm. Rostrum about 1.6–1.8cm.

N.W. Spain: Cantabrian mountains.

Introduced into cultivation by R. McBeath (no. 232, Picos de Europa, 1978) (Clifton, 1998)) and by T. Schulz in 1993 (Schulz, 1995). McBeath's stock was available from Edrom Nursery soon after its introduction (Clifton, 1998). Typically, this is one of the most vigorous members of the group but a dwarf form, collected also in the Picos de Europa by C. Sandes, is in cultivation. The flower-size measurements given here do not cover those given by Aedo (1996): he found larger sepals and fruit and smaller petals.

139. *G. dolomiticum* Rothmaler
Similar to 138. *G. subargenteum* but stems not normally more than 25cm; leaf-blades less

Figure 9.139. (A) *G. subargenteum*: cult. D. Victor (R. McBeath 232), 7cm wide; (B) *G. makmelicum*: from W.K. Aslet, 1974, coll. Lebanon: Mt. Lebanon; (C) *G. palmatipartitum*: E.M. Rix, 1972, coll. Turkey: Sivas Prov., x $^2/_3$; (D) the same, another plant; (E) *G. petri-davisii*: cult. Edinburgh, coll. P.H. Davis (D 20169); 7cm wide

deeply cut, their upper and lower surfaces similar, with small hairs; flowers smaller, filaments apparently not coloured at apex; rostrum slightly shorter.

N.W. Spain: Montes Aquilianos.

This is another extremely rare species, known from only two localities 3km apart and within the range of 138. *G. subargenteum*. Not separated from 140. *G. subcaulescens* and 142. *G. austro-apenninum* in my key, though typically quite distinct from them.

140. *G. subcaulescens* De Candolle (*G. cinereum* Cavanilles var. *subcaulescens* (De Candolle) Knuth) (Figure 9.137F–I, Plate 56)

Rootstock ranging from very compact to quite elongated. Leaf-blades rather dark green, with minute or quite long and loose hairs, not more than 5cm wide, divided as far as $^3/_4$ or nearly to the base into 5 or 7; divisions lobed for $^1/_3$–$^1/_2$ their length; lobes as broad as long and obtuse or up to two or more times as long as broad and acute, with occasional teeth. Inflorescences with 6 or 8 flowers. Sepals 6–8.5mm; mucro 0.5–1mm. Petals 12–15mm, nearly as wide as long, notched or rounded at apex, triangular or constricted at base, brilliant or dull deep purplish red, often paler towards base but usually with a blackish, rayed spot at the extreme base, or with a dark red zone at base formed by the converging veins; veins very dark red, reaching $^1/_2$–$^3/_4$ of the way up the petal, sometimes netted. Filaments blackish red; anthers black. Stigmas black or nearly so. Mericarps 5–6mm. Rostrum 18–20 or as little as 14mm.

Balkan peninsula and central and N.E. Turkey.

A really splendid plant for those not afraid to admire a dazzling colour. However, to quote Ingwersen (1946), "some assert that the typical plant verges dangerously on magenta, a barbaric colour disliked especially by ladies".

G. subcaulescens is extremely variable, but in my view it comprises all forms with rather dark leaves, deep purplish red petals, more or less dark at the base, and blackish stamens and stigmas. Plants from southern Italy appear to have rather paler petals and still paler stamens and stigmas, and I have therefore omitted this area from the statement of natural distribution. These have been separated as *G. austro-apenninum* by Aedo (1996) on the basis of flower colour and possession of teeth on the leaf-lobes (i.e. divisions cut into more than three segments). At least for plants in cultivation this distinction cannot be sustained, since some stocks known or believed to have come from the Balkan peninsula have toothed leaf-blades or petals without a black basal blotch (as collected by Lionel Bacon on Mount Ossa, Greece). It is remarkable that plants with black-centred flowers reappear in central and eastern

Turkey; they were assigned by Davis and Roberts (1955) partly to var. *subcaulescens* (which also, in their view, includes paler-flowered plants from S.W. Turkey) and partly to var. *ponticum* Davis & Roberts, now accepted as a species by Aedo (see no. 144. for my comments).

Pale-flowered Greek forms were collected on Mount Kithairon (Attiki) by Heldreich in 1856 and S.C. Atchley in 1936 and were photographed in the Varnous Mountains, Dhytiki, northern Greece, by Sebastian Payne in 1987. They were also found in the Peloponnese in 1998 at low frequency among normal forms by Robinson (1998). The first has very pale pink notched petals with darker, unbranched veins, white filaments and pink stigmas. The second has very pale pink rounded petals with weak darker veins and blackish basal spot, blackish stamens and stigmas but yellow pollen. The third has pink petals, strongly veined and with a "crushed strawberry" base.

G. subcaulescens was cultivated in Central Europe at the beginning of the twentieth century, having been used by Sündermann in a cross with 132. *G. argenteum* (*G. x lindavicum* Knuth, 1912). It was brought to Britain independently by two expeditionary parties in 1929, one composed of Mr Walter Ingwersen and Dr P.L. Giuseppi, who collected it at Korab, and the other of Dr R. Seligman and "H.R.S." (?H.R. Spivey), who collected it on Mount Kaimachkalan in Serbia (*Alpine Garden Society Bulletin*, 2, 195, 1934). This is doubtless the reason why there is even now a clone in circulation named after Dr Giuseppi, although when the name was first coined, I do not know. A second cultivar, 'Splendens', has emerged comparatively recently. The latter has been grown at Cambridge and is distinct from three other stocks also grown there, namely one supplied by Mr Alan Bloom (Blooms of Bressingham) (Figure 9.137F), one collected by Dr Alexis Vlasto near Tetovo in Yugoslavia (his no. 28, 1959), and one collected as seed by Akeroyd, Mellors & Preston (no. 375, 1976) (Figure 9.137I).

All stocks seem to be propagated quite easily from cuttings or divisions, and at least Dr Vlasto's sometimes reproduced itself from seed (but is now lost).

G. subcaulescens 'Giuseppii' has the petals moderately broad and varying from rounded to weakly notched at the apex even in the same flower, not quite magenta in colour, and with no distinct black basal spot, but merely a dark area formed by the convergent bases of the veins; the ground-colour becomes pale just above the base. The name has been persistently mis-spelt as 'Guiseppii'; it is sometimes applied to plants in which there is no fading of the ground-colour towards the dark basal area but I suspect that this is incorrect. (For origin, see above.)

G. subcaulescens 'Splendens' (Figure 9.137H, Plate 56) has broad, rounded, weakly notched petals of a brilliant but not harsh colour, slightly iridescent, with a distinct blackish red basal blotch, well-marked dark veins and a white zone along each margin for a short distance above the basal blotch; the leaves have shallow blunt lobes, some of them toothed, also bluntly. A most charming plant, but not so easily suited in cultivation as other forms. Said by Clifton (1979) to have been introduced by J. Stormonth about 1936 and offered again in 1974 by Stanton Alpine Nurseries.

The species has given rise to some important hybrids (see 133. *G.* x *lindavicum* and 141. *G. cinereum* x *G. subcaulescens*).

141. *G. cinereum* Cavanilles x *G. subcaulescens* De Candolle (Figure 9.137D, Plate 54)

Blades of basal leaves not more than 5cm wide, divided as far as $^1/_5$ or $^1/_6$ into 7; divisions lobed for $^1/_3$ to nearly half of their length, the lobes often with a tooth; tips of lobes and teeth obtuse. Leaf-blades a slightly greyish green. Stem leaves paired, rather well developed, with 5 divisions, their lobes occasionally toothed, more or less acute. Stems with about 4 pairs of leaves and about 8 flowers. Flowers to 32mm wide. Sepals 7–10mm, recurved at tips, with mucro about 0.5mm. Petals 18 x 16mm, drawn out into a long point at base, narrowly notched at apex, ground-colour pale purplish pink, fading towards base, marked with a close network of strong, fine, dark red veins which converge to form a very dark red V-shaped basal zone; base with hairs across front and a strong tuft on either edge. Stamens blackish red. Stigmas red.

A hybrid raised by Blooms of Bressingham, Diss, Norfolk. It received a Preliminary Commendation of the Royal Horticultural Society in 1961 and an Award of Merit in 1976. Although a few good seeds are formed, the plant seems to be largely sterile, which may partly account for its prolonged flowering season. The flowers are dramatically rather than vividly coloured. 'Ballerina' is easily propagated by cuttings or by division. Blooms introduced three cultivars, two of which appear in Plate 54.

G. cinereum x *G. subcaulescens*: 'Artistry' has a clearer pink ground-colour in the flowers than the other two.

G. cinereum x *G. subcaulescens*: 'Ballerina', the best known of the group, lacks this ground colour and has rather uniformly coloured petals that are not frilly.

G. cinereum x *G. subcaulescens*: 'Laurence Flatman' (corrected spelling) is very similar to 'Ballerina' but more vigorous, with less regular, slightly frilly, petals in which there is a triangle of darker ground-colour at the apex with its tip pointing towards the base; this is not present in all flowers, presumably depending on age.

142. *G. austro-apenninum* Aedo

Said to be distinguishable from *G. subcaulescens* by the leaf-divisions having more than 3 lobes (or with teeth additional to 3 lobes), no dark basal spot on the petals and stamens less dark. Unfortunately, *G. subcaulescens* sometimes shows these characters. The very coarse hair-clothing may help to distinguish *G. austro-apenninum*.

The southern half of the Apennine range in Italy.

143. *G. thessalum* Franzén

Leaf-blades to 3.7cm wide, divided as far as $^4/_5$–$^5/_7$ into 5 or 7; divisions narrow, with open sinuses between them, the terminal entire, bilobed or trilobed, the laterals bilobed, the basal usually entire, untoothed; upper surface hairy, lower silky, looking paler than the upper. Stem with spreading hairs. Inflorescence with up to 5 pairs of flowers. Sepals 8–10mm, silky, without long hairs on the margin; mucro 0.75–1.25mm. Petals 12–17 x 10–12mm, slightly notched, pinkish purple with purple veins and white base. Stamens perhaps sometimes purple, otherwise filaments pale yellow, anthers deep yellow. Stigmas white. Mericarps 6–7.5mm. Rostrum *c.* 25mm.

Greece: one mountain in the northern province of Kozania.

This species was first discovered in 1979. It is peculiar in the very sparse segmentation of the leaves. Unlike 140. *G. subcaulescens* it has a pale centre to the flower. On paper it seems very like 148. *G. palmatipartitum* but the actual plant looks quite different. It has been cultivated at Lund.

144. *G. ponticum* (Davis & Roberts) Aedo

Resembling *G. subcaulescens* in its intensely coloured flowers with blackish purple centres, but said to differ in having the leaf-lobes toothed, which it does; however, 140. *G. subcaulescens* sometimes has this character too, at least in cultivation. There are slight differences in the size-ranges of floral parts but only that of the sepal mucro (1.5–2.5mm here) seems significant. Very wide, strongly overlapping, petals are shown in a photograph by Aitchison (1995b).

Bacon (Bacon, 1993), showing it to be neat and low-growing. Flower said to be 25mm wide. The dark-coloured anthers are probably more than usually persistent. Reintroduced by Dr D. Évrard and Dr E.M. Rix in 1997 (but this importation not seen by me).

136. G. subacutum (Boissier) Aedo

Plant usually not more than about 10cm. Leaf-blades to 3.6cm wide, divided as far as $^1/_2$–$^3/_4$ into 5 or 7; divisions broadest at apex, giving a kidney-shaped outline, wedge-shaped with more or less open sinuses between them, palmately 3-lobed at the apex; lobes as long as broad or less, entire or with an occasional tooth; teeth and tips of lobes acute; upper and lower surfaces similar in colour. Flowers few. Sepals 6–9mm. Petals 13–15 x 8–10mm, slightly notched, white or pale pink with dark veins. Filaments apparently pale or unpigmented; anthers yellowish to brown or purple. Stigmas pink to purple. Mericarps about 4.5mm. Rostrum about 18mm.

Central Turkey, and possibly S.W. Turkey (depending on the ultimate assignment of specimens included in *G. subacutum* by Aedo).

As explained under 148. *G. palmatipartitum*, I exclude plants with strongly coloured petals from *G. subacutum*.

137. G. cinereum Cavanilles (Figures 9.137E & 9.138, Plate 53)

Leaf-blades not more than 5cm wide, divided as far as $^3/_4$ or $^4/_5$ into 5 or 7; divisions wedge-shaped, usually 3-lobed for $^1/_5$–$^1/_3$ of their length, the lobes about as broad as long, more or less acute, without teeth, the lateral more or less bent upwards. Leaf-blades greyish green, an effect not produced by hairs, which are small and sparse. Stems with up to 5 pairs of leaves but inflorescence usually with 10 or fewer flowers. Sepals 7.5–9.5mm; mucro 1mm or less. Petals about 17mm, notched, translucent white or pale pink

Figure 9.138. *G. cinereum*: from Spetchley Park Gardens, 1960. (A) plant beginning to flower, x $^2/_3$; (B) branch bearing cymule with immature fruit, x $^2/_3$; (C) petal, with pigmentation, x 2; (D) base of front surface of petal, x 4; (E) flower in male stage with petals and two sepals removed, x 4; (F) stamen of outer whorl, x 4; (G) fruit in pre-explosive interval, x 2; (H) seed, x 4

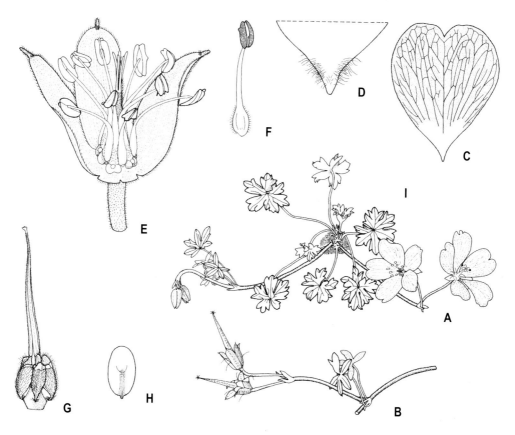

with a dense network of fine, sharply defined, pinkish purple veins. Filaments white; anthers yellowish. Stigmas 2mm, green. Mericarps about 5.5mm. Rostrum 1.7–1.9cm.

Central Pyrenees.

Can be propagated by division or from seeds if grown in isolation from other members of the *G. cinereum* group. The strongly coloured plants which are recommended to be grown by Ingwersen (1946) must be hybrids, though a degree of variation in the ground-colour occurs naturally.
G. cinereum 'Album' has completely white flowers.

For hybrids see 141. *G. cinereum* x *G. subcaulescens* ('Ballerina' etc.) and remarks on the Cinereum Group.

138. *G. subargenteum* Lange (Figure 139A)
Stems to 60cm but trailing. Leaf-blades to 8cm wide, divided as far as $^5/_6 - ^7/_8$ into 5 or 7; divisions broadest at or near apex, giving a nearly rounded outline, overlapping, with partly open or closed sinuses, more or less palmately lobed for about $^1/_3$ to nearly $^1/_2$ their length, toothed; teeth 1–2 times as long as broad; teeth and tips of lobes acute; lower surface velvety or silky, greyish, upper very finely and more sparsely hairy, much greener. Inflorescences with several pairs of small leaves and up to about 10 pairs of flowers. Sepals 8–9mm, finely hairy to greyish velvety-hairy, mucro 1–1.5mm. Petals to 21 x 13mm, distinctly notched, medium purple with fine dark occasionally forking or closely netted veins. Filaments white at base, same colour as petals at apex, anthers violet or bluish. Stigmas pink or yellowish-pink. Mericarps 5.5mm. Rostrum about 1.6–1.8cm.

N.W. Spain: Cantabrian mountains.

Introduced into cultivation by R. McBeath (no. 232, Picos de Europa, 1978) (Clifton, 1998)) and by T. Schulz in 1993 (Schulz, 1995). McBeath's stock was available from Edrom Nursery soon after its introduction (Clifton, 1998). Typically, this is one of the most vigorous members of the group but a dwarf form, collected also in the Picos de Europa by C. Sandes, is in cultivation. The flower-size measurements given here do not cover those given by Aedo (1996): he found larger sepals and fruit and smaller petals.

139. *G. dolomiticum* Rothmaler
Similar to 138. *G. subargenteum* but stems not normally more than 25cm; leaf-blades less

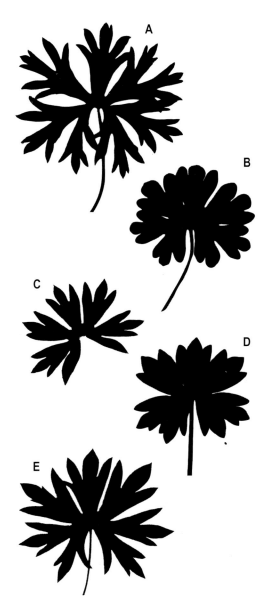

Figure 9.139. (A) *G. subargenteum*: cult. D. Victor (R. McBeath 232), 7cm wide; (B) *G. makmelicum*: from W.K. Aslet, 1974, coll. Lebanon: Mt. Lebanon; (C) *G. palmatipartitum*: E.M. Rix, 1972, coll. Turkey: Sivas Prov., x $^2/_3$; (D) the same, another plant; (E) *G. petri-davisii*: cult. Edinburgh, coll. P.H. Davis (D 20169); 7cm wide

deeply cut, their upper and lower surfaces similar, with small hairs; flowers smaller, filaments apparently not coloured at apex; rostrum slightly shorter.

N.W. Spain: Montes Aquilianos.

This is another extremely rare species, known from only two localities 3km apart and within the range of 138. *G. subargenteum*. Not separated from 140. *G. subcaulescens* and 142. *G. austro-apenninum* in my key, though typically quite distinct from them.

140. *G. subcaulescens* De Candolle (*G. cinereum* Cavanilles var. *subcaulescens* (De Candolle) Knuth) (Figure 9.137F–I, Plate 56)

Rootstock ranging from very compact to quite elongated. Leaf-blades rather dark green, with minute or quite long and loose hairs, not more than 5cm wide, divided as far as $^3/_4$ or nearly to the base into 5 or 7; divisions lobed for $^1/_3$–$^1/_2$ their length; lobes as broad as long and obtuse or up to two or more times as long as broad and acute, with occasional teeth. Inflorescences with 6 or 8 flowers. Sepals 6–8.5mm; mucro 0.5–1mm. Petals 12–15mm, nearly as wide as long, notched or rounded at apex, triangular or constricted at base, brilliant or dull deep purplish red, often paler towards base but usually with a blackish, rayed spot at the extreme base, or with a dark red zone at base formed by the converging veins; veins very dark red, reaching $^1/_2$–$^3/_4$ of the way up the petal, sometimes netted. Filaments blackish red; anthers black. Stigmas black or nearly so. Mericarps 5–6mm. Rostrum 18–20 or as little as 14mm.

Balkan peninsula and central and N.E. Turkey.

A really splendid plant for those not afraid to admire a dazzling colour. However, to quote Ingwersen (1946), "some assert that the typical plant verges dangerously on magenta, a barbaric colour disliked especially by ladies".

G. subcaulescens is extremely variable, but in my view it comprises all forms with rather dark leaves, deep purplish red petals, more or less dark at the base, and blackish stamens and stigmas. Plants from southern Italy appear to have rather paler petals and still paler stamens and stigmas, and I have therefore omitted this area from the statement of natural distribution. These have been separated as *G. austro-apenninum* by Aedo (1996) on the basis of flower colour and possession of teeth on the leaf-lobes (i.e. divisions cut into more than three segments). At least for plants in cultivation this distinction cannot be sustained, since some stocks known or believed to have come from the Balkan peninsula have toothed leaf-blades or petals without a black basal blotch (as collected by Lionel Bacon on Mount Ossa, Greece). It is remarkable that plants with black-centred flowers reappear in central and eastern

Turkey; they were assigned by Davis and Roberts (1955) partly to var. *subcaulescens* (which also, in their view, includes paler-flowered plants from S.W. Turkey) and partly to var. *ponticum* Davis & Roberts, now accepted as a species by Aedo (see no. 144. for my comments).

Pale-flowered Greek forms were collected on Mount Kithairon (Attiki) by Heldreich in 1856 and S.C. Atchley in 1936 and were photographed in the Varnous Mountains, Dhytiki, northern Greece, by Sebastian Payne in 1987. They were also found in the Peloponnese in 1998 at low frequency among normal forms by Robinson (1998). The first has very pale pink notched petals with darker, unbranched veins, white filaments and pink stigmas. The second has very pale pink rounded petals with weak darker veins and blackish basal spot, blackish stamens and stigmas but yellow pollen. The third has pink petals, strongly veined and with a "crushed strawberry" base.

G. subcaulescens was cultivated in Central Europe at the beginning of the twentieth century, having been used by Sündermann in a cross with 132. *G. argenteum* (*G. x lindavicum* Knuth, 1912). It was brought to Britain independently by two expeditionary parties in 1929, one composed of Mr Walter Ingwersen and Dr P.L. Giuseppi, who collected it at Korab, and the other of Dr R. Seligman and "H.R.S." (?H.R. Spivey), who collected it on Mount Kaimachkalan in Serbia (*Alpine Garden Society Bulletin*, 2, 195, 1934). This is doubtless the reason why there is even now a clone in circulation named after Dr Giuseppi, although when the name was first coined, I do not know. A second cultivar, 'Splendens', has emerged comparatively recently. The latter has been grown at Cambridge and is distinct from three other stocks also grown there, namely one supplied by Mr Alan Bloom (Blooms of Bressingham) (Figure 9.137F), one collected by Dr Alexis Vlasto near Tetovo in Yugoslavia (his no. 28, 1959), and one collected as seed by Akeroyd, Mellors & Preston (no. 375, 1976) (Figure 9.137I).

All stocks seem to be propagated quite easily from cuttings or divisions, and at least Dr Vlasto's sometimes reproduced itself from seed (but is now lost).

G. subcaulescens 'Giuseppii' has the petals moderately broad and varying from rounded to weakly notched at the apex even in the same flower, not quite magenta in colour, and with no distinct black basal spot, but merely a dark area formed by the convergent bases of the veins; the ground-colour becomes pale just above the base. The name has been persistently mis-spelt as 'Guiseppii'; it is sometimes applied to plants in which there is no fading of the ground-colour towards the dark basal area but I suspect that this is incorrect. (For origin, see above.)

G. subcaulescens 'Splendens' (Figure 9.137H, Plate 56) has broad, rounded, weakly notched petals of a brilliant but not harsh colour, slightly iridescent, with a distinct blackish red basal blotch, well-marked dark veins and a white zone along each margin for a short distance above the basal blotch; the leaves have shallow blunt lobes, some of them toothed, also bluntly. A most charming plant, but not so easily suited in cultivation as other forms. Said by Clifton (1979) to have been introduced by J. Stormonth about 1936 and offered again in 1974 by Stanton Alpine Nurseries.

The species has given rise to some important hybrids (see 133. *G.* x *lindavicum* and 141. *G. cinereum* x *G. subcaulescens*).

141. *G. cinereum* Cavanilles x *G. subcaulescens* De Candolle (Figure 9.137D, Plate 54)

Blades of basal leaves not more than 5cm wide, divided as far as $^1/_5$ or $^1/_6$ into 7; divisions lobed for $^1/_3$ to nearly half of their length, the lobes often with a tooth; tips of lobes and teeth obtuse. Leaf-blades a slightly greyish green. Stem leaves paired, rather well developed, with 5 divisions, their lobes occasionally toothed, more or less acute. Stems with about 4 pairs of leaves and about 8 flowers. Flowers to 32mm wide. Sepals 7–10mm, recurved at tips, with mucro about 0.5mm. Petals 18 x 16mm, drawn out into a long point at base, narrowly notched at apex, ground-colour pale purplish pink, fading towards base, marked with a close network of strong, fine, dark red veins which converge to form a very dark red V-shaped basal zone; base with hairs across front and a strong tuft on either edge. Stamens blackish red. Stigmas red.

A hybrid raised by Blooms of Bressingham, Diss, Norfolk. It received a Preliminary Commendation of the Royal Horticultural Society in 1961 and an Award of Merit in 1976. Although a few good seeds are formed, the plant seems to be largely sterile, which may partly account for its prolonged flowering season. The flowers are dramatically rather than vividly coloured. 'Ballerina' is easily propagated by cuttings or by division. Blooms introduced three cultivars, two of which appear in Plate 54.

G. cinereum x *G. subcaulescens*: 'Artistry' has a clearer pink ground-colour in the flowers than the other two.

G. cinereum x *G. subcaulescens*: 'Ballerina', the best known of the group, lacks this ground colour and has rather uniformly coloured petals that are not frilly.

G. cinereum x *G. subcaulescens*: 'Laurence Flatman' (corrected spelling) is very similar to 'Ballerina' but more vigorous, with less regular, slightly frilly, petals in which there is a triangle of darker ground-colour at the apex with its tip pointing towards the base; this is not present in all flowers, presumably depending on age.

142. *G. austro-apenninum* Aedo

Said to be distinguishable from *G. subcaulescens* by the leaf-divisions having more than 3 lobes (or with teeth additional to 3 lobes), no dark basal spot on the petals and stamens less dark. Unfortunately, *G. subcaulescens* sometimes shows these characters. The very coarse hair-clothing may help to distinguish *G. austro-apenninum*.

The southern half of the Apennine range in Italy.

143. *G. thessalum* Franzén

Leaf-blades to 3.7cm wide, divided as far as $^4/_5$–$^5/_7$ into 5 or 7; divisions narrow, with open sinuses between them, the terminal entire, bilobed or trilobed, the laterals bilobed, the basal usually entire, untoothed; upper surface hairy, lower silky, looking paler than the upper. Stem with spreading hairs. Inflorescence with up to 5 pairs of flowers. Sepals 8–10mm, silky, without long hairs on the margin; mucro 0.75–1.25mm. Petals 12–17 x 10–12mm, slightly notched, pinkish purple with purple veins and white base. Stamens perhaps sometimes purple, otherwise filaments pale yellow, anthers deep yellow. Stigmas white. Mericarps 6–7.5mm. Rostrum *c.* 25mm.

Greece: one mountain in the northern province of Kozania.

This species was first discovered in 1979. It is peculiar in the very sparse segmentation of the leaves. Unlike 140. *G. subcaulescens* it has a pale centre to the flower. On paper it seems very like 148. *G. palmatipartitum* but the actual plant looks quite different. It has been cultivated at Lund.

144. *G. ponticum* (Davis & Roberts) Aedo

Resembling *G. subcaulescens* in its intensely coloured flowers with blackish purple centres, but said to differ in having the leaf-lobes toothed, which it does; however, 140. *G. subcaulescens* sometimes has this character too, at least in cultivation. There are slight differences in the size-ranges of floral parts but only that of the sepal mucro (1.5–2.5mm here) seems significant. Very wide, strongly overlapping, petals are shown in a photograph by Aitchison (1995b).

N.E. Turkey, more widespread than 145. *G. lazicum.*

Details of its introduction to cultivation are as for 145. *G. lazicum.*

145. *G. lazicum* (Woronow) Aedo
Leaf-blades to 4.5cm wide, divided as far as $3/4$ or $4/5$ into 5 or 7; divisions broadest just below the apex, giving a moderately angled outline, lobed for about $1/4$–$1/3$ of their length; lobes toothed; teeth and tips of lobes obtuse or broadly pointed; upper surface shortly hairy, lower silvery-silky. Cymules few. Sepals 7–8mm, silky, with mucro 0.7–1.5mm. Petals 12–15 x 8–11mm, slightly notched, very pale pink to darker purplish pink, with a white basal area of variable size, and with dark veins variously developed or none. Anthers yellow or purple. Stigmas pale. Mericarps 7mm. Rostrum 20–22mm.

N.E. Turkey.

Occurs in the same area as 144. *G. ponticum* but differs in having the leaves silky beneath, sepals silky and petals without a dark basal spot. It was introduced into cultivation in Britain by Dr C. Aitchison in 1994 (Aitchison, 1995b). A colour photograph of it was published by Clifton (Anon. 1996).

146. *G. makmelicum* Aedo (*G. cinereum* Cavanilles var. *obtusilobum* Bornmüller) Yeo) (Figure 9.139B)
Rootstock prolifically branched. Leaf-blades light green, velvety above, more or less woolly beneath, not more than 3cm wide, divided as far as about $2/3$ into 5 or 7; divisions 3-lobed for $1/3$ of their length, the lobes obtuse or, in late-season growth, more or less acute. Flowers bowl-shaped. Sepals 6.5–8.5mm; mucro 0.5mm or less. Petals about 17mm, tending to be oblong, apex notched, ground-colour white, faintly tinged with pink around the edges, inconspicuously marked with fine reddish purple veins, forking towards their extremities. Filaments white; anthers yellowish brown. Stigmas pink. Mericarps about 5.5mm. Rostrum 12–16mm.

Lebanon, Syria.

This species was introduced by Mr Ken Aslet from Mount Lebanon about 1974. One wonders whether he knew of Walter Ingwersen's commendation of it as a desirable plant (Ingwersen, 1946), which proved to be fully justified. In colouring it recalls 137. *G. cinereum* but is quite different in character, with its tiny blunt-lobed leaves and flowers held well above them. The rootstock is profusely branched and propagation is very easy. It is reproducible from seed by self-fertilisation.

At Cambridge this produced hybrids with other members of the Cinereum Group when seed has been sown, and from self-sown seed.

147. *G. petri-davisii* Aedo (*G. cinereum* Cavanilles var. *elatius* Davis) (Figure 139E)
Like a very large *G. palmatipartitum* (no. 148), with stems to 50cm, leaves mostly 5–7cm wide and flowers more numerous. Slightly differing also in that the dark veins of the petals are continued on to the pale basal part and there converge.

S. central Turkey: known only from the type locality.

Originally listed by Davis & Roberts (1955) as *G. cinereum* var. *subcaulescens* by which time it was already in cultivation. I have not heard of its being still in cultivation.

148. *G. palmatipartitum* (Knuth) Aedo (*G. cinereum* Cavanilles var. *palmatipartitum* Knuth) (Figure 9.139C, D)
Leaf-blades not more than 5cm wide, divided as far as about $4/5$ into 5 or 7; divisions lobed for about $1/3$ of their length, the lobes entire, acute, variable in breadth, unequal, sometimes some of them considerably reduced or occasionally suppressed so that the division is narrowly elliptic instead of wedge-shaped. Leaf-blades generally silver-grey and velvety, underside less green than upper. Inflorescence usually with 6 or 8 flowers. Sepals 8–11mm; mucro 0.5–1mm. Flowers somewhat bowl-shaped. Petals about 18mm, varying in width, not significantly notched, clear rose-pink in the outer half, fading gently to nearly white about the middle, marked with fine dark veins which are slightly feathered towards the tips. Filaments white at base, coloured more darkly than the petals at the tips; anthers purplish red. Stigmas 1.5–2mm, dull crimson. Mericarps 7.5mm. Rostrum 24–28mm.

E. central Turkey.

I use the strong flower-colour of *G. palmatipartitum* and the weak colour of *G. subacutum* in drawing the line between the two and therefore classify some specimens differently from Aedo (1996). This results in allowing more variation in leaf-segmentation. Knuth described the leaf lamina of *G. palmatipartitum* as palmately divided into oblong-ovate, acutish, entire lobes (our "divisions"). The illustration shows the terminal leaf-division and sometimes one or both of the laterals as entire and elliptic (his "oblong-ovate"), the remaining divisions having just one lateral lobe, giving the total number of segments as 7–9. This condition is allowed for in my description. However, Knuth allows for the leaves to be 5–12-partite (i. e. 5–12-segmented in my sense). The rest of Knuth's description tells us that the plant is robust (to 15cm tall), densely tufted and having a clear rose-red corolla. The occurrence of more than 9 leaf segments suggests that the plant occurs in a form with more normal leaf outline than that shown in the drawing. Davis & Roberts (1955) accept this possibility, saying that the leaf segments (our "divisions") are entire and acute or deeply divided into 2–3 acute lobes (similar wording appears in Davis (1967)). Such a plant is Rix 2083 (from Yildiz Da. in the Turkish province of Sivas), the original of which is in the Cambridge University Herbarium. Three clones, recognisably different in leaf cutting, details of flower colouring and breadth of petals,

were grown in the Cambridge Botanic Garden but all are now dead. The most beautiful lasted the longest and several expert growers took cuttings, so someone may be growing it. All seedlings raised, with one possible exception (which does not match the parent in beauty), have been hybrids.

Rix's plants key out to *G. subacutum* in Aedo (1996). The specimen of *G. palmatipartitum* figured by Aedo (1996) is about the same size as that illustrated for *G. subacutum*, which is typically a smaller species.

If *G. palmatipartitum* should ever be collected again, a number of clones should be obtained (or seeds collected), and once plants are established, they should be pollinated among themselves in isolation from other members of the Cinereum Group before the collection is dispersed.

Glossary

This glossary defines terms as they are used in this book or as they apply to *Geranium*. Some of the definitions do not have validity in a wider context, while some terms have additional or wider meanings not mentioned here. Reference to Chapters 4 or 5 means that the term is defined in greater detail or illustrated there.

annual a plant which completes its life-cycle from seed to seed in less than a year.

anther the terminal part of a stamen, containing the pollen.

anthocyanin a class of plant pigments, ranging in colour from blue through purple to red, imparting these colours to flowers and often suffusing the chlorophyll-containing (green) parts of the plant.

appressed pressed up against a surface (as hairs on a leaf, leaves on the ground) or organ (as stamens against the style).

awn used in this book for a particular floral part (see Chapter 4, p. 24).

axil the angle between the base of a leaf and the part of the stem that forms the next internode above it.

axillary situated in an axil.

back-cross a cross between a hybrid and one of its parents; to make such a cross.

biennial a plant that completes its life-cycle from seed to seed in a period of more than one year but less than two.

bilaterally symmetric (of a flower) with a single plane of symmetry, along which it can be divided into halves which are mirror-images of each other.

bract a leaf found in the inflorescence and having a reduced size and modified shape (see Chapter 4, p. 21).

bracteate furnished with bracts.

bracteole a small bract; in *Geranium* it applies to the small bracts at the bases of the pedicels in a cymule (see Chapter 4, p. 22).

calyx collective term for all the sepals of one flower.

carpel one of the hollow structures in the centre of the flower that contain the ovules, each bearing a style.

carpel-projection a term adopted in this book for one of the methods of seed-dispersal found in *Geranium* (see Chapter 5, p. 28).

central column (of a fruit) see Chapter 4, p. 24.

chromosome one of the microscopic thread-like or rod-like bodies, consisting of nucleic acid and containing the genes, that appear in a cell-nucleus shortly before cell-division.

claw the stalk of a stalked petal (see Chapter 4, p. 24).

clone the sum-total of the plants derived from vegetative reproduction of an individual and having the same genetic constitution.

cotyledon one of the two leaves preformed in the seed.

cultivar a variant of horticultural interest that is not conveniently treated as one of the categories (such as subspecies, variety) in a botanical classification (its name is written in single quotation marks and with capital initial letters).

cuspidate with a sharp, shortly tapered point on an otherwise blunt apex.

cymule see Chapter 4, p. 22.

dense (of an inflorescence) see Chapter 4, p. 23.

diffuse (of an inflorescence) see Chapter 4, p. 22; (of coloured veins on a petal) smudgy.

diploid a set of chromosomes the various members of which can be matched up in pairs; a diploid plant is one in which each of the vegetative cells contains a diploid chromosome set.

division (of a leaf) see Chapter 4, p. 25.

eglandular hairs see Chapter 4, p. 25.

endemic confined, as a native, to a named (usually small) area.

Erodium-type term adopted in this book for one of the methods of seed-dispersal found in *Geranium* (see Chapter 5, p. 28).

female stage (of a flower) see Chapter 4, p. 24.

filament the slender part of a stamen which bears the anther at its tip (see stamen).

glandular hairs see Chapter 4, Figure 4.5.

haploid a set of chromosomes, the members of which cannot be paired off; two haploid sets go to make a diploid set (see *diploid*).

hexaploid a set of chromosomes, the various members of which can be matched up in sets of six (compare diploid).

inflorescence see Chapter 4, p. 21.

internode a length of stem extending from one node to the next.

inverted flowers see Chapter 4, p. 25.

lobe (of a leaf) see Chapter 4, p. 25.

lobulate bearing a series of small lobes.

male stage (of a flower) see Chapter 4, p. 24.

mericarp see Chapter 4, p. 24.

mucro (of leaf-teeth and lobes) a short narrow point at the tip; (of a sepal) in this book used of the narrow point at the tip, regardless of length.

mucronate provided with a short narrow point at the tip.

nectar passage a tube or orifice formed above each nectary by the shaping of the petal bases.

nectary see Chapter 4, p. 24.

nodding flowers (see Chapter 4, p. 25).

node the point on a stem at which a leaf or pair of leaves is attached.

opposite (of leaves) see Chapter 4, p. 21.

palmate a group of leaf-divisions, leaf-lobes or veins all radiating from the same point.

palmato-pinnate (of a leaf-division) see Chapter 4, p. 25.

pedicel see Chapter 4, p. 22.

peduncle see Chapter 4, p. 22.

peltate (in our context) a leaf in which the stalk is attached to the surface (not the margin).

petal see Chapter 4, Figure 4.5.

pinnate an arrangement in which leaf-lobes or veins arise at intervals on either side of a leaf-division or central vein.

radially symmetric (of a flower) with the parts alike and arranged in circles, so that the flower can be divided into identical halves, which are mirror-images of each other, along a number of planes passing through the centre (this number being five in the case of *Geranium* which has floral parts in fives).

rhizome a horizontal stem, situated underground or on the substratum, with roots arising from

some or all of its nodes (see also *stolon*).

rootstock see Chapter 4, p. 22.

rosette see Chapter 4, p. 21.

rostrum see Chapter 4, p. 24.

seed-ejection a term adopted in this book for one of the methods of seed-dispersal found in *Geranium* (see Chapter 5, p. 28).

segment (of a leaf) see Chapter 4, p. 25.

sepal see Chapter 4, Figure 4.5.

solitary (of leaves) see Chapter 4, p. 22.

stamen the organ of the flower which produces the pollen, there being 10 of them in a flower of *Geranium* (Figure 4.5; see also *filament* and *anther*).

stigma see Chapter 4, p. 24.

stipule one of the pair of small appendages found beside the base of the leaf-stalk.

stolon a far-creeping, more or less slender above-ground or underground rhizome giving rise to a new plant at its tip and sometimes at intermediate nodes.

stylar portion (of the rostrum) see Chapter 4, p. 26.

style see Chapter 4, Figure 4.5.

subtending leaf the leaf in the axil of which named organ is situated.

taxon a named assemblage of plants, regardless of rank, such as a family, species or variety (see Chapter 3, p. 17).

tetraploid a set of chromosomes, the various members of which can be matched up in sets of four (compare diploid).

triploid a set of chromosomes, the various members of which can be matched up in sets of three (compare diploid).

tuber a swollen underground stem or root used for food-storage.

type specimen see Chapter 3, p. 17.

umbel-like see Chapter 4, p. 23.

whorl a circlet of 3 or more similar organs (e. g. petals, leaves) attached at the same level.

References

There are a number of small publications on *Geranium* produced by botanic gardens, horticultural societies and individuals. These are not obtainable through booksellers and they are distinguished here by the fact that the number of pages they contain is indicated.

Aedo, C. (1996) 'Revision of *Geranium* Subgenus Erodioidea (Geraniaceae)', *Systematic Botany Monographs, 49*, 1–104

__(2000) 'The genus *Geranium* L. (Geraniaceae) in North America. I. Annual species', *Anales Jardín Botánico de Madrid, 58*, 39–82

Aedo, C., Aldasoro, J.J., & Navarro, C. (1998) 'Taxonomic revision of *Geranium* Sections Batrachioidea and Divaricata (Geraniaceae)', *Annals of the Missouri Botanical Garden, 85*, 594–630

Aedo, C., Muñoz Garmendia, F., & Pando, F. (1998) 'World checklist of Geranium L. (Geraniaceae)', *Anales Jardín Botánico de Madrid, 56*, 211–252

Aitchison, C. (1994) 'High alpines of Morocco', *Rock Garden, 23*, 433–439

__(1995a) 'Plant hunting indoors [*Geranium nanum*]', *Rock Garden, 24*, 248–250

__(1995b) '*Geranium cinereum* in the Kackar Mountains [*ponticum* and *lazicum*]', *Rock Garden, 24*, 297–299

__(1997) '*Geranium nanum*: flower colour', *Geraniaceae Group News, 67*, 15–16

__(1998a) 'Hybridising in the *G. cinereum* group', *Geraniaceae Group News, 69*, 14–15

Aiton, W. (1789) *Hortus Kewensis, 2*, London

Allan, H.H. (1961) *Flora of New Zealand, 1*, Wellington

Anon [R. Clifton] (1996) '*Geranium cinereum*, south & east Mediterranean', *Geraniaceae Group News, 61*, 10–13

__[R. Clifton] (1997) '*Geranium atlanticum*', *Geraniaceae Group News, 65*, 18–20

__[R. Clifton] (2000) '*Geranium wallichianum* 21 colour forms', *Geraniaceae Group News, 79*, 26–28

Anton-Smith, J. (1997) 'Plant portraits from the seedlist', *Geraniaceae Group News, 64*, 8

Bacon, L. (1993) 'Geraniums for the rock garden [incl. colour photo of *G. cazorlense*]', *Quarterly Bulletin of the Alpine Garden Society, 61*, 171–190

Baker, H.G. (1956) '*Geranium purpureum* Vill. and *G. robertianum* L. in the British flora. II. Geranium robertianum', *Watsonia, 3*, 270–279

__(1957) 'Genecological studies in *Geranium* (Section Robertiana). General considerations and the races of *G. purpureum* Vill.', *New Phytologist, 56*, 172–192

Baltensperger, U. (1997) *Geranium*, Stammheim, 56 pages

Bath, T., & Jones, J. (1994) *The Gardener's Guide to Growing Hardy Geraniums*, David & Charles

Berrisford, J.M. (1963) *Gardening on Lime*, London

Bobrov, E.G. (1949) 'Geraniaceae', in B.K. Shishkin & E.G. Bobrov, *Flora of USSR, 14*, Moscow and Leningrad

Bøcher, T.W. (1947) 'Cytogenetic and biological studies in *Geranium robertianum*', *Biologiske Meddelelser, 20 (8)*, 1–29

Bowles, E.A. (1914) *My Garden in Summer*, London

__(1921) 'Hardy geraniums for the wild garden, woodland and border', *The Garden, 85*, 308, 321, 344–345, 369

Bremner, A. (1991) 'Some hybridisations in *Geranium*', *Geraniaceae Group News, 41*, 12–16

__(1997) 'Experiments in breeding new Geraniums', *New Rare and Unusual Plants, 3(2)*, 54–57

__(1997) 'Experiments in breeding new Geraniums', *New Rare and Unusual Plants, 3(3)*, 112–113

Buczacki, S., & [special photography] Lawson, A., (1998) *Best Geraniums [and Pelargoniums]* Hamlyn (Amateur Gardening), London

Burman, J. (1738–9) *Rariorum africanorum plantarum*, Amsterdam

Carolin, R.C. (1964) 'The genus *Geranium* L. in the south western Pacific area', *Proceedings of the Linnean Society of New South Wales, 89*, 326–361

Clement, E. (1976) 'Adventive news 5', *BSBI News, 13*, 33–34

Clifton, R. (1979) *Hardy Geraniums (Cranesbills) Today*, Farnham, Surrey (British Pelargonium and Geranium Society), 16 pages

Clifton, R. (1998) '*Geranium subargenteum*', *Geraniaceae Group News*, 69, 17–19

Clifton, R.T.F. (1992) *Geranium Family, Species Check List*, 4th edn., part 2, Geranium, Dover

Dahlgren, K.V.O. (1923) '*Geranium bohemicum* L. x *G. bohemicum *deprehensum* Erik Almq., ein grün-weiss-marmorierter Bastard', *Hereditas*, 4, 239–249

__(1925) 'Die reziproken Bastarde zwischen *Geranium bohemicum* L. und seiner Unterart *deprehensum* Erik Almq.', *Hereditas*, 6, 237–256

Davis, P.H. (1967) '*Geranium*' in P.H. Davis, J. Cullen and M.J.E. Coode (eds.), *Flora of Turkey*, 2, 451–474, Edinburgh

__(1970) '*Geranium* sect. *Tuberosa*, revision and evolutionary interpretation', *Israel Journal of Botany*, 19, 91–113

Davis, P.H., & Roberts, J. (1955) 'Materials for a Flora of Turkey, I–Geraniaceae', *Notes from the Royal Botanic Garden Edinburgh*, 22, 9–27

De Candolle, A.P. (1824) *Prodromus Systematis Naturalis Regni Vegetabilis*, 1, Paris

Duthie, J.F. (1906) '*Geranium platyanthum* Duthie n. sp.', *Gard. Chron. ser. 3*, 39, 52

Edgeworth, M.P., & Hooker, J.D. (1874) 'Geraniaceae' in J.D. Hooker, *Flora of British India*, 1, 426–440, London

Évrard, D. (1997) *L'essentiale sur les géranium vivaces*, Paris

Farrer, R. (1917) *On the Eaves of the World*, 2, London

Feltwell, J. (2001) *Geraniums and Pelargoniums*, Collins & Brown, London

Gams, H. (1923–4) 'Geraniaceae' in G. Hegi, *Illustrierte Flora von Mittel-Europa*, 1st edn, IV (3), 1656–1725, Munich

Goldblatt, P., *et al.* (1985–1996) 'Index to Plant Chromosome Numbers', *Missouri Botanical Garden Monographs in Systematic Botany nos. 5, 8, 13, 23, 30, 40, 51 and 58*

Greuter, W., *et al.* (eds.) (2000) *International Code of Botanical Nomenclature (Saint Louis Code)*, Königstein

Grigson, G. (1955) *The Englishman's Flora*, London

Hara, H., Stearn, W.T., & Williams, L.H.J. (1979) *An Enumeration of the Flowering Plants of Nepal*, 2, London

Harz, K. (1921) '*Geranium phaeum* L. + *G. reflexum* L.= *G. monacense* Harz', *Mitteilungen der Bayerischen Botanischen Gesellschaft*, 4, 7

Hibberd, D. (1992) 'Some recently introduced

Geranium cultivars', *Geraniaceae Group News*, 44, 3–8

Hibberd, D. (1994) *Hardy Geraniums*, a Wisley Handbook, London

Hilliard, O.M., & Burtt, B.L. (1985) 'A revision of Geranium in Africa south of the Limpopo', *Notes from the Royal Botanic Garden, Edinburgh*, 42, 171–225

Hooker, J.D. (1879) '*Geranium atlanticum*', *Curtis's Botanical Magazine*, 105, tab. 6452

Hylander, N. (1960) *Vara Prydnadsväxters Namn*, revised edn, Boras

__(1961) 'Kungsnävan, vara trädgardars praktfullaste *Geranium*', *Lustgarden, 1961*, 109–14

Ingwersen, W. (1946) *The Genus Geranium*, East Grinstead, 31 pages

Jansen, C. (1997) Geranium für den Garten, transl. H. Duggen, Stuttgart

Jeffrey, C. (1989) *Biological Nomenclature*, 3rd edn., London

__(1982) *An Introduction to Plant Taxonomy*, 2nd edn., Cambridge

Johnson, A.T. (1937) *A Woodland Garden*, London, New York

Jones, C.N., & Jones, F.J. (1943) 'A revision of the perennial species of *Geranium* of the United States and Canada', *Rhodora*, 45, 5–53

Jones, J., *et al.* (1992) *Hardy Geraniums for the Garden*

Kent, D.H. (1959) '*Geranium retrorsum* L'Hérit. ex DC.', *Proceedings of the Botanical Society of the British Isles*, 3, 284

Kitamura, S., & Murata, G. (1961) *Coloured Illustrations of Herbaceous Plants of Japan, Choripetalae*, Osaka

Knuth, R. (1912) 'Geraniaceae' in A. Engler, *Das Pflanzenreich, IV. 129*, Leipzig

Kokwaro, J.O. (1971) 'The family "Geraniaceae" in North-east Tropical Africa', *Webbia*, 25, 623–669

Lawrence, W.J.C. (1948) *Practical Plant Breeding*, 2nd edn., London

Linnaeus, C. (1753) *Species Plantarum*, 2 vols.

Llewellyn, J., Hudson, B., & Morrison, G.C. (1981) *Growing Geraniums and Pelargoniums in Australia and New Zealand*, Kenthurst

Loudon, J.C. (1830) *Hortus Britannicus* (and 2nd edn., 1832)

Lousley, J.E. (1962) '*Geranium retrorsum* L'Hérit', *Proceedings of the Botanical Society of the British Isles*, 4, 413–414

Lundström, E. (1914) 'Plantae in horto botanico bergiano annis 1912–1913 critice examinatae, *Geranium*', *Acta Horti Bergiani, 5(3)*, 50–77

McClintock, D. (1980) *A Guide to the Naming of Plants with Special Reference to Heathers*, 2nd edn., Leicester, 37 pages

Moore, H.E. (1943) 'A revision of the genus *Geranium* in Mexico and Central America', *Contributions from the Gray Herbarium, 146*
__(1963) '*Geranium campii* and *G. durangense* – two new species', *Brittonia, 15,* 92–95
Moss, R. (1997) 'The Alan Bremner Geranium hybrids', *Geraniaceae Group News, 64,* 15–20
Nakai, T. (1912) 'Notulae ad plantas Japonicae et Coreae VII. *Geranium Coreanum,* Japonicum et Sachalinense', *The Botanical Magazine [Tokyo], 26,* 251–266
__(1912) 'Notulae ad plantas Japoniae et Koreae VII', *Botanical Magazine (Tokyo), 24,* 251–266
Nasir, Y.J. (1983) 'Geraniaceae', in E. Nasir & S.I. Ali, *Flora of Pakistan, 149,* 1–43, Islamabad
Ohwi, J. (1965) *Flora of Japan,* Washington
Olsen, O. (2000) 'Norway: *Geranium napuligerum*', *Geraniaceae Group News, 77,* 15
Paterson, A. (1981) *Plants for Shade,* London
Rix, M., & Phillips, R. (1981) *The Bulb Book,* London
Robertson, K.R. (1972) 'The genera of Geraniaceae in the southeastern United States', *Journal of the Arnold Arboretum, 53,* 182–201
Robinson, A. (1998) 'A holiday in Greece', *Geraniaceae Group News, 70,* 15–16
Rostanski, K., & Tokarski, M. (1973) '*Geranium wilfordii* Maxim. an ephemerophyte new to the Polish flora', *Fragmenta Floristica et Geobotanica, 19,* 385–388 (in Polish with English summary)
Rowley, G.D. (1980) *Name That Succulent,* Cheltenham
Royal Botanic Gardens, Kew (1902) *Hand-List of Herbaceous Plants Cultivated in the Royal Botanic Gardens,* 2nd edn., London
Royal Horticultural Society Colour Chart (1966), London
Sansome, F.W. (1936) 'Experiments with *Geranium* species', *Journal of Genetics, 33,* 359–363
Schönbeck-Temesy, E. (1970), 'Geraniaceae' in K.H. Rechinger (ed.), *Flora Iranica, 69,* 1–67, Graz
Schulz, T. (1995) 'A trip to northern Spain: *Geranium subargenteum*', *Geraniaceae Group News, 57,* 15–21
Schwarz, O. (1936) '*Geranium microrrhizum* (Freyn) Schwz., ein verkannter Storchschnabel Dalmatiens', *Feddes Repertorium, 40,* 349–352 & t.
Stace, C.A. (1975) *Hybridization and the Flora of the British Isles,* London, New York, San Francisco

Stapf, O. (1926) '*Geranium farreri*', *Curtis's Botanical Magazine, 151,* tab. 9092
Stephens, J. (1967) 'A new hybrid Geranium', *Journal of the Royal Horticultural Society, 92,* 491
Sweet, R. (1820–30) *Geraniaceae,* 5 vols., London
Thomas, G.S. 'Geraniums for ground cover', *Gardeners Chronicle, 147,* 480–481, 504, 508–509
__(1976) *Perennial Garden Plants,* 1st edn., London
__(1977) *Plants for Ground-Cover,* 2nd edn., London (and revisions, 1984 & 1990)
__(1982) *Perennial Garden Plants,* 2nd edn., London
Thompson, D. (1982) *Hardy Geraniums,* Seattle, 24 pages
Tokarski, M. (1972) 'Morphological and taxonomical analysis of fruits and seeds of the European and Caucasian species of the genus *Geranium* L.' *Monographiae Botanicae, 36* (in Polish with English captions and summary)
Townsend, C.C. (1964) 'More on the introduced Bordon and Alderney geraniums', *Proceedings of the Botanical Society of the British Isles, 5,* 224–226
Trehane, P., *et al.* (1995) *International Code of Nomenclature for Cultivated Plants – 1995 (issued as Regnum Vegetabile,* vol. 133), Wimborne, UK
Tsyrenova, D.Y. [A.I. Gertseva Pedagog. Inst., Leningrad] (1985) 'Geranium erianthum and closely related species', *Botanicheskii Zhurnal (Leningrad), 70,* 476–482
Van Loon, J.C. (1984b) 'Chromosome numbers in *Geranium* from Europe I. The perennial species', *Proceedings of the Koninklijke Nederlandse Akademie van Wetenschappen, Series C, 87,* 263–277
__(1984a) 'Chromosome numbers in Geranium from Europe II. The annual species', *Proceedings of the Koninklijke Nederlandse Akademie van Wetenschappen, Series C, 87,* 263–277
__(1984c) 'Hybridization experiments in *Geranium*', *Genetica, 65,* 167–171
Veldkamp, J.F. & Moerman, A. (1978) 'A review of the Malesian species of *Geranium* L. (Geraniaceae)', *Blumea, 24,* 463–477
Voss, E.G., *et al.* (1983) *International Code of Botanical Nomenclature,* Utrecht, etc.
Walters, S.M., *et al.* (eds.) (1984) *The European Garden Flora, 2,* & (1986) vol. 1, (1989–2000) vols. 3–6, Cambridge, London, New York, New Rochelle, Melbourne, Sydney
Warburg, E.F. (1938) 'Taxonomy and relationship in the Geraniales in the light of their

cytology', *New Phytologist, 37*, 130–159, 189–210

Webb, D.A., & Ferguson, I.K. (1968) 'Geraniaceae' in T.G. Tutin et al. (eds.), *Flora Europaea, 2*, 193–204, Cambridge

Widler-Kiefer, H., & Yeo, P.F. (1987) 'Fertility relationships of *Geranium* (Geraniaceae): sectt. Ruberta, Anemonifolia, Lucida and Unguiculata', *Plant Systematics and Evolution, 155*, 283–306

Wilson, R.F. (1939 and 1942) *Horticultural Colour Chart*, 2 vols., London

Wolley Dod, C. (1903) 'Geraniums', *Flora and Sylva, 1*, 54–57

Yeo, P.F. (1970) 'The *Geranium palmatum* group in Madeira and the Canary Isles', *Journal of the Royal Horticultural Society, 95*, 410–414, and correction (1971), *ibid., 96*, 44

__(1973) '*Geranium procurrens*', *Curtis's Botanical Magazine, 139*, tab. 644

__(1975) '*Geranium* species from Mount Victoria, Burma', *Notes from the Royal Botanic Garden, Edinburgh, 34*, 195–200

__(1983) '*Geranium candicans* and *G. yunnanense* of gardens', *The Garden, 109*, 36–37

__(1984a) '*Geranium pylzowianum*, the ricegrain geranium and its mysterious ally', *Kew Magazine, 1*, 111–118 (colour plates have captions transposed)

__(1984b) 'Fruit-discharge type in *Geranium* (Geraniaceae): its use in classification and its evolutionary implications', *Botanical Journal of the Linnean Society, 89*, 1–36

__(1985) *Hardy Geraniums*, London

__(1988) *Geranium: Freiland-Geranien für Garten und Park* transl. M. Zerbst. With a contribution by H. Simon, Stuttgart

__(1988) '*Geranium sessiliflorum* x *G. traversii*: 'Stanhoe', a new cultivar name', *Geraniaceae Group News, 28*, 2–5

__(1989) '*Geranium swatense* continued', *Geraniaceae Group News, 32*, 5–6

__(1990) 'The classification of Geraniaceae', *Proceedings of the International Geraniaceae Symposium ...Stellenbosch, 24–26 September, 1990*, 1–22

__(1992) 'A revision of *Geranium* L. in south-west China', *Edinburgh Botanical Journal, 49*, 123–211

__(1995) '*Geranium antrorsum* stocks in cultivation', *Geraniaceae Group News, 58*, 12

__(1998) 'Not *G[eranium] tripartitum* [nor *G. yesoense* var. *lobatodentatum*] but *G. yoshinoi*', *Geraniaceae Group News, 68*, 20

__(2000) '*Geranium sanguineum*: validation of a cultivar name', *Geraniaceae Group News, 78*, 17

__reported anonymously by R. Clifton (1996) Meeting on 8 October 1996: paragraph on *Geranium pyrenaicum* 'Isparta', *Geraniaceae Group News, 63*, 11–12

Appendix I
Place of Publication and Meaning of Scientific Names

Numbers in bold type are those of species (etc.) in Chapter 9; the "equals" sign (=) indicates a synonym mentioned under the number cited. Author citations are given in full; elsewhere in the book author-names followed by "ex" or preceded by "in" are omitted.

I have seen most references for names. Most others are cited in a recent compendium (Aedo et al., 1998) and can be taken as verified; a few remain unverified and are asterisked.

G. aconitifolium L'Héritier, in Aiton, *Hort. Kew.*, 2, 435 (1789), = **10** (with leaves like *Aconitum*, monkshood)

G. albanum Bieberstein, *Fl. Taur.-Cauc.*, 2, 137 (1808), **112** (pertaining to Albania, Roman province on Caspian Sea, now Daghestan)

G. albidum Rydberg ex Hanks & Small, *N. Amer. Fl.*, 25, 19 (1907), before **80** (whitish)

G. albiflorum Ledebour, *Icon. Fl. Pl. Ross.*, 1, 6 (1829), **13** (white-flowered)

G. alpestre Schur, *Verh. Mitt. Siebenb. Ver. Naturw.*, 10, 131 (1859), not Chaix (1785), = **8** (found in the lower alps)

G. alpicola Loesener, *Bull. Herb. Boiss.*, ser. 2, 3, 92 (1903), before **82** (an inhabitant of alps)

G. anemonifolium L'Héritier, in Aiton, *Hort. Kew.*, 2, 432 (1789), = **126** (anemone-leaved)

G. angulatum Curtis, *Bot. Mag.*, 6, tab. 203 (1792), = **8** (angled, referring to the stem)

G. x antipodeum Yeo, *this volume, Appendix II* (2001) **59**, (on the opposite side of the earth)

G. antrorsum Carolin, *Proc. Linn. Soc. N.S.W.*, ser. 2, 89, 357 (1965), **61**, (forwardly directed [hairs on pedicels])

G. arboreum A. Gray, *Bot. U.S. Expl. Exped., Phan. 1*, 315 (1854) before **127** (tree-like)

G. argenteum Linnaeus, *Cent. Pl.*, 2, 25 (1756), **132** (silvery, referring to the leaves, etc.)

G. aristatum Freyn & Sintenis ex Freyn, *Bull. Herb. Boiss.*, 5, 587 (1897), **131** (bristled, referring to sepal-mucro)

G. armenum Boissier, *Fl. Or.*, 1, 878 (1867), = **14** (pertaining to Armenia, territory in N.E. Turkey and S.W. Transcaucasia)

G. asphodeloides N.L. Burman, *Spec. Bot. Geran.*, 28 (1759), **86/86a** (like asphodel, referring to the roots)

G. asphodeloides N.L. Burman subsp. *crenophilum* (Boissier) Bornmüller, *Feddes Repert. Beih.*, 89 (3), 134 (1938), **86b** (spring-loving; "spring" in the sense of a source of water)

G. asphodeloides N.L. Burman subsp. *sintenisii* (Freyn) Davis, *Notes Roy. Bot. Gard. Edinb.*, 28, 36 (1967), **86c** (P.E.E. Sintenis, plant-collector, Germany)

G. atlanticum Boissier, *Diagn. Pl. Or. Nov., 1 (1)*, 59 (1843), **9** (pertaining to the Atlas Mountains, N.W. Africa)

G. atropurpureum A. Heller, *Bull. Torrey Bot. Club 25*, 195 (1898), **79b** (blackish purple)

G. austro-apenninum Aedo, *Anal. Jard. Bot. Madrid 52*, 105 (1994), **142** (of the southern apennines)

G. backhouseanum Regel, *Acta Horti Petrop.*, 2, 432 (1873), = **14** (James Backhouse, nurseryman, Britain)

G. bellum Rose, *Contr. U.S. Nat. Herb.*, 10, 108 (1906), before **82** (beautiful)

G. x bergianum Lundström, *Acta Horti Berg.*, 5 (3), 69 (1914), under **15** (from the Latin name of Stockholm Botanic Garden: Hortus Bergianus)

G. bicknellii Britton, *Bull. Torrey Bot. Club*, 24, 92 (1897), **75** (E.P. Bicknell, botanist, USA)

G. biuncinatum Kokwaro, *Webbia*, 25, 639 (1971), **108** (two-hooked, referring to the mericarps)

G. bohemicum Linnaeus, *Cent. Pl.*, 2, 25 (1756), **99** (pertaining to Bohemia)

G. bohemicum Linnaeus subsp. *depraehensum* Almquist, *Svensk Bot. Tidskr.*, 10, 411 (1916), = **100** (detected, discovered, presumably as distinct from *G. bohemicum* proper)

G. brutium Gasparrini, *Rendic. Accad. Sci. (Napoli), 1*, 49 (1842), **115** (the Bruttii or Brutii, inhabitants of S. Italy)

G. brycei N.E. Brown, *Kew Bull. 175/177*, 120 (1901), **65** (name of collector)

G. caeruleatum Schur, *Enum. Pl. Transs.*, 136 (1866), **11** (made blue)

G. caespitosum E. James, *Account Exped. Pittsburgh to Rocky Mts., 1819–20 under Maj. S.H. Long. London, 3 vols., Philadelphia, 2 vols* (1823), **79a** (tufted)

G. caespitosum E. James var. *fremontii* (A. Gray) Dorn, **79** (see *G. fremontii*)

G. caffrum Ecklon & Zeyher, *Enum. Pl. Afr. Austral.*, 58 (1834–5), **69** (of the Kaffirs)

G. californicum Jones & Jones, *Rhodora 45*, 38 (1943), **81**, (of California)

G. canariense Reuter, *Cat. Graines Jard. Bot. Genève*, 1857, no. 3 (1858), **97** (inhabiting the Canary Isles)

G. candicans Knuth, in Engler, *Pflanzenreich, IV, 129*, 580 (1912), = **35** (becoming pure white)

G. x cantabrigiense Yeo, *Hardy Geraniums*, 188 (1985), **120** (inhabiting Cambridge)

G. carolinianum Linnaeus, *Sp. Pl.*, 682 (1753), **76** (pertaining to Carolina, USA)

G. carolinianum Linnaeus var. *confertiflorum* Fernald, *Rhodora, 37*, 298 (1935), **76** (densely flowered)

G. cataractarum Cosson, *Not. Pl. Crit., 3*, 99 (1851), **122** (of cataracts)

G. cataractarum Cosson subsp. *pitardii* Maire, *Bull. Soc. Hist. Nat. Afr. Nord 15*, 96 (1924), **122**, (C.-J.M. Pitard, France, collecting in Morocco)

G. cazorlense Heywood, *Bull. Brit. Mus. (Bot.) 1*, 112 (1954), **135** (Cazorla, district of S. Spain)

G. christensenianum Handel-Mazzetti, *Symbolae Sinicae 7(3)*, 621 (1933), **26** (C.F.A. Christensen, pteridologist, Denmark)

G. chumbiense Knuth, *Feddes Repert., 19*, 228 (1923), = **25** (inhabiting Chumbi, part of Tibet between Sikkim and Bhutan)

G. cinereum Cavanilles, *Monad. Class. Diss. Dec., 4*, 204 (1787), **137** (ashy in colour, referring to the leaves, etc.)

G. cinereum Cavanilles var. *elatius* Davis, *Notes Roy. Bot. Gard. Edinb., 28*, 36 (1967), = **147** (taller)

G. cinereum Cavanilles subsp. *nanum* (Cosson) Maire, *Mem. Soc. Sci. Nat. Maroc, nos. 21-22*, 29 (1929), = **134** (dwarf, adj.)

G. cinereum Cavanilles var. *obtusilobum* (Bornmüller) Yeo, *Hardy Geraniums*, 189 (1985), = **146** (blunt-lobed, referring to the leaves)

G. cinereum Cavanilles var. *palmatipartitum* Knuth, in Engler, *Pflanzenreich, IV, 129*, 94 (1912), = **148** (palmately split, referring to the leaves)

G. cinereum Cavanilles var. *ponticum* Davis & Roberts, *Notes Roy. Bot. Gard. Edinb., 22*, 23 (1955), = **144** (pertaining to the Pontus, Latin name of a region of N.E. Turkey)

G. cinereum Cavanilles var. *subcaulescens* (L'Héritier ex De Candolle) Knuth, in Engler, *Pflanzenreich, IV, 129*, 92 (1912), = **140** (slightly stem-forming)

G. clarkei Yeo, *Hardy Geraniums*, 188 (1985), **19**

(C.B. Clarke, botanist, Britain)

G. collinum Willdenow, *Sp. Pl., 3*, 705 (1800), **15** (of hills)

G. columbinum Linnaeus, *Sp. Pl.*, 682 (1753), **51** (pertaining to a dove, the foot of which is supposedly resembled by the leaf)

G. crenophilum Boissier, *Diagn. Pl. Or. Nov., 2 (8)*, 117 (1849), = **86b** (spring-loving; "spring" in the sense of a source of water)

G. dahuricum De Candolle, *Prodr., 1*, 642 (1824), **45** (Dahuria, a Latinised name for a region of S.E. Siberia, former USSR)

G. dalmaticum (Beck) Rechinger, *Magyar Bot. Lapok, 33*, 28 (1934), **121** (Dalmatia, Latin name for an Adriatic Province)

G. x decipiens Haussknecht, *Mitt. Thür. Bot. Ver., 5*, 65 (1893) (deceptive)

G. delavayi Franchet, *Bull. Soc. Bot. Fr., 33*, 442 (1886), **32** (P.J.M. Delavay, missionary and plant collector, France)

G. deltoideum Rydberg ex Hanks & Small as cit. by Moore 1943, *in Underw. & Britt. (eds.), N. Amer. Fl., 25(1)*, 18 ["Rydberg sp. nov."] (1907), **83** (leaves delta-shaped)

G. dissectum Linnaeus, *Cent. Pl., 1*, 21 (1755), **87** (cut-up, referring to the leaves)

G. divaricatum Ehrhart, *Beiträge zur Naturkunde, 7*, 164, (1792)

G. dolomiticum Rothmaler, *Boll. Soc. Esp. Hist. Nat. 34*, 151 (1934), **139** (occurring on dolomite rock)

G. donianum Sweet, *Geraniaceae, 4*, sub tab. 338 (1827), **39** (D. Don, botanist, Britain)

G. drakensbergense Hilliard & Burtt, *Notes Roy.Bot. Gard. Edinb., 42*, 190 (1985), under **68b** (inhabiting the Drakensberg, high mountain range in Republic of South Africa and Lesotho)

G. endressii Gay, *Ann. Sci. Nat., 26*, 228 (1832), **1** (P.A.C. Endress, plant collector, Germany)

G. endressii Gay var. *armitageae* Turrill, *Gard. Chron., 85*, 164 (1929), = **2** (Miss E. Armitage, horticulturist, Britain)

G. endressii Gay var. *thurstonianum* Turrill, *Jour. Bot. (London), 66*, 46 (1928), = **2** (E. Thurston, horticulturist, Britain)

G. erianthum De Candolle, *Prodr., 1*, 641 (1824), **23** (woolly-flowered)

G. eriostemon Fischer ex De Candolle, *Prodr., 1*, 641 (1824), = **22** (woolly-stamened)

G. eriostemon Fischer ex De Candolle var. *reinii* (Franchet & Savatier) Maximowicz, *Bull. Acad. Imp. Sci. Pétersb., 26*, 464 (1880), = **22** (J.J. Rein, geographer and geologist, Germany)

G. eriostemon Fischer ex De Candolle var. *reinii* (Franchet & Savatier) Maximowicz forma *onoei* (Franchet & Savatier) Hara, = **22** (M.

Ono, botanist, Japan)

G. farreri Stapf, *Bot. Mag., 151*, tab. 9092 (1926), **36** (R.J. Farrer, plant collector and horticulturist, Britain)

G. favosum Hochstetter, *in G.W. Schimper, Iter Abyss. Sect. II*, no. 806, on labels, with description (1842), **111**, (describes mericarp surface)

G. favosum Hochstetter ex A. Richard, *Tent. Fl. Abyss., 1*, 117 (1847), **111** (honeycombed, referring to the mericarps)

G. flanaganii Schlechter ex Knuth, *Bot. Jahrb. 40*, 69 (1908), **71** (H.G. Flanagan, plant collector in South Africa and Zimbabwe)

G. forrestii Knuth, in Engler, *Pflanzenreich, IV, 129*, 578 (1912), = **32** (G. Forrest, botanist and plant collector, Britain)

G. forrestii Stapf, *Bot. Mag., 151*, sub tab. 9092 (1926), = **42** (G. Forrest, botanist and plant collector, Britain)

G. fremontii Torrey ex Gray, *Pl. Fendl.*, 26 (1849) (*Mem. Amer. Acad. ser. 2, 4,* 26 (1849)), **79** (J.C. Frémont, explorer and plant collector, USA)

G. fremontii Gray var. *parryi* Engelmann, *Amer. Jour. Sci., ser. 2(33)*, 405 (1862), **79a** (see *G. parryi*)

G. glaberrimum Boissier & Heldreich, in Boissier, *Diagn. Pl. Or. Nov., 2 (8)*, 116 (1849), **118** (quite without hairs)

G. gracile Ledebour ex Nordmann, *Bull. Sci. Acad. Imp. Pétersb., 2*, 314 (1837), **101** (slender, graceful)

G. grandiflorum Edgeworth, *Trans. Linn. Soc. London, 20*, 42 (1846), not Linnaeus (1753) **20** (large-flowered)

G. grandiflorum Edgeworth var. *alpinum* (Regel) Knuth, in Engler, *Pflanzenreich, IV, 129*, 188 (1912), = **18** (alpine)

G. grevilleanum Wallich, *Pl. Asiat. Rar., 3*, 4 (1832), = **24** (R.K. Greville, botanist, Britain)

G. gymnocaulon De Candolle, *Prodr., 1*, 640 (1824), **95** (naked-stemmed)

G. harveyi Briquet, *Annu. Cons. Jard. Bot. Genève 11/12*, 183 (1908), **67** (named after part-author of *Flora Capensis*)

G. hayatanum Ohwi, *Acta Phytotax. Geobot. 2*, 152 (1933), **47**, (B. Hayata, Japan)

G. herrerae Knuth, *Feddes. Repert. 38*, 1 (1930), **84** (name of collector)

G. himalayense Klotzsch, in Klotzsch & Garcke, *Bot. Ergeb. Reise Waldem.*, 122 (1862), **20** (inhabiting the Himalaya Mountains)

G. hispidissimum (Franchet) Knuth, *in Engler, Pflanzenreich IV, 129*, 183 (1912), **105** (very bristly)

G. homeanum Turczaninov, *Bull. Soc. Nat. Moscou 36*, 591 (1863), **before 63**, (Sir James

Everard Home, Australia, New Zealand)

G. x hybridum Haussknecht, *Mitt. Geogr. Ges. Bot. Ver. Thür., 3*, 278 (1885), not Linnaeus (1767) (hybrid, adj.)

G. x hybridum F.A. Lees, *Bot. Loc. Rec. Club, Rep. 1884, 1885, 1886*, 118 (1887), not Linnaeus (1767) (hybrid, adj.)

G. hyperacrion Veldkamp, *Blumea, 24*, 470 (1978) (over the mountains)

G. ibericum Cavanilles, *Monad. Class. Diss. Dec., 4*, 209 (1790), **93** (Iberia, Latin name for Georgia in the Caucasus, now Gruziya)

G. ibericum Cavanilles subsp. *jubatum* (Handel-Mazzetti) Davis, *Notes Roy. Bot. Gard. Edinb., 22*, 24 (1955), **93** (maned [sic], possibly from the very long hairs in the inflorescence)

G. ibericum Cavanilles var. *platypetalum* (Fischer & Meyer) Boissier, *Fl. Or., 1*, 876 (1867), = **92** (flat-petalled, referring to the petals of a flower collectively)

G. incanum N.L. Burman, *Spec. Bot. Geran.*, 28 (1759), **68** (white or hoary, referring to stems and undersides of leaves)

G. incanum N.L. Burman var. *multifidum* (Sweet) Hilliard & Burtt, *Notes Roy. Bot. Gard. Edinb., 42*, 197 (1985), **68** (much cleft, referring to the leaves)

G. incisum (Torrey & Gray) Brewer & Watson, *Bot. Calif., 1*, 94 (1880), not Andrews (1799), = **74**; under **77** (deeply cut, referring to the leaves)

G. x intermedium Sündermann ex Knuth in Engler, *Pflanzenreich, IV, 129*, 220 (1912), not Colla (1834), hybrids between **132 & 137** (see under **132**) (intermediate)

G. kariense Knuth, in Engler, *Pflanzenreich, IV, 129*, 577 (1912), = **32** (inhabiting the Kari Pass, Yunnan, China)

G. kerberi Knuth, *Knuth, in Engler, Pflanzenreich, IV, 129*, 200 (1912), **before 84** (A.E. Kerber, collector in Mexico and elsewhere)

G. kishtvariense Knuth, *Feddes Repert., 19*, 229 (1923), **28** (district of Kishtwar in Kashmir)

G. koreanum Komarov, *Acta Horti Petrop. 18*, 433 (1899, teste Nakai) (1901) **41**, (Korean)

G. krameri Franchet & Savatier, *Enum. Pl. Jap., 2*, 306 1878), **44** (Kramer, collector for Savatier)

G. lambertii Sweet, *Geraniaceae, 4*, tab. 338 (1827), **25** (A.B. Lambert, botanist, Britain)

G. lanuginosum Lamarck, *Encycl. Méth. Bot., 2*, 655 (1788), **100** (woolly)

G. lazicum (Woronow) Aedo, *Anal. Jard. Bot. Madrid 52*, 105 (1994), **145** (from Lazistan, now in N.E. Turkey)

G. libani Davis, *Notes Roy. Bot. Gard. Edinb., 22*, 25 (1955), **98** (of Lebanon)

G. libanoticum (Boissier) Boissier, *Fl. Or., 1*, 877 (1867), not Schenk (1840), = **98** (Lebanese)

G. x *lindavicum* Sündermann ex Knuth, in Engler, *Pflanzenreich, IV, 129*, 220 (1912), **133** (Lindau on Lake Constance)

G. lindleyanum Royle, *Ill. Bot. Himal. Mount.*, 150 (1835), (J. Lindley, botanist, Britain)

G. linearilobum De Candolle, *Fl. Fr., ed. 3, 5*, 629 (1815), **90** (with linear lobes, referring to the leaves)

G. linearilobum De Candolle subsp. *transversale* (Karelin & Kirilow) Davis, *Israel Jour. Bot., 19*, 105 (1970), **90** (transverse, possibly referring to the wide leaves)

G. londesii Fischer ex Link, *Enum. Hort. Berol. Alt., 2*, 196 (1822), under **15** (F.W. Londes, botanist, Germany/Russia)

G. lucidum Linnaeus, *Sp. Pl.*, 682 (1753), **117** (shining)

G. macrorrhizum Linnaeus, *Sp. Pi.*, 680 (1753), **119** (large-rooted)

G. macrostylum Boissier, *Diagn. Pl. Or. Nov., 1 (1)*, 58 (1843), **89** (large-styled)

G. maculatum Linnaeus, *Sp. Pl.*, 681 (1753), **73** (spotted, from the yellowish marks in the notches of the leaves)

G. maderense Yeo, *Bol. Mus. Munic. Funchal, 23*, 26 (1969), **127** (inhabiting Madeira)

G. x *magnificum* Hylander, *Lustgarden, 1961*, 114 (1961), **94** (magnificent)

G. magniflorum Knuth, *Bot. Jahrb, 40*, 68 (1907), **68a** (large-flowered)

G. makmelicum Aedo, *Anal. Jard. Bot. Madrid 52*, 105 (1994), **146** (Makmel mountain range, Lebanon)

G. malviflorum Boissier & Reuter, *Pugillus*, 27 (1852), **91** (mallow-flowered)

G. mascatense Boissier, *Diagn. Pl. Or. Nov., 1 (1)*, 59 (1842), **110** (inhabitant of Sultanate of Mascat)

G. maximowiczii Regel & Maack ex Regel, *Tent. Fl. Ussur.*, 38 (1861)*, under **23** & **41** (C.J. Maximowicz, botanist, Russia)

G. meeboldii Briquet, *Annu. Cons. Jard. Bot. Genève, 11/12*, 184 (1908), = **20** (Meebold, personal name, presumably Swiss)

G. melanandrum Franchet, *Pl. Delav.*, 112 (1889), = **33** (with black anthers)

G. molle Linnaeus, *Sp. Pl.*, 682 (1753), **116** (soft, referring to the hairiness of the plant)

G. x *monacense* Harz, *Mitt. Bayer. Bot. Ges., 4 (1)*, 7 (1921), **129** (inhabiting Monachium, Latinised form of Munich or München)

G. x *monacense* Harz nothovar. *anglicum* Yeo, *Hardy Geraniums*, 188 (1985), **129** (English)

G. multifidum D. Don, *Prodr. Fl. Nepal.*, 207 (1825), = **39** (much cleft, referring to the leaves)

G. nakaoanum Hara, *Acta Phytotax. Geobot. 16*, 1 (1955), **103** (S. Nakao, collector in the Himalayas, Japan)

G. nanum Cosson ex Battandier, *in Batt. & Trabut, Fl. Algér. (Dicot.)*, 119 (1888), **134** (dwarf)

G. napuligerum Franchet, *Pl. Delav.*, 115 (1889), under **36** (bearing turnips, referring to the shape, but not the size, of the roots)

G. nepalense Sweet, *Geraniaceae, 1*, tab. 12 (1820), **55** (inhabiting Nepal)

G. nepalense Sweet var. *thunbergii* (Siebold ex Lindley & Paxton) Kudo, *Medic. Pl. Hokkaido*, tab. 55 (1922)*, = **52** (C.P. Thunberg, botanist, Sweden)

G. nervosum Rydberg, *Bull. Torrey Bot. Club, 28*, 34 (1901), **77** (nerved, probably referring to the petals)

G. niuginiense Veldkamp, *Blumea, 24*, 473 (1978) (inhabiting New Guinea)

G. nodosum Linnaeus, *Sp. Pl.*, 681 (1753), **5** (knotty, referring to the swollen joints of the stem)

G. ocellatum Cambessèdes, in Jacquemont, *Voy. Inde, 4 (Bot.)*, 33 (1841?)*, **109** (eyed or eyeletted, referring to the dark centre of the flower)

G. omphalodeum Lange, *Ind. Sem. Horti Haun.*, 27 (1865), **106** (like *Omphalodes*, a genus of Boraginaceae, from the resemblance in the mericarps)

G. oreganum Howell, *Fl. N. W. Amer.*, 106 (1897), **74** (Oregon)

G. orientali-tibeticum Knuth, *Feddes Repert., 19*, 230 (1923), **49** (E. Tibet, now W. Sichuan)

G. ornithopodioides Hilliard & Burtt, *Notes Roy. Bot. Gard. Edinb., 42*, 220 (1985), **under 72** (like *ornithopodum/on*)

G. ornithopodon Ecklon & Zeyher, *Enum. Pl. Afr. Austral. 1*, 59 (1834), **72** (bird's foot, from supposed resemblance in leaf-outline)

G. x *oxonianum* Yeo, *Hardy Geraniums*, 187 (1985), **2** (pertaining to Oxford)

G. pallens Bieberstein, *Fl. Taur.-Cauc., 2*, 138 (1808), = **86a** (pale, referring to the flower-colour)

G. palmatipartitum (Haussknecht ex Knuth) Aedo, *Anal. Jard. Bot. Madrid 52*, 105 (1994), **148** (palmately split, referring to the leaves)

G. palmatum Cavanilles, *Monad. Class. Diss. Dec., 4*, 216 (1787), **126** (palmate, referring to the leaf-form)

G. palustre Linnaeus, *Cent. Pl., 2*, 25 (1756), **37** (found in marshes)

G. papuanum Ridley, *Trans. Linn. Soc. London (Bot.) 9*, 22 (1916), **62** (Papuan)

G. parryi (Engelmann) A. Heller, *Cat. N. Amer. Plants, ed. 2*, 7 (1900), = **79a** (C.C. Parry, collector in west N. America, Britain, USA)

G. *patagonicum* J.D. Hooker, *Fl. Antarct. 2*, 252 (1845), **85** (of Patagonia)

G. *peloponnesiacum* Boissier, *Diagn. Pl. Or. Nov. 3 (1)*, 110 (1853), **97** (the Peloponnese, the part of Greece S. of the Gulf of Corinth)

G. *peloponnesiacum* Boissier var. *libanoticum* Boissier, *Diagn. Pl. Or. Nov., 3 (5)*, 73 (1856), = **98** (Lebanese)

G. *petri-davisii* Aedo, *Anal. Jard. Bot. Madrid 52*, 105 (1994), **147** (of Peter H. Davis, author of Flora of Turkey)

G. *phaeum* Linnaeus, *Sp. Pl.*, 681 (1753), **128** (dusky)

G. *phaeum* Linnaeus var. *lividum* (L'Héritier) Persoon, *Syn. Pl., 2*, 235 (1806), **128** (livid)

G. *platyanthum* Duthie, *Gard. Chron., 39*, 52 (1906), **22** (flat-flowered)

G. *platypetalum* Fischer & Meyer, *Ind. Sem. Horti Petrop., 1*, 28 (1835)*, **92** (flat-petalled, referring to the petals of a flower collectively)

G. *platypetalum* Franchet, *Pl. Delav.*, 111 (1889), = **31** (flat-petalled)

G. *pogonanthum* Franchet, *Pl. Delav.*, 111 (1889), **34** (with a bearded flower)

G. *polyanthes* Edgeworth & J.D. Hooker, in J.D. Hooker, *Fl. Brit. Ind.*, 1 431 (1874), **102** (many-flowered)

G. *ponticum* (Davis & Roberts) Aedo, *Anal. Jard. Bot. Madrid 52*, 106 (1994), **144** (part of N.E. Turkey known as Pontus in Roman times)

G. *potentilloides* L'Héritier ex De Candolle, *Prodr., 1*, 639 (1824), **63** (like a *Potentilla*, presumably referring to the flowers)

G. *potentilloides* L'Héritier var. *abditum* Carolin, *Proc. Linn. Soc. N.S.W., 89*, 340 (1964), (removed)

G. *pratense* Linnaeus, *Sp. Pl.*, 681 (1753), **16** (inhabiting meadows)

G. *pratense* Linnaeus forma *albiflorum* Opiz, *Seznam Rostlin Kvéteny Ceské*, 47 (1852), **16** (white-flowered)

G. *pratense* Linnaeus var. *album* Weston, *The Universal Botanist and Nurseryman, 2*, 353 (1771), = **16** (white)

G. *pratense* Linnaeus subsp. *stewartianum* Y. Nasir var. *stewartianum*, *Fl. Pak., 149*, 19 (1983), **16** (R.R. Stewart, botanist, USA/Pakistan)

G. *pratense* Linnaeus subsp. *stewartianum* Y. Nasir var. *schmidii* Y. Nasir, *Fl. Pak., 149*, 21 (1983), under **16** (F. Schmid, botanist, Germany)

G. *procurrens* Yeo, *Bot. Mag., 179*, tab. 644 (1973), **27** (running forth)

G. *pseudosibiricum* J. Mayer, *Abh. Böhm. Ges. Wiss., 1786*, 238 (1786), **12** (false sibiricum)

G. *psilostemon* Ledebour, *Fl. Ross., 1*, 465

(1842), **14** (with bare, i.e. hairless, stamens)

G. *pulchrum* N.E. Brown, *Kew Bull. 1895*, 143 (1895), **66** (beautiful)

G. *purpureum* Villars, in Linnaeus, *Syst. Pl. Eur., 1, Fl. Delph.*, 72 (1785), under & before **123** (purple)

G. *purpusii* Knuth, *Feddes Repert., 12*, 40 (1913), = **82** (C.A. Purpus, plant collector, Germany)

G. *pusillum* Linnaeus, *Syst. Nat., ed. 10, 2*, 1144 (1759), **114** (puny, slender)

G. *pylzowianum* Maximowicz, *Bull. Acad. Imp. Sci. Pétersb., 26*, 452, 466 (1880), **48**

G. *pyrenaicum* N.L. Burman, *Spec. Bot. Geran.*, 27 (1759), **113** (Pyrenean)

G. *pyrenaicum* N.L. Burman forma *albiflorum* Schur, *Verh. Naturf. Verein Brunn, 15*, 161 (1877)*, **113** (white-flowered)

G. *pyrenaicum* N.L. Burman subsp. *lusitanicum* (Sampaio) S. Ortiz, *Anal. Jard. Bot. Madrid 47*, 244 (1990), **113** (of Lusitania, old name for Portugal)

G. *pyrenaicum* N.L. Burman var. *majus* Pau ex Merino, *Flora Galicia 1*, 283 (1905), **113** (larger)

G. *pyrenaicum* N.L. Burman forma *pallidum* Gilmour & Stearn, *Jour. Bot. (London), 70, suppl.*, 6 (1932), **113** (pale coloured, of petals)

G. *rectum* Trautvetter, *Bull. Soc. Nat. Moscou, 33*, 459 (1860), **6** (straight, referring to the stem or the [sometimes] upright pedicels)

G. *reflexum* Linnaeus, *Mantissa Alt.*, 257 (1771), **130** (reflexed, referring to the sepals and petals)

G. *refractum* Edgeworth & J.D. Hooker, in J.D. Hooker, *Fl. Brit. India, 1*, 428 (1874), **33** (bent backwards, referring to the pedicels)

G. *regelii* Nevski, *Acta Inst. Bot. Acad. Sci. U.R.S.S., 4*, 304 1937), **18** (E. Regel, botanist, Switzerland/Russia)

G. *renardii* Trautvetter, in Trautvetter, Regel, Maximowicz & Winkler, *Decas Pl. Nov.*, 5 (1882), **96** (K.I. Renard, naturalist, Russia)

G. *retrorsum* L'Héritier ex De Candolle, *Prodr. 1*, 644 (1824), **before 63** (turned back, of the hairs on the pedicels)

G. *reuteri* Aedo & Muñoz Garmendia, *Kew Bull. 53*, 726 (1997), **125**, (G.F. Reuter, botanist, Switzerland)

G. *richardsonii* Fischer & Trautvetter, *Ind. Sem. Horti Petrop., 4*, 37 (1838)*, **80** (Sir John Richardson, explorer and naturalist, Britain)

G. x *riversleaianum* Yeo, *Hardy Geraniums*, 187 (1985), **3** (Riverslea Nursery near Christchurch, England)

G. *rivulare* Villars, *Prosp. Pl. Dauph.*, 40 (1779), **10** (found by rivers or streams, a misnomer)

G. *robertianum* Linnaeus, *Sp. Pl.*, 681 (1753), **123** (Robert or Ruprecht, see Chapter 1)

G. robertianum Linnaeus forma *bernettii* ?A. Schwarz, ex Gams [Hegi] (1926)*, [*teste* Clifton] **123**

G. robertianum Linnaeus subsp. *celticum* Ostenfeld, *Rep. Bot. Exch. Club Brit. Is., 5*, 551 (1920), **123** (Celtic)

G. robertianum Linnaeus var. *celticum* (Ostenfeld) Druce, *Brit. Pl. List, ed. 2*, 21 (1928), **123** (Celtic)

G. robertianum Linnaeus forma *leucanthum* Dumortier ex Beckhaus, *Jahresb. Westfäl. Prov. Ver. Wiss. Kunst, 5*, 178 (1878), **123** (white-flowered)

G. robertianum Linnaeus subsp. *maritimum* (Babington) H.G. Baker, *Watsonia, 3*, 272 (1956), **123** (maritime)

G. robustum Kuntze, *Revis. Gen. 3*, 32 (1898), **64**, (robust)

G. rotundifolium Linnaeus, *Sp. Pl.*, 683 (1753), **7** (round-leaved)

G. rubescens Yeo, *Bol. Mus. Munic. Funchal, 23*, 26 (1969), **124** (reddish or becoming reddish, referring to the stems and leaf-stalks)

G. rubifolium Lindley, *Bot. Reg., 26*, tab. 67 (1840), **29** (bramble-leaved)

G. sanguineum Linnaeus, *Sp. Pl.*, 683 (1753), **50** (bloody, blood-red, referring, inaccurately, to the colour of the petals)

G. sanguineum Linnaeus var. *lancastrense* (Miller) Druce, *List of British Plants*, 14 (1908), = **50** (Lancashire, English county) (later homonym of *G. s. lancastriense* G. Nicholson)

G. sanguineum Linnaeus *lancastriense* G. Nicholson, *Ill. Dict. Gard., 2*, 64 (1885), name published without indication of rank, = **50** (Lancashire, English county)

G. sanguineum Linnaeus var. *prostratum* (Cavanilles) Persoon, *Syn. Pl., 2*, 234 (1806), = **50** (prostrate)

G. sanguineum Linnaeus var. *striatum* Weston, *The Universal Botanist and Nurseryman, 2*, 353 (1771), **50** (striped, referring to the veiny petals)

G. saxatile Karelin & Kirilow, *Bull. Soc. Nat. Moscou 15*, 177 (1842), **21** (growing on stones/rocks)

G. schiedeanum Schlechtendal, *Linnaea, 10*, 253 (1836), **82** (C.J.W. Schiede, botanist and plant collector)

G. schlechteri Knuth, *in Engler, Pflanzenreich IV, 129*, 207 (1912), **70** (R. Schlechter, botanist, Germany)

G. schrenkianum Trautvetter ex Becker, *Bull. Soc. Nat. Moscou, 57*, 53 (1882), before **51** (A.G. von Schrenk, botanist)

G. sessiliflorum Cavanilles, *Monad. Class. Diss. Dec., 4*, 198 (1787), **60** (sessile-flowered,

referring to the pedicels arising from the rootstock)

G. sessiliflorum Cavanilles subsp. *brevicaule* (J.D. Hooker) Carolin, *Proc. Linn. Soc. N.S.W., 89*, 357 (1964), **60** (short-stemmed)

G. sessiliflorum Cavanilles subsp. *novaezelandiae* Carolin, *Proc. Linn. Soc. N.S.W., 89*, 356 (1964), **60** (of New Zealand)

G. shikokianum Matsumura, *Bot. Mag. Tokyo, 15*, 123 (1901), **40** (Shikoku, S. Japan, the smallest of the five main islands of Japan)

G. shikokianum Matsumura var. *quelpaertense* Nakai, *Bot. Mag. Tokyo, 26*, 260 (1912), **40** (Quelpart Island, S. Korea, also called Cheju do)

G. sibiricum Linnaeus, *Sp. Pl.*, 683 (1753), **56** (Siberian)

G. sinense Knuth, in Engler, *Pflanzenreich, IV, 129*, 577 (1912), **31** (inhabiting Sina, Latinised form of China)

G. soboliferum Komarov, *Acta Horti Petrop., 18*, 433 (1901), **43** (bearing runners or long rhizomes, see Chapter 9)

G. solanderi Carolin, *Proc. Linn. Soc. N.S.W., 89*, 357 (1965), **before 63** (Daniel Solander, botanist, Sweden, Britain)

G. stapfianum Handel-Mazzetti, *Symbolae Sinicae, 7 (3)*, 620 (1933), **42** (O. Stapf, botanist, Germany/Britain)

G. stenorrhizum Stapf, *Bot. Mag., 151*, sub tab. 9092 (1926), = **39** (slender-rooted)

G. stepporum Davis, *Notes Roy. Bot. Card. Edinb., 28*, 35 (1967), = **88** (of steppes)

G. striatum Linnaeus, *Amoen. Acad., 4*, 282 (1759), = **4** (striped)

G. strictipes Knuth, *in Engler, Pflanzenreich IV, 129*, 581 (1912), **104** (slender foot [= stalk, in this case pedunc. & pedic.])

G. strigosius St John, *Fl. S.E. Wash. Adj. Idaho*, 243 (1937), = **77** (more strigose; erroneously written *strigosior* when published. See *G. strigosum*)

G. strigosum Franchet not N.L. Burman, *Bull. Soc. Bot. Fr. 33*, 42 (1886), = **104** (with stiff appressed hairs)

G. strigosum Rydberg, *Bull. Torrey Bot. Club, 29*, 243 (1902), not N. L. Burman (1768), = **77** (with stiff appressed hairs)

G. subacutum (Boissier) Aedo, *Anal. Jard. Bot. Madrid 52*, 106 (1994), **136** (almost acute, of the leaf-segments)

G. subargenteum Lange in Willkomm & Lange, *Prodr. Fl. Hispan. 3*, 525 (1878), **138** (silvery beneath [of the leaves])

G. subcaulescens L'Héritier ex De Candolle, *Prodr., 1*, 640 (1824), = **140** (slightly stem-forming)

G. submolle Steudel, misapplied, *Flora 39*, 438

(1856), = **84** (rather soft)

G. subulato-stipulatum Knuth, *in Engler, Pflanzenreich, IV, 129*, 199 (1912), **before 84** (awl-shaped stipules)

G. suzukii Masamune, *Jour. Soc. Trop. Agric. 33*, 392 (1931), **57**, (plant collector, presumably Japan)

G. swatense Schönbeck-Temesy, *in Rech. fil. (ed.) Fl. Iran. 69*, 22 (1970), **30** (inhabitant of Swat, N. Pakistan)

G. sylvaticum Linnaeus, *Sp. Pl.*, 681 (1753), **8** (pertaining to woods)

G. sylvaticum Linnaeus forma *albiflorum* A.G. Blytt, *Haandb. Norges Fl.*, 478 (1965), **8** (white-flowered)

G. sylvaticum Linnaeus var. *alpestre* Thaiss. ex Domin & Podpera in Polívka, Domin & Podpera, *Kliç k Uplné Kvetene Republicky Çeskoslovenské, ed. 2*, 111 (1928), = **8** (found in the lower alps)

G. sylvaticum Linnaeus subsp. *caeruleatum* (Schur) Webb & Ferguson, *Feddes Repert., 74*, 25 (1967), = **11** (made blue)

G. sylvaticum Linnaeus subsp. *pseudosibiricum* (J. Mayer) Webb & Ferguson, *Feddes Repert., 74*, 26 (1967), = **12** (false *sibiricum*)

G. sylvaticum Linnaeus subsp. *rivulare* (Villars) Rouy, *Fl. Fr., 4*, 81 (1897), = **10** (found by rivers or streams, a misnomer)

G. sylvaticum Linnaeus forma *roseum* Murr, **8** (rose-coloured)

G. sylvaticum var. *wanneri* Briquet, *Bull. Soc. Bot. Genève, 5*, 201 (1889), **8** (Monsieur Wanner, botanist, Switzerland)

G. thessalum Franzén, *Nordic Jour. Bot. 2*, 549 (1983), **143** (of Thessaly, Greece)

G. thodei Schlechter ex Knuth, *Bot. Jahrb., 40*, 70 (1907), under **68a** (J. Thode, collector for Schlechter)

G. thunbergii Siebold ex Lindley & Paxton, *Paxton's Flower Garden, 1*, 186 (1851), **52** (C.P. Thunberg, botanist, Sweden)

G. transbaicalicum Sergievskaya, *Sist. Zametki Mater. Gerb. Tomsk. Univ., 1*, 4 (1934), **17** (beyond Lake Baikal)

G. traversii J.D. Hooker, *Handb. N. Zeal. Flora*, 726 (1867), **58** (W.T.L. Travers, ornithologist)

G. traversii J.D. Hooker var. *elegans* Cockayne, *Trans. N. Zeal. Inst., 34*, 320 (1902), **58** (elegant)

G. trilophum Boissier, *Diagn. Pl. Or. Nov., 1 (6)*, 30 (1845), **107** (three-crested, referring to the mericarps)

G. tuberosum Linnaeus, *Sp. Pl.*, 680 (1753), **88** (tuberous)

G. tuberosum Linnaeus subsp. *linearifolium* (Boissier) Davis, *Notes Roy. Bot. Gard. Edinb., 22*, 26 (1956), **88** (linear-leaved, but

probably referring to the divisions of the upper leaves)

G. tuberosum Linnaeus subsp. *micranthum* Schönbeck-Temesy, in K.H. Rechinger, *Flora Iranica, 69*, 7 (1970), **88** (small-flowered)

G. versicolor Linnaeus, *Cent. Pl., 1*, 21 (1755), **4** (variously coloured)

G. viscosissimum Fischer & Meyer, *Ind. Sem. Horti Petrop., 9, suppl.*, 18 (1846)*, **78** (very sticky, from the glandular hairs)

G. viscosissimum Fischer & Meyer var. *nervosum* (Rydberg) C.L. Hitchcock, in C.L. Hitchcock et al., *Vasc. Pl. Pacific Northwest, 3*, 383 (1961), = **77** (nerved, probably referring to the petals)

G. vulcanicola Small, *in Underw. & Britt. (eds.), N. Amer. Fl., 25(1)*, 12 (1907), **before 84** (inhabitant of volcanoes!)

G. wakkerstroomianum Knuth, *Feddes Repert. 45*, 62 (1938), **under 70** (Wakkerstroom, a district of S. Transvaal)

G. wallichianum D. Don, in Sweet, *Geraniaceae, 1*, tab. 90 1821), **24** (N. Wallich, surgeon and botanist, Denmark/Britain/India)

G. wilfordii Maximowicz, *Bull. Acad. Imp. Sci. Pétersb., 26*, 453 (1880), **53** (C. Wilford, botanist and plant collector, Britain)

G. wlassovianum Fischer ex Link, *Enum. Horti Berol. Alt., 2*, 197 (1822), **38** G. Vlassov, Governor of the Russian town of Doroninsk

G. yemense in the sense of Knuth, in Engler, *Pflanzenreich IV, 129*, 60 (1912), = **108** (inhabiting the Yemen)

G. yeoi Aedo & Muñoz Garmendia, *Kew Bull. 52*, 726 (1977) **124**, (name of botanist)

G. yesoense Franchet & Savatier, *Enum. Pl. Jap., 2*, 305 (1878), **46** (inhabiting Yeso or Yezo, old name of Hokkaido, the northernmost large island of Japan)

G. yesoense Franchet & Savatier var. *lobatodentatum* Takeda, *not traced**, **under 54**, (with lobed teeth)

G. yesoense Franchet & Savatier var. *nipponicum* Nakai, *Bot. Mag. Tokyo, 26*, 266 (1912), **46** (Nippon, another name for Japan)

G. yoshinoi Makino ex Nakai, *Bot. Mag. (Tokyo) 26*, 258 (1912), **54** (Z. Yoshino, botanist, Japan)

G. yunnanense Franchet, *Pl. Delav.*, 114 (1889), **35** (inhabiting Yunnan, China)

Appendix II
A New Name and a Discussion of a Taxonomic Problem

TAXONOMY OF "*Geranium* sp. Pamirs" OF GARDENS: its identification with *G. saxatile* Karelin & Kirilow

The following names are available for plants from approximately the area where the plant designated as A.C. Leslie 6/80B, and treated as 21. *G. saxatile* in Chapter 9, was collected.

G. saxatile Karelin & Kirilow (1842) ("plants collected in the desert of Songoria and in the high passes of mount Alatau")

G. ferganense Bobrov, Addenda Fl. URSS 13 (actually in v. 14, p. 713); I have noted: "does not agree with anything in **CGG** [=Cambridge Botanic Garden herbarium]"

G. wakhanicum (Paulsen) Ikonnikov (1971) or *G. collinum* var. *wakhanicum* Paulsen (1906); Schönbeck-Temesy associates this with *G. collinum*

G. humifusum Knuth (1904) (syn. of *G. collinum* var. *eglandulosum* in Knuth, Pflanzenreich, 1912, p. 186, where date of name is given as 1903)

G. pamiricum Ikonnikov name in Herb. **LE** [Komarov Herbarium, St. Petersburg]

G. candidum Komarov Trav. Soc. Nat. St Pétersbourg, Sect. Bot., 26: 151 (1896) (*G. collinum* var. *candidum* (Kom.) Knuth ["Dwarf, tufted, almost stemless. Sepals flushed with red" so nothing like our plant])

Of these, *humifusum*, *candidum* and *wakhanicum* seem to be firmly associated with *G. collinum*, whereas *pamiricum* may not yet have been validly published. As stated above, the description of *ferganense* rules out our plant. The original description of *G. saxatile*, on the other hand, has a number of points in common with our plant.

These are:
  _ numerous stems from a creeping rootstock,
  _ stems, peduncles and carpels with backwardly appressed hairs
  _ filaments widened at the base
  _ "related to *G. pratense* but .... with much sparser hairs" (leaf-divisions also shorter but this is given in the "reconcilable" group, below)

_ petals entire, bearded at the base.

There are some characters that do not agree perfectly but may be reconcilable with those of our plant:
  _(basal) leaves with 5 divisions – 5 or 7 in ours
  _(basal) leaves with divisions "abbreviatis, ovato-subrotundis, inciso-pinnatifidis" – but rhombic, palmately to palmato-pinnately lobed in my description
  _(basal) leaves with divisions half as long as those of *G. pratense* – but even less than half as long as those of *G. pratense* in our plant
  _calyx aristate – probably agreeing with my description of mucro 1–1.5mm
  _petals twice as long as calyx (calyx length not stated) – petals around $2^{1}/_2$ times as long as calyx in our plant
  _no mention of glandular hairs – ours has a few in addition to small eglandular hairs on the carpels
  _petals pale blue or light blue – but ours mid-blue-violet becoming mid-purple.

There are some characters totally in conflict:
  _peduncles bent back (this probably never happens in *Geranium* and the statement should be applied to the pedicels, but this is not true of our plant)
  _filaments glabrous (finely hairy in our plant; as the hairs are so fine, and as glabrous filaments are very rare, perhaps unknown, in *Geranium* section *Geranium*, K. & K. may have missed them, so this obstacle can be disregarded).

In addition, the plant gives the impression that it would behave as a dwarf in a natural alpine situation, and this is said to be the case for *G. saxatile* by Bobrov (1949).

The almost horizontal to slightly declined pedicels of the cultivated plant hardly show as such in dried specimens; they are mostly angled upwards.

If K. & K.'s statement that the filaments are glabrous is an error, then there is only one character completely opposed to those of our plant.

I have been supplied with photographs of the type specimen of *G. saxatile* and other authentic specimens of this species held in the Komarov Herbarium, St Petersburg, Russia, by the kindness of Dr Galina Gussarova. These show a plant virtually indistinguishable from that which we are growing. The peduncles are more or less erect and the pedicels with immature fruit (not many available) a little above to a little below the horizontal, and not reflexed. Thus I think our plant is *G. saxatile*, although that species was associated in *Flora Iranica* with *G. collinum* (Schönbeck-Temesy, 1970).

What is surprising is that the area from which the original *G. saxatile* was collected is several hundred kilometres from the Fergana area and yet the plants are so similar. The original locality for *G. saxatile* was stony alps and sub-alps on the rivers Lepsa, Baskan and Sarachan in the Alatau. The River Lepsa (and presumably the others) flows north from the Dzungarskiy (Songarian) Alatau range into Lake Balkhash which lies in the desert to the north-west.

THE TAXONOMY OF A PLANT SIMILAR TO *G. saxatile* THAT WAS INTRODUCED ABOUT THE SAME TIME

G. affine **saxatile**

The plant similar to the presumed *G. saxatile* discussed above that is mentioned under 21. *G. saxatile* in Chapter 9 was collected in Uzbekistan by Dr A.C. Leslie (no. ACL 6/80A, Cambridge accession 1980.0496) (locality: Chimgan, N.E. of Tashkent).

It differs from my supposed *G. saxatile*, firstly, by the hair-clothing of the stems, petioles and pedicels, which consists of very small glandular hairs and longer but unequal, spreading, eglandular hairs, secondly, by the velvety hair-clothing of the leaf-blades and, thirdly, by the horizontal floral axis and downwardly directed post-floral pedicels and immature fruits. Less specifically it also differs in its looser rootstock, different leaf-cutting, larger maximum leaf-size and slight deviation in most other size characters.

In this stock the anthers are barren and the fruit-set is low. A male or hermaphrodite plant might have larger flowers.

A NEW NAME FOR AN INTERSPECIFIC HYBRID

Geranium x *antipodeum* P.F. Yeo, nothosp. nov.

As explained in Chapter 3, an interspecific hybrid may be referred to by a hybrid formula or by a binary name. There is no obligation to provide a binary name for a plant recognised as a hybrid and,

indeed, it is wise to avoid a proliferation of such names. However, there are times when it is useful to have them for convenience of citation, especially when, as here, the hybrid has crossed with many other species and hybrids. At the prompting of Alan Bremner I have therefore provided the name below in conformity with the *International Code of Botanical Nomenclature* (see Chapter 3).

Hybrida partim fertilis inter *G. sessiliflorum* et *G. traversii*, in hortis orta. Herba perennis caespitosa foliis basalibus numerosis caulibusque multis foliosis ad 20cm longis praedita. Folia basalia lamina ad 6cm lata, usque ad $^3/_5$ septempartita, segmentis congestis, non complanatis, late cuneiformibus, ad apicem nec profunde nec acute trilobum latissimis, lobis plerisque dentes unum vel duos parvos obtusos ferentibus. Folia caulina opposita, maxime inaequalia, interdum solitaria, plerumque 7–20mm lata, segmentis pro parte majore ellipticis. Caules, petioli, pedunculi, pedicelli pilis retroappressis coacti. Laminae breviter appressopilosae, vivide virides vel brunneosuffusae. Cymulae uniflorae, stipite bracteam longe sub medio ferente. Flores subinfundibulares. Sepala 5–6mm longa, acuminata, colore brunneo vel purpureobrunneo suffusa, mucrone circa 1mm longo praedita. Petala 10 x 6–8mm longa, pallide rosea, ad basin alba, vel admodum impellucide alba, ad apicem rotundata, ad basin unguiculata, in margine parce ciliata. Staminum filamenta alba, in dimidio proximali satis dilatata et ibi ciliolata; antherae pallide violaceae vel violaceomarginatae. Stigmata circa 1.5mm longa. Fructus 11–14mm longi; rostra vix partem stylarem habentia, coacta.

Epitheton antipodeum huic hybridae ob specierum parentalium originem in Europae borealioccidentalis antipodibus et ob illorum coitum in Australasiae antipodibus pariter datur.

The epithet *antipodeum* is given to this hybrid equally on account of the origin of its parent species in the antipodes of north-west Europe and of their cross-breeding in the antipodes of Australasia.

TYPUS. *G. sessiliflorum* Cav. ssp. *novae-zelandiae* x *G. traversii* Hook.f. var. *elegans* Cock.: 'Stanhoe', cult. University Botanic Garden, Cambridge, accession no. 1998.0471 Beckett, 2.xi.1979 (**K**) (from K. and G. Beckett, Bramley Cottage, Stanhoe, near King's Lynn, Norfolk. Det. P.F. Yeo). Latinisation of description by Philip Oswald, Cambridge, 10 February 2001.

This plant is no. 59 in Chapter 9 of this book.

Appendix III
Interspecific Hybrids of Geranium

This list comprises the records known to me of hybrids involving two to four parent species that have a reasonably simple and straightforward genealogy. For each cross the parents are placed in alphabetical order. Only hybrids that have flowered are included, and, of these, feeble or short-lived progeny are excluded. The records are grouped into five sets covering four taxonomic groups within which hybrids can be formed, and a fifth group in which the parent species represent two different subgenera.

Sources: Aitchison = Aitchison, 1998a, 1998b, 2001; Bremner = ms information supplied in 1998 and 1999 by Alan Bremner of St Ola, Kirkwall, Orkney; Dahlgren = Dahlgren, 1923, 1925; Kiefer = Widler-Kiefer & Yeo, 1987; Van Loon = Van Loon, 1984; Yeo = Yeo, 1973, 1984, 1985 and specimens in CUBG herbarium.

Group 1: *Parent species in Subgenus Geranium, Section Geranium*

albiflorum x sylvaticum (Bremner).
x antipodeum x endressii (Bremner).
 incl. 'Black Ice', 'Sea Spray', 'Stanhoe'.
x antipodeum x herrerae (Yeo).
 first parent was 'Stanhoe'.
x antipodeum x kishtvariense (Bremner).
x antipodeum x x oxonianum (Bremner).
 incl. 'Elizabeth Ross', 'Orkney Pink'.
x antipodeum x rubifolium (Bremner).
x antipodeum x sessiliflorum (Bremner).
 2 ways.
x antipodeum x sibiricum (Bremner).
x antipodeum x sp. Chile (Bremner).
 antipodeum used sessiliflorum 'Porter's Pass'.
x antipodeum x swatense (Bremner).
x antipodeum x transbaicalicum (Yeo).
 spont.; first parent was 'Stanhoe'; in CUBG
 herbarium; plant died.
x antipodeum x versicolor (Bremner).
bicknellii x carolinianum (Yeo).
 spont., Cambridge B.G.
caffrum x platyanthum (Bremner).
carolinianum x endressii (Bremner).
carolinianum x herrerae (Bremner).
carolinianum x oreganum (Bremner).

carolinianum x x oxonianum (Bremner).
carolinianum x platyanthum (Bremner).
carolinianum x procurrens (Bremner).
carolinianum x rotundifolium (Bremner).
carolinianum x sessiliflorum (Bremner).
carolinianum x sibiricum (Bremner).
carolinianum x sp. Chile (Bremner).
carolinianum x traversii (Bremner).
carolinianum x versicolor (Bremner).
clarkei x collinum (Bremner, CUBG spont.).
 spont.; incl. 'Nimbus'.
clarkei x himalayense (Bremner, spont. CUBG).
clarkei x pratense (Bremner, Kiefer).
 2 ways; incl. 'Brookside', 'Kashmir Blue',
 'Prima Donna' &, using subsp. stewartianum
 and 'Kashmir White', 'Scheherazade'.
clarkei x regelii (Bremner).
clarkei x saxatile (Bremner).
clarkei x transbaicalicum (Bremner).
 2 ways.
(clarkei x pratense) x regelii (Bremner).
collinum x dahuricum (Lundström).
 spont.; named G. x bergianum.
collinum x himalayense (Bremner).
collinum x pratense (Bremner, Lundström).
 2 ways; incl. 'Distant Hills', 'Harmony'.
collinum x psilostemon (Bremner).
collinum x regelii (Bremner).
collinum x transbaicalicum (Bremner).
dahuricum x pratense (Lundström).
dahuricum x yesoense (Bremner).
delavayi x sinense (spont.).
 spont.; reported by Yeo (1992).
endressii x herrerae (Bremner).
endressii x potentilloides (Bremner).
endressii x psilostemon (Bremner).
 2 ways; incl. 'Patricia'.
endressii x sessiliflorum (Bremner, O. Folkard).
 spont.; incl. 'Kate'.
endressii x sibiricum (Bremner).
endressii x subulato-stipulatum (Bremner).
endressii x sylvaticum (I.R.& J.Grout).
 source Évrard (1997); incl. 'Mary Mottram'.
endressii x traversii (Bremner, spont.).
 named G. x riversleaianum; incl. 'Russell
 Prichard' and 'Mavis Simpson', both spont.
endressii x versicolor (spont.+J. Innes
 [Sansome 1936]).

named G. x oxonianum, spont.; incl. 'A.T. Johnson',
'Claridge Druce', 'Lady Moore', 'Miriam Rundle', 'Southcombe Double', 'Southcombe Star', 'Winscombe', etc.
endressii x wallichianum (Bremner).
erianthum x platyanthum (Bremner).
2 ways.
farreri x kishtvariense (Bremner).
farreri x wallichianum (Bremner).
flanaganii x magniflorum (Bremner).
flanaganii x pulchrum (Bremner).
flanaganii x robustum (Bremner).
fremontii x viscosissimum (Bremner).
2 ways.
herrerae x sessiliflorum (Bremner).
2 ways.
herrerae x sibiricum (Bremner).
herrerae x traversii (Bremner).
herrerae x versicolor (Bremner).
herrerae x wilfordii (Bremner).
himalayense x pratense (Bremner, Kiefer, A.T. Johnson).
incl. 'Johnson's Blue', spont.
himalayense x regelii (Bremner).
2 ways.
himalayense x saxatile (Bremner).
himalayense x transbaicalicum (Bremner).
homeanum x x oxonianum (Bremner).
homeanum x sessiliflorum (Bremner).
homeanum x traversii (Bremner).
kishtvariense x x oxonianum (Bremner).
kishtvariense x rubifolium (Bremner).
2 ways.
kishtvariense x wallichianum (Bremner).
(kishtvariense x wallichianum) x (rubifolium x wallichianum) (Bremner).
lambertii x potentilloides (Bremner).
lambertii x procurrens (Bremner, Strangman).
spont. in E. Strangman's garden, named 'Salome'.
lambertii x retrorsum (Bremner).
lambertii x sessiliflorum (Bremner).
incl. 'Libretto'.
lambertii x swatense (Bremner).
lambertii x thunbergii (Bremner).
lambertii x traversii (Bremner).
incl. 'Coombland White', 'Joy'.
(lambertii x procurrens) x x oxonianum (B.& S. Wynn-Jones).
incl. 'Sue Crûg'.
(lambertii x procurrens) x psilostemon (Bremner).
(lambertii x procurrens) x sanguineum (Bremner).
first parent is 'Salome'.
(lambertii x procurrens) x traversii (Bremner).
first parent is 'Salome'.

magniflorum x robustum (Bremner).
orientali-tibeticum x herrerae (Bremner).
orientali-tibeticum x vulcanicola (Bremner).
x oxonianum x herrerae (Bremner).
x oxonianum x potentilloides (Bremner).
x oxonianum x psilostemon (Bremner).
incl. 'Nicola'.
x oxonianum x retrorsum (Bremner).
x oxonianum x sessiliflorum (Bremner).
incl. 'Red Dwarf', 'Rothbury Redneck' [unregistered name]
'Sea Fire', 'Sea Pink'.
x oxonianum x sibiricum (Bremner).
x oxonianum x subulato-stipulatum (Bremner).
x oxonianum x traversii (Bremner).
incl. 'Little Gem'.
x oxonianum x versicolor (Bremner).
x oxonianum x vulcanicola (Bremner).
x oxonianum x wallichianum (Bremner).
platyanthum x psilostemon (Bremner).
pogonanathum x (sinense x yunnanense) (Bremner).
pogonanthum x sinense (Bremner).
pogonanthum x yunnanense (Bremner).
potentilloides x sessiliflorum (Bremner, R. Carolin).
2 ways; spont. in New South Wales.
potentilloides x sibiricum (Bremner).
potentilloides x traversii (Bremner).
potentilloides x versicolor (Bremner).
pratense x psilostemon (Bremner).
incl. 'Eva'.
pratense x regelii (Bremner).
pratense x saxatile (Bremner).
2 ways; incl. 'Natalie'.
pratense x swatense (Bremner).
pratense x sylvaticum (R. D. Nutt).
spont. in Alps.
pratense x transbaicalicum (Bremner).
procurrens x psilostemon (Bremner).
spont. incl. 'Ann Folkard', 'Anne Thomson'.
procurrens x sanguineum (Bremner).
incl. 'Dilys'.
procurrens x sanguineum (Bremner).
sanguineum var. striatum used.
pseudosibiricum x rivulare (Bremner).
psilostemon x rotundifolium (Bremner).
psilostemon x sanguineum (Bremner).
incl. 'Little David' (using sanguineum 'Minutum').
psilostemon x swatense (Bremner).
psilostemon x transbaicalicum (Bremner).
psilostemon x wallichianum (Bremner).
pulchrum x robustum (Bremner).
regelii x saxatile (Bremner).
regelii x transbaicalicum (Bremner).
retrorsum x herrerae (Bremner).

retrorsum x sessiliflorum (Bremner).
   2 ways.
retrorsum x thunbergii (Bremner).
retrorsum x traversii (Bremner).
rivulare x sylvaticum (Gams).
rubifolium x sessiliflorum (Bremner).
   incl. 'Aria'.
rubifolium x traversii (Bremner).
rubifolium x wallichianum (Bremner).
    incl. 'Nora Bremner' (using wallichianum
    'Buxton's Variety').
(rubifolium x wallichianum) x farreri (Bremner).
(rubifolium x wallichianum) x traversii
   (Bremner).
sanguineum x swatense (Bremner).
sanguineum x swatense (Bremner).
   sanguineum 'Album' used.
saxatile x transbaicalicum (Bremner).
sessiliflorum x sibiricum (Bremner).
   2 ways.
sessiliflorum x sp. Chile (Bremner).
sessiliflorum x sp. New Guinea (Bremner).
sessiliflorum x subulato-stipulatum (Bremner).
sessiliflorum x suzukii (Bremner).
   incl. 'Welsh Guinness'.
sessiliflorum x swatense (Bremner).
sessiliflorum x traversii (Bremner, spont.).
   2 ways; named G. x antipodeum; incl.
   'Sea Spray' (using sessiliflorum
   'Nigricans'), 'Stanhoe'.
sessiliflorum x versicolor (Bremner).
   incl. 'Sonata'.
sessiliflorum x wilfordii (Bremner).
sibiricum x thunbergii (Bremner).
sibiricum x traversii (Bremner).
sinense x yunnanense (Bremner).
   2 ways; incl. 'Pagoda'.
soboliferum x wlassovianum (Bremner).
sp. Chile x subulato-stipulatum (Bremner).
   sp. Chile might be sessiliflorum subsp.
   sessiliflorum (based on Bremner's
   description).
sp. Chile x traversii (Bremner).
sp. Costa Rica x subulato-stipulatum
   (Bremner).
sp. Costa Rica x versicolor (Bremner).
subulato-stipulatum x suzukii (Bremner).
subulato-stipulatum x traversii (Bremner).
subulato-stipulatum x versicolor (Bremner).
subulato-stipulatum x vulcanicola (Bremner).
thunbergii x yoshinoi (Yeo)
swatense x traversii (Bremner).
traversii x versicolor (Bremner).
traversii x wilfordii (Bremner).

total hybrids in this group: 165
total binary hybrids: 130

Group 2: *Parent species in Subgenus Geranium,*
Section Tuberosa (hybrids are confined to
Subsection Mediterranea)
bohemicum x lanuginosum (Bremner, K. Dahlgren).
   2 ways.
gracile x ibericum (Bremner).
   incl. 'Sirak'.
gracile x (platypetalum x renardii) (Bremner).
gracile x renardii (Bremner).
   incl. 'Chantilly'.
gymnocaulon x ibericum (Bremner).
gymnocaulon x platypetalum (Bremner).
ibericum x libani (Bremner).
ibericum x platypetalum (Bremner, spont.).
   2 ways; spont. clones have been named
   G. x magnificum;
   incl. 'Hylander', 'Peter Yeo', 'Rosemoor'.
ibericum x (platypetalum x renardii) (Bremner).
ibericum x renardii (Bremner).
   2 ways.
libani x peloponnesiacum (Bremner).
libani x renardii (Bremner).
   2 ways.
peloponnesiacum x renardii (Bremner).
platypetalum x renardii (Bremner, Bobrov).
   incl. 'Philippe Vapelle'.

total hybrids in this group: 15
total binary hybrids: 12

Group 3: *Parent species in Subgenus Robertium*

brutium x molle (Bremner).
   2 ways.
canariense x palmatum (Bremner).
canariense x robertianum (Bremner, Kiefer).
canariense x rubescens (Kiefer, Baker).
   2 ways; Kiefer F1, Baker, F2.
cataractarum x maderense (Yeo, Kiefer).
   Yeo, 1973, p. 318, and edn.1; Kiefer. 1974.
dalmaticum x macrorrhizum (Bremner, Kiefer,
   H. Simon).
   2 ways, named G. x cantabrigiense; incl.
   'Berggarten', 'Cambridge', 'Karmina',
   'St Ola', etc.
maderense x palmatum (Yeo, Kiefer).
maderense x robertianum (Kiefer).
purpureum x robertianum (Yeo, Kiefer, Baker).
   2 ways. Baker in Yeo, 1973, p. 314, Yeo edn.1,
   Widler-Kiefer & Yeo, 1987.
pusillum x pyrenaicum (Bremner).
robertianum x rubescens (Kiefer, spont.
   CUBG).

total hybrids in this group: 11
total binary hybrids: 11

Group 4: *Parent species in Subgenus Erodioidea (no crosses between Sections Erodioidea and Subacaulia are known)*

argenteum x cinereum (Yeo).
  incl. 'Apple Blossom'.
argenteum x nanum (Aitchison).
  Both ways.
argenteum x subcaulescens (Bremner, Knuth).
  2 ways; named G. x lindavicum; incl.
  'Alanah', 'Gypsy', 'Lissadel', 'Purpureum'.
cinereum x x lindavicum (Bremner).
cinereum x makmelicum (Bremner).
cinereum x nanum (Aitchison).
cinereum x subcaulescens (Bremner).
  incl. 'Artistry', 'Ballerina', 'Laurence
  Flatman'.
x lindavicum x makmelicum (Bremner).
makmelicum x ponticum (Aitchison).
  2 ways.
makmelicum x subcaulescens (Bremner).
nanum x makmelicum (Aitchison).
  2 ways.
nanum x subcaulescens (Aitchison).
  2 ways.
nanum x subcaulescens (Aitchison).
phaeum x reflexum (Bremner, spont.).
  2 ways, spont. plants have been named
  G. x monacense nothovars.
  monacense & anglicum; incl. 'Eric Clement',
  'Muldoon', 'Rose Madder'.

total hybrids in this group: 14
total binary hybrids: 12

Group 5: *Parent species in different subgenera: Erodioidea and Geranium (confined to Sections Subacaulia and Geranium respectively)*

x antipodeum x argenteum (Bremner).
x antipodeum x makmelicum (Yeo).
  in CUBG herbarium.
x antipodeum x subcaulescens (Bremner).
argenteum x sessiliflorum (Bremner).
argenteum x traversii (Bremner).
  incl. 'Silver Pink'.
cinereum x herrerae (Bremner).
cinereum x traversii (Bremner).
herrerae x subcaulescens (Bremner).
x lindavicum x herrerae (Bremner).
x lindavicum x traversii (Bremner).
retrorsum x subcaulescens (Bremner).
sessiliflorum x subcaulescens (Bremner).
subcaulescens x traversii (Bremner).

total hybrids in this group: 13
total binary hybrids: 8

Index

This
book
provided
by

The Laramore
Literacy Fund

BOOK D
READING FOR CONCEPTS

"All things change; nothing perishes."   Ovid

BOOK D
READING

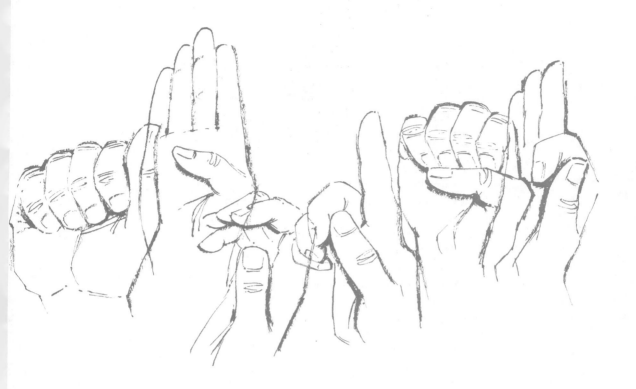

FOR CONCEPTS

Third Edition

Phoenix Learning Resources
New York

Reading for Concepts
Third Edition
Book D

Contributing Authors for the Reading for Concepts Series

Linda Barton, feature writer for St. Louis Today
Roberta H. Berry, elementary school teacher, writer
Barbara Broeking, journalist and educational publications editor
Eth Clifford, author of many volumes of fiction and poetry for youth
Ellen Dolan, juvenile book author
Betsy Feist, juvenile book author and reading specialist
Barbara R. Frey, Professor of Education, State University College, Buffalo, N.Y.
Ruth Harley, author and editor of young people's periodicals
Phyllis W. Kirk, children's book editor
Richard Kirk, author of science, social studies, and reading books for youth
Thomas D. Mantel, attorney and juvenile author
Marilyn F. Peachin, journalist and editor
James N. Rogers, author-editor of science and social studies resource books
James J. Pflaum, author and editor of current events periodicals
Gloria S. Rosenzweig, writer of children's books
Jean Shirley, author of juvenile books
Rosemary Winebrenner, editor of children's books
Jean White, journalist and writer of young people's reference materials

Vocabulary
Cynthia Merman, Reading and Language Specialist

Project Management and Production
Kane Publishing Services, Inc.

Cover Design
Pencil Point Studios

Text Design
Jim Darby

Illustrators
James Cummings; Tony Giamis, GAI; Paul Weiner

Cover Photograph
Johnny Sundby/Dakota Skies Photography

ISBN 0–7915–2106–0

3 4 5 6 7 8 9 0 05 04 03

TABLE OF CONTENTS

TO THE TEACHER

Purpose

This book is one of eight in the series "Reading for Concepts." It was designed to provide an opportunity for young readers to grow in reading experience while exploring a wide variety of ideas contained in the major academic disciplines.

Three basic underlying concepts are reflected in this book. They are: *Different patterns of life are found in the world; Different communities need and use different ways to reach the same goal;* and *Communities establish patterns of behavior.* The overriding concept in this book is ways in which things organize to allow for change. To illustrate these concepts, stories have been written around intriguing pieces of information that reflect these ideas. Content has been drawn from disciplines of art, history, biology, economics, ecology, engineering, sociology, anthropology, mathematics, and geography. In this way, a wide array of content for meeting various interests has been assured.

A narrative follows stories 24, 48, and 72. The narratives, largely drawn from folk literature, will provide a change of pace and are "just for fun" types of stories.

Teaching Procedure

Detailed suggestions for presenting the selections in this book will be found on pages 15 and 16 in the Teacher's Guide. Difficult words, with grade-level definitions, are listed by story on pages 6-12. Important content-area proper nouns not defined in the text are included in this listing.

Following each article is a test, which is especially designed to improve specific skills in reading. The test items were created to incorporate the thinking skills reflected in Benjamin S. Bloom's *Taxonomy of Educational Objectives*, which is explained on pages 6-7 in the Teacher's Guide.

Concept Recapitulations

After students have completed each of the three sections of this book, you may conduct a discussion to tie together the information carried in the individual articles in terms of the overall concept. Guiding questions are found on page 13 for Concept I, on page 65 for Concept II, and page 117 for Concept III.

Have a few priming possibilities ready to suggest, or shape them out of earlier offerings from the group. Sophisticated statements and a review of specifics are not to be expected. Look for signs of mental play and the movement of information from one setting to another. It is perfectly reasonable to conclude with unanswered questions for students to ponder in retrospect. However, it is important to give students the satisfaction of enthusiastic acceptance of their early attempts at this type of open-ended speculation.

STEPS FOR THE READER

A. Turn to page 14. Look at the picture. Read the title. Think about what the story will say.

B. Study the words for this page on the list beginning on page 6.

C. Read the story carefully.

D. Put your name and the title of the story on a sheet of paper.

Number from one to nine. Begin the test on the page next to the story.

1. This question asks you to remember something the story has told you. Which of the four choices is correct for this sentence?

2. The question asks you to find the word in the story that means the same as the words in italics. The question gives you a paragraph number. Read that part again to be sure you have the right word.

3. Reread the paragraph given. Which word is described by the words given in the question? The given words must modify or explain the noun you select.

4. This question wants you to think about the story. The answer is not in your book. Read the choices. Choose the one that is the very best guess you might make from the ideas you have just read.

5. The question tests your memory for a detail. Which of the choices agees with the story?

6. The question requires that you confirm whether or not an idea was actually presented in the story you have just read. If the sentence is wrong according to the information, you have just read, choose No. If the information was not given at all, be sure to answer *Does not say.*

7. The question asks you to choose a statement about the entire story. Don't select an idea that fits only one small part. Your answer should fit all of the story.

8. The story gives you the information you need. Refer to it again to be sure which of the given choices is the best explanation.

9. On the basis of the story, which of the choices is most likely to be

4

true? The answer is not in the story. You will have to think about the ideas and draw your own conclusions.

E. Check your work. The answers for the first test are given below. Your teacher may let you use the answer key for other tests.

F. Put the number correct at the top of your paper. Now go back and recheck the answers that were wrong. Do you see now how the correct answer was better? How can you get ready to do the next test better?

G. Turn to page 170. The directions tell you how to put your score onto a record chart. Your teacher will tell you if you may write in the book. If not, he or she will help you make a copy.

Looking for the Big Idea

The first 24 stories in this book lead you to see one big idea, which we call a concept. Before each group of 24 stories, there is an opening page. This page asks you a few questions to keep in mind as you read. Think about the way each story might be pointing out the big idea. Do you agree with the idea? Do you find places that suggest it could be wrong?

Just for Fun

Your book has three longer stories that are just for fun. These stories, beginning on pages 62, 114, and 166, are from old folktales. There are no questions to answer.

Answers for Practice Test, page 15

1. c	2. charge	3. Indian stirrup
4. b	5. d	6. No
7. b	8. a	9. b

5

Vocabulary Words and Definitions

PAGE 14
force power; strength
invention discovery of something
spears sticks with a sharp point at the end
stirrups parts of a horse's saddle that hold the rider's feet

PAGE 16
borrowed learned from
evergreens trees whose leaves stay green all year long
recent not many years ago
science studying or inventing new things
waterfall streams of water that fall from a higher place

PAGE 18
alphabet the letters of a language that make up words
alphabetic writing that uses letters instead of pictures
centuries one hundred years
easily not difficult; without any trouble
manner the way of doing something
traders people who buy and sell things
travels trips

PAGE 20
beetle a small insect or bug
dragonfly an insect with big wings
praying mantis an insect that puts its front legs together and looks like it is praying
scoop to pick up
stinger sharp part of an insect
stun to hurt and make sleepy
victims animals or people hurt by others
wasp an insect like a bee

PAGE 22
moss a plant that looks like very short grass
motions movements
sly smart and sneaky
spiders small animals with eight legs
webs homes that spiders make; webs look like lace

PAGE 24
echoes sounds that come back so you hear them again
ink-black very, very dark black
ledge a narrow piece of rock, like a shelf
oilbird a kind of bird that flies at night
owl-like like an owl, a bird that flies at night

PAGE 26
barter trading something you don't want to get something you do want
Congo a country in southern Africa
game animals used for food
goods and services things and help that you need to live
Mbuti (∂m bōōʹtē) native people of the Congo

PAGE 28
exporting selling things you make to people in other countries
famous well-known
grown got bigger; became an adult
importing buying things you need from other countries
industry business; making things
products things people or a country makes
steel-making putting iron together with other things to make the metal steel

PAGE 30
communities groups of people who live together
reservations places where Native Americans live together
themselves those people
travel moving from place to place
wealth riches; a lot of money or other things

PAGE 32
language the words people use to talk and write
photograph a picture taken with a camera
products items made by people
sandwich two pieces of bread with meat, cheese, or vegetables in between
smog a weather condition mostly found in cities, consisting of heavy smoke combined with fog in the air

6

PAGE 34

chat (shat) the French word for "cat"

example one of a group of things

per each one

probably likely but not for sure

spoken said out loud

syllables parts of a word; each syllable has a different sound

television a machine that shows pictures with sound

throughout in all places

vocabulary all the words of a language

PAGE 36

announcers people who tell what will happen

automobile car

freight car part of a train that carries things but not people

overpass a road that goes over another road

pronounce say

subway a train that travels under the ground

PAGE 38

colorful with a lot of different colors

curving rounded; not straight

decorate to make pictures on

decoration pictures

designs pictures

imaginations ideas and thoughts

Middle East part of the world that includes Iran, Iraq, and Arabia

Mohammed the Moslem God

palm tree with large leaves

PAGE 40

ceremonies things done on a special day; a wedding is a kind of ceremony, and so is a birthday party

cowhide the skin of a cow

materials things

medicine man a doctor who is also a priest

Southwest the part of the United States consisting of Texas, Oklahoma, New Mexico, and Arizona

watercolors paints made with water and dyes

PAGE 42

cedar a kind of tree

dugout canoes boats made by digging out the inside of a tree trunk

objects small things

totem pole a tall piece of wood that has animals and faces carved in it

PAGE 44

canvas a kind of cloth that artists paint pictures on

complicated not simple; with many parts

customs ways of doing things

professional doing work you get paid for

routes ways to get from one place to another

settlement a place where people live

style the way something looks

PAGE 46

materials things needed to do something

medical center a hospital; place where sick people go to get better

stadium a place where teams play sports

turban a scarf wound around the head

PAGE 48

celebrating having a party

festive very happy; like a party

treasure to make special; to remember

PAGE 50

archeologists scientists who dig up and study the remains of people and places from long ago

chemicals natural and man-made things, like sugar, salt, air, water; everything is made of chemicals

coffin a box to bury someone in

decaying rotting; falling apart

moisture water

mummies bodies of dead people that have not decayed

Osiris (ō sī´rəs) Egyptian god of the underworld, where people went after death

preserved kept in one piece; not falling apart

tomb (tüm) place where dead people are buried

underworld place where Egyptians believed people went after death

PAGE 52
diseases sicknesses
jungles hot, wet places with lots of plants and trees and animals
malaria a disease spread by mosquito bites
mosquitoes insects that sting; some insects carry diseases
shortcut a shorter way to get from one place to another

PAGE 54
approaching getting closer to
state a part of a country
towers tall buildings

PAGE 56
ancestors people who lived long ago
decide choose to do something
reborn born again
secret not told to anyone else
sneeze to blow air out of the nose
spirits the souls of dead people

PAGE 58
appointment a date to meet someone
exact correct
programs music or talk shows

PAGE 60
almonds nuts
dragon a make-believe animal like a giant lizard with fire coming out of its nose
fireworks exploding colors in the sky
harvest moon a full moon in September
reunions parties of family members from far away
pastries cookies and cakes
traditional the way things were done in the past

PAGES 62–64
chariot a cart with wheels pulled by animals
fierce powerful and angry
ointment a cream that is rubbed on the skin
sacred very important to a religion
succeed to do something correctly
warriors fighters; army

PAGE 66
abacus a Chinese tool for adding numbers
accurately correctly; all right
East Asia; China, Japan and other countries
engineers people who build things
marketplaces places where things are bought and sold; malls
merchants people who sell things
monuments buildings and statues to honor important people

PAGE 68
architect someone who decides how houses and buildings will look
depth distance
Middle Ages the years from A.D. 500 to 1500
overlapped one on top of the other
realistic lifelike; the way things really are
Renaissance the years from 1300 to 1600, when there was a lot of art in Europe
stylized shapes and colors that don't look like real things
technique a way of drawing or painting

PAGE 70
container a can or box to hold something
corked put a top on a bottle
gases not liquids or solids; air is a gas
germs things that make people sick
Napoleon a ruler of France many years ago
soldering using melted metal to seal a can
spoil rot; go bad

PAGE 72
female girl
stickleback a kind of fish
wolves wild animals that are related to dogs

PAGE 74
badgers small, furry animals
chimpanzees small monkeys
chorus singing together
howl to yell loudly
otters furry animals that live in the water and like to play
rhythm a beat, as in music
sundown late afternoon when the sun sets

8

PAGE 76
flocks groups of birds
rattling a sound like marbles in a tin can

PAGE 78
generations many years
livestock animals raised on a farm
plot a small piece of land
supplies provides; grows
wealthy rich

PAGE 80
climate weather; how cold or hot and how wet or dry a place is
inland away from the ocean
pioneers the first people to live somewhere
rangeland large areas of land where cows and other animals live
regions areas of a country
similar a lot alike
temperatures how hot or cold it is

PAGE 82
operates works
scientific using science or facts
whereas but; on the other hand

PAGE 84
although no matter that; even though
code pictures or symbols that stand for letters
imagine pretend
injured hurt
invented made up; was the first to think of
inventor someone who invents things
struck hit
workshop place where things are made

PAGE 86
communicate to share ideas
forefinger the finger next to the thumb
movements actions of the body

PAGE 88
characters pictures that stand for words
difficult hard; not easy

PAGE 90
beaded with small balls attached
flutes hollow tubes with holes in them that you blow into to make music
headdresses big hats
pretend make believe
statues stones, wood, or metal in the shape of people

PAGE 92
instruments things that people use to make music; pianos and drums are instruments
musical like music; with a pretty sound
popular well liked
reed a plant with a long, hollow stem
strum to move the fingers over strings on an instrument

PAGE 94
ability knowing how to do something
actors people who pretend to be other people in plays
eyebrows the hair above the eyes
perform act; pretend to be someone else
wigs make-believe hair

PAGE 96
birch a kind of tree
furnace an oven that heats a room
perspire to sweat
relax to sit down and rest
sauna a room full of hot steam

PAGE 98
air-conditioned cooled with cold air
midday noon; 12 o'clock
restaurant a place that serves food

PAGE 100
aside apart
geysers hot air and water that shoot up from deep in the Earth
hike to take a long walk
Northwest part of the United States that contains Idaho, Wyoming, and Montana

9

PAGE 102
account (takes into) thinks about
apply use; put on
data facts; information
ensure make sure that something happens
fertilizers chemicals put on plants to make them grow better

PAGE 104
cartons boxes
electric using electricity
gallons amounts equal to four quarts

PAGE 106
adults grown-ups
habitat a place in nature where animals live
medicine something that cures disease
territory an area owned or used by a group of people or animals

PAGE 108
bank accounts money in a bank that belongs to different people
bonds promises to pay back loans, plus extra money
businesses stores and other places that do work to earn money
convince to make someone agree with you
interest the extra money you get back when you make a loan
invest to buy part of a company
loans money given to someone for a short time; they must return it, plus extra money
producers people who make things
profit earning more money than is spent
stock a piece of paper that says you own part of a company

PAGE 110
exhaust (ig zôst´) blow out smoke
fumes (fyümz) smoke that smells bad and makes people sick
pollution dirt in the air or in water
U.S. Congress a group of people who are elected to make laws
waste garbage; trash; things people throw out

PAGE 112
entire whole; all of
ourselves us
scars marks left by cuts

PAGES 114–116
gobbled ate very quickly
parrot a big bird with colorful feathers
polite use good manners
raisins small, sweet fruits
sidewise not straight ahead

PAGE 118
castes classes of people showing how important they are
create make; bring about
religious believing in God

PAGE 120
afford have enough money
collects gets; takes
Colonial the early days of the United States, the 1600s and 1700s
education learning; going to school
property what you own or what belongs to you
usually most of the time

PAGE 122
boundary where one person's land ends and another person's land begins
crime an act that breaks the law
earliest times very long ago
guilty committed a crime; did something wrong
jury people who decide if someone broke a law
thief (thēf) someone who steals; robber
trial test to decide if someone has committed a crime
witnesses people who saw what happened or know the facts

PAGE 124
females women or girls
social friendly; like to be with others
termites insects that eat wood
wasp a stinging flying insect

10

PAGE 126
defended made safe from enemies
selected chosen; decided to live in
supply amount; how many

PAGE 128
carefully paying close attention
contest game to see who is stronger
perch place to sit
whatever of any kind at all

PAGE 130
craft job; what someone does for a living
guilds (gildz) groups of people who do the same
     work; labor unions
labor work
makers people who make something
skilled able to do something very well
unions groups of people who do the same work

PAGE 132
chained tied to with metal ropes
cruel very mean
factories buildings where things are made or
     produced
government the people who make the laws

PAGE 134
band to come together as a group
conditions how people are treated
demand insist; say you must have

PAGE 136
concerned worried; unhappy
control keep order; make students behave
disciplines school subjects
license permission to do something, such as
     teach or drive a car
pranks silly jokes

PAGE 138
automatic done by a machine, not by people
customers people who do business with a bank
identification something that tells who someone
     is; a name is a kind of identification
signatures names written in script
tellers people who work in banks

PAGE 140
forum a place where people talk to each other
status importance; power

PAGE 142
remind make you think of or remember
     something
Southwest area of the United States that
     includes Arizona and New Mexico

PAGE 144
capital the most important city
collection a lot of the same thing
colony a place that doesn't have its own govern-
     ment and is ruled by a nation far away
governor a person elected to be in charge of an
     area
lawmakers people who decide what laws you
     must obey
museum a building that contains art or other
     things; museums are open to the public
Rockefeller, John D., Jr. a very rich
     businessman

PAGE 146
midwestern a town in the middle of the
     United States
New England states in the northeastern
     United States
sheriff a person who makes sure that people
     obey the laws
someday at some time in the future
study learn about
studios places where movies are made

PAGE 148
Lake Erie a lake between Canada and New York
     and Pennsylvania
sources beginnings; where things come from

PAGE 150
creations things people make
dyed changed the color
elaborate very fancy
featuring showing off
literally really; in fact

PAGE 150 continued

noblemen important people, such as kings and princes

pageboy a hairstyle that is shoulder-length and curled under, sometimes with bangs on the forehead

Roman Empire all the countries ruled by Rome, Italy, two thousand years ago

upper-class rich and important people

variety differences

PAGE 152

adopt take care of

careless not paying attention

credit thanks

Department of Transportation part of a state or national government that deals with roads, trains, planes, etc.

highway a large road

public-spirited caring about other people

recognition praise

sponsor pay people to do something

trash garbage; things people don't want and throw away

PAGE 154

designated certain places decided in advance

electronically through computers

instantly right now; without waiting

post letters sent by mail

relays people taking turns

satellite TV the way worldwide television receives signals, through orbiting manmade space objects

PAGE 156

Bolivia a country in central South America

model copy

mold shape with the hands

sculptors people who make things out of stone or clay

wander walk all around

PAGE 158

electricity power to make machines work

invisible cannot be seen with the eyes

PAGE 158 continued

Newfoundland Canada's easternmost province

receive hear from far away

signals sounds

wireless without electric wires

PAGE 160

Africa the continent south of Europe

differently in another way

Eskimos group of native people who live in Canada and Alaska; Eskimos are also called Inuit

evil bad

misfortune bad luck

polar living near the North Pole

spirit ghost

PAGE 162

castle a big stone house

fuss trouble

hereby now

knights men from long ago who fought; armies

serious important

squire an important person in England

PAGE 164

community people living together

host a person who has guests

invited asked to join

manners ways of behaving

PAGES 166–169

awoke stopped sleeping

dragging pulling behind

stupid not smart

wrestler a person who fights without hitting

12

I

Different Patterns of Life Are Found in the World

In this section, you will read about new and different patterns of life that are found in the world. You will read about these things from the standpoint of history, biology, economics, sociology, art, geography, engineering, and anthropology.

Keep these questions in mind when you are reading.

1. How does life in the United States differ from life in Europe?

2. How do different life patterns affect people in our country?

3. Do these differences affect you?

4. Do our life patterns affect people in other countries?

5. Is it good that there are differences in life patterns?

Look on pages 6-8 for help with words in this section you don't understand

Soldiers in Stirrups

1   A long time ago, soldiers fought wars on foot. Then they began to ride horses to battle. Until the invention of the stirrup, though, men could not fight well with swords or spears while on horseback.

2   Without stirrups, soldiers had no place to put their feet. They could not stand up to use their swords without falling off their horses. They could throw spears only with the force of their arms.

3   Using stirrups, a soldier could stand up in his saddle. He could put a spear under the top part of his arm and charge with the force of his horse. He could use force when fighting with a sword. And he could win most fights against soldiers who did not use stirrups.

4   The first stirrups were made in India. Because the weather was warm, people did not wear shoes. The Indian stirrup was made of rope. It fit around the big toes. Later, the Chinese made a foot stirrup of wood. Because the Chinese lived in a colder country, the stirrup had to fit around shoes. Still later, around A.D. 700, soldiers in Asia used strong iron foot stirrups.

14

FIND THE ANSWERS

1. Stirrups were first made in
   - a. China.　　　　　　　　c. India.
   - b. Japan.　　　　　　　　d. Korea.

2. The word in paragraph 3 that means *to attack* or *to rush into battle*

   is _____ .

3. The words "made of rope" in paragraph 4 tell about the

   _____ _____ .

4. The story does not say so, but it makes you think that stirrups were invented before
   - a. saddles.　b. guns.　c. rope.

5. Around A.D. 700, the soldiers in Asia used stirrups made of
   - a. wood.　　　　　　　　c. shoes.
   - b. rope.　　　　　　　　d. iron.

6. Wars were first fought on horseback.
   - Yes　　　　　　No　　　　　　Does not say

7. On the whole, this story is about
   - a. the soldiers in warm and cold countries.
   - b. an invention that changed man's way of fighting wars.
   - c. how to throw a spear.

8. How did the stirrup help soldiers fight better? (Check the story again.)
   - a. They could now stand in their saddles to throw spears.
   - b. They looked better when they were using stirrups.
   - c. Horses were safer.

9. Which of these sentences do you think is right?
   - a. There were no wars 2,000 years ago.
   - b. Men were fighting 2,000 years ago.
   - c. War is something new.

A Different Kind of Beauty

1   Japan is made up of a chain of islands that lie off the coast of Asia. People came to live in Japan from the nearby countries of China and Korea. From these older countries, the Japanese borrowed ideas, inventions, and habits.

2   For many years, the Japanese built buildings like those in China. They dressed like the Chinese. From China came their way of writing and their habit of drinking tea.

3   In more recent times, the Japanese have borrowed from the United States. They have a government like ours. They do much work in science, as we do. Baseball is a favorite sport in Japan, just as it is here.

4   Things change when they come to Japan. The Japanese improve on almost everything they borrow. The art of garden-making came from Korea or China, but Japanese gardens are special. Each garden has a waterfall, a pond, and small bridges. There are few flowers in Japanese gardens. But the gardens are green during all seasons because they have many evergreens. Japanese gardens have a different kind of beauty.

16

FIND THE ANSWERS

1. The Japanese borrowed ideas from
   - a. South America.
   - b. Canada.
   - c. England.
   - d. China.

2. The word in paragraph 4 that means *to make better* is

   _____.

3. The words "green during all seasons" in paragraph 4 describe the

   _____ _____.

4. The story does not say so, but it makes you think that
   - a. Japanese gardens are different from Chinese gardens.
   - b. Japan is older than China.
   - c. the Japanese cannot grow crops because their soil is poor.

5. Each Japanese garden has
   - a. many flowers.
   - b. few evergreens.
   - c. a pond.
   - d. vegetables.

6. Things change when they come to Japan.

   Yes   No   Does not say

7. On the whole, this story is about
   - a. the Japanese.   b. tea.   c. clothing.

8. Why do the Japanese change the things that they borrow? (Check the story again.)
   - a. They don't like them the way they are.
   - b. They try to make them better.
   - c. They want visitors to like their changes.

9. Which of these sentences do you think is right?
   - a. There are few gardens in Japan.
   - b. Peoples from many countries came to live in Japan.
   - c. The Japanese invented the habit of drinking tea.

17

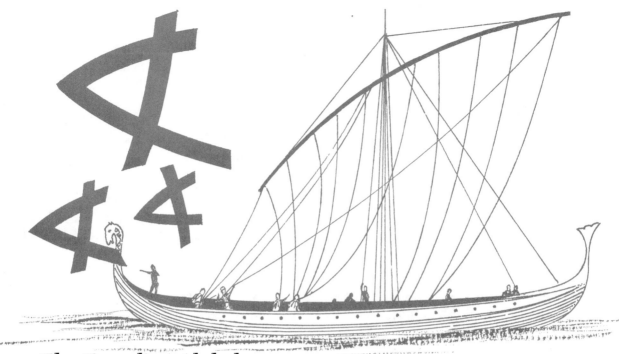

The Traveling Alphabet

1   Three thousand years ago, Phoenicia (fə nish′ ə) was one of the small countries along the Mediterranean Sea. The Phoenicians were sailors and traders who rowed in large sailboats to countries along the Mediterranean.

2   They traded goods with other countries. They also traded ideas with the people they met. In their travels, the Phoenicians came across a people who used an alphabet. Alphabetic writing has a letter for each sound.

3   In those days, most writing was made up of signs. The signs stood for whole words. It was hard to remember and to write so many words. The Phoenicians needed a good way to keep business records. With the letters of an alphabet, the Phoenicians could write any word they wanted. They could keep records more easily with the help of their borrowed alphabet.

4   As the Phoenician traders went from country to country, the alphabet traveled with them. Other people liked the idea of using letters, too. Many began to use the same way of writing.

5   In this manner, the alphabet spread to many lands. The letters were changed slowly over the centuries. But the alphabet we use today comes from the one used by the Phoenicians long ago.

18

FIND THE ANSWERS

1. The Phoenician traders traveled in
   a. rowboats.   c. sailboats.
   b. steamboats.   d. clipper ships.

2. The word in paragraph 5 that means *way* or *method* is

   _____.

3. The words "made up of signs" in paragraph 3 describe the word

   _____.

4. The story does not say so, but it makes you think that the Phoenicians
   a. borrowed records.
   b. were good businessmen.
   c. lived on an island.

5. Alphabetic writing uses
   a. letters.   c. ideas.
   b. signs.   d. boats.

6. The Phoenicians learned about an alphabet during their travels.
   Yes   No   Does not say

7. On the whole, this story is about
   a. sailors.   b. Phoenicia.   c. an alphabet.

8. Why did the Phoenicians start using an alphabet? (Check the story again.)
   a. They did not know how to make signs.
   b. They wanted a better way to keep records.
   c. They wanted to trade it for valuable goods.

9. Which of these sentences do you think is right?
   a. An alphabet made writing easier and quicker.
   b. The Phoenicians rowed their boats around the world.
   c. The sea was not important to the Phoenicians.

19

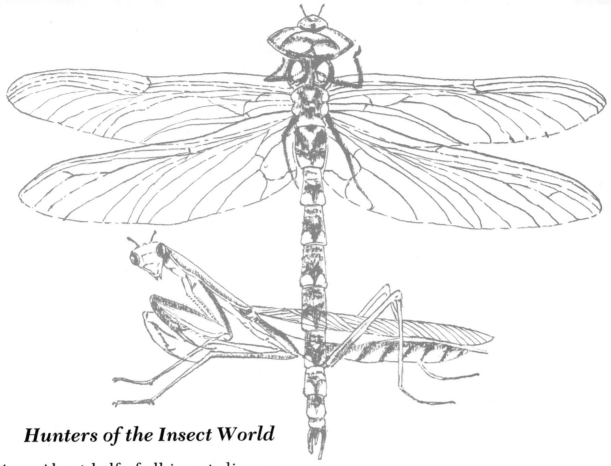

Hunters of the Insect World

1   About half of all insects live on plants. The rest catch and kill other insects for food. They are the hunters of the insect world.

2   Each kind of hunter insect has a weapon. The dragonfly uses its legs as a basket to scoop up other insects. The sand wasp has a stinger it uses to stun its victims.

3   Some hunter insects set traps. The tiger beetle digs a small hole and gets in. Only its head is at the top of the hole. The tiger beetle can pop its head out like a jack-in-the-box. It catches its victims by surprise.

4   The ant lion digs a hole in the sand and waits at the bottom. When an ant or other insect gets near the hole, the sand gives way. The victim slides down into the jaws of the waiting ant lion.

5   The praying mantis is a large insect that looks as if it has arms. Its "arms" are really legs, but they are not used for walking. They are used to grab and hold its victims.

6   We fight to keep down the number of insects that eat our food. Can you see how hunter insects help people?

FIND THE ANSWERS

1. Each kind of hunter insect
   - a. picks a leader.
   - b. has a weapon.
   - c. eats plants.
   - d. has a basket.

2. The word in paragraph 2 that means *to make helpless* is

   _____.

3. The words "looks as if it has arms" in paragraph 5 refer to the

   _____ _____.

4. The story does not say so, but it makes you think that hunter insects
   - a. eat our food.
   - b. are dangerous to people and animals.
   - c. catch insects that damage crops.

5. The dragonfly uses its legs to
   - a. scoop up insects.
   - b. grab insects.
   - c. stab insects.
   - d. sting insects.

6. The tiger beetle is gold with black stripes.
   - Yes   No   Does not say

7. On the whole, this story is about
   - a. insects that use stingers.
   - b. insects that hunt other insects.
   - c. ants and lions.

8. What is meant by the sentence, "The tiger beetle can pop its head out like a jack-in-the-box"?
   - a. The tiger beetle makes noises.
   - b. The tiger beetle moves quickly.
   - c. The tiger beetle is funny.

9. Which of these sentences do you think is right?
   - a. About half of all insects are hunter insects.
   - b. People fight the hunter insects.
   - c. All hunter insects dig holes to trap their victims.

A Spider Without a Web

1   Most spiders build webs to trap other insects. But the trap-door spider has another way of hunting. First, she digs a hole about ten inches deep and an inch and a half wide. Next, she makes a lid of dirt and webbing. This trap door must fit over the upper end of the hole like a cork fits in a bottle.

2   Finally, the spider hides her nest by spreading dirt over the lid. Then the trap door looks like the earth around it. Sometimes she even plants moss on top. She is as sly as a fox.

3   The trap-door spider hunts at night. For hours, she stays hidden right below her door. She holds it open just a crack as she waits for insects.

4   When something comes near her door, she can sense the motions above her nest. She pushes the lid open quickly. But the trap door is so strong that she could be locked out. So she leaves her hind legs and a part of her body under the open lid. Then the spider grabs the surprised insect in her jaws. Down they go into her nest! The trap-door spider does not need a web.

FIND THE ANSWERS

1. A spider that does not build a web to catch its food is the
   a. garden spider.   c. trap-door spider.
   b. wolf spider.   d. lace spider.

2. The word in paragraph 2 that means *tiny green plants* is

   _____.

3. The words "a lid of dirt and webbing" in paragraph 1 refer to the

   _____.

4. The story does not say so, but it makes you think that the trap-door spider
   a. plants a small garden.
   b. eats other insects for food.
   c. leaves the nest at night.

5. The trap-door spider hunts
   a. after dark.   c. when the moon is out.
   b. during the day.   d. in the winter.

6. The trap door is so strong that it could lock the spider out.
   Yes   No   Does not say

7. On the whole, this story is about
   a. spiders that build webs.
   b. materials that spiders use to hunt.
   c. spiders that do not build webs.

8. What is meant by the sentence, "She is as sly as a fox"?
   a. The trap-door spider is tricky.
   b. The trap-door spider is playful.
   c. The trap-door spider is brown.

9. Which of these sentences do you think is right?
   a. The trap-door spider is afraid to leave its nest.
   b. The spider builds a nest to keep out other insects.
   c. The trap-door spider moves quickly when hunting.

23

Birds That "See" with Their Ears

1   Most birds live in places where it is light during the day. They can use their eyes to see where they are going. The oilbirds of South America live in dark caves. They use their ears to help them find their way.

2   The oilbird is a brown bird with owl-like eyes. It nests on a high ledge in an ink-black cave. It only leaves the cave at night to hunt for food and returns before dawn.

3   The oilbird flies in circles in its dark cave. There is not enough light for it to see clearly with its large eyes. As the oilbird flies, it uses its voice to make sharp, clicking sounds. These clicks bounce off the cave walls and become echoes.

4   The oilbird listens to the echoes it has made. If the echoes take a long time to come back, the bird knows it is far from the wall. If they return quickly, the bird is close to it. In this way, the oilbird hears how far it is from the wall.

5   Oilbirds spend their lives in the dark, yet they never bump into the walls of their cave homes. We say that oilbirds "see" with their ears.

24

FIND THE ANSWERS

1. Oilbirds live
   - a. on mountain tops.
   - b. in dark caves.
   - c. on the ground.
   - d. in nests in trees.

2. The word in paragraph 2 that means *a shelf* or *a ridge of rock* is

   _____.

3. The words "owl-like" in paragraph 2 describe the oilbird's

   _____.

4. The story does not say so, but it makes you think that
   - a. oilbirds do not like light.
   - b. oilbirds are blind.
   - c. most birds sing only in the dark.

5. Oilbirds leave their caves at night to
   - a. exercise.
   - b. play.
   - c. hunt for food.
   - d. see their friends.

6. Oilbirds make clicking sounds that become echoes.

   Yes   No   Does not say

7. On the whole, this story is about
   - a. echoes that are heard in caves.
   - b. owls that live in the dark.
   - c. the oilbirds of South America.

8. How do the clicking sounds help an oilbird inside a cave? (Check the story again.)
   - a. They are signals to other birds.
   - b. They become echoes that help it find its way.
   - c. They mean the bird is getting ready to eat.

9. Which of these sentences do you think is right?
   - a. Oilbirds have good hearing.
   - b. Oilbirds live near oil wells.
   - c. Oilbirds often bump into the cave walls.

One Way of Doing Business

1   The Mbuti people of Congo live deep in an African forest. The forest takes care of most of their needs. The men hunt for game that lives in the forest. The game there is different from what you would find in American forests, including such animals as elephants and monkeys. The women gather plants and nuts and also catch insects and fish.

2   The Mbuti also need things that they cannot find in the forest. To get these things, they trade with farmers who live in villages just beyond the forest. They give the farmers meat, and in exchange the farmers give the Mbuti crops, tools, and cloth.

3   Before the invention of money, people received goods and services by trading in this way. Such trading is called barter. Even though we have money, we still sometimes use barter. When you trade baseball cards with a friend, you are bartering. You are also bartering if you offer to let your brother play your CDs, if he takes your turn washing the dishes. Of course, we mostly use money to get the things we need. The Mbuti, on the other hand, must barter for things they cannot find in their forest.

26

FIND THE ANSWERS

1. The Mbuti trade with farmers to get
   - a. barter.
   - b. monkeys.
   - c. cloth.
   - d. CDs.

2. The word in paragraph 1 that means *animals people hunt for* is

   _____.

3. The words "who live in villages" in paragraph 2 refer to

   _____.

4. The story does not say so, but it makes you think that
   - a. the Mbuti don't have money.
   - b. the Mbuti hunt for deer.
   - c. the Mbuti don't get along with their neighbors.

5. People who trade baseball cards
   - a. don't have any money.
   - b. live like the Mbuti.
   - c. are being stingy.
   - d. are bartering.

6. The Mbuti eat insects.

   Yes   No   Does not say

7. On the whole, this story is about
   - a. how the Mbuti get the things they need.
   - b. the animals that live in the African forest.
   - c. everyday life in the Congo.

8. Why do the Mbuti barter with farmers? (Check the story again.)
   - a. They cannot get everything they need in the forest.
   - b. The farmers don't know how to hunt.
   - c. They like to have a reason to get together with their neighbors.

9. Which of these sentences do you think is right?
   - a. Everybody in Congo gets the things they need by bartering.
   - b. The Mbuti don't do any farming.
   - c. Americans usually barter for what they want.

Business Between Countries

1   People within a country do business together. They buy goods, or products, from one another and sell products to others.

2   Different countries do business together, too. One country may buy and bring in things from another country. This is called importing products. The same country may also sell and send things to another country. This is called exporting products.

3   The Netherlands is a small country better known to us as Holland. It lies in the low country of Europe on the North Sea.

4   Holland has a steel-making industry which needs iron. This ore is found in some parts of the world, but Holland has none. The little country must import it. Ships carry the ore to the Netherlands from places like Canada and Africa.

5   Holland grows millions of flower bulbs every year. The country is famous for the beautiful tulips grown from these bulbs. Large numbers of tulip bulbs are dug up, dried, and exported to many countries.

6   Do you have tulips growing in your garden? Perhaps they are growing from bulbs brought from Holland.

28

FIND THE ANSWERS

1. Holland is a small country on the
   a. Pacific Ocean.
   b. North Sea.
   c. Atlantic Ocean.
   d. Mediterranean Sea.

2. The words "sell and send things to another country" in paragraph 2 explain the word _____.

3. The words "this ore" in paragraph 4 refer to the word

   _____.

4. The story does not say so, but it makes you think that
   a. Holland is much smaller than the United States.
   b. Holland is one of the largest countries in Asia.
   c. Holland does not have any industry.

5. Every year Holland grows millions of
   a. trees.
   b. vegetables.
   c. grains.
   d. flower bulbs.

6. Holland imports iron ore from the United States.
   Yes   No   Does not say

7. On the whole, this story is about
   a. tulips.
   b. importing and exporting.
   c. the low countries in Europe.

8. Why does Holland import some things? (Check the story again.)
   a. The people there like to trade things.
   b. Holland needs some things from other countries.
   c. There are not enough people in Holland who like tulips.

9. Which of these sentences do you think is right?
   a. Holland depends on other countries to keep its industry going.
   b. Holland does not trade with other countries.
   c. Holland is a large country with many natural resources.

Animals Mean Wealth

1   Different things are important in different communities. What a community thinks is important can change the way it lives and carries on its business.

2   The Navaho Indians live on large reservations in Arizona, New Mexico, and Utah. They raise sheep and horses as a business. The animals feed on grass growing on Navaho land.

3   The Navaho got sheep and horses from the Spaniards in the 1600s. Later, the sheep and horses became important to the Navaho for wool, meat, and travel. But the animals were also a sign of wealth. A family with many sheep or horses was important in the community.

4   At one time, the Navaho had more than a million animals. But the sheep were eating the grass down to the ground. Each horse ate more grass than five sheep. Even the roots of the grass were dying, and the ground was beginning to wash away in the rain. There were too many animals. Without grass to eat, the animals would die. The Navaho themselves would not have enough food.

5   The government wanted to help. It asked the Navaho to make their herds smaller. It was a sad time for the people. Large herds were very important to them.

30

FIND THE ANSWERS

1. The Navaho Indians live in
   - a. Mexico.
   - b. California.
   - c. Arizona.
   - d. Colorado.

2. The word in paragraph 2 that means *places where Native Americans live* is

   _____.

3. The words "were eating the grass down to the ground" in paragraph 4 tell about the word _____.

4. The story does not say so, but it makes you think that
   - a. the Navaho need more animals.
   - b. too many animals can kill the grass.
   - c. the Navaho grow many crops.

5. The Navaho Indians raise
   - a. pigs and chickens.
   - b. corn and wheat.
   - c. cows and goats.
   - d. sheep and horses.

6. The Navaho raise sheep just for food.
   Yes   No   Does not say

7. On the whole, this story is about
   - a. the government in Mexico.
   - b. the Navaho and their animals.
   - c. Native American reservations.

8. Why did the Navaho want to keep large herds of animals? (Check the story again.)
   - a. Large herds were important to the Navaho.
   - b. The Navaho eat a lot.
   - c. The Navaho need the hides of the animals for clothing.

9. Which of these sentences do you think is right?
   - a. The Navaho were running out of food for their animals.
   - b. The Navaho did not have enough animals.
   - c. The Navaho liked small herds of animals.

31

A Changing Language

1 The English language is different from any other language. Yet, like most other languages, ours is always changing. We need new words for new inventions and new ideas. Different words come into use, or older words are used in a new way.

2 English can change by borrowing words from other languages. *Tomato* was borrowed from Mexico and *pajamas* from India. The word *coffee* came from Turkey, and *tea* came from China. Now new space and science words are being borrowed from other countries, too.

3 New words are also made by adding two words together. *Strawberry, popcorn,* and *grandfather* are words made up of two parts.

4 Sometimes new words are shorter forms of older words. The word *photo* was made from *photograph* by cutting off the end of the longer word. *Plane* was made by cutting off the front part of *airplane. Smog* was made by using only the first two and last two letters from the words *smoke* and *fog.*

5 The names of people and products can become new words. Our *sandwich* was named after a man named Sandwich. Scotch Tape, Band-Aid, and Jell-O were names made up by the companies that first made the products.

32

FIND THE ANSWERS

1. The English language needs new words for new
   a. books and magazines.
   b. movies and TV plays.
   c. inventions and ideas.
   d. stories and fairy tales.

2. The word in paragraph 2 that means *taking* or *using as one's own* is

   _____.

3. The words "always changing" in paragraph 1 refer to our

   _____.

4. The story does not say so, but it makes you think that
   a. all new words are borrowed.
   b. languages do not stay the same.
   c. all new words come from company names.

5. Scotch tape was named by
   a. a Scotchman.
   b. a country.
   c. a child.
   d. a company.

6. Other languages borrow words from English.
   Yes   No   Does not say

7. On the whole, this story is about
   a. borrowing other languages.
   b. the English language.
   c. naming new products.

8. Why is the English language always changing? (Check the story again.)
   a. People get tired of using the same words.
   b. We need new words for new inventions and ideas.
   c. English must become more like French and German.

9. Which of these sentences do you think is right?
   a. New words come about in different ways.
   b. There are no new words in our language.
   c. People in space talk a different language.

chat **cat** fatze

Thousands of Sounds

1   Most people in our country speak English. In some lands, people speak other languages. There are over 2,000 languages spoken throughout the world.

2   You probably know that every language has its own words, or vocabulary. If you want to learn a foreign language, you must learn its vocabulary. For example, our word "cat" is *chat* (shä) in French and *Katze* (kät′ zə) in German.

3   You must learn what the words mean, and you must say them in the right way. Words are made up of sounds, and different languages have different sounds. There are thousands of language sounds. When you speak English, you are using only about fifty of them.

4   Have you ever heard a foreign language spoken on television? Did it sound as if it was spoken very fast? Maybe it was. Some languages are spoken faster than others. English is spoken more slowly than French. French people speak about 350 syllables per minute. Using English, we speak 220. But some South Seas peoples speak only fifty syllables per minute.

5   Women speak faster than men. In America, women speak about 175 words per minute, but men speak only 150. How many words per minute do you speak?

34

FIND THE ANSWERS

1. The main language spoken in the United States is
   a. French.
   b. German.
   c. foreign.
   d. English.

2. The word in paragraph 2 that means *something from another country* is _____.

3. The words "speak faster than men" in paragraph 5 refer to the word _____.

4. The story does not say so, but it makes you think that
   a. learning another language takes time.
   b. all languages use the same sounds.
   c. most people in the world speak English.

5. Words are made up of
   a. language.
   b. English.
   c. sounds.
   d. pictures.

6. There is a word for "cat" in French.
   Yes   No   Does not say

7. On the whole, this story is about
   a. how fast people talk.
   b. traveling in foreign countries.
   c. the many sounds of many languages.

8. What must you do if you want to learn a foreign language? (Check the story again.)
   a. You must learn its vocabulary.
   b. You must live in the foreign country.
   c. You must learn to speak French first.

9. Which of these sentences do you think is right?
   a. Men speak faster than women.
   b. All foreign languages are spoken faster than English.
   c. English is only one of many languages.

English Can Be Strange

1   Have you ever heard someone speak in a language that you couldn't understand? Perhaps it was French. But it could have been English!

2   At times, English can sound as different as another language. It is spoken by one out of ten people in the world. Yet there are many differences between the "Queen's English" and American English.

3   In England, the Queen's English is the way radio and TV announcers say words. It is thought to be the most correct way to pronounce words. When the doctor asks you to say "ah," you are using the sound that the English use in

the words *bath* and *dance.*

4   Words can have different meanings, too. English children go to a "sweets shop." American children would visit a candy store. They watch the "telly." Americans watch TV. The English go to "flicks," while we go to movies.

5   Railroad tracks are "metals." A freight car is a "goods wagon." They call the subway the "underground." A "flyover" is our overpass. They call an automobile hood a "bonnet." Our car trunk is a "boot" to them, and our horn is a "hooter."

6   If you went to England, could you understand the language?

FIND THE ANSWERS

1. In England, the "Queen's English" is spoken by all
   a. Americans.
   b. announcers.
   c. people.
   d. children.

2. The word in paragraph 3 that means *to speak* or *to say* is

   _____ .

3. The words "can sound as different as another language" in paragraph

   2 refer to the word _____ .

4. The story does not say so, but it makes you think that
   a. people watch television in both England and America.
   b. English children never eat candy.
   c. the same language always sounds the same.

5. The Americans call them movies, but the English call them
   a. metals.   b. sweets   c. goods wagons.   d. flicks.

6. English is spoken by three out of ten people in the world.
   Yes   No   Does not say

7. On the whole, this story is about
   a. going to see an English doctor.
   b. American and English television programs and movies.
   c. differences between American and English speech.

8. Why might an American have trouble understanding the English?
   (Check the story again.)
   a. Some of the words the English use are different.
   b. The English speak a foreign language.
   c. The people in England speak only to their Queen.

9. Which of these sentences do you think is right?
   a. The English do not have cars or television sets.
   b. The English and the Americans cannot understand one another.
   c. The "Queen's English" would be easier to understand than
      French.

Artists Who Didn't Draw People

1   Moslems (moz' ləmz) are people who believe in the teachings of a man called Mohammed. Mohammed lived in the 600s. One of the things he said was that no one should make copies of living things.

2   In the 600s and 700s, the Moslems took over the Middle East. The artists of the Middle East had to follow the laws of Mohammed. For many years, they could not copy living figures. They could not draw people.

3   Do you wonder what the Moslem artists did? They used their imaginations to make many beautiful and colorful designs. To make designs, they often used the shapes of flowers. Sometimes they used the curving lines of vines and palm leaves.

4   The Moslem artists used designs to decorate many different things. They decorated the walls of buildings and the pages of books. Decoration became the most important part of Moslem art.

5   After a while, some Moslem artists could paint pictures with people in them. In Persia in the 1400s, the artists made beautiful paintings for books. Even then, decoration still filled the pictures. The people in the pictures looked strange. They looked as if they were living in a dream world.

38

FIND THE ANSWERS

1. People who believe in the teachings of Mohammed are called
   - a. artists.
   - b. Americans.
   - c. Moslems.
   - d. Persians.

2. The word in paragraph 3 that means *forms* or *outlines* is

   _____.

3. The words "beautiful and colorful" in paragraph 3 refer to the word

   _____.

4. The story does not say so, but it makes you think that
   - a. artists of the Middle East could not paint.
   - b. Moslem artists drew pictures using only straight lines.
   - c. Moslem artists used curving lines to make designs.

5. For many years, Moslem artists could not draw
   - a. figures.
   - b. lines.
   - c. buildings.
   - d. mountains.

6. Decoration became the most important part of Moslem art.
   Yes   No   Does not say

7. On the whole, this story is about
   - a. Moslem artists. b. Persia. c. a dream world.

8. What is meant by the sentence, "The people looked as if they were living in a dream world"?
   - a. The people did not seem to be real.
   - b. The people were dreaming about another world.
   - c. The people were asleep.

9. Which of these sentences do you think is right?
   - a. Art in the Middle East changed after the Moslems took over.
   - b. The artists of the Middle East would not obey the Moslems.
   - c. Moslem artists painted with palm leaves.

Paintings from the Earth

1   Have you ever used watercolors to make a picture? Have you made designs with finger paints? Many pictures are made by putting colored paint on paper or cloth. Pictures painted in this way will last a long time.

2   The Navaho (nav′ ə hō) Indians in the Southwest make paintings that last less than one day. These designs are called sand paintings. They are different from all other paintings.

3   Using bits of powdered and colored rock, the Navahos "paint" on a large cowhide or on smooth sand. Sand flows through their fingers to make paintings. The designs are often of their Indian gods. They also use pieces of flowers or meal and other vegetable materials.

4   Once, sand paintings were made only by a medicine man when someone was ill. The medicine man hoped the Navaho gods would like his design and make the sick well.

5   Today, most sand paintings are made for special Indian ceremonies. These beautiful paintings are always destroyed before the sun sets. They are not painted for people to enjoy. They are painted to please the Navaho gods.

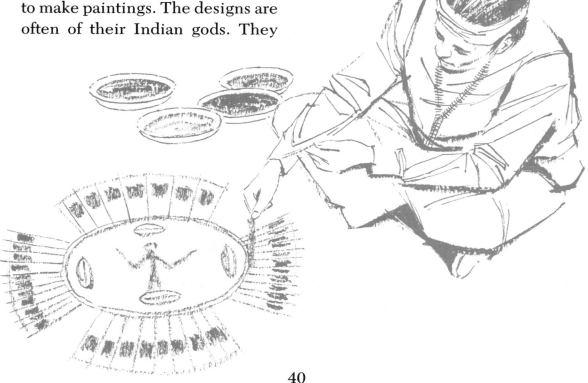

40

FIND THE ANSWERS

1. The Navaho Indians make paintings that last
   - a. one week.
   - b. less than a year.
   - c. less than a day.
   - d. a long time.

2. The word in paragraph 5 that means *torn apart* or *ruined* is

   _____.

3. The words "The designs are often of their Indian gods" in paragraph

   3 refer to _____ _____.

4. The story does not say so, but it makes you think that sand paintings
   - a. are done to make money.
   - b. are made every day.
   - c. are not meant to last.

5. Sand paintings are made of
   - a. powdered rock.
   - b. finger paints.
   - c. sand from the beach.
   - d. oil paints.

6. Sand paintings are made for the Navahos to enjoy.
   - Yes　　　　　No　　　　　Does not say

7. On the whole, this story is about
   - a. Indian sand paintings.
   - b. the Southwest.
   - c. beautiful sunsets.

8. Why do the Navahos make sand paintings? (Check the story again.)
   - a. They want to show they are fine artists.
   - b. They want to please their Indian gods.
   - c. They want to help the medicine man.

9. Which of these sentences do you think is right?
   - a. Sand paintings make people ill.
   - b. Sand paintings are made for people to enjoy.
   - c. Sand paintings have special meanings for the Navahos.

41

They Carved Totem Poles

1 The Haida people live in Alaska and Northwest Canada. The Haida are well known for their dugout canoes and their wood carvings. Most people know about their carvings of animals and people on tall poles. These decorated posts are called totem poles.

2 The Haida carved on wood long before other peoples came to their land. They carved designs on their canoes and on wooden boxes. They decorated everything they made.

3 The designs told stories and were thought to bring good luck. For carving, the Haida used sharp stones, pieces of bone, and shells. Think how hard it must have been to carve wood with a stone tool!

4 Later, the Haida got metal tools from visitors. These metal tools made carving easier.

5 The early 1800s, was the time the Haida produced their best work. They carved many totem poles, using logs from cedar trees. The poles were 40 to 70 feet high. But in 1880 a serious disease struck the Haida islands, and many of them died. Most of the others moved away.

6 Today, the remaining Haida still carve beautiful objects to sell to visitors, but the totem poles they carved almost 200 years ago are the ones now looked upon as valuable works of art.

42

1. The Haida are well known for their carvings made of
   a. ivory.
   b. wood.
   c. soap.
   d. bone.

2. The word in paragraph 2 that means *made designs on or made beautiful* is

   _____.

3. The word "serious" in paragraph 5 refers to the word

   _____.

4. The story does not say so, but it makes you think that the Haida
   a. took a long time to carve with stone tools.
   b. carved designs on the doors of every house.
   c. carved designs on the trees in the forests.

5. The Haida once carved with
   a. wooden poles.
   b. axes.
   c. pieces of bone.
   d. their teeth.

6. Today, the Haida show visitors how they do their carving.
   Yes   No   Does not say

7. On the whole, this story is about
   a. how to carve.   b. cedar logs.   c. Haida carvings.

8. Why did the Haida carve designs on everything they made? (Check the story again.)
   a. They thought their carvings would bring good luck.
   b. They liked to work with stone tools.
   c. They made decorated canoes to sell to neighbors.

9. Which of these sentences do you think is right?
   a. The Haida carve for fun.
   b. The most valuable Haida totem poles are very old.
   c. The Haida learned to carve from other people.

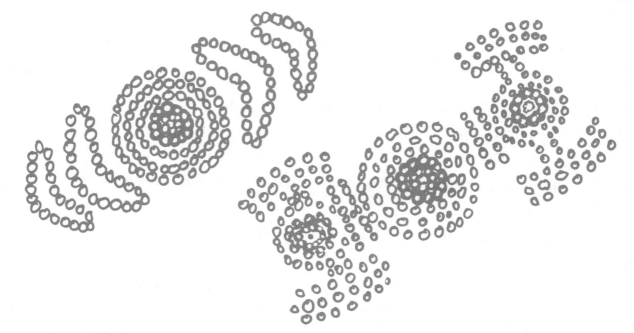

Artists of the Western Desert

1   The western desert of Australia is not an easy place to live. The early people of this area had to move from place to place to find food and water. They used sand paintings as kinds of maps to remember their routes through the desert and to explain them to others. Some of these tribes, such as the Pintupi, continued to live as nomads until the 1960s.

2   Even now that the tribes have moved into different settlements, they follow old customs. Parents teach their children by making drawings in the sand. The drawings show designs of dots, circles, and straight and U-shaped lines. Sometimes they are decorated with feathers and flower petals. They tell tales of ancient places and illustrate dreams. Everybody learns to make the sand paintings, but until recently, no one thought of himself or herself as an *artist*.

3   In the early 1970s, some people at the Papunya settlement started painting on canvas. Very soon they became professional artists, selling their paintings for money and putting on art shows. Their paintings now hang in museums all over the world. These artists' pictures tell the old stories, still using designs of dots, circles, and straight and U-shaped lines. But the work is more complicated and the artists now use many different kinds and colors of paint.

4   In 1986, the artists explained their work. They said, "The style has changed but not the message."

FIND THE ANSWERS

1. People at the Papunya settlement first started painting on canvas in the
   a. 1960s.
   b. 1970s.
   c. 1980s.
   d. desert.

2. The word in paragraph 1 that means *roads* is _____.

3. The words "such as the Pintupi" in paragraph 1 refer to
   _____.

4. The story does not say so, but it makes you think that
   a. the paintings are hard to understand unless explained.
   b. today the desert is a favorite place to live.
   c. it's a waste of time to draw in the sand.

5. The desert tribes used sand paintings to
   a. earn money for food.
   b. show what birds and flowers look like.
   c. remember places in the dessert.
   d. hang in museums.

6. Sand paintings sometimes have real bird feathers in them.
   Yes   No   Does not say

7. On the whole, this story is about
   a. sand paintings.
   b. the western desert.
   c. artists at the Papunya settlement.

8. Why did the desert tribes move from place to place? (Check the story again.)
   a. They needed to find food and water.
   b. They were nomads.
   c. They got lost easily.

9. Which of these sentences do you think is right?
   a. Sand paintings show realistic landscapes.
   b. Canvas paintings are more colorful than sand paintings.
   c. Only people from the Pintupi tribe are artists.

The Mayor Wore a Turban

1   Many cities in the world have a mayor, who is head of the city government. Doña Felisa Rincón del Guatier was a strong mayor of San Juan, the capital city of Puerto Rico. To the people of San Juan, Doña Fela was not only a mayor but also a warm friend.

2   Like other mayors, Doña Fela wanted good things for her city. Puerto Ricans like to play baseball. Doña Fela saw that they got a large stadium. Many of the poor people in San Juan needed help when they got sick. Doña Fela's favorite work was the building of a new medical center.

3   Unlike other mayors, Doña Fela usually wore a turban and often carried a fan. She held parties for old women. She gave candy and toys to children. When a poor man had a hole in his roof, he went to see Doña Fela. She helped him get materials to build a new roof.

4   The weather in San Juan is always warm, and many children there never see snow. One winter, Doña Fela had a plane full of snow flown to San Juan for the children to enjoy.

5   Doña Fela took care of big problems in her city, but she also remembered the little ones.

46

FIND THE ANSWERS

1. San Juan is a
   - a. country.
   - b. river.
   - c. city.
   - d. state.

2. The word in paragraph 2 that means *a large building where games are played* is _____.

3. The words "who is head of the city government" in paragraph 1 refer to _____.

4. The story does not say so, but it makes you think that
   - a. Doña Fela liked children.
   - b. Doña Fela liked candy.
   - c. Doña Fela liked big hats.

5. Puerto Ricans liked to play
   - a. baseball.
   - b. soccer.
   - c. football.
   - d. basketball.

6. Doña Fela wanted bad things for her city.

   Yes   No   Does not say

7. On the whole, the story is about
   - a. a senator   b. a president.   c. a mayor.

8. Why was a new medical center built in San Juan? (Check the story.)
   - a. Doctors like to work in new buildings.
   - b. Many poor people needed help when they got sick.
   - c. There were not enough doctors in San Juan.

9. Which of these sentences do you think is right?
   - a. San Juan is in the Pacific Ocean.
   - b. It does not snow in San Juan.
   - c. San Juan is a small city.

Celebrating Sunlight

1   In Sweden, the winters are long, cold, and dark. In fact, during this season the northern part of the country has very few hours of sunlight. Summers, on the other hand, are short but full of light.

2   On the longest day of the year—the summer solstice—there are 18 hours of sunshine in southern Sweden. And in the north, it never gets completely dark. No wonder Swedish people have a holiday on the summer solstice! After the winter, they are ready to celebrate. They call this holiday Midsummer Day, because it comes in the middle of their summer, June 21. It's a day for people to be outside.

3   Swedes decorate poles with flowers and ribbons, and children dance around the poles and sing. They also play special games, such as one in which the children pretend to be small animals. In the evening, it's time for the adults to celebrate. They make a festive meal. For dessert, they have a special summer treat: strawberries and cream. Afterward, they dance. Many Swedes stay awake until the sun comes up, which is earlier than you might think. In the north, the sun rises at 3 a.m. in the summer.

4   It is not surprising that Midsummer Day is a favorite holiday in Sweden. Summer is a time to treasure for the people who live so far north.

48

1. On Midsummer Day, some Swedish children pretend to be
   a. flowers and ribbons.
   b. adults.
   c. lions.
   d. small animals.

2. The word in paragraph 3 that means *grown-ups* is

   _____.

3. The words "longest day of the year" in paragraph 2 refer to the

   _____   _____.

4. The story does not say so, but it makes you think that
   a. people in Sweden like cold weather best.
   b. the Swedes enjoy summertime.
   c. they don't celebrate Christmas in Sweden.

5. On the summer solstice in the far north of Sweden,
   a. the children stay up all night.
   b. sometimes it rains.
   c. there are 18 hours of sunlight.
   d. it never gets completely dark.

6. The adults eat potatoes at their festive dinners.
   Yes   No   Does not say

7. On the whole, this story is about
   a. Swedish holidays.
   b. Midsummer Day.
   c. summer in Sweden.

8. Why do people who live in the north like summer so much? (Check the story again.)
   a. Winters are long and hard.
   b. They can eat all the strawberries they want.
   c. The children sing, dance, and play games.

9. Which of these sentences do you think is right?
   a. Children like Midsummer Day better than adults do.
   b. It is colder in the north of Sweden than in the south.
   c. People all over the world celebrate the summer solstice.

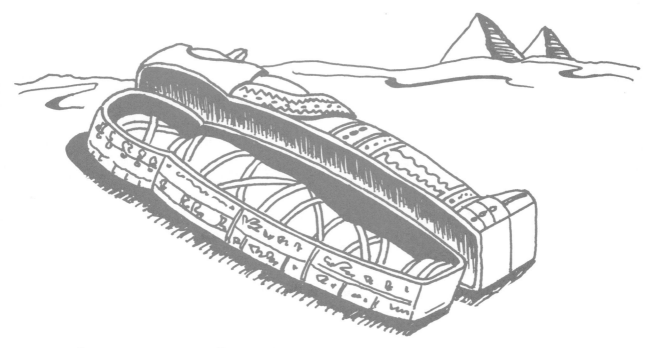

The Mummies of Osiris

1   The people of ancient Egypt believed in life after death. When people died, they went to live with Osiris, the god of the underworld. In the underworld, they would keep the same bodies they had before they died. The priests of Osiris knew how to keep bodies from decaying. They used chemicals to take the moisture out of the body. Then they washed the body and spread oil over it. Finally, they wrapped the body in cloth, making it into a mummy. Once the mummy was wrapped, it was placed in a coffin.

2   Egyptians thought they would need the same kinds of things in the afterlife as they did before they died. Therefore, people surrounded the coffin with useful objects such as bowls, pots, and clothing, and with beautiful objects such as gold and jewelry.

3   When a king died, the mummy was placed in a stone tomb called a pyramid. Modern archeologists have found some of these tombs. They are filled with wonderful treasures as well as household goods. And, of course, they also contain the mummies of long-dead kings.

4   Thousands of years after they died, these kings are teaching us about their world. The mummies are so well preserved that scientists can tell what they ate and how their doctors set broken bones. We owe a great deal to the priests of Osiris.

50

FIND THE ANSWERS

1. The Egyptian mummies were made by
   a. priests.   c. kings.
   b. Osiris.   d. scientists.

2. The word in paragraph 1 that means *very old* is _____.

3. The words "filled with wonderful treasures" in paragraph 3 describe the
   _____.

4. The story does not say so, but it makes you think that
   a. it was easy to make mummies.
   b. the ancient Egyptians had some knowledge of chemistry.
   c. the priests of Osiris acted as doctors to the kings.

5. The people in Egypt believed
   a. that science was more important than religion.
   b. in life after death.
   c. in witches and goblins.
   d. in burying their kings underground.

6. The mummies were put into coffins.
   Yes   No   Does not say

7. On the whole, this story is about
   a. Egyptian ideas about the afterlife.
   b. Egyptian mummies.
   c. archeologists.

8. Why did the Egyptians make mummies? (Check the story again.)
   a. They wanted to preserve bodies for future scientists.
   b. The priests said Osiris demanded that they make them.
   c. They believed that people needed their bodies in the afterlife.

9. Which of these sentences do you think is right?
   a. The ancient Egyptians believed in many gods.
   b. Just about everybody in ancient Egypt understood how mummies were made.
   c. Making mummies was a waste of time and skill.

A Shortcut Between Two Oceans

1   In 1904, Americans began the hardest building task they had ever tried. They started to dig the Panama Canal.

   As you know, our country lies between the Atlantic and the Pacific Oceans. There was no easy way for ships to go from ocean to ocean. They had to sail almost 8,000 miles around South America.

2   The country of Panama lies between North and South America. In one place, Panama is only 28 miles wide. Americans wanted to build a canal across this narrow piece of land.

3   Panama had high mountains and thick jungles. It also had mosquitoes which carried yellow fever and malaria. Men working there often became sick and died.

4   First, our country sent men to destroy as many mosquitoes and their eggs as they could. Then doctors used drugs to fight the diseases. At last, big earth-moving machines were sent to Panama, and hundreds of men began to build the Canal.

5   Work went slowly as thousands of tons of earth were moved. After ten years, the Panama Canal was finally opened. The first ship passed through the Canal in 1914. Today, ships from many lands use the Canal. It is a shortcut between two oceans.

52

FIND THE ANSWERS

1. The Americans began to build the Panama Canal in
   a. 1940.　　　　　　　　　　　c. 1914.
   b. 1904.　　　　　　　　　　　d. 1900.

2. The word in paragraph 1 that means *job* or *thing to be done* is

   _____.

3. The words "carried yellow fever and malaria" in paragraph 3 refer to

   the word _____.

4. The story does not say so, but it makes you think that the Panama Canal
   a. was easy to build.
   b. gave the workers no problems.
   c. helped speed up trade.

5. Before building the Canal, our country sent men to destroy many
   a. wild animals.　　　　　　　c. mosquitoes.
   b. snakes.　　　　　　　　　　d. villages.

6. Panama is flat, desert country.
   Yes　　　　　　　No　　　　　　　Does not say

7. On the whole, this story is about
   a. building the Panama Canal.
   b. malaria and yellow fever.
   c. doctors and drugs.

8. The Panama Canal was built in order to
   a. divide Panama in half.
   b. make a shortcut between the Atlantic and Pacific Oceans.
   c. help doctors destroy the mosquitoes.

9. Which of these sentences do you think is right?
   a. The people of Panama asked America to build the Canal.
   b. The Panama Canal is hundreds of miles long.
   c. Panama lies between the Atlantic and Pacific Oceans.

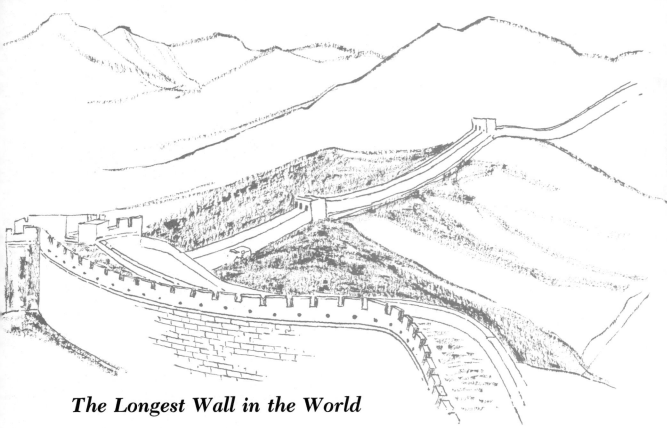

The Longest Wall in the World

1   The Great Wall of China winds across the country like a giant stone snake. It is 1,500 miles long.

2   The wall crosses mountains and rivers. It reaches from the ocean on the east to the desert on the west.

3   The Chinese began their wall more than 2,000 years ago. They worked on it for hundreds of years. The Chinese wanted to keep out their enemies.

4   At the bottom, the wall is 25 feet wide. At the top, it is about 15 feet wide. The sides of the wall are made of stone and brick, while the inside is filled with earth.

5   Parts of the wall rise as high as a three-story building. Placed 100 yards apart are tall towers. Lookouts could stand in the towers to watch for enemies approaching. The road on top of the wall is wide enough for two wagons to pass.

6   If we were to build such a wall now, we would use modern machines. But the Chinese had to build the wall by hand. If the wall were in our country, it would reach from the state of New York to Nebraska. The Great Wall of China is the longest wall ever built.

FIND THE ANSWERS

1. The Great Wall of China is
   a. 15,000 inches long.   c. 10,500 yards long.
   b. 150 feet long.   d. 1,500 miles long.

2. The word in paragraph 5 that means *coming near* or *coming up to* is

   _____.

3. The words "the longest wall ever built" in paragraph 6 refer to the

   _____ _____ _____ _____.

4. The story does not say so, but it makes you think that the Great Wall
   a. was hard to build.
   b. has a gate every 100 yards.
   c. is used as a road for cars today.

5. The inside of the Great Wall is filled with
   a. iron.   c. brick.
   b. earth.   d. stone.

6. The Great Wall of China was built by hand.
   Yes   No   Does not say

7. On the whole, this story is about
   a. tall towers.
   b. the Great Wall of China.
   c. Chinese lookouts.

8. What is meant by the sentence, "The Great Wall winds across the country like a giant stone snake"?
   a. It stops the wind from blowing.
   b. It can move.
   c. It has many curves.

9. Which of these sentences do you think is right?
   a. The Great Wall of China was built with modern machinery.
   b. The Great Wall was like a long fort.
   c. The Great Wall goes from New York to Nebraska.

Naming Children

1   Among most peoples in the world, children are given names. In the United States children have a family name, or a "last name," and a first name. Most also have a middle name. However, not all people name children in the same way.

2   Some peoples believe that the spirits of those who have died are reborn in babies. To name a baby, the parents begin by saying the names of the child's ancestors. The baby may sneeze, smile, or cry when a certain name is said. The parents think that means the ancestor is reborn in the baby. The baby is given that name.

3   Some peoples change their names. Navaho Indians change their names when they want new ones. The Navaho can decide to use the mother's last name rather than the father's. They may want an English name in place of a Native American one. Or they may change their English name into a Navaho name. The Navaho do not think it important to keep the same name.

4   In some parts of Africa, a baby's name is kept secret. No strangers are allowed to learn it. People there believe that the name is part of the child. They think that anyone who learns the name will have power over the child.

56

FIND THE ANSWERS

1. In the United States most children have
   a. a first name.
   b. only a last name.
   c. three names.
   d. a middle and a last name.

2. The word in paragraph 4 that means *kept from others* is

   _____ .

3. The words "sneeze, smile, or cry" in paragraph 2 refer to the

   _____ .

4. The story does not say so, but it makes you think that
   a. parents everywhere tell all their friends the name of their baby.
   b. peoples have different reasons for choosing a baby's name.
   c. all children are named after their ancestors.

5. In some parts of Africa, strangers are not told the name of
   a. a baby.
   b. the family.
   c. the ancestors.
   d. the mother.

6. Navaho Indians always change their names.
   Yes   No   Does not say

7. On the whole, this story is about
   a. giving ancestors a name.
   b. changing the name of an African child.
   c. how people are given their names.

8. Why is it easy for Navaho Indians to change their name? (Check the story.)
   a. They feel that it is not important to keep the same name.
   b. Whenever they sneeze, they change their names.
   c. They believe a name is part of them.

9. Which of these sentences do you think is right?
   a. Children's names are not important to many parents.
   b. The parents in each country have different customs.
   c. Babies' names are always kept secret.

They Don't Watch Clocks

1   In cities in the United States, there are clocks in most stores, factories, and other buildings. Radio announcers give the correct time during the day. People here think that it is important to know the time. Most Americans have watches. They want to do certain things at certain times. They don't want to be late.

2   Time is not so important to peoples everywhere. Suppose you visit a country in South America. You would find that people living there do not like to rush. If you had an appointment with some friends, they would probably be late. They would not want to arrive on time.

3   In South America, even the radio programs may not begin right on time. Nor do the radio people think it important to announce the exact time.

4   In South America, many people think of a clock as a machine. They feel that people who do everything on time are letting clocks run their lives. They don't want a clock or any machine to have that much power over their lives.

58

FIND THE ANSWERS

1. There are clocks in most stores and factories in
   a. South America.
   c. India.
   b. the United States.
   d. South Africa.

2. The word in paragraph 3 that means *to tell* or *to let it be known* is

   _____.

3. The words "is not so important to peoples everywhere" in paragraph 2

   tell about the word _____.

4. The story does not say so, but it makes you think that
   a. people in South America are in a hurry.
   b. people in South America do not make appointments.
   c. there are fewer clocks in South America than in America.

5. The people of South America think of the clock as a
   a. machine.
   c. friend.
   b. radio.
   d. person.

6. Radio programs always begin on time in South America.
   Yes   No   Does not say

7. On the whole, this story is about
   a. factories in the United States.
   b. radio announcers in South America.
   c. peoples' feelings about time.

8. Why isn't time too important to the people of South America? (Check the story again.)
   a. It is too hot there to hurry to appointments.
   b. They don't want a machine to run their lives.
   c. They don't know how to tell time.

9. Which of these sentences do you think is right?
   a. Time means different things to different peoples.
   b. In the United States, it is a good idea to be late.
   c. Time is more important in South America than in America.

Hall of Apricot Forests

1   Would you like to buy bread from a store that was called *Garden of the Golden Valley*? Could you find a box of bandages in a shop called *Hall of Apricot Forests*?

2   When the Chinese people first came to the United States and opened stores, each store had a wonderful name. The names made even ordinary places such as grocery stores and drugstores sound interesting.

3   Although these Chinese were eager to learn about the United States, they also wished their children to know and remember things from China. Even today, some Chinese-American children go to school for a few hours at night to learn the history, writing, and languages of China.

4   Many Chinese-Americans also celebrate traditional Chinese holidays. Most people's favorite is the Chinese New Year. This seven-day celebration is known for music, food, fireworks, and dragon parades. The holiday is so much fun that many people besides Chinese-Americans enjoy it.

5   The Moon Festival is a much quieter holiday. It takes place in the fall—at the time of the harvest moon. During the Moon Festival, many Chinese-American families hold reunions just as their ancestors did in China. During the Moon Festival, people give each other moon cakes. These round pastries are filled with such things as dates, red beans, pineapple, and almonds.

60

1. Chinese people have interesting names for their
   a. rivers.   c. stores.
   b. children.   d. cities.

2. The word in paragraph 2 that means *regular* is _____.

3. The word "they" in paragraph 3 refers to the _____.

4. The story does not say so, but it makes you think that
   a. Chinese-Americans eat a lot of pastries.
   b. Chinese-Americans are proud of both their countries.
   c. Chinese-Americans do not like stores.

5. During the Moon Festival, people
   a. march in parades.   c. watch fireworks.
   b. go to school at night.   d. hold family reunions.

6. Many Chinese-American children give moon cakes to their teachers.
   Yes   No   Does not say

7. On the whole, this story is about
   a. Indians.
   b. Chinese-Americans.
   c. South Americans.

8. Why do people whose families are not from China celebrate the Chinese New Year? (Check the story.)
   a. The holiday is a lot of fun.
   b. They like eating moon cakes.
   c. They want to learn about life in China.

9. Which of these sentences do you think is right?
   a. Chinese children do not go to school during the day.
   b. The Moon Festival is not so widely celebrated as Chinese New Year.
   c. Most Chinese-Americans own stores.

Medea
(A Tale from Greek Mythology)

Medea was a beautiful princess who lived in the land of Colchis near the Black Sea. She was the granddaughter of the Sun, and so she had many magic powers.

Medea's father, Aeëtes, was the King of Colchis. He kept careful watch over his favorite treasure, the Golden Fleece. This was the golden wool of a sacred ram. The Golden Fleece hung from a tree in a dark forest in Colchis. A fierce dragon guarded the Fleece. No one had been able to touch the Golden Fleece because the dragon never went to sleep.

Then one day, a young man, Jason, came to Colchis in search of the Golden Fleece. Jason and his men came in a ship, the *Argos*, and they

62

were called *Argonauts*. If Jason could bring the Golden Fleece home, he would become king of his country.

Medea fell in love with Jason at once and wanted to help him. But her father was very angry that these strangers should land in Colchis. Jason said he would do anything the king wanted if he would give him the Golden Fleece. The king did not want to lose the Golden Fleece, so he decided to trick Jason.

"Very well," said Aeëtes. "Tomorrow, between sunrise and sunset, you must harness my fire-breathing bulls. You must plow a field and sow it with dragons' teeth. If you succeed, you may have the Golden Fleece. If you fail, I will cut out your tongue."

Aeëtes knew that no man could stand the terrible heat that blew from the noses of the bulls.

Medea understood what her father was trying to do, but she was not going to let anything happen to Jason. Late that night, she went to a dark cave. Carefully she mixed a magic ointment and gave it to Jason.

"Use this ointment tomorrow," said Medea. "For one day, neither fire nor iron can harm you."

Jason was very grateful. He promised to take Medea home with him and make her his queen.

Early the next morning, Jason went straight to the field. Because of Medea's ointment, he was able to harness the bulls and plow the field. Then he scattered the dragon's teeth. At once a crop of warriors sprang up. Jason threw a rock in the middle of them and they began to fight among themselves. By dark, all the warriors were dead.

Jason had done what the king asked, but Aeëtes still would not give up the Golden Fleece. Secretly, he decided to kill Jason and his men at dawn. When Medea learned this, she went straight to Jason.

"You have earned the Golden Fleece, but my father will never give it to you," said Medea. "You must take the Fleece and sail away before dawn. I will help you."

Medea led Jason into the forest where the shining Golden Fleece hung. The dragon guarding the Fleece roared, but Medea was not afraid. She cast a magic spell on the dragon and it fell asleep.

Quickly Jason reached up and took the Golden Fleece from the tree branch. He and Medea ran to the *Argos*. They woke the *Argonauts* and sailed safely away.

After many adventures, Jason and Medea brought the Golden Fleece home to Jason's land. But it gave them no real happiness. More and more, Medea began to use her magic pow-ers to do evil things. At last, she got in a chariot drawn by two dragons. Medea rode off into a dark cloud and was never seen again. The Golden Fleece was hung in a Delphi temple.

602 words

II

Different Communities Need and Use Different Ways to Reach the Same Goal

In this section, you will read about how different communities need and use different ways to reach the same goals. You will read about these things from the standpoint of history, biology, economics, mathematics, sociology, art, geography, engineering, and anthropology.

Keep these questions in mind when you are reading.

1. Do all people approach a problem in the same way?

2. What are some of the problems that are common to all people?

3. What are some different ways that these problems are met?

4. Do other people's solutions to problems benefit us?

5. What are some things that cause people to use different ways to reach the same goals?

Look on pages 8-10 for help with words in this section you don't understand.

65

Math Machines

1   Before people could trade with neighbors, build cities and monuments, and learn about the world, they needed to know mathematics. As life became more complicated, they needed ways to solve problems quickly and accurately.

2   Somewhere in ancient Asia people came up with a powerful tool—the abacus—which may have been invented as early as 2300 b.c. The abacus is a frame containing sets of beads (or counters) strung on wires. Each group of beads on the same wire has the same value. The first group usually stands for units, or ones; the second for tens; the third for hundreds; and so on. With this simple tool, people could work out problems in a flash.

3   In marketplaces throughout the East, merchants used the abacus to do business. Scientists used it to gain knowledge about our planet and our solar system. Engineers used it to build better structures and to create better tools.

4   Until the calculator and computer were invented, the abacus remained an important tool in Asia, Russia, and the Middle East. In fact, the Russians used an abacus when they designed the first space satellite in 1957. Today, calculators and computers have become common. But you can still find people who use the abacus.

66

FIND THE ANSWERS

1. The first group of counters on an abacus is usually for
   a. units.
   b. values.
   c. tens.
   d. hundreds.

2. The word in paragraph 2 that means *having great strength* is

   _____.

3. The words "remained an important tool" in paragraph 4 tell about the

   _____.

4. The story does not say so, but it makes you think that
   a. towns did not have marketplaces until after the abacus was invented.
   b. engineers use math to design bridges.
   c. NASA uses the abacus to launch satellites.

5. The first space satellite was launched by
   a. Russians.
   b. the United States.
   c. Asians.
   d. scientists.

6. The abacus was invented by a Russian.
   Yes   No   Does not say

7. On the whole, this story is about
   a. the abacus.
   b. the importance of math.
   c. how to use a calculator.

8. Why did people need to invent math tools? (Check the story again.)
   a. Merchants were having trouble making change for customers.
   b. They didn't know how to read and write.
   c. They needed to solve problems quickly and accurately.

9. Which of these sentences do you think is right?
   a. Scientists used abacuses more often than merchants did.
   b. The abacus can be used to do addition and subtraction.
   c. There are no problems that couldn't be solved with an abacus.

New Art

1   During the Middle Ages art, was seen mainly in churches, in the form of paintings that told stories from the Bible. These pictures, which were flat like the walls and boards they were painted on, did not make things look realistic. The backgrounds were simple and stylized. Artists overlapped objects and people to show that one was actually behind another, but these efforts didn't really show depth.

2   After the Middle Ages came the Renaissance—a period of great change. People began to look at themselves and the world in new ways, and artists wanted to show how the world truly appeared. They wanted their pictures to show depth. But how could they show depth on a flat wall? An Italian architect named Filippo Brunelleschi used geometry to find a way. When he drew two straight lines slanting toward each other, they seemed to be moving farther away from the viewer.

3   Another Italian architect, Leone Battista Alberti, found a different way to show depth. He realized that far-away objects looked smaller than the ones up close. So, if he drew two trees, the smaller one looked farther away than the bigger one.

4   In this way, the artists of the Renaissance developed a technique of drawing that we still use today, over 400 years later.

1. Filippo Brunelleschi was
   a. a mathematician.
   b. an architect.
   c. a philosopher.
   d. a doctor.

2. The word in paragraph 4 that means *method* is _____.

3. The words "a period of great change" in paragraph 2 refer to the

   _____.

4. The story does not say so, but it makes you think that
   a. art was very important in Italy during the Renaissance.
   b. during the Middle Ages, artists didn't show people in their pictures.
   c. during the Renaissance, artists painted only pictures that told stories from the Bible.

5. Leone Battista Alberti showed depth by
   a. using geometry.
   b. making objects different sizes.
   c. overlapping objects
   d. making lines come together.

6. Brunelleschi and Alberti knew each other.
   Yes   No   Does not say

7. On the whole, this story is about
   a. how Renaissance artists showed depth.
   b. the differences between the Middle Ages and the Renaissance.
   c. Filippo Brunelleschi and Leone Battista Alberti.

8. Why did the Renaissance artists want to show depth? (Check the story again.)
   a. They wanted to show they were better than the artists in the Middle Ages.
   b. They wanted to show how the world truly appeared.
   c. They wanted to teach about religious ideas.

9. Which of these sentences do you think is right?
   a. Other Renaissance artists began using Brunelleschi's and Alberti's ways of showing depth.
   b. After the Renaissance, artists stopped using Brunelleschi's and Alberti's methods.
   c. Art from the Middle Ages is very realistic.

A Bottle of Peas

1   We know that we need to eat a variety of foods in order to stay healthy. Yet some foods grow only at certain times of year, and they spoil quickly. Before the invention of canning, people did not eat green vegetables or fruit except during their growing season.

2   With canning, fresh food is put into a container. Any gases are removed before the container is sealed, then the container is heated to kill any germs.

3   The cans we know are metal. The earliest cans, however, were made of glass. In fact, the very first can was actually a bottle. A Frenchman named Nicolas Alpert used it when he invented canning in 1795. He filled the bottle with cooked peas, then heated and corked it. Napoleon used Alpert's invention to help feed the French army.

4   The first tin can came along in 1810. It was invented by an Englishman—Peter Durand. His tin cans were made by hand. In 1847, a machine for cutting the tin was invented, and in 1876 one for shaping and soldering the can came along.

5   Today, we are able to preserve foods by freezing or freeze-drying them. Even so, canning is still important. Just think of all the different kinds of canned foods there are in your supermarket.

70

FIND THE ANSWERS

1. Canning was invented in
   - a. 1795.
   - b. 1810.
   - c. 1847.
   - d. 1876.

2. The word in paragraph 3 that means *put a stopper in* is
   _____.

3. The word "spoil" in paragraph 1 describes _____.

4. The story does not say so, but it makes you think that
   - a. canning is the best way to preserve foods.
   - b. before canning many people couldn't get vegetables in the winter.
   - c. the cans we use today are made out of tin.

5. The very first can Nicolas Alpert made was filled with
   - a. peas.
   - b. beans.
   - c. tuna fish.
   - d. gases.

6. The earliest cans were made of glass.
   Yes   No   Does not say

7. On the whole, this story is about
   - a. inventions.
   - b. ways to keep food fresh.
   - c. the history of canning.

8. Why do the cans need to be heated? (Check the story again.)
   - a. The heat takes out the gases.
   - b. The heat kills microorganisms.
   - c. The heat seals the cans.

9. Which of these sentences do you think is right?
   - a. Canned vegetables are better for you than fresh vegetables.
   - b. Canning hasn't changed much since Nicolas Alpert's day.
   - c. Canning was an important invention.

Who Takes Care of the Young?

1   Who takes care of young animals until they are old enough to care for themselves? Different animals have different ways to care for their young.

2   The female bear feeds, protects, and teaches her cubs for over a year. Male bears do not like cubs and have been known to kill them. So the mother must keep the cubs away from their father.

3   Among some living things, it is the father who is in charge of the young. The male stickleback fish builds a nest in water weeds. As soon as the female has laid her eggs in the nest, she leaves.

4   The male stickleback guards the eggs. After the eggs hatch, the male watches over the young fish. If they go too far from the nest, their father carries them back in his mouth.

5   Wolves live together as a family. Both parents help raise the young. Both bring food to the pups and show them how to hunt. Both father and mother fight to protect their young against bears or other enemies.

72

FIND THE ANSWERS

1. The female bear
   a. leaves her cubs alone.   c. doesn't like cubs.
   b. gives her cubs away.   d. protects her cubs.

2. The word in paragraph 2 that means *guards from danger* is

   _____.

3. The words "do not like cubs" in paragraph 2 tell about the

   _____ _____.

4. The story does not say so, but it makes you think that
   a. most young animals are well taken care of.
   b. only wolves know how to care for their young properly.
   c. young animals must care for themselves.

5. The female stickleback fish
   a. builds a nest.   c. guards the nest.
   b. lays the eggs.   d. watches over the young.

6. Young stickleback fish never try to leave their nests.
   Yes   No   Does not say

7. On the whole, this story is about
   a. wild animals.
   b. animal parents.
   c. bears and fish.

8. How do wolves care for their young? (Check the story again.)
   a. They leave them alone.
   b. Both parents feed and watch over them.
   c. Only the female wolf protects the young.

9. Which of these sentences do you think is right?
   a. All animals of one kind live together as families.
   b. All young animals are cared for by their mothers.
   c. Young animals are cared for in different ways.

73

Animal Games

1   Children around the world like to play games. But did you know that many animals play games, too? Some of these games are almost like those you play.

2   In the winter, otters coast on ice. When they find a snowbank, they stop and slide down it again and again. In the summer, otters have just as much fun. They make their slides on the banks of rivers and ponds.

3   Some animals like to sing and dance in groups. Wolves gather on a hill when the moon is out and make a chorus as they howl to-gether. Chimpanzees like to march in single file. They keep in step as they march around. Each chimpanzee comes down hard on one foot. Then, in a kind of rhythm, they shake their heads.

4   Other animals have favorite games like tag. Some kinds of fish and birds play follow-the-leader. English badgers play king-of-the castle. At sundown, the badgers go to the stump of a fallen tree. When one badger climbs to the top, the others try to climb up, too, and pull down the king.

74

FIND THE ANSWERS

1. In the winter, otters coast on
   - a. river banks.
   - b. ice.
   - c. logs.
   - d. sleds.

2. The word in paragraph 3 that means *to cry long and loudly* is

   _____.

3. The words "march in single file" in paragraph 3 refer to

   _____.

4. The story does not say so, but it makes you think that
   - a. animals play games with children.
   - b. animals learn to play games by watching children.
   - c. some kinds of animals seem to have favorite games.

5. English badgers play
   - a. tag.
   - b. follow-the-leader.
   - c. marching games.
   - d. king-of-the-castle.

6. Cats and dogs also have favorite games.

   Yes   No   Does not say

7. On the whole, this story is about
   - a. games animals play.
   - b. how animals hunt.
   - c. singing and dancing.

8. Animals seem to play games in order to
   - a. stay awake during the day.
   - b. have fun like children.
   - c. practice being children.

9. Which of these sentences do you think is right?
   - a. Animals play games by themselves.
   - b. Animals play games in groups.
   - c. All animals play the same games.

"Fly Home with Me"

1   If your mother wants to tell you something, she uses words. Birds cannot talk as we do. But some birds can make sounds to warn their young of danger. They have their own ways to make the young birds do certain things.

2   The jackdaw is a kind of blackbird that lives in Europe. Jackdaws live together in flocks. Young jackdaws do not know their enemies. When an older jackdaw sees a dog, it makes a loud, rattling sound. The younger birds know this sound means an enemy is nearby. The sound warns them and teaches them to know their enemies.

3   If a young jackdaw is in a dangerous place, a jackdaw parent flies over him from behind. The parent bird flies low over the young bird's back. The parent's tail feathers move quickly from side to side. It is trying to say, "Follow me."

4   At the same time, the parent calls out, "Key-aw, key-aw." The parent means, "Fly home with me." The younger bird then follows the older one home.

5   Young jackdaws do not have to learn what certain sounds mean. They know the meaning of these sounds from the time they hatch.

76

FIND THE ANSWERS

1. The jackdaw lives in
   - a. America.
   - b. Europe.
   - c. Africa.
   - d. Australia.

2. The word in paragraph 2 that means *groups of birds* is

   _____.

3. The words "a kind of blackbird" in paragraph 2 refer to the

   _____.

4. The story does not say so, but it makes you think that
   - a. jackdaws have to be taught to know their enemies.
   - b. birds do not have their own language.
   - c. jackdaws have to learn what certain sounds mean.

5. When an older jackdaw sees a dog, it
   - a. flies away.
   - b. fights the dog.
   - c. calls out, "Follow me."
   - d. makes a loud sound.

6. Parent jackdaws can use their tail feathers to warn of danger.
   Yes   No   Does not say

7. On the whole, this story is about
   - a. ways in which people can talk to birds.
   - b. the nests of jackdaws.
   - c. the way jackdaws warn their young of danger.

8. Why did the parent jackdaw signal, "Fly home with me"? (Check the story again.)
   - a. Danger was near.
   - b. It was time to eat.
   - c. The parent was playing a game.

9. Which of these sentences do you think is right?
   - a. All animal parents can talk to their young.
   - b. The dog is not an enemy of the jackdaw.
   - c. Birds can give certain information to one another.

Who Owns the Land?

1   Farmland is very important to every country in the world. Farmland supplies the food needed by people everywhere. Who owns this land?

2   Farmland may be owned by the farmers who work the land. It may be owned by people who have others farm it. In some places, a government owns the farmland.

3   In England, many farmers rent their land. Some families have farmed a piece of land for generations without owning it. In Chile, most farmland was once owned by a few wealthy landowners. Workers farmed the land for them. But during the 1940s, many landowners divided their land into small farms and sold it. Today, there are fewer large farms but many smaller ones.

4   In China, large groups of farmers own most of the land together. The families in each group agree to raise certain crops and livestock. Each family also owns a small plot for its own use. In the United States, most farmland is owned by the families who farm the land. A few farmers rent their land from others. In the 1990s, almost 90 percent of American farmers owned all or part of the land they farmed.

FIND THE ANSWERS

1. Farmland supplies
   a. farms.
   b. food.
   c. farmers.
   d. landowners.

2. The word in paragraph 2 that means *to get land ready to plant crops* is

   _____.

3. The words "many farmers rent their land" in paragraph 3 refer to farmers
   in _____.

4. The story does not say so, but it makes you think that
   a. you have to be 21 to own farmland.
   b. ownership of farmland is important government policy.
   c. farming is not popular in our country.

5. In Chile during the 1940s many landowners
   a. divided their farms.
   b. gave their farms away.
   c. ran out of money.
   d. built factories on their land.

6. Most farmers rent their land.
   Yes   No   Does not say

7. On the whole, this story is about
   a. 100 farmers.
   b. different countries in Asia.
   c. owning farmland.

8. Why is farmland important all over the world? (Check the story again.)
   a. Farmers work the land to supply people with food.
   b. Most people visit farms during their summer vacations.
   c. It is where new cities will be built.

9. Which of these sentences do you think is right?
   a. English farm families move often.
   b. Farmlands are owned in different ways in different countries.
   c. Small farms are best.

The Outback

1   In the United States, there are different kinds of farmland. The land is planted with crops in many places. Only in the western part of our country do we have dry rangeland where cattle are raised.

2   But most of Australia's farmland has a dry climate similar to our rangeland. Less than 20 inches of rain fall each year. The land does not get enough rain for farmers to grow crops. So most farmland in Australia is used to raise sheep and cattle. Australia raises more sheep than any other country in the world.

3   In Australia, all large cities are on the coast. The people of Australia call the empty inland regions of their country the "outback." In the outback are huge sheep and cattle ranches called "stations." One station may cover thousands of miles.

4   The men and women of the outback are like the pioneers who first settled the American West. Some families live 400 miles from the nearest town. Herds going to market are driven hundreds of miles to the nearest railroad.

5   Sometimes it does not rain for years. The temperatures can go as high as 130°. These outback families often lead hard and lonely lives.

80

FIND THE ANSWERS

1. The outback has
   a. jungles.
   b. many large rivers.
   c. high temperatures.
   d. freezing winds.

2. The word in paragraph 3 that means *very big* or *very large* is

   _____.

3. The words "empty inland regions" in paragraph 3 refer to the word

   _____.

4. The story does not say so, but it makes you think that
   a. few people live in the outback.
   b. outback stations are always near railroads.
   c. American pioneers moved to Australia.

5. Most farmland in Australia is used to raise
   a. crops.
   b. sheep and cattle.
   c. kangaroos.
   d. corn and potatoes.

6. The United States raises more sheep than any other country.
   Yes   No   Does not say

7. On the whole, this story is about
   a. growing crops in Australia.
   b. railroads in Australia.
   c. farmland in Australia.

8. Why are sheep and cattle raised in the outback? (Check the story again.)
   a. The people who live there don't know how to raise crops.
   b. Sheep and cattle are easy to raise.
   c. The land is too dry to grow crops.

9. Which of these sentences do you think is right?
   a. Life in the outback is easy.
   b. Families in the outback have to get along on their own.
   c. It rains often in the outback and causes flooding.

Fewer Farmers but More Food

1   Today, most Americans live in cities and towns. People who live in cities do not raise their own food. Instead, they depend on our farmers for it.

2   In the 1800s, there were fewer people in the United States. However, more people were farmers then. In the 1900s, many people left their farms to work in big cities. Now fewer than three out of every 100 Americans work on farms.

3   Although there are fewer farmers today, there are larger farms. In 1900, the average farm covered 150 acres, whereas the average farmer in the 1990s owned 467 acres of land.

Farmers can raise more crops now with the help of science and modern machines.

4   Farmers can use scientific methods to protect crops from weeds and insects. They can buy large machines that will help them do their work. Some farm equipment contains computer parts so it operates very fast and accurately.

5   Now farmers in the United States produce more food than ever before. In 1820, one farm worker could feed himself or herself and three other people. In the 1990s, a farm worker could grow enough food for eighty people.

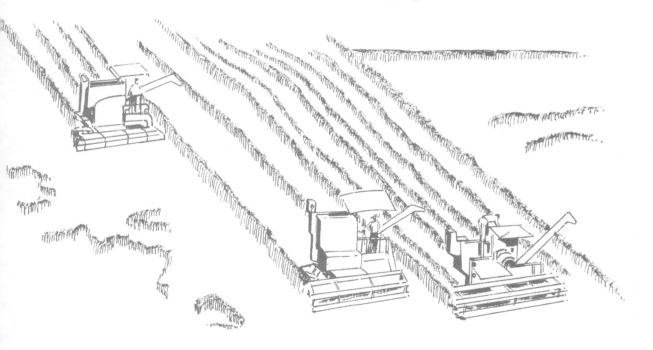

FIND THE ANSWERS

1. Farmers today
   a. live in towns and cities.
   b. have less land.
   c. grow more food.
   d. feed only themselves.

2. The word in paragraph 4 that means *keep safe* is _____.

3. The words "produce more food" in paragraph 5 refer to the _____.

4. The story does not say so, but it makes you think that
   a. methods of farming have changed.
   b. the people of today eat more.
   c. farmers cannot grow enough food to feed everyone.

5. In the 1990s, a farm worker could grow enough food for
   a. eighty people.
   b. three people.
   c. twenty people.
   d. thirteen people.

6. Farmers can grow more crops with the help of modern machines.
   Yes   No   Does not say

7. On the whole, this story is about
   a. farmers in the 1800s.
   b. going to school.
   c. modern farmers.

8. Why do people who live in cities depend on farmers for food? (Check the story again.)
   a. They do not raise their own food.
   b. They do not like the food that is grown in cities.
   c. Food produced by farmers is cheaper.

9. Which of these sentences do you think is right?
   a. We need more farmers in the United States.
   b. Farmers produce more food with the help of modern machines.
   c. Farms today are smaller than they used to be.

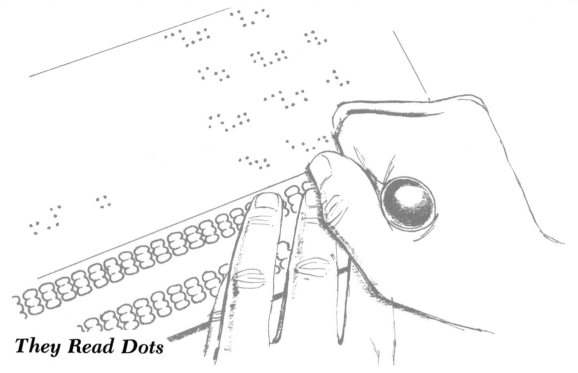

They Read Dots

1   To read this page, you must use your eyes. The blind can read, too, but they must use their fingers.

2   Over 100 years ago in France, a young boy was playing in his father's workshop. He was making holes in a piece of leather with a pointed tool. All at once, the tool flew from his hands and struck his face. This child, Louis Braille, had injured his eyes. Soon he was blind.

3   In those days, few blind people could read. Then, years later, Louis Braille had an idea. He remembered the holes he had once made in leather. If he pushed the tool only part way through the leather, he could feel raised dots on the other side. Using from one to five raised dots, he made up an alphabet.

4   Although only fifteen, Louis Braille had found a way for the blind to read. He had invented a kind of code that the fingers and the mind could learn. Named after its inventor, this new way to read was called Braille.

5   Today, many books are printed in Braille. Look below. Imagine that the dots are raised. Do you think your fingers could learn Braille?

a b c d e f g h i j k l m

n o p q r s t u v w x y z

84

FIND THE ANSWERS

1. People who read Braille
   a. have poor hearing.
   b. can't read English.
   c. are blind.
   d. have good eyesight.

2. The word in paragraph 2 that means *hurt* or *harmed* is

   is _____.

3. The words "new way to read" in paragraph 4 tell about the word

   _____.

4. The story does not say so, but it makes you think that
   a. few blind people can learn Braille.
   b. many blind people can learn Braille.
   c. anyone can read Braille.

5. The Braille alphabet is made up of
   a. round letters.
   b. raised dots.
   c. thin lines.
   d. square holes.

6. Louis Braille found a way for blind to read.
   Yes   No   Does not say

7. On the whole, this story is about
   a. making holes in leather.
   b. Louis Braille and an alphabet.
   c. using your eyes to read faster.

8. How does Braille help the blind? (Check the story again.)
   a. It gives them a way to read.
   b. It gives their fingers something to do.
   c. It helps them work with leather.

9. Which of these sentences do you think is right?
   a. Young children should not play with leather.
   b. Braille is read with the toes.
   c. Before Braille, few blind people could read.

85

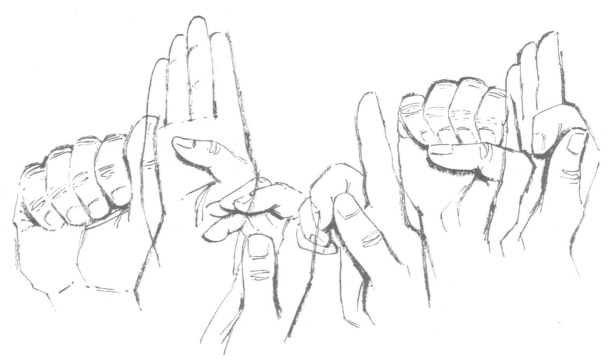

They Speak with Their Hands

1   For many years, no one could communicate with people who had been born without hearing. These deaf people were not able to use a spoken language.

2   But, beginning in the 1700s, the deaf were taught a special language. Using this language, they could share thoughts and ideas with others. The language they used was a language without sound. It was a sign language.

3   How did this sign language work? The deaf were taught to make certain movements using their hands, faces, and bodies. These movements stood for things and ideas. People might move their forefingers across their lips. This meant, "You are not telling the truth." They might tap their chins with three fingers. This meant "my uncle."

4   The deaf were also taught to use a finger alphabet. They used their fingers to make the letters of the alphabet. In this way, they spelled out words. Some deaf people could spell out words at a speed of 130 words per minute.

5   Sign language and finger spelling are not used as much as they once were. Today, the deaf are taught to understand others by watching their lips. They are also taught how to speak.

86

FIND THE ANSWERS

1. In the 1700s, the deaf were taught
   a. to speak.
   b. to watch others.
   c. sign language.
   d. Braille.

2. The word in paragraph 3 that means *the finger next to the thumb* is

   _____.

3. The words "a language without sound" in paragraph 2 tell about a

   _____ _____.

4. The story does not say so, but it makes you think that
   a. the deaf must have special teachers.
   b. there is still no way to communicate with the deaf.
   c. deaf people make signs to earn a living.

5. A tap on the chin with three fingers means
   a. "hello."
   b. "come here."
   c. "I have a toothache."
   d. "my uncle."

6. Sign language is used as much today as it once was.
   Yes   No   Does not say

7. On the whole, this story is about
   a. how the deaf communicate.
   b. learning to spell.
   c. teaching the deaf to speak.

8. How did sign language help the deaf? (Check the story again.)
   a. It helped them learn to read.
   b. The deaf could understand Indian sign language.
   c. It helped them communicate with other people.

9. Which of these sentences do you think is right?
   a. Deaf people draw signs.
   b. Deaf people read with their fingers.
   c. Many deaf people now can speak.

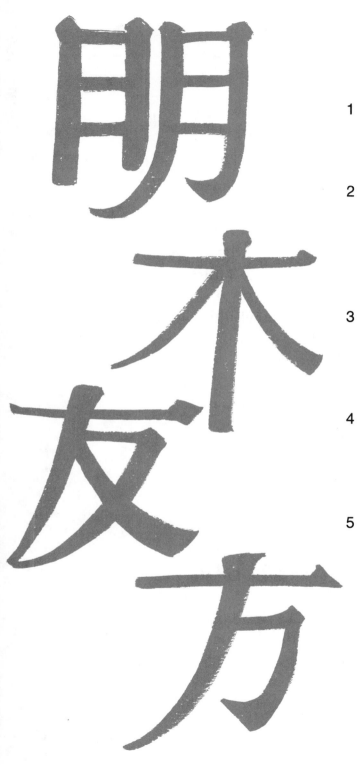

They Read Pictures

1   The Chinese began writing their language over 3,000 years ago. Their way of writing is very different from ours.

2   Until a few years ago, the Chinese did not have an alphabet. Their language was written in characters. These characters were a little like pictures. Each one stood for a different word.

3   Probably the first characters had been pictures. The character for "sun" was a circle with a dot in the center. The character for "man" looked like a body with two legs.

4   As time went on, the characters changed. New ones were added. A person could no longer tell what a character meant just by looking at it.

5   In order to read or write, people had to learn thousands of characters. Even to read a newspaper, they had to know 2,000 different characters. Learning so many characters was difficult. Many people in China could not read or write. In fact, there were letter writers in front of Chinese post offices. These people sat at tables and were paid to write letters for others.

FIND THE ANSWERS

1. The first Chinese characters were probably
   a. letters.
   b. circles.
   c. people.
   d. pictures.

2. The word in paragraph 3 that means *no doubt* or *it was likely* is

   _____.

3. The words "a little like pictures" in paragraph 2 refers to the word

   _____.

4. The story does not say so, but it makes you think that
   a. few Chinese wrote their own letters.
   b. the Chinese alphabet is very old.
   c. it is easy to read a Chinese newspaper.

5. Learning many Chinese characters was
   a. difficult.
   b. silly.
   c. fun.
   d. easy.

6. The character for "sun" was a square.
   Yes   No   Does not say

7. On the whole, this story is about
   a. Chinese post offices.
   b. Chinese characters.
   c. characters in a play.

8. Why did the Chinese need to know so many characters to write? (Check the story again.)
   a. Chinese has more words than other languages.
   b. Each character stood for a different word.
   c. They liked to write long letters.

9. Which of these sentences do you think is right?
   a. Chinese characters looked more like drawings than letters.
   b. The Chinese invented an alphabet hundreds of years ago.
   c. Chinese characters did not change through the years.

A Noisy Dance

1   Young people in most countries like to dance. Different peoples have different kinds of dances.

2   Pretend that you are in Africa. You are visiting the Kikuyu (kə kü′ yü) tribe.

3   Hear the drums beat! Listen to the flutes! Almost 2,000 Kikuyus are meeting for the most important dance of the year.

4   First, the Kikuyus choose a large, flat place for their dance. For hundreds of years, they have danced on a fall night when the moon is full. The moon and the glow from small fires light the dancers.

5   Older people watch from the side while young men and women gather at the dancing place. The girls wear beaded leather skirts and tops. The men wear fancy headdresses and carry spears. The dancers' skin and clothes are colored by light red chalk. The chalk and the firelight make the dancers look like statues.

6   The dancers act out stories of good and bad deeds. The dances tell stories of lion hunts and other adventures. In one dance, the girls stand on the boys' feet. The girls are pretending to be afraid of snakes.

7   All night the drums beat and the fires burn. But the dancers never seem to get tired.

90

FIND THE ANSWERS

1. The place where the Kikuyu tribe dances is
   a. flat.
   b. small.
   c. hilly.
   d. square.

2. The word in paragraph 2 that means *make believe* is

   _____.

3. The words "look like statues" in paragraph 5 describe the

   _____.

4. The story does not say so, but it makes you think that
   a. few people go to Kikuyu dances.
   b. the Kikuyu dance is an old custom.
   c. the Kikuyu girls and boys dance to band music.

5. The dancers' skin and clothes are covered with
   a. paint.
   b. dust.
   c. feathers.
   d. chalk.

6. The dancing area is lit by electric lights.
   Yes   No   Does not say

7. On the whole, this story is about
   a. the beat of drums.
   b. an African dance.
   c. African storytelling.

8. What do the Kikuyu dances tell? (Check the story again.)
   a. The dances tell the story of drum beats.
   b. The dances tell about adventures.
   c. The dances tell funny jokes.

9. Which of these sentences do you think is right?
   a. The Kikuyus do not often get together.
   b. Dancing is important to the Kikuyus.
   c. The most important event is a singing group.

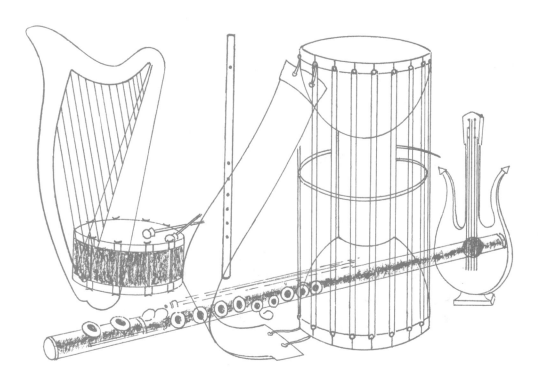

Harps, Flutes, and Drums

1   People from all countries have played musical instruments at some time in their history. But not all people have made music in the same way. In olden times, as today, there were many kinds of musical instruments. There were rattles to shake and flutes to blow. There were drums to beat and harps to strum.

2   In the Middle East, people played instruments with strings. Their first stringed instrument was a hunting bow. People played tunes on it by using the bow string. From the musical bow was to come the idea for the harp.

3   Long ago in Greece, people made music by blowing into a hollow reed or pipe called a flute. The flute was a very popular instrument. It was played during boxing matches and foot races. On Greek ships, flute players kept time for the men rowing.

4   In Africa, the most important musical instrument was the drum. Hundreds of years ago, the Africans learned to make drums by stretching animal skins over hollow logs. They used drums to keep time as they danced. They also beat out codes on their drums. In this way, they sent messages through the jungle.

1. Instruments with strings were played in
   a. Africa.
   b. Greece.
   c. the Middle East.
   d. South America.

2. The word in paragraph 1 that means *something that music is played on*

   is _____.

3. The words "first stringed instrument" in paragraph 2 refer to the

   _____ _____.

4. The story does not say so, but it makes you think that
   a. people all over the world like music.
   b. everyone plays the same kind of instrument.
   c. drummers kept time for the men rowing.

5. Drums were made from
   a. hunting bows.
   b. empty gourds.
   c. hollow reeds.
   d. hollow logs.

6. The idea for the harp came from the musical bow.
   Yes   No   Does not say

7. On the whole, this story is about
   a. stretching animal skins.
   b. sending messages.
   c. musical instruments.

8. How was the flute played? (Check the story again.)
   a. It was played by hitting the strings.
   b. It was played by blowing on a hollow reed.
   c. It was played by shaking and beating the instrument.

9. Which of these sentences do you think is right?
   a. Different peoples often play different instruments.
   b. Musical instruments have not changed over the years.
   c. The Middle East has the best musical instruments.

A Different Kind of Play

1   Maybe your class in school has given a play. People throughout the world like to act in plays. In Japan, actors perform in Kabuki (kə bü′ kē) plays. The word is made up of three Japanese words meaning song, dance, and ability.

2   Kabuki actors do not look like the actors in American plays. American actors dress and look like real people. In Kabuki plays, the actors wear bright-colored robes and wigs. Their robes are very large, and their wigs do not look like real hair.

3   American actors wear make-up, but their make-up does not often hide their faces. Kabuki actors paint their faces chalk white. They draw black eyebrows above their real eyebrows. They outline their eyes in black or red. Their mouths are bright red. They look as if they are wearing masks.

4   An actor performing in an American play must make his face look happy, sad, or angry. Make-up helps the Kabuki actor show his feelings. If an actor is going to show anger, he paints dark blue or red lines on his face. His make-up makes him look angry.

5   American and Kabuki actors perform in different ways. But they both try to please the people who watch them.

94

FIND THE ANSWERS

1. Most Kabuki plays are given in
   - a. China.
   - b. Japan.
   - c. Korea.
   - d. India.

2. The word in paragraph 1 that means *to act* is _____.

3. The words "look as if they are wearing masks" in paragraph 3 refer to

   _____ _____ .

4. The story does not say so, but it makes you think that
   - a. Kabuki actors are afraid to show their real faces.
   - b. American actors don't wear make-up.
   - c. make-up helps a Kabuki actor look sad.

5. To show anger, a Kabuki actor paints
   - a. dark lines on his face.
   - b. hair on his head.
   - c. his costume blue.
   - d. his eyebrows black.

6. Kabuki actors wear bright-colored robes and wigs.
   Yes   No   Does not say

7. On the whole, this story is about
   - a. how the Japanese sing and dance.
   - b. why actors look sad or happy.
   - c. a kind of Japanese play.

8. Why do Kabuki actors wear so much make-up? (Check the story again.)
   - a. They do not want anyone to know who they are.
   - b. It helps them show their feelings during a play.
   - c. They think it makes them look better.

9. Which of these sentences do you think is right?
   - a. Americans are not used to seeing Kabuki plays.
   - b. Kabuki actors and American actors are much the same.
   - c. American actors wear more make-up than Kabuki actors.

A Very Hot Air-Bath

1   In Finland, most houses have a sauna. The sauna is a small wood hut or a room with a furnace inside. Stones piled over the furnace are heated red-hot. After the stones are heated, the sauna is used for taking a sauna bath.

2   The temperature in the sauna is sometimes over 190 degrees. People taking a sauna bath sit or lie on a wood platform in the hot, dry air. The hot air makes them perspire. From time to time, they pour water on the hot stones to make clouds of steam.

3   People in the sauna sometimes beat themselves with branches from a birch tree. They do this to make themselves perspire more. Then they wash with soap and water. After washing, they cool off in cold water.

4   The sauna is often built near a lake so people can go from the hot sauna into the cold water. If it is winter, they may roll in the snow. After cooling off, they rest.

5   In Finland, most families take a sauna bath at least once a week. For Finns, this bath is more than a way to get clean. It is a healthful way to relax and enjoy themselves.

96

FIND THE ANSWERS

1. The Finns often build saunas near a lake because they
   a. do not like to walk far.
   b. like to cool off in the water.
   c. can get a drink there.
   d. think lakes are beautiful.

2. The word in paragraph 2 that means to *give off liquid through the skin* is

   _____.

3. The words "heated red-hot" in paragraph 1 refer to the

   _____.

4. The story does not say so, but it makes you think that the sauna
   a. is important to the Finns.
   b. is a waste of time.
   c. is used only in the winter.

5. The temperature in the sauna is
   a. as cold as snow.
   b. the same as the temperature outside.
   c. below zero.
   d. much warmer than a hot day.

6. The Finns also have bathtubs.
   Yes   No   Does not say

7. On the whole, this story is about
   a. rolling in the snow.
   b. the sauna bath.
   c. life in Finland.

8. People in a sauna beat themselves with birch branches in order to
   a. make themselves perspire more.
   b. stop the itching caused by the heat.
   c. punish themselves.

9. Which of these sentences do you think is right?
   a. The sauna is in a special building or room.
   b. People take a sauna bath to get warm.
   c. People take a sauna bath because they have nothing else to do.

97

The Siesta

1   In Mexico many people stop working for several hours in the afternoon. These Mexicans eat a big lunch and visit with friends. Later they may have time to lie down and enjoy a quiet rest.

2   The custom of resting in the afternoon is an old one. The weather in Mexico is very warm. Many years ago, people could not work outside in the middle of the day. It was too hot. They had a time of rest at midday called the siesta. Now, professional people usually work in air-conditioned buildings, but some of them still take time off from work at midday.

3   In Mexico lunch is the biggest meal of the day for most people. Office workers usually have about two hours for lunch. There are few quick-lunch counters to visit for a fast snack. If people do not want to go home, they eat in a hotel or restaurant. Outside of the large cities most people go home for lunch so the whole family can eat together.

4   Mexicans want a long lunchtime. They do not like to hurry. They want to enjoy the meal and to visit with family and friends. They want time for a siesta.

FIND THE ANSWERS

1. A Mexican eats a lunch that is
   a. small.
   b. big.
   c. fast.
   d. just a snack.

2. The word in paragraph 2 that means *12:00 noon* is

   _____.

3. The words "a time of rest at midday" in paragraph 2 refer to the

   _____.

4. The story does not say so, but it makes you think that
   a. there are many people in Mexico who do not go home for lunch.
   b. people going home for lunch cause traffic jams in cities.
   c. Mexicans are in a hurry at lunchtime.

5. In Mexico the biggest meal of the day is
   a. breakfast.
   b. an evening snack.
   c. dinner.
   d. lunch.

6. There are many quick-service lunch counters in Mexico.
   Yes   No   Does not say

7. On the whole, this story is about
   a. Mexican food.
   b. the weather in Mexico.
   c. lunchtime in Mexico.

8. Why do the Mexicans like to have a long lunchtime? (Check the story again.)
   a. They don't like to work in air-conditioned buildings.
   b. They like time to visit with their family and friends.
   c. It takes a long time to eat the many foods that are served.

9. Which of these sentences do you think is right?
   a. Mexicans do not like to eat quick lunches.
   b. Even with air-conditioning, it is too hot to work in Mexico.
   c. Mexican families do not often eat together.

Beautiful Parks

1   As our cities grow bigger, more land is taken up by buildings. For miles on each side of many big cities, buildings take the place of trees.

2   But even people who live in cities can enjoy America's parks and forests. Found in different parts of America, these parks are owned by our government. No one can build houses or stores there. The parks are kept so that people can hike, camp, and picnic. They can relax there.

3   One of the most popular American parks is Yellowstone National Park in the Northwest. It is the oldest of all the parks owned by the government. In 1872, it was set aside for the people to enjoy. Each year, thousands of people come to Yellowstone. They see high mountains, beautiful waterfalls, and thousands of hot water springs called geysers. Yellowstone has more geysers than all the rest of the world together.

4   Forests were not always open to all the people. In England long ago, the forests belonged to the king. It was against the law for the people to go there.

5   Most people in America like to go to parks. They are glad that their parks are kept open for everyone to use and enjoy.

100

FIND THE ANSWERS

1. Near many cities, buildings take the place of
   - a. streets.
   - b. geysers.
   - c. trees.
   - d. parks.

2. The word in paragraph 2 that means *to be happy with* or *to like to use*

   is _____.

3. The words "one of the most popular American parks" in paragraph 3

   refer to _____ _____ _____.

4. The story does not say so, but it makes you think that
   - a. England does not have parks.
   - b. there are few parks in America.
   - c. parks often have trees.

5. Yellowstone has many
   - a. cities.
   - b. stores.
   - c. buildings.
   - d. geysers.

6. Forests in England once belonged to the king.

   Yes   No   Does not say

7. On the whole, this story is about
   - a. big cities.
   - b. parks and forests.
   - c. American cities.

8. The government has set aside land to be kept as parks in order to
   - a. stop building.
   - b. let people relax somewhere.
   - c. help keep cities small.

9. Which of these sentences do you think is right?
   - a. The United States is the only country that has parks.
   - b. People do not often visit Yellowstone.
   - c. It is important to have parks that everyone can use.

The Modern Farmer

1 How do farmers decide if it's time to plant the wheat? Not so long ago they went by the calendar, but now they use computers. Since conditions vary from year to year, the best time to plant is not exactly the same every year. A computer can read all the data and find the best time.

2 The computer also helps farmers know what crops to plant. It takes into account weather conditions, soil types, and the amount of water in the soil. It also uses information about the prices crops are getting and how much is being grown.

3 Farmers also use computers to help them buy the right amount of seed and fertilizers. This saves farmers money because they don't over-buy, "just in case." Computers go out into the fields with the farmers. Computers on tractors make certain that seeds are planted in the right places and that the right number are planted in each place. Computers are also found on the trucks used to spread fertilizer to ensure that farmers apply exactly the right amount.

4 With their computers, farmers have joined the modern work force in order to do a better job of growing the foods we need.

FIND THE ANSWERS

1. Farmers use trucks to
   - a. plant seeds.
   - b. spread fertilizer.
   - c. save money.
   - d. read data.

2. The word in paragraph 3 that means *make certain that* is

   _____.

3. The words "takes into account" in paragraph 2 refer to

   _____.

4. The story does not say so, but it makes you think that
   - a. farmers started using computers fairly recently.
   - b. farmers who raise animals don't use computers.
   - c. before computers, farming was all guesswork.

5. Computers can help farmers save money by helping them avoid
   - a. using fertilizer.
   - b. buying new tractors.
   - c. planting wheat.
   - d. overbuying.

6. Modern plows have computers on them.

   Yes   No   Does not say

7. On the whole, this story is about
   - a. how computers are used on farms.
   - b. how farming has changed over the years.
   - c. the best way to grow crops.

8. Why isn't it best to plant wheat at the same time every year? (Check the story again.)
   - a. Computers need to read all the data.
   - b. Some seeds grow more quickly than others.
   - c. Conditions change from year to year.

9. Which of these sentences do you think is right?
   - a. The more fertilizer a farmer uses, the better the crops will be.
   - b. Crops grow best when the seeds are planted in the right places.
   - c. Farmers don't need to worry about what crops other farmers are planting.

From Farm to Family

1. Everyone knows cows give milk. But did you know that machines get the milk from farm to family?

2. At one time, a farmer had to milk his cows by hand. Today, many farmers have electric milking machines to do the work for them. A milking machine can milk two or more cows at one time. And it does the job in a matter of minutes.

3. From the milking machine, the milk flows through pipes into a big metal tank. There, the milk is kept cool until a large tank truck stops at the farm. The tank truck can hold 2,000 gallons of milk and keep it cold. The tank truck may go to a dairy more than 100 miles away.

4. At the dairy, the milk is heated to kill germs. It is also put into bottles. Bottling machines do the work of many hands. They wash and scrub thousands of bottles inside and out. When the bottles are clean, they are carried on a moving belt to a bottle-filling machine. This machine fills each bottle with the right amount of milk. Then it puts on the cap.

5. Other machines put milk into paper cartons. After the milk has been put into bottles or cartons, it is ready for your family.

104

FIND THE ANSWERS

1. Milking machines are run by
   - a. hand.
   - b. germs.
   - c. electricity.
   - d. cows.

2. The word in paragraph 3 that means *measures of a liquid* is

   _____.

3. The words "They wash and scrub thousands of bottles" in paragraph 4

   refer to the _____ _____.

4. The story does not say so, but it makes you think that
   - a. machines help keep milk free of germs.
   - b. cows are afraid of milking machines.
   - c. milk can be made by machines.

5. Tank trucks pick up milk at the
   - a. factory.
   - b. farm.
   - c. store.
   - d. machine.

6. Machines get the milk ready for the family.
   Yes   No   Does not say

7. On the whole, this story is about
   - a. how much milk cows give.
   - b. tank trucks.
   - c. milk and machines.

8. What happens to the milk when it is in a big metal tank? (Check the story again.)
   - a. It is kept warm.
   - b. It is kept cool.
   - c. It is made into ice cream.

9. Which of these sentences do you think is right?
   - a. Machines are important in getting milk to your kitchen.
   - b. Milk is made at the dairy by many machines.
   - c. Milk is ready for your family when it comes from the cow.

Life Among the Trees

1   Orangutans are most at home in forests. These large and interesting apes move through the trees by swinging among branches. They sleep in trees too, in nests they make from branches and leaves. They eat the fruit, leaves, and bark of the trees.

2   Most orangutans are found on two Southeast Asian islands, Borneo and Sumatra. They live in groups made up of 10 to 12 adults and their young. A group occupies about a square mile of the forest. Within the area, each adult group member has its own territory.

3   Orangutans need large forests to follow this way of life, but the forests in Borneo and Sumatra are shrinking. The local people have been clearing the forests to make farmland. Huge forest fires have destroyed much of the habitat. Sometimes the forest that remains is too small for the orangutans.

4   Scientists from the Wildlife Conservation Society are trying to help the orangutans. But in order to help, they must first capture the animals. So as not to hurt them, the scientists use darts that have sleeping medicine on the tips. Once the orangutans are asleep, the scientists take them to forests that are large enough for them to live comfortably. However, the orangutans are still in danger. Care must be taken to control forest fires, and also to help the people to live together with these animals as good neighbors.

106

FIND THE ANSWERS

1. Each group of orangutans lives in an area of about
   - a. 1 mile.
   - b. 10 to 12 miles.
   - c. 1 square mile.
   - d. 100 square miles.

2. The word in paragraph 3 that means *cutting all the trees down* is
   _____.

3. The words "these large and interesting apes" in paragraph 1 refer to
   _____.

4. The story does not say so, but it makes you think that
   - a. young orangutans live by themselves.
   - b. orangutans don't spend much time walking around on the ground.
   - c. Because their territory is so large, most orangutans hardly ever see another orangutan.

5. Orangutans are being helped by
   - a. scientists.
   - b. the United Nations.
   - c. farmers.
   - d. local people.

6. Orangutans eat nuts.
   Yes   No   Does not say

7. On the whole, this story is about
   - a. the Wildlife Conservation Society.
   - b. how orangutans live.
   - c. the forests of Borneo and Sumatra.

8. Why are the forests of Borneo and Sumatra shrinking? (Check the story again.)
   - a. The forests are too small for the orangutans.
   - b. The orangutans are eating all the bark off the trees.
   - c. Because of forest fires and local people clearing them.

9. Which of these sentences do you think is right?
   - a. Without help, the orangutans might die out.
   - b. The people of Borneo and Sumatra want to get rid of the orangutans.
   - c. Scientists are helping the orangutans to change the way they live.

Money at Work

1   Go to a city anywhere in the United States. In it you will find people who own businesses, people who work in businesses, and people who buy products and services from businesses. One thing keeps the products and services flowing from producers to buyers: money. Workers use the money they earn to buy things they need and want. Companies use that money to make more things that people need and want.

2   People who start companies also have to convince other people to invest in them. To get people to invest, companies offer them a chance to make money. They can do this in a number of ways.

3   Some companies sell stock. The people who buy stock own a piece of the company. If the company makes a profit, so will the stockholders. If the company does not do well, stockholders may lose their money.

4   Businesses can also sell bonds. People who buy bonds lend their money to the company. To make it worthwhile for lenders, companies pay interest on the money.

5   Businesses also get loans from banks. They pay interest to the bank. The bank uses the money in people's bank accounts to make loans. It pays them interest in exchange for using their money.

1. People are lending money to a business when they buy
   a. products.
   b. interest.
   c. stock.
   d. bonds.

2. The word in paragraph 5 that means *the giving of one thing for something else* is _____.

3. The words "who buy stock" in paragraph 3 refer to _____.

4. The story does not say so, but it makes you think that
   a. a great many people can own one business.
   b. all businesses sell stocks and bonds.
   c. banks lend money only to businesses.

5. When businesses borrow money from banks, they have to
   a. open an account.
   b. make a profit.
   c. buy bonds.
   d. pay interest.

6. People who keep money in the bank earn interest on it.
   Yes   No   Does not say

7. On the whole, this story is about
   a. how businesses get money.
   b. what banks do.
   c. stocks and bonds.

8. Why do people buy stocks in a business? (Check the story again.)
   a. They want to own the business.
   b. They needed the business's products and services.
   c. They hope to make money.

9. Which of these sentences do you think is right?
   a. Small cities do not have banks.
   b. You need money in order to start a business.
   c. The only way to earn money is by working.

Clearing the Air

1   In an American city many years ago, a large number of paintings was damaged by "bad" air. In New York City 168 people died and thousands became ill from fumes in the air in one year—1966.

2   Air pollution, or dirty air, is caused by many things. Great clouds of smoke come from factory chimneys. Cars send smoke and fumes into the air. Burning waste fills the air with bits of dirt. Even burning leaves add smoke to the air. Smoke of all kinds is bad to breathe and can do great harm to the body.

3   We still have a problem with air pollution. However, things have gotten better. In 1970, the U.S. Congress passed the Clean Air Act. This law limits the amount of fumes cars can exhaust into the air. It also sets limits on pollution from power plants and factories. Although scientists have not yet been able to stop air pollution, they have found ways to make cars and factories burn fuel more cleanly. People are also more careful than they once were. For example, they have stopped burning fallen leaves in the autumn. We still have a long way to go. But if we all work together, we can solve the problem.

110

1. Scientists are now working on ways to
   a. make new paintings.
   b. help people breathe dirty air.
   c. build safer cars.
   d. stop air pollution.

2. The word in paragraph 1 that means *gas* or *smoke* is

   _____.

3. The words "dirty air" in paragraph 2 describe _____.

4. The story does not say so, but it makes you think that
   a. stopping air pollution is hard.
   b. dirty air is blown away by the wind.
   c. there has always been air pollution.

5. Air pollution is caused by
   a. clouds.
   b. breathing.
   c. smoke and fumes.
   d. paintings.

6. Works of art have been damaged by dirty air.
   Yes   No   Does not say

7. On the whole, this story is about
   a. dirty air.
   b. electric power.
   c. burning oil.

8. Why do burning leaves add to air pollution? (Check the story again.)
   a. They could cause a dangerous fire.
   b. They leave ashes behind.
   c. They add smoke to the air.

9. Which of these sentences do you think is right?
   a. More ways to stop pollution must be found.
   b. Air is clean.
   c. It is good for our lungs to breathe smoke.

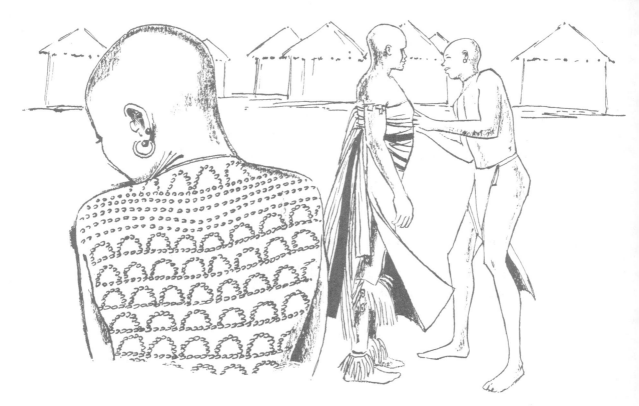

Decorating Themselves

1 When we want to look our best, we dress up in our nicest clothes. We are using the clothes to decorate ourselves.

2 The Nubas in the African country of Sudan do not dress up in fancy clothes. They use another kind of decoration. They have scars which form designs on their skin.

3 You may wonder how a Nuba gets these scars. First, a design is cut into the skin. Then a kind of oil is rubbed into the wounds. When the wounds heal, scars are left. The scars rise in bumps above the skin and form designs.

4 The scarring of a Nuba girl begins when she is seven or eight. Sometimes a women's entire body is covered by designs.

5 The Nuba men also decorate themselves. Their cuts are deeper, so their scars stand out more.

6 The Nubas use many different designs, and some are favorites. A young woman likes to have three rows of scars across her left shoulder. A Nuba man sometimes has the figure of an animal carved on his chest.

7 The Nubas are proud of their decorations. They want to look their best.

112

FIND THE ANSWERS

1. The Nubas decorate themselves with
   - a. scars.
   - b. clothes.
   - c. beads.
   - d. fancy hats.

2. The word in paragraph 3 that means *stand up* is _____.

3. The words "form designs on their skin" in paragraph 2 refer to the Nubas' _____.

4. The story does not say so, but it makes you think that
   - a. women have more designs than young girls.
   - b. men do not scar themselves.
   - c. all the scars are made at one time.

5. The Nubas make designs on their
   - a. clothes.
   - b. skin.
   - c. shirts.
   - d. houses.

6. The Sudan is in Africa.
   Yes   No   Does not say

7. On the whole, this story is about
   - a. long-headed women.
   - b. Nuba men.
   - c. Nuba decorations.

8. Why do the Nubas scar themselves? (Check the story again.)
   - a. They want to see who can make the best designs.
   - b. It is the way to punish their children.
   - c. They believe it makes them look their best.

9. Which of these sentences do you think is right?
   - a. Nubas wear clothes that have fancy designs on them.
   - b. People decorate themselves in different ways.
   - c. Nuba men and women use the same designs.

The Hungry Cat
(An Indian Folktale)

A cat and a parrot were once good friends.

"You must come to my house for dinner," said the cat.

"Thank you," said the parrot. "Then you must be my guest for dinner."

When the parrot went to the cat's house, the cat prepared a very poor meal. There was nothing that the parrot liked, but he was too polite to say so.

Next, the cat went to the parrot's house for dinner. The parrot had worked all day. He roasted a big piece of meat. He had a pot of tea and a basket of fruit. He baked 500 little cakes with raisins in them.

The parrot put all the food before the cat except two little cakes with

114

raisins in them. He kept those for himself. "Two cakes are all I want," he said.

The cat gobbled up all her food. Then she said, "I'm hungry. Where is my dinner?"

The parrot tried to be polite. "You may have my two cakes with raisins in them."

The cat ate the cakes. "Is that all you have?" she asked.

"It is," said the angry parrot, "unless you wish to eat me!"

"All right," said the cat. And she ate the parrot.

An old woman had seen the whole thing. "Cat!" she called out. "You should not have eaten your friend!"

"Mind your own business," said the cat. "I think I will eat you, too." And she ate the old woman.

The cat walked down the road. She met a man and his donkey. "Out of my way, cat!" shouted the man. "My donkey may step on you!"

"What do I care?" said the cat. "I have just eaten 500 cakes, a parrot, and an old woman. I think I will eat you, too." And she ate both the man and the donkey and walked on.

The King and Queen were coming down the road. Behind them came all the soldiers and dozens of elephants marching two by two.

The happy King spoke kindly.

"Stand aside, pussy cat. My elephants might hurt you."

"Hurt *me*?" said the hungry cat. "I have just eaten 500 cakes, a parrot, an old woman, and a man and his donkey! I think I will eat you, too!" And the cat ate the King, the Queen, the soldiers, and all the elephants marching two by two.

The cat walked on, a little more slowly. She met two land crabs. They were walking sidewise in the dust, as crabs will do.

"Out of our way, Puss," said the land crabs.

"Out of *your* way?" said the cat. "I have just eaten 500 cakes, a parrot, an old woman, a man and his donkey, a King and Queen, all the soldiers, and his elephants marching two by two. I think I will eat you, too." And she ate the crabs.

When the land crabs were inside the cat, they looked around. It was very dark, but they could see the King holding the Queen's hand. The elephants were trying to line up two by two. The soldiers were stepping on each other's toes. The old woman was talking to the old man and the donkey. The parrot was sitting on a big pile of cakes with raisins in them.

The crabs cut a hole in the side of the cat with their sharp claws. They walked out sidewise, as crabs will

do. After them came the King, the Queen, the soldiers, the elephants marching two by two, the man and his donkey, the old woman and, last of all, the parrot. The parrot was carrying two cakes with raisins in them.

"Two cakes are all I want," he said.

The hungry cat went off to find a needle and thread to sew up the hole in her coat.

And that is why cats and parrots are no longer friends.

648 words

116

III

Communities Establish Patterns of Behavior

In this section, you will read about how communities establish patterns of behavior. You will read about these things from the standpoint of history, ecology, biology, economics, sociology, art, geography, engineering, and anthropology.

Keep these questions in mind when you are reading.

1. What are some things that cause us to develop certain customs?

2. Are these things established quickly or slowly?

3. Are well-established customs always good?

4. How do customs affect us?

5. Why is it good to study about other peoples?

Look on pages 10-12 for help with words in this section you don't understand.

The Castes of India

1   Long ago, around 1500 B.C., warriors from the north came down into the country we now call India. They fought their way through mountain passes. Finally, these warriors, the Aryans, became the rulers of the country.

2   The Aryans thought that they were more important than the people who had lost. So they kept their subjects separate from themselves.

3   They divided their subjects into four groups, or classes. The people in each class made their living in a different way. Some were religious leaders, and some were soldiers. Others were farmers. Most were workers.

And some people were thought to be so low they were not in a class at all. These people were called Untouchables.

4   Separate classes became a part of Indian life. These classes were called castes. Indians of different castes could not eat or work together. They could not marry each other. The people believed that they were born into castes, and they could never leave them.

5   In many country villages people still live this way. But most modern Indians do not pay much attention to the castes. An Untouchable even become president of India!

118

FIND THE ANSWERS

1. The Aryans came to India through
   - a. heavy snows.
   - b. deep rivers.
   - c. mountain passes.
   - d. separate classes.

2. The word in paragraph 5 that means *present day* or *not long ago* is

   _____.

3. The words "these warriors" in paragraph 1 refer to the _____.

4. The story does not say so, but it makes you think that
   - a. the Aryans ruled over the American Indians.
   - b. all modern Indians believe in separate castes.
   - c. India is a very old country.

5. Aryan warriors came to India from the
   - a. sea.
   - b. north.
   - c. cities.
   - d. south.

6. The Aryans had a king.
   - Yes   No   Does not say

7. On the whole, this story is about
   - a. country villages.
   - b. castes in India.
   - c. Indians in the United States.

8. How were castes different from one another? (Check the story again.)
   - a. One caste was made up of women and the others of men.
   - b. All the tall people were in one caste and the short people in another.
   - c. Each caste made their living in a different way.

9. Which of these sentences do you think is right?
   - a. The caste system is very old, and it is hard to change.
   - b. The Aryans were not important in the early history of India.
   - c. All the people made their living in the same way.

Education for All

1   Today, all fifty states in America have many laws about education. One of these laws says all children must go to school. Each state collects tax money from people who own property. Taxes are used to build schools, buy books, and pay teachers. In that way, everyone can go to school.

2   In Colonial days, it was different. Usually, people had to pay to send children to school. Not everyone could afford to send their children, and many young people never went to school. In school, most children were taught only to read and write. Children from rich families had a better education.

3   During the early 1800s, people began to think it was important for all children to have an education. In 1852, Massachusetts passed a law which said that all children must go to school. Then other states passed education laws. At first, children only had to go to school four or five years. There were no high schools.

4   Now children must remain in school until they are sixteen. In some states, they must stay in school until they are eighteen. Schools are paid for by tax money. All children have a chance to learn.

120

FIND THE ANSWERS

1. In America, there are education laws
   - a. nowhere.
   - b. in every state.
   - c. in some states.
   - d. only in the East.

2. The word in paragraph 4 that means *stay* or *keep on* is _____.

3. The words "are paid for by tax money" in paragraph 4 tell about the word _____.

4. The story does not say so, but it makes you think that
   - a. only a few children can go to school today.
   - b. there are no education laws.
   - c. Massachusetts was the first state to pass education laws.

5. In some states, children must stay in school until they are
   - a. ten.
   - b. twelve.
   - c. twenty-one.
   - d. eighteen.

6. Taxes pay teachers, buy books, and build schools.
   Yes   No   Does not say

7. On the whole, this story is about
   - a. Massachusetts.
   - b. education.
   - c. property taxes.

8. Why did states pass laws saying that all children must go to school? (Check the story again.)
   - a. They wanted children to stop bothering their mothers.
   - b. They wanted to raise more taxes.
   - c. They believed that all children should go to school.

9. Which of these sentences do you think is right?
   - a. Children from poor families do not have a chance to learn.
   - b. Education laws have not helped schools very much.
   - c. Americans believe that education is important.

Trial by Jury

1   In the United States everyone has the right to a trial by jury. If a person is charged with a crime but says, "I am not guilty," there will be a trial. The person is brought before a jury made up of twelve people. The members of the jury listen to facts about the crime. They decide if the person is guilty or not guilty.

2   The earliest juries in England were used mostly to get facts about a crime. An English country-woman might see a thief stealing a sheep. She would tell the judge who the thief was. If the judge did not know the boundary line of the royal land, a member of the jury would go get the facts. These jury members were like witnesses or detectives.

3   In the 1100s, trial by jury began in England. Under King Henry II, the first juries for a trial were chosen. Slowly, different kinds of juries spread to Europe and to North and South America.

4   Today, a person who knows something special about the crime cannot be a member of the jury. Why do you think this is so?

122

FIND THE ANSWERS

1. In the United States everyone has the right to
   a. a trial by jury.
   b. bring a sheep into court.
   c. a trial without a jury.
   d. a trial in England.

2. The word in paragraph 1 that means *to make up their minds* or *to settle*

   is _____.

3. The words "made up of twelve people" in paragraph 1 describe the

   word _____.

4. The story does not say so, but it makes you think that
   a. jury members steal sheep.
   b. people in England still have trial by jury.
   c. King Henry II did not like boundary lines.

5. In the earliest juries, members were more like
   a. judges.
   b. criminals.
   c. lawyers.
   d. witnesses.

6. People in Japan have the right to a trial by jury.
   Yes   No   Does not say

7. On the whole, this story is about
   a. changing crimes.
   b. changing kings.
   c. changes in trials.

8. What spread to Europe and to North and South America? (Check the
   story again.)
   a. Different kinds of crimes.
   b. Different kinds of juries.
   c. Different kinds of witnesses.

9. Which of these sentences do you think is right?
   a. People in England have always had trial by jury.
   b. A jury is chosen by the president.
   c. Fair trials came about slowly.

A King and a Queen

1   Termites are small insects that live together in groups. They are called "social insects." Wasps, bees, and ants are the only other social insects.

2   Termites eat wood and live in dark tunnels in trees or underground. Most of the termites in a nest are small males and females without wings. These are the workers. They build the nest and care for the king and queen, the soldiers, and the eggs.

3   The termite soldiers are males and females. They are larger than the workers and have such big jaws that they cannot feed themselves. Food must be put in their mouths by the workers. The soldiers come to any part of the nest that is in danger. To warn the other termites, they bang their heads against the wood and make a loud sound.

4   In a different room in the nest live a little king and a large queen. The queen is sometimes four inches long and very fat. Her only work is laying eggs. From most of these eggs come workers and soldiers. But a few of the eggs become termites with wings. These termites fly off and become the kings and queens of new nests.

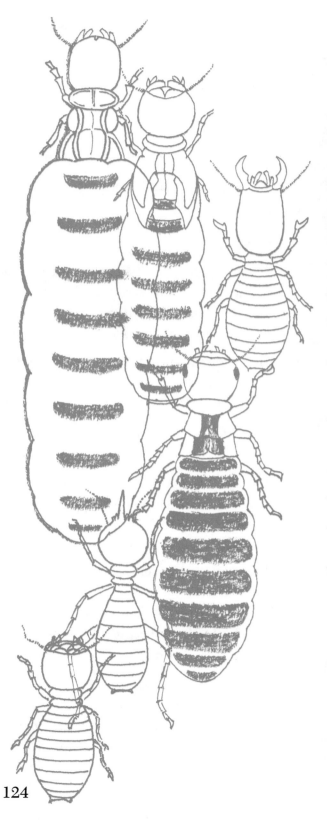

124

FIND THE ANSWERS

1. Termites live
   a. in caves.
   b. in tunnels.
   c. in water.
   d. in dens.

2. The word in paragraph 3 that means *to signal* or *to tell someone* is

   _____.

3. The words "they build the nest" in paragraph 2 refer to the

   _____.

4. The story does not say so, but it makes you think that
   a. termites eat other insects.
   b. termites live with wasps, bees, and ants.
   c. termites with wings become kings and queens.

5. Termite soldiers
   a. feed themselves.
   b. are smaller than the workers.
   c. have large jaws.
   d. are all males.

6. The queen's only job is to lay eggs.
   Yes   No   Does not say

7. On the whole, this story is about
   a. termites as social insects.
   b. kinds of social insects.
   c. underground tunnels.

8. Why do the soldier termites bang their heads against wood? (Check the story again.)
   a. They like the sound it makes.
   b. They are warning other termites of danger.
   c. They are trying to make the nest bigger.

9. Which of these sentences do you think is right?
   a. All termites are alike.
   b. Termites work together as a group.
   c. The termite soldiers do the most work.

He Saw It First

1　Did you know that birds could be "property owners," too? In the spring, the male robin looks for a place to build a nest. A tree near a green lawn that has many worms suits him best. When he finds the right place, he sings loudly. He tells other birds that this place is his property.

2　At the same time, other birds are choosing places for their nests. A robin does not mind if swallows nest nearby because swallows eat insects. They leave his worms alone. But other robins are different. They would eat the worm supply he needs for his own family.

3　When another male robin comes near, the robin owner sings to warn him away. The property owner looks cross and fierce. He raises his head feathers and holds his tail high.

4　If the owner cannot frighten away the new robin, he attacks. The two fight until one is the winner. The new bird often gives up and flies away. So the first bird has defended his property. He now has the right to build a nest in the place he selected.

126

FIND THE ANSWERS

1. The male robin looks for a place to build a nest
   a. near swallows.
   b. near other male robins.
   c. near a lawn with worms.
   d. in the woods.

2. The word in paragraph 1 that means *pleases* or *satisfies* is

   _____.

3. The words "cross and fierce" in paragraph 3 refer to a robin

   _____ _____.

4. The story does not say so, but it makes you think that
   a. robins chase away all other birds.
   b. robins do not care where they build their nests.
   c. robins are careful when choosing a place to nest.

5. Robins eat
   a. worms.
   b. insects.
   c. fruit.
   d. berries.

6. Robins will nest near swallows.
   Yes   No   Does not say

7. On the whole, this story is about
   a. what robins eat.
   b. robins finding a nesting place.
   c. robins finding friends.

8. Why does the male robin raise his head feathers and hold his tail high?
   (Check the story again.)
   a. He wants to scare away another male robin.
   b. He is getting ready to hunt for worms.
   c. He is too warm.

9. Which of these sentences do you think is right?
   a. The first robin that chooses a tree can build there.
   b. Female robins select the nesting places.
   c. Swallows always help robins defend their property.

The Pecking Order

1   Birds of one kind often stay together in one group, or flock. In every flock, some birds are more important than others. Each bird has its own place. This order goes from the most important to the least important. It is called the "pecking order."

2   In a flock of hens in a barnyard, one hen becomes the most important of the group. She eats first and gets the best perch. She can peck all the other hens. The least important hen is pecked by all the others. She has no other hen to peck. She usually eats last and takes whatever space is left on the perch.

3   To get a place in the pecking order, hens have a pecking contest among themselves. A hen may lose or back away from a fight. Then she becomes less important than the winner and can be pecked by her. Each hen knows which hens to fear and which to peck.

4   Do you have a bird feeder at home or outside your school window? If you do, watch carefully when a group of birds comes to feed. The most important bird in the pecking order will be the first to eat.

FIND THE ANSWERS

1. In every flock of birds,
   - a. some are more important.
   - b. all are equal.
   - c. the males fight the females.
   - d. there are many small groups.

2. The word in paragraph 3 that means *a kind of fight* is _____.

3. The words "from the most important to the least important" in paragraph 1 refer to the _____ _____.

4. The story does not say so, but it makes you think that
   - a. hens do not fight.
   - b. the most important hen can do as she pleases.
   - c. hens are the only kind of bird that have a pecking order.

5. The most important hen
   - a. eats last.
   - b. eats at a bird feeder.
   - c. never fights.
   - d. gets the best perch.

6. Each bird has its own place in a pecking order.
   Yes   No   Does not say

7. On the whole, this story is about
   - a. bird feeders in the barnyard.
   - b. flocks of birds in the sky.
   - c. the order of birds in a flock.

8. Why do hens have pecking contests among themselves? (Check the story again.)
   - a. It is a kind of game that chickens play.
   - b. Hens fight to get a place in the pecking order.
   - c. They like to have contests.

9. Which of these sentences do you think is right?
   - a. Many kinds of birds have pecking orders.
   - b. Birds in a flock never fight with each other.
   - c. The least important bird must leave the flock.

Craft Guilds

1   Today, many people who are skilled at a trade belong to labor unions. As long ago as the Middle Ages, people in western Europe also belonged to a kind of union. These early unions were called guilds.

2   From the 1300s to the 1700s, people who knew a trade joined a craft guild. Guilds were made up of groups of people who did the same kind of work. Shoemakers belonged to the shoemakers' guild. Nail makers belonged to a guild of nail makers.

3   Craft guilds were important in those days. If people were not members of a guild, they could not find work.

4   To become a guild member, a person first had to be an apprentice, or learner. A learner received no pay. Next the person became a journeyman and received pay. At last a person became a master and could open a shop.

5   In the 1800s Candace Wheeler, an artist and maker of American cloth, became interested in women's problems. Many women had good educations but could not earn enough money to live. Candace opened the Women's Exchange, a kind of guild, in New York.

6   At the Exchange women could sell their beautiful handmade dresses and tablecloths. It helped them earn enough to live.

FIND THE ANSWERS

1. Today, many people skilled at a trade belong to
   a. a shoemakers' guild.   c. a labor union.
   b. the Boy Scouts.   d. a group of masters.

2. The word in paragraph 4 that means *a person who is learning a trade* is

   _____.

3. The words "a kind of union" in paragraph 1 describe the word

   _____.

4. The story does not say so, but it makes you think that
   a. journeymen were very skilled.
   b. apprentices did not have much money to spend.
   c. guilds were made up of people who lived in the same town.

5. One kind of union began as long ago as
   a. the Stone Age.   c. the Atomic Age.
   b. the Revolutionary War.   d. the Middle Ages.

6. It was hard for people who were guild members to find work.
   Yes   No   Does not say

7. On the whole, this story is about
   a. becoming a craft guild member.
   b. people going on journeys.
   c. masters who made nails and shoes.

8. Why did people want to belong to craft guilds? (Check the story again.)
   a. By belonging, they could find jobs.
   b. They wanted to make shoes and nails.
   c. They wanted to work where their friends worked.

9. Which of these sentences do you think is right?
   a. The Women's Exchange sold bread.
   b. The Women's Exchange sold handwork.
   c. The Women's Exchange lost tablecloths.

131

Working Children

1   Almost since time began children have helped their parents at home. In the 1700s, a great change was taking place in England. Cloth and other things which had been made by hand in homes were now made by machines in factories. New inventions caused this change, which was called the Industrial Revolution. Children then began to work outside their homes.

2   Factory owners liked children to work for them. They had small hands and could work the cloth-making machines quicker than an adult. They worked for little money and did as they were told.

3   But the factory owners were often cruel to the children. Five- and six-year-old children were chained to their machines. They often worked as long as 16 hours a day. They did not have nice places to live and were not fed enough. They did not go to school. Sometimes they were taken away from their parents and did not see them again.

4   At last, the government in England began to make laws that helped the children. One of these laws was passed in 1819. It said that children under nine years old could not work in factories. In time, the laws of most countries protected their children.

132

FIND THE ANSWERS

1. A great change was taking place in England in the
   - a. 1400s.
   - b. 700s.
   - c. 1700s.
   - d. 1800s.

2. The word in paragraph 3 that means *to cause pain or suffering* is

   _____.

3. The words "had small hands" in paragraph 2 refer to the word

   _____.

4. The story does not say so, but it makes you think that
   - a. children were kept in cages.
   - b. children had many vacations.
   - c. few children lived at home.

5. Children often worked as long as
   - a. 10 hours a week.
   - b. 16 hours a day.
   - c. 12 hours a month.
   - d. 20 hours a month.

6. Children who worked in factories had a hard life.

   Yes   No   Does not say

7. On the whole, this story is about
   - a. cloth-making machines.
   - b. children who worked in factories.
   - c. the government of England.

8. Why did the government of England begin to make laws to help children? (Check the story again.)
   - a. They wanted the children chained to their machines.
   - b. They wanted the children to work for the government.
   - c. They wanted the children to be treated better.

9. Which of these sentences do you think is right?
   - a. Children liked to work in factories.
   - b. Children who worked in factories lived with their parents.
   - c. At one time, children did much of the factory work.

Labor Unions

1   The Industrial Revolution brought great changes in both England and the United States. Many workers were needed to work the new machines. People from the country went to the cities to find jobs in factories.

2   Sometimes these factory workers were not well treated. Their working days were very long. Their pay was small. The bosses did not listen to the demands of one or two workers. In America, the workers began to band together into groups called "labor unions." These groups were the first unions in the world.

3   A labor union could demand better working conditions. If its demands were not met, the people in the union would not work. They went "on strike" until they had what they wanted.

4   At first, unions were small groups in their own cities. If they had strikes that did not work, the unions fell apart. Next, all the unions in a city grouped together. All the people in all the unions were able to help one another.

5   At last, unions from all over the country banded together into very large groups. Then the unions were a more powerful group. People felt that they had help when they asked for better working conditions.

134

FIND THE ANSWERS

1. The new machines of the Industrial Revolution needed
   - a. many workers.
   - b. new parts.
   - c. no repairs.
   - d. too much oil.

2. The word in paragraph 2 that means *to get together in groups* is

   _____.

3. The words "people in the union would not work" in paragraph 3

   explain the words _____.

4. The story does not say so, but it makes you think that
   - a. labor unions were formed to help one or two workers.
   - b. people on strike did not belong to a union.
   - c. the United States had labor unions before other countries.

5. Labor unions are found
   - a. just in the country.
   - b. just city-wide.
   - c. nowhere.
   - d. all across the country.

6. People who were not in the unions could not get what they demanded.
   - Yes   No   Does not say

7. On the whole, this story is about
   - a. cities.
   - b. the growth of labor unions.
   - c. working conditions in factories.

8. Why did so many people find jobs in factories? (Check the story.)
   - a. The factories paid their workers a lot of money.
   - b. New machines made many more jobs open to workers.
   - c. They didn't like to live in the country.

9. Which of these sentences do you think is right?
   - a. Labor unions helped people get better working conditions.
   - b. Workers have always had short hours and high pay.
   - c. Union members never go on strike.

"I Love Teaching"

1 Judy Krecek has been teaching for twenty-four years. She teaches social studies, language arts, computer skills, and other disciplines. Students in her class read and write, as all students do. Like all elementary school students, they also play pranks on their teacher. (Ms. Krecek's says they do it out of love.)

2 Still, in some ways Ms. Krecek's classroom is not like other classrooms. When students do not recognize words, they spell them out loud instead of pointing to them. Students listen to recorded stories instead of stories read by their teacher. Their tests are recorded, too. Students must always sit in the same seats for every class. In addition, Ms. Krecek uses a talking clock calculator. She does things this way because she is blind.

3 When Ms. Krecek first got her teaching license, she had trouble getting a job. Many people did not think a blind person could control a class. The principal who hired Ms. Krecek wasn't concerned. All he wanted to know was if she could teach.

4 Ms. Krecek is a tough teacher who pushes her students to do their best. To them, she is simply the teacher—not the blind teacher.

5 Here's how Judy Krecek feels about her job. "I love teaching because I can touch children's lives and make a difference."

FIND THE ANSWERS

1. Judy Krecek teaches
   - a. blind children.
   - b. elementary school.
   - c. high school.
   - d. college.

2. The word in paragraph 1 that means *fields of study* is

   _____.

3. The words "are recorded, too" in paragraph 2 refer to

   _____.

4. The story does not say so, but it makes you think that
   - a. Judy Krecek is a good teacher.
   - b. Judy Krecek's students don't learn how to read.
   - c. Judy Krecek teaches fourth grade.

5. When Ms. Krecek's students don't recognize words, they
   - a. sound them out.
   - b. point to them in their books.
   - c. ask a classmate.
   - d. spell them to her.

6. Judy Krecek teaches health education.
   - Yes　　　　　No　　　　　Does not say

7. On the whole, this story is about
   - a. Judy Krecek's job.
   - b. an elementary school class.
   - c. what it's like to be blind.

8. Why did Judy Krecek have trouble getting a job? (Check the story again.)
   - a. Many other people also had gotten teaching licenses that year.
   - b. She didn't know how to use a computer.
   - c. Many people thought she wouldn't be able to control her class.

9. Which of these sentences do you think is right?
   - a. The children in Ms. Krecek's class are especially well behaved.
   - b. Judy Krecek had to face many challenges to become a teacher.
   - c. Several teachers in Ms. Krecek's school are blind.

The Face Is Familiar

1   At one time, most people lived in small towns where everybody knew everybody else. When people went to the bank, the tellers recognized them. Therefore, the tellers didn't need to ask for identification.

2   As towns grew larger and many people moved to cities, things changed. Tellers didn't know their customers so they checked customers' signatures against signatures they kept on file. To make life easier, banks started giving customers identification cards. People got used to handing their bank cards to the tellers.

3   Then banks put in automatic teller machines, or ATMs. People didn't have to wait for a teller any more and they could do their banking at any time. Customers still used bank cards to identify themselves, however. To do this, they fed their card into the ATM. But if the card was stolen, a thief could use it to empty the customer's bank account. Banks found a way to protect their customers by giving them "Personal Identification Numbers," or PINs. They could identify themselves by entering their PINs on the keypad.

4   New technology makes it possible for computers to recognize people's faces. Someday we may be identifying ourselves to ATMs by simply smiling at built-in TV cameras.

138

FIND THE ANSWERS

1. Numbers people use as identification are
   a. ATMs.
   b. keys.
   c. IDs.
   d. PINs.

2. The word in paragraph 2 that means *the way people sign their names* is

   _____.

3. The words "built-in" in paragraph 4 describe _____.

4. The story does not say so, but it makes you think that
   a. automatic teller machines are not very convenient.
   b. people change their habits as the world they live in changes.
   c. banks don't need tellers anymore.

5. Bank cards are used for
   a. writing checks.
   b. identification.
   c. entering PINs.
   d. taking pictures.

6. ATMs can be used only during the hours when banks are open.
   Yes   No   Does not say

7. On the whole, this story is about
   a. changes in how banks identify customers.
   b. how to use automatic teller machines safely.
   c. the job of a bank teller.

8. How did small town tellers identify their customers? (Check the story again.)
   a. They asked for their bank cards.
   b. They checked their signatures.
   c. They recognized them.

9. Which of these sentences do you think is right?
   a. Someday people won't need PINs to use ATMs.
   b. Tellers should make an effort to know all their customers.
   c. You can take money out of your bank account at an ATM, but you can't put money in it.

A Club for Working Women

1   In India, many women belong to a club called Working Women's Forum. Most of these women work at jobs such as washing clothes, sewing, selling fruits and vegetables, and running small shops. Working Women's Forum members want to make life better for themselves and their families. They help each other in many ways. They also work together to improve conditions in their communities.

2   To do their work successfully, these women often need to buy equipment and materials. If they do not have enough money to purchase these things, they cannot earn enough to take care of their families and help their communities. One answer is to borrow the money from banks. However, most banks don't lend money in small amounts. The Working Women's Forum solved this problem. The Forum borrows large amounts from a bank, then lends small amounts to members.

3   The women who borrow money often turn their work into larger businesses where they will earn more money. They can then use this money to buy more and better food, find better housing, and go to school. These things lead to a higher status for the women. Forum women can then use their new status to work for better conditions for all Indian women.

140

FIND THE ANSWERS

1. The women in the story need money to buy
   a. small shops.
   b. cloth.
   c. tools and equipment.
   d. fruits and vegetables.

2. The word in paragraph 2 that means *in a way that turns out well* is

   _____.

3. The words "small amounts" in paragraph 2 refer to

   _____.

4. The story does not say so, but it makes you think that
   a. most women in the Working Women's Forum are poor.
   b. most women in the Working Women's Forum own stores.
   c. most women in the Working Women's Forum are not married.

5. Members of the Working Women's Forum
   a. borrow money from banks.
   b. borrow money from the Forum.
   c. lend each other money.
   d. put their savings in bank accounts.

6. Some women in the Working Women's Forum earn money by weaving mats.
   Yes   No   Does not say

7. On the whole, this story is about
   a. Indian women.
   b. banking in India.
   c. the Working Women's Forum.

8. How do women use their improved status? (Check the story again.)
   a. They turn their work into businesses.
   b. They work for better conditions for all Indian women.
   c. They move into better housing.

9. Which of these sentences do you think is right?
   a. The Working Women's Forum helps only a few women in India.
   b. The Working Women's Forum has made life better for many people.
   c. There is no longer a need for the Working Women's Forum.

141

Buildings from the Past

1   Many people visiting the Southwest stop at Santa Fe, New Mexico. There, they see long, low buildings that have flat roofs. Most houses are only one story high. They have beautiful small gardens with walls around them.

2   The buildings are tan and brown like the earth because they are made of adobe (ə dō' bē). Adobe is a Spanish word that means "sundried brick." It is made by mixing clay soil, straw, and water. Its cost is low. Houses built of adobe stay cool in the summer heat and warm in winter.

3   Santa Fe is one of the oldest cities in North America. About 1610, Spanish settlers gave Santa Fe its name. Centuries before the Spanish came, the Pueblo (pweb' lō) Indians lived there. The city's adobe buildings are much like those the Indians lived in long ago. The gardens are like those built by the early Spanish settlers.

4   The people of Santa Fe liked their early Spanish-American buildings. So they passed a law in 1953. It said that all new buildings in the older part of town had to look like the adobe buildings. Now a part of Santa Fe will remind people of the city's long history.

142

FIND THE ANSWERS

1. In Santa Fe, New Mexico, there are many
   - a. Japanese buildings.
   - b. adobe buildings.
   - c. English gardens.
   - d. pointed roofs.

2. The word in paragraph 4 that means *to help someone remember something* is _____.

3. The words "sun-dried brick" in paragraph 2 describe the word

   _____.

4. The story does not say so, but it makes you think that
   - a. Santa Fe has never changed its name.
   - b. adobe is a new kind of brick.
   - c. the Indians built many gardens.

5. Santa Fe was named by
   - a. the Pueblo Indians.
   - b. visitors.
   - c. Spanish settlers.
   - d. the government.

6. People make their own adobe bricks.
   Yes   No   Does not say

7. On the whole, this story is about
   - a. North American gardens.
   - b. Spanish-American laws.
   - c. adobe buildings in Santa Fe.

8. Why did the people of Santa Fe pass a law about adobe buildings? (Check the story again.)
   - a. There were too many people living in new buildings.
   - b. They wanted to make the city modern.
   - c. They wanted one part of town to stay the same.

9. Which of these sentences do you think is right?
   - a. The people in Santa Fe are proud of their city's history.
   - b. The people in Santa Fe like modern buildings.
   - c. Pueblo Indians are the only people who live in Santa Fe.

The Town That Woke Up

1   In 1699 the governor of Virginia made plans for a new capital for his colony. The new capital city was called Williamsburg. It was built with wide streets and beautiful houses. The buildings and governor's home were the finest in the colony. Williamsburg was a busy place until 1780. Then the capital was moved to Richmond, and Williamsburg went to sleep.

2   When the capital moved, the people moved away, too. The old houses began to need paint, roofs caved in, and gardens became thick with weeds.

3   Almost 150 years later, John D. Rockefeller, Jr., became interested in the town. He gave money to re-build Williamsburg just as it had been. In 1926 work began.

4   Rockefeller's wife, Abby Aldrich Rockefeller, liked American folk art. When the town was rebuilt, Mrs. Rockefeller gave her collection of early American paintings and dolls to a museum there.

5   Today, the homes and gardens look as they did when the town was new. Many people dress as people dressed long ago. They make shoes and candles, as people did in the past. Thousands of people visit Williamsburg each year. They see a beautiful American town of two centuries ago. It is the town that woke up.

144

FIND THE ANSWERS

1. Williamsburg is in the state of
   a. New York.   c. Virginia.
   b. Richmond.   d. America.

2. The word in paragraph 1 that means *the city where the head of the government is found* is _____.

3. The words "wide streets and beautiful houses" in paragraph 1 refer to the word _____.

4. The story does not say so, but it makes you think that
   a. much money is needed to rebuild a town.
   b. Williamsburg is now the capital of our country.
   c. few people visit Williamsburg.

5. When Williamsburg was built, its streets were
   a. filled with weeds.   c. caved in.
   b. wide.   d. in need of paint.

6. Williamsburg is a new American city.
   Yes   No   Does not say

7. On the whole, this story is about
   a. John D. Rockefeller, Jr.
   b. people moving away.
   c. Williamsburg, Virginia.

8. Why did the people leave Williamsburg after 1780? (Check the story again.)
   a. They ran out of food.
   b. The town was burned to the ground.
   c. The capital was moved to Richmond.

9. Which of these sentences do you think is right?
   a. Williamsburg helps visitors learn about early America.
   b. The capital of Virginia is Williamsburg.
   c. Thousands of people live in Williamsburg.

145

Make-Believe Towns

1   The movie cowboy is being chased by a band of Indians. The horse gallops through the streets of an old Western town.

2   Chances are that the cowboy is not riding through a real town! The buildings probably have false fronts and no backs. The town is a movie set.

3   Most movie studios keep one or more "towns" on the studio grounds. Someday, you may visit a movie studio. Then you can see these sets. There is the old Western town with its sheriff's office and general store. There is a small midwestern town that has a church and town hall. Walking down the streets of another set, you may think you are in a large city.

4   The buildings on a set must fit the time and place of the movie being filmed. Perhaps a movie's story is supposed to take place in a New England town of the 1800s. The people who make sets must take time to learn what such a town would be like. They study books and pictures. They make a trip to a real New England town. The set must not look like a make-believe town. It must look true to life.

146

FIND THE ANSWERS

1. The people who make sets study
   - a. other sets.
   - b. churches and town halls.
   - c. books and pictures.
   - d. studio grounds.

2. The word in paragraph 2 that means *not real* is _____.

3. The words "it must look true to life" in paragraph 4 refer to a

   _____.

4. The story does not say so, but it makes you think that
   - a. many movies are not filmed in real towns.
   - b. most movies take place in small midwestern towns.
   - c. it is easy to build make-believe towns.

5. Buildings on a set often are
   - a. Indian teepees.
   - b. books and pictures.
   - c. real towns.
   - d. false fronts.

6. People can visit movie studios.
   Yes   No   Does not say

7. On the whole, this story is about
   - a. sets made by movie studios.
   - b. movies that are filmed in large cities.
   - c. cowboys and Indians.

8. Why do people who make sets go to real towns? (Check the story.)
   - a. They like to travel to different places.
   - b. They want to see how to make sets look real.
   - c. They get tired of make-believe towns.

9. Which of these sentences do you think is right?
   - a. All movie studios have dozens of sets.
   - b. You can tell when you see a movie with a make-believe set.
   - c. When you see a movie, the buildings in it look real.

The Lake That Almost Died

1　We must have water to live, and if the water we use is not clean, it can make us ill. The animals that live in and around lakes and rivers must also have clean water.

2　Our rivers and lakes supply most of our water, but the clear, blue water found by the first Americans has changed. Many of our water sources now are polluted. They are filled with dirt and waste, which is hard to get rid of. In many places, water is not safe for most uses.

3　Lake Erie was once a beautiful lake, but then people dumped waste from their homes and factories into it. Fish could not live in much of its polluted water. People called it "a dying lake."

4　Things began to change in the 1970s. Towns were forced by law to stop dumping waste into the lake, and slowly it began to come back to life. Now fish live in Lake Erie again. People still need to be careful about eating them, though. It will be a long time before these fish are free of chemicals.

5　Water cannot be made in a factory. We have learned that once water is polluted, it is hard to make it clean and safe. We must remember to take care of the water we now have.

148

1. Most of our water supply comes from
   a. oceans.
   c. springs and wells.
   b. factories.
   d. rivers and lakes.

2. The word in paragraph 2 that means *starting points* is

   _____.

3. The words "a dying lake" in paragraph 3 refer to _____.

4. The story does not say so, but it makes you think that
   a. we have an endless supply of clean water.
   b. all kinds of life need clean water.
   c. polluted waters are beautiful to look at.

5. Our lakes are often polluted by
   a. waste.
   c. rocks.
   b. fish.
   d. salt water.

6. It is easy to make polluted water safe again.
   Yes   No   Does not say

7. On the whole, this story is about
   a. polluted water.
   b. Lake Erie.
   c. going fishing.

8. We must learn to take care of the water we now have because
   a. factories need time to learn how to make water.
   b. we must have water we can use in the future.
   c. fish from polluted water tastes strange.

9. Which of these sentences do you think is right?
   a. Water pollution is a problem today.
   b. Our water is now clean and safe.
   c. People need clean water more than animals do.

A Headful of Beauty

1   People have always wanted to look beautiful. One way people try to look beautiful is by how they wear their hair.

2   During the Roman Empire, upper-class men put colored powder or gold dust on their hair. Their wives dyed their hair blond and wore elaborate hairdos of braids and curls. During the early Middle Ages, noblemen wore their hair short. Later on, they wore it in what we call a pageboy style. Women often kept their hair hidden inside a net called a *caul*, or a hood called a *wimple.*

3   After the Middle Ages, there was more variety in hair styles, with dif-ferent countries featuring their own favorites. For example, Queen Elizabeth of England had red hair, so many people in her country dyed their hair red. Perhaps the high point, literally, in hair design came in the late 17th century. During that time, men and women spent many hours arranging hairdos as high as three feet tall. These creations were built on wire frames.

4   Today, many different hair styles are in fashion at the same time. People choose the ones they favor for the same reason as always: they want to look beautiful.

150

1. People put gold dust in their hair during the
    a. Roman Empire.   c. late Middle Ages.
    b. early Middle Ages.   d. 17th century.

2. The word in paragraph 2 that means *worked out in great detail* is

    _____.

3. The words "called a *caul*" in paragraph 2 refer to a _____.

4. The story does not say so, but it makes you think that
    a. most people in ancient Rome wore powder in their hair.
    b. throughout history, women have worn more elaborate hairstyles than men.
    c. people in different social classes wear different hairdos.

5. During the 17th century some people had hairdos that were
    a. three feet tall.   c. dyed red.
    b. worn with a caul.   d. many colors.

6. During the Roman Empire some women braided their hair.
    Yes   No   Does not say

7. On the whole, this story is about
    a. unusual hair styles.
    b. hair styles through the ages.
    c. the Middle Ages.

8. Why did many people in England dye their hair red? (Check the story again.)
    a. They wanted to look like ancient Romans.
    b. Red hair is beautiful.
    c. Queen Elizabeth had red hair.

9. Which of these sentences do you think is right?
    a. Some hair styles are always in fashion.
    b. People's ideas about what is beautiful change over time.
    c. People look basically the same, no matter how they wear their hair.

Litter-Free Landscapes

1   When careless people drop trash on the sides of the roads, the rest of us must put up with the results: litter.

2   In 1985, the Texas Department of Transportation gave people a way to do something about litter. A community group could "adopt" a stretch of highway. Members of the group would keep "their" road clean. In exchange, the Department would put up a sign giving the group credit.

3   Many kinds of groups signed on. They included youth groups, public-spirited clubs such as the Elks, and local businesses. Each group agreed to pick up the trash on a regular schedule, such as once a month. The Department gave each group large trash bags and other tools they would need. It also hauled away the trash the groups collected.

4   The idea, known as the "Adopt-A-Highway" program, spread across the country. Now groups all over the United States either pick up litter themselves or sponsor others to do the job. People happily take on this work for many reasons: their groups get recognition, and working as part of a group makes the work fun. Most importantly, they are doing something to make their communities a better place to live.

FIND THE ANSWERS

1. The Department of Transportation gave the groups
   a. trash bags.
   b. fast food.
   c. medals.
   d. litter.

2. The word in paragraph 2 that means *praise* is _____.

3. The word "happily" in paragraph 4 refers to the word

   _____.

4. The story does not say so, but it makes you think that
   a. groups get paid for picking up trash along highways.
   b. only a few people care what our roadsides look like.
   c. roadsides are cleaner than they used to be.

5. The Adopt-A-Highway program was started
   a. in 1995.
   b. by youth groups.
   c. by businesses.
   d. in Texas.

6. There is an Adopt-A-Highway program in France.
   Yes   No   Does not say

7. On the whole, this story is about
   a. roadside litter.
   b. the Adopt-A-Highway program.
   c. the Texas Department of Transportation.

8. Why do people have to put up with the sight of litter along the highways?
   (Check the story again.)
   a. Careless people drop trash on the sides of the road.
   b. Fast-food restaurants are often located along highways.
   c. There are no trash cans on country roads.

9. Which of these sentences do you think is right?
   a. Cleaning up other people's trash is a thankless job.
   b. A Scout troop could adopt a stretch of highway.
   c. The Texas Department of Transportation runs all the Adopt-A-Highway programs.

From Pony Express to E-Mail

1   In the mid-nineteenth century, it took about two weeks for a letter to get from the East to the West. First, the letter went to Saint Joseph, Missouri. Then Pony Express riders carried it west in relays, each rider taking the mail for a part of the journey. At designated points, new riders would take over. Riders changed horses every 10 to 15 miles. It took eight days for the riders to cover 2,000 miles.

2   Settlers had to wait all that time for letters and newspapers from home. The news would be two weeks old when it reached the West. Businesses ran at a slower pace, too. Store-keepers waited weeks for the goods they sold to arrive. And the companies they bought from waited as long to be paid.

3   Today, satellite TV carries news around the world instantly. We contact friends and family by fax and E-mail almost as quickly. Businesses place orders the same way, and thanks to airplanes and computers, they can receive goods the next day. Payment can also be immediate, because banks can send money around the world electronically.

4   Now that we are used to speed, we want it all the time! That's why we call letters sent by post "snail mail."

154

FIND THE ANSWERS

1. We can see news from around the world right away by
   - a. fax.
   - b. snail mail.
   - c. E-mail.
   - d. satellite TV.

2. The word in paragraph 4 that means *mail* is _____.

3. The words "almost as quickly" in paragraph 3 refer to the verb _____.

4. The story does not say so, but it makes you think that
   - a. once people moved west, they never heard from their families again.
   - b. people in the nineteenth century didn't have telephones.
   - c. nobody sent letters from the West to the East.

5. Pony Express riders changed horses
   - a. every 10 to 15 miles.
   - b. at designated points.
   - c. every day.
   - d. at Saint Joseph, Missouri.

6. Each Pony Express rider traveled 100 miles.

   Yes   No   Does not say

7. On the whole, this story is about
   - a. how much faster communication is now than it used to be.
   - b. the Pony Express.
   - c. why people today are more impatient than people were in the nine-teenth century.

8. What makes it possible for businesses to receive goods overnight? (Check the story again.)
   - a. Airplanes and computers
   - b. E-mail and faxes
   - c. The relay system

9. Which of these sentences do you think is right?
   - a. Satellite TV is used only for foreign news.
   - b. Letters still take two weeks to go from the East to the West.
   - c. It would be hard to run a business today without a computer and a fax machine.

155

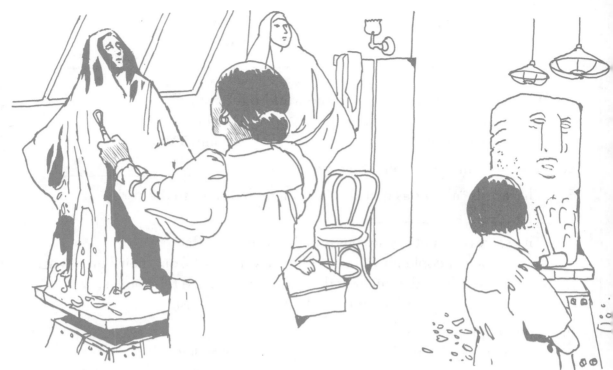

Two Sculptors

1   Have you ever made a turtle or an elephant out of clay? This is the way many sculptors begin work on a large statue. They make a small model out of clay. Then they follow the same lines as they carve or mold their large pieces.

2   Sculptors often carve things they see around them. This might be a person or an animal. Some carve figures that show feeling, such as sorrow or happiness. Still others carve figures that tell of an idea, such as "power."

3   Marina Núñez del Prado, a famous sculptor of Bolivia, liked to make statues of figures from Bolivian Indian stories. Her work reminds us of long ago times.

4   Edmonia Lewis was a sculptor from New York. She had a black father and an Indian mother. Her Indian name was *Wildfire*. Edmonia wanted her statues to show feelings.

5   One of her statues is called *Hagar in the Wilderness*. Hagar, a woman of the Bible, and her son were forced to wander in the desert. Hagar's face looks tired and sad. People who look at Edmonia's statue understand how all women felt who have suffered.

6   Can you think of a statue that shows an idea?

FIND THE ANSWERS

1. Marina Núñez del Prado is a famous
   - a. teacher.
   - b. soldier.
   - c. sculptor.
   - d. artist.

2. The word in paragraph 1 that means *people who make statues* is

   _____.

3. The words "a woman of the Bible" in paragraph 5 refer to

   _____.

4. The story does not say so, but it makes you think that
   - a. many good sculptors are women.
   - b. sculptors always make statues of people.
   - c. all sculptors live in New York.

5. Sculptors' models are often made of
   - a. stone.
   - b. wood.
   - c. clay.
   - d. sand.

6. Edmonia Lewis's Indian name was *Wildfire.*
   - Yes   No   Does not say

7. On the whole, this story is about
   - a. American Indians.
   - b. the Bible.
   - c. two sculptors.

8. How does Hagar's face look? (Check the story.)
   - a. Sunburned.
   - b. Pleased.
   - c. Tired and sad.

9. Which of these sentences do you think is right?
   - a. Sculpture is an art form.
   - b. Clay statues will last forever.
   - c. Nobody makes statues of animals.

Invisible Messages

1   It would be difficult to imagine a world without radio. Some of us even carry small radios in our pockets. Before radio, the best way to send messages a long way was by wire.

2   By 1838, Samuel F. B. Morse had invented a working telegraph. He had also invented a new alphabet made up of dots and dashes. This alphabet was called Morse Code.

3   The telegraph uses electricity and wire. Messages in Morse Code could go only where there were telegraph wires.

4   Scientists knew that radio waves moved through the air. They believed that radio messages could be sent without wires. No one knew how to do it.

5   The man who found a way to send wireless messages was Guglielmo Marconi (gü lyel' mō mär kō' nē) of Italy. His first signals went only a few miles, but he wanted to send messages across the Atlantic Ocean. Marconi went to Newfoundland to try to receive signals from England.

6   Late in 1901, the letter "S" was sent out in Morse code from England. "Dot, dot, dot" came the signal. Marconi picked it up on his set.

7   In a short time, wireless was in use everywhere. Americans call it radio. It can send invisible messages around the world.

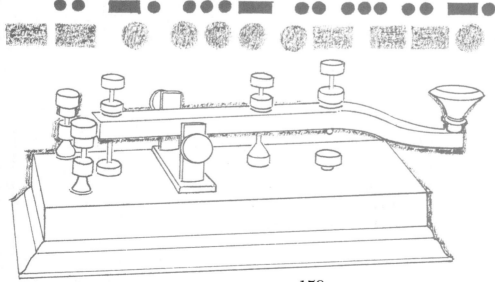

158

FIND THE ANSWERS

1. A working telegraph was invented by
   a. Guglielmo Marconi.   c. Thomas A. Edison.
   b. Samuel F. B. Morse.   d. George Washington.

2. The word in paragraph 7 that means *cannot be seen* is

   _____.

3. The words "a new alphabet made up of dots and dashes" in paragraph 2

   refer to the _____ _____.

4. The story does not say so, but it makes you think that
   a. telegraph messages are sent to a satellite.
   b. radio messages can be sent where telegraph messages cannot.
   c. wireless messages can go only a few miles.

5. Marconi wanted to send wireless messages
   a. to a satellite in space.   c. across the Atlantic Ocean.
   b. to the moon.   d. to Samuel F. B. Morse.

6. Radio waves move along wires.
   Yes   No   Does not say

7. On the whole, this is a story about
   a. scientists and alphabets.
   b. England, Italy, and Newfoundland.
   c. the telegraph and the radio.

8. Why was the wireless important? (Check the story again.)
   a. Wire could be used in other ways.
   b. Radio messages could be sent where there were no wires.
   c. Wireless changed the alphabet.

9. Which of these sentences do you think is right?
   a. The wireless made sending messages quicker.
   b. Morse and Marconi worked together on the wireless.
   c. Radio waves cannot be sent without wires.

Taboos

1 There are certain things that people think they must not do. These are called taboos. People who have a taboo act in a certain way. They think that to act differently would bring bad luck. Some people think that walking under a ladder will bring bad luck.

2 For the people of one tribe in Africa, it was taboo to count anything. If people wanted to know how many goats they had, they looked quickly. Then they guessed how many goats were there. They thought something bad would happen to the goats if they counted them.

3 For another tribe in Africa, it was taboo to talk about the misfortune of an ancestor. These people thought the ancestor's spirit would hear them and become angry. Then the spirit would punish them.

4 Saying their own names was taboo for Polar Eskimos. They believed evil spirits were always listening when they spoke. It would not be safe to say their names out loud. Evil spirits would cause bad luck. If someone asked, "Who is there?" an Eskimo would answer, "It is I." Eskimos would never give their names.

160

FIND THE ANSWERS

1. For Polar Eskimos it was taboo to
   - a. walk under a ladder.
   - b. say their names.
   - c. talk to anyone.
   - d. count anything.

2. The word in paragraph 1 that means *to do* or *to behave* is

   _____ .

3. The words "certain things that people think they must not do" in

   paragraph 1 tell about the word _____ .

4. The story does not say so, but it makes you think that
   - a. everyone should walk under ladders.
   - b. goats bring bad luck.
   - c. different peoples have different taboos.

5. One tribe in Africa believed that they should not
   - a. speak to spirits.
   - b. listen to others.
   - c. ask questions.
   - d. count their goats.

6. Polar Eskimos live in tribes.
   Yes   No   Does not say

7. On the whole, this story is about
   - a. the weather in Africa.
   - b. the clothes of a Polar Eskimo.
   - c. taboos among different peoples.

8. Why wouldn't Polar Eskimos say their names out loud? (Check the story.)
   - a. They couldn't remember their names.
   - b. They believed that their ancestors would hear them.
   - c. They thought it would bring bad luck.

9. Which of these sentences do you think is right?
   - a. Taboos are something to eat.
   - b. Many peoples have taboos.
   - c. Evil spirits are always listening to what you say.

From Page to Knight

1   During the Middle Ages in England, all boys from important families were expected to become knights. But first, they had to learn many things.

2   When a boy was seven, he was sent to a friend's castle. There, he started his training as a page. He began by doing all kinds of small tasks. He also learned to ride a horse. He had to do his work well and without a fuss.

3   After seven years, a page became a squire. As a squire, he learned to use weapons and to hunt. In time, he could fight beside his master in battle.

4   When they were twenty-one, squires who had done well were made knights in long, serious ceremonies. Sometimes a squire became a knight after he had been very brave in battle. Then the ceremony was quick. The squire's master might say, "I hereby make you a knight." To finish the ceremony, the master gave the new knight a slap on the shoulder or the cheek.

5   All knights had to promise certain things. They promised to tell the truth and to be brave. They had to be kind to women and children. Above all, they promised to serve God and their king.

1. A page learned to
   a. fight in battle.
   b. use weapons.
   c. make a fuss.
   d. ride a horse.

2. The word in paragraph 4 that means *special acts for special times* is

   _____.

3. The words "learned to use weapons and to hunt" in paragraph 3 refer

   to a _____.

4. The story does not say so, but it makes you think that
   a. all boys did not become knights.
   b. a page had a lot of free time for play.
   c. pages did not know how to ride a horse.

5. Knights promised to
   a. be brave and kind.
   b. fight and hunt.
   c. be a page.
   d. own a castle.

6. The ceremony of a squire becoming a knight was always quick.
   Yes   No   Does not say

7. On the whole, this story is about
   a. boys in America.
   b. girls in the Middle Ages.
   c. becoming a knight.

8. How did a squire become a knight? (Check the story again.)
   a. He talked to the king about it.
   b. He took part in a special ceremony.
   c. He slapped himself on the cheek.

9. Which of these sentences do you think is right?
   a. It took many years of hard work to become a knight.
   b. Knights did not have to follow rules or keep promises.
   c. Knights became kings.

Eskimo Good Manners

1   You say "please" when you ask someone for something and "thank you" when you get it. You are using good manners. Polar Eskimos had their own ways to show good manners.

2   Polar Eskimos liked to visit with one another. When Eskimos had good hunting, they put aside the best meat to serve guests. Then they invited the other families in the community to dinner. While visiting, both the Eskimo host and the Eskimo guests used good manners.

3   The Eskimo hosts were eager to be thought good hosts. Being good hosts made Eskimos important in the community. The hosts served the best meat. However, it would have been bad manners to say so. It was good manners for them to say they wished they could have served better. The hosts said they did not hunt well and that their meat was not good.

4   The guests then used their good manners. They told the hosts they were great hunters. They said the food was the best anywhere. They made noises to show how much they enjoyed the food. They ate until they could not eat another bite.

FIND THE ANSWERS

1. Eskimos like to
   - a. live alone.
   - b. use bad manners.
   - c. be good hosts.
   - d. serve tough meat.

2. The word in paragraph 3 that means *neighborhood* or *area* is

   _____.

3. The words "used their good manners" in paragraph 4 refer to the

   _____.

4. The story does not say so, but it makes you think that
   - a. Eskimos do not like meat when it is cooked.
   - b. Eskimo life is very different from ours.
   - c. Eskimos are unfriendly to each other.

5. When Eskimo families visited one another,
   - a. everyone used good manners.
   - b. they ate a little snack.
   - c. they just talked.
   - d. they sat around a fire.

6. Being a good host made an Eskimo important in the community.
   Yes   No   Does not say

7. On the whole, this story is about
   - a. the Middle Ages.
   - b. how to be a great hunter.
   - c. good manners among the Polar Eskimos.

8. Why did Polar Eskimos invite other families to dinner? (Check the story.)
   - a. They had so much meat that they couldn't eat it all.
   - b. They didn't want to be alone.
   - c. They liked to visit with friends.

9. Which of these sentences do you think is right?
   - a. Good manners are different in different places.
   - b. Eskimos are bad hunters.
   - c. The Polar Eskimos do not like to have guests.

165

The Noodlehead and the Pumpkin
(A Persian Folktale)

There was once a strong young man who was a great wrestler. He lived alone in the woods near the small village of Hums.

The wrestler was as strong as a bear. Sometimes, just for fun, he pulled up hundred-year-old trees by the roots.

Now, the people of Hums were so stupid that they were called Noodleheads. Of all the people in Hums, the wrestler was the most stupid.

166

One day, the wrestler decided to go to the city. "Maybe I can find someone who will wrestle with me," he said. And he started out.

Hums was a tiny town, and the wrestler had never seen many people before. When he came to the city, he saw hundreds and thousands of people. He was afraid that he would get lost.

"Suppose I forget who I am?" he thought. "I couldn't find myself in these crowds."

The wrestler saw a man selling pumpkins. He bought the biggest pumpkin he could find. He tied it by a string to his right leg. He could not get lost now! He walked along, dragging the pumpkin.

"Good day," said a young man. "Where do you come from?"

"I come from Hums," said the wrestler.

The young man knew that Hums was the home of the Noodleheads. "Why do you have a pumpkin tied to your leg?" he asked.

"There are so many people here that I might not know who I am," said the wrestler. "As long as I have a pumpkin tied to my leg, I know that I am I. When it is time to leave, I'll know that I am the one who goes home to Hums."

"Come home with me," said the young man. He thought it would be fun to play a trick on this stupid Noodlehead. "Be my guest for awhile," he said.

"Thank you," said the wrestler, and he followed the young man to his home. They ate a good dinner and went to bed. As soon as the wrestler was asleep, the young man took the pumpkin from the wrestler's leg and tied it on his own.

Early the next morning, the wrestler awoke. The pumpkin was gone! He went to find his new friend. He saw a young man who was still asleep with a pumpkin tied to one leg.

The wrestler rubbed his head. It felt like his head, but how could it be? He could see that he was still in bed. "How wise I was to buy that pumpkin!" he said to himself. "There I am asleep, and I thought I was awake! If that's the wrestler, then I'm the man who owns this house."

He went outside and sat on a rock. "This city is no place to live," he decided. "I've heard that Hums is the best place to live. I think I'll go there." He looked at the fine house. "I guess I'll sell it," he said.

168

Soon a man and his wife came by. They were carrying heavy loads of furniture. Behind them came seven children.

The wrestler felt sorry for them. "May I help you carry something?" he asked.

"I'm looking for a house to buy," said the man.

"You have come to the right place," said the wrestler. "This house is for sale."

The man took a bag from his pocket. "All the money I have is this bag of gold," he said.

"That will be fine," said the wrestler. He took the gold and started to leave. Then he remembered something.

"Inside your house you will find a man with a pumpkin tied to his leg," said the wrestler. "He won't stay long. He's a Noodlehead." And the wrestler went home to Hums.

618 words

169

KEEPING CHARTS ON SKILLS

Fill in your record chart after each test. Beside the page numbers, put a one for each correct question. Put zero in the box of each question you missed. At the far right, put your total. Nine is a perfect score for each test.

When you finish all the tests in a concept, total your scores by question. The highest possible score for each question in one concept is the number of stories.

When you have taken several tests, check to see which questions you get right each time. Which ones are you missing? Find the places where you need help. For example, if you are missing Question 3 often, ask for help in learning to use directing words.

As you begin each concept, copy the chart onto lined paper. Down the left side are the test page numbers. Across the top are the question numbers and the kinds of questions. For example, each Question 1 in this book asks you to recall a fact. Your scores for each question show how well you are learning each skill.

Your Reading Scores
Concept I

Question Page 15	1 fact	2 vocabulary	3 modification	4 inference	5 fact	6 confirming content	7 main idea	8 cause and effect	9 inference	Total for Page
17										
19										
21										
23										
25										
27										
29										
31										
33										
35										
37										
39										
41										
43										
45										
47										
49										
51										
53										
55										
57										
59										
61										
Totals by question										

170

Your Reading Scores
Concept III

Question	fact 1	vocabulary 2	modification 3	inference 4	fact 5	confirming content 6	main idea 7	cause and effect 8	inference 9	Total for Page
Page 119										
121										
123										
125										
127										
129										
131										
133										
135										
137										
139										
141										
143										
145										
147										
149										
151										
153										
155										
157										
159										
161										
163										
165										
Totals by question										

Your Reading Scores
Concept II

Question	fact 1	vocabulary 2	modification 3	inference 4	fact 5	confirming content 6	main idea 7	cause and effect 8	inference 9	Total for Page
Page 67										
69										
71										
73										
75										
77										
79										
81										
83										
85										
87										
89										
91										
93										
95										
97										
99										
101										
103										
105										
107										
109										
111										
113										
Totals by question										